PRESENTED BY

SWEDENBORG SOCIETY

(INCORPORATED)

INSTITUTED IN LONDON 1810 · INCORPORATED 1925

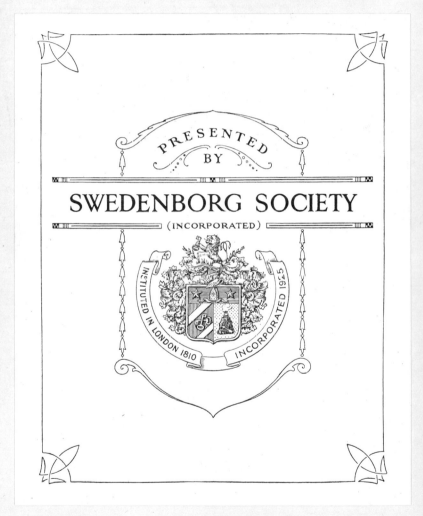

CONJUGIAL LOVE

THE DELIGHTS OF WISDOM

RELATING TO

CONJUGIAL LOVE

AFTER WHICH FOLLOW

THE PLEASURES OF INSANITY

RELATING TO

SCORTATORY LOVE

FROM THE LATIN

OF

EMANUEL SWEDENBORG

THE SWEDENBORG SOCIETY (INCORPORATED)
SWEDENBORG HOUSE
20 HART STREET, BLOOMSBURY SQUARE
LONDON, W.C.1

Printed in Great Britain
by Turnbull & Spears, Edinburgh

TRANSLATOR'S PREFATORY NOTE.

The present translation of the Work on *Conjugial Love* was commenced, in the first instance, as a mere revision of the edition issued in 1876. The amount of alteration found necessary was, however, so great as to resolve itself into an entirely new version, which in its turn has been carefully compared with the Latin and further corrected in passing through the press.

The extent of the alterations made in the text has necessitated the reconstruction of the Index of Subjects. An Index of Scripture passages has, for the first time, been added; and a few critical notes on the text. Footnotes have also been inserted giving reference to parallel passages in other Works of Swedenborg where the Memorable Relations are repeated.

Into both the text and the Indexes, the subdivisional reference numbers first adopted in the Rev. J. F. Potts' *Swedenborg Concordance,* and kindly supplied for this purpose by the author of that work, have been introduced.

The translator has been greatly assisted in his exceptionally difficult task by the Rev. R. L. Tafel, whose many valuable suggestions have contributed materially towards making this translation accurate. The correctness of the work has likewise been enhanced by a careful collation with M. le Boys des Guays' excellent French translation of *Conjugial Love,* and with the able translations scattered throughout the *Swedenborg Concordance,* as far as that work has been published. Among the renderings adopted from the latter may be mentioned the use of capital initial letters to distinguish Latin neuter adjectives when used as substantives; the rendering of the phrase *omnia et singula* by "each and all things;" and the distinguishing of *cognitio* from *scientia* by the use of a capital initial when the word "knowledge" (which is used to translate both terms) stands for *cognitio*.

It cannot, of course, be claimed that the present translation is perfect; much indeed necessarily remains to be done by the painstaking and enlightened translator of the future, in the direction of a more happy rendering of many phrases into idiomatic English; but it is believed that at least the true meaning of the original has been faithfully and accurately rendered.

A. H. SEARLE.

LONDON, 5*th June* 1891.

CONTENTS.

*** These "Contents" have been translated from two separate tables which in the original Latin edition are placed at the end of the volume, and entitled, respectively, "General Index" and "Index of the Memorable Relations:" The items from the latter Index are here distinguished by the use of Italic type.

PART THE FIRST.

PART THE SECOND.

THE DELIGHTS OF WISDOM

RELATING TO

CONJUGIAL LOVE

A.

PRELIMINARIES.

THE JOYS OF HEAVEN AND THE WEDDINGS THERE.

1. * I FORESEE that many who read these things that follow, and the Memorable Relations at the end of the chapters, will believe that they are inventions of the imagination; but I asseverate in Truth that they are not inventions, but have of a truth been done and seen; and that they have been seen, not in any dozing state of the mind, but in a state of full wakefulness. For it has pleased the Lord to manifest Himself to me, and to send me to teach those things which will belong to the New Church, which is meant by the "New Jerusalem" in the Apocalypse. For the sake of this end He has opened the interiors of my mind and spirit; by virtue of which it has been given me to be in the spiritual world with the angels, and at the same time in the natural world with men, and this now for twenty-five years.†

2. ‡ On a certain time I saw an angel flying underneath the eastern heaven, who had a trumpet in his hand and at his mouth, which he sounded towards the north, towards the west, and towards the south. He was clad in a cloak, which streamed behind him as he flew; and he was girt with a girdle which as it were flamed and shone with fiery stones and sapphires. He flew downwards, and let himself slowly down on to the earth, near where I was standing. As soon as he touched the earth, he stood erect on his feet, and paced to and fro; and then, seeing me, he directed his steps towards me. I was in the spirit, and was standing, in the spirit, on a hill in the southern quarter.

When he was near me, addressing him I asked, "What is the matter now? I heard the sound of your trumpet, and saw your descent through the air."

The angel replied, "I have been sent to call together those who are the most celebrated for learning, the most clear-sighted in genius, and the most eminent in the renown of wisdom, who are on this part of the earth from the kingdoms of the Christian world, that they may assemble on this hill where you are standing, and from the heart utter their minds, as to what had been

* This paragraph, in the original Latin edition, is enclosed in inverted commas. It is repeated in the *True Christian Religion*, no. 851.

† The original Work was published in the year 1768.

‡ The following Memorable Relation, extending from nos. 2 to 25, is repeated in the *True Christian Religion*, nos. 731 to 752.

their thought, understanding, and wisdom, while in the world, concerning HEAVENLY JOY, and concerning ETERNAL HAPPINESS.
2 The cause of my mission was this, that some new-comers from the world, having been admitted into our heavenly society, which is in the east, have informed us, that not a single person in the whole Christian world knows what heavenly joy is, and what eternal happiness is, nor, consequently, what heaven is. My brethren and companions wondered much at this, and said to me, 'Go down, call together and assemble the wisest in the world of spirits, (into which all mortals are first collected after their departure out of the natural world,) to the end that we may know of a certainty, from the mouth of many, whether it be the Truth that there is such thick darkness, or dense ignorance, among Christians, concerning the future life.'"

And he said, "Wait a little while, and you will see companies of the wise ones flocking hither; the Lord will prepare a house of assembly for them."

3 I waited, and lo! after half an hour, I saw two troops from the north, two from the west, and two from the south; and, as they came, they were introduced by the angel of the trumpet into the house prepared for them, where they took the places assigned them according to the quarters. There were six troops or companies; and there was a seventh from the east, which, by reason of its light, was not seen by the others. When they were gathered together, the angel explained the reason of their being called together, and desired that the companies in order would utter their wisdom concerning HEAVENLY JOY, and concerning ETERNAL HAPPINESS. Then each company formed themselves into a ring, with their faces turned towards each other, in order that they might recall that subject according to the ideas which they had conceived in the former world, and then examine it, and that, after having examined it, and consulted together, they might state what they thought about it.

3. After consultation, the FIRST COMPANY, which was from the north, said that heavenly joy and eternal happiness are one with the very life of heaven; wherefore every one who enters heaven, enters into its festivities as to the life; no otherwise than as a person who goes to a wedding enters into its festivities. "Is not heaven before our sight, above us, and consequently in a place? and are there not there, and nowhere else, states of bliss on states of bliss, and pleasures on pleasures? Into these blissful states and pleasures a man is introduced, both as to the perception of the mind and as to every sensation of the body, in consequence of the fulness of the joys of that place, when he is admitted into heaven; wherefore, heavenly happiness, which is also eternal happiness, consists solely in admission into heaven, and admission into heaven depends on the Divine favour."

When they had said this, the SECOND COMPANY from the 2
north uttered this conjecture from their wisdom: "Heavenly joy and eternal happiness consist solely in most delightful social gatherings with angels, and sweetest conversations with them, whence the faces are kept continually expanded with gladnesses, and the lips of the whole company are kept continually in pleasant smiles at kind speeches and pleasantries. What else are heavenly joys, than the variations of such things to eternity?"

The THIRD COMPANY, which was the first of the wise ones from 3
the western quarter, gave utterance to the following opinion from the thoughts of their affections: "In what else do heavenly joy and eternal happiness consist than in feasting with Abraham, Isaac, and Jacob, on whose tables there will be delicate and rich foods, and generous and noble wines, and after the banquets games and dances of maidens and young men dancing to the music of symphonies and flutes, with sweetest songs and odes interspersed; and lastly in the evening stage performances; and this again to be followed by feasts, and so on every day to eternity?"

When they had said these things, the FOURTH COMPANY, which 4
was the second from the western quarter, expressed their opinion, saying, "We have entertained many ideas concerning heavenly joy, and concerning eternal happiness; and we have explored a variety of joys, and compared them one with another, and have come to the conclusion that heavenly joys are paradisiacal joys. What is heaven but a paradise, whose extension is from the east to the west, and from the south to the north, wherein are trees of fruits, and flowers of delights, in the midst of which is the magnificent tree of life, around which the blessed will sit, eating fruits of delicate flavour, and adorned with garlands of the sweetest smelling flowers? These fruits and flowers, under the influence of a perpetual spring, are renewed, and renewed again, every day, with infinite variety; and by their perpetual growth and blossoming, and at the same time by reason of the constantly vernal temperature of the atmosphere, the minds (*animus*) of the blessed, being continually renewed, cannot but attract and breathe daily new joys, and thus be restored to the flower of age, and thereby to the primitive state, into which Adam and his wife were created, and thus be led back into their paradise, which has been transferred from earth to heaven."

The FIFTH COMPANY, which was the first of the men of genius 5
from the southern quarter, pronounced the following opinion: "Heavenly joys and eternal happiness consist solely in most exalted power, and overflowing treasuries, and thus in more than kingly magnificence, and splendour beyond that of the greatest nobles. That the joys of heaven, and their continual enjoyment, which is eternal happiness, consist in these things, we have

clearly perceived from the case of those persons in the former world who have possessed them; and especially from this circumstance, that the happy in heaven are to reign with the Lord, and to be kings and princes, because they are the sons of Him Who is King of kings and Lord of lords; and that they are to sit on thrones and be ministered to by angels. The magnificence of heaven we have clearly perceived from this fact, that the New Jerusalem, whereby is described the glory of heaven, is to have gates, each of which will consist of a single pearl, and streets of pure gold, and a wall founded upon precious stones; consequently, that every one who is received into heaven will have a palace of his own, glittering with gold and precious materials, and that the government will pass in orderly succession from one to another. And since we know that in such things joys are innate, and happiness is inherent, and that they are the promises of God, which cannot fail, we could not deduce the most happy state of heavenly life from any other source."

5 After this, the SIXTH COMPANY, which was the second from the southern quarter, raised their voice, and said, "The joy of heaven and its eternal happiness consist solely in a perpetual glorification of God, a never-ceasing festival of praise, and most blessed worship, with songs and shouts of joy, and thus in a constant elevation of the heart towards God, with a full reliance on His acceptance of the prayers and praises for the Divine bounty in imparting blessedness to them." Some of this company added, that this glorification would be attended with magnificent illuminations, with most fragrant incense, and with stately processions, preceded by a high pontiff with a great trumpet, who would be followed by primates and office-bearers, great and small, and, after these, by men carrying palms, and by women with golden images in their hands.

4. The SEVENTH COMPANY, which, by reason of its light, was not seen by the rest, was from the east of heaven; they were angels of the same society as the angel of the trumpet. When these heard in their heaven, that not a single person in the Christian world knew what the joy of heaven and eternal happiness were, they said one to another, "Surely this cannot be the truth: such thick darkness, and such dulness of mind, cannot prevail among Christians. Let us also go down and hear whether it be the truth; for if it be the truth, it is indeed a monstrous thing."

2 Then those angels said to the angel of the trumpet, "You know that every man that had desired heaven, and had thought anything definite concerning the joys there, is introduced after death into the joys of his imagination; and that, after they have found out the quality of those joys, in that they are according to the idle ideas of their mind, and according to the

ravings of their own phantasy, they are led away from them, and instructed. This happens in the world of spirits to most of those who in the former life had meditated about heaven, and had drawn some conclusion concerning the joys there, till they desired to possess these joys."

On hearing these things, the angel of the trumpet said to the six companies of the wise ones of the Christian world who had been called together, "Follow me; and I will introduce you into your joys, and consequently into heaven."

5. Having said this, the angel went before them; and he was first accompanied by the company of those who had persuaded themselves that heavenly joys consisted solely in most delightful social gatherings and sweetest conversations. These the angel introduced to companies in the northern quarter, who, in the former world, had considered the joys of heaven to be no other than these. There was there a spacious house, into which such had been gathered together. In the house there were more than fifty rooms, distinguished according to the various kinds of conversation. In some of these rooms they conversed about such matters as they had seen and heard in the public places of resort and in the streets; in others they spoke about the various charms of the beautiful sex, with a mixture of pleasantries, so that the countenances of all in the company were expanded in cheerful merriment; in others they talked about the news relating to courts, administrations, and the body politic, and to various matters which had transpired from privy councils, with reasonings and conjectures of their own about the outcomes of such councils; in others again they conversed about business matters; in others about literature; in others about such things as belong to statesmanship and moral life; and in others about affairs relating to the Church, and about the sects; and so forth.

It was given me to look into that house; and I saw people running from one room to another, seeking such company as best suited their own affection and consequent joy; and in the different companies I saw three kinds of persons; some as it were panting to speak, some eager to ask questions, and some greedy to listen.

The house had four doors, one towards each quarter; and 2
I observed that many broke away from their company, and hastened to go out. I followed some of them to the east door, and I saw several sitting by it with sad countenances. I went up to them, and asked why they were sitting thus sadly; and they replied, "The doors of this house are kept shut against those who would go out, and this is the third day since we entered, and we have completely exhausted the life of our desire in company and conversation, and are so tired out

with continual conversations, that we can scarcely bear to hear a murmur of the sounds which come from them; wherefore, we have betaken ourselves in weariness to this door; and we knocked, but it was answered us, that the doors of this house are not opened to those who would go out, but only to those who would enter, and that we must remain and enjoy the joys of heaven; from which answer we concluded, that we are to remain here to eternity: hence sorrow has come over our minds, and now our breast begins to be oppressed, and anxiety begins to arise."

3 The angel then spoke to them, and said: "This state is the death of your joys, which you had believed to be the only heavenly joys, when yet they are only accessories of heavenly joys."

And they asked the angel, "What then is heavenly joy?"

And the angel replied briefly thus: "It is the delight of doing something that is of use to oneself and others; and the delight of use derives its essence from love, and its existence from wisdom. The delight of use, originating in love through wisdom, is the
4 soul and life of all heavenly joys. In the heavens there are most delightful social gatherings, which exhilarate the minds (*mens*) of the angels, amuse their lower minds (*animus*), delight their breasts, and recreate their bodies; but they hold these gatherings after they have done uses in their respective function and work. From these uses there is soul and life in all their gladnesses and delights; but if you take away that soul or life, the accessory joys gradually cease to be joys, becoming first indifferent, then as it were trifles, and at last sorrowful and anxious."

When he had said these things, the door was opened, and those who were sitting near it bounded out, and fled home, each one to his own function, and to his own work, and they were warmed into life again.

6. After this the angel addressed those who had deluded themselves with the idea that the joys of heaven, and eternal happiness, consisted in feasts with Abraham, Isaac, and Jacob, succeeded by sports and public shows, and these by other feasts, and so on to eternity. He said unto them: "Follow me, and I will introduce you into the happinesses of your joys:" and he led them through groves into a plain floored with planks, on which were set tables, fifteen on one side and fifteen on the other.

They asked, "Why are there so many tables?" and the angel replied: "The first table is for Abram, the second for Isaac, the third for Jacob, and by the side of them, in a series, are the tables of the twelve apostles. On the other side are the same number of tables for their wives; the first three are for Sarah, Abram's wife, for Rebecca, the wife of Isaac, and for Leah and

Rachel, the wives of Jacob; and the other twelve are for the wives of the twelve apostles."

2 After a slight delay, all the tables appeared covered with dishes, the little spaces between which were adorned with little pyramids holding sweetmeats. Those who were about to feast stood around the tables waiting to see the presidents of the tables; after they had waited a little while, these were seen entering in order of procession, from Abram to the last of the apostles; and then each president, going up to his own table, reclined on a couch at the head thereof; and they said thence to the bystanders, "Recline ye also with us;" and the men reclined with the patriarchs [and apostles], and the women with their wives: and they ate and drank in gladness, and with reverence.

After the repast, the patriarchs [and apostles] went out: and then were introduced games, and dances of maidens and young men, and after these there were public shows.

At the conclusion of these entertainments, they were again invited to feasts, but with this restriction, that on the first day they should eat with Abram, on the second with Isaac, on the third with Jacob, on the fourth with Peter, on the fifth with James, on the sixth with John, on the seventh with Paul, and with the rest in order till the fifteenth day, when the banquets should be renewed again in like order, only changing their seats, and so on to eternity.

3 After these events the angel called together the men of the company, and said to them, "All those whom you have seen at the tables, had been in a similar imaginary thought as yourselves, concerning the joys of heaven, and thus concerning eternal happiness; and it is with the intent that they may see the vanity of their ideas, and be led away from them, that such representations of banquets have been appointed and permitted by the Lord. Those personages whom you saw at the head of the tables, were old men in feigned characters, many of them of the peasant class, who wore long beards, and on account of their comparative wealth were exceedingly haughty, who were deluded by the phantasy that they were those ancient patriarchs. But follow me to the ways that lead out of this place of sports."

4 They accordingly followed, and saw groups of fifty here and fifty there, who had surfeited themselves with dainties to the point of vomiting, and who wished above all things to return to their domestic employments, some to their professional duties, some to their business affairs, and some to their works; but many of them were detained by the keepers of the grove, and questioned concerning the days they had feasted, and whether they had as yet eaten at table with Peter and Paul; and it was represented to them that it would be unbecoming and a shame of them to go out before they had done so. But most of them answered, "We have exhausted our joys; our food has become

insipid to us, and its flavour dry; the stomach loathes it, and we cannot bear to taste it: we have spent some days and nights in that luxury: we earnestly request to be set free." Then being set free, they fled home with panting breath and at full speed.

5 After this the angel called the men of the company, and in
the way he taught them the following particulars concerning
heaven:—"There are in heaven, the same as in the world, both
foods and drinks, both banquets and feasts; and at the houses
of the more distinguished there are tables on which are the
richest foods, dainties and delicacies, wherewith the minds (*animus*)
are exhilarated and recreated. There are also sports and public
shows, concerts of music, vocal and instrumental, and all these
things in the highest perfection. Such things are a source of
joys to them, but not of happiness; for happiness ought to be
within joys, and consequently to flow from them. The happiness
within the joys causes them to be joys; it enriches them, and
prevents their becoming worthless and loathsome; and every
6 one has this happiness from the use in his own function. There
is a certain vein latent in the affection of the will of every angel,
which attracts his mind (*mens*) to do something: by this his
mind calms itself, and is satisfied. This satisfaction and that
calmness constitute a state of mind capable of receiving the love
of use from the Lord; and from the reception of this love comes
heavenly happiness, which is the life of the above-mentioned
joys. Heavenly food in its essence is nothing else than love,
wisdom, and use together; that is, use done through wisdom
out of love; wherefore food for the body is given to every one
in heaven according to the use which he performs; sumptuous
food to those who are in eminent use; moderate, but of an
exquisite flavour, to those who are in use of a middle degree;
and common to those who are in common use; but none at all
to the slothful.

7. After this the angel called to him the company of the so-called wise ones, who had placed heavenly joys, and the eternal happiness flowing thence, in most exalted power and overflowing treasuries, and in more than kingly magnificence, and splendour beyond that of the greatest nobles, because it is said in the Word, that they are to be kings and princes, and to reign with Christ to eternity, and to be ministered unto by angels: with many other similar expressions.

The angel said unto them, "Follow me, and I will introduce you into your joys." And he introduced them into a colonnade constructed of pillars and pyramids: in front there was a palace of lowly structure, through which there was an open entrance into the colonnade; through this palace he introduced them, and lo! there were seen people in groups of twenty. So they waited, and suddenly there stood present a certain one who had the appearance of an angel, and he said to them, "The way to heaven is through this colonnade: wait a little while and prepare yourselves; for the elder ones of you are to be kings, and the younger ones princes."

When he had said this, there appeared beside each pillar 2
a throne, and on each throne a silken cloak, and on each cloak a sceptre and a crown: and beside each pyramid there appeared a chair of state raised three cubits from the ground, and on each chair of state a chain of links of gold, and the badges of an order of knighthood, fastened at the ends with diamond clasps. And then they heard a voice saying, "Go now, and array yourselves in your robes; be seated, and wait:" and instantly the elder ones ran to the thrones, and the younger ones to the chairs of state; and they arrayed themselves in their robes and seated themselves. And then there appeared as it were a mist rising up from below, which, on being inhaled by those who sat on the thrones and chairs of state, made their faces puff up and their breasts swell out, and caused themselves to be fully persuaded that now they were kings and princes. That mist was an aura of the phantasy with which they were inspired. And suddenly several young men flew down as it were from heaven; and two of them stood in waiting behind each throne, and one behind each chair of state: and then by turns acclamation was made by a herald, in these words: "Ye kings and princes, wait a little longer; your palaces in heaven are now being made ready for you; your courtiers and guards will soon come, and introduce you." They waited and waited, till their spirits were exhausted, and they grew weary with desire.

After a space of three hours, the heaven above their 3
heads was opened, and the angels looked down in pity upon them, and said, "Why sit ye here like doltheads playing comedy? They have made a mockery of you, and have changed you from men into mere images, because you have induced on your hearts the phantasy, that you should reign with Christ as kings and princes, and that angels should then minister unto you. Have you forgotten the Lord's words, that whosoever would be great in heaven must become a servant? Learn therefore what is meant by being kings and princes, and what by reigning with Christ; that it means being wise and doing uses. For the kingdom of Christ, which is heaven, is a kingdom of uses; inasmuch as the Lord loves all, and consequently wishes good to all; and good is use; and because the Lord does goods or uses mediately through angels, and in the world through men, therefore, to those who do uses faithfully, he gives the love of use, and its reward, which is internal blessedness; and this is
eternal happiness. There are in the heavens, as in the earths, 4
lofty administrative positions, and overflowing treasuries; for

there are governments and forms of government, and consequently greater and lesser Powers and dignities. Those of the highest rank have palaces and courts, which for magnificence and splendour exceed the palaces and courts of the emperors and kings of the earth; and they derive honour and glory from the number of their courtiers, ministers, and retinue, and their magnificent vestments. But these persons of the highest rank are chosen from those whose heart is in the public welfare, and only their bodily senses in the dignity of magnificence for the sake of obedience: and as it is for the public welfare that every one should be of some use in society, as in the common body, and as all use is from the Lord, and is done through angels and men as if by them, it is manifest that this is meant by reigning with the Lord."

On hearing these things out of heaven, the kings and princes descended from their thrones and chairs of state, and cast away their sceptres, crowns, and cloaks; and the mist in which was the aura of phantasy, departed from them, and a bright white cloud, in which there was the aura of wisdom, covered them, whence soundness returned to their minds.

8. After this the angel returned to the house of assembly of the wise ones from the Christian world, and called to him those who had persuaded themselves that the joys of heaven and eternal happiness consisted in paradisiacal delights.

To these he said, "Follow me, and I will introduce you into a paradise, your heaven, so that you may enter upon the blessednesses of your eternal happiness." And he introduced them through a lofty gate, constructed of the boughs and shoots of noble trees woven together. After their entrance, he led them through winding paths from one quarter to another. The place was actually a paradise, in the first entrance to heaven, into which are admitted those who in the world had believed that the whole heaven is a single paradise, because it is called paradise, and had impressed on themselves the idea that after death there would be a perfect rest from all kinds of labour, and that this rest would consist in inhaling the very souls of delights, walking on roses, being gladdened with the most delicate vintages (*mustum*) of grapes, and frequenting festive gatherings; and that this life did not exist except in a heavenly paradise.

2 Led by the angel, they saw a great multitude of both old and young men and boys, and also of women and girls, sitting by threes and tens on banks of roses; some wreathing garlands to adorn the heads of the old men, the arms of the young men, and in festoons the bosoms of the boys; others gathering fruits off the trees, and bearing them in baskets to their companions; others pressing the juice (*mustum*) out of grapes, cherries, and currants, into cups, and drinking jovially; some inhaling with their nostrils the fragrant smells that exhaled, and were diffused

around, from flowers, fruits, and odoriferous leaves: others singing sweet odes, by which they charmed the hearing of those present, others sitting by fountains, and diverting the waters of the leaping jets into various forms; others walking, conversing together, and jesting; others running, playing games, dancing in one place minuets, in another round dances; others retiring into little summer-houses to lie on couches; besides many other paradisiacal enjoyments.

After these things had been seen, the angel led his companions 3
by roundabout ways hither and thither, and at last led them to a most beautiful bank of roses, surrounded by olive, orange, and citron trees: here there were some persons sitting disconsolate, with their hands under their cheeks, mourning and weeping. The companions of the angel accosted them, and said, "Why are you sitting thus?" and they replied, "This is the seventh day since we came into this paradise: when we entered, our mind seemed to be as it were elevated into heaven, and admitted into the inmost blissfulnesses of its joys; but after three days those blissfulnesses began to pall, and in our minds they began to decay and to become tasteless, and consequently to become no blissfulnesses; and when our imaginary joys had thus died out, we were afraid of losing all the delightsomeness of our life, and began to doubt whether any such thing as eternal happiness existed. We then wandered through the ways and paths, in search of the gate through which we had entered; but we wandered round and round about, and asked those we met, some of whom said that it was impossible to find the gate, because this paradisiacal garden is a spacious labyrinth of such a nature, that whoever wants to go out, enters further and further into it; 'wherefore,' said they, 'you cannot but remain here to eternity; you are in the middle of the garden, where all delights are centred.'" They further said to the angel's companions, "We have now been sitting here for a day and a half, and as we are without hope of finding the way out, we have sat down on this bank of roses, where we view around us olives, grapes, oranges, and citrons, in abundance; but the longer we look at them, the more our sight is wearied with seeing, our smell with smelling, and our taste with tasting: and this is the cause of the dejection, sorrow, and weeping, in which you now see us."

On hearing this, the angel of the company said to them, "This paradisiacal labyrinth is truly an entrance into heaven; I know the way out; and I will lead you out." When he had said this, those who were sitting down rose up, and embraced the angel, and accompanied him, together with his company. And the angel, as they went, taught them what heavenly joy, and eternal happiness flowing thence, were; that they do not consist in external paradisiacal delights, unless together with these there are also internal paradisiacal delights: "external paradisiacal delights are merely delights of the senses of the body; but internal paradisiacal delights are delights of the affections of the soul: unless the latter be in the former, these have no heavenly life, because they have no soul; and every delight without its corresponding soul, forthwith becomes feeble and dull, and fatigues the lower mind (*animus*) more than labour. There are everywhere in heaven paradisiacal gardens, and from these also the angels derive joys; and in so far as in these joys there is a delight of the soul, in the same proportion those joys are joys to them."

5 On hearing this, they all asked, "What is the delight of the soul, and whence is it?"

The angel replied, "The delight of the soul is from love and wisdom from the Lord; and as love is the efficient, and as it is the efficient through wisdom, therefore the seat of both love and wisdom is in the effect, and the effect is use. This delight inflows from the Lord into the soul, and descends through the higher and lower parts of the mind into all the senses of the body, and fulfils itself in them: thus joy becomes joy, and becomes eternal from the Eternal Being from Whom it is. You have just now seen paradisiacal places; and I assure you that there is nothing therein, not even the smallest leaf, which is not from the marriage of love and wisdom in use; wherefore if a man be in this marriage, he is in a heavenly paradise, and consequently in heaven."

9. After this, the angel conductor returned to the house of assembly, to those who had firmly persuaded themselves that heavenly joy and eternal happiness consist in a perpetual glorification of God, and an unceasing festival [of worship] to eternity; because they had believed in the world that they should then see God, and because the life of heaven, by reason of the worship of God, is called a perpetual sabbath.

To these the angel said, "Follow me, and I will introduce you into your joy." And he introduced them into a little city, in the midst of which was a temple, and all the houses were called sacred abodes or chapels. In that city they saw a concourse of people flocking together from all parts of the surrounding country, and among them a number of priests, who received and saluted them on their arrival, and taking them by the hand led them to the gates of the temple, and from thence into some of the chapels around it, and initiated them into the unceasing worship of God; telling them that the city was an entrance-hall to heaven, and that the temple of the city was an entrance to a magnificent and most spacious temple in heaven, where God is glorified by the angels with prayers and praises to eternity. "It is ordered," said they, "both here and in heaven, that you shall first enter into the temple, and remain there three days and three nights: and that after this initiation you shall enter the houses of this city, which are so many chapels consecrated by us, and that you shall go from chapel to chapel, and, in communion with those who are gathered together there, pray, give praise, and repeat chants; take heed, above all things, that ye think within yourselves, and speak with your companions, nothing but what is holy, pious, and religious."

After this the angel introduced his companions into the temple, 2
which was filled and crowded with many of those who in the world had been in great dignity, and also with many of the common people: guards were stationed at the doors to prevent any one from going out until he had stayed there three days. And the angel said, "To-day is the second day since the present congregation entered the temple: examine them, and you will see their glorification of God." And they examined them, and saw that most of them were asleep, and that those who were awake were gaping and yawning; and some of them, in consequence of their thoughts being so continually elevated towards God, and not allowed to relapse into the body, seemed to themselves, and thence also to others, as if their faces were cut off or separated from their bodies; some had wild and raving eyes, on account of their being constantly kept raised upwards; in a word, all of them had an oppression at the chest, and great weariness of spirits from irksomeness, and they had turned away from the pulpit, and were crying out, "Our ears are stunned: put an end to your sermon; we no longer hear your voice, and the very sound of it begins to disgust us." They then all rose up, and ran in a body to the doors, broke them open, and pressed hard on the guards, and drove them off.

On seeing this, the priests followed them, and placed themselves 3
at their sides, teaching and teaching, praying, sighing, and saying, "Celebrate the festival, glorify God, sanctify yourselves; in this entrance-hall of heaven we will inaugurate you into the eternal glorification of God in that magnificent and most spacious temple which is in heaven, and thus [introduce you] to the enjoyment of eternal happiness." These words, however, were unheeded by them, and scarcely heard, on account of the dulness caused by two days' inactivity of mind, and detention from household and public affairs. But when they attempted to pull themselves away from the priests, the priests caught hold of their arms and also of their garments, in order to force them back again into the chapels to a repetition of their prayers and chants; but in vain: they cried out, "Let us alone; we have a sensation in the body as of fainting."

As they said this, lo! there appeared four men (*vir*) in shining 4
white garments, with mitres on their heads; one of them in the world had been an archbishop, and the three others, bishops; they had now become angels. They called the priests together, and

addressing them, said, "We have seen from heaven how you feed
these sheep. Ye feed them so that they become insane. You
do not know what is meant by the glorification of God. It
means bringing forth the fruits of love, that is, doing the work
of one's function faithfully, sincerely, and diligently, for this
is of the love of God, and of the love of the neighbour; and this
is the bond of society, and its good. Thereby God is glorified, and
in that case He is glorified by worship at stated times. Have you
never read these words of the Lord, "*Herein* is My Father glorified,
that ye bring forth much fruit; and ye shall become My disciples"
5 (John xv. 8)? Ye priests are able to be in the glorification of
worship, because this is your office, and from it you derive
honour, glory, and remuneration; but even you could not be in
that glorification more than they, unless honour, glory, and
remuneration were annexed to your office."

Having said this, the bishops ordered the doorkeepers to let all in and out freely: "for there is such a multitude of people, who could think of no other heavenly joy than the perpetual worship of God, because they have known nothing of the state of heaven."

10. After this the angel returned with his companions to the place of assembly, from whence the companies of the wise ones had not yet departed, and there he called to him those who believed that heavenly joy and eternal happiness consist only in admission into heaven, and this out of Divine favour; and that then they would have joy, just as do those in the world who enter into the courts of kings on days of festivity, or into weddings to which they have been invited.

To these the angel said, "Wait here a little while, and I will sound the trumpet, and hither will come those who have been most renowned for wisdom in the spiritual things of the church." After some hours, there were present nine men (*vir*), each wearing a wreath of laurel as a mark of his renown: these the angel introduced into the house of assembly, in which there were present all those who had been called together at the first: in the presence of these the angel addressed the nine laureates, and said, "I know that by your desire, formed according to your idea, it has been given you to ascend into heaven, and that you have returned to this lower or sub-celestial earth, with a full knowledge concerning the state of heaven: relate therefore what sort of a place heaven appeared to you."

2 And they replied in order. And the FIRST said: "My idea of
heaven from my earliest childhood to the end of my life in the world
was, that it was a place abounding with all blessings, blissfulnesses,
delightsomenesses, pleasantnesses, and pleasures; and that if I were
admitted, I should be encompassed by the aura of such felicities,
and should imbibe them with a full breast, like a bridegroom
when he celebrates his nuptials, and when he enters the bridal

chamber with his bride. With this idea I ascended into heaven, and passed the first guard, and also the second; but when I came to the third, the chief of the guard accosted me and said, 'Who are you, friend?' and I answered, 'Is not this heaven? I have come up hither by reason of the longing of my desire; admit me, I pray you:' and he admitted me. And I saw angels in white garments, and they came about me, and examined me, and muttered, 'Behold a new guest, who is not clothed with a garment of heaven,' and I heard this and thought, This seems to me to be a similar case to his of whom the Lord says that he came in unto the wedding without a wedding garment: and I said, 'Give me such garments;' and they laughed; and then one came running from the government-house with this command: 'Strip him naked, cast him out, and cast his garments after him'; and so I was cast out."

The SECOND in order said: "I believed as he did, that if I were 3
but admitted into heaven, which was over my head, I should there be encompassed with joys, and inhale them to eternity. I also gained my desire; but the angels on seeing me fled away, and said one to another, 'What prodigy is this? how came this bird of night here?' and I really felt as if I had undergone some change, and was no longer a man: although I was not changed, but the feeling arose from breathing the heavenly atmosphere. Presently, however, there came one running from the government-house with an order that two attendants should lead me out, and conduct me back by the way I had ascended, till I reached my own house; and when I was at home, I appeared to others and to myself as a man."

The THIRD said: "My constant idea of heaven was derived 4
from place, and not from love; wherefore, when I came into this world, I desired heaven with a great desire. And I saw some who were ascending thither, and I followed them, and was admitted, but not beyond a few paces. But when I wanted to gladden my mind (*animus*) according to my idea of the joys and blessednesses in heaven, a stupor, caused by the light of heaven, which was as white as snow, and whose essence is said to be wisdom, seized on my mind (*mens*), and a consequent darkness seized on my eyes, and I began to go mad: and thereupon, by reason of the heat of heaven, which corresponded with the brightness of that light, and whose essence is said to be love, my heart palpitated, anxiety seized me, and I was tortured with inward pain, and threw myself prostrate on the ground. While I lay prostrate, one of the attendants came out of the government-house with an order that they should carry me slowly down into my own light and heat; and when I came into my own light and heat, my spirit and my heart returned."

The FOURTH said, that he also had been in the idea of place 5 and not in the idea of love [when thinking] about heaven. "As soon," said he, "as I came into the spiritual world, I enquired of the wise ones whether it was allowed to ascend into heaven, and they said to me, that it is allowed to all, but that there was need to beware lest they should be cast down again. At this I laughed, and ascended, believing, as did the others, that all in the whole world were capable of receiving the joys of heaven in all their fulness; but, as a matter of fact, when I was within I was almost deprived of life, and by reason of the pain and the consequent torture in my head and body, I threw myself prostrate on the ground, where I writhed about like a snake when it is brought near the fire: and I crawled to the brink of a precipice, from which I cast myself down: and I was afterwards taken up by those who were standing below, and carried to an inn, where health returned to me."

6 The OTHER FIVE also related wonderful things about their ascents into heaven, and compared the changes of the states of their life with the state of fish when raised out of the waters into the air, and with the state of birds in the ether; and they said that after those hard experiences they no longer desired heaven, but only a suitable life among their like wherever they might be. "We know," added they, "that in the world of spirits, where we now are, all are previously prepared, the good for heaven, and the evil for hell; and that when they are prepared, they see ways opened for them to societies of their like, with whom they are to remain to eternity; and that they then enter these ways with delight, because they are the ways of their love."

When all of the first assembly heard these relations, they likewise confessed that they had had no other idea of heaven than as of a place, where with open mouth they should be drinking in to eternity the joys that surrounded them.

7 After this the angel of the trumpet said to them: "You see now that the joys of heaven, and eternal happiness, do not belong to a place, but to the state of a man's life; and a state of heavenly life is derived from love and wisdom; and since use is the containant of love and wisdom, a state of heavenly life is derived from the conjunction of love and wisdom in use. It is the same if we call them charity, faith, and a good work; for charity is love, faith is truth whence wisdom proceeds, and a good work is a use. Moreover, in our spiritual world there are places as in the natural world; otherwise there could be no habitations and distinct abodes; nevertheless place there is not place, but an appearance of place according to the state of love
8 and wisdom, or of charity and faith. Every one who becomes an angel carries his own heaven within himself, because he carries within himself the love of his own heaven. For a man is, by creation, a least effigy, image, and type of the great heaven;

the human form is nothing else. Wherefore, every one comes into that society of heaven of whose form he is an effigy in particular; therefore, when he enters into that society he enters into a form corresponding to his own; thus he enters from his own individual self, as it were, into a society of his own self (*sicut a se in se-illam*), and from this society of his own individual self, as it were, into that same society in himself (*sicut ab illa in illam in se*), and inhales its life as his own life, and his own life as that of the society; every society is as one common body, and the angels in it are as the like parts, from which the common body co-exists. Hence, then, it follows, that those who are in evils and consequent falsities, have formed in themselves an effigy of hell, and this is tortured in heaven by reason of the influx and violence of the activity of one opposite upon another; for infernal love is opposite to heavenly love, and consequently the delights of those two loves come into collision with each other like enemies, and whenever they meet they destroy each other."

11. After these occurrences a voice was heard from heaven, saying to the angel of the trumpet, "Choose ten out of all those who have been called together, and introduce them to us. We have heard from the Lord that He will prepare them so that, during the space of three days, the heat and light, or the love and wisdom, of our heaven, shall not do them any injury."

Ten were then chosen, and they followed the angel. They ascended by a steep foot-path up a certain hill, and from thence up a mountain, on which was the heaven of those angels, which had before appeared to them at a distance like an expanse in the clouds. The gates were opened for them: and after they had passed through the third gate, the angel introducer hastened to the prince of that society or heaven, and announced their arrival; and the prince answered, "Take some of my attendants, and tell them that they are welcome, and introduce them into my antechamber, and apportion to each a separate room with a bed-chamber, and appoint some of my courtiers and servants to minister unto them, and do their bidding." And it was done so.

On being introduced by the angel, they asked whether they might go and see the prince; and the angel replied, "It is now morning, and it is not permissible to go and see the prince before noon; till that time all are engaged in their particular duties and works: but you are invited to dinner, and then you will sit at table with our prince; in the meantime I will introduce you into his palace, where you will see magnificent and splendid things."

12. When they were led to the palace, they first viewed it from without. It was large, and built of porphyry, with a foundation of jasper; and before the gates were six lofty

columns of lapis lazuli; the roof was of plates of gold; the lofty windows, of the most transparent crystal, also had frames of gold. After viewing the outside, they were introduced within, and were conducted from one room to another; and they saw ornaments of inexpressible beauty,—on the ceilings, decorations of inimitable carving; near the walls they saw set silver tables overlaid with gold, on which were placed various utensils made of precious stones and of entire gems in heavenly forms, and many other things such as no eye had ever seen on earth, and consequently such as no one could bring himself to believe existed in heaven.

While they were in astonishment at these magnificent sights, the angel said, "Be not surprised; the things which you now see were not made and fashioned by any angelic hand, but were framed by the Maker of the universe, and presented as a gift to our prince; wherefore the architectonic art is here in its very art, and from it are derived all the rules of that art in the world." The angel said further, "You may possibly suppose that such things charm our eyes and infatuate them to such an extent, that we believe them to be the joys of our heaven: but because our hearts are not in these things, they are only accessory to the joys of our hearts; therefore, so far as we contemplate them as accessory, and as the workmanship of God, so far we contemplate in them the Divine omnipotence and clemency"

13. After this the angel said to them, "It is not yet noonday: come with me into the garden of our prince, which is near this palace." So they went; and as they were entering, he said, "Behold the most magnificent of all the gardens in this heavenly society!"

But they replied, "What do you say? there is no garden here. We see only one tree, and on its branches and at its top as it were fruits of gold, and as it were leaves of silver, with their edges adorned with emeralds, and beneath the tree little children with their nurses."

At this, the angel said, with an inspired voice, "This tree is in the midst of the garden; and by us it is called the tree of our heaven, and by some the tree of life. But advance, and approach nearer, and your eyes will be opened, and you will see the garden."

They did so, and their eyes were opened, and they saw trees most heavily laden with fruits of fine flavour, entwined about with tendrilled vines, whose tops with their fruits inclined towards the tree of life in the midst.

2 These trees were set in a continuous series, which began from a point and was continued into endless rings or gyres, as of a perpetual spiral. It was a perfect arboreal spiral, in which species followed species without a break, according to the noblenesses of the fruits. The beginning of the circum-

gyration was at a considerable distance from the tree in the midst, and the intervening space glittered with a beam of light, which caused the trees of the gyre to shine with a graduated splendour that was continued from the first to the last. The first trees were the most excellent of all, being laden with the choicest fruits, and were called paradisiacal trees, being such as are never seen in the earths of the natural world, because they do not, and can not, exist there; after these came trees of oil; after these trees of wine; after these trees of fragrance; and lastly, trees of wood, useful for building. Here and there in this arboreal spiral or gyre, there were seats formed of the young shoots of the trees behind, brought forward and entwined together, and enriched and adorned by their fruits. In this perpetual ring of trees, there were gates which opened into flower-gardens, and from these into greenswards, laid out in borders and beds.

At the sight of all these things the companions of the angel 3
exclaimed, "Behold heaven in form! wherever we turn the glances of our eyes, there flows in something heavenly-paradisiacal, which is inexpressible."

On hearing this the angel rejoiced, and said, "All the gardens of our heaven are representative forms or types of heavenly blessednesses in their origins; and because the influx of these blessednesses elevated your minds, therefore you exclaimed, 'Behold heaven in form!' but those who do not receive that influx, regard these paradisiacal things no otherwise than as things of the forest; and all those who are in the love of use receive the influx; whereas those who are in the love of glory, not proceeding from use, do not receive it. He afterwards explained and taught what the particular things of that garden represented and signified.

14. While they were thus employed, there came a messenger from the prince, who invited them to eat bread with him; and at the same time two attendants of the court brought garments of fine linen, and said, "Put on these; for no one is admitted to the prince's table unless he be clothed in the garments of heaven."

So they girded themselves, and accompanied their angel, and were introduced into an open court of the palace, where there was a promenade, where they waited for the prince; and there the angel introduced them to the company and conversation of the magnates and ministers, who were also waiting for the prince. And lo! in about an hour the doors were opened, and through a wider door on the west, they saw the prince entering in order and pomp of procession. His privy-councillors went before him, after them his councillors of the treasury, and next the chief officers belonging to the court: in the midst of these was the prince; after him followed courtiers of various ranks, and lastly the guards; in all they amounted to one hundred and twenty.

2 Then the angel, placing himself before the ten new-comers, who by their dress now appeared like inmates of the place, approached with them towards the prince, and respectfully introduced them; and the prince, without stopping the procession, said to them, "Come with me to bread."

So they followed him into the dining-hall, and they saw a table magnificently laid out, having in the middle a tall golden pyramid, with a hundred salvers arranged in three rows on their forms or stands, containing sweet-cakes, and wine-jellies, with other delicacies made of bread and wine; and through the middle of the pyramid, there gushed as it were a leaping fountain of wine sweet as nectar, whose jet fell in different directions from the top of the pyramid, and filled the cups. At the sides of this high pyramid were various heavenly forms of gold, on which were dishes and plates loaded with food of every kind: these heavenly forms on which were the dishes and plates, were forms of art derived from wisdom, and can neither be produced in the world by any art, nor described by any words. The dishes and plates were of silver, engraved in relief, on their surface, with forms similar to those on their supports; the cups were of transparent gems. Such was the splendid furniture of the table.

15. The dress of the prince and his ministers was as follows: The prince was clad in a long robe, reaching to the ankles, of a crimson colour, set with stars of a silver colour wrought in needle-work; and under this robe he was girded with a tunic of bright silk of a purple colour; this was open about the breast, where there appeared the fore part of a kind of zone with the ensign of his society: the ensign was an eagle brooding over her young at the top of a tree; this ensign was of shining gold surrounded with diamonds. The privy-councillors were dressed after nearly the same manner, but without the ensign; instead of which they wore cut sapphires, hanging from their necks by a golden necklace. The courtiers were in cloaks of a chestnut colour, on which were wrought flowers surrounding young eagles; the vests which they wore under these were of silk of an opaline colour; so also were their breeches and stockings. Such was their apparel.

16. The privy-councillors and councillors of the treasury, and the ministers, stood around the table, and at the order of the prince folded their hands together, and at the same time uttered in a low voice a devout thanksgiving to the Lord, and after this, at the prince's bidding, reclined themselves on couches at the table; and the prince said to the ten strangers, "Do you also

recline with me; behold, there are your seats:" and they reclined; and the courtiers who had previously been sent by the prince to minister unto them, stood behind them. Then the prince said unto them, 'Take each of you a plate from its ring, and afterwards a salver from the pyramid;" and they did so, and lo! instantly new plates and salvers appeared in the place of those that were taken away; and their cups were filled with wine from the fountain that leaped out of the great pyramid; and they ate and drank.

When dinner was about half ended, the prince addressed the ten 2
guests, and said, "I have heard that you were called together in the earth which is under this heaven, to disclose your thoughts concerning the joys of heaven and the eternal happiness thence resulting, and that you expressed different opinions, each according to the delights of the senses of his body. But what are the delights of the senses of the body, without the delights of the soul? It is the soul that enjoys them. The delights of the soul are in themselves imperceptible blessednesses; but they become more and more perceptible as they descend into the thoughts of the mind, and from these into the sensations of the body. In the thoughts of the mind they are perceived as blissfulnesses, in the sensations of the body as delightsomenesses, and in the body itself as pleasures. Eternal happiness is derived from the latter and the former together; but from the latter alone there results a happiness not eternal but temporary, which comes to an end and passes away, and in some cases becomes unhappiness. You have now seen that all your joys are also joys of heaven, and that these are far more excellent than you could have conceived: but still these joys do not inwardly affect our minds (*animus*).
There are three things which flow in as a one from the Lord into our 3
souls; these three as a one, or this trine, are love, wisdom, and use. Love and wisdom exist only ideally, because they exist only in the affection and thought of the mind; but in use they exist really, because they exist at the same time in an act and work of the body; and, where they exist really, there they also subsist. And, since love and wisdom exist and subsist in use, it is uses that affect us; and use consists in faithfully, sincerely, and diligently discharging the works of one's own function. The love of use, and a consequent busying oneself in use, keeps the mind together and prevents it from melting away, and from wandering about, and imbibing all the lusts which flow in through the senses with allurements from the body and the world, whereby the truths of religion and the truths of morality, with their goods, become scattered to every wind; but the busying of the mind in use keeps and binds those truths together, and disposes the mind into a form capable of receiving the wisdom derived from those truths; and then it exterminates from the sides the idle sports and pastimes both of falsities and of vanities. But

you will hear more on these subjects from the wise ones of our society, whom I will send to you in the afternoon."

So saying, the prince arose, and the guests with him, and said grace, and charged their angel conductor to lead them back to their rooms, and to shew them all the honours of civility, and also to summon men (*vir*) of urbanity and affability to entertain them with conversation on the various joys of the society.

17. When they were returned, it was done so, and those who had been summoned from the city to entertain them with conversation concerning the various joys of the society, arrived, and, after courteous greetings, spoke in choice and elegant phrases with them, walking up and down the while. But their angel conductor said, "These ten men were invited into this heaven to see its joys, and to receive thus a new idea concerning eternal happiness: recount therefore some of its joys which affect the senses of the body; and afterwards some wise ones will come, who will mention some of the things which render those joys blissful and happy."

On hearing this, those who had been summoned from the city, related the following particulars:—

"1. There are here days of festivity appointed by the prince, in order that the lower minds (*animus*) may be relaxed from the weariness which the lust of emulation may have brought upon some. On these days there are concerts of music and singing in the public places, and outside the city there are games and shows: in the public places at such times there are raised orchestras, enclosed by barriers, formed of vines entwined together, from which hang clusters of grapes; within these barriers in three rows, one above another, sit the musicians, with stringed instruments and with wind instruments, both alto and bass, loud-toned and soft, and at the sides there are male and female singers, who entertain the citizens with most pleasant solos and part songs, varied at intervals. These concerts continue there on those days of festivity from morning till noon, and afterwards till evening.

2 "2. Moreover, every morning from the houses around the public places are heard the sweetest songs of maidens and girls, with which the whole city resounds. It is one affection of spiritual love, which is sung every morning, that is, sounded by modifications of the singing voice, or by modulations, and that affection in the song is perceived as the affection itself; it flows in into the souls of the hearers, and excites them to a correspondence with it: such is heavenly singing. The singers say, that the sound of their song is as it were self-inspired and self-animated from within, and exalted delightfully according to its reception by the hearers. When this is ended, the windows of the houses of the public places, and at the same time of the houses of the streets,

are shut, and so also are the doors; and then the whole city is silent, and no noise is heard in any part of it, nor is any person seen loitering about: all then are strictly performing the duties of their employments.

"3. At noon-time the doors are opened, and in the afternoon 3
the windows also in some houses, and boys and girls are seen playing in the streets, while their nurses and tutors sit in the porches of the houses, keeping them within bounds.

"4. At the outskirts of the city, there are various sports of 4
boys and youths; there are races, and games with balls; there are games with little balls which are struck back, called rackets; there are trials of skill among the boys, in order to discover which is the quickest, and which the most backward, in speaking, acting, and perceiving; and the quickest receive some leaves of laurel as a reward; besides many other things of a like nature, designed to call forth the latent abilities of the boys.

"5. Moreover outside the city there are dramatic entertain- 5
ments, in theatres, by actors who represent the various honourable qualities and virtues of moral life, among whom there are lesser actors for the sake of [representing] relatives."

And one of the ten asked, "What is meant by 'for the sake of relatives'?"

And they replied, "No virtue, with its honourable qualities and beauties (*decus*), can be exhibited to the life except by means of relatives, from the greatest of them to the least; the lesser actors represent the least of them, even till they become none; but it has been decreed by law, that nothing of the opposite, which is called dishonourable and unbecoming, should be exhibited, except figuratively and as it were from afar. The reason for this decree is, that nothing that is honourable and good in any virtue can by successive progressions pass over to what is dishonourable and evil, but only to its least till it perishes; and when it perishes the opposite commences; wherefore heaven, where all things are honourable and good, has nothing in common with hell, where all things are dishonourable and evil."

18. During this conversation an attendant came running, and announced that eight wise ones, by order of the prince, were present, and wished to enter; on hearing which, the angel went out, and received them, and brought them in; and presently the wise ones, after the customary and becoming formalities of introduction, spoke with them, first concerning the beginnings and increase of wisdom, with which they intermixed various things concerning its progression, shewing, that with the angels wisdom never has an end or ceases to be, but that it grows and increases to eternity.

On hearing this, the angel of the company said to them, "Our prince at table spoke with them concerning the seat of wisdom, as being in use: will you also be pleased to speak with them on the same subject."

And they said, "Man, at his first creation, was imbued with wisdom and its love, not for the sake of himself, but that he might communicate it to others from himself. Hence it is inscribed on the wisdom of the wise, that no one is wise, or lives, for himself alone, but for others at the same time: this is the origin of society, which otherwise could not exist. Living for others consists in doing uses. Uses are the bonds of society, and these bonds are as many in number as there are good uses; and uses are infinite in number. There are spiritual uses, which belong to love to God and to love towards the neighbour, there are moral and civil uses, which belong to the love of the society and city in which a man is, and of his companions and fellow-citizens with whom he is; there are natural uses, which belong to the love of the world and its necessities; and there are corporeal uses, which belong to the love of self-
2 preservation for the sake of higher uses. All these uses are inscribed on man, and follow in order one after another; and when they are together, one is in the other. Those who are in the first uses, which are spiritual, are also in the following ones, and these persons are wise; but those who are not in the first, and yet are in the second, and thus in the following ones, are not so wise, but only appear to be so by virtue of external morality and civility. Those who are in neither the first nor the second, but only in the third and fourth, are not wise in the least, for they are satans, since they love only the world, and themselves for the sake of the world; but those who are only in the fourth, are the least wise of all, for they are devils, because they live for themselves alone, and if they live for others, it is
3 only for the sake of themselves. Moreover, every love has its own delight; for love lives by means of its delight: and the delight of the love of uses is a heavenly delight, which enters into the following delights in order, and according to the order of succession exalts them and makes them eternal." After this they enumerated the heavenly delights proceeding from the love of use, and they said, that there are myriads of myriads of them; and that those who enter heaven enter into those delights. With further wise conversation on the love of use, they passed the day with them until the evening.

19. Towards evening there came a courier clothed in linen, to the ten strangers, the companions of the angel, and invited them to a wedding which was to be celebrated the next day; and the strangers were very glad that they were also to see a wedding in heaven. After this they were conducted to the house of one of the privy-councillors, and supped with him; and after supper

they returned to the palace, and separated, each one to his own bedroom, and slept till morning.

And when they awoke in the morning, they heard the singing of the maidens and young girls from the houses around the public place, which singing was mentioned above. That morning there was sung the affection of conjugial love; the sweetness of which so affected and moved the hearers, that they perceived a blessed pleasantness instilled into their joys, which elevated and renewed them.

When it was time, the angel said, "Gird yourselves, and put on the garments of heaven, which our prince sent you." So they put them on, and lo! the garments shone as from a flaming light; and they asked the angel, "Whence is this?" He replied, "Because you are going to a wedding: on such occasions our garments shine, and become wedding garments."

20. After this the angel conducted them to the house of the wedding, and the door-keeper opened the doors; and presently within the threshold they were received and greeted by an angel sent by the bridegroom, and were brought in and led to the seats assigned to them: and soon after they were invited into a room adjoining the bridal-chamber, in the middle of which they saw a table on which was placed a magnificent candlestick fitted with seven branches and sconces of gold: against the walls there were hung lamps of silver, which being lighted made the atmosphere appear golden: and they saw at the sides of the candlestick two tables, on which were placed loaves in three rows; and in the four corners of the room there were tables, on which were crystal cups.

While they were surveying these things, lo! a door opened 2
from a chamber near the bridal-chamber, and they saw six maidens coming out, and after them the bridegroom and bride, holding each other by the hand, and leading each other towards a seat which was placed opposite to the candlestick: on this seat they placed themselves, the bridegroom on the left, and the bride on his right, and the six maidens stood at the side of the seat near the bride. The bridegroom was dressed in a cloak of bright crimson, and a vest of fine shining linen, with an ephod, on which there was a thin golden plate set all round with diamonds, and on the plate was engraved a young eagle, the wedding-badge of this heavenly society; and on his head he wore a mitre. The bride was dressed in a scarlet robe, under which was an embroidered gown that reached from her neck to her feet, and below her breast she wore a golden girdle, and on her head a crown of gold set with rubies.

When they were thus seated, the bridegroom turned himself 3
towards the bride, and placed a golden ring on her finger, and he produced bracelets and a necklace of pearls, and fastened the

bracelets on the wrists of her hands, and the necklace around her neck, and said, "Accept these pledges;" and when she accepted them, he kissed her, and said, "Now thou art mine," and he called her his wife.

When this was done, the guest cried out, "May there be a blessing!" This was first cried out by each one separately, and afterwards by all together. One who had been sent by the prince as his representative also joined in this cry; and at that instant the room adjoining the bridal-chamber was filled with an aromatic smoke, which was a sign of blessing from heaven.

Then the ministers took loaves from the two tables near the candlestick, and cups, now filled with wine, from the tables in the corners, and gave to each guest his own loaf and his own cup, and they ate and drank.

After this the husband and his wife rose up, and the six maidens followed with the silver lamps, now lighted, in their hands, as far as the threshold; and the married pair entered the bridal-chamber, and the door was shut.

21. Afterwards the angel conductor spoke with the guests about his ten companions, telling them that he had by command introduced them, and shewed them the magnificent things of the prince's palace, and the wonders there; and that they had dined at table with him, and afterwards had conversed with the wise ones of the society; and he requested that they might be allowed to enjoy some conversation with them also. So they approached, and conversed with them.

And a wise one of the men at the wedding said, "Do you understand the signification of what you have seen?"

They replied, that in some little degree they did; and then they asked him why the bridegroom, now a husband, had been dressed in that particular manner.

He answered, "That the bridegroom, now a husband, represented the Lord, and the bride, now a wife, represented the church, because weddings in heaven represent the marriage of the Lord with the church. Hence it is that he wore a mitre on his head, and was dressed in a cloak, a vest, and an ephod, like Aaron; and that the bride, now a wife, wore a crown on her head, and wore a robe like a queen; but to-morrow they will be dressed differently, because this representation lasts only to-day."

2 They asked further, "Since he represented the Lord, and she the church, why did she sit at his right hand?"

The wise one replied, "Because there are two things which constitute the marriage of the Lord and the church—love and wisdom; the Lord is love, and the church is wisdom; and wisdom is at the right hand of love. For the man of the church is wise as of himself, and in proportion as he is wise he receives love from the Lord. The right hand also signifies power; and love has power by means of wisdom: but, as was just now said, after the wedding the representation is changed; for then the husband represents wisdom, and the wife the love of his wisdom. This love, however, is not a primary love, but a secondary love, which the wife has from the Lord through the wisdom of the husband. The love of the Lord, which is the primary love, is the love of being wise with the husband; wherefore after the wedding, both together, the husband and his wife, represent the church."

They asked again, "Why did not you men stand beside the 3
bridegroom, now the husband, as the six virgins stood beside the bride, now the wife?"

The wise one answered, "Because to-day we are numbered among the virgins; and the number six signifies all and what is complete."

But they said, "What does this mean?"

He replied, "Virgins signify the church; and the church consists of both sexes: wherefore also we, as to the church, are virgins. That this is the case, is evident from these words in the Apocalypse: '*These are they who have not been polluted with women; for they are* VIRGINS; *and they follow the Lamb whithersoever he goeth*' (chap. xiv. 4). And because virgins signify the church, therefore the Lord *likened it to ten virgins invited to a wedding* (Matt. xxv. 1). And because by Israel, Zion, and Jerusalem is signified the church, therefore mention is so often made in the Word of the VIRGIN AND DAUGHTER OF ISRAEL, ZION, AND JERUSALEM. The Lord also describes His marriage with the church in these words in David: 'AT THY RIGHT HAND [DID STAND] THE QUEEN *in fine gold of Ophir: her garment is of brocades of gold: she shall be brought unto the king in* GARMENTS OF NEEDLEWORK: THE VIRGINS AFTER HER, *her friends, shall come into the king's palace*' (Psalm xlv. 9–16)."

Afterwards they said, "Is it not expedient that some priest 4
be present and minister at the wedding?"

The wise one answered, "This is expedient in the earths, but not in the heavens, on account of the representation of the Lord Himself and the church. On the earths they do not know this; but even with us a priest administers at betrothals, and hears, receives, confirms, and consecrates the consent. Consent is the essential of marriage; and all the things which follow are its formalities."

22. After this the angel conductor went to the six maidens, and gave them an account of his companions, and requested that they would favour them with their company. And they approached; but when they were near, they suddenly retired, and entered into the women's apartment, where also were the maidens their friends.

On seeing this, the angel conductor followed them, and asked why they had retired so suddenly without speaking with them; and they replied, "We could not approach." He said, "Why not?" and they answered, "We do not know; but we perceived something which repelled us and drove us back again: we hope they will excuse us."

The angel then returned to his companions, and told them of this answer, and added, "I conjecture that you do not possess the chaste love of the sex. In heaven we love maidens on account of their beauty and the elegance of their manners; and we love them very much, but chastely." On this his companions laughed, and said, "You conjecture aright: who can see such beauties near and not feel some desire?"

23. After this festive companionship, all those who had been invited to the wedding departed, and also those ten men with their angel: the evening was far advanced, and they went to bed.

At daybreak they heard a proclamation, "TO-DAY IS THE SABBATH"; and they arose and asked the angel what it meant. He replied, "It is for the worship of God, which returns at stated times, and is proclaimed by the priests. It is performed in our temples, and lasts about two hours; wherefore, if it please you, go with me, and I will take you there."

So they dressed themselves, and accompanied the angel, and entered the temple. It was a large temple, capable of containing about three thousand persons. It was of a semicircular form: the benches or seats were continuous, being carried round in a circular sweep according to the shape of the temple; and the back seats were raised higher than the front ones. The pulpit in front of the seats was drawn back a little from the centre; there was a door behind the pulpit, on the left.

The ten strangers entered with their angel conductor, and he pointed out to them the places where they were to sit, saying to them, "Every one who enters into the temple knows his own place; he knows it by virtue of what is innate; nor can he sit anywhere else: if he sits anywhere else, he hears nothing and perceives nothing, and he also disturbs order; and when order is disturbed, the priest is not inspired."

24. When the congregation had assembled, the priest ascended the pulpit, and preached a sermon full of the spirit of wisdom. The sermon was about the holiness of the Sacred Scripture, and the conjunction of the Lord with both worlds, the spiritual and the natural, by means thereof. In the illustration in which he was, he fully proved, that that holy Book was dictated by Jehovah the Lord, and that consequently He is in it, so far that He is the wisdom therein; but that the wisdom which is Himself therein, lies concealed under the sense of the

letter, and is opened only to those who are in the truths of doctrine, and at the same time in the goods of life, and thus who are in the Lord, and the Lord in them. To his sermon he added a devout prayer, and descended.

As the audience were going out, the angel requested the priest to speak a few words of peace with his ten companions; so he drew near to them, and they conversed together for half an hour; and he spoke about the Divine Trinity, that it is in Jesus Christ, in Whom all the fulness of the Divinity dwells bodily, according to the declaration of the Apostle Paul; and afterwards about the union of charity and faith; but he said the union of charity and truth (*veritas*), because faith is truth.

25. After expressing their thanks, they returned home; and there the angel said to them, "This is now the third day since your ascent into the society of this heaven, and you were prepared by the Lord to remain here three days; wherefore, it is time that we separate; put off, therefore, the garments sent you by the prince, and put on your own;" and when they were in their own garments, they were inspired with a desire to depart; so they departed, and descended, the angel accompanying them to the place of assembly; and there they gave thanks to the Lord for vouchsafing to bless them with knowledge, and thereby with intelligence, concerning heavenly joys and concerning eternal happiness.

26. * I again asseverate in truth, that these things were done and said as they are related; the former in the world of spirits which is intermediate between heaven and hell, and the latter in the society of heaven to which the angel of the trumpet, who acted as conductor, belonged. Who in the Christian world would have known anything about heaven, and the joys and happiness there, the knowledge of which is also the knowledge of salvation, unless it had pleased the Lord to open to some person the sight of his spirit, and to shew and teach [him]? That similar things exist in the spiritual world appears very manifestly from the things which were seen and heard by the Apostle John, and which are described in the Apocalypse; as, that he saw the Son of man in the midst of the seven candlesticks [chap. i. 12, 13]; also a tabernacle, temple, ark, and altar in heaven [xv. 5, 8; xi. 19; vi. 9; viii. 3; ix. 13]; a book sealed with seven seals; the book opened, and horses going forth thence [v. 1; vi. 1, 2, 4, 5, 8]; four animals around the throne [iv. 6]; twelve thousand chosen out of each tribe [vii. 4–8]; locusts ascending out of the abyss [ix. 3, 7]; the dragon, and his combat with Michael [xii. 7]; a woman bringing forth a male son, and fleeing

* This paragraph, in the original Latin edition, is enclosed in inverted commas. It is repeated, with slight variations, in the *True Christian Religion*, no. 851.

into the wilderness on account of the dragon [xii. 1, 2, 5, 6]; two beasts, one ascending out of the sea, the other out of the earth [xiii. 1, 11]; a woman sitting upon a scarlet beast [xvii. 3]; the dragon cast out into a pool of fire and brimstone [xx. 3, 10]; a white horse, and the great supper [xix. 11, 17]; a new heaven and a new earth, and the holy Jerusalem descending, described as to its gates, wall, and the foundations of the wall [xxi. 1, 2, 12, 14, 17–20]; also a river of the water of life, and trees of life bearing fruits every month [xxii. 1, 2]; besides many other things, all which were seen by John, while as to his spirit he was in the spiritual world and in heaven. Not to mention the things which were seen by the apostles after the Lord's resurrection; and the things which were afterwards seen by Peter (Acts xi.); also the things which were seen and heard by Paul. Besides the things which were seen and heard by the prophets; as by EZEKIEL, who saw four animals which were cherubs (chapter i. and chapter x.); a new temple and a new earth, and an angel measuring them (chapters xl.–xlviii.); and was led away to Jerusalem, and there saw abominations; and also into Chaldea into captivity (chapter viii. and chapter xi.). The case was similar with ZECHARIAH, who saw a man riding among the myrtle trees (chapter i. 8 and following verses); also four horns; and afterwards a man with a measuring-line in his hand (chapter ii. 5 [1] and following verses); likewise a candlestick and two olive-trees (chapter iv. 2, and following verses); also a flying roll, and an ephah (chapter v. 1, 6); also four chariots going forth between two mountains, and horses (chapter vi. 1 and following verses). So likewise with DANIEL, who saw four beasts ascending out of the sea (chapter vii. 1 and following verses); also combats of a ram and a goat (chapter viii. 1 and following verses); who also saw the angel Gabriel, and spoke much with him (chapter ix.). The youth of Elisha saw chariots and horses of fire round about Elisha; and he saw them when his eyes were opened (2 Kings vi. 17). From these and many other instances in the Word, it is evident, that the things which exist in the spiritual world appeared to many both before and after the Lord's coming; what wonder, then, is it, that the same things should now also be seen when the church is commencing, or when the New Jerusalem is coming down from the Lord out of heaven?

MARRIAGES IN HEAVEN.

27. THAT there are marriages in the heavens, cannot enter into the faith of those who believe that a man after death is a soul or spirit, and who conceive of a soul or spirit as of a thin ether or breath of air: who believe also, that a man will not live as a man till after the day of the last judgment; and, in general, of those who know nothing about the spiritual world, in which angels and spirits are, consequently in which the heavens and hells are: and because that world has been heretofore unknown, and it has been altogether unknown that the angels of heaven are men in perfect form, and in like manner the spirits of hell, but in imperfect form, therefore it was impossible for anything to be revealed concerning marriages in that world; for they would have said, "How can a soul be conjoined with a soul, or a breath of air with a breath of air, as one married partner with another on earth?" besides many other things, which, the instant they were said, would take away and dispel all faith concerning marriages in the other world. But now, since many things have been revealed concerning that world, and its quality has also been described in the Work on *Heaven and Hell*, and also in the *Apocalypse Revealed*, the fact that marriages take place there, can be confirmed, even before the reason, by the following propositions:—

I. *Man lives a man after death.*

II. *The male then is a male, and the female a female.*

III. *Every one's own love remains with him after death.*

IV. *The love of the sex, especially, remains; and with those who come into heaven, as those do who become spiritual on earth, conjugial love remains.*

V. *These things fully confirmed by personal observation.*

VI. *Consequently there are marriages in the heavens.*

VII. *Spiritual weddings are meant by the Lord's words, that after the resurrection they are not given in marriage.*

Now follows an explanation of these propositions in their order.

28. I. MAN LIVES A MAN AFTER DEATH. That man lives a man after death, has been heretofore unknown in the world, for the reasons mentioned just now; and, what is surprising, it has been unknown even in the Christian world, where there is the Word, and enlightenment thence concerning eternal life,

and where the Lord Himself teaches, "*that all the dead rise again; and that God is not the God of the dead but of the living*" (Matt. xxii. 31, 32; Luke xx. 37, 38). Moreover, man, as to the affections and thoughts of his mind, is in the midst of angels and spirits, and he is so consociated with them, that he cannot be separated from them without dying. It is still more surprising that this is unknown, when yet every man that has died since the first creation, after death has come and still comes to his own, or, as it is said in the Word, has been gathered and is gathered to his own. Besides, man has a common perception, which is the same thing as the influx of heaven into the interiors of his mind, by virtue of which he inwardly in himself perceives truths, and as it were sees them, and especially this truth, that he lives a man after death, a happy man if he has lived well, and an unhappy one if he has lived ill. For who does not think this, when he elevates his mind a little above the body, and above the thought which is nearest to its senses; as is the case when he is more interiorly in Divine worship, and when he lies on his death-bed waiting for the end; in like manner when he hears of those who are deceased, and about their lot? I have related thousands of particulars about the departed, as in what sort of lot were the brethren, married partners, and friends of certain persons. I have also written concerning the lot of the English, the Dutch, the Papists, the Jews, the Gentiles, and likewise concerning the lot of Luther, Calvin, and Melancthon; and hitherto I have never heard any one say, "How can such be their lot, when they are not yet risen out of their graves, for the last judgment has not yet taken place? Are they not in the meantime souls which are breaths of air, and which reside in some indefinite place?" Such things I have never yet heard said by anyone; and from this circumstance I have been able to conclude, that every one perceives in himself that he lives a man after death. What man (*vir*) who has loved his married partner and his children, will not say to himself, when they are dying or are dead (if his thought be elevated above the sensuals of the body) that they are in the hand of God, and that he shall see them again after his own death, and again be conjoined with them in a life of love and joy?

29. Who cannot see from reason, if he be willing to see, that man after death is not a breath of air, of which there is no other idea than as of a puff of wind, or as of air and ether, and that it constitutes or contains the soul of the man, which desires and waits for conjunction with its own body, in order that it may enjoy the senses, and their delights, as before in the world? Who cannot see, that if this were the case with man after death, his state would be more contemptible than that of the fishes, birds, and animals of the earth, whose souls do not live, and consequently

are not in such anxiety by reason of desire and expectation? If man after death were such a breath of air, and thus a puff of wind, he would either float about in the universe, or, according to the traditions of some, would be reserved in some indefinite place, or in the *limbo* of the Fathers, until the last judgment. Who cannot from reason conclude thence, that those who have lived since the first creation, which is computed to have been six thousand years ago, must be still in a similar anxious state, and progressively more anxious, because all expectation from desire produces anxiety, and from time to time increases it; consequently that they must still be either floating about in the universe, or be kept confined in some indefinite place, and thus in extreme misery; and that the case must be similar with Adam and his wife, with Abraham, Isaac, and Jacob, and with all who have lived since that time? Hence it follows, that nothing would be more deplorable than to be born a man. But on the contrary, it has been provided by the Lord, Who is Jehovah from eternity, and the Creator of the universe, that the state of the man who conjoins himself with Him by means of a life according to His precepts, becomes more blessed and happy after death than before it in the world; and that it is more blessed and happy from this circumstance, that the man then is spiritual, and a spiritual man feels and perceives spiritual delight, which is super-eminent in comparison with natural delight, because it exceeds the latter a thousand times.

30. That angels and spirits are men, may be manifest from those seen by Abraham, Gideon, Daniel, and the prophets, and especially by John when he wrote the Apocalypse, and also by the women in the Lord's sepulchre; yea, from the Lord Himself being seen by the disciples after His resurrection. The reason of their being seen was, that the eyes of the spirit of those who saw them were opened at the time; and when the eyes of the spirit are opened, angels appear in their own form, which is the human form; but when the eyes of the spirit are closed, that is, when they are veiled by the sight of the eyes [of the body], which derive from the material world all that pertains to them, then they do not appear.

31. It must, however, be known, that a man after death is not a natural, but a spiritual man; and that, nevertheless, he still appears in all respects like what he was before; so like, indeed, that he knows no otherwise than that he is still in the natural world: for he has a similar body, a similar face, similar speech, and similar senses; because he has a similar affection and thought, or a similar will and understanding. He is indeed actually not similar, because he is a spiritual, and consequently an interior man; but the difference does not appear to him,

because he cannot compare his state with his previous natural state, for he has put off the latter, and is in the former; wherefore, I have often heard such persons say, that they know no otherwise than that they are in the former world, with only this difference, that they no longer see those whom they have left in that world; but that they see those who have departed out of that world, or have died. The reason why they now see the latter and not the former, is, that they are not natural, but spiritual or substantial men; and a spiritual or substantial man sees a spiritual or substantial man, as a natural or material man sees a natural or material man, but not contrariwise, on account of the difference between what is substantial and what is material, which is like the difference between what is prior and what is posterior; and what is prior, because in itself it is purer, cannot appear to what is posterior, which in itself is grosser; nor can what is posterior, because it is grosser, appear to what is prior, which in itself is purer; consequently an angel cannot appear to a man of this world, nor a man of this world to an angel. The reason why a man after death is a spiritual or substantial man, is, that this spiritual or substantial man lay concealed inwardly in the natural or material man; this natural or material man was to it as a covering, or as a skin about to be cast off; and when the covering or skin is cast off, the man comes forth spiritual or substantial, and thus purer, more interior, and more perfect. That the spiritual man is still a perfect man, although he does not appear to the natural man, was plainly evidenced from the Lord's appearing to the apostles after His resurrection, in that He appeared, and presently did not appear; and yet He was a man like to Himself both when seen and when not seen: they also said that, when they saw Him, their eyes were opened.

32. II. THE MALE THEN IS A MALE, AND THE FEMALE A FEMALE. Since a man lives a man after death, and man is male and female, and there is such a distinction between the masculine and the feminine that the one cannot be changed into the other, it follows, that after death the male lives a male, and the female a female, both being a spiritual man. It is said that the masculine cannot be changed into the feminine, nor the feminine into the masculine, and that therefore after death the male is a male, and the female a female. But because it is not known in what the masculine essentially consists, and in what the feminine, therefore it shall here be stated in a few words. The difference consists essentially in this, that the inmost in the male is love, and its covering is wisdom; or, what is the same thing, the male is love covered or veiled by wisdom; and that the inmost in the female is that wisdom of the male, and its covering is love thence derived; but this love is feminine love, and it is given by the

Lord to the wife through the wisdom of the husband; whereas the former love is masculine love, and is the love of growing wise, and it is given by the Lord to the husband according to the reception of wisdom. Hence it is that the male is the wisdom of love, and the female, the love of that wisdom; wherefore from creation there has been implanted in both the love of conjunction into a one; but of these things more will be said in the following pages. That the feminine is from the masculine, or that the woman was taken out of the man (*vir*) is manifest from these words in Genesis: "*Jehovah God took one of the ribs of the man* (vir), *and closed up the flesh in the place thereof; and He built the rib, which He had taken out of the man* (homo), *into a woman; and He brought her to the man; and the man said, This is bone of my bones, and flesh of my flesh; hence she shall be called Ishshah* (woman), *because she was taken out of the man* (vir, *Hebrew* Ish) (chap. ii. 21–23): the signification of a rib, and of flesh, will be stated elsewhere.

33. From this primitive formation it follows, that the male is born intellectual, and that the female is born voluntary; or, what is the same thing, that the male is born into the affection of knowing, understanding, and growing wise, and that the female is born into the love of conjoining herself with that affection in the male. And because the interiors form the exteriors to their own likeness, and the masculine form is the form of intellect, and the feminine form is the form of the love of that intellect, therefore the male and the female differ as to the features of the face, the tone of the voice, and the form of the body; the male having harder features, a harsher tone of voice, and a stronger body, and also a bearded chin, and in general a form less beautiful than that of the female; they differ also in their gestures and manners; in a word, there is nothing alike; but still there is conjunctiveness in every particular; yea, the masculine in the male is masculine in every part of his body, even the smallest part, and also in every idea of his thought, and in every spark of his affection; so, likewise, the feminine in the female; and since thus the one cannot be changed into the other, it follows, that after death the male is a male, and the female a female.

34. III. Every one's own love remains with him after death. Man knows that love is, but he does not know what love is. He knows that love is, from common conversation, as from its being said: such a one loves me, a king loves his subjects, and the subjects love the king; a husband loves his wife, and a mother her children, and conversely; also, such or such a person loves his country, his fellow-citizens, his neighbour; in like manner of things abstractedly from person, as when it is said, that a person loves this or that thing. But although love

is so universal in conversation, scarcely any one knows what love is. While meditating on the subject, as he is not then able to form any idea of thought concerning it, and thus to convey it into the light of the understanding, because it is a matter not of light but of heat, he either says that it is not anything, or else that it is merely something that flows in from sight, hearing, and conversation, and thus moves [the spirit]. He is altogether ignorant that love is his very life, not only the general life of his whole body, and the general life of all his thoughts, but also the life of all their particulars. A wise man can perceive this from queries like these: if you remove the affection of love, can you think anything, and can you do anything? Do not thought, speech, and action grow cold in proportion as the affection which belongs to the love grows cold? And do they not grow warm in proportion as the affection which belongs to the love grows warm? Love therefore is the heat of man's life, or his vital heat. The heat of the blood, and also its redness, are from no other source. The fire of the angelic sun, which is pure love, effects this.

35. That every one has his own love, or a love distinct from the love of another; that is, that no two men have exactly the same love, may be manifest from the infinite variety of faces: the faces are the types of the loves; for it is known that the faces are changed and varied according to the affections of love; a man's desires also, which belong to his love, and likewise his joys and sorrows, shine forth thence. From this consideration it is evident, that a man is his own love; yea, that he is the form of his own love. It must, however, be known, that the interior man, which is the same as his spirit which lives after death, is the form of his own love, but not so the exterior man in the world, because the latter has learnt from childhood to conceal the desires of his love, yea, to make a pretence and show of desires which are different from his own.

36. The reason why every one's own love remains with him after death, is, that, as was said just above, no. 34, love is the life of man; and hence it is the man himself. A man also is his own thought, thus his own intelligence and wisdom; but these make a one with his love. For a man thinks, yea, if he be in freedom, speaks and acts, from his love, and according to it; whence it may be seen, that love is the Esse or essence of a man's life, and that thought is the existere or existence of his life thence derived; wherefore, speech and action, which flow from the thought, do not flow from the thought, but from the love through the thought. From much experience it has been given me to know, that a man after death is not his own thought, but that he is his own affection and consequent thought; or, that he

is his own love and consequent intelligence; also that a man after death puts off everything which does not agree with his love; yea, that he successively puts on the face, the tone of voice, the speech, the gestures, and the manners of the love of his life. Hence it is, that the universal heaven is arranged in order according to all the varieties of the affections of the love of good, and the universal hell according to all the affections of the love of evil.

37. IV. THE LOVE OF THE SEX, ESPECIALLY, REMAINS; AND WITH THOSE WHO COME INTO HEAVEN, WHO ARE THOSE WHO BECOME SPIRITUAL ON EARTH, CONJUGIAL LOVE REMAINS. The reason why the love of the sex remains with man after death, is, that the male then is a male and the female a female; and the masculine in the male is masculine in the whole and in every part thereof; and in like manner the feminine in the female; and there is a conjunctiveness in all their singulars, yea, even their veriest singulars. Now, since this conjunctiveness was implanted by creation, and hence is perpetually within, it follows, that the one desires and breathes conjunction with the other. Love, considered in itself, is nothing else than a desire and a consequent effort for conjunction; and conjugial love for conjunction into a one. For the male human being and the female human being have been so created, that out of two they may become as it were one human being, or one flesh; and when they become one, then, taken together, they are a human being in his fulness; but without such conjunction, they are two, and each of them is like a divided or half a human being. Now, since this conjunctiveness lies inmostly latent in every singular of the male, and in every singular of the female, and the faculty and desire for conjunction into a one is in every singular, it follows, that the mutual and reciprocal love of the sex remains with human beings after death.

38. It is said, the love of the sex and conjugial love, because the love of the sex is different from conjugial love. The love of the sex is with the natural man, but conjugial love with the spiritual man. The natural man loves and desires only external conjunctions, and the pleasures of the body arising therefrom; whereas the spiritual man loves and desires an internal conjunction, and the blissfulnesses of the spirit arising thence, and these blissfulnesses he perceives are possible with one wife, with whom he can be perpetually more and more conjoined into a one: and the more he is thus conjoined, the more he perceives his blissfulnesses ascending in a like degree, and enduring to eternity. But the natural man does not think so. Hence then it is that it is said, that after death conjugial love remains with those who come into heaven, who are those who become spiritual on earth.

39. V. THESE THINGS FULLY CONFIRMED BY PERSONAL OBSERVATION. That man lives a man after death, and that the male then is a male, and the female a female; and that every one's own love remains with him, and especially the love of the sex and conjugial love, are positions which I have thus far endeavoured to confirm by such things as belong to the understanding, and are called rational things. But, since man from his childhood has obtained from his parents and masters, and afterwards from the learned and the clergy, the belief that he will not live a man after death till after the day of the last judgment, in the expectation whereof they have now been for six thousand years; and since many have alleged that this is one of the articles of faith which ought to be embraced in faith and not by the understanding, it was necessary that the above positions should be confirmed also by the proofs of personal observation; otherwise, a man who believes only the senses, would say, from the faith previously impressed on him:—"If men lived men after death, I should see and hear them: who has ever descended out of heaven, or ascended out of hell, and related such things?" But, whereas it never was possible, nor can it ever be possible, for any angel of heaven to descend, or for any spirit of hell to ascend, and speak with any man, except with those who have the interiors of the mind, which are the interiors of the spirit, opened by the Lord; and this opening of the interiors cannot be fully effected except with those who have been prepared by the Lord to receive the things which belong to spiritual wisdom,—therefore it has pleased the Lord thus to prepare me, so that the state of heaven and hell, and the state of the life of men after death, might not remain unknown, and be laid asleep in ignorance, and at length buried in denial. Nevertheless, the proofs of personal experience on the subjects above mentioned, cannot, by reason of their abundance, be adduced here; but they have been already adduced in the Work on *Heaven and Hell,* and afterwards in the *Continuation concerning the Spiritual World,* and lastly in the *Apocalypse Revealed;* and especially in the Memorable Relations which follow after the paragraphs or chapters of the present Work.

40. VI. CONSEQUENTLY THERE ARE MARRIAGES IN HEAVEN. Since these positions have been confirmed by reason, and at the same time by experience, they need no further demonstration.

41. VII. SPIRITUAL WEDDINGS ARE MEANT BY THE LORD'S WORDS, THAT AFTER THE RESURRECTION THEY ARE NOT GIVEN IN MARRIAGE. In the Evangelists the following words are read: "*Certain of the Sadducees, who deny the resurrection, asked Jesus, saying, Master, Moses wrote, If any one's brother die, having a*

wife, and he be childless, his brother shall take his wife, and raise up seed unto his brother. There were seven brethren, of whom one after the other took the wife; but they died childless; last of all the woman died also; in the resurrection therefore whose wife shall she be of the seven? But Jesus answering, said unto them, The sons of this age marry and are given in marriage; but those who shall be held worthy to attain to another age and the resurrection from the dead, shall neither marry nor be given in marriage, for they can die no more; for they are like unto the angels, and are sons of God, being sons of the resurrection. But that the dead rise again, Moses also shewed at the bramble-bush, when he called the Lord the God of Abraham, and the God of Isaac, and the God of Jacob; for He is not the God of the dead, but of the living; for all live unto Him" (Luke xx. 27–38; Matt. xxii. 22–31 [23–32]; Mark xii. 18–27). There are two things which the Lord taught by these words: first, that man rises again after death; and secondly, that in heaven they are not given in marriage. That man rises again after death, He taught by these words, "that God is not the God of the dead, but of the living, and that Abraham, Isaac, and Jacob are alive": and further in the parable concerning the rich man in hell, and Lazarus in heaven (Luke xvi. 22–31).
Secondly, that in heaven they are not given in marriage, He 2
taught by these words, "that those who shall be held worthy to attain to another age, neither marry nor are given in marriage." That none other than spiritual weddings are here meant, appears manifestly from the words which immediately follow, "that they can no more die; because they are like unto the angels, and are sons of God, being sons of the resurrection." By spiritual weddings is meant conjunction with the Lord, and this is effected on earth; and when it is effected on earth, it is also effected in the heavens; wherefore in the heavens they are not married again, nor again given in marriage: this is also meant by these words, "The sons of this age marry and are given in marriage; but those who are held worthy to attain to another age neither marry nor are given in marriage." These are also called by the Lord, "sons of the wedding" (Matt. ix. 15; Mark ii. 19); and in this passage, "angels," "sons of God," and "sons of the
resurrection." That making a wedding denotes being conjoined 3
with the Lord, and that entering into a wedding denotes being received into heaven by the Lord, is manifest from the following passages:—"*The kingdom of the heavens is like unto a man, a king, who made a wedding for his son, and sent out servants and invited to the wedding*" (Matt. xxii. 2–14). "*The kingdom of the heavens is like unto ten virgins, who went forth to meet the bridegroom; of whom five being prepared entered in unto the wedding*" (Matt. xxv. 1 and following verses). That the Lord here meant Himself, is evident from verse 13 of that chapter, where it is said, "*Watch ye; because ye know not the day and the hour in*

which the Son of man will come:" also from the Apocalypse: "*The time of the wedding of the Lamb is come, and His wife hath made herself ready: blessed are those who are called to the wedding supper of the Lamb*" (xix. 7, 9). That there is a spiritual meaning in each and all things that the Lord spoke, has been fully shewn in the *Doctrine of the New Jerusalem concerning the Sacred Scripture,* published at Amsterdam in the year 1763.

42. To the above I shall add two Memorable Relations out of the spiritual world. The first is as follows:—

One morning I looked up into heaven, and I saw above me expanse above expanse; and I saw that the first expanse, which was the nearest, opened, and then the second, which was above it, and lastly the third, which was the highest; and, from enlightenment thence, I perceived, that upon the first expanse were the angels of whom the first or ultimate heaven consists; upon the second expanse were the angels of whom the second or middle heaven consists; and upon the third expanse were the angels of whom the third or highest heaven consists.

I wondered at first what this meant, and why it happened: and presently there was heard out of heaven a voice as of a trumpet saying, "We have perceived, and now see, that you have been meditating on CONJUGIAL LOVE; and we know that as yet no one on earth knows what truly conjugial love is in its origin and in its essence; and yet it is of importance that it should be known: wherefore it has pleased the Lord to open the heavens to you, in order that enlightening light and perception thence may flow in into the interiors of your mind. With us in the heavens, especially in the third heaven, our heavenly delights are principally from conjugial love; wherefore, in consequence of leave having been given us, we will send down to you a married pair, in order that you may see."

2 And lo! there then appeared a chariot descending out of the highest or third heaven, in which there appeared one angel; but as it approached, there appeared therein two. The chariot at a distance glittered before my eyes like a diamond, and to it were harnessed young horses white as snow; and they who sat in the chariot held in their hands two turtle-doves; and they called out to me, "Do you wish us to come nearer to you? but in that case take heed, lest the coruscation (*coruscum*) which flashes out of the heaven whence we have descended, and is flaming, penetrate interiorly; by its influx the higher ideas of your understanding, which in themselves are heavenly, are indeed enlightened; but these ideas are inexpressible in the world in which you dwell: wherefore receive rationally what you are about to hear, and explain it rationally to the understanding."

I replied, "I will take heed; come nearer."

And they came nearer; and lo! it was a husband and his

wife; and they said, "We are married partners: we have lived happy in heaven from the first age, which by you is called the golden age, and we have lived perpetually in the same flower of age in which you see us to-day."

I observed them both attentively, because I perceived that they 3
represented conjugial love in its life and in its attire; in its life in their faces, and in its attire in their garments; for all angels are affections of love in human form. The ruling affection itself shines forth out of their faces; and garments are allotted to them, from the affection, and according to it: wherefore it is said in heaven, that every one is invested with his own affection. The husband appeared of age intermediate between youth and young manhood: from his eyes darted forth sparkling light by reason of the wisdom of love, from which light his face was as it were inmostly radiant; and in consequence of the radiance the surface of his skin as it were shone: hence his whole face was one resplendent beauty (*decor*). He was dressed in a garment reaching down to his feet, and underneath it was a garment of a purple colour, girt about with a golden girdle, upon which were three precious stones, two sapphires at the sides, and a fiery stone in the middle: his stockings were of shining linen, with threads of silver interwoven, and his shoes were all of silk. This was the representative form of conjugial love with the
husband. But with the wife it was as follows:—her face was 4
seen by me, and it was not seen; it was seen as beauty itself, and it was not seen because this beauty was inexpressible; for in her face there was a splendour of flaming light, such as the angels in the third heaven have, and this light dimmed my sight; wherefore I was simply lost in astonishment.

Observing this, she spoke to me, saying, "What do you see?"

I replied, "I see nothing but conjugial love and the form thereof; but I see, and I do not see."

Hereupon she turned herself sideways from her husband; and then I was able to observe her more attentively. Her eyes sparkled from the light of her own heaven, which light, as was said, is flammeous, and therefore is derived from the love of wisdom; for the wives in that heaven love their husbands from their wisdom and in their wisdom, and the husbands love their wives from that love and in that love towards themselves: and thus they are united. This was the origin of her beauty, which was such that it would be impossible for any painter to imitate and exhibit it in its form, for there is no such lustre in his colours; nor is such beauty expressible in his art. Her hair was arranged in beautiful order according to its correspondence with her beauty; and in it were inserted flowers of diadems; she had a necklace of fiery stones, from which hung a rosary of chrysolites; and she had bracelets of pearls. She was arrayed in a scarlet robe, and underneath it she had a crimson stomacher, fastened in front with clasps of rubies; but what surprised me was, that the colours varied according to her aspect towards her husband, and according thereto sparkled sometimes more and sometimes less; in mutual aspect, [or face to face,] more, and in sideways aspect, less.

5 When I had seen these particulars, they again spoke with me; and when the husband was speaking, he spoke at the same time as from his wife; and when the wife was speaking, she spoke at the same time as from her husband; for such was the union of their minds from whence their speech flowed: and then also I heard the tone of voice of conjugial love, that inwardly it was simultaneous, and also that it proceeded from the delights of a state of peace and innocence.

At length they said, "We are recalled; we must depart." And then they again appeared to be conveyed in a chariot as before. They were conveyed by a paved way between flower-beds, from the beds of which arose olive-trees, and trees full of oranges: and when they were near their own heaven, maidens came to meet them, and received them and led them in.

43. After this an angel appeared to me out of that heaven, holding in his hand a parchment, which he unrolled, saying, "I saw that you were meditating about conjugial love. In this parchment there are arcana of wisdom concerning that love, which have never yet been disclosed in the world. They must now be disclosed, because it is of importance that they should be. Those arcana abound more in our heaven than in the rest, because we are in the marriage of love and wisdom; but I foretell that no others will appropriate that love to themselves but those who are received by the Lord into the New Church, which is the New Jerusalem." Having said this, the angel let down the unrolled parchment, which a certain angelic spirit took, and laid on a table in a certain chamber, which he instantly locked, and held out the key to me, and said, "Write."

44. The second Memorable Relation:—

I once saw three novitiate spirits from the world, who were wandering about, examining everything, and asking questions about it. They were in wonderment on finding that men lived altogether as before, and that they saw similar things as they had seen before; for they knew that they had departed out of the former or natural world, and that in that world they had believed that they should not live as men until after the day of the last judgment, when they should again be clothed with the flesh and bones that had been laid in their graves; wherefore, in order that they might be freed from all doubt that they were really and truly men, they by turns viewed and touched themselves and others, and felt objects, and by a thousand proofs convinced themselves that they were now men as in the former world; besides which they saw each other in a brighter light, and objects in a greater brilliance, and thus more perfectly.

Just then, two angelic spirits happened to meet them, and 2
stopped them, saying, "Whence are you?"

They replied, "We have departed out of a world, and again we live in a world; thus we have migrated from a world into a world; this surprises us."

Then the three novitiates questioned the two angelic spirits concerning heaven; and as two of the three novitiates were youths, and from their eyes there flashed forth as it were a fiery ardour of lust for the sex, the angelic spirit said, "Possibly you have seen some women;" and they replied, "We have." And as they made inquiry about heaven, the angelic spirits made the following statement: "In heaven there are all kinds of magnificent and splendid things, and such things as the eye had never seen; there are also maidens and young men; maidens of such beauty that they may be called beauties in beauty's own form, and young men of such morality that they may be called moralities in morality's own form; and the beauties of the maidens and the moralities of the young men correspond to each other, as forms mutually related to and fitted for each other."

And the two novitiates asked, "Are there in heaven human forms exactly similar to those which are in the natural world?"

And answer was made, "They are exactly similar; nothing is taken away out of the man (*vir*), and nothing out of the woman; in a word, the man (*vir*) is a male, and the woman a woman, in all the perfection of form in which they were created: retire, if you like, and examine yourself, whether anything is wanting to make you less a man (*vir*) than before."

Again, the novitiates said, "We have heard in the world from 3
which we have departed, that in heaven they are not given in marriage, because they are angels: does the love of the sex, therefore, not exist there?"

And the angelic spirits replied, "Your love of the sex does not exist in heaven; but the angelic love of the sex, which is chaste, and devoid of all allurement from lust."

To this the novitiates said, "If there exists a love of the sex devoid of all allurement, what in that case is the love of the sex?" And while they were thinking about this love, they sighed, and said, "Oh, how dry is the joy of heaven! What young man, if this be the case, can possibly wish for heaven? Is not such a love barren and devoid of life?"

To this the angelic spirits replied, smiling, "The angelic love of the sex, or such a love of the sex as exists in heaven, is nevertheless full of inmost delights: it is a most pleasant expansion of all things of the mind, and consequently of all things of the breast, and inwardly in the breast, it is as if the heart sported with the

lungs, from which sport proceeds a respiration, a tone of voice, and a speech which cause the social gatherings among the sexes, or among young men and maidens, to be heavenly sweetnesses
4 themselves, which are pure. All novitiates, on ascending into heaven, are explored as to the quality of their chastity, for they are let into the company of maidens, the beauties of heaven, who perceive, from their tone of voice, their speech, their face, their eyes, their gesture, and their exhaling sphere, of what quality they are as to the love of the sex; if their love be unchaste, they flee away from them, and tell their companions that they have seen satyrs or priapuses. The new comers also undergo a change, and before the eyes of the angels appear rough and hairy, and with feet like those of calves or leopards, and presently they are cast down, lest by their lust they should pollute the heavenly aura."

5 On hearing this, the two novitiates again said, "So there is no love of the sex in heaven; what is the chaste love of the sex but a love emptied of the essence of its life? And thus, does not the intercourse of young men and maidens in heaven consist of dry joys? We are not stocks and stones, but perceptions and affections of life."

On hearing this the two angelic spirits indignantly replied, "You are utterly ignorant what the chaste love of the sex is, because as yet you are not chaste. That love is the very delight itself of the mind, and hence of the heart, and not at the same time of the flesh beneath the heart. Angelic chastity, which is common to both sexes, prevents the passing of that love beyond the enclosure of the heart; but within that enclosure, and above it, the morality of a young man is delighted with the beauty of a maiden in the delights of the chaste love of the sex; which delights are too interior, and too abundant in pleasantness, to be described in words. The angels have this love of the sex, because they have conjugial love only; and this love cannot exist together with the unchaste love of the sex. Truly conjugial love is chaste love, and has nothing in common with unchaste love: it is restricted to one only of the sex, and removed from all others; for it is a love of the spirit and thence of the body, and not a love of the body and thence of the spirit; that is, it is not a love which infests the spirit."

6 On hearing this, the two novitiate youths rejoiced, and said, "There still exists in heaven the love of the sex; what else is conjugial love?"

But to this the angelic spirits replied, "Think more deeply, weigh the matter well, and you will perceive, that your love of the sex is an extra-conjugial love, and that conjugial love is altogether different; and that the latter is as distinct from the former, as wheat is from chaff, or rather as the human is from the bestial. If you were to ask the women in heaven, 'What is

extra-conjugial love?' I asseverate that they would reply, 'What
is this? What are you talking about? How can you utter such
an expression which so wounds our ears? How can a love not
created be generated in man?' If you were then to ask them,
'What is truly conjugial love?' I know they would reply, 'It
is not the love of the sex, but the love of one of the sex; and
it comes into existence no otherwise than when a young man
sees a maiden provided by the Lord, and a maiden a young man,
and both feel what is conjugial being kindled in their hearts,
and perceive, he that she is his, and she that he is hers, for love
meets love, and causes them to know each other, and instantly
conjoins their souls, and afterwards their minds, and thence
enters their bosoms, and after the wedding penetrates further,
and thus becomes a full love, which grows every day into conjunction, till they are no longer two, but as it were one.' I 7
know also that they would swear that they do not know any
other love of the sex; for they say, 'How can the love of the
sex exist, unless it be so mutual and reciprocal as to breathe
after an eternal union, which consists in two being one flesh?'"
To this the angelic spirits added, "In heaven they are utterly
ignorant what whoredom is; nor do they know that it exists, or
that its existence is possible. The angels grow cold all over the
body at unchaste or extra-conjugial love; and, on the other hand,
they grow warm all over the body from chaste or conjugial love.
With the men (*viri*) there, all the nerves are unstrung at the sight
of a whore, and recover their tension at the sight of a wife."

The three novitiates, on hearing this, asked, "Is there a 8
similar love between married partners in the heavens as in the
earths?"

And the two angelic spirits replied, that it was exactly
similar. And as they perceived that the novitiates wished to
know whether in heaven there were similar ultimate delights,
they said, that they were exactly similar, but much more blessed,
because angelic perception and sensation are much more exquisite
than human perception and sensation: "and what," added they,
"is the life of that love unless [derived] from the vein of potency?
When this vein fails, does not that love fail and grow cold?
Is not this virtue the very measure, degree, and basis of that
love? Is it not its beginning, its support, and its fulfilment?
It is a universal law, that primary things exist, subsist, and
persist, from ultimate things; this applies also to that love;
wherefore, unless there were ultimate delights, there would be no
delights of conjugial love at all." 9

The novitiates then asked, whether offspring were born from
the ultimate delights of that love in heaven; and if not, of what
use were those delights?

The angelic spirits replied, that no natural offspring were
born, but spiritual offspring.

And the novitiates asked, "What are spiritual offspring?"

They replied, "Two married partners by means of the ultimate delights are more united in the marriage of good and truth, and the marriage of good and truth is the marriage of love and wisdom; and love and wisdom are the offspring which are born of that marriage; and since in heaven the husband is wisdom, and the wife is the love thereof, and both are spiritual, therefore no other than spiritual offspring can be conceived and begotten there. Hence it is that the angels, after the delights, do not become sad, as some do on earth, but cheerful; and this they have from a continual influx of fresh powers (*vires*) succeeding the former ones, which renovate, and at the same time enlighten: for all who come into heaven, return into their vernal youth, and into the powers (*vires*) of that age, and remain so to eternity."

10 The three novitiates, on hearing this, said, "Is it not read in the Word, that in heaven they are not given in marriage, because they are angels?"

To this the angelic spirits replied, "Look up into heaven, and an answer will be given you."

And they asked why they should look up into heaven.

The angelic spirits said, "Because thence we have all interpretations of the Word. The Word is inwardly spiritual, and the angels, because they are spiritual, will teach the spiritual understanding of it."

After a little while the heaven over their heads was opened, and two angels came within sight of them, and said, "There are weddings in the heavens, as on earth; but for no others in the heavens than those who are in the marriage of good and truth; nor are any others angels; wherefore, it is spiritual weddings, which are of the marriage of good and truth, that are meant in the Word. These spiritual weddings take place on earth, but not after death, thus not in the heavens; as it is said of the five foolish virgins, who were also invited to the wedding, that they could not enter, because they did not possess the marriage of good and truth; for they had no oil, but only lamps. By oil is meant good, and by lamps truth; and being given in marriage denotes entering into heaven, where the marriage of good and truth is."

The three novitiates were made glad on hearing this, and being filled with a desire of heaven, and with the hope of wedding there, they said, "We will diligently practise morality and virtue (*decor*) of life, that we may obtain what we wish for."

THE STATE OF MARRIED PARTNERS AFTER DEATH.

45. THAT there are marriages in the heavens, has been shewn just above; it remains now to be shewn, whether the marriage-covenant which has been contracted in the world will remain and be in force after death, or not. As this is a matter not of judgment but of experience, and as experience has been given me by consociation with angels and spirits, it must be adduced by me; but yet in such a manner that reason also may assent thereto. It is also among the wishes and desires of married persons to know this; for men (*viri*) who have loved their wives, and likewise wives who have loved their husbands, wish to know whether (if they are dead) it be well with them, and whether they shall ever meet again. Many married pairs also wish to know beforehand whether they will be separated after death, or whether they will live together: those who disagree in their dispositions wish to know whether they will be separated; and those who agree, whether they will live together. Since these answers are wished for, they shall be given, and in the following order:—

I. *The love of the sex remains with every man* (homo) *after death, such as it had been interiorly, that is, such as it had been in his interior will and thought in the world.*

II. *Conjugial love likewise remains.*

III. *The two married partners most generally meet after death, recognize each other, again consociate, and for some time live together: this takes place in the first state, thus while they are in externals as in the world.*

IV. *But successively, as they put off their externals, and enter into their internals, they perceive what had been the quality of their love and inclination for each other mutually, and consequently whether they can live together, or not.*

V. *If they can live together, they remain married partners; but if they cannot, they separate; sometimes the husband* (vir) *from the wife, sometimes the wife from the husband, and sometimes both mutually from each other.*

VI. *Then there is given to the man a suitable wife, and to the woman likewise a suitable husband.*

VII. *Married partners enjoy similar intercourse with each other as in the world, but more delightful and blessed; yet without prolification, for which, or in place of which, they have spiritual prolification, which is that of love and wisdom.*

VIII. *This takes place with those who come into heaven; but it is otherwise with those who go into hell.*

Now follows the explanation, by which these articles are illustrated and confirmed.

46. I. THE LOVE OF THE SEX REMAINS WITH EVERY MAN AFTER DEATH, SUCH AS IT HAD BEEN INTERIORLY, THAT IS, SUCH AS IT HAD BEEN IN HIS INTERIOR WILL AND THOUGHT IN THE WORLD. Every love follows man after death, because it is the esse of his life; and the ruling love, which is the head of all the others, remains with man to eternity, and together with it the subordinate loves. The reason why they remain, is, that love belongs properly to the spirit of man, and to the body from the spirit; and a man after death becomes a spirit, and so carries his love with him; and, as love is the esse of man's life, it is evident, that such as a man's life has been in the world, such does his lot become after death. As regards the love of the sex, it is the universal of all loves, for it has been implanted from creation in the very soul of man, from which the essence of the whole man is, and this for the sake of the propagation of the human race. The reason why this love especially remains, is, that after death a man (*vir*) is a man, and a woman a woman; and that there is nothing in the soul, in the mind, and in the body, which is not masculine in the male, and feminine in the female; and these two have been so created, that they have a powerful striving for conjunction, yea, for conjunction so as to become a one. This effort or striving is the love of the sex, which precedes conjugial love. Now, since the conjunctive inclination is inscribed on each and all things of the male and of the female, it follows, that this inclination cannot be obliterated, or die, with the body.

47. The reason why the love of the sex remains such as it had been interiorly in the world, is, that with every man there is an Internal and an External, which are also called the internal and external man; and hence there is an internal and an external will and thought. A man, when he dies, leaves his External behind, and retains his Internal; for externals, strictly speaking, belong to his body, and internals, strictly speaking, belong to his spirit. Now, since a man is his own love, and love resides in his spirit, it follows, that the love of the sex remains with him after death, such as it had been interiorly with him; as for example, if that love interiorly had been conjugial or chaste, it remains conjugial and chaste after death; but if it had been interiorly scortatory, it remains such also after death. But it ought to be known, that the love of the sex is not the same with one person as with another; its differences are infinite: nevertheless, such as it is in the spirit of any one, such also it remains.

48. II. CONJUGIAL LOVE LIKEWISE REMAINS, SUCH AS IT HAD BEEN INTERIORLY; THAT IS, SUCH AS IT HAD BEEN IN THE MAN'S INTERIOR WILL AND THOUGHT IN THE WORLD. Since the love of the sex is one thing, and conjugial love another, therefore a distinct name is given to each, and it is said, that the latter also remains after death such as it has been with a man, while he lived in the world, in his internal man. But as few know the difference between the love of the sex and conjugial love, therefore, on the threshold of this Treatise, I will preface something about it. The love of the sex is a love towards several, and with several of the sex; but conjugial love is only towards one, and with one of the sex. Love towards several and with several is a natural love; for it is common [to man] with beasts and birds, which are natural. But conjugial love is a spiritual love, and it is peculiar and proper to men, because men were created, and therefore are born, in order that they may become spiritual; wherefore, in the proportion in which a man becomes spiritual, he puts off the love of the sex, and puts on conjugial love. In the beginning of marriage the love of the sex appears as if conjoined with conjugial love; but in the progress of marriage they are separated; and then, with those who are spiritual, the love of the sex is exterminated, and conjugial love is insinuated; but with those who are natural, the contrary takes place. From what has now been said, it is evident, that the love of the sex, because it is a love with several, and in itself natural, yea, animal, is impure and unchaste, and, because it is roving and unlimited, it is scortatory: but that conjugial love is altogether otherwise. That conjugial love is spiritual, and, strictly speaking, human, will manifestly appear from what follows.

47 [b]. III. THE TWO MARRIED PARTNERS MOST GENERALLY MEET AFTER DEATH, RECOGNIZE EACH OTHER, CONSOCIATE, AND FOR A TIME LIVE TOGETHER: THIS TAKES PLACE IN THE FIRST STATE, THUS WHILE THEY ARE IN EXTERNALS AS IN THE WORLD. There are two states into which man enters after death, an external and an internal state. He comes first into his external state, and afterwards into the internal; and while in the external state, married partners, if they have both died, meet each other, recognize each other, and if they have lived together in the world, consociate again, and for some time live together; and when they are in this state, they do not know the inclination of each to the other, because this conceals itself in the internals. But afterwards, when they come into their internal state, the inclination manifests itself; if it is concordant and sympathetic, they continue their conjugial life; but if it is discordant and antipathetic, they dissolve their conjugial life. If a man has had several wives, he conjoins himself with them successively, while he is in the external state; but when he enters the

internal state, in which he perceives the inclinations of his love, as to their quality, he then either adopts one, or leaves them all; for in the spiritual world, as well as in the natural, it is not allowable for any Christian to marry several wives, because this infests and profanes religion. The case is the same with a woman who has had several husbands: nevertheless the women do not adjoin themselves to their husbands; they only present themselves, and the husbands adjoin them to themselves. Be it known, that husbands rarely recognize their wives, but that wives well recognize their husbands: the reason is, that women have an interior perception of love, and men (*viri*) only an exterior perception.

48 [b]. IV. BUT SUCCESSIVELY, AS THEY PUT OFF THEIR EXTERNALS, AND ENTER INTO THEIR INTERNALS, THEY PERCEIVE WHAT HAD BEEN THE QUALITY OF THEIR LOVE AND INCLINATION FOR EACH OTHER MUTUALLY, AND CONSEQUENTLY WHETHER THEY CAN LIVE TOGETHER, OR NOT. There is no need to explain this further, because it follows from what was explained in the preceding article; here it shall merely be shewn how a man after death puts off his externals and puts on his internals. Every one after death is first introduced into the world which is called the world of spirits, and which is intermediate between heaven and hell; and in that world he is prepared, the good man for heaven, and
2 the evil man for hell. This preparation has for its end, that the Internal and External may agree together and make a one, and not disagree and make two: in the natural world they make two, and only make a one with those who are sincere at heart. That they make two is manifest from the deceitful and the cunning; especially from hypocrites, flatterers, dissemblers, and liars. But in the spiritual world it is not allowable thus to have a divided mind, but he who has been evil in internals must also be evil in externals; likewise, he who has been good in internals must be
3 good in externals. For every man after death becomes such as he had been interiorly, and not such as he had been exteriorly. For the sake of this end, he is let alternately into his External and his Internal: and every man, while he is in his External, is wise, that is, he wishes to seem wise, even if he be an evil man; but an evil man is insane in his Internal. By those changes he is able to see his insanities, and to repent of them: but if he had not repented in the world, he cannot afterwards; for he loves his insanities, and wishes to remain in them: wherefore he forces his External also to be insane likewise; thus his Internal and his External become a one; and when this is effected, he is prepared
4 for hell. But it is otherwise with a good man: such a one, because in the world he had looked unto God and had repented, was more wise in his Internal than in his External: in his External also, through the allurements and vanities of the

world, he had sometimes raved; wherefore his External is likewise reduced to agreement with his Internal, which, as was said, is wise; when this is effected, he is prepared for heaven. From these considerations it plainly appears, how the putting off the External, and the putting on the Internal, after death, is effected.

49. V. IF THEY CAN LIVE TOGETHER, THEY REMAIN MARRIED PARTNERS; BUT IF THEY CANNOT, THEY SEPARATE, SOMETIMES THE HUSBAND (*vir*) FROM THE WIFE, SOMETIMES THE WIFE FROM THE HUSBAND, AND SOMETIMES BOTH FROM EACH OTHER. The reason why separations take place after death is, that the conjunctions which are made on earth are seldom made from any internal perception of love, but from an external perception, which hides the internal. The external perception of love derives its cause and origin from such things as belong to the love of the world and of the body. Wealth and possessions especially are objects of worldly love, and dignities and honours are objects of the love of the body: and besides these things, there are also various allurements that entice, such as beauty and a counterfeit grace of manners, and sometimes even unchastity. Besides, matrimonies are contracted within the district, city, or village, in which the parties were born, or where they live, and even there the choice is confined and limited to the families that are known, and, among these, to such as are of a corresponding condition of life. Hence it is, that marriages contracted in the world are for the most part external, and not at the same time internal; when yet it is the internal conjunction, which is the conjunction of souls, which constitutes marriage itself; and this conjunction is not perceptible until man puts off the External and puts on the Internal, which takes place after death. Hence now it is that separations take place then, and afterwards new conjunctions with similar and homogeneous partners; unless these conjunctions have been provided on earth, as takes place with those who from early manhood have loved, wished for, and asked of the Lord a lawful and loving companionship with one woman, and who spurn and detest wandering lusts.

50. VI. THEN THERE IS GIVEN TO THE MAN A SUITABLE WIFE, AND TO THE WOMAN LIKEWISE A SUITABLE HUSBAND. The reason is, that no other married partners can be received into heaven, so as to remain there, than those who are interiorly united, or are capable of being united as into a one. For in heaven two married partners are not called two, but one angel; this is meant by the Lord's words, "that they are no longer two, but one flesh." The reason why no other married partners are received into heaven is, that no others can dwell together in heaven, that is, be together in one house, and in one bedchamber and bed; for

all who are in the heavens are consociated according to affinities and relationships of love, and have habitations according to these. For in the spiritual world there are not spaces, but there are appearances of spaces; and these appearances are according to the state of life of those who are there, and states of life are according to states of love. Wherefore, in that world no one can dwell but in his own house, which is provided for him and assigned to him according to the quality of his love: if he dwells in any other, he is distressed in his breast and breathing; and it is not possible for two to dwell together in the same house unless they are likenesses; and married partners are absolutely unable to do so unless they are mutual inclinations; if they are external inclinations, and not at the same time internal, the very house or place itself separates, rejects, and expels them. This is the reason why, for those who after preparation are introduced into heaven, there is provided a marriage with a consort whose soul inclines to union with the soul of the other, so that they no longer wish to be two lives, but one life. This is the reason why after separation there is given to the man a suitable wife, and to the woman likewise a suitable husband.

51. VII. Married partners enjoy similar intercourse with each other as in the world, but more delightful and blessed; yet without prolification, for which, or in place of which, they have spiritual prolification, which is that of love and wisdom. The reason why married partners enjoy similar intercourse as in the world, is, that after death the male is a male, and the female a female, and there has been implanted in both from creation an inclination to conjunction; and this inclination with man belongs to his spirit and thence to his body; wherefore after death, when man becomes a spirit, the same mutual inclination remains, and this cannot exist without similar intercourse. For after death man is a man as before; neither is there anything wanting either in the male or in the female: as to the form they are like themselves, and also as to the affections and thoughts; what else, then, follows thence, but that they must enjoy similar intercourse? and also that, since conjugial love is chaste, pure, and holy, this intercourse must be full? but on this subject see the several particulars in the Memorable Relation, in no. 44. The reason why the intercourse then is more delightful and blessed, is, that when conjugial love becomes of the spirit, it becomes more interior and pure, and consequently more perceptible; and every delightsomeness grows according to the perception, and grows even until its blessedness is discernible in its delightsomeness.

52 The reason why marriages in the heavens are without prolification, and that instead thereof there is spiritual prolifi-

cation, which is that of love and wisdom, is, that with those who are in the spiritual world, the third [degree], which is the Natural, is wanting; and it is this which is the containant of spiritual things; and spiritual things without their containant have no consistence, like the things which are procreated in the natural world. Moreover, spiritual things, considered in themselves, have relation to love and wisdom; wherefore love and wisdom are the things which are born of marriages in the heavens. It is said that love and wisdom are born, because conjugial love perfects an angel, for it unites him with his consort; whence he becomes more and more a human being; for, as was said above, two married partners in heaven are not two, but one angel. Wherefore, by means of the conjugial unition they become filled with the Human, which consists in willing to become wise, and in loving that which belongs to wisdom.

53. VIII. This takes place with those who come into heaven; but it is otherwise with those who go to hell. The statements that after death a suitable wife is given to the man (*vir*), and a suitable husband to the wife, and that they enjoy delightful and blessed intercourse, but without any other prolification than spiritual prolification, must be understood of those who are received into heaven and become angels; the reason is, that these are spiritual, and marriages in themselves are spiritual, and hence holy. But those who go to hell are all natural; and merely natural marriages are not marriages, but conjunctions which originate in unchaste lust. The quality of these conjunctions will be stated in the following pages, where the chaste and the unchaste [principles] are treated of, and further where scortatory love is treated of.

54. To what has been above related concerning the state of married partners after death, the following statements must be added. I. That all those married partners who are merely natural, are separated after death; the reason is, that with them the love of marriage is cold, and the love of adultery is warm. Nevertheless after separation they sometimes consociate as married partners with others; but after a short time they withdraw from each other: and this in many cases is done repeatedly; and at length the man is made over to some whore, and the woman to some adulterer, which is effected in an infernal prison (which is treated of in the *Apocalypse Revealed*, no. 153 § 10), where promiscuous whoredom is forbidden to both of
them under a penalty. II. Married partners, of whom one is 2
spiritual and the other natural, are also separated after death; and to the spiritual one is given a suitable partner; but the natural one is consigned to places of lasciviousness among his or
her like. III. But they who in the world have lived unmarried, 3

and have altogether alienated their mind from marriage, if they are spiritual, remain unmarried; but if they are natural, they become whoremongers. It is otherwise with those who in their celibacy have desired marriage, and especially with those who have solicited it without success; for these, if they are spiritual, blessed marriages are provided, but not until they
4 are in heaven. IV. They who in the world have been shut up in monasteries, both virgins and men, at the conclusion of the monastic life, which continues some space of time after death, are set free and discharged, and obtain the wished-for liberty of their desires, whether they are desirous of living in a married state or not: if they are desirous of living in a married state, this is granted them; but if not, they are conveyed to the unmarried at the side of heaven; but those who have burned
5 with forbidden lust, are cast down. V. The reason why the unmarried are at the side of heaven, is, that the sphere of perpetual celibacy infests the sphere of conjugial love, which is the very sphere of heaven; and the reason why the sphere of conjugial love is the very sphere of heaven, is, that it descends from the heavenly marriage of the Lord and the church.

55. To the above I shall add two Memorable Relations. The first is this:

On a certain time there was heard out of heaven a very sweet tune: there were there wives with virgins, who were singing a song. The sweetness of their singing was like the affection of some love flowing forth harmoniously. Heavenly songs are nothing else than sonorous affections, or affections expressed and modified by sounds; for as thoughts are expressed by speech, so affections are expressed by song: from the symmetry and fluency of the melody or modulation, the angels perceive the subject of the affection.

On this occasion there were many spirits about me; and some of them informed me that they heard this very sweet tune, and that it was the tune of some loving affection, the subject of which they did not know: they therefore made various conjectures about it, but in vain. Some conjectured that the singing expressed the affection of a bridegroom and bride when they are betrothing themselves, some that it expressed the affection of a bridegroom and bride when they are going to their wedding; and some that it expressed the primitive love of a husband and wife.

2 But at that moment there appeared in the midst of them an angel out of heaven, and he said, that they were singing the chaste love of the sex.

Hereupon the bystanders asked, "What is the chaste love of the sex?"

And the angel said, "It is the love of a man (*vir*) towards a maiden or wife who is beautiful in form and graceful in manners, free from any idea of lasciviousness, and the same love experienced by a maiden or wife towards a man." Having said this the angel vanished.

The song continued; and as the bystanders then knew the subject of the affection which it expressed, they heard it with much variety, each one according to the state of his love. Those who looked upon women chastely, heard that song as a symphonious and sweet song; those who looked upon women unchastely, heard it as a disharmonious and melancholy song; and those who looked upon women with loathing, heard it as a discordant and hoarse song.

At that moment the area on which they were standing was 3
suddenly changed into a lecture-hall, and a voice was heard, saying, "DISCUSS THIS LOVE."

And suddenly there were present spirits from various societies, and in the midst of them some angels in white. The latter then spoke and said, "We in this spiritual world have inquired into every species of love, not only into the love of a man (*vir*) towards a man, and of a woman towards a woman; and into the reciprocal love of husband and wife; but also into the love of a man (*vir*) towards women, and of a woman towards men; and it has been granted us to pass through societies and explore them, and we have never yet found the general love of the sex chaste, except with those who from truly conjugial love are in continual potency, and these are in the highest heavens. It has also been granted us to perceive the influx of this love into the affections of our hearts, and we have experienced that in sweetness it exceeds every other love, except the love of two married partners whose hearts are a one: but we ask you to discuss this love, because to you it is new and unknown; and since it is pleasantness itself, it is called, by us in heaven, heavenly sweetness."

When, therefore, they discussed it, those spoke first who were 4
unable to think of chastity in relation to marriages, and they said, "Who, when he beholds a beautiful and lovely maiden or wife, can so chastise and purify the ideas of his thought from concupiscence, as to love the beauty and yet have no desire to take a taste of it, if he is allowed to? Who can convert the concupiscence which is innate in every man, into such chastity, thus into what is not itself, and yet love? Can the love of the sex, when it enters from the eyes into the thoughts, stop short at the face of a woman? Does it not instantly descend into the breast, and beyond? The angels spoke unmeaning words when they said, that this love exists chaste, and yet is the sweetest of all loves, and that it can only exist with husbands who are in truly conjugial love, and thence in supereminent potency with their wives. Are those husbands more able than other men, when

they see beautiful women, to keep the ideas of their thought on high, and as it were to suspend them, so that they shall not descend and proceed to that which constitutes that love?"

5 Afterwards those spoke who were both in cold and in heat; in cold towards their wives, and in heat towards the sex; and they said, "What is the chaste love of the sex? Is not the love of the sex a contradiction in terms when chastity is added to it? What is the contradiction involved in the added term, except that the subject is deprived of its predicate, and then is not anything? How can the chaste love of the sex be the sweetest of all loves, when chastity deprives it of its sweetness? You all know where the sweetness of that love resides; when therefore the idea of conjunction [which is usually associated] with that love, is banished, where and whence then is the sweetness?"

Then some others took up the word, and said, "We have been with the most beautiful women and have felt no desire; wherefore we know what the chaste love of the sex is."

But their companions, who were acquainted with their lasciviousnesses, replied, "You were then in a state of loathing towards the sex, by reason of impotence; and this is not the chaste love of the sex, but the ultimate of unchaste love."

6 On hearing what had been said, the angels were indignant, and
requested those who stood on the right, or to the south, to speak.
These said, "There is the love of a man (*vir*) and a man, and also
of a woman and a woman; and there is the love of a man for a
woman, and of a woman for a man; and these three pairs of loves
totally differ from each other. The love of a man and a man is
as the love of understanding and understanding; for the man
was created, and consequently is born, to become understanding:
the love of a woman and a woman is as the love of affection and
affection of the understanding of men; for the woman was
created and is born to become the love of the understanding of
a man. These loves, namely, of a man and a man, and of a
woman and a woman, do not enter deeply into the breasts, but
stand without and only touch each other: thus they do not interiorly
conjoin the two: wherefore also two men, by their
antagonistic reasonings, combat together like two wrestlers; and
two women, by their antagonistic concupiscences, deal blows at
7 each other like two pugilists. But the love of a man and a woman
is the love of the understanding and its affection; and this love
enters deeply and conjoins, and this conjunction is that love.
But the conjunction of minds, and not at the same time of bodies,
or the effort towards that conjunction alone, is spiritual love, and
consequently chaste love; and this love exists only with those
who are in truly conjugial love, and thence in eminent potency,
because these, on account of their chastity, do not admit the
influx of love from the body of any other woman than their own
wife; and as they are in supereminent potency, they cannot do

otherwise than love the sex, and at the same time hold unchastity in aversion. Hence they have the chaste love of the sex, which, considered in itself, is interior spiritual friendship, which derives its sweetness from eminent but still chaste potency. They possess eminent potency in consequence of a total renunciation of whoredom: and as the wife alone is loved, the potency is chaste. Now, since that love with those does not partake of the flesh, but only of the spirit, it is chaste; and as the beauty of a woman, from innate inclination, at the same time enters into the mind, that love is sweet."

On hearing this, many of the bystanders put their hands to 8
their ears, saying, "Those statements offend our ears: and what you have spoken is of no account to us." These bystanders were unchaste.

Then again was heard that song out of heaven, and sweeter now than before; but to those unchaste ones it sounded so discordant that, because of the grating of the discord, they rushed out of the lecture-hall and fled, leaving behind them the few who from wisdom loved conjugial chastity.

56. The second Memorable Relation:—

Once when I was speaking with angels in the spiritual world, I was inspired with a pleasant desire to see the TEMPLE OF WISDOM, which I had seen once before; and I asked them the way to it. They said, "Follow the light, and you will find it."

I said, "What do you mean by following the light?"

They said, "Our light grows brighter and brighter as we draw near to that temple; wherefore, follow the light according to the increase of its brightness; for our light proceeds from the Lord as a sun, and hence considered in itself it is wisdom."

I then, in company with two angels, directed my course according to the increase of the brightness of the light, and ascended by a steep path to the summit of a hill which was in the southern quarter. There was a magnificent gate there, and the keeper, on seeing the angels with me, opened it; and lo! there was seen an avenue of palm-trees and laurels, according to which we directed our course. It was a winding avenue, and terminated in a garden, in the midst of which was the TEMPLE OF WISDOM.

On arriving there I looked about me, and I saw several smaller buildings, just like the temple, in which were the wise. We drew near to one of them, and in the doorway we spoke to the person who dwelt there, and told him the occasion of our coming, and the manner of our approach: and he said, "You are welcome; enter and sit down, and let us discourse together about wisdom."

I saw the little building within, that it was divided into two, 2
and yet was one: it was divided into two by a transparent wall;

but it appeared as one by reason of its transparence, which was like that of the purest crystal. I inquired why it was so.

He said, "I am not alone; my wife is with me, and we are two; but yet we are not two, but one flesh."

But I said, "I know that you are a wise one; and what has a wise one or a wisdom to do with a woman?"

At this our host, from a certain indignation, changed countenance, and beckoned with his hand, and lo! instantly other wise ones came out of the neighbouring buildings, to whom he said jocosely, "Our stranger here asked this question, 'What has a wise one or a wisdom to do with a woman?'"

At this they all smiled and said, "What is a wise one or a wisdom without a woman, or without love? A wife is the love of a wise man's wisdom."

3 But our host said, "Let us now discourse together about wisdom; let the conversation be about causes, and at present about the cause of the beauty of the feminine sex."

Then they spoke in order; and the first assigned as the cause, that women were created by the Lord affections of the wisdom of the men (*viri*), and the affection of wisdom is beauty itself.

The second assigned as the cause, that woman was created by the Lord through the wisdom of the man, because from the man; and that hence she is a form of wisdom inspired with the affection of love; and as the affection of love is life itself, the female is the life of wisdom, and the male is wisdom; and the life of wisdom is beauty itself.

The third assigned as the cause, that to women there has been given a perception of the delights of conjugial love: and as their whole body is an organ of that perception, it cannot be otherwise than that the habitation of the delights of conjugial love with its perception, should be beauty.

4 The fourth assigned as the cause, that the Lord has taken away beauty and elegance of life from the man, and transcribed it into the woman; and that hence the man without reunion with his beauty and elegance in the woman, is grim, austere, dry, and unlovable, and is not wise except for himself alone, and such a one is foolish: but when a man is united with his beauty and elegance of life in a wife, he becomes agreeable, pleasant, lively, and lovable, and thereby wise.

The fifth assigned as the cause, that women were created beauties, not for the sake of themselves, but for the sake of the men; in order that the men, who of themselves are hard, might be softened; that their minds (*animi*), of themselves harsh, might become gentle; and that their hearts, of themselves cold, might become warm; which effects take place when they become one flesh with their wives.

5 The sixth assigned as the cause, that the universe was created by the Lord a most perfect work: and that nothing was created

in it more perfect than a woman beautiful in face and graceful in manners, for this reason, that man might render thanks to the Lord for this bounty, and repay it by the reception of wisdom from Him.

After these and many other similar things had been said, the wife [of our host] appeared on the other side of the crystal wall, and said to her husband, "Speak, if it please you;" and when he spoke, the life of wisdom from the wife was perceived in his discourse; for in the tone of his speech was the love of her: thus experience testified to the Truth.

After this we went over the temple of wisdom, and also the paradisiacal places around it, and being thereby filled with joy we departed, and passed through the avenue to the gate, and descended by the way we had ascended.

TRULY CONJUGIAL LOVE.

57. Conjugial love is of infinite variety; it does not exist exactly the same in any two persons. It appears indeed as if it were the same with many; but it so appears before the judgment of the body, and as this judgment is gross and obtuse, man has but little discernment from it in such matters. By the judgment of the body is meant the judgment of the mind from the external senses. But to those who see from the judgment of the spirit, the differences are apparent; and more distinctly to those who are able to elevate the sight of this judgment higher, which is effected by withdrawing it from the senses, and exalting it into a higher light; these can at length confirm themselves in understanding, and thus see, that conjugial love does not exist the same in any two persons. Nevertheless no one can see the infinite varieties of this love in any light even of the elevated understanding, unless he first knows what is the quality of that love in its very essence and integrity, thus what was its quality when, together with life from God, it was imparted to man. Unless this its state, which was most perfect, be known, it is in vain to attempt to discover its differences by any investigation: for there is no fixed point, from which as a beginning, those differences may be deduced, and to which as their focus they may be referred, and thus may appear in a true, and not in a fallacious light. This is the reason why we here proceed to describe that love in its genuine essence; and as it was in this essence when, together with life from God, it was infused into man, we proceed to describe it as to its quality in its primeval state; and as in this state it was truly conjugial, therefore this section is entitled, TRULY CONJUGIAL LOVE. This description of it shall be made in the following order:—

I. *There exists a truly conjugial love, which at the present day is so rare that it is not known what its quality is, and scarcely that it exists.*

II. *The origin of that love is from the marriage of good and truth.*

III. *There is a correspondence of that love with the marriage of the Lord and the church.*

IV. *That love, on account of its origin and on account of its correspondence, is celestial, spiritual, holy, pure, and clean, above every other love which from the Lord is with the angels of heaven and with the men of the church.*

V. *It is also the fundamental love of all celestial and spiritual loves, and hence of all natural loves.*

VI. *And into that love are collected all joys and all delights from primes to ultimates, or from first to last.*

VII. *But none others come into that love, and are able to be in it, but those who approach the Lord, and love the truths of the church, and do its goods.*

VIII. *This love was the love of loves with the Ancients, who lived in the golden, silver, and copper ages; but afterwards it successively departed.*

The explanation of these articles now follows.

58. I. THERE EXISTS A TRULY CONJUGIAL LOVE WHICH AT THE PRESENT DAY IS SO RARE THAT IT IS NOT KNOWN WHAT ITS QUALITY IS, AND SCARCELY THAT IT EXISTS. That there exists such a conjugial love as is described in the following pages, may indeed be acknowledged from the first state of that love, when it insinuates itself and enters into the hearts of a bachelor and a maiden; thus from its first state with those who begin to love one alone of the sex, and to desire that one as a bride; and still more [from its state] during the time of betrothal, while it lasts, and as it progresses toward the wedding; and lastly on the wedding-day and the first few days after. At such times, who does not acknowledge and consent to the following statements:—that that love is the fundamental of all loves, and also that into it are collected all joys and delights from first to last? And who does not know that, after this pleasant time, those gladnesses successively pass away and depart, till at length they are scarcely felt? In this case, if it be said as before, that that love is the fundamental of all loves, and that into it are collected all joys and gladnesses, these statements are neither agreed to nor acknowledged, and possibly it is said that they are nonsense or transcendental mysteries. From these considerations it is evident, that the primitive love of marriage emulates truly conjugial love, and presents it to view in a certain image. The reason of this is, that then the love of the sex, which is unchaste, is cast away, and in place of it, the love of one of the sex, which is truly conjugial love, and chaste, remains implanted. Who does not then regard other women with a look of indifference, and his only one with a look of love?

59. The reason why truly conjugial love is, nevertheless, so rare that its quality is not known, and scarcely its existence, is, that the state of pleasantnesses before the wedding is afterwards changed into a state of indifference, owing to an insensibility to those pleasantnesses. The causes of this change of state are too numerous to be here adduced; but they shall be adduced in a future part of this Work, where the causes of colds, separations,

and divorces, will be disclosed in their order; from which it will be seen, that with most people at the present day that image of conjugial love is so far abolished, and with the image the Knowledge thereof, that it is not known what its quality is, and scarcely that it exists. It is known, that every man, when he is born, is merely corporeal, and that from corporeal he becomes more and more interiorly natural, and thus rational, and at length spiritual. The reason why he thus progressively advances is, that the Corporeal is like ground, into which natural, rational, and spiritual things are implanted in their order; thus a man
2 becomes more and more a man. The case is nearly similar when he enters upon marriage: a man then becomes a fuller man, because he is conjoined with a consort, with whom he acts as one man: but this is effected in a certain image, in the first state spoken of above. At that time, likewise, he commences from the Corporeal, and proceeds to the Natural, but as to conjugial life, and thus as to conjunction into a one. Those who then love corporeal natural things, and rational things only from them, cannot be conjoined with a consort as into a one, except as to those externals: and when those externals fail, cold invades the internals and disperses the delights of that love, as from the mind so from the body, and afterwards as from the body so from the mind: and this until there is left nothing of the remembrance of the primeval state of their marriage, consequently no Knowledge concerning it. Now since this takes place with most people at the present day, it is evident that it is not known what is the quality of truly conjugial love, and that it is scarcely known that such a love exists. The case is different with those who are spiritual. With these the first state is an initiation into perpetual blissfulnesses, which are heightened in proportion as the Spiritual Rational of the mind, and from thence the Natural Sensual of the body, in each party, become conjoined and united with the same in the other party. But these cases are rare.

60. II. THE ORIGIN OF THAT LOVE IS FROM THE MARRIAGE OF GOOD AND TRUTH. That all things in the universe have relation to good and truth, is acknowledged by every intelligent man, because it is a universal truth. That likewise in each and all things of the universe good is conjoined with truth, and truth with good, cannot but be acknowledged, because this also is a universal truth, which coheres with the former truth. The reason why all things in the universe have relation to good and truth, and why good is conjoined with truth, and truth with good, is, that both proceed from the Lord, and they proceed from Him as a one. The two things which proceed from the Lord are love and wisdom, because these are Himself, thus from Himself; and all things which are of love are called goods, and all things

which are of wisdom are called truths; and as those two proceed from Him as the Creator, it follows that they are in the created things. This may be illustrated by the heat and light which proceeds from the sun. From these are all things of the Earth, for they germinate according to the presence of heat and light, and according to their conjunction; and moreover, natural heat corresponds to spiritual heat, which is love; and natural light corresponds to spiritual light, which is wisdom.

61. That conjugial love proceeds from the marriage of good and truth, will be demonstrated in the following section or paragraph: the fact is mentioned here only in order that it may be seen that that love is celestial, spiritual, and holy, because it is from a celestial, spiritual, and holy origin. In order that it may be seen that the origin of conjugial love is from the marriage of good and truth, it is of importance that the matter should here be stated in a short summary. It was said just above, that in all created things, in general and particular, there is a conjunction of good and truth; and conjunction does not exist unless it be reciprocal; for conjunction from the one part, and not from the other in return, is dissolved of itself. Now, since there is a conjunction of good and truth, and, indeed, a reciprocal conjunction, it follows that there is a truth of good, or a truth from good, and that there is a good of truth, or a good from truth. That the truth of good, or the truth from good, is in the male, and that it is the very masculine principle, and that the good of truth, or good from truth, is in the female, and that it is the very feminine principle; also that between these two there is a conjugial union, will be seen in the following section; it is here only mentioned in order to give some preliminary idea on the subject.

62. III. THERE IS A CORRESPONDENCE OF THAT LOVE WITH THE MARRIAGE OF THE LORD AND THE CHURCH; that is, as the Lord loves the church, and desires that the church should love Him, so husband and wife mutually love one another. That there is a correspondence between these two cases, is known in the Christian world; but the quality of that correspondence is not as yet known; wherefore that correspondence shall be explained in one of the following paragraphs.* It is here mentioned in order that it may be seen that conjugial love is celestial, spiritual, and holy, because it corresponds to the celestial, spiritual, and holy marriage of the Lord and the church. This correspondence also follows from the origin of conjugial love from the marriage of good and truth (which was treated of in the preceding article), because the marriage of good and truth is the church with man: for the marriage of good and truth is the

* See nos. 116–131.

same as the marriage of charity and faith, because good belongs to charity, and truth to faith. That this marriage constitutes the church, cannot but be acknowledged, because it is a universal truth; and every universal truth is acknowledged as soon as it is heard, which [immediate acknowledgment] comes from the Lord's influx, and at the same time from the confirmation of heaven. Now, since the church is the Lord's, because it is from the Lord, and since conjugial love corresponds to the marriage of the Lord and the church, it follows that that love is from the Lord.

63. But in what manner the church is formed by the Lord with the two married partners, and, through the church, conjugial love, shall be illustrated in the paragraph spoken of above: at present it shall merely be stated, that the church is formed by the Lord with the man (*vir*) and through the man with the wife; and that after it has been formed with both, the church is a full church; for then there is effected a full conjunction of good and truth; and the conjunction of good and truth is the church. That the conjunctive inclination, which is conjugial love, is in the same degree as the conjunction of good and truth, which is the church, will be confirmed by demonstrative arguments in what follows in the series.

64. IV. THAT LOVE, ON ACCOUNT OF ITS ORIGIN, AND ON ACCOUNT OF ITS CORRESPONDENCE, IS CELESTIAL, SPIRITUAL, HOLY, PURE, AND CLEAN, ABOVE EVERY OTHER LOVE WHICH IS FROM THE LORD WITH THE ANGELS OF HEAVEN AND WITH THE MEN OF THE CHURCH. That conjugial love, from its origin, which is the marriage of good and truth, is such, was confirmed above by a few arguments, but the subject was merely touched upon there: it was likewise briefly confirmed above, that that love is such on account of its correspondence with the marriage of the Lord and the church. These two marriages, from which conjugial love descends as an offshoot, are essentially holy; wherefore if it be received from its Author, who is the Lord, holiness from Him follows, which continually decants and purifies it: if there be then in the man's will a desire and effort towards it, that love becomes perpetually cleaner and purer from day to day. Conjugial love is called celestial and spiritual, because it is with the angels of heaven; celestial, with the angels of the highest heaven, because those angels are called celestial angels; and spiritual, with the angels beneath that heaven, because these angels are called spiritual angels. Those angels are so called, because the celestial are loves and hence wisdoms, and the spiritual are wisdoms and hence loves. Their conjugial [quality] is similar. Now, since conjugial love s with the angels of both the higher and the lower heavens, as was also shewn in the first

paragraph concerning "Marriages in Heaven," it is manifest that it is holy and pure. The reason why that love, considered in its essence and from its derivation, is holy and pure above every other love with angels and with men, is, that it is as the head of the other loves. Concerning this its eminence, something shall be said in the following article.

65. V. IT IS ALSO THE FUNDAMENTAL LOVE OF ALL CELESTIAL AND SPIRITUAL LOVES, AND HENCE OF ALL NATURAL LOVES. The reason why conjugial love, considered in its essence, is the fundamental love of all the loves of heaven and the church, is, that its origin is from the marriage of good and truth, and from this marriage proceed all the loves which constitute heaven and the church with man. The good of this marriage constitutes love, and its truth constitutes wisdom; and when love draws near to wisdom, or conjoins itself therewith, then love becomes love; and when wisdom in return draws near to love, and conjoins itself therewith, then wisdom becomes wisdom. Truly conjugial love is nothing else than the conjunction of love and wisdom. Two married partners, between or in whom at the same time this love is, are an effigy and form of it: all likewise in the heavens, where the faces are genuine types of the affections of each one's own love, are likenesses of it; for, as was shewn above, it is in them in general and in every part. Now, since two married partners are that love in effigy and form, it follows that every love which proceeds from the form of love itself, is a resemblance thereof; wherefore if conjugial love be celestial and spiritual, the loves proceeding from it are also celestial and spiritual. Conjugial love therefore is as the parent, and all other loves are as the offspring. Hence it is, that from the marriages of the angels in the heavens are generated spiritual offspring, which are those of love and wisdom, or of good and truth; concerning which generation see above (nos. 51 and 52).

66. The same manifestly appears from the creation of men into that love, and from their formation afterwards from it. The male was created to become wisdom from the love of growing wise, and the female was created to become the love of the male from his wisdom, and consequently was created according to that wisdom; from which consideration it is evident that two married partners are the very forms and effigies of the marriage of love and wisdom, or of good and truth. It ought to be well known, that there does not exist any good or truth which is not in a substance as in its subject: abstract goods and truths do not exist; for they are nowhere, because they have no abode, yea, neither can they appear [even] as fleeting things; wherefore they are merely entities, concerning which reason seems to itself to think abstractedly; but nevertheless it cannot think of them

except as being in subjects; for every idea of man, however sublimated, is substantial, that is, affixed to substances. It ought moreover to be known, that there does not exist any substance without a form; an unformed substance is not anything, because nothing can be predicated of it; and a subject without predicates is also an entity of no reason. These philosophical considerations have been added in order that thereby also it may be seen that two married partners who are in truly conjugial love, are actually forms of the marriage of good and truth, or of love and wisdom.

67. Since natural loves flow forth from spiritual loves, and spiritual loves flow forth from celestial loves, therefore it is said that conjugial love is the fundamental love of all celestial and spiritual loves, and *hence of all natural loves.* Natural loves have relation to the loves of self and of the world; but spiritual loves have relation to love towards the neighbour; and celestial loves have relation to love to the Lord; and since the relations of loves are such, it is evident in what order they follow, and in what order they are present with man. When they are in this order, then natural loves live from spiritual loves, and these from celestial loves, and all in this order from the Lord, from Whom they are.

68. VI. INTO THAT LOVE ARE COLLECTED ALL JOYS AND DELIGHTS FROM PRIMES TO ULTIMATES. All delights whatsoever that are felt by man are of his love; the love manifests itself, yea, comes into existence and lives, by means of them. It is known that delights exalt themselves in the proportion that the love exalts itself, and also in proportion as the incident affections touch the reigning love more nearly. Now, since conjugial love is the fundamental love of all good loves, and since it is inscribed on the veriest singulars of man, as was shewn above, it follows that the delights of that love exceed the delights of all other loves, and also that it delights these loves according to its presence, and at the same time conjunction, with them; for it expands the innermost parts of the mind, and at the same time the innermost parts of the body, as the delicious current of its fountain flows through and opens them. The reason why all delights from primes to ultimates are collected into this love, is on account of the surpassing excellence of its use: its use is the propagation of the human race, and hence of the angelic heaven; and as this use was the end of ends of creation, it follows that all the blessednesses, blissfulnesses, delightsomenesses, pleasantnesses, and pleasures, which could possibly be conferred upon man by the Lord the Creator, are collected into this his love. That delights follow the use, and are in man according to the love of use, is evident from the delights of the five senses, sight, hearing, smell, taste, and touch. Each of these senses has delights with variations accord-

ing to its specific uses. What then must be the delight belonging to the sense of conjugial love, the use of which is the complex of all other uses?

69. I know that few will acknowledge that all joys and delights from primes to ultimates are collected into conjugial love; because truly conjugial love, into which they are collected, is at this day so rare, that it is not known what its quality is, and scarcely that it exists, according to what was explained and confirmed above (nos. 58, 59); for those joys and delights do not exist in any other than genuine conjugial love; and as this is so rare on earth, it is impossible to describe its supereminent felicities from any other source than from the mouth of angels, because they are in it. They have said that the innermost delights of this love, which are of the soul, into which the conjugial quality of love and wisdom, or of good and truth from the Lord, first flows in, are imperceptible and consequently ineffable, because they are at the same time the delights of peace and innocence; but that in their descent they become more and more perceptible, in the higher parts of the mind as blessednesses, in the lower parts of the mind as blissfulnesses, in the breast as delightsomenesses derived from those, and that from the breast they diffuse themselves into each and all things of the body, and at last unite themselves in ultimates into the delight of delights. Moreover, the angels have related wonderful things about these delights, saying also that the varieties of these delights in the souls of married partners, and from their souls in their minds, and from their minds in their breasts, are infinite and also eternal; and that they are exalted according to the wisdom with the husbands; and this, because they live to eternity in the flower of their age, and because nothing is more blessed to them than to grow wiser and wiser. But more about those delights from the mouth of the angels, may be seen in the Memorable Relations, especially in those added to some of the following chapters.

70. VII. BUT NONE OTHERS COME INTO THAT LOVE, AND ARE ABLE TO BE IN IT, BUT THOSE WHO APPROACH THE LORD, AND LOVE THE TRUTHS OF THE CHURCH, AND DO ITS GOODS. The reasons why no others come into that love but those who approach the Lord, are, that monogamous marriages, which are of one man (*vir*) with one wife, correspond to the marriage of the Lord and the church, and, that the origin of those marriages is from the marriage of good and truth; on which subject see above (nos. 60 and 62). That from this origin, and from that correspondence, it follows, that truly conjugial love is from the Lord, and is for those who approach Him directly, cannot be fully confirmed unless those two arcana be treated of in detail, as shall be done in

the sections which immediately follow this one, one of which will treat of the origin of conjugial love from the marriage of good and truth, and the other, of the marriage of the Lord and the church, and of the correspondence of that marriage. That hence it follows, that conjugial love with man is according to the state of the church with him, will also be seen in those sections.

71. The reason why none others can be in truly conjugial love except those who receive it from the Lord, who are they who approach Him directly, and from Him live the life of the church, is, that that love, looked at from its origin, and from its correspondence, is celestial, spiritual, holy, pure, and clean, above every love which is with the angels of heaven and the men of the church, as was shewn above (no. 64); and these its attributes cannot possibly exist except with those who are conjoined with the Lord, and by Him are consociated with the angels of heaven. For these shun, as injuries to the soul and as hell-pools, extra-conjugial loves [*i.e.*, loves beyond, or outside of, conjugial love], which are conjunctions with others than one's own married partner: and in proportion as married partners shun those conjunctions, even as to the lusts of the will and the intentions thence, in the same proportion that love is purified with them, and becomes successively spiritual, first while they live on earth,
2 and afterwards in heaven. It is not however possible for any love to become perfectly pure either with men or with angels; consequently neither this love: but since the intention which is of the will is primarily regarded by the Lord, therefore in proportion as man is in this intention, and perseveres in it, in the same proportion he is initiated into its purity and holiness, and successively advances therein. The reason why no others can be in spiritual conjugial love, but those who are such from the Lord, is, that heaven is in this love; and the natural man, with whom that love derives its pleasure (*volupe*) only from the flesh, cannot approach to heaven, nor to any angel, nor even to any man, in whom that love is, for it is the fundamental love of all
3 celestial and spiritual loves (see above, nos. 65 to 67). That this is so, has been confirmed to me by experience. I have seen genii in the spiritual world who were being prepared for hell, approach to an angel who was being delighted with his consort; and at a distance, as they approached, they became like furies, and sought out caverns and ditches as asylums, into which they cast themselves. That evil spirits love that which is homogeneous to their affection, however unclean it is, and hold in aversion the spirits of heaven, as that which, because it is pure, is heterogeneous to them, may be concluded from what was related in the "Preliminaries" in no. 10.

72. The reason why those who love the truths of the church

and do its goods, come into this love and are capable of being in it, is, that none others are received by the Lord; for these are in conjunction with Him, and consequently can be kept in that love by Him. There are two things which constitute the church, and hence heaven, with man, the truth of faith and the good of life. The truth of faith effects the Lord's presence, and the good of life according to the truths of faith effects conjunction with Him, and, thus, the church and heaven. The reason why the truth of faith effects presence, is, that it is of light: spiritual light is nothing else. The reason why the good of life effects conjunction, is, that it is of heat: spiritual heat is nothing else, for it is love; and the good of life is of love; and it is known, that all light, even the light of winter, causes presence, and that heat united to light causes conjunction; for gardens and flower-beds appear in all degrees of light, but they do not flower and bear fruits except when heat becomes conjoined with light. From these considerations the conclusion is evident, that not those are gifted by the Lord with truly conjugial love, who merely know the truths of the church; but those who know them, and do its goods.

73. VIII. THIS LOVE WAS THE LOVE OF LOVES WITH THE ANCIENTS, WHO LIVED IN THE GOLDEN, SILVER, AND COPPER AGES. That conjugial love was the love of loves with the Most Ancient people and with the Ancient people, who lived in the first ages thus named, cannot be known from histories, because their writings are not extant: those which are extant are of writers who lived after those ages; for they are mentioned by these, and the purity and integrity of their life is also described, and likewise its successive decrease, which is as the decrease of gold to iron. But an account of the last or iron age, which commenced from those writers, may, as to some part, be gathered from the historical records of the lives of some of their kings, judges, and wise men, who, in Greece and elsewhere, were called Sophi. That this age, however, would not endure, as iron endures in itself, but that it would be like iron mixed with clay, which do not stick together, is foretold by Daniel (chapter ii. 40–43). Now, since the ages which were named the golden, silver, and copper ages, had passed away before the time of written documents, and thus no Knowledge concerning their marriages is possible on earth, it has pleased the Lord to make those marriages known to me through a spiritual way, by conducting me to the heavens where the dwellings of those who lived in those ages are, so that I might learn from their own mouth of what quality the marriages with them had been, during their life in their several eras: for all who have departed out of the natural world since the creation, are in the spiritual world, and all as to their loves are still like unto themselves, and remain such to eternity. As

these things are worthy of being known and related, and confirm the holiness of marriages, I purpose to make them public as they were shewn me in a wakeful state of my spirit, and afterwards recalled to my remembrance by an angel, and thus described. And as they are from the spiritual world, like the other accounts annexed to the preceding chapters, I have decided to arrange them into six Memorable Relations according to the progression of the ages.

74. *These six Memorable Relations which are from the spiritual world, concerning conjugial love, reveal what was the quality of that love in the first eras, and what was its quality afterwards, and what its quality is at the present day; whence it is manifest that that love has successively fallen away from its holiness and purity, until it has become scortatory; but that nevertheless there is a hope of its being brought back again to its primeval or ancient holiness.

75. The first Memorable Relation:—

†Once while I was meditating on conjugial love, my mind was seized with a desire of knowing what had been the quality of that love among those who lived in the GOLDEN AGE, and what it had been afterwards among those who lived in the following ages, which are called after silver, copper, and iron: and as I knew that all who had lived well in those ages are in the heavens, I prayed to the Lord that I might be allowed to speak with them and be instructed.

And lo! an angel stood near me, and said, "I have been sent by the Lord to be your guide and companion: I will first guide and accompany you to those who lived in the first era or age, which is called the golden age." And he said, "The way to them is arduous; it lies through a dark forest, which none can pass through except with a guide given by the Lord."

2 I was in the spirit, and girded myself for the journey; and we turned our faces towards the east; and as we advanced I saw a mountain, whose height extended beyond the region of clouds. We passed through a great wilderness, and came into the forest crowded with various kinds of trees and rendered dark by their density, of which the angel had foretold me. That forest was divided by several narrow foot-paths; and the angel said that they were so many windings and intricacies of error: and that unless his eyes were opened by the Lord, so as to see olive-trees engirded with tendrilled vines, and his steps were directed from olive-tree to olive-tree, the traveller would go

* This paragraph, in the original Latin edition, is enclosed in inverted commas.

† This Memorable Relation is also given, with a few slight variations, in *Coronis*, no. 37.

astray into Tartarus, which is round about at the sides. This forest is such, to the end that the passage may be guarded; for no other nation than the Primeval one dwells upon that mountain.

After we had entered the forest, our eyes were opened, 3
and we saw here and there olive-trees intertwined with vines, from which hung clusters of grapes of a dark blue colour, and the olive-trees were arranged in perpetual gyres; wherefore we directed our circuitous journey as they presented themselves to our view; and at length we saw a grove of tall cedars, and on their branches some eagles; on seeing which the angel said, "We are now on the mountain not far from its summit."

And we went on, and lo! behind the grove was a round plain, where there were feeding lambs and ewe lambs, which were representative forms of the state of innocence and peace of the mountaineers.

We passed through this plain, and lo! we saw tabernacles on tabernacles, to the number of several thousands, in front and at the sides as far as the sight could reach. And the angel said, "We are now in the camp, where are the armies of the Lord Jehovih: so they call themselves and their habitations. These Most Ancient people, while they were in the world, dwelt in tabernacles; wherefore now also they dwell in tabernacles. But let us bend our way to the south, where the wiser of them are, that we may meet some one with whom we may converse."

On the way I saw at a distance three boys and three girls 4
sitting at the door of a certain tent; but when we approached, the boys and girls appeared like men (*viri*) and women of a middle stature; and the angel said, "All the inhabitants of this mountain appear at a distance like little children because they are in a state of innocence; and childhood is the appearance of innocence."

These men (*viri*), on seeing us, ran up to us, and said, "Whence are you; and how came you here? Your faces are not of the faces of our mountain."

And the angel replied, and related the means of access through the forest, and what the cause of our coming was.

On hearing this, one of the three men invited and introduced us into his tabernacle. The man was dressed in a robe of a purple colour, and a vest of white wool: and his wife was dressed in a crimson gown, with a stomacher under it of fine linen wrought with needlework.

And as in my thought there was a desire of knowing the 5
state of marriage among the Most Ancient people, I looked by turns on the husband and the wife, and observed as it were the unity of their souls in their faces; and I said, "You two are one."

And the man answered, "We are one; her life is in me, and mine in her; we are two bodies, but one soul. The union between us is like that of the two sanctuaries in the breast, which are called the heart and the lungs; she is my heart and I am her lungs; but as by the heart we here mean love, and by the lungs wisdom, she is the love of my wisdom, and I am the wisdom of her love; wherefore her love from without veils my wisdom, and my wisdom from within is in her love. Hence, as you said, there is an appearance of the unity of our souls in our faces."

6 I then asked, "If the union is such, are you able to look at any other woman than your own?"

He replied, "I am able to; but as my wife is united to my soul, we both look together, and then nothing of lust can enter; for while I behold the wives of others, I behold them through my own wife, whom alone I love: and as my own wife has the faculty of perceiving all my inclinations, she, as an intermediate, directs my thoughts, and removes everything discordant, and at the same time infuses a cold and horror for everything unchaste; wherefore it is as impossible for us to look at the wife of a fellow-being from lust as it is to look at the light of our heaven from the shades of Tartarus; therefore neither does there exist with us any idea of thought, and still less any expression of speech, for the allurements of libidinous love." He could not utter the word whoredom, because the chasity of their heaven opposed it.

Hereupon my angel guide said to me, "You hear now the speech of the angels of this heaven, that it is the speech of wisdom, because they speak from causes."

7 After this, I looked around, and saw their tabernacle as it were overlaid with gold; and I asked, "Whence is this?"

He replied, "It is in consequence of a flaming light, which, like gold, glitters, irradiates, and tinges the curtains of our tabernacle while we are in conversation about conjugial love; for the heat from our sun, which in its essence is love, at such times bares itself, and tinges the light, which in its essence is wisdom, with its colour, which is golden; and this takes place because conjugial love in its origin is the sport of wisdom and love; for the man (*vir*) was born to be wisdom, and the woman to be the love of the man's wisdom: hence are the delights of that sport in conjugial love, and from it, between us and our wives. We have seen clearly for thousands of years in our heaven, that those delights as to abundance, degree, and power (*virtus*), are excellent and eminent according to the worship among us of the Lord Jehovih from Whom inflows that heavenly union or marriage, which is the union or marriage of love and wisdom."

8 When he had said this, I saw a great light upon the hill in the midst among the tabernacles; and I inquired, "Whence is that light?"

He said, "It is from the sanctuary of the tabernacle of our worship."

And I asked whether I might approach it; and he said that I might. I approached therefore, and saw the tabernacle without and within, answering exactly to the description of the tabernacle which was built for the sons of Israel in the wilderness; the form of which was shewn to Moses on Mount Sinai (Exod. xxv. 40; xxvi. 30). I then asked, "What is there within that sanctuary, from whence so great a light proceeds?"

He replied, "There is a tablet on which is this inscription: THE COVENANT BETWEEN JEHOVAH AND THE HEAVENS." He said no more.

And as by this time we were ready to depart, I asked, "Did any 9
of you, while you were in the natural world, live with more than one wife?"

He replied, "I know not one; for we could not think of more. We have been told by those who had thought of more, that instantly the heavenly blessednesses of their souls withdrew from the innermosts to the extremes of their bodies, even to the nails, and together therewith the distinguished marks of virility: when this was perceived, they were cast out of our land."

Having said this, the man ran to his tabernacle, and returned with a pomegranate, in which there was an abundance of seeds of gold: and he gave it me, and I brought it away with me, as a sign that we had been with those who lived in the golden age. And then, after a salutation of peace, we went away, and returned home.

76. The second Memorable Relation:—

The next day the same angel came to me, and said, "Do you wish me to guide and accompany you to the peoples who lived in the SILVER ERA or AGE, that we may hear from them concerning the marriages of their time?" And he added that access to these also can only be had of the Lord's auspices.

I was in the spirit as before, and accompanied my guide. We first came to a hill on the confines between the east and the south; and while we were ascending its heights, he shewed me a far stretch of country: we saw at a distance an eminence as it were mountainous, between which and the hill on which we stood was a valley, and beyond the valley a plain, and from the plain a rising ground of easy ascent.

We descended the hill to pass through the valley, and we saw here and there on the sides pieces of wood, and stones, carved into the figures of men, and of various beasts, birds, and fishes; and I asked the angel "What are these? are they idols?"

He replied, "By no means: they are representative configurations of various moral virtues and spiritual verities. The peoples of that age possessed the science of correspondences; and as every man, beast, bird, and fish, corresponds to some quality, therefore each carved figure represents partially some virtue or verity, and several together represent the virtue or verity itself in a general extended form. These are what in Egypt were called hieroglyphics."

2 We proceeded through the valley, and when we entered the plain, lo! we saw horses and chariots; horses variously harnessed and caparisoned, and chariots of different forms; some carved like eagles, some like whales, and some like stags with horns, and like unicorns; and likewise at the further end some carts, and stables round about at the sides; and when we approached, both horses and chariots disappeared, and instead thereof we saw men, in pairs, walking, talking, and reasoning. And the angel said to me, "The different species of horses, chariots, and stables, seen at a distance, are appearances of the rational intelligence of the men of that era; for a horse, by reason of correspondence, signifies the understanding of truth, a chariot, its doctrine, and stables, instructions: you know that in this world all things appear according to correspondences."

3 But we passed these things by, and ascended by a long acclivity, and at length saw a city, which we entered; and in walking through the streets and public places we viewed the houses: they were so many palaces built of marble, having steps of alabaster in front, and at the sides of the steps pillars of jasper: we also saw temples of precious stones of the colour of the sapphire and the lapis lazuli. And the angel said to me, "Their houses are of stones, because stones signify natural verities, and precious stones spiritual verities; and all those who lived in the silver era had intelligence from spiritual verities, and thence from natural verities: silver also has a similar signification."

4 While wandering through the city, we saw here and there consorts in pairs: and as they were husbands and wives, we expected that we should be invited somewhere; and while this expectation was in our mind (*animus*), as we were passing by, we were called back by two into their house; and we went up and entered: and the angel, speaking for both, explained to them the cause of our coming into this heaven; saying that it was "for the sake of instruction concerning the marriages among the Ancients, of whom you in this heaven are."

They replied, "We were from the peoples in Asia; and the chief pursuit of our age was the study of verities through which we had intelligence. This was the study of our soul and mind (*mens*); but the study of the senses of our bodies was the representations of verities in forms; and the science of correspondences conjoined the sensuals of our bodies with the perceptions of our minds, and procured us intelligence."

5 On hearing this, the angel asked them to give some account of the marriages among them.

So the husband said, "There is a correspondence between spiritual marriage, which is that of truth with good, and natural marriage, which is that of a man (*vir*) with one wife; and as we have studied correspondences, we have seen that the church, with its truths and goods, can by no means exist with any others except those who live in truly conjugial love with one wife; for the marriage of good and truth is the church with man. Wherefore all we in this heaven say that the husband is truth, and the wife the good thereof; and that good cannot love any other truth than its own, neither can truth love in return any other good than its own. If any other were loved, internal marriage, which constitutes the church, would perish, and marriage would become only external, to which idolatry and not the church corresponds. Therefore marriage with one wife we call sacrimony; but if it should take place among us with more than one wife, we should call it sacrilege."

As he said this, we were introduced into a room adjoining 6
the bridal-chamber, where there were many designs on the walls, and little images as it were molten of silver; and I enquired, "What are those?"

They said, "They are pictures and forms representative of the many qualities, properties and delightsomenesses which belong to conjugial love. These represent the unity of souls, these, the conjunction of minds (*mens*), these, the concord of breasts, these, the delights thence arising."

While we were surveying these things, we saw as it were a rainbow on the wall, consisting of three colours, crimson, purple, and white; and we saw how the crimson colour passed through the purple, and tinged the white with a dark blue colour, and that this colour flowed back through the purple into the crimson and raised this as it were into a flaming beam.

And the husband said to me, "Do you understand this?"

I replied, "Instruct me."

So he said, "The crimson colour, from its correspondence, 7
signifies the conjugial love of the wife, the white colour the intelligence of the husband, the purple colour the beginning of conjugial love in the perception of the husband from the wife, and the dark blue colour, with which the white was tinged, signifies the conjugial love then in the husband; and this colour flowing back through the purple into the crimson, and raising it as it were into a flaming beam, signifies the conjugial love of the husband flowing back to the wife. Such things are represented on those walls, while from meditation on conjugial love, its mutual, successive, and simultaneous union, we look with attentive eyes at the rainbows there."

To this I said, "These things are more than mystical at the present day; for they are appearances representative of the arcana of the conjugial love of one man with one wife."

And he replied, "They are so; yet to us in this heaven they are not arcana, and consequently neither are they mystical."

8 As he said this, there appeared at a distance a chariot drawn by small white cobs, on seeing which the angel said, "That chariot is a sign for us to depart;" and then, as we were descending the steps, our host gave us a bunch of white grapes clinging to the vine leaves: and lo! the leaves became silver; and we brought them down with us for a sign that we had spoken with the people of the silver age.

77. The third Memorable Relation:—

After one day, the angel guide and companion came to me and said, "Gird thyself, and let us go to the heavenly inhabitants in the west, who are of the men that lived in the third age, or in the COPPER AGE. Their habitations are from the south by the west towards the north; but they do not reach unto the north."

Having girded myself, I accompanied him, and we entered their heaven on the southern side. There was there a magnificent grove of palm trees and laurels. We passed through this, and then on the very confines of the west we saw giants of twice the ordinary stature of men.

They asked us, "Who let you in through the grove?"

The angel said, "The God of heaven."

And they replied, "We are guards to the western Ancient heaven; but pass on."

2 We passed on, and from an eminence we saw a mountain reaching to the clouds, and, between us on the eminence and the mountain, villages on villages, with gardens, groves, and plains between them. We passed through the villages to the mountain, which we ascended; and lo! its summit was not a point but a plain, on which was an extensive and spacious city. All the houses of the city were built of the wood of resinous trees, and their roofs consisted of beams.

And I asked, "Why are the houses here made of wood?"

The angel replied, "Because wood signifies natural good; and the men of the third age of the Earth were in this good; and as copper also signifies natural good, therefore the age in which they lived the ancients named from copper. Here there are also sacred buildings constructed of the wood of the olive, and in the midst of them is the sanctuary, where there lies in an ark the Word that was given to the inhabitants of Asia before the Israelitish Word; the historical books of which are called the WARS OF JEHOVAH, and the prophetic books, THE ENUNCIATIONS; both mentioned by Moses (Numb. xxi. 14, 15, 27–30). This Word at the present day is lost in the kingdoms of Asia, and is only preserved in Great Tartary."

The angel then led me to one of the sacred buildings, which we looked into, and saw in the midst of it that sanctuary, the whole in the brightest white light; and the angel said,

"That light is from that ancient Asiatic Word; for all Divine truth in the heavens gives forth light."

As we were going out of the building, we heard that it had 3
been reported in the city that two strangers had arrived there; and that they were to be examined as to whence they came, and what their business there was; and immediately an officer came running out of the court, and took us before the judges: and on being asked whence we came, and what our business there was, we replied, "We have passed through the grove of palm-trees, and also the abodes of the giants who are the guards of your heaven, and afterwards the region of villages; from which circumstances you may conclude, that we have not come hither of ourselves, but of the God of heaven. The business on which we came is, that we may be instructed concerning your marriages, whether they be monogamous or polygamous."

And they replied, "What are polygamous marriages? Are they not scortatory?"

And then the bench of judges deputed an intelligent person to 4
instruct us in his own house on this matter: and when we were in his house, he set his wife by him and spoke as follows: "We have preserved among us the precepts concerning marriages, from the Primeval or Most Ancient people, who were in truly conjugial love, and consequently excelled all others in the power (*virtus*) and potency of that love in the world, and are now in a most blessed state in their heaven, which is in the east. We are their posterity, and they, as fathers, gave to us, as their sons, canons of life, among which is the following concerning marriages: '*Sons, if you wish to love God and the neighbour, and if you wish to become wise, and to be happy to eternity, we counsel you to live monogamists; if you depart from this precept, all heavenly love will pass away from you, and therewith internal wisdom; and you will be exterminated.*' This precept of our fathers we have obeyed as sons, and have perceived its verity, which is, that in the proportion in which any one loves his own married partner alone, he becomes celestial and internal, and that in the proportion in which any one does not love his own married partner alone, he becomes natural and external; and such a one loves only himself and the images of his own mind, and is silly and foolish. Hence it is, that all of us in this heaven are mono- 5
gamists, and because we are such, all the borders of our heaven are guarded against polygamists, adulterers, and whoremongers. If polygamists invade us, they are cast out into the darkness of the north; if adulterers, they are cast out into the fire-places of the west; and if whoremongers, they are cast out into the illusory lights of the south."

On hearing this, I asked, what he meant by the darkness of the north, the fire-places of the west, and the illusory lights of the south.

He answered, "The darkness of the north is dulness of mind and ignorance of verities; the fire-places of the west are the loves of evil; and the illusory lights of the south are the falsifications of truth, which are spiritual whoredoms."

6 After this, he said, "Follow me to our museum of treasures." So we followed him, and he shewed us that the writings of the Most Ancient people were on tablets of wood and stone, and afterwards on thin tablets of polished wood; and that the second age set down its writings on parchments; he brought me a parchment, on which were copied the canons of the Primeval people from their tablets of stone, among which also was the precept concerning marriages.

Having seen these and other remarkable things of Antiquity itself, the angel said, "It is now time for us to be going;" and then our host went out into the garden, and plucked some twigs off a tree, and bound them into a bunch, and gave them to us, saying, "These twigs are from a tree, which is native of or peculiar to our heaven, and whose juice has a balsamic fragrance." We brought this bunch down with us, and descended by the way by the east, which was not guarded; and lo! the twigs were changed into shining brass, and their tips into gold; as a sign that we had been with the people of the third age, which is named from copper or brass.

78. The fourth Memorable Relation:—

After two days the angel again spoke to me, saying, "Let us complete the period of the ages; the last age still remains, which is named from IRON. The people of this era dwell in the north on the side of the west, inwards, that is, in the direction of latitude: they are all from the ancient inhabitants of Asia, among whom was the Ancient Word, and worship from it; consequently they were before the time of our Lord's coming into the world. This is evident from the writings of the Ancients, in which those times are so named. These same Eras are meant by the statue seen by Nebuchadnezzar, of which the head was of gold, the breast and arms of silver, the belly and thighs of brass, the legs of iron, and the feet of iron and also of clay (Dan. ii. 32, 33)."

2 These things the angel said to me in the way, which was shortened and anticipated by changes of state induced on our minds according to the genius of the inhabitants whom we passed; for spaces and consequently distances in the spiritual world are appearances according to the states of the minds. When we raised our eyes, lo! we were in a wood consisting of beeches, chestnuts, and oaks; and on looking around us, there appeared bears to the left and leopards to the right: and when I wondered at this, the angel said, "They are neither bears nor leopards, but men, who guard these inhabitants of the north; with their nostrils they scent the spheres of life of those

who pass by, and they rush violently on all who are spiritual, because the inhabitants are natural. Those who only read the Word, and derive thence nothing of doctrine, appear at a distance like bears; and those who confirm falsities thence, appear like leopards." But when they saw us, they turned away, and we passed on.

After the forest there appeared thickets, and afterwards 3
fields of grass divided into plots bordered with box: after these the land sloped down into a valley, wherein were cities on cities. We passed by some of them, and entered into one great one: its streets were irregular; so were the houses; the latter were built of bricks, with beams between, and plastered over.

In the public places were temples of hewn lime-stone; the substructure of which was below the earth, and the superstructure above. We descended into one of them by three steps, and saw round about at the walls idols of various forms, and a crowd on their knees paying adoration to them: in the midst was the choir, out of which the head of the tutelary god of that city projected. As we were going out, the angel said to me that those idols, with the Ancients who lived in the silver age, who have been treated of above, were images representative of spiritual verities and moral virtues; and that when the science of correspondences was forgotten and extinct, those images first became objects of worship, and afterwards were adored as deities: hence came idolatry.

When we were outside the fane, we observed the men and 4
their dress. Their faces were like steel, of a grey colour, and they were dressed like comedians, with aprons round about their loins hanging from a vest fitting closely to the breast; and on their heads they wore caps with the brims rolled up so as to make them resemble boats.

But the angel said, "Enough of this; let us seek instruction concerning the marriages of the peoples of this era."

So we entered into the house of one of the authorities, who wore on his head a tower-shaped cap. He received us kindly, and said, "Enter, and let us converse together."

We entered into the hall, and there seated ourselves; and I asked him about the marriages of this city and country. He said, "We do not live with one wife, but some with two and three, and some with more, because we are delighted with variety, obedience, and honour as of majesty; and these we receive from our wives according to their number. With one wife there would be no delight from variety, but weariness from sameness; there would be no flattering from obedience, but annoyance from equality; neither would be any blissfulness from domination and the honour thence derived, but vexation from wrangling about superiority. And what is a woman? Is she not born subject to the man's will; to serve and not to rule? Wherefore in this place every husband in his own house enjoys as it were royal majesty; and as this is of our love, it is also the blessedness of our life."

5 But I asked, "In such a case where is conjugial love, which from two souls makes one soul, and conjoins minds, and renders man blessed? This love cannot be divided; for if it be divided it becomes a heat which effervesces and passes away."

To this he replied, "I do not understand what you say; what else renders a man (*homo*) blessed, but the emulation of wives for the honour of the first place in their husband's favour?"

As he said this, a man (*vir*) entered into the women's apartment, and opened the two doors; and there issued thence a libidinous effluvium, which smelt like mire; this arose from polygamous love, which is connubial, and at the same time scortatory; wherefore I rose and shut the doors.

6 Afterwards I said, "How can you subsist upon this earth, when you do not possess any truly conjugial love, and also when you worship idols?"

He replied, "As to connubial love, we are so extremely jealous of our wives, that we do not suffer any one to enter further within our houses than the hall; and where there is jealousy, there also is love. As to idols, we do not worship them; but we are not able to think of the God of the universe, except by means of appearances presented before our eyes; for we cannot elevate our thoughts above the sensuals of the body, nor think of God above the things which are within its range of vision."

I then asked him again, "Are not your idols of different forms? How then can they excite the mental vision of one God?"

To this he replied, "This is a mystery to us; something of the worship of God lies concealed in each form."

I then said, "You are merely sensual corporeal men; you possess neither the love of God, nor the love of a married partner which partakes anything of what is spiritual; and these loves together form a man (*homo*), and from sensual make him celestial."

7 As I said this, there appeared through the gate as it were lightning; and I asked what it meant.

He said, "Such lightning is a sign to us that there will come the Ancient one from the east, who teaches us about God, that He is one, that He alone is omnipotent, Who is the First and the Last; he also admonishes us not to worship idols, but only to look upon them as images representative of the virtues proceeding from the one God, which together form the worship of Him. This ancient one is our angel, whom we revere and to whom we hearken. He comes to us, and raises us up, when we are falling into obscure worship of God by reason of mere fancies respecting images."

8 On hearing this, we went out of the house and the city; and

in the way, from what we had seen in the heavens, we drew some conclusions about the circle and progression of conjugial love; of its circle, that it had passed from the east to the south, from the south to the west, and from the west to the north; of its progression, that it had decreased according to its circulation, namely, that in the east it was celestial, in the south spiritual, in the west natural, and in the north sensual; and also that it had decreased in a like degree with the love and worship of God. From which considerations this conclusion is made, that this love in the first era was like gold, in the second like silver, in the third like brass, and in the fourth like iron, and that at length it ceased to be.

Then the angel, my guide and companion, said, "Nevertheless I am nourished by the hope that this love will be raised up again by the God of heaven, Who is the Lord, because it is capable of being so raised up again."

79. The fifth Memorable Relation:—

The angel who had been my guide and companion to the Ancients who had lived in the four ages—the golden, the silver, the copper, and the iron—again came and said to me, "Do you wish to see the age which succeeded those Ancient ones, and to know what its quality was, and still is? Follow me and you shall see. They are those of whom Daniel thus prophesied: '*A kingdom shall arise after those four, in which iron shall be mixed with clay of mire: they shall mingle themselves by the seed of man; but they shall not cohere one with the other, as iron is not mixed with clay*' (Dan. ii. 41–43)": and he said, "By the seed of man, whereby iron shall be mixed with clay, and still they shall not cohere, is meant the truth of the Word falsified."

When he had said this, I followed him, and in the way he 2
related to me these particulars: "They dwell in the borders between the south and the west, but at a great distance beyond those who lived in the four former ages, and also at a greater depth."

We then proceeded through the south to the region bordering on the west, and passed through a dreadful forest; for in it there were pools, out of which crocodiles raised their heads, and gaped at us with their wide jaws beset with teeth; and between the pools were terrible dogs, some of which were three-headed like Cerberus, some two-headed, all looking at us as we passed by, with a horrible hungry look and fierce eyes. We entered the western tract of this region, and saw dragons and leopards, such as are described in the Apocalypse, chap. xii. 3, and chap. xiii. 2.

Then the angel said to me, "All those wild beasts which you 3
have seen, are not wild beasts, but correspondences, and thus representative forms, of the cupidities in which are the inhabi-

tants whom we shall visit. The cupidities themselves are represented by those horrible dogs; their deceits and cunning by the crocodiles; their falsities and depraved inclinations to the things which are of worship, by the dragons and leopards. But the inhabitants represented do not live just behind the forest, but behind a great wilderness which is intermediate, in order that they may be fully withheld and separated from the inhabitants of the antecedent ages; for they are utterly alien or diverse from them. They have indeed heads above their breasts, and breasts above their loins, and loins above their feet, like the primeval men; but in their heads there is not anything of gold, nor in their breasts anything of silver, nor in their loins anything of brass, no, nor in their feet anything of pure iron; but in their heads is iron mixed with clay, in their breasts, both mixed with brass, in their loins also, both mixed with silver, and in their feet they are mixed with gold. Through this inversion they have been changed from men into graven images of men, in which inwardly nothing coheres: for that which had been the highest has been made the lowest, thus that which had been the head has become the heel, and contrariwise. They appear to us from heaven like acrobats, who lie upon their elbows with the body inverted, and thus advance; or like beasts, which lie on their backs, and lift the feet upwards, and out of the head, which they bury in the earth, look towards heaven."

4 We passed through the forest and entered the wilderness, which was not less terrible: it consisted of heaps of stones, and ditches between them, out of which hydras and vipers crept, and fire-serpents flew out. This whole wilderness sloped down gradually: we descended by a long slope, and at length came into the valley inhabited by the inhabitants of that region and age.

There were here and there huts, which at last appeared to meet, and to be joined together into the form of a city. We entered this city, and lo! the houses were built of scorched branches of trees, cemented together with mud, and roofed with black slates. The streets were irregular; all of them at the entrance were narrow, but they widened out as they extended, and at the end were spacious, where the places of public resort were: hence there were as many places of public resort as there were streets.

As we entered the city it became dark, because the sky did not appear; we therefore looked up, and light was given us, and we saw; and then I asked those we met, "Are you able to see, because the sky above you does not appear?"

They replied, "What a question is this! we see clearly; we walk in full light."

On hearing this, the angel said to me, "Darkness to them is light, and light darkness, as is the case with birds of night; for they look downwards and not upwards."

We entered into some of the cottages, and saw in each a man 5
with his woman, and we asked them, "Do all here live in their own houses with one wife only?"

To this they replied with a hissing, "What do you mean by one wife only? Why do not you ask, whether we live with one harlot? What is a wife but a harlot? By our laws it is not allowable to commit fornication with more than one woman; but still we do not hold it dishonourable or unbecoming to do so with several, but away from home; we boast of this among ourselves: thus we rejoice in licentiousness, and the pleasure of it, more than polygamists. Why is a plurality of wives denied us, when yet it has been granted, and at the present day is granted in all the countries round about us? What is life with one woman only, but captivity and imprisonment? But we in this place have broken down the bolts of this prison, and rescued ourselves from slavery, and made ourselves free: who is angry with a prisoner for asserting his freedom when he can?"

To this we replied, "You speak, friend, as if you were devoid 6
of religion. Who that is imbued with any reason does not know that adulteries are profane and infernal, and that marriages are holy and heavenly? Do not adulteries exist with the devils in hell, and marriages with the angels in heaven? Did you never read the sixth commandment of the Decalogue? and in Paul, that adulterers can by no means come into heaven [1 Cor. vi. 9]?"

Hereupon our host laughed most heartily, and regarded me as a simpleton, and almost as a madman.

But just then there came in haste a messenger from the ruler of the city, and said, "Bring the two strangers into court; and if they will not come, drag them there: we have seen them in a shade of light; they have entered in secret; they are spies."

Hereupon the angel said to me, "The reason why we were seen in a shade, is, that the light of heaven in which we have been, is shade to them, and the shade of hell is light to them; and this is because they consider nothing as sin, not even adultery: hence they see falsity altogether as truth; and falsity shines in hell before satans, and truth darkens their eyes like the shade of night."

We said to the messenger, "We will not be pressed, still less 7
will we be dragged into court; but we will go with you of our own accord."

So we went: and lo! there was there a great crowd, out of which came some lawyers, and whispered into our ears, "Take heed to yourselves lest you speak anything against religion, the form of our government, and good morals."

And we replied, "We will not speak against them, but for them and from them."

Then we asked, "What is your religion concerning marriages?"

At this the crowd murmured, and said, "What have you to do here with marriages? Marriages are marriages."

Again we asked, "What is your religion concerning whoredoms?"

At this also the crowd murmured, saying, "What have you to do here with whoredoms? Whoredoms are whoredoms: let him that is guiltless cast the first stone."

And we asked thirdly, "Does your religion teach that marriages are holy and heavenly, and that adulteries are profane and infernal?"

Hereupon several in the crowd laughed aloud, jested, and jeered, saying, "Inquire of our priests, and not of us, as to what concerns religion. We acquiesce entirely in what they say, because nothing of religion is referred to the judgments of the understanding. Have you never heard that the understanding is without any discernment in the mysteries of which the whole of religion consists? And what have deeds to do with religion? Is not the soul made blessed by the muttering of words from a devout heart concerning expiation, satisfaction, and imputation, and not by works?"

8 But just then some of the wise ones of the city, so called, approached us, and said, "Retire hence; the crowd grows angry; a tumult will soon burst out: let us talk in private on this subject; there is a walk behind the court; let us withdraw thither; come with us."

So we followed them; and then they asked us whence we came, and what our business there was.

And we said, "To be instructed about marriages, whether they are holy with you, as they were with the Ancients who lived in the golden, silver, and copper ages; or whether they are not holy."

And they replied, "What do you mean by holy things? Are not marriages works of the flesh and of the night?"

And we answered, "Are they not also works of the spirit? and what the flesh does from the spirit, is not that spiritual; and all that the spirit does, it does from the marriage of good and truth. Is not this marriage spiritual, which enters the natural marriage which is that of husband and wife?"

To this the wise ones, so called, made answer, "You refine and sublimate this subject too much: you ascend far above rational principles to spiritual ones: and who can begin there, descend thence, and thus form a judgment of anything?" To this they added with a smile of ridicule, "Perhaps you have the wings of an eagle, and can fly in the highest region of heaven, and have a clear sight of these things: we cannot."

9 We then asked them to tell us, from the height or region in which the winged ideas of their minds fly, whether they knew, or were able to know, that there exists such a thing as the

conjugial love of one man with one wife, into which are collected all the blessednesses, blissfulnesses, delights, pleasantnesses, and pleasures of heaven; and that this love is from the Lord according to the reception of good and truth from Him, and thus according to the state of the church?"

On hearing this, they turned away, and said, "These men are 10
out of their senses; they enter the ether with their judgment, and scatter about vain conjectures like nuts." After this they turned to us, saying, "We will give a direct answer to your windy conjectures and dreams;" and they said, "What has conjugial love in common with religion and inspiration from God? Is not this love with every one according to the state of his potency? Is it not the same with those who are outside of the church as with those who are within it, the same with Gentiles as with Christians, yea, the same with the impious as with the pious? Has not every one the strength of this love either hereditarily, or from health, or from temperance of life, or from the heat of the climate? By medicines also it can be strengthened and stimulated. Is not the case similar with the beasts, and especially with the birds which love in pairs? Is not this love carnal? and what has that which is carnal in common with the spiritual state of the church? Does this love, as to its ultimate effect with a wife, differ at all from love as to that effect with a harlot? Is not the lust similar, and the delight similar? Wherefore it is wrong to deduce the origin of conjugial love from the holy things of the church."

On hearing this, we said to them, "You reason from the 11
burning heat of lasciviousness, and not from conjugial love; you are utterly ignorant what conjugial love is, because it is cold with you. From what you have said we are convinced that you are of the age which has its name from, and consists of, iron and clay, which do not cohere, according to the prophecy in Daniel ii. 43; for you make conjugial love and scortatory love one thing. Do these two cohere any more than iron and clay? You are believed to be wise, and you are called wise, and yet you are as far as possible from being wise."

On hearing this they were kindled with anger, and cried out, and called the crowd together to cast us out; but at that instant, by virtue of power given us by the Lord, we stretched out our hands, and lo! the fire-serpents, vipers, and hydras, and also the dragons from the wilderness, approached, and invaded and filled the city; at which the inhabitants being terrified fled away.

And the angel said to me, "Into this region new comers from the Earth daily enter, and the former inhabitants are by turns banished and cast down into the gulfs of the west, which appear at a distance like pools of fire and brimstone. All there are spiritual and natural adulterers."

80. The sixth Memorable Relation:—

When the angel had said this, I looked to the end of the west, and lo! there appeared as it were pools of fire and brimstone; and I asked the angel, "Why do the hells there appear so?"

He replied, "They appear as pools on account of the falsifications of truth, because water in the spiritual sense denotes truth; and there appears as it were fire around them, and in them, on account of the love of evil, and as it were brimstone, on account of the love of falsity. Those three things, the pool, the fire, and the brimstone, are appearances, because they are correspondences of the evil loves in which they are. All there are shut up in eternal workhouses, where they labour for food, clothing, and a bed; and when they do evil, they are grievously and miserably punished."

2 I further asked the angel, "Why didst thou say that in that quarter are spiritual and natural adulterers, and not, rather, evil doers and impious?"

He replied, "Because all those who account adulteries as nothing, that is, who believe and commit them from confirmation and thus from set purpose that they are not sins, are at heart evil doers and impious; for the human conjugial [state] and religion proceed together at the same pace; and every step and every advance from religion, and into religion, is also a step and advance from the conjugial state, and into the conjugial state which is peculiar and proper to the Christian man."

To the question what that conjugial [state or principle] was, he said, "It is the desire to live with one wife only; and a Christian man has this desire according to his religion."

3 I was afterwards grieved in spirit to think that marriages, which in the Ancient eras had been most holy, were so hopelessly changed into adulteries.

The angel said, "It is the same at the present day with religion; for the Lord says, '*In the consummation of the age there will be the abomination of desolation foretold by Daniel. And there will be great affliction, such as there has not been from the beginning of the world*' (Matt. xxiv. 15, 21). The abomination of desolation signifies the falsification and deprivation of all truth; affliction signifies the state of the church infested by evils and falsities; and the consummation of the age, concerning which those things are said, signifies the last time or end of the church. The end is now, because there does not remain a truth which has not been falsified; and the falsification of truth is spiritual whoredom, which acts in unity with natural whoredom, because they cohere."

81.* As we were conversing and grieving together about these

* This paragraph, with some slight variations, is inserted as a complete Memorable Relation in the *True Christian Religion*, no. 625.

things, there suddenly appeared a beam of light, which affetced my eyes strongly; wherefore I looked up: and lo! the whole heaven above us appeared luminous; and from the east to the west in a long series there was heard a GLORIFICATION.

And the angel said to me, "That is a glorification of the Lord on account of His coming, and it is made by the angels of the eastern and western heavens."

From the southern and northern heavens nothing was heard but a gentle murmur.

As the angel understood everything, he told me first, that glorifications and celebrations of the Lord are made from the Word, because then they are made from the Lord; for the Lord is the Word, that is, the Divine truth itself therein; and he said, "Now in particular they are glorifying and celebrating the Lord by these words which were said through Daniel the prophet, '*Thou sawest iron mixed with clay of mire; they shall mingle themselves together by the seed of man; but they shall not cohere. But in those days the God of the heavens shall cause a kingdom to arise, which shall not perish for ages. It shall bruise and consume all those kingdoms; but itself shall stand for ages*' (Dan. ii. 43, 44)."

After this, I heard as it were the voice of singing, and further 2
in the east I saw a flashing of light more resplendent than the former; and I asked the angel what they were glorifying there.

He said that "they were glorifying by these words in Daniel: '*I was seeing in the visions of the night, and lo! with the clouds of heaven there was coming as it were the* SON OF MAN: *and to Him was given dominion and a kingdom; and all peoples and nations shall worship Him. His dominion is the dominion of an age, which shall not pass away; and His kingdom that which shall not perish*' (Dan. vii. 13, 14).

"Besides that, they are celebrating the Lord from these words in the Apocalypse: '*To* JESUS CHRIST *be glory and strength: behold He cometh with the clouds. He is the alpha and the omega, the beginning and the end, the first and the last; Who is, Who was, and Who is to come, the Almighty. I, John, heard this from the* SON OF MAN, *out of the midst of the seven candlesticks*' (Apoc. i. 5–13; xxii. 13; and also from Matt. xxiv. 30, 31)."

I looked again into the eastern heaven; it was enlightened on 3
the right side, and the luminosity entered the southern expanse, and I heard a sweet sound; and I asked the angel what [attribute] of the Lord they were glorifying there.

He said, "These words in the Apocalypse: '*I saw a new heaven and a new earth; and I saw the holy city, New Jerusalem, coming down from God out of heaven, prepared as a* BRIDE *for her* HUSBAND: *and the angel spoke with me, and said, Come, I will shew thee the* BRIDE, THE LAMB'S WIFE: *and he carried me away in the spirit upon a great and high mountain, and shewed me the city, the holy*

Jerusalem' (Apoc. xxi. 1, 2, 9, 10): also these words, 'I JESUS *am the bright and morning star; and the spirit and the bride say,* COME; AND HE SAID, YEA, I COME QUICKLY; *Amen: even so* COME, LORD JESUS' (Apoc. xxii. 16, 17, 20)."

4 After these and several others, there was heard a general glorification from the east to the west of heaven, and also from the south to the north; and I asked the angel, "What now is the subject?"

He said, "These words from the prophets; '*Let all flesh know that* I, JEHOVAH, AM THY SAVIOUR AND THY REDEEMER' (Isaiah xlix. 26). '*Thus saith* JEHOVAH, *the King of Israel and* HIS REDEEMER, JEHOVAH ZEBAOTH, *I am the first and the last,* and BESIDES ME THERE IS NO GOD' (Isaiah xliv. 6). '*It shall be said in that day,* LO! THIS IS OUR GOD, *whom we have expected to deliver us;* THIS IS JEHOVAH WHOM WE HAVE EXPECTED' (Isaiah xxv. 9). '*The voice of him that crieth in the wilderness, Prepare a way for* JEHOVAH. *Behold* THE LORD JEHOVIH *cometh in strength. He shall feed his flock like a* SHEPHERD' (Isaiah xl. 3, 5, 10, 11). '*Unto us a Child is born; unto us a Son is given; Whose name is Wonderful, Counsellor,* GOD, *Hero,* FATHER OF ETERNITY, *Prince of Peace*' (Isaiah ix. 5, [6]). '*Behold the days will come, and I will raise up to David a righteous Branch, Who shall reign a king: and this is His name,* JEHOVAH OUR RIGHTEOUSNESS' (Jeremiah xxiii. 5, 6; xxxiii. 15, 16). 'JEHOVAH ZEBAOTH *is His name, and* THY REDEEMER, *the Holy one of Israel;* THE GOD OF THE WHOLE EARTH SHALL HE BE CALLED' (Isaiah liv. 5). IN THAT DAY SHALL JEHOVAH BE FOR A KING OVER THE WHOLE EARTH; IN THAT DAY THERE SHALL BE ONE JEHOVAH, AND HIS NAME ONE' (Zech. xiv. 9)."

5 On hearing and understanding these words, my heart exulted, and I went home with joy; and there I returned out of the state of the spirit into the state of the body; in which latter state I committed to writing what I had seen and heard: to which I now adjoin the following particular: That conjugial love, such as it was among the Ancients, will be raised up again by the Lord after His coming; because that love is from the Lord Alone, and it is with those who by Him, through the Word, are made spiritual.

82. After this, a man (*vir*) came running in great haste from the northern quarter, and looked at me with a threatening countenance, and addressing me in a passionate tone of voice, said, "Art thou he that would seduce the world by establishing a New church, which thou understandest by the New Jerusalem coming down out of heaven from God; and by teaching, that the Lord will gift with truly conjugial love those who embrace the doctrinals of that church; the delights and felicity of which love thou exaltest even to heaven? Is not this a mere fiction?

and dost thou not hold it forth as a bait and enticement for others to accede to thy new [doctrinals]? But tell me briefly, what are those doctrinals of the New Church, and I will see whether they agree or disagree."

I replied, "The doctrinals of the church, which is meant by the New Jerusalem, are these:—I. That there is one God, in Whom is a Divine Trinity, and that He is the LORD JESUS CHRIST. II. That saving faith consists in believing on Him. III. That evils ought to be shunned, because they are of the devil and from the devil. IV. That goods ought to be done, because they are of God and from God. V. That these things ought to be done by a man as from himself; but that it ought to be believed, that they are done by the Lord with him and through him."

On hearing these things, his fury abated for some moments; 2
but after some deliberation he again looked at me with a stern countenance, and said, "Are these five precepts the doctrinals of the faith and charity of the New Church?"

I replied, "They are."

He then asked sharply, "How can you demonstrate the FIRST, 'That there is one God in Whom there is a Divine Trinity; and that He is the Lord Jesus Christ?'"

I said, "I demonstrate it thus: Is not God one and indivisible? Is not there a trinity? If God is one and indivisible, is not He one person? If He is one person, is not the trinity in that person? That He is the LORD JESUS CHRIST, is evident from these considerations, that He was conceived from God the Father (Luke i. 34, 35); and thus that as to His soul He is God; and hence, as He Himself says, that the Father and He are one (John x. 30); that He is in the Father, and the Father in Him (John xiv. 10, 11); that he who seeth Him and knoweth Him, seeth and knoweth the Father (John xiv. 7, 9); that no one seeth and knoweth the Father, except He Who is in the bosom of the Father (John i. 18); that all things of the Father are His (John iii. 35; xvi. 15); that He is the Way, the Truth, and the Life; and that no one cometh to the Father but through Him (John xiv. 6), thus from Him, because He is in Him; and, according to Paul, that all the fulness of the Godhead dwelleth bodily in Him (Coloss. ii. 9); and moreover, that He hath Power over all flesh (John xvii. 2); and that He hath all power in heaven and in earth (Matt. xxviii. 18): from which declarations it follows, that He is the God of heaven and earth."

He afterwards asked how I prove the SECOND, "that saving 3
faith consists in believing on Him?"

I said, "I prove it by these words of the Lord Himself: 'This is the will of the Father, that every one who BELIEVETH ON THE SON should have eternal life' (John vi. 40). 'God so loved the world, that He gave His only-begotten Son, that every one who BELIEVETH ON HIM should not perish, but have eternal life'

(John iii. 15, 16). 'He who believeth on the Son hath eternal life; but he who believeth not the Son shall not see life; but the wrath of God abideth on him' (John iii. 36)."

He afterwards said, "Demonstrate also the THIRD, and the following ones.

I replied, "What need is there to demonstrate 'that evils ought to be shunned, because they are of the devil and from the devil; and that goods ought to be done, because they are of God and from God;' also, 'that these things ought to be done by man as from himself; but that it ought to be believed that they are done by the Lord with him and through him?' That these three doctrinals are true, is confirmed by the whole Sacred Scripture from beginning to end; for what else is therein insisted upon in general, than the shunning of evils and the doing of goods, and a believing on the Lord God? And besides, without these three doctrinals there is no religion; for does not religion belong to life? and what is life but shunning evils and doing goods? and how can a man do the latter and believe the former but as from himself? Wherefore if you remove these doctrinals from the church, you remove from it the Sacred Scripture, and you also remove religion; and when these are removed, the church is not a church."

The man on hearing these things retired, and mused, but still he departed in indignation.

THE ORIGIN OF CONJUGIAL LOVE FROM THE MARRIAGE OF GOOD AND TRUTH.

83. THERE are both internal and external origins of conjugial love, and the internal ones are many, and likewise the external; nevertheless there is but one inmost or universal origin of all. That this origin is the marriage of good and truth, shall be demonstrated in what now follows. The reason why no one heretofore has deduced the origin of that love thence, is, that it has been unknown, that there is an union between good and truth; and it has been unknown, because good does not appear in the light of the understanding, as truth does, and hence the Knowledge of it has concealed itself and evaded investigation: and as from this circumstance good is among the unknown things, it was impossible for any one to conjecture that there was any marriage between it and truth: yea, before the natural rational sight, good appears so distant from truth, that no conjunction between them can be supposed. That this is the case, may be seen from the forms of speech used whenever they are mentioned; as when it is said, "This is good," truth is not at all thought of; and when it is said, "This is true," neither is good at all thought of; wherefore at the present day it is believed by many, that truth is quite a different thing from good; and by many also, that a man is intelligent and wise, and thus a man, according to the truths which he thinks, speaks, writes, and believes, and not at the same time according to goods. That nevertheless there does not exist any good without truth, nor any truth without good, consequently that there exists an eternal marriage between them; also that this marriage is the origin of conjugial love, shall now be explained, and in the following order:—

I. *Good and truth are the universals of creation, and hence are in all created things; but in the created subjects they are according to the form of each.*

II. *There does not exist solitary good, nor solitary truth, but they are everywhere conjoined.*

III. *There is the truth of good, and from this the good of truth; or, the truth from good, and the good from that truth: and in those two there has been implanted from creation an inclination to become conjoined into a one.*

IV. *In the subjects of the animal kingdom, the truth of good, or the truth from good, is masculine; and from that the good of truth, or the good from that truth, is feminine.*

V. *From the influx of the marriage of good and truth from the Lord, there is the love of the sex, and there is conjugial love.*

VI. *The love of the sex belongs to the external or natural man, and hence it is common to every animal.*

VII. *But conjugial love belongs to the internal or spiritual man; and hence this love is peculiar to man.*

VIII. *With man conjugial love is in the love of the sex, as a gem in its matrix.*

IX. *The love of the sex with man is not the origin of conjugial love, but its first [manifestation]; thus it is like the natural external into which the spiritual internal is implanted.*

X. *When conjugial love has been implanted, the love of the sex inverts itself, and becomes the chaste love of the sex.*

XI. *The male and the female were created to be the very form of the marriage of good and truth.*

XII. *They are that form in their inmosts, and hence in the things that are derived from those inmosts, in proportion as the interiors of their mind are opened.*

Now follows the explanation of these articles.

84. I. GOOD AND TRUTH ARE THE UNIVERSALS OF CREATION, AND HENCE ARE IN ALL CREATED THINGS; BUT IN THE CREATED SUBJECTS THEY ARE ACCORDING TO THE FORM OF EACH. The reason why good and truth are the universals of creation, is that they two are in the Lord God the Creator; yea, they are Himself; for He is Divine good itself and Divine truth itself. But this falls more clearly into the perception of the understanding, and thus into the idea of thought, if instead of good one says love, and instead of truth one says wisdom; consequently that in the Lord God the Creator there are Divine love and Divine wisdom, and that they are Himself, that is, that He is love itself and wisdom itself; for these two are the same as good and truth. The reason is, that good is of love, and truth is of wisdom; for love consists of goods, and wisdom of truths. Since the two latter and the two former are one and the same thing, therefore in the following pages sometimes the latter and sometimes the former set of terms shall be used, and by both the same is understood. This preliminary observation is here made, lest different meanings should be attached to the expressions when they occur in the following pages.

85. Since therefore the Lord God the Creator is love itself and wisdom itself, and since the universe was created by Him, which thus is as a work proceeding from Him, it cannot but be, that in each and all created things there is something of good and truth from Him; for whatever is done and proceeds from any one, derives a similar quality from him. That this is the case, reason also may see from the order in which

each and all things in the universe were created; which order is, that one exists for the sake of another, and that consequently one depends upon another, like the links of a chain. For all things are for the sake of the human race, that from it there may be an angelic heaven through which creation returns to the Creator Himself, from Whom it was. Hence there is a conjunction of the created universe with its Creator, and by means of the conjunction everlasting preservation. Hence it is that good and truth are called the universals of creation. That this is the case, is evident to every one who considers the matter from reason: he sees in every created thing something which relates to good, and something which relates to truth.

86. The reason why good and truth in the created subjects are according to the form of each, is, that every subject receives influx according to its form. The preservation of the whole consists in nothing else than the perpetual influx of Divine good and Divine truth into forms created by them; for thus subsistence or preservation is perpetual existence or creation. That every subject receives influx according to its form, may be illustrated by various things, as, by the influx of heat and light from the sun into plants of every kind: each of these receives influx according to its form; thus every tree and shrub according to its form, every herb and every blade of grass according to its form: the influx is alike into all, but the reception, because it is according to the form, causes every species to continue the same species. The same thing may also be illustrated by the influx into animals of every kind according to the form of each. That the influx is according to the form of each thing, may also be seen by the most unlettered person, if he attends to the various instruments of sound, as pipes, flutes, trumpets, horns, and organs, which give forth sound from the same blowing or influx of air, according to their forms.

87. II. There does not exist solitary good, nor solitary truth, but they are everywhere conjoined. Whoever wants from any of the senses to acquire an idea about good, cannot possibly find it without some attribute which exhibits and manifests it: good without this is an entity of no name; that by which it is exhibited and manifested, has relation to truth. Pronounce the word good only, and say nothing at the same time of this or that thing with which it is connected; or define it abstractedly, or without any characteristic attribute, and you will see that it is not anything, and that it becomes something with its attribute: and if you bring the acuteness of your reason to bear upon the subject, you will perceive that good, without some attribute, is a term of no predication, and thus of no relation, of no affection, and of no state; in a word, of no quality. The case is

similar with truth, if it be pronounced and heard without something inwardly joined with it; that that which is inwardly joined with it, has relation to good, may be seen by cultivated reason.
2 But since goods are innumerable, and each ascends to its greatest, and descends to its least, as by the steps of a ladder, and also varies its name according to its progression, and according to its quality, it is difficult for any but the wise to see the relation of good and truth to their objects, and their conjunction in them. That nevertheless there does not exist good without truth, nor truth without good, is evident from common perception, when it is first acknowledged that each and all things in the universe have relation to good and truth; as was shewn in
3 the foregoing article (nos. 84, 85). That there does not exist solitary good, nor solitary truth, may be illustrated and at the same time confirmed by various considerations; as by the following: that there does not exist an essence without a form, nor a form without an essence; and good is an essence or esse, and truth is that by means of which the essence is formed and the esse comes into outward existence. Again, in a man there are the will and the understanding. Good is of the will, and truth is of the understanding; and the will alone does nothing except through the understanding; nor does the understanding alone do anything except from the will. Again, in a man there are two fountains of the life of the body, the heart and the lungs. The heart cannot produce any sensitive and motory life without the respiration of the lungs; neither can the lungs without the heart. The heart has relation to good, and the respiration of the
4 lungs to truth: there is also a correspondence. The case is similar in each and all things of the mind, and in each and all things of the body, with man; but we have not leisure to produce further confirmations in this place. These subjects may however be seen confirmed more fully in *Angelic Wisdom concerning the Divine Providence* (nos. 3–16), where they are explained in the following order: I. The universe, with all its created things, is from Divine love through Divine wisdom; or, what is the same thing, from Divine good through Divine truth. II. Divine good and Divine truth proceed as a one from the Lord. III. This one is, in a certain image, in every created thing. V. Good is not good, except in proportion as it is united with truth; and truth is not truth, except in proportion as it is united with good. VII. The Lord does not suffer that anything should be divided; wherefore a man must either be in good and at the same time in truth, or in evil and at the same time in falsity. Besides many other things.

88. III. THERE IS THE TRUTH OF GOOD, AND FROM THIS THE GOOD OF TRUTH; OR, THE TRUTH FROM GOOD, AND THE GOOD FROM THAT TRUTH; AND IN THOSE TWO THERE HAS BEEN IMPLANTED

FROM CREATION AN INCLINATION TO BECOME CONJOINED INTO A ONE. It is necessary that some distinct idea be procured concerning these things; because on this depends the Knowledge about the essential origin of conjugial love: for, as is stated below, the truth of good, or truth from good, is masculine, and the good of truth, or good from that truth, is feminine. But this may be comprehended more distinctly, if instead of good one says love, and instead of truth wisdom; which are one and the same, as may be seen above, no. 84. Wisdom cannot exist with man, except by means of the love of becoming wise; if this love be taken away, man is utterly unable to become wise. Wisdom from this love is meant by the truth of good, or by truth from good: but when a man from that love has procured to himself wisdom, and loves that wisdom in himself, or himself on account of that wisdom, he then forms a love, which is the love of wisdom, and is meant by the good of truth, or the good from that truth. There are, therefore, two loves with a man (*vir*), whereof one, which is prior, is the love of becoming wise; and the other, which is posterior, is the love of wisdom; but this latter love, if it remains with the man (*vir*), is an evil love, and is called conceit, or the love of one's self-intelligence. That it was provided from the creation, that this love should be taken out of the man (*vir*), lest it should destroy him, and that it should be transcribed into woman, in order that it might become conjugial love, which restores the man to integrity, will be confirmed in the following pages. Something about those two loves, and the transcription of the posterior love into the woman, may be seen above, nos. 32, 33, and in the "Preliminaries," no. 20. If therefore instead of love is understood good, and instead of wisdom truth, it is manifest, from what has been already said, that there exists the truth of good, or the truth from good, and from this the good of truth, or the good from that truth.

89. The reason why in these two there has been implanted from creation an inclination to become conjoined into a one, is, that the one was formed from the other; wisdom being formed from the love of becoming wise, or, truth from good; and the love of wisdom being formed from that wisdom, or, the good of truth from that truth: from which formation it may be seen, that there is a mutual inclination to become reunited, and conjoined into a one. But this takes place with men (*viri*) who are in genuine wisdom, and with women who are in the love of that wisdom in the husband; thus with those who are in truly conjugial love. But concerning the wisdom which ought to exist with the man, and which should be loved by the wife, more will be said in what follows.

90. IV. IN THE SUBJECTS OF THE ANIMAL KINGDOM, THE TRUTH OF

GOOD, OR THE TRUTH FROM GOOD, IS MASCULINE; AND THE GOOD OF TRUTH FROM THAT TRUTH OF GOOD, OR THE GOOD FROM THAT TRUTH, IS FEMININE. That from the Lord, the Creator and Supporter of the universe, there flows in a perpetual union of love and wisdom, or marriage of good and truth, and that created subjects receive it, each one according to its form, was shewn above, nos. 84–86: but, that the male from this marriage, or from that union, receives the truth of wisdom, and that the good of love is conjoined to it by the Lord according to the reception, and that this reception takes place in the intellect or understanding, and that hence the male is born to become intellectual,—reason, by virtue of its own lumen, can see from various things in him, espe-
2 cially from his affection, application, manners, and form. From the AFFECTION of the male, which is the affection of knowing, understanding, and becoming wise; the affection of knowing in childhood, the affection of understanding in adolescence and early manhood, and the affection of becoming wise from this early manhood even to old age: from which it is evident, that his nature or inborn disposition inclines to form the intellect; consequently, that he is born to become intellectual: but as this cannot be effected except through love, therefore the Lord adjoins love to him according to his reception, that is, according to his disposition
3 and willingness to become wise. From his APPLICATION, which is to such things as belong to the intellect, or in which the intellect predominates, many of which are public matters, and regard uses in public. From his MANNERS, which all partake of the predominance of the intellect; in consequence whereof the acts of his life, which are meant by manners, are rational; and if they are not, he still wants them to appear so; masculine rationality is also discernible in every one of his virtues. From his FORM, which is different and altogether distinct from the female form; on which subject see also what was said above, no. 33. Add to this, that the prolific principle is in him, which is from no other source than the intellect; for it is from the truth from good in the intellect: that the prolific principle is from this source will be seen in the following pages.

91. But that the female is born to be voluntary, but voluntary from the intellectual of the man (*vir*), or, what is the same, to be the love of the man's wisdom, because she was formed through his wisdom (on which subject see above, nos. 88, 89), may also be manifest from the female's affection, application, manners, and form. From her AFFECTION, which is the affection of loving knowledge, intelligence, and wisdom, nevertheless not in herself, but in the man, and thus of loving the man: for the man (*vir*) cannot be loved merely on account of his form, in that he appears as a man (*homo*), but on account of the quality which is in him, which causes him to be man. From her APPLICATION,

which is to such things as are works of the hands, and are called knitting, needlework, and the like, serving for adornment, both to decorate herself, and to exalt her beauty; and moreover to various duties which are called domestic, which adjoin themselves to the duties of men, which, as was said, are called public. They are led to these duties by an inclination to marriage, in order that they may become wives, and thus one with their husbands. That the same appears also from their MANNERS and FORM, is evident without explanation.

92. V. FROM THE INFLUX OF THE MARRIAGE OF GOOD AND TRUTH FROM THE LORD, THERE IS THE LOVE OF THE SEX, AND THERE IS CONJUGIAL LOVE. That good and truth are the universals of creation, and thus are in all created subjects; and that they are in created subjects according to the form of each; and that good and truth proceed from the Lord not as two but as one, was shewn above, nos. 84 to 87. From these considerations it follows, that the UNIVERSAL CONJUGIAL SPHERE proceeds from the Lord, and pervades the universe from its primes to its ultimates, thus from angels even to worms. The reason why such a sphere of the marriage of good and truth proceeds from the Lord, is, that it is also the sphere of propagation, that is, of prolification and fructification; and this sphere is the same with the Divine providence for the preservation of the universe by means of successive generations. Now, since this universal sphere, which is that of the marriage of good and truth, flows in into subjects according to the form of each (see no. 86), it follows that the male receives it according to his form, thus in the intellect, because he is an intellectual form; and that the female receives it according to her form, thus in the will, because she is a voluntary form from the intellectual of the man; and since that sphere is also the sphere of prolification, it follows that the love of the sex is thence.

93. The reason why conjugial love also is thence, is, that that sphere flows in into the form of wisdom with men, and also with angels; for man is able to grow in wisdom to the end of his life in the world, and afterwards to eternity in heaven; and in proportion as he grows in wisdom, in the same proportion his form is perfected; and this form receives not the love of the sex, but the love of one of the sex; for with one of the sex it can be united to the inmosts in which heaven is with its felicities: and this union is conjugial love.

94. VI. THE LOVE OF THE SEX BELONGS TO THE EXTERNAL OR NATURAL MAN, AND HENCE IT IS COMMON TO EVERY ANIMAL. Every man is born corporeal, and becomes more and more interiorly natural, and in proportion as he loves intelligence he

becomes rational, and afterwards, if he loves wisdom, he becomes spiritual. What the wisdom is through which man becomes spiritual, will be stated in the following pages, at no. 130. Now, as a man progresses from knowledge into intelligence, and from intelligence into wisdom, so also his mind changes its form; for it is opened more and more, and conjoins itself more closely with heaven, and through heaven with the Lord; hence it becomes more enamoured of truth, and more studious of the good of life. If therefore he halts at the threshold in the progression to wisdom, the form of his mind remains natural; and this receives the influx of the universal sphere, which is that of the marriage of good and truth, in no other way than it is received by the lower subjects of the animal kingdom, which are called beasts and birds; and as these are merely natural, that man becomes like them, and thus loves the sex just as they do. This is what is meant by the statement that the love of the sex belongs to the external or natural man, and that hence it is common to every animal.

95. VII. BUT CONJUGIAL LOVE BELONGS TO THE INTERNAL OR SPIRITUAL MAN; AND THIS LOVE IS PECULIAR TO MAN. The reason why conjugial love belongs to the internal or spiritual man is, that the more intelligent and wise man becomes, the more internal or spiritual he becomes, and in the same proportion the form of his mind is perfected; and this form receives conjugial love: for he perceives and feels in this love a spiritual delight, which is full of blessedness within, and from this a natural delight, which derives its soul, life, and essence from the former.

96. The reason why conjugial love is peculiar to man, is, that man only can become spiritual, for he can elevate his understanding above his natural loves, and from that state of elevation see them beneath him, and judge of their quality, and also amend, chastise, and remove them. No animal can do this; for the loves of animals are entirely united with their connate knowledge; wherefore this knowledge cannot be elevated into intelligence, and still less into wisdom; in consequence of which circumstance an animal is led along by the love implanted in its knowledge, as a blind man is led through the streets by a dog. This is the reason why conjugial love is peculiar to man. It may also be called native and germane to man, because in man there is the faculty of becoming wise, with which faculty this love makes a one.

97. VIII. WITH MAN CONJUGIAL LOVE IS IN THE LOVE OF THE SEX AS A GEM IN ITS MATRIX. As this however is merely a comparison, it shall be explained in the article which immediately follows; this comparison also illustrates what was shewn

just above, nos. 94, 95, that the love of the sex belongs to the external or natural man, and conjugial love to the internal or spiritual man.

98. IX. THE LOVE OF THE SEX WITH MAN IS NOT THE ORIGIN OF CONJUGIAL LOVE, BUT ITS FIRST [MANIFESTATION]; THUS IT IS LIKE THE NATURAL EXTERNAL, IN WHICH THE SPIRITUAL INTERNAL IS IMPLANTED. The subject here treated of is truly conjugial love, and not the common love which also is called conjugial, and which with some is nothing but the limited love of the sex. Truly conjugial love exists only with those who earnestly desire wisdom, and who therefore progress more and more into wisdom. These the Lord foresees, and for them He provides conjugial love. This love indeed commences with them from the love of the sex, or rather by means of it, but still it does not originate in it; for it originates in the proportion in which wisdom advances and progresses into the light with it; for wisdom and that love are inseparable companions. The reason why 2
conjugial love commences by means of the love of the sex, is that, before a consort is found, the sex is loved in a general way, and regarded with a loving eye, and it is treated with courteous morality: for the young man has to make his choice; and at that time from an innate inclination to marriage with one woman, which lies concealed in the inmost recesses of his mind, his external receives a gentle warmth. A further reason is, that the determinations to marriage are delayed from various causes even to the middle of the age of manhood, and in the meantime the beginning of that love is as lust, which with some passes off into the love of the sex actually; yet even with them its bridle is relaxed no further than is conducive to health. This, however, is said of the male sex, because it has allurements which actually inflame; but not of the female sex. From these considerations it is evident that the love of the sex is not the origin of truly conjugial love; but that it is its first [manifestation] as to time, yet not as to end; for what is first as to end, is first in the mind and its intention, because it is primary; but to this first there is no approach except successively through media, and these are not primes or first things in themselves, but only conducive to what is first in itself.

99. X. WHEN CONJUGIAL LOVE HAS BEEN IMPLANTED, THE LOVE OF THE SEX INVERTS ITSELF, AND BECOMES THE CHASTE LOVE OF THE SEX. It is said that the love of the sex then inverts itself, because when conjugial love has arrived at its origin, which is in the interiors of the mind, it sees the love of the sex not before itself but behind, or not above itself but beneath, and thus as something which it has passed by and left. The case herein is similar to that of a person who climbs from one office

to another till he reaches one which exceeds the rest in dignity, and afterwards looks back behind or beneath himself upon the offices through which he had passed; or as when a person intends a journey to the palace of some king, after his arrival he inverts his view in regard to what he had seen in the way. That in this case the love of the sex remains, and becomes chaste, and yet, to those who are in truly conjugial love, sweeter than it was before, may be seen from the description given of it by those who are in the spiritual world, in the two Memorable Relations, nos. 44 and 55.

100. XI. THE MALE AND THE FEMALE WERE CREATED TO BE THE VERY FORM OF THE MARRIAGE OF GOOD AND TRUTH. The reason is, that the male was created to be the understanding of truth, thus truth in form; and the female was created to be the will of good, thus good in form; and there has been implanted in each, from their inmosts, an inclination towards conjunction into a one (see above, no. 88); thus the two make one form, which emulates the conjugial form of good and truth. It is said to emulate it, because it is not the same, but is like it; for the good which conjoins itself with the truth in the man (*vir*) is from the Lord immediately; and the good of the wife, which conjoins itself with the truth in the man, is from the Lord mediately through the wife; wherefore there are two goods, one which is internal, and another which is external, which conjoin themselves with the truth in the husband, and cause him to be constantly in the understanding of truth, and hence in wisdom through truly conjugial love; but on this subject more will be said in the following pages.

101. XII. THE TWO MARRIED PARTNERS ARE THAT FORM IN THEIR INMOSTS, AND THENCE IN THOSE THINGS THAT ARE DERIVED FROM THOSE INMOSTS, IN PROPORTION AS THE INTERIORS OF THEIR MIND ARE OPENED. There are three things of which every man consists, and which follow in order with him, the soul, the mind, and the body: his inmost is the soul, his mediate is the mind, and his ultimate is the body. Everything which flows in from the Lord into man, flows in into his inmost, which is the soul, and descends thence into his mediate, which is the mind, and through this into his ultimate, which is the body. In this manner does the marriage of good and truth flow in from the Lord with man: it flows in immediately into his soul, and thence proceeds to the succeeding parts, and through these to the extremes; and thus conjointly these things constitute conjugial love. From the idea of this influx it is evident, that the two married partners are that form in their inmosts, and thence in those things that are derived from the inmosts.

102. But the reason why married partners become that form in proportion as the interiors of their minds are opened, is, that the mind is successively opened from infancy even to extreme old age. For man is born corporeal; and in proportion as the mind is opened proximately above the body, he becomes Rational; and in proportion as this rational is purified, and as it were decanted of the fallacies which flow in from the senses of the body, and of the concupiscences which flow in from the allurements of the flesh, in the same proportion it is opened; and this is effected solely by wisdom: and when the interiors of the rational mind are opened, the man becomes a form of wisdom; and this form is the receptacle of truly conjugial love. *The wisdom which constitutes this form, and receives this love, is rational, and at the same time moral, wisdom. Rational wisdom looks upon the truths and goods which appear inwardly in man, not as its own, but as flowing in from the Lord; and moral wisdom shuns evils and falsities as leprosies, especially lasciviousnesses, which contaminate its conjugial love.

103. To the above I shall add two Memorable Relations; the first is this:—

One morning before sunrise I was looking towards the east in the spiritual world, and I saw four horsemen as it were flying out of a cloud refulgent with the flame of the dawn. On their heads there appeared crested helmets, on their arms as it were wings, and around their bodies light orange-coloured tunics; thus clad as for expedition, they rose in their seats, and gave their horses the rein, which thus ran as if they had wings to their feet. I followed their course or flight with my eye, desiring to know whither they were going; and lo! three of the horsemen spread themselves abroad towards three different quarters, the south, the west, and the north; and the fourth in a short space of time halted in the east.

Wondering at all this, I looked up into heaven, and asked 2
where those horsemen were going. I received for answer, "To the wise men in the kingdoms of Europe, who discriminate matters with penetrating reason and with sharp-sighted discernment, and were celebrated in their own countries as men of genius, that they may come and solve the secret concerning THE ORIGIN OF CONJUGIAL LOVE, AND CONCERNING ITS VIRTUE OR POTENCY."

And they said from heaven, "Wait a little, and you will see twenty-seven chariots; three, in which are Spaniards; three, in which are Frenchmen; three, in which are Italians; three, in which are Germans; three, in which are Batavians or Dutchmen; three, in which are Englishmen; three, in which are Swedes;

* The words that here follow, to the end of the pargaraph, are, in the original Latin edition, enclosed in inverted commas.

three, in which are Danes; and three, in which are Poles." And after two hours I saw these chariots, drawn by cobs of a light bay colour, with remarkable trappings: they passed rapidly along towards a spacious house on the confines of the east and south, around which all alighted from their several chariots, and entered in with much confidence.

Then it was said to me, "Go, and do thou also enter, and thou wilt hear."

3 I went and entered. On examining the house within, I saw that it was square, the sides looking to the four quarters: in each side there were three high windows of crystalline glass, the frames of which were of olive-wood; on each side of the frames were projections from the walls, like chambers vaulted above, in which there were tables. The walls of these chambers were of cedar, the roof of the noble thyine wood, and the floor of poplar beams. At the eastern wall, where no windows were seen, there was set a table overlaid with gold, on which was placed a TIARA set about with precious stones, which was to be given as a prize or reward to him who should trace out the secret about to be propounded.

4 While my attention was directed to the chamber projections, which were like closets near the windows, I saw five men in each chamber from each kingdom of Europe, who were ready and waiting to know the object for the exercise of their judgments.

At that instant an angel stood in the midst of the palace, and said, "The object for the exercise of your judgments shall be CONCERNING THE ORIGIN OF CONJUGIAL LOVE, AND CONCERNING ITS VIRTUE OR POTENCY. Investigate this and come to a decision about it; and write your decision on a piece of paper, and put this paper into the silver urn which you see placed near the golden table, and subscribe the initial letter of the kingdom from which you come; as F for Frenchmen, B for Batavians or Dutchmen, I for Italians, A for English (*Angli*), P for Poles, G for Germans, H for Spaniards (*Hispani*), D for Danes, and S for Swedes." As he said this, the angel departed, saying, "I will return."

Then the five fellow-countrymen in each closet by the windows, took into consideration the proposed subject, examined it attentively, and came to a decision according to the excellence of the qualities of their judgments, wrote it on a piece of paper, and put it in the silver urn, having first subscribed the initial letter of their kingdom. This business being accomplished in about three hours, the angel returned, and drew the papers in order from the urn, and read them before the assembly.

104. From the FIRST PAPER which he happened to lay hold of, he read as follows: "We five natives of the same country, in our closet have come to the decision that the origin of conjugial

love is from the Most Ancient people in the golden age, and with them, from the creation of Adam and his wife; hence is the origin of marriages, and with marriages the origin of conjugial love. As regards the virtue or potency of conjugial love, we derive it from no other source than the climate, or the direction of the sun, and the consequent heat of the country. We have come to this conclusion, not by vain conjectures of reason, but by evident proofs of experience, as by the case of the people who live under the line, or the equinoctial, where the heat of the day is intense, and by the case of those who live nearer to the line, or more distant from it; and also from the co-operation of the sun's heat with the vital heat in the animals of the earth and the birds of heaven, in the time of spring when they are prolific. Moreover, what is conjugial love but heat, which becomes virtue or potency if supplementary heat from the sun be added to it?" To this decision was subscribed the letter H, the initial of the kingdom from which they were.

105. After this he put his hand into the urn a SECOND TIME, and took thence a paper from which he read as follows; "We, natives of the same country, in our lodge have agreed that the origin of conjugial love is the same with the origin of marriages, which have been sanctioned by the laws in order to restrain man's connate concupiscences towards adulteries, which ruin the soul, pollute the reason of the mind, defile the morals, and infect the body with disease. For adulteries are not human but bestial, not rational but brutish, and thus not in any respect Christian but barbarous: for the sake of the condemnation of such adulteries, marriages originated, and at the same time a conjugial love. The case is similar with the virtue or potency of this love; for it depends on chastity, which consists in abstinence from roving whoredoms: the reason is, that the virtue or potency, with him who loves his married partner alone, is reserved for one, and is thus collected and as it were concentrated; and then it becomes refined like a quintessence from which all defilements have been removed, which would otherwise be dispersed and cast away in every direction. One of us five, who is a priest, has also added predestination as a cause of that virtue or potency, saying, 'Are not marriages predestinated? and if they are, are not the prolifications thence, and the efficacy thereto, predestinated also?' He insisted on this cause because he had sworn to it." To this decision was subscribed the letter B.

On hearing this a certain one said in a derisive voice, "How beautiful an apology for defect or impotence is predestination!"

106. Next, he took out of the urn, the THIRD TIME, a paper from which he read as follows: "We, natives of the same country, in our cell have thought over the causes of the origin

of conjugial love, and have seen this to be the principal one, that it is the same with the origin of marriage, because conjugial love had no existence before marriage; and it comes into existence because, when any one desperately loves a maiden, he desires in heart and soul to own her as a possession loveable above all things; and as soon as she promises herself to him he regards her as if his own self were looking at another self. That this is the origin of conjugial love, is clearly evident from the fury of every man against his rivals, and from his jealousy against violators. We afterwards thought over the origin of the virtue or potency of that love; and the opinion of three prevailed against that of the other two, that virtue or potency with a married partner is from some licentiousness with the sex. They said that they knew from experience that the potency of the love of the sex is greater than the potency of conjugial love." To this decision was subscribed the letter I.

On hearing this they cried from the tables, "Remove this paper and draw another out of the urn."

107. And instantly he drew out a FOURTH, from which he read as follows: "We, natives of the same country, under our window have come to the decision, that the origin of conjugial love and of the love of the sex is the same, because the former is from the latter; only that the love of the sex is unlimited, indeterminate, loose, promiscuous, and roving, whereas conjugial love is limited, determinate, restricted, settled, and constant; and that this love therefore has been sanctioned and established by the prudence of human wisdom, because otherwise no empire, kingdom, commonwealth, nor even society, would exist; for without it men would wander about like droves of cattle in fields and forests, with whores and ravished females, and would fly from one habitation to another to avoid the bloody murders, violations, and robberies, whereby the whole human race would be in danger of being extirpated. This is our judgment concerning the origin of conjugial love. But the virtue or potency of conjugial love we deduce from the continual lasting of the health of the body from birth to old age; for the man who is always well and possessed of sound health does not fail in vigour; his fibres, nerves, muscles, and cremasters [muscles peculiar to the male] do not become stiff, relaxed, nor feeble, but retain the full strength of their powers: farewell." To this decision was subscribed the letter A.

108. FIFTHLY, he drew out of the urn a paper, from which he read as follows: "We, natives of the same country, at our table, according to the rationality of our minds have examined into the origin of conjugial love, and into the origin of its virtue or potency; and from all the reasons which we have considered, we

have seen and confirmed no other origin of conjugial love than this—that every man, from incentives and consequent incitements which are concealed in the adytum of his mind and body, after indulging in various lusts of his eyes, at length fixes his mind and inclination on one woman of the sex, until his passion is determined entirely to her: from this time his heat goes from flame to flame, until at length it becomes a conflagration; in this state the lust of the sex is banished, and conjugial love takes its place. A youthful bridegroom under the influence of this conflagration, knows no otherwise than that the virtue or potency of that love will never cease; for he lacks experience and consequently knowledge of the state of the failure of his powers, and of the chilling of love which then succeeds the delights. The origin of conjugial love therefore is from this first ardour before the wedding; and from the same also comes its virtue or potency; but this virtue or potency changes its aspect after the wedding, and decreases and increases; yet still it lasts with regular changes, or with decrease and increase, even to old age, by means of moderations from prudence, and by bridling the lusts which burst forth from the recesses of the mind not yet thoroughly purified; for lust precedes wisdom. This is our judgment concerning the origin and continuance of conjugial virtue or potency." To this decision was subscribed the letter P.

109. SIXTHLY, he drew out a paper, from which he read as follows: "We, natives of the same country, from our fellowship have attentively considered the causes of the origin of conjugial love, and have agreed on two; one of which is the right education of children, and the other the distinct possession of inheritances. We have chosen these two, because they aim at and regard the same goal, which is the public good; and this is obtained, because infants conceived and born from conjugial love become one's very own and true children; and these, in consequence of the love of children (*storge*) being heightened by the consideration that they are legitimate, are educated to be heirs of all their parents' possessions, both spiritual and natural. That the public good is founded on the right education of children and on the distinct possession of inheritances, is seen by reason. There is the love of the sex, and there is conjugial love; the latter love appears as if it were one with the former, but it is distinctly different; neither is the one love near to the other, but within it; and what is within is more excellent than what is without: and we have seen that conjugial love from creation is within, and lies hidden in the love of the sex, just as an almond does in its shell; wherefore when conjugial love is set free from its shell, which is the love of the sex, it glitters before the angels like a gem, a beryl, and an astroites. This takes place because on conjugial

love is inscribed the well-being of the whole human race, which is what we mean by the public good. This is our judgment concerning the origin of this love. With respect to the origin of its virtue or potency, from a consideration of its causes, we have come to the conclusion that it is the setting free and separation of conjugial love from the love of the sex, which is effected by the husband (*vir*) by means of wisdom, and by the wife by means of the love of the husband's wisdom; for the love of the sex is common [to men] with beasts, and conjugial love is peculiar to men (*homines*). Wherefore in the proportion in which conjugial love is set free and separated from the love of the sex, a man is a man and not a beast; and a man acquires virtue or potency from his love, as a beast does from his." To this decision was subscribed the letter G.

110. SEVENTHLY, he drew out a paper from which he read as follows: "We, natives of the same country, in the chamber under the light of our window, have exhilarated our thoughts and thence our judgments by meditating on conjugial love. Who is not exhilarated by that love, for while it is in the mind, it is at the same time in the whole body? We judge of the origin of that love from its delights: who ever knows or has known the footsteps of any love except from its delight and pleasurableness? The delightsomenesses of conjugial love in their origins are felt as blessednesses, blissfulnesses, and happinesses, in their derivations as pleasantnesses and pleasures, and in their ultimates as the delights of delights. The love of the sex therefore originates when the interiors of the mind, and thence the interiors of the body, are opened for the influx of those delightsomenesses; but conjugial love originated at the time when, through betrothals which had taken place, the primitive sphere of that love ideally promoted those delights. As regards the virtue or potency of that love, it arises from the capacity of that love of passing, with its current, from the mind into the body; for the mind, from the head, is in the body when it feels and acts, especially when it is being delighted from this love: hence we judge of the degrees of its potency and the constancies of its alternations. Moreover we also deduce the virtue of potency from the stock: if this be noble on the father's side, it becomes also by transmission noble with his offspring. That that nobility is engendered, inherited, and descends by transmission, is assented to by reason with experience." To this decision was subscribed the letter F.

111. The EIGHTH time he drew out a paper, from which he read as follows: "We, natives of the same country, in our place of assembly have not discovered the real origin of conjugial love, because it lies deeply concealed in the sanctuaries of the mind.

The most consummate wisdom cannot, by any stretch of the understanding, reach that love in its origin. We have made many conjectures; but after pondering in vain over subtleties, we have been in doubt whether our conjectures might not be called rather trifling than judicious; wherefore whoever wants to extract the origin of that love from the sanctuaries of the mind, and to exhibit it clearly before his eyes, let him go to Delphi. We have contemplated that love beneath its origin, and have seen that in the minds it is spiritual, and as the fountain of a sweet stream, whence it flows down into the bosom, where it becomes delightful, and is called bosom love, which, regarded in itself is full of friendship and full of confidence by reason of its full inclination to mutuality; and that when it has passed the bosom, it becomes genial love. When a young man is revolving these and similar considerations in his thoughts, as he does when he chooses for himself one of the sex, they kindle in his heart the fire of conjugial love; which fire, because it is the primitive fire of that love, is its origin. We acknowledge no other origin of its virtue or potency than that love itself, for they are inseparable companions; yet still they are such that sometimes the one precedes and sometimes the other. When the love precedes and the virtue or potency follows it, both are noble, because in this case the potency is the virtue of conjugial love; but if the potency precedes and the love follows, then both are ignoble, because in this case the love belongs to the potency of the flesh. We therefore judge of the quality of each from the order in which the love descends or ascends, and thus proceeds from its origin to its goal." To this decision was subscribed the letter D.

112. Lastly, or NINTHLY, he took up a paper, from which he read as follows: "We, natives of the same country, from our place of meeting have exercised our judgment on the two points proposed, namely, the origin of conjugial love, and the origin of its virtue or potency. When weighing the subtleties respecting the origin of conjugial love, in order to avoid obscurity in our reasonings, we have distinguished between the spiritual, the natural, and the carnal love of the sex; and by the spiritual love of the sex we have understood truly conjugial love, because this is spiritual: and by the natural love of the sex we have understood polygamous love, because this is natural; and by the merely carnal love of the sex we have understood scortatory love, because this is merely carnal. When we had carefully examined truly conjugial love with our judgments, we clearly saw that this love exists only between one male and one female, and that from creation it is heavenly and inmost, and the soul and father of all good loves, being inspired into the first parents, and capable of being inspired into Christians; it is also of such a conjunctive nature that through it two minds may

become one mind, and two human beings (*homines*) [*i.e.* one man and one woman] as it were one man (*homo*), which is meant by becoming one flesh. That this love was inspired at the creation, is evident from these words in the Book of the Creation, '*And a man* (vir) *shall leave father and mother, and shall cleave to his wife; and they shall become one flesh*' (Gen. ii. 24). That it can be inspired into Christians, is evident from these words, '*Jesus said, Have ye not read, that He who made them from the beginning, made them male and female, and said, For this cause shall a man leave father and mother, and cleave to his wife; and they two shall become one flesh? Wherefore they are no longer two but one flesh*' (Matt. xix. 4–6). So far in regard to the origin of conjugial love. But as to the origin of the virtue or potency of truly conjugial love, we surmise that it proceeds from likeness of minds, and unanimity; for when two minds are conjugially conjoined, their thoughts spiritually kiss each other, and inspire into the body their virtue or potency." To this decision was subscribed the letter S.

113. There were standing behind an oblong gallery in the palace, erected before the doors, some strangers from Africa, who cried out to the natives of Europe, "Permit one of us also to give his opinion on the origin of conjugial love, and on its virtue or potency."

And all the tables gave signs of assent with their hands that it should be allowed.

Then one of them entered, and stood at the table on which the tiara was placed. He said, "You Christians deduce the origin of conjugial love from love itself; but we Africans deduce it from the God of heaven and earth. Is not conjugial love a chaste, pure, and holy love? Are not the angels of heaven in that love? Is not the whole human race, and thus the whole angelic heaven, the seed of that love? And can such a super-eminent thing derive its existence from any other source than from God Himself, the Creator and Supporter of the universe? You Christians deduce conjugial virtue or potency from various rational and natural causes; but we Africans deduce it from the state of man's conjunction with the God of the universe. This state we call the state of religion, but you call it the state of the church: for when the love is from that state, and is stable and perpetual, it must needs produce its own virtue, which is like it, and thus also is stable and perpetual. Truly conjugial love is known only to those few who are near to God; consequently the potency also of that love is known to no others. This potency with that love is described by the angels in the heavens as the delight of a perpetual spring."

114. As he said these words, they all arose, and lo! behind

the golden table on which lay the tiara, there appeared a window that had not been seen before; and through it was heard a voice, saying, "THE AFRICAN SHALL HAVE THE TIARA." The angel then placed it into his hand, but not upon his head; and he went home with it.

The inhabitants of the kingdoms of Europe then went out and entered their chariots, in which they returned to their own homes.

115. The second Memorable Relation:*—

Awaking from sleep at midnight, I saw at some height towards the east an angel holding in his right hand a paper, which appeared in a bright whiteness by reason of the light flowing from the sun. In the middle of the paper there was a writing in golden letters, and I saw that there was written thereon "THE MARRIAGE OF GOOD AND TRUTH." From the writing there darted forth a splendour which formed a wide circle around the paper: this circle or encompassing splendour appeared like the dawn in spring-time.

After this I saw the angel descending with the paper in his hand; and as he descended the paper became less and less lucid, and the writing, which was "THE MARRIAGE OF GOOD AND TRUTH," changed from a golden into a silver colour, afterwards into a copper colour, next into an iron colour, and at length into the colour of iron and copper rust: and finally, the angel was seen to enter a dark mist, and pass through the mist to the earth; and there the paper was not seen although the angel still held it in his hand. This happened in the world of spirits, in which all human beings first assemble after death.

The angel then spoke to me, saying, "Ask those who come 2
hither whether they see me, or anything in my hand."

There came a great number; one company from the east, another from the south, another from the west, and another from the north; and I asked those who came from the east and from the south, who were those who in the world had applied themselves to learning, "Do you see any one here with me, and anything in his hand?" They all said, that they saw nothing at all.

I then put the same question to those who came from the west and from the north, who were those who in the world had believed in the words of the learned. These also said that they did not see anything: nevertheless the last of them, who in the world had been in simple faith from charity, or in some truth from good, when the rest were gone away, said that they saw a man (*vir*) with a paper, the man in a beautiful dress, and the paper with letters written upon it: and when they applied their eyes nearer to it, they said that they read these words, "*The marriage*

* This Memorable Relation is repeated in the *True Christian Religion*, no. 624.

of good and truth"; and they addressed the angel, entreating him to tell them what this meant.

3 He said, "All things which exist in the whole heaven, and all things which exist in the whole world, are nothing else than a marriage of good and truth; for all things whatsoever, both those which live and possess a soul and those which do not live and do not possess a soul, were created from the marriage of good and truth, and into that marriage. There does not exist anything that has been created into truth alone, nor anything that has been created into good alone: solitary good or solitary truth is not anything; but by means of marriage they come into existence and become such a thing as the marriage itself is. In the Lord the Creator there is Divine good and Divine truth in its very substance: the Esse of His substance is Divine good, and its Existere is Divine truth: in Him also they are in their very union; for in Him they infinitely constitute a one. Since these two in the Creator Himself are a one, therefore also they are a one in each and all things that have been created by Him; thereby also the Creator is conjoined in an eternal covenant as
4 of marriage with all things created by Himself." The angel further said, that the Sacred Scripture, which has proceeded immediately from the Lord, is in general and in particular the marriage of good and truth; and since the church, which is formed by means of the truth of doctrine, and religion, which is formed by means of the good of life according to the truth of doctrine, are, among Christians, derived solely from the Sacred Scripture, therefore it may be manifest that the church in general and in particular is the marriage of good and truth (*that this is the case, may be seen in the The Apocalypse Revealed*, nos. 373, 483). What has just been said concerning the marriage of good and truth, is also said of the MARRIAGE OF CHARITY AND FAITH; for good belongs to charity, and truth to faith.

Some of those above-mentioned, who did not see the angel and the writing, being still near, and hearing these things, said in an undertone, "*That is so; we apprehend that.*"

But the angel then said to them, "Turn aside a little from me, and speak in like manner."

They turned aside and said aloud, "*It is not so.*"

5 After this the angel spoke of the MARRIAGE OF GOOD AND TRUTH with married partners, saying, that "if their minds were in that marriage, the husband being truth and the wife the good thereof, they would both be in the delights of the blessedness of innocence, and thence in the happiness in which the angels of heaven are; and in this state the prolific principle of the husband would be in a continual spring, and thus in the endeavour and power (*virtus*) of propagating its truth, and the wife would be in a continual reception thereof from love. The wisdom which is with men (*viri*) from the Lord, is sensible of

nothing more delightful than to propagate its truths; and the love of wisdom which is with wives from the Lord is sensible of nothing more pleasant than to receive those truths as it were in the womb, and thus to conceive them, carry them in the womb, and bring them forth. Spiritual prolifications with the angels of heaven are of this sort; and if you are willing to believe it, natural prolifications also are from the same origin."

The angel, after a salutation of peace, raised himself up from the earth, and passing through the mist ascended into heaven; and then the paper shone as before according to the degrees of ascent; and behold! the circle, which had before appeared as the dawn, descended, and dispelled the mist which had caused darkness on the earth, and a bright sunshine succeeded.

THE MARRIAGE OF THE LORD AND THE CHURCH, AND ITS CORRESPONDENCE.

116. THE reason why the marriage of the Lord and the church, together with its correspondence, is here also treated of, is, that without knowledge and intelligence on this subject, scarcely any one can know that conjugial love in its origin is holy, spiritual, and celestial, and that it is from the Lord. It is indeed said by some in the church, that marriages have relation to the marriage of the Lord with the church; but the quality of this relation is not known. In order therefore that this relationship may be exhibited in some light of the understanding so as to be seen, it is necessary to treat particularly of that holy marriage which exists with and in those who are the Lord's church: these also, and no others, possess truly conjugial love. But for the elucidation of this arcanum, this chapter must be divided into the following articles:

I. *The Lord in the Word is called the Bridegroom and Husband, and the church the bride and wife; and the conjunction of the Lord with the church, and the reciprocal conjunction of the church with the Lord, is called marriage.*

II. *The Lord is also called the Father, and the church the mother.*

III. *The offspring from the Lord as the husband and father, and from the church as the wife and mother, are all spiritual; and in the spiritual sense of the Word are meant by sons and daughters, brothers and sisters, sons-in-law and daughters-in-law, and by the other names of relationship.*

IV. *The spiritual offspring, which are born from the marriage of the Lord with the church, are truths, from which there are understanding, perception, and all thought; and goods, from which there are love, charity, and all affection.*

V. *From the marriage of good and truth, which proceeds from the Lord, and flows in, man receives truth, and to this the Lord conjoins good; and thus the church is formed by the Lord with man.*

VI. *The husband does not represent the Lord, and the wife the church; because both together, the husband and the wife, constitute the church.*

VII. *Therefore there is no correspondence of the husband with the Lord, and of the wife with the church, in the marriages of angels in the heavens, and of human beings on earth.*

VIII. *But there is a correspondence with conjugial love, fecundation, prolification, the love of children, and similar things which are in marriages and from marriages.*

IX. *The Word is the medium of conjunction, because it is from the Lord, and thus is the Lord.*

X. *The church is from the Lord, and is with those who come to Him, and live according to His precepts.*

XI. *Conjugial love is according to the state of the church, because it is according to the state of wisdom, with man.*

XII. *And, since the church is from the Lord, conjugial love also is from Him.*

Now follows the explanation of these articles.

117. I. THE LORD IN THE WORD IS CALLED THE BRIDEGROOM AND HUSBAND, AND THE CHURCH THE BRIDE AND WIFE; AND THE CONJUNCTION OF THE LORD WITH THE CHURCH, AND THE RECIPROCAL CONJUNCTION OF THE CHURCH WITH THE LORD, IS CALLED MARRIAGE. That the Lord in the Word is called the Bridegroom and Husband, and the church the bride and wife, may be manifest from the following passages: "*He Who hath the* BRIDE *is the* BRIDEGROOM; *but the friend of the* BRIDEGROOM, *who standeth and heareth Him, rejoiceth with joy because of the* BRIDEGROOM'S *voice*" (John iii. 29); this was said of the Lord by John the Baptist. "*Jesus said, So long as the* BRIDEGROOM *is with them, the* SONS OF THE WEDDING *cannot fast: the days will come when the* BRIDEGROOM *will be taken away from them, and then they will fast*" (Matt. ix. 15; Mark ii. 19, 20; Luke v. 34, 35). "*I saw the holy city, New Jerusalem, prepared as a* BRIDE *adorned for* HER HUSBAND" (Apoc. xxi. 2): that by the New Jerusalem is meant the Lord's New Church, may be seen in the *Apocalypse Revealed*, nos. 880, 881. "*The angel said to John, Come, and I will shew thee the* BRIDE, THE LAMB'S WIFE: *and he shewed him the holy city, [New] Jerusalem*" (Apoc. xxi. 9, 10). "*The time of the* WEDDING OF THE LAMB *is come, and* HIS WIFE *hath made herself ready. Blessed are those who are called to the supper of the* WEDDING OF THE LAMB" (Apoc. xix. 7, 9). By the BRIDEGROOM, whom the five virgins that were ready went forth to meet, and with whom they entered in to the WEDDING (Matt. xxv. 1–10) is meant the Lord, as is evident from verse 13, where it is said, "*Watch, therefore; because ye know neither the day nor the hour in which the* SON OF MAN *will come.*" Besides many passages in the Prophets.

118. II. THE LORD IS ALSO CALLED THE FATHER, AND THE CHURCH THE MOTHER. That the Lord is called the Father, is manifest from the following passages: "*Unto us a Child is born; unto us a Son is given; and His name shall be called Wonderful, Counsellor,* GOD, THE FATHER OF ETERNITY, *the Prince of Peace*"

(Isaiah ix. 5 [6]). "*Thou,* JEHOVAH, *art* OUR FATHER, *our* REDEEMER; *Thy name is from eternity*" (Isaiah lxiii. 16). "*Jesus saith, he that seeth* ME, *seeth the* FATHER *Who sent* ME" (John xii. 45). "*If ye had known* ME, *ye had known My* FATHER *also; and henceforth ye have known Him, and have seen Him*" (John xiv. 7). "*Philip said, Shew us the* FATHER: *Jesus said unto him, He that seeth Me, seeth the* FATHER; *how sayest thou then, Shew us the* FATHER?" (John xiv. 8, 9). "*Jesus said, The* FATHER *and* I *are one*" (John x. 30). "*All things that the* FATHER *hath are* MINE" (John xvi. 15; chap. xvii. 10). "*The* FATHER *is in* ME, *and* I IN THE FATHER" (John x. 38; chap. xiv. 10, 11, 20). That the Lord and His Father are one, as the soul and the body are one, and that God the Father descended from heaven, and assumed the Human, to redeem and save human beings, and that His Human is what is called the Son, who was sent into the world, has been fully shewn in the *Apocalypse Revealed.*

119. That the church is called the mother, is manifest from the following passages: "*Jehovah said, Contend with* YOUR MOTHER: *she is not* MY WIFE, *and I am not her* HUSBAND" (Hosea ii. 2, 5). "*Thou art thy* MOTHER'S *daughter, that loatheth her* HUSBAND" (Ezek. xvi. 45). "*Where is the bill of thy* MOTHER'S *divorcement, whom I have put away?*" (Isaiah l. 1). "*Thy* MOTHER *was like a vine planted by the waters, bearing fruit*" (Ezek. xix. 10): these things are said of the Jewish church. "*Jesus stretching out His hand to the disciples, said,* MY MOTHER *and My brethren are those who hear the Word of God, and do it*" (Luke viii. 21; Matt. xii. 49 [49, 50]; Mark iii. 33–35): by the Lord's disciples is meant the church. "*There was standing at the cross of Jesus, His mother: and Jesus, seeing His mother and the disciple whom He loved, standing by, saith unto His mother, Woman, behold thy son: and He saith to the disciple, Behold thy mother: wherefore from that hour the disciple took her unto his own*" (John xix. 25–27): by this is meant that the Lord did not acknowledge Mary as a mother, but the church; wherefore he calls her Woman, and the disciple's mother. The reason why the Lord called her the mother of this disciple, or of John, was, that John represented the church as to the goods of charity, which are the church in very effect; therefore it is said that he took her unto his own. That Peter represented Truth and faith, James charity, and John the works of charity, see the *Apocalypse Revealed*, nos. 5, 6, 790, 798, 879; and that the twelve disciples together represented the church as to all its [constituents], see nos. 233, 790, 903, 915.

120. III. THE OFFSPRING FROM THE LORD AS THE HUSBAND AND FATHER, AND FROM THE CHURCH AS THE WIFE AND MOTHER,

ARE ALL SPIRITUAL; AND IN THE SPIRITUAL SENSE OF THE WORD ARE MEANT BY SONS AND DAUGHTERS, BROTHERS AND SISTERS, SONS-IN-LAW AND DAUGHTERS-IN-LAW, AND BY THE OTHER NAMES OF RELATIONSHIP. That no other than spiritual offspring are born of the church from the Lord, needs no demonstration, because reason sees it without; for it is the Lord from Whom all good and truth proceeds, and it is the church which receives them and puts them into effect; and all the spiritual things of heaven and the church relate to good and truth. Hence it is that by sons and daughters in the Word, in its spiritual sense, are meant truths and goods; by sons, truths conceived in the spiritual man and born in the natural; and by daughters, goods in like manner: wherefore those who are regenerated by the Lord, are called in the Word sons of God, sons of the kingdom, born of Him: and the Lord called the disciples sons: by the male child that the woman brought forth, and that was caught up to God (Apoc. xii. 5) nothing else is signified; see the *Apocalypse Revealed*, no 543. Since by daughters are signified the goods of the church, therefore in the Word mention is so frequently made of the daughter of Zion, the daughter of Jerusalem, the daughter of Israel, and the daughter of Judah; by whom is signified not any daughter, but the affection of good, which is an affection of the Church; see also the *Apocalypse Revealed*, no. 612. The Lord also calls those who are of His church, brethren and sisters (Matt. xii. 40 [49, 50]; xxv. 40; xxviii. 10; Mark iii. 35; Luke viii. 21).

121. IV. THE SPIRITUAL OFFSPRING, WHICH ARE BORN FROM THE MARRIAGE OF THE LORD WITH THE CHURCH, ARE TRUTHS, FROM WHICH THERE ARE UNDERSTANDING, PERCEPTION, AND ALL THOUGHT; AND GOODS, FROM WHICH THERE ARE LOVE, CHARITY, AND ALL AFFECTION. The reason why truths and goods are the spiritual offspring, which are born from the Lord by the church, is, that the Lord is good itself and truth itself, and these in Him are not two but one; also, that nothing can proceed from the Lord but what is in Him, and is Himself. That the marriage of good and truth proceeds from the Lord, and flows in with men, and is received according to the state of the mind and life of those who are of the church, was shewn in the foregoing section on the "Marriage of Good and Truth." The reason why by means of truths man has understanding, perception, and all thought, and, by means of goods, love, charity, and all affection, is, that all things of man relate to truth and good; and there are two things in man which constitute him, the will and the understanding; the will is the receptacle of good, and the understanding is the receptacle of truth. That love, charity, and affection belong to the will, and that perception and thought belong to the understanding, has no need of light from demonstration; for there is a light from

the understanding itself by which this proposition is seen as soon as it is stated.

122. V. FROM THE MARRIAGE OF GOOD AND TRUTH, WHICH PROCEEDS FROM THE LORD, AND FLOWS IN, MAN RECEIVES TRUTH, AND TO THIS THE LORD CONJOINS GOOD; AND THUS THE CHURCH IS FORMED BY THE LORD WITH MAN. The reason why man receives truth from the good and truth which proceed as a one from the Lord, is, that he receives this as his own, and appropriates it to himself as his own; for he thinks truth as from himself, and likewise speaks from it; and this takes place because truth is in the light of the understanding, and therefore he sees it; and whatever he sees in himself, or in his mind, he knows not whence it is; for he does not see the influx, as he sees those things which come within the range of the sight of the eye; hence he supposes that it [the truth] is in himself. That it should appear thus, is given to man by the Lord, in order that he may be a man, and that he may have a reciprocal principle of conjunction. Add to this, that man is born a faculty of knowing, understanding, and becoming wise; and this faculty receives truths, by means of which he has knowledge, intelligence, and wisdom: and since the female was created by means of the truth of the male, and is formed into the love thereof more and more after marriage, it follows, that she also receives her husband's truth in herself, and conjoins it with her own good.

123. The reason why the Lord adjoins and conjoins good to the truths which man receives, is, that man cannot take good as of himself, for it is invisible to him, because it is not a matter of light, but of heat, and heat is felt and not seen. Wherefore, when a man sees truth in his thought, he seldom reflects upon the good which flows in from the love of the will into the truth, and gives it life. Neither does a wife reflect upon the good with her, but upon the inclination of her husband towards her, which is according to the ascent of his understanding towards wisdom; the good which is with her from the Lord, she applies, without the husband's knowing anything about that application. From these considerations, the Truth is now manifest, that man receives truth from the Lord, and that the Lord adjoins good to that truth, according to the application of the truth to use, consequently as the man is willing to think wisely, and hence to live wisely.

124. The reason why the church is thus formed with man by the Lord, is, that he is then in conjunction with the Lord, in good from Him, and in truth as from himself. Thus man is in the Lord, and the Lord in him, according to the Lord's words in John xv. 4, 5. The case is similar if instead of good you say

charity, and instead of truth, faith; because good belongs to charity, and truth belongs to faith.

125. VI. THE HUSBAND DOES NOT REPRESENT THE LORD, AND THE WIFE THE CHURCH; BECAUSE BOTH TOGETHER, THE HUSBAND AND THE WIFE, CONSTITUTE THE CHURCH. It is a common saying within the church, that as the Lord is the Head of the church, so the husband is the head of the wife: whence it would follow, that the husband represents the Lord, and the wife the church. But the Lord is the Head of the church; and man (*homo*),—a man (*vir*) and a woman,—are a church; and still more a husband and wife together. With these the church is first implanted in the man (*vir*), and through the man in the wife, because the man receives the truth of the church with his understanding, and the wife receives it from the man. But if it happens contrariwise, it is not according to order; although it does sometimes happen so, but then it is with men (*vir*) who either are not lovers of wisdom, and consequently are not of the church, or else depend like slaves on the will of their wives. Something on this subject may be seen in the "Preliminaries," no. 21.

126. VII. THEREFORE THERE IS NO CORRESPONDENCE OF THE HUSBAND WITH THE LORD AND OF THE WIFE WITH THE CHURCH, IN THE MARRIAGES OF ANGELS IN THE HEAVENS, AND OF MEN ON EARTH. This follows from what has just been said. To this nevertheless it must be added, that it appears as if truth was the primary of the church, because it is its first in time. It is in consequence of this appearance that the prelates of the church have given the palm to faith, which belongs to truth, in preference to charity, which belongs to good. The learned have likewise given the palm to thought, which belongs to the understanding, in preference to affection, which belongs to the will. Wherefore the knowledge of what the good of charity and the affection of the will are, lies deeply buried as in a tomb, and some even cast earth upon them, as upon the dead, to prevent their rising again. That the good of charity nevertheless is the primary of the church, may be plainly seen by those who have not closed the way from heaven to their understandings, by confirmations in favour of faith, as the sole constituent of the church, and in favour of thought, as the sole constituent of man. Now, since the good of charity is from the Lord, and the truth of faith is with a man as from himself, and these two cause such a conjunction of the Lord with man, and of man with the Lord, as is understood by the Lord's words, that "He is in them and they in Him" (John xv. 4, 5), it is evident that this conjunction constitutes the church.

127. VIII. BUT THERE IS A CORRESPONDENCE WITH CONJUGIAL

LOVE, FECUNDATION, PROLIFICATION, THE LOVE OF CHILDREN, AND SIMILAR THINGS WHICH ARE IN MARRIAGES AND FROM MARRIAGES. These, however, are arcana of too deep a nature to enter the understanding with any degree of light, unless preceded by Knowledge about correspondence; nor is it possible so to explain them as to make them comprehensible, unless this Knowledge be disclosed to the understanding. But what correspondence is, and that it is of natural things with spiritual things, has been abundantly shewn in the *Apocalypse Revealed,* also in the *Arcana Cœlestia,* and specifically in the *Doctrine of the New Jerusalem concerning the Sacred Scripture,* and particularly in a Memorable Relation about it in the following pages [no. 532]. Before some Knowledge about it has been imbibed, only these few things shall be stated before the understanding, in a shade:—conjugial love corresponds to the affection of genuine truth, its chastity, purity, and holiness; fecundation corresponds to the potency of truth; prolification corresponds to the propagation of truth; and the love of children corresponds to the protection of truth and good. Now, since truth with man appears as his own, and good is adjoined thereto by the Lord, it is evident that those correspondences are of the natural or external man with the spiritual or internal man. But some light shall be shed on these subjects in the Memorable Relations which follow.

128. IX. THE WORD IS THE MEDIUM OF CONJUNCTION, BECAUSE IT IS FROM THE LORD, AND THUS IS THE LORD. The reason why the Word is the medium of conjunction of the Lord with man, and of man with the Lord, is, that in its essence it is Divine truth united with Divine good, and Divine good united with Divine truth: that this unition exists in each and all things of the Word in its celestial and spiritual sense, may be seen in the *Apocalypse Revealed,* nos. 373, 483, 689, 881; whence it follows, that the Word is the perfect marriage of good and truth; and as it is from the Lord, and what is from Him is also Himself, it follows, that while a man reads the Word; and takes truths out of it, the Lord adjoins good. For man does not see the goods which affect him, because he reads the Word from the understanding, and the understanding imbibes thence only such things as are its own, that is, truths. That good is adjoined to the truths by the Lord, the understanding feels from the delight which flows in when it is enlightened. But this does not take place interiorly with any others except those who read the Word with the object of becoming wise; and they have the object of becoming wise who are willing to learn the genuine truths in the Word, and to form the church with themselves by means of these truths. Whereas those who read the Word only with a view to gain the reputation of learning, and also those who read it from the opinion that the mere reading or hearing of

it inspires faith and conduces to salvation, do not receive any good from the Lord: because the object of these latter is to save themselves by the mere expressions in the Word, in which there is nothing of truth; and the object of the former is to be distinguished for their learning; with which object there is not conjoined any spiritual good, but only the natural delight arising from worldly glory. As the Word is the medium of conjunction, it is therefore called the Old and the New Covenant: and a covenant signifies conjunction.

129. X. THE CHURCH IS FROM THE LORD, AND IS WITH THOSE WHO APPROACH HIM, AND LIVE ACCORDING TO HIS PRECEPTS. It is not denied at the present day that the church is the Lord's, and that, because it is the Lord's, it is from the Lord. The reason why it exists with those who approach Him, is, that His church in the Christian world is from the Word: and the Word is from Him, and in such a manner from Him, that it is Himself: the Divine truth therein is united with the Divine good, and this also is the Lord. Nothing else is meant by the Word, "*which was with God, and which was God; from which men have life and light, and which was made flesh*" (John i. 1–14). Moreover, the reason why the church exists with those who approach Him, is, that it exists with those who believe on Him; and to believe that He is God the Saviour and Redeemer, Jehovah our Righteousness, that He is the Door through which we are to enter into the sheepfold, that is, into the church, that He is the Way, the Truth, and the Life, and that no one comes to the Father but through Him, that the Father and He are one, besides many other things which He Himself teaches;—to believe these things, I say, no one is able except from Him; and the reason why this is impossible unless He be approached, is, that He is the God of heaven and earth, as He also teaches. Who else is to be approached, and who else can be approached? The reason why the church exists with those who live according to His precepts, is, that there is no conjunction with any others, for He says, "*He who hath My precepts, and doeth them, he it is who loveth Me; and I will love him, and will make My abode with him: but he who doth not love Me, doth not keep My precepts*" (John xiv. 21–24). Love is conjunction; and conjunction with the Lord is the church.

130. XI. CONJUGIAL LOVE IS ACCORDING TO THE STATE OF THE CHURCH, BECAUSE IT IS ACCORDING TO THE STATE OF WISDOM, WITH MAN. That conjugial love is according to the state of wisdom with man, has been often said above, and will often be repeated in the following pages: here therefore it shall be illustrated what wisdom is, and that it makes one with the church.

*With man there are knowledge, intelligence, and wisdom: knowledge (*scientia*) belongs to Knowledges (*cognitiones*), intelligence belongs to reason, and wisdom belongs to life. Wisdom, considered in its fulness, belongs at the same time to Knowledges, reason, and life; Knowledges precede, reason is formed by means of them, and wisdom by means of both; as is the case when a man lives rationally according to the Truths which are Knowledges. Wisdom therefore belongs at the same time both to reason and to life, and it becomes wisdom when it belongs to reason and hence to life; but it is wisdom when it has become a matter of life and hence of reason. The Most Ancient people in this world acknowledged no other wisdom than the wisdom of life: this was the wisdom of those who were formerly called SOPHI: but the Ancient people, who succeeded the Most Ancient, acknowledged the wisdom of reason as wisdom; and these were called PHILOSOPHERS. At the present day, however, many call even knowledge, wisdom; for the learned, the erudite, and the merely knowing, are called wise; thus wisdom has fallen from its
2 mountain-top to its valley. But it shall be briefly stated what wisdom is in its rise, in its progress, and thence in its full state. The things which belong to the church, and are called spiritual things, reside in the inmosts with man; those which belong to the commonwealth, and are called civil things, hold a place below these; and those which belong to science, experience, and art, and are called natural things, constitute their resting-place. The reason why the things which belong to the church, and are called spiritual things, reside in the inmosts with man, is, that they conjoin themselves with heaven, and through heaven with the Lord; for no other things enter with man from the Lord through heaven. The reason why the things which belong to the commonwealth, and are called civil things, occupy a place underneath spiritual things, is, that they are conjoined with the world, for they belong to the world; for they are statutes, laws, and rules, which bind men together, so that from them there may be formed a settled and well-organized society and state. The reason why the things which belong to science, experience, and art, and are called natural things, constitute their basis or resting-place, is, that they are closely conjoined with the five senses of the body; and these senses are the ultimates on which the interior things which belong to the mind, and the inmost
3 things which belong to the soul, as it were sit or rest. Now, since the things which belong to the church, and are called spiritual things, reside in the inmosts, and the things which reside in the inmosts constitute the head, and the succeeding things beneath them, which are called civil things, constitute the body, and the ultimate things, which are called natural things,

* In the original Latin edition the remainder of this paragraph is enclosed in inverted commas.

constitute the feet,—it is manifest, that when these three kinds of things follow in their order, the man is a perfect man; for they then flow in in the same manner as the things which belong to the head flow in into the body, and through the body into the feet; thus spiritual things flow in into civil things, and through civil things into natural things. Now, since spiritual things are in the light of heaven, it is evident that by their light they enlighten the things which follow in order, and by their heat, which is love, animate them; and when this is the case the man has wisdom. As wisdom belongs to life, and hence to reason, as 4
was said above, it may be asked, What is wisdom of life? In a summary statement, it consists in shunning evils, because they are injurious to the soul, injurious to the commonwealth, and injurious to the body; and in doing goods, because they are profitable to the soul, to the commonwealth, and to the body. This is the wisdom which is meant by the wisdom with which conjugial love binds itself; for it binds itself therewith by shunning the evil of adultery as the pestilence of the soul, of the commonwealth, and of the body; and since this wisdom springs from the spiritual things which belong to the church, it follows, that conjugial love is according to the state of the church, because it is according to the state of wisdom, with man. By this is also meant, what has been repeatedly stated above, that in proportion as a man becomes spiritual, in the same proportion he is in truly conjugial love; for a man becomes spiritual by means of the spiritual things of the church. More about the wisdom with which conjugial love conjoins itself, may be seen below, nos. 163–165.

131. XII. AND SINCE THE CHURCH IS FROM THE LORD, CONJUGIAL LOVE ALSO IS FROM HIM. As this follows as a consequence from what has been said above, I dispense with further confirmation of it. Moreover, that truly conjugial love is from the Lord, all the angels of heaven testify; and also that that love is according to the state of wisdom, and that the state of wisdom is according to the state of the church with them. That the angels of heaven testify those things is evident from the Memorable Relations annexed to the chapters, which are things that have been seen and heard in the spiritual world.

132. To the above I shall add two Memorable Relations. The first is this:*—

I was once speaking with two angels: one was from the eastern heaven, and the other from the southern heaven; who when they perceived that I was meditating on the arcana of wisdom relating to conjugial love, said, "Dost thou know anything about the SCHOOLS OF WISDOM in our world?"

* The following Memorable Relation is repeated in the *True Christian Religion*, no. 48.

I replied, "Not as yet."

And they said, "There are many; and those who love truths from spiritual affection, or because they are truths, and because they are the means of attaining wisdom, meet together on a given signal, and discuss and draw conclusions about such things as are matters of deeper understanding."

They then took me by the hand, saying, "Follow us: and thou shalt see and hear: to-day the signal for meeting is given."

I was led across a plain to a hill; and lo! at the foot of the hill was an avenue of palm-trees continued even to its head; this avenue we entered, and ascended: on the head or top of the hill was seen a grove, the trees of which on an elevated piece of ground, formed as it were a lecture-hall, within which was a level space paved with variously coloured stones: around it in a square form were placed seats, on which the lovers of wisdom were seated; and in the middle of the hall was a table on which was laid a sealed paper.

2 Those who sat on the seats invited us to sit down where there was room: and I replied, "I was led here by the two angels to see and hear, and not to sit down."

The two angels then went into the middle of the level space to the table, and broke the seal of the paper, and read, in the presence of those who were seated, the arcana of wisdom written on the paper, which they were now to discuss and unfold. They had been written by angels of the third heaven, and let down upon the table. There were three arcana, FIRST, What is the image of God, and what the likeness of God, into which man was created? SECOND, Why is man not born into the knowledge of any love, when yet beasts and birds, both noble and ignoble, are born into the knowledges of all their loves? THIRD, What is signified by the tree of life, and what by the tree of the knowledge of good and evil, and what by eating of them? Under these was written, "Collect these three into one sentence, write it on a fresh sheet of paper, and place it on this table, and we shall see it: if the opinion on being weighed appear fairly balanced and just, a prize of wisdom shall be given to each of you." Having read out these things, the two angels withdrew, and were taken up into their own heavens.

3 Then those who sat on the seats began to discuss and unfold the arcana proposed to them; and they spoke in order, first those who sat towards the north, next those towards the west, afterwards those towards the south, and lastly those towards the east. They took up the first subject of discussion, which was, WHAT IS THE IMAGE OF GOD, AND WHAT THE LIKENESS OF GOD, INTO WHICH MAN WAS CREATED? But first, the following words from the Book of the Creation were read out in the presence of them all: "*God said, Let us make man into* OUR IMAGE, *according to* OUR LIKENESS: *and God created man into* HIS

IMAGE; *into the* IMAGE OF GOD *created He him*" (Gen. i. 26, 27). "*In the day that God created man, into the* LIKENESS OF GOD *made He him*" (Gen. v. 1).

Those who sat towards the north spoke first, saying, "The image of God and the likeness of God are the two lives breathed into man by God, which are the life of the will and the life of the understanding; for it is written, '*Jehovah God breathed into Adam's nostrils the soul of* LIVES; *and man became a living soul*' (Gen. ii. 7): into the nostrils denotes into the perception, that the will of good and the understanding of truth, and thus the soul of lives, was in him; and since life from God was breathed into him, the image and likeness of God signify integrity from wisdom and love, and from justice and judgment in him."

These sentiments were favoured by those who sat towards the west; only they added, that the state of integrity breathed in by God is continually breathed into every man since the first man; but that it is in man as in a receptacle; and man, as he is a receptacle, is an image and likeness of God.

4 After this, the third in order, who were those that were seated towards the south, said: "The image of God and the likeness of God are two distinct things; but in man they are united from creation; and we see, as from an interior light, that the image of God may be destroyed by man, but not the likeness of God. This appears as through a lattice from the fact that Adam retained the likeness of God after he had lost the image of God; for it is written after the curse, '*Behold the man is as one of us, knowing good and evil*' (Gen. iii. 22); and afterwards he is called a likeness of God, and not an image of God (Gen. v. 1). But we will leave to our associates who sit towards the east, and are consequently in a higher light, to say what is properly meant by the image of God, and what by the likeness of God."

5 And then, after silence had been obtained, those who sat towards the east arose up from their seats, and looked up to the Lord, and afterwards sat down again, and said: "The image of God is the receptacle of God; and since God is love itself and wisdom itself, the image of God is the receptacle of love and wisdom from God in man; but the likeness of God is the perfect likeness and full appearance, as if love and wisdom were in man, and therefore altogether as his own; for man feels no otherwise than that he loves from himself, and is wise from himself, or that he wills good and understands truth from himself; when nevertheless he does not in the least do so from himself, but from God. God alone loves from Himself and is wise from Himself, because God is love itself and wisdom itself. The likeness or appearance that love and wisdom, or good and truth, are in man as his own, causes man to be man, and makes him capable of being

conjoined with God, and thereby of living to eternity: from which consideration it follows, that man is man from this circumstance, that he is able to will good and understand truth altogether as from himself, and yet know and believe that it is from God; for as he knows and believes this, God places His image in him, which He could not do if the man believed that he did thus from himself and not from God."

6 When they had said this, being overpowered with zeal from the love of Truth, they spoke as follows: "How can man receive anything of love and wisdom, and retain it, and reproduce it, unless he feel it as his own? And how can there be conjunction with God through love and wisdom, unless there be given to man some reciprocality of conjunction? For without reciprocality no conjunction is possible; and the reciprocality of conjunction is, that man should love God, and be wise in the things which are of God, as from himself, and yet believe that it is from God. Again, how can man live to eternity, unless he be conjoined with the eternal God? Consequently how can man be man without that likeness of God in him?"

7 These words met with the approbation of all, and they said, Let the following conclusion be made from what has been said: "Man is a receptacle of God, and a receptacle of God is an image of God; and since God is love itself and wisdom itself, man is a receptacle of love and wisdom; and a receptacle becomes an image of God in proportion to reception. And man is a likeness of God from this, that he feels in himself that the things which are of God are in him as his own; but still from that likeness he is only so far an image of God, as he acknowledges that love and wisdom, or good and truth, are not his own in him, and thus are not from him, but that they are only in God, and thus from God."

133. After this, they took up the second subject of discussion, WHY IS NOT MAN BORN INTO THE KNOWLEDGE OF ANY LOVE, WHEN YET BEASTS AND BIRDS, BOTH NOBLE AND IGNOBLE, ARE BORN INTO THE KNOWLEDGES OF ALL THEIR LOVES? They first confirmed the Truth of the proposition by various considerations; as in regard to man, that he is born into no knowledge, not even into the knowledge of conjugial love; and they inquired, and were informed by those who had investigated the subject, that an infant from connate knowledge cannot even move itself to the mother's breast, but has to be moved thereto by the mother or nurse; and that it knows only how to suck, and that it has acquired this in consequence of continual suction in the womb; and that afterwards it does not know how to walk, or to articulate sound into any human voice; no, nor even to express by tone of voice the affection of its love, as the beasts do: and further, that it does not know what is salutary for it in the

way of food, as all beasts do, but catches at whatever comes in its way, whether it be clean or unclean, and puts it into its mouth. Those who had investigated the matter said, that man without instruction does not even know the distinction of sex, and knows absolutely nothing of the ways of loving it; and that neither maidens nor young men have any knowledge thereof without instruction from others, notwithstanding their being educated into various sciences. In a word, man is born corporeal like a worm; and he remains corporeal, unless he learns to know, understand, and be wise, from others. After this, 2
they gave proofs that beasts, both noble and ignoble, as the animals of the earth, the birds of the heaven, reptiles, fishes, the small creatures called insects, are born into all the knowledges of the loves of their life, as into the knowledge of all things relating to nourishment, to habitation, to the love of the sex and prolification, and to the rearing of their young. This they confirmed by wonderful things which they recalled to remembrance from things seen, heard, and read, in the natural world, (so they called our world, in which they had formerly lived,) in which there exist not representative but real beasts. When the Truth of the proposition was thus fully proved, they exerted their minds to investigate and find out the ends and causes by which they might unfold and disclose this arcanum; and they all said, that only from the Divine wisdom could these things exist, to the end that a man may be a man, and a beast, a beast; and thus, that the imperfection of man at his birth becomes his perfection, and the perfection of a beast at its birth is its imperfection.

134. Those on the NORTH then began to declare their mind, and said, "A man is born without knowledges, in order that he may receive all knowledges; whereas if he were born into knowledges, he could not receive any but those into which he was born, and in this case neither could he appropriate any to himself." This they illustrated by the following comparison: "A man when first born is like ground in which no seeds are implanted, but which nevertheless is capable of receiving all seeds, and of bringing them forth and fructifying them; whereas a beast is like ground already sown, and filled with grasses and herbs, which receives no other seeds than those which have been sown in it, or if it received any others it would choke them. Hence it is, that a man requires many years to grow to maturity; during which time he can be cultivated like ground, and bring forth as it were grain, flowers, and trees of every kind; whereas a beast arrives at maturity in a few years, during which it cannot be cultivated into any other [faculties] than those which are connate with it."

Afterwards, those on the WEST spoke, and said, "Man is not 2 born knowledge, as a beast is; but he is born faculty and inclination; faculty to know, and inclination to love: and he is born faculty not only to know but also to understand and be wise: he is likewise born the most perfect inclination to love not only the things which are of self and the world, but also those which are of God and heaven; consequently man, by birth from his parents, is an organ which lives merely in the external senses, and at first not in any internal senses, to the end that he may successively become man, first natural, afterwards rational, and lastly spiritual; which could not be the case if he was born into knowledges and loves, as the beasts are: for connate knowledges and affections limit that progression, but connate faculty and inclination limit nothing: wherefore man is capable of being perfected in knowledge, intelligence, and wisdom, to eternity."

3 Those on the SOUTH next took up the discussion, and expressed their opinion, saying, "It is impossible for a man to take any knowledge from himself, since he has no connate knowledge; but he may take it from others; and as he cannot take any knowledge from himself, so neither can he take any love; for where there is no knowledge there is no love; knowledge and love are inseparable companions, and no more capable of separation than the will and the understanding, or affection and thought, yea, no more than essence and form: wherefore, as a man takes knowledge from others, so love adjoins itself thereto as its companion. The universal love which adjoins itself is the love of knowing, understanding, and being wise: this love belongs to man alone, and not to any beast, and it flows in from God.
4 We agree with our companions from the west, that a man is not born into any love, and consequently not into any knowledge; but that he is only born into an inclination to love, and thence into a faculty to receive knowledges, not from himself, but from others, that is, through others: we say, through others, because neither have these received anything of knowledge from themselves, but from God. We agree also with our companions to the north, that a man when first born is like ground in which no seeds are sown, but in which all seeds, both noble and ignoble, can be sown. To these considerations we add, that beasts are born into natural loves, and consequently into knowledges corresponding to them; and that yet they do not at all know, think, understand, and possess wisdom from knowledges, but are led by means of them by their loves, almost as blind men are led through the streets by dogs, for as to understanding they are blind; or rather like sleep-walkers, who do what they do from blind knowledge, while the understanding is asleep."

5 Lastly, those on the EAST spoke, and said, "We agree with what our brethren have said, that man knows nothing from himself, but from others and through others, to the end that he may know and acknowledge that everything which he knows and

understands, and as to which he is wise, is from God; and that a man cannot otherwise be conceived, born, and generated of the Lord, and become an image and likeness of Him. For he becomes an image of the Lord by acknowledging and believing that he has received and does receive from the Lord, all the good of love and charity, and all the truth of wisdom and faith, and not the least portion thereof from himself; and he becomes a likeness of the Lord by his feeling those things in himself, as from himself. This he feels, because he is not born into knowledges, but receives them; and what he receives, appears to him as if it were from himself. To feel thus is also given to man by the Lord, to the end that he may be a man and not a beast, since by willing, thinking, loving, knowing, understanding, and being wise, as from himself, he receives knowledges, and exalts them into intelligence, and, through the uses of them, into wisdom. Thus the Lord conjoins man with Himself, and man conjoins himself with the Lord. This could not have been the case, unless it had been provided by the Lord, that man should be born in total ignorance."

When they had said this, it was the desire of all present, that a 6
conclusion should be formed from what had been discussed; and the following was made: "That a man is born into no knowledge, in order that he may come into all knowledge, and advance into intelligence, and through this into wisdom; and that he is born into no love, in order that he may come into all love, by applications of the knowledges from intelligence, and into love to the Lord through love towards the neighbour, and may thereby be conjoined with the Lord, and thereby become a man and live to eternity."

135. After this they took the paper, and read the third subject of discussion, which was, WHAT IS SIGNIFIED BY THE TREE OF LIFE, WHAT BY THE TREE OF THE KNOWLEDGE OF GOOD AND EVIL, AND WHAT BY EATING THEREOF? and all requested that those who were from the east would unfold this arcanum, because it was a matter of a deeper understanding; and because those who are from the east are in flaming light, that is, in the wisdom of love; and this wisdom is meant by the garden of Eden, in which those two trees were placed.

They replied, "We will state the matter; but, as man does not take anything from himself but from the Lord, therefore we will state it from Him; but yet from ourselves as of ourselves." And then they said, "A tree signifies a man, and the fruit thereof the good of life; hence by the tree of life is signified a man living from God, or God living in man; and since love and wisdom, and charity and faith, or good and truth, constitute the life of God in man, therefore these are signified by the tree of life, and hence man has eternal life: the like is signified by the

tree of life, of which it will be given to eat (Apoc. ii. 7; chap.
2 xxii. 2, 14). By the tree of the knowledge of good and evil is
signified a man who believes that he lives from himself and not
from God; thus that in man love and wisdom, charity and faith,
that is, good and truth, are his own and not God's; believing this,
because he thinks and wills, and speaks and acts, to all likeness
and appearance as from himself: and as a man from this faith
persuades himself, that God has imparted Himself, or infused His
Divine into him, therefore the serpent said, '*God doth know, in the
day that ye eat of the fruit of that tree your eyes will be opened, and*
3 *ye will be as God, knowing good and evil*' (Gen. iii. 5). By eating of
those trees is signified reception and appropriation; by eating of the tree of life, the reception of eternal life, and by eating of the tree of the knowledge of good and evil, the reception of damnation; therefore also both Adam and his wife, together with the serpent, were cursed. By the serpent is meant the devil as to the love of self and the conceit of self-intelligence. This love is the possessor of that tree; and the men who are in conceit from that love, are those trees. They, therefore, are in enormous error who believe that Adam was wise and did good from himself, and that this was his state of integrity; when yet Adam himself was cursed on account of that belief; for this is signified by eating of the tree of the knowledge of good and evil: wherefore he then fell from the state of integrity in which he had been in consequence of believing that he was wise and did good from God and not at all from himself; for this is meant by eating of the tree of life. The Lord alone, when He was in the world, was wise from Himself and did good from Himself; because the Divine Itself from birth was in Him and was His own; wherefore also from His own proper power He became the Redeemer and Saviour."

4 From all these considerations they came to this conclusion, "That by the tree of life and the tree of the knowledge of good and evil, and by eating thereof, is signified that life for man is God in him, and that then he has heaven and eternal life; but that death for man is the persuasion and belief that life for him is not God but himself; whence he has hell and eternal death, which is damnation."

136. After this they looked at the paper left by the angels upon the table, and saw written underneath, COLLECT THESE THREE INTO ONE SENTENCE. Then they collected them, and saw that those three cohered in one series, and that the series or sentence was this, "That man was created to receive love and wisdom from God, and yet to all likeness as from himself; and this for the sake of reception and conjunction: and that therefore a man is not born into any love, or into any knowledge, and also not into any power of loving and becoming wise from

himself; wherefore if he ascribes all the good of love and truth of wisdom to God, he becomes a living man; but if he ascribes them to himself, he becomes a dead man."

These words they wrote on a fresh piece of paper, and placed it on the table: and lo! on a sudden the angels were present in bright light, and carried the paper away into heaven.

And after it had been read there, those who sat on the seats heard from thence voices saying: "Well, well, well;" and instantly there appeared one angel as it were flying from heaven, with two wings about his feet, and two about his temples, having in his hand prizes, consisting of robes, caps, and wreaths of laurel; and he let himself down, and gave to those who sat towards the north robes of an opaline colour; to those who sat towards the west robes of a scarlet colour; to those who sat towards the south caps whose borders were adorned with fillets of gold and pearls, and the upper part of the left side with diamonds cut in the form of flowers; but to those who sat towards the east he gave wreaths of laurel in which there were rubies and sapphires. Then all of them, adorned with these prizes, went home from the school of wisdom; and when they shewed themselves to their wives, their wives came to meet them, being adorned also with ornaments given to them from heaven, at which circumstance their husbands wondered.

137. The second Memorable Relation:—

When I was meditating on conjugial love, lo! there appeared at a distance two naked little children with baskets in their hands, and turtle-doves flying around them; and when they were nearer, they seemed as if they were naked, and becomingly adorned with garlands; chaplets of flowers adorned their heads, and festoons of lilies and roses of a hyacinthine colour, hanging obliquely from the shoulders to the loins, adorned their bosoms; and round about both of them there was as it were a common band woven of small leaves interspersed with olives. But when they came nearer, they did not appear as little children, nor naked, but as two human beings in the first flower of age, wearing robes and vests of shining silk, in which were woven flowers most beautiful to behold; and when they were near me, there breathed forth from heaven through them a vernal heat, with a fragrant odour, like that which arises from the earliest spring flowers in gardens and fields. They were two married partners from heaven. They then accosted me; and because I was thinking about what I had just seen, they inquired, "What didst thou see?"

And when I told them that at first they appeared to me as 2
naked little children, afterwards as little children adorned with garlands, and lastly as grown-up persons arrayed in garments interwoven with flowers, and that instantly there breathed on

me a vernal influence with its delights, they smiled pleasantly, and said, "In the way we did not seem to ourselves as little children, nor naked, nor adorned with garlands, but constantly in the same appearance as now: thus at a distance was represented our conjugial love; its state of innocence by our appearing like naked little children, its delights by the garlands, and the same delights now by the flowers woven in our robes and vests; and as thou saidst that, as we approached, a vernal heat, with its pleasant fragrances as from a garden, breathed on thee, we will explain the reason of all this."

3 So they said, "We have now been married partners for ages, and constantly in the flower of age in which thou now seest us. Our first state was like the first state of a virgin and a bachelor, when they become consociated in marriage; and we then believed, that this state was the very blessedness of our life; but we were informed by others in our heaven, and have since perceived ourselves, that it was a state of heat not tempered with light; and that it is successively tempered in proportion as the husband is perfected in wisdom, and the wife loves that wisdom in the husband; and that this is effected by means of, and according to, the uses which both, by mutual aid, perform in the society; also that delights succeed according to the due proportion of heat and light, or of wisdom and its love.

4 The reason why, when we approached, there breathed on thee as it were a vernal heat, is, that conjugial love and that heat act as a one in our heaven; for heat with us is love, and the light, with which the heat is united, is wisdom; and use is as it were the atmosphere which contains both in its bosom. What are heat and light without that which contains them? And so what are love and wisdom without their use? There is no conjugial principle in them, because the subject in which they might be does not exist. In heaven, where there is vernal heat, there is truly conjugial love; because the vernal heat exists only where heat is equally united with light, or where heat and light are in equal proportion; and it is our opinion, that as heat is delighted with light, and light in return with heat, so love is delighted with wisdom, and wisdom, in return, with love."

5 He said further, "With us in heaven there is perpetual light, and never the shades of evening, still less is there darkness, because our sun does not set and rise like yours, but remains constantly in a middle altitude between the zenith and the horizon, which, as you express it, is at an elevation of 45 degrees. Hence it is, that the heat and light proceeding from our sun cause perpetual spring, and that a perpetual vernal influence breathes into those with whom love is united with wisdom in equal proportion; and our Lord, through the eternal union of heat and light, breathes forth nothing but uses. Hence also come the germinations of your Earth, and the pairing of your birds and animals in time of spring;

for the vernal heat opens their interiors even to the inmosts, which are called their souls, and affects them, and imparts to them its conjugial principle, and causes their [principle of] prolification to come into its delights, in consequence of a continual endeavour to produce fruits of use, which use is the propagation of their kind. But with men there is a perpetual influx of 6
vernal heat from the Lord; wherefore they are capable of enjoying marriage delights at all times, even in the midst of winter; for men (*viri*) were created receptions of light, that is, of wisdom from the Lord, and women were created receptions of heat, that is, of the love of the wisdom of the man (*vir*) from the Lord. Hence then it is, that, as we approached, there breathed on thee a vernal heat with a sweet fragrance, like that from the earliest spring flowers in gardens and fields."

As he said this, the man (*vir*) gave me his right hand, and 7
conducted me to houses where there were married partners in a like flower of age as himself and his partner; and he said, "These wives, who now seem like virgins, were in the world infirm old women; and their husbands, who now seem like youths, were in the world decrepit old men; and all of them have been restored by the Lord to this flower of age, because they mutually loved each other, and from religion shunned adulteries as enormous sins:" and he said, "No one knows the blessed delights of conjugial love, except he who rejects the horrid delights of adultery; and no one is able to reject those delights, except he who is wise from the Lord; and no one is wise from the Lord unless he does uses from the love of uses."

I also saw on this occasion their household utensils, which were all in celestial forms, and glittered with gold, which had a flaming appearance by reason of the rubies with which they were studded.

THE CHASTE AND THE NON-CHASTE.

138. As I am, as yet, only just beginning to treat of conjugial love in detail, and as conjugial love cannot be cognized in detail, except indistinctly and thus obscurely, unless its opposite, which is the unchaste, also in some measure appear; and as this unchaste appears in some measure, or in shade, when the chaste is described together with the non-chaste, non-chastity being only the removal of what is unchaste from what is chaste [; therefore I will now proceed to treat of the chaste and the non-chaste]. But the unchaste which is altogether opposite to the chaste, is treated of in the latter part of this Work, where it is described in its fulness and with its varieties under the title *The Pleasures of Insanity relating to Scortatory Love.* But what the chaste is, and what the non-chaste, and with what persons each of these exists, shall be illustrated in the following order:

I. *The chaste and the non-chaste are predicated only of marriages, and of such things as belong to marriage.*

II. *The chaste is predicated only of monogamous marriages, or of the marriage of one man with one wife.*

III. *The Christian conjugial [principle] alone is chaste.*

IV. *Truly conjugial love is chastity itself.*

V. *All the delights of truly conjugial love, even the ultimate ones, are chaste.*

VI. *With those who are made spiritual by the Lord, conjugial love is more and more purified and made chaste.*

VII. *The chastity of marriage comes into existence by means of a total renunciation of whoredoms on account of religion.*

VIII. *Chastity cannot be predicated of little children, nor of boys and girls, nor of youths and maidens before they feel in themselves the love of the sex.*

IX. *Chastity cannot be predicated of eunuchs so born, nor of eunuchs so made.*

X. *Chastity cannot be predicated of those who do not believe adulteries to be evils of religion; and still less of those who do not believe adulteries to be hurtful to society.*

XI. *Chastity cannot be predicated of those who abstain from adulteries only for various external reasons.*

XII. *Chastity cannot be predicated of those who believe marriages to be unchaste.*

XIII. *Chastity cannot be predicated of those who have renounced marriages by vowing perpetual celibacy, unless there be and remain in them the love of a truly conjugial life.*

XIV. *The state of marriage is to be preferred to the state of celibacy.*

Now follows an explanation of these articles.

139. I. THE CHASTE AND THE NON-CHASTE ARE PREDICATED [ONLY] OF MARRIAGES, AND OF SUCH THINGS AS BELONG TO MARRIAGE. The reason is, that truly conjugial love is chastity itself, as now follows, and the love opposite to it, which is called scortatory, is unchastity itself; so far therefore as any one is purified from the latter love, so far he is chaste, for so far the opposite, which is destructive of chastity, is taken away; whence it is evident that the purity of conjugial love is what is called chastity. There exists, however, a conjugial love which is not chaste, and yet is not unchastity, as, for example, that between married partners who, for various external reasons, abstain from the effects of lasciviousness so far as not to think about them; yet if that love is not purified in their spirits, it is still not chaste; its form is chaste, but it has not a chaste essence in it.

140. The reason why the chaste and the non-chaste are predicated of such things as belong to marriage, is, that the conjugial principle is inscribed on both sexes from the inmosts to the ultimates; and a man as to his thoughts and affections, and consequently inwardly as to his bodily actions and behaviour, is according thereto. That this is the case, appears more evidently from such as are unchaste. The unchaste element that is seated in their minds is heard from the tone of their voice in conversation, and from their applying whatever is said, even though it be chaste, to wanton things; (the tone of the voice is from the affection of the will, and the voice or speech itself is from the thought of the understanding;) which is a proof, that the will, with everything belonging to it, and the understanding, with everything belonging to it, consequently the whole mind, and hence everything of the body, from the inmosts to the ultimates, abound with unchaste elements. I have heard from the angels that, with the greatest hypocrites, the unchaste is perceivable from hearing their conversation, however chastely they may talk, and is also felt from the sphere that issues from them; which circumstance also is a proof that unchastity resides in the inmosts of their minds, and hence in the inmosts of their bodies, and that these inmosts are exteriorly covered over like a shell painted with figures of various colours. That a sphere of lasciviousness issues forth from those who are unchaste, is evident from the statutes among the sons of Israel, that everything should be unclean that was merely touched with the hand by those who were defiled by such impurities. From these

considerations it may be concluded that the case is similar with those who are chaste, namely, that with them each and all things are chaste from the inmosts to the ultimates, and that this is effected by the chastity of conjugial love. Hence it is, that in the world it is said that to the clean all things are clean, and to the unclean all things are unclean.

141. II. THE CHASTE IS PREDICATED ONLY OF MONOGAMOUS MARRIAGES, OR OF THE MARRIAGE OF ONE MAN WITH ONE WIFE. The reason why what is chaste is predicated of these only is, that with them conjugial love does not reside in the natural man, but enters into the spiritual man, and successively opens to itself a way to the spiritual marriage itself, which is the marriage of good and truth, which is its origin, and conjoins itself therewith; for that love enters according to the increase of wisdom, and this increase is according to the implantation of the church by the Lord, as has been shewn above in many places. This cannot be effected with polygamists, for they divide conjugial love; and this love, when divided, is not unlike the love of the sex, which in itself is natural. But on this subject something worthy of attention will be seen in the section on "Polygamy."

142. III. THE CHRISTIAN CONJUGIAL [PRINCIPLE] ALONE IS CHASTE. The reasons are, that truly conjugial love keeps pace with the state of the church in man, and, that the state of the church is from the Lord, as has been shewn in the foregoing section (nos. 130, 131), and elsewhere; also, that the church in its genuine truths is in the Word, and the Lord is present there in those truths. From these considerations it follows, that the chaste conjugial principle exists nowhere but in the Christian world, and that, if it does not exist, still there is a possibility of its existing. By the Christian conjugial principle is meant the marriage of one man with one wife. That this conjugial principle can become implanted in Christians, and transmitted hereditarily into the offspring from parents who are in truly conjugial love, and that, from it, both the faculty and the inclination to become wise in the things which belong to the church and heaven may become connate, will be seen in its proper place. That Christians, if they marry more wives than one, commit not only natural adultery, but also spiritual adultery, will be shewn in the section on "Polygamy."

143. IV. TRULY CONJUGIAL LOVE IS CHASTITY ITSELF. The reasons are, 1. That it is from the Lord, and corresponds to the marriage of the Lord and the church. 2. That it descends from the marriage of good and truth. 3. That it is spiritual, in proportion as the church is with man. 4. That it is the fundamental love and the head of all celestial and spiritual loves. 5. That it

is the legitimate seminary of the human race, and thence of the angelic heaven. 6. That on this account it also exists with the angels of heaven, and from it with them there are born spiritual offspring, which are love and wisdom. 7. And that thus its use is more excellent than the other uses of creation. From these considerations it follows, that truly conjugial love, considered from its origin and in its essence, is so pure and holy, that it may be called purity and holiness, consequently chastity itself: but that nevertheless it is not altogether pure, either with men or angels, may be seen below in article VI., no. 146.

144. V. ALL THE DELIGHTS OF TRULY CONJUGIAL LOVE, EVEN THE ULTIMATE ONES, ARE CHASTE. This follows from what was explained above, that truly conjugial love is chastity itself; moreover, delights constitute the life of that love. That the delights of this love ascend and enter heaven, and in the way pass through the delights of the heavenly loves in which the angels of heaven are; as also that they conjoin themselves with the delights of the conjugial love of the angels, has been mentioned above. Moreover, I have heard from the angels, that they perceive those delights with themselves to be exalted and fulfilled, when they ascend from chaste married partners on earth; and for the sake of some bystanders who were unchaste, on the question being put whether [this is the case as to] the ultimate delights also, they signified assent by nodding, and said silently, "How should it be otherwise? Are not these the delights of truly conjugial love in their fulness?" The origin and quality of the delights of this love, may be seen above, no. 69; and also in the Memorable Relations, especially in those which follow.

145. VI. WITH THOSE WHO ARE MADE SPIRITUAL BY THE LORD CONJUGIAL LOVE IS MORE AND MORE PURIFIED AND MADE CHASTE. The reasons are, 1. That the first love, by which is meant the love previous to the wedding and immediately after the wedding, partakes somewhat of the love of the sex, and thus of the ardour belonging to the body not as yet moderated by the love of the spirit. 2. That man from natural successively becomes spiritual; for he becomes spiritual in the proportion in which his Rational, which is the medium between heaven and the world, begins to derive a soul from the influx out of heaven, which is the case in the proportion in which it is affected and gladdened by wisdom (concerning which wisdom see above, no. 130); and in proportion as this is done, in the same proportion his mind is elevated into a higher aura, which is the continent of the heavenly light and heat, or, what is the same, of the wisdom and love, in which the angels are; for heavenly light acts in unity with wisdom, and heavenly heat with love; and in

proportion as wisdom and the love of it increase with married pairs, in the same proportion the conjugial love with them is purified; and as this is effected successively, it follows that conjugial love is made more and more chaste. This spiritual purification may be compared with the purification of natural spirits, which is effected by the chemists, and is called defecation, rectification, castigation, cohobation, intensification (*acutio*), decantation, and sublimation: and wisdom purified may be compared with alcohol, which is spirit most highly rectified. 3. Now, as spiritual wisdom in itself is such that it grows warmer and warmer with the love of becoming wise, and by virtue of this love grows to eternity; and as this is effected in proportion as it is perfected, as it were by defecations, castigations, rectifications, intensifications, decantations, and sublimations, and as these latter processes are effected by the freeing and withdrawing of the understanding from the fallacies of the senses, and of the will from the allurements of the body,—it is evident that conjugial love, whose parent is wisdom, is in like manner made successively more and more pure, and thus chaste. That the first state of love between married partners is a state of heat not yet tempered by light, but that it is successively tempered in proportion as the husband is perfected in wisdom, and the wife loves the wisdom in her husband, may be seen in the Memorable Relation, no. 137.

146. It should however be known, that altogether chaste or pure conjugial love does not exist either with men or with angels; there is still something not chaste or not pure which adjoins or subjoins itself to it; but this is of a different nature from that which gives rise to what is unchaste: for with them the chaste is above and the non-chaste beneath, and there is as it were a door with a hinge interposed by the Lord, which is opened by determination, and is carefully prevented from standing open, lest the one principle should pass into the other, and they should mix together. For the Natural of man from birth is contaminated and surcharged with evils; whereas his Spiritual is not so, because its birth is from the Lord, for this is regeneration: and regeneration is a successive separation from the evils which are ingrained in the inclinations from birth. That no love with either men or angels is altogether pure, or can become so, but that the end, purpose, or intention of the will, is primarily regarded by the Lord, and that therefore so far as a man is in the end, purpose, or intention, and perseveres therein, so far he is initiated into purity, and so far he progressively approaches towards purity, see above at no. 71.

147. VII. THE CHASTITY OF MARRIAGE COMES INTO EXISTENCE BY MEANS OF A TOTAL RENUNCIATION OF WHOREDOMS ON ACCOUNT

OF RELIGION. The reason is, that chastity is the removal of unchastity; for it is a universal rule that in proportion as any one removes evil, so far an opportunity is given for good to succeed in its place; and further, in proportion as evil is hated, good is loved; and also contrariwise; consequently, in proportion as whoredom is renounced, the chastity of marriage enters in. That conjugial love is purified and rectified according to the renunciation of whoredoms, every one sees from common perception as soon as it is stated and heard, thus before confirmations; but as all have not common perception, it is of importance that the subject should also be illustrated by means of confirmations. These confirmations are, that conjugial love becomes cold as soon as it is divided, and this coldness causes it to perish; for the heat of unchaste love extinguishes it; for two opposite heats cannot exist together, but one must needs reject the other and deprive it of its power. When therefore the heat of conjugial love removes and casts away the heat of scortatory love, conjugial love begins to grow pleasantly warm, and from a sense of its delights to bud and flourish, like an orchard and rose-garden in spring time; the latter from the vernal temperateness of the light and heat from the sun of the natural world, but the former from the vernal temperateness of the light and heat from the sun of the spiritual world.

148. There is implanted in every man from creation, and consequently from birth, an internal conjugial and an external conjugial [principle]. The internal is spiritual, and the external natural. Man comes first into the latter, and as he becomes spiritual, he comes into the former. If, therefore, he remains in the external or natural conjugial, the internal or spiritual conjugial is veiled or covered over until he knows nothing about it, yea, until he calls it an empty idea. But if a man becomes spiritual, he then begins to know something about it, and afterwards to perceive something of its quality, and successively to feel its pleasantnesses, delights, and deliciousnesses; and in proportion as this is the case, the veil or covering between the external and internal, spoken of above, begins to be attenuated, and afterwards as it were to melt, and lastly to be dissolved and dissipated. When this effect has taken place, the external conjugial indeed remains; but it is continually purged and purified from its dregs by the internal; and this until the external becomes as it were the face of the internal, and derives its delight from the blessedness which is in the internal, and at the same time its life, and the delights of its potency. Such is the renunciation of whoredoms, by means of which the chastity of marriage comes into existence. It may be imagined, that the 2
external conjugial, which remains after the internal has separated itself from it, or it from itself, is like the external not separated:

but I have heard from the angels that they are utterly unlike;
for that the external from the internal, which they called the
external of the internal, was devoid of all lasciviousness, because
the internal cannot be lascivious, but can only be chastely delighted, and that it imparts the same disposition to its external,
wherein it feels its own delights. The case is altogether otherwise
with the external separated from the internal; this, they said,
3 was lascivious in the whole and in every part. They compared
the external conjugial from the internal to excellent fruit, whose
pleasant taste and flavour insinuate themselves into its rind or
skin, and form this into correspondence with themselves. They
also compared the external conjugial from the internal to a
granary, whose store is never diminished, but is constantly being
renewed in proportion as it is drawn upon; and they compared
the external, separate from the internal, to wheat in a winnow-
ing shovel, for when it is cast forth all around, the chaff only
remains, which is dispersed by the wind. Thus it is with conjugial
love, unless the scortatory principle be renounced.

149. The reason why the chastity of marriage does not come into existence through the renunciation of whoredoms, unless this renunciation be made on account of religion, is, that without religion man does not become spiritual, but remains natural, and if the natural man renounces whoredoms, still his spirit does not renounce them; and thus, although it seems to himself that he is chaste through that renunciation, still unchastity lies hidden within like corrupt matter in a wound which is only outwardly healed. That conjugial love is according to the state of the church with man, see above, no. 130. More on this subject may be seen in the exposition of article XI., below.

150. VIII. CHASTITY CANNOT BE PREDICATED OF LITTLE CHILDREN, NOR OF BOYS AND GIRLS, NOR OF YOUTHS AND MAIDENS BEFORE THEY FEEL IN THEMSELVES THE LOVE OF THE SEX. The reason is that the chaste and the unchaste are predicated only of marriages, and of such things as belong to marriage (see above, no. 139); and with those who know nothing of the things belonging to marriage, there is no predication of chastity, for it is as nothing with them, and of nothing there can be no affection or thought; but after that nothing there arises something, when the first of marriage is felt, which is the love of the sex. That maidens and youths, before they feel in themselves the love of the sex, are commonly called chaste, is owing to ignorance of what chastity is.

151. IX. CHASTITY CANNOT BE PREDICATED OF EUNUCHS SO BORN, NOR OF EUNUCHS SO MADE. By eunuchs so born are meant those especially with whom the ultimate of love is wanting from

birth; and as in such a case the first and the mediate are without a foundation on which they may subsist, they have therefore no existence; and if they exist, the persons in whom they exist have no concern to distinguish between the chaste and the unchaste, for both principles are indifferent to them; but of these persons there are several kinds. The case is nearly the same with eunuchs so made as with some eunuchs so born; but eunuchs so made, because they are both men and women, cannot possibly regard conjugial love any otherwise than as a phantasy, and the delights of it as fables. If they have any inclination, it is rendered of a neuter quality, which is neither chaste nor unchaste; and what is neither chaste nor unchaste, derives no denomination from either the one or the other.

152. X. CHASTITY CANNOT BE PREDICATED OF THOSE WHO DO NOT BELIEVE ADULTERIES TO BE EVILS OF RELIGION, AND STILL LESS OF THOSE WHO DO NOT BELIEVE ADULTERIES TO BE HURTFUL TO SOCIETY. The reason why chastity cannot be predicated of these is, that they do not know what chastity is, nor even that it exists; for chastity belongs to marriage, as was shewn in the first article of this chapter. Those who do not believe adulteries to be evils of religion, make even marriages unchaste, when yet the religion with married partners constitutes their chastity; thus such persons have nothing chaste in them, wherefore it is in vain to talk to them of chastity: these are adulterers from confirmation. But those who do not believe adulteries to be hurtful to society, know still less than the others, either what chastity is, or even that it exists: for they are adulterers from set purpose. If they say that marriages are less unchaste than adulteries, they say so merely with the mouth, but not with the heart, because marriages with them are cold, and those who speak from this cold concerning chaste heat, cannot have an idea of chaste heat with reference to conjugial love. The quality of these persons, and the quality of the ideas of their thought, and hence the quality of the interiors of their speech, will be seen in the Second Part of this Work, which treats of the Insanities of Adulterers.

153. XI. CHASTITY CANNOT BE PREDICATED OF THOSE WHO ABSTAIN FROM ADULTERIES ONLY FOR VARIOUS EXTERNAL REASONS. Many believe that the mere abstinence from adulteries in the body is chastity, when yet this is not chastity, unless at the same time there is abstinence in the spirit. The spirit of man, by which is here meant his mind as to the affections and thoughts, makes what is chaste and what is unchaste, for it is from the mind that what is chaste and what is unchaste is in the body; for the body is altogether such as the mind or spirit is. Hence it follows, that neither they who abstain

from adulteries in the body and not from the spirit, nor they who abstain from them in spirit from the body, are chaste. There are many causes which make a man desist from adulteries in the body, and also in the spirit from the body; but still, he who does not desist from them in the body from the spirit, is unchaste; for the Lord says, "*That whosoever looketh upon another man's woman, so as to lust after her, hath already committed*
2 *adultery with her in his heart*" (Matt. v. 28). It is impossible to enumerate all the causes of abstinence from adulteries in the body only, for they are various according to states of the marriage and also according to states of the body; for there are some persons who abstain from them from fear of the civil law and its penalties; some from fear of the loss of reputation and of honour thence; some from fear of diseases which may be thereby contracted; some from fear of domestic quarrels on the part of the wife, whereby the quiet of their lives may be disturbed; some from fear of revenge on the part of the husband or relations; some from fear of being beaten or whipped by the servants of the family; some also abstain from poverty, avarice, or weakness arising either from disease, abuse, age, or impotence. Among these there are also some who, because they are not able or do not dare to commit adulteries in the body, condemn them also in the spirit, and thus speak morally against adulteries, and in favour of marriages; but these persons, if they do not in spirit, and the spirit does not from religion, hold adulteries as accursed, they are still adulterers, for although they do not commit them in the body, yet they do in the spirit; wherefore after death when they become spirits, they speak openly in favour of them. Hence it is evident, that even a wicked person may shun adulteries as hurtful, but that none but a Christian can shun them as sins. Hence then the Truth of the proposition is manifest, that chastity cannot be predicated of those who abstain from adulteries merely for various external reasons.

154. XII. CHASTITY CANNOT BE PREDICATED OF THOSE WHO BELIEVE MARRIAGES TO BE UNCHASTE. These persons do not know either what chastity is, or even that it exists; and in this respect they are like those who were spoken of just above, no. 152 [*a*], and like those who make chastity to consist merely in celibacy, who now come to be treated of.

155. XIII. CHASTITY CANNOT BE PREDICATED OF THOSE WHO HAVE RENOUNCED MARRIAGE BY VOWING PERPETUAL CELIBACY. UNLESS THERE BE AND REMAIN IN THEM THE LOVE OF A TRULY CONJUGIAL LIFE. The reason why chastity cannot be predicated of these is, that after a vow of perpetual celibacy, conjugial love is cast forth; and yet it is of this love alone that chastity is predicated. A further reason is, that there still remains within, from

creation, and consequently from birth, an inclination towards the sex; and when this inclination is restrained and subdued, it must needs pass away into heat, and with some into a burning heat, which, in rising from the body into the spirit, infests it, and with some defiles it; and it is possible that the spirit thus defiled may defile also the principles of religion, and cast them down from their internal abode, where they are in holiness, into the externals, where they become mere matters of talk and gesture; wherefore it has been provided by the Lord, that that kind of celibacy should exist only with those who are in external worship, in which worship they are because they do not approach the Lord, or read the Word. With such, eternal life is not so much endangered by vows of celibacy together with a solemn promise of chastity, as it is with those who are in internal worship. Moreover, in many instances that state of life is not entered upon from any freedom of the will, many entering upon it before they are in freedom from reason, and some in consequence of
alluring causes from the world. Of those who adopt that state 2
for the sake of the withdrawal of their minds from the world, that they may be free to devote themselves to Divine worship, those only are chaste with whom the love of a truly conjugial life either preceded that state, or follows it, and remains; for the love of a truly conjugial life is that of which chastity is predicated. Wherefore also, after death, all who have lived in monasteries are at length freed from their vows, and set at liberty, in order that, according to the interior vows and desires of their love, they may be led to choose a life either conjugial or extra-conjugial: if they then enter into conjugial life, those who have loved also the spiritual things of worship are given in marriage in heaven; but those who enter into extra-conjugial life are sent
to their like, who dwell at the sides of heaven. I have asked the 3
angels, whether those who have devoted themselves to piety, and given themselves up entirely to Divine worship, and thus withdrawn themselves from the snares of the world and the concupiscences of the flesh, and for that reason have vowed perpetual virginity, are received into heaven, and there become especially happy among the blessed, according to their faith. But the angels have replied, that such are indeed received into heaven; but when they feel the sphere of conjugial love there, they become sad and anxious, and then, some of their own accord, some by asking leave, and some by command, depart and are sent away; and when they are outside of that heaven, a way is opened for them to their consociates, who had been in a similar state of life in the world; and then from being anxious they become cheerful, and become glad together.

156. XIV. THE STATE OF MARRIAGE IS TO BE PREFERRED TO THE STATE OF CELIBACY. This is manifest from what has thus far

been said about marriage and celibacy. The state of marriage is to be preferred because it is the state ordained from creation; because its origin is the marriage of good and truth; because its correspondence is with the marriage of the Lord and the church; because the church and conjugial love are constant companions; because its use is more excellent than the uses of all the other things of creation, for thence according to order is the propagation of the human race, and also of the angelic heaven, for this is from the human race: add to this, that marriage is the fulness of man; for by means of it man becomes a full man, as will be proved in the following chapter. All these things are wanting in celibacy. But if the proposition be granted, that the state of celibacy is more excellent than the state of marriage, and if this proposition be subjected to a strict examination, to be assented to and established by confirmations, then the conclusion must be, that marriages are not holy, neither can they be chaste; yea, that chastity in the female sex belongs only to those who abstain from marriage and vow perpetual virginity; and moreover, that those who have vowed perpetual celibacy are meant by the eunuchs who make themselves eunuchs for the sake of the kingdom of God (Matt. xix. 12); besides many other such conclusions, which, being deduced from a proposition that is not true, are also not true. By the eunuchs who make themselves eunuchs for the sake of the kingdom of God, are meant spiritual eunuchs, who are those who in marriages abstain from the evils of whoredoms. That Italian eunuchs are not meant, is evident.

151 [a]. To the above I shall add two Memorable Relations. The first is this:—

*As I was going home from the school of wisdom spoken of above, no. 132, I saw in the way an angel in a hyacinthine garment. He joined me and walked by my side, and said, "I see that you are come from the school of wisdom, and that you have been gladdened by what you heard there; and as I perceive that you are not a full inhabitant of this world, because you are at the same time in the natural world, and therefore know nothing of our Olympic Gymnasia, where the ancient Sophi meet together, and by the information they collect from every new comer from thy world, learn what changes and successions wisdom has undergone and is still undergoing;—if you are willing I will conduct you to the place where several of those ancient Sophi and their sons, that is, their disciples, dwell."

So he led me to the confines between the north and east; and while I was looking that way from an eminence, lo! there appeared a city, and on one side of it two small hills: that

* The following Memorable Relation is repeated in the *True Christian Religion*, no. 692.

which was nearer to the city was lower than the other. And he said to me, "That city is called Athens, the lower hill, Parnassus, and the higher, Helicon. They are so called, because in the city and around it dwell the ancient wise men who lived in Greece, as Pythagoras, Socrates, Aristippus, Xenophon, with their disciples and scholars."

On my asking about Plato and Aristotle, he said, "They and their followers dwell in another region, because they taught rational things which belong to the understanding; whereas the former taught morals which belong to the life."

He further said, that from the city of Athens there were 2
frequently deputed some of the students to learn from the literati of the Christians what they think at the present day about God, the creation of the universe, the immortality of the soul, the state of man relatively to the state of beasts, and other subjects which belong to interior wisdom: and he added, that a herald had that day announced an assembly, which was a token that the emissaries had met with some new-comers from the earth, from whom they had heard some curious things.

We then saw many persons going out of the city and its suburbs, some having wreaths of laurel on their heads, some holding palms in their hands, some with books under their arms, and some with pens under the hair of the left temple. We mixed with them, and ascended the hill with them: and lo! on the top was an octagonal palace, which they called the Palladium, into which we entered: and lo! within there were eight hexangular recesses, in each of which was a bookcase and a table: at these recesses were seated the laureates, and in the Palladium itself there were seen seats cut out of the rock, on which the rest sat down.

A door on the left was then opened, through which the two 3
new-comers from the earth were introduced; and after they had been greeted, one of the laureates asked them, "WHAT NEWS FROM THE EARTH?"

They said, "This is new, that men like beasts have been found in the woods, or beasts like men: from their face and body they were known to have been born men, and to have been lost or left in the forests when they were two or three years old; it was reported that they were not able to give utterance to any thought, nor to learn to articulate the voice into any expression; neither did they know the food suitable for them as the beasts do, but put greedily into their mouths whatever they found in the forest, whether it was clean or unclean; besides many other particulars of a like nature: from which some of the learned among us have formed several conjectures and conclusions, concerning the state of men relatively to that of beasts."

On hearing this, some of the ancient Sophi asked, "What 4
were the conjectures and conclusions formed from those facts?"

The two strangers replied, "There were many; but they may all be comprised under the following: 1. That a man in consequence of his nature, and also by birth, is more stupid and consequently viler than any beast; and that he remains so, unless he be instructed. 2. That he is capable of being instructed, because he learned to make articulate sounds, and so to speak, and thereby began to express his thoughts, and this successively more and more perfectly, until he could express the laws of society; many of which, however, are impressed on beasts from their birth. 3. That beasts have rationality equally with men. 4. Therefore, that if beasts could speak, they would reason on every subject as cleverly as men; a proof of which is, that they think from reason and sagacity just as men do. 5. That the understanding is only a modification of the light from the sun, the heat co-operating by means of the ether, so that it is only an activity of interior nature; and that this activity may be exalted to such an extent as to appear like wisdom. 6. That therefore it is ridiculous to believe that a man lives after death any more than a beast; unless perchance, for some days after his decease, in consequence of an exhalation of the life of the body, he may appear as a mist under the form of a spectre, before he is dissipated into nature; hardly otherwise than as a burnt twig, when taken out of the ashes, appears in the likeness of its own form. 7. Consequently, that religion, which teaches a life after death, is a mere invention to keep the simple inwardly in bonds by its laws, as they are kept outwardly in bonds by the laws of the state."

To this they added, that "people of mere ingenuity reason in this manner, but not so the intelligent."

They asked what the intelligent thought on the subject.

They said that they had not heard, but that they only thought so.

152 [a]. On hearing this relation, all those who were sitting at the tables said, "Alas! what times are come on the earth! What changes has wisdom undergone! How is she changed into a fatuous ingenuity! The sun is set, and is beneath the earth in direct opposition to his meridian. From the case of such as have been left and found in woods, who cannot know that an uninstructed man is such? Is he not just as he is instructed? Is he not born in greater ignorance than the beasts? Must he not learn to walk and to speak? Supposing he never learnt to walk, would he ever stand upright on his feet? And if he never learnt to speak, would he be able to express anything of thought? Is not every man such as instruction makes him,—insane from falsities, or wise from truths? and is not he that is insane from falsities, entirely possessed with the phantasy that he is wiser than he who is wise from truths? Do there not

exist foolish and insane men, who are no more men than those who have been found in the woods? Are not such as have been deprived of memory like unto these? From all these considerations we conclude, that a man without instruction is neither a man nor a beast; but that he is a form, which is capable of receiving in itself that which constitutes a man; and thus that he is not born a man, but that he becomes a man; and that a man is born such a form as to be an organ receptive of life from God, to the end that he may be a subject into which God can introduce all good, and, by union with Himself, make him blessed to eternity. We have perceived from your conversation, that wisdom at the present day is extinguished or infatuated to such an extent, that nothing at all is known about the state of the life of men relatively to the state of the life of beasts; and hence it is that the state of the life of man after death is not known: but those who are capable of knowing this, and yet are not willing to know it, and consequently deny it, as many of your Christians do, we may liken to such as are found in the woods: not that they have become so stupid from a want of instruction, but that they have made themselves so by the fallacies of the senses, which are the darkness of Truths."

153 [*a*]. At that moment a certain person standing in the middle of the Palladium, and holding in his hand a palm, said, "Pray unfold this arcanum, 'How could man, created the form of God, be changed into a form of the devil?' I know that the angels of heaven are forms of God, and that the angels of hell are forms of the devil, and that the two forms are opposite to each other, the latter being insanities, the former wisdoms. Tell me, therefore, how man who was created a form of God, could pass from the day into such a night, as to be capable of denying God and eternal life."

To this the teachers replied in order; first the Pythagoreans, 2
next the Socratists, and afterwards the rest.

But among them there was a certain Platonist, who spoke last; and his opinion prevailed, which was to this effect: "That the men of the Saturnian or golden era knew and acknowledged that they were forms receptive of life from God; and that on this account wisdom was inscribed on their souls and hearts, and hence they saw truth from the light of truth, and through truths perceived good from the delight of the love of it. But as the human race in the following ages receded from the acknowledgment that all truth of wisdom, and the consequent good of love with them, continually flowed in from God, they ceased to be dwellings of God; and then also discourse with God and consociation with the angels ceased: for the interiors of their minds were bent from their direction, which had been elevated upwards to God from God, into a direction more and

more oblique, outwards into the world, and thus to God from God through the world, and at length inverted into an opposite direction, which is downwards to self; and as God cannot be beheld by a man interiorly inverted, and thus averted, men separated themselves from God, and were made forms of hell or
3 of the devil. From these considerations it follows, that in the first eras they acknowledged in heart and soul, that all the good of love and the consequent truth of wisdom were derived to them from God, and also that they were God's in them; and thus that they were mere receptacles of life from God, and hence were called images of God, sons of God, and born of God; but that in the succeeding eras they did not acknowledge this in heart and soul, but by a certain persuasive faith, afterwards by a historical faith, and lastly only with the mouth; and this kind of acknowledgment is no acknowledgment at all; yea, it is a denial at heart. From these considerations it may be seen what is the quality of the wisdom on the earth among Christians at the present day, when they do not know the difference between a man and a beast, notwithstanding their being in possession of a written revelation, whereby they may be inspired by God: and hence many believe, that if a man lives after death, a beast must live also; or that, because a beast does not live after death, neither will a man. Is not our spiritual light, which enlightens the sight of the mind, become thick darkness with them? and is not their natural light, which only enlightens the sight of the body, become brightness to them?"

154 [*a*]. After this they all turned towards the two strangers, and thanked them for their visit, and for the relation they had given, and begged them to report to their brethren what they had heard. The strangers replied that they would endeavour to confirm their brethren in this Truth, that in proportion as they attribute all the good of charity and the truth of faith to the Lord, and not to themselves, in the same proportion they are men, and in the same proportion become angels of heaven.

155 [*a*]. The second Memorable Relation:—

One morning very sweet singing, which was heard from some height above me, awoke me; and in consequence, during the first wakefulness, which is more internal, peaceful, and sweet than the rest of the day, I was able to be kept for some time in the spirit as it were out of the body, and to attend carefully to the affection which was being sung. The singing of heaven is nothing else than an affection of the mind, sent forth through the mouth as melody; for it is the tone of voice, separate from the discourse of the speaker, and flowing from the affection of love, that gives life to the speech. In that state I perceived that it was the affection of the delights of conjugial love which was made musical by wives in heaven: that this was the case I observed from the tone of the song, in which those delights were varied in a wonderful manner.

After this I arose, and looked out into the spiritual world; and lo! in the east, beneath the sun, there appeared as it were a GOLDEN SHOWER. It was the early morning dew descending in great abundance, which, catching the sun's rays, exhibited before my sight the appearance of a golden shower. Becoming still more fully awake in consequence of this appearance, I went forth in the spirit, and asked an angel whom I then happened to meet whether he saw a golden shower descending from the sun.

He replied, that he saw one as often as he meditated on con- 2
jugial love; and at the same time turning his eyes thither, he said, "That shower falls over a palace, in which are three husbands with their wives, who dwell in the midst of an eastern paradise. Such a shower is seen falling from the sun over that palace, because with those husbands and wives there resides wisdom concerning conjugial love and its delights; with the husbands concerning conjugial love, and with the wives concerning its delights. But I perceive that you are in meditation concerning the delights of conjugial love: wherefore I will lead you to that palace, and introduce you."

He led me through paradisiacal scenes to houses which were built of olive wood, having two pillars of cedars before the gate, and introduced me to the husbands, and asked that I might be allowed to speak with their wives in their presence.

They consented, and called their wives.

These looked into my eyes searchingly; and I asked, why they did so.

They said, "We are able exquisitely to see what is your inclination and consequent affection, and your thought from affection, concerning the love of the sex; and we see that you are meditating intensely, but still chastely, concerning that love." And they added, "What do you wish us to tell you on the subject?"

I replied, "Pray tell me something about the delights of conjugial love."

The husbands assented, saying, "If you are so disposed, give them some information about those delights: their ears are chaste."

They asked, "Who taught you to question us about the delights 3
of that love? Why did you not question our husbands?"

I replied, "This angel, who is with me, told me aside, that wives are the receptacles and sensories of those delights, because they are born loves; and all delights belong to love."

To this they replied with a smile, "Be prudent, and declare nothing of the sort except in an ambiguous sense, because it is a wisdom deeply reserved in the hearts of our sex, and is not disclosed to any husband, unless he be in truly conjugial love. There are many reasons for this, which we keep entirely to ourselves."

Then the husbands said, "Our wives know all the states of our minds, neither is anything hidden from them; they see, perceive, and feel whatever proceeds from our will. We, on the other hand, know nothing of what passes with our wives. This is given to wives, because they are most tender loves, and as it were burning zeals for the preservation of friendship and conjugial confidence, and thus of the happiness of life both of their husbands and themselves, which they carefully watch over both for their husbands and themselves, by virtue of a wisdom implanted in their love, which wisdom is so full of prudence, that they are unwilling to say, and consequently cannot say, that they love, but that they are loved."

I asked why they were unwilling, and consequently unable, to say so?

They replied, "If the least hint of the kind were to escape from the mouth of the wives, cold would invade their husbands, and would separate them from bed, bed-chamber, and sight: but this takes place only with those who do not hold marriages to be holy, and therefore do not love their wives from spiritual love. It is otherwise with those who do. In the minds of the latter that love is spiritual, and by derivation thence in the body is natural. We in this palace are in the latter love by derivation from the former; wherefore we trust our husbands with the secrets about our delights of conjugial love."

4 I then courteously asked them to disclose to me some of those secrets.

Hereupon they looked towards a window in the southern quarter, and lo! there appeared a bright white dove, whose wings glistened as if they were of silver, and its head was adorned with a crown as of gold: it was standing upon a branch out of which there went forth an olive; and while it was in the attempt to spread out its wings, the wives said, "We will disclose something: while that dove appears it is a sign to us that it is allowed." "Every man (*vir*)," they continued, "has five senses, sight, hearing, smell, taste, and touch; but we have likewise a sixth, which is the sense of all the delights of the conjugial love of the husband; and this sense we have in the palms of our hands, when we touch the breasts, arms, hands, or cheeks of our husbands, especially their breasts; and also when we are touched by them. All the gladnesses and pleasantnesses of the thoughts of their mind (*mens*), all the joys and delights of their lower mind (*animus*), and all the festive and cheerful states of their bosoms, pass from them into us, and put on form, and become perceptible, sensible, and tangible; and we discern them as exquisitely and distinctly as the ear does the melody of a song, and the tongue the tastes of delicacies: in a word, the spiritual delightsomenesses of our husbands put on with us a kind of natural embodiment; wherefore we are called by our husbands the sensory organs of chaste conjugial love, and hence its delights. But this sense of our sex exists, subsists, persists, and is exalted in the degree in which our husbands love us from wisdom and judgment, and in which we in return love them from the same qualities in them. This sense of our sex is called in the heavens the sport of wisdom with its love, and of love with its wisdom."

This information excited in me the desire of asking further 5
questions, as, concerning the variety of delights.

They said, "It is infinite; but we are unwilling and therefore unable to say more; for the dove at our window, with the olive branch under his feet, has flown away."

I waited for its return, but in vain. In the meantime I asked the husbands, "Have you a like sense of conjugial love?"

They replied, "We have a like sense in general, but not in particular. We enjoy a general blessedness, a general delight, and a general pleasantness, arising from the particulars of our wives; and this general, which we derive from them, is as the serenity of peace."

As they said this, lo! through the window there appeared a swan standing on a branch of a fig-tree, and it spread out his wings and flew away. On seeing this, the husbands said, "This is a sign for us to be silent about conjugial love: come again some other time, and perhaps more things may be disclosed."

They then withdrew, and we departed.

THE CONJUNCTION OF THE SOULS AND MINDS BY MEANS OF MARRIAGE, WHICH IS MEANT BY THE LORD'S WORDS, THAT THEY ARE NO LONGER TWO, BUT ONE FLESH.

156 [*a*]. That at creation there was implanted in man and woman an inclination and also a faculty of conjunction as into a one, and that this inclination and faculty are still in man and woman, is manifest from the Book of the Creation, and at the same time from the Lord's words. In the Book of the Creation, which is called GENESIS, it is read, "*Jehovah God built the rib which He had taken from the man* (homo), *into a woman, and brought her to the man. And the man said, This now is bone of my bones, and flesh of my flesh. Her name shall be called Woman* (Ishshah) *because she was taken out of man* (Ish, vir): *therefore shall a man* (vir) *leave his father and his mother, and cleave to his wife; and they shall become one flesh*" (chap. ii. 22–24). The Lord also said something similar in Matthew, "*Have ye not read, that He who made them from the beginning, made them male and female, and said, Therefore shall a man* (homo) *leave father and mother, and cleave to his wife; and* THEY TWO SHALL BECOME ONE FLESH? WHEREFORE THEY ARE NO LONGER TWO, BUT ONE FLESH" (chap.
2 xix. 4–6). From this it is evident, that the woman was created out of the man (*vir*), and that both have an inclination and faculty to become reunited into a one. That such reunion means into one man (*homo*), is also evident from the Book of the Creation, where both together are called man (*homo*); for it is read, "*In the day that God created man* (homo), *male and female created He them, and called their name Man* (homo)" (chap. v. 1, 2). It is there read, He called their name Adam; but Adam and man are one expression in the Hebrew language; moreover, both together are called man in the same Book (chap. i. 27; chap. ii. 22–24). By one flesh is also signified one man; as is evident from the passages in the Word where mention is made of all flesh, by which is meant every man, as Gen. vi. 12, 13, 17, 19; Isaiah xl. 5, 6; xlix. 26; lxvi. 16, 23, 24; Jer. xxv. 31; xxxii.
3 27; xlv. 5; Ezek. xx. 48; xxi. 4, 5; and other passages. But what is meant by the rib of the man (*vir*), which was built into a woman; what by the flesh, which was closed up in the place thereof, and thus what by bone of my bones, and flesh of my flesh; and what by the father and the mother, whom a man (*vir*)

shall leaveafter marriage; and what by cleaving to his wife, has been shown in the *Arcana Cœlestia;* in which work the two books, Genesis and Exodus, are explained as to the spiritual sense. It is there proved that a rib does not mean a rib,—nor flesh, flesh,—nor a bone, a bone,—nor cleaving to, cleaving to; but that they mean spiritual things, which correspond to them, and consequently are signified by them. That spiritual things are meant, which from two make one man (*homo*), is evident from this, that conjugial love conjoins them, and this love is spiritual. That the love of the wisdom of the man (*vir*) is transcribed into the wife, has been occasionally stated above, and will be more fully confirmed in the following sections: at present we may not digress from the subject proposed, which is, the conjunction of the two married partners into one flesh through the union of their souls and minds. This union shall be elucidated in the following order:—

I. *From creation there has been implanted in both sexes a faculty and inclination, whereby they are able and willing to be conjoined as into a one.*

II. *Conjugial love conjoins two souls, and hence two minds, into a one.*

III. *The will of the wife conjoins itself with the understanding of the man, and hence the understanding of the man conjoins itself with the will of the wife.*

IV. *The inclination to unite the man to herself is constant and perpetual with the wife, but inconstant and fluctuating with the man.*

V. *Conjunction is inspired into the man by the wife according to her love, and is received by the man according to his wisdom.*

VI. *This conjunction is effected successively from the first days of marriage; and, with those who are in truly conjugial love, it is effected more and more thoroughly to eternity.*

VII. *The conjunction of the wife with the rational wisdom of the husband is effected from within, but with his moral wisdom from without.*

VIII. *For the sake of this conjunction as an end, there has been given to the wife a perception of the affections of the husband, and also the utmost prudence in governing them.*

IX. *The wives conceal this perception with themselves, and hide it from their husbands, on account of causes which are necessities, in order that conjugial love, friendship, and confidence, and thus the blessedness of dwelling together, and the happiness of life, may be secured.*

X. *This perception is the wisdom of the wife; and this wisdom is not possible with the man: neither is the rational wisdom of the man possible with the wife.*

XI. *The wife, from love, is continually thinking about the man's inclination towards her, with the purpose of conjoining him with herself; it is otherwise with the man.*

XII. *The wife conjoins herself with the man, by means of applications to the desires of his will.*

XIII. *The wife is conjoined with her husband by means of the sphere of her life, which goes out from her love.*

XIV. *The wife is conjoined with the husband by means of the appropriation of the forces of his virtue or manhood; but this is effected according to their mutual spiritual love.*

XV. *Thus the wife receives into herself the image of her husband, and hence perceives, sees, and feels his affections.*

XVI. *There are duties proper to the man, and duties proper to the wife; and the wife cannot enter into the duties proper to the man, nor the man into the duties proper to the wife, and perform them rightly.*

XVII. *These duties, according to mutual aid, also conjoin the two into a one, and at the same time constitute one house.*

XVIII. *Married partners, according to the above-named conjunctions, become one man* (homo) *more and more.*

XIX. *Those who are in truly conjugial love, feel that they are a united man, and as it were one flesh.*

XX. *Truly conjugial love, considered in itself, is a union of the souls, a conjunction of the minds, and an effort for conjunction in the bosoms, and hence in the body.*

XXI. *The states of this love are innocence, peace, tranquillity, inmost friendship, full confidence, and a desire of the disposition and of the heart to make all good mutual to each other; and the states arising from all these are blessedness, blissfulness, delightsomeness, and pleasure; and from the eternal enjoyment of these is heavenly felicity.*

XXII. *These things can by no means exist except in the marriage of one man with one wife.*

Now follows the explanation of these articles.

157. I. FROM CREATION THERE HAS BEEN IMPLANTED IN BOTH SEXES A FACULTY AND INCLINATION, WHEREBY THEY ARE ABLE AND WILLING TO BE CONJOINED AS INTO A ONE. That the woman was taken out of the man, was shewn just above from the Book of the Creation; hence it follows, that there is in both sexes a faculty and inclination to become conjoined into a one. For that which is taken out of anything, derives and retains of its peculiarity, which it makes its own; and as this derivation is of a similar nature with that from which it was derived, it breathes after reunion; and when it has been reunited, it is as in itself when it is in that from whence it came, and contrariwise. That there is a faculty of conjunction of the one sex with the other, or that they are capable of being united, admits of no doubt; and also that there is an inclination to become conjoined; for personal experience teaches both.

158. II. CONJUGIAL LOVE CONJOINS TWO SOULS, AND HENCE TWO MINDS, INTO A ONE. Every man consists of a soul, a mind, and a body. The soul is his inmost, the mind his mediate, and the body his ultimate. Since the soul is a man's inmost, it is, from its origin, celestial; as the mind is his mediate, it is, from its origin, spiritual; and as the body is his ultimate, it is, from its origin, natural. Those things which, from their origin, are celestial and spiritual, are not in space, but in the appearances of space. This also is known in the world, wherefore it is said, that neither extension nor place can be predicated of spiritual things. Since therefore spaces are appearances, distances also and presences are appearances. That the appearances of distances and presences in the spiritual world are according to proximities, propinquities, and affinities of love, has been frequently pointed out and confirmed in small treatises concerning that world. These things are said in order that it may be known that the souls and minds of men are not in space like their bodies; because the former, as was said above, are from their origin celestial and spiritual; and as they are not in space, they can be conjoined as into a one, although their bodies may not be so conjoined at the same time. This is the case especially with married partners, who love each other inmostly: but as the woman is from the man (*vir*), and that conjunction is a kind of reunition, it may be seen from reason that it is not a conjunction into a one, but an adjunction, close and near according to the love, and amounting to contact with those who are in truly conjugial love. This adjunction may be called spiritual dwelling together, and this takes place with married partners who love each other tenderly, however distant they may be from each other in the body. Many proofs of experience exist, even in the natural world, which confirm these statements. Hence it is evident, that conjugial love conjoins two souls and minds into one.

159. III. THE WILL OF THE WIFE CONJOINS ITSELF WITH THE UNDERSTANDING OF THE MAN, AND HENCE THE UNDERSTANDING OF THE MAN CONJOINS ITSELF WITH THE WILL OF THE WIFE. The reason is, that the male is born to become understanding, and the female to become will, loving the understanding of the male; from which it follows, that conjugial conjunction is that of the will of the wife with the understanding of the man, and the reciprocal conjunction of the understanding of the man with the will of the wife. Every one sees that there is a very close conjunction of the understanding and the will; and that it is such, that the one faculty can enter into the other, and be delighted from the conjunction, and in it.

160. IV. THE INCLINATION TO UNITE THE MAN TO HERSELF IS CONSTANT AND PERPETUAL WITH THE WIFE, BUT INCONSTANT AND

FLUCTUATING WITH THE MAN. The reason is, that love cannot do otherwise than love, and unite itself in order that it may be loved in return; its essence and life is nothing else; and women are born loves, whereas men, with whom they unite themselves in order that they may be loved in return, are receptions. Besides, love is continually efficient; it is like heat, flame, and fire, which perish if their efficiency is checked. Hence it is that the inclination to unite the man to herself is constant and perpetual with the wife. But the reason why there is not a similar inclination with the man towards the wife is, that the man is not love, but only a recipient of love; and as a state of reception is absent or present according to intruding cares, and according to the changes of heat and want of heat in the mind from various causes, and according to the increase and decrease of the powers in the body, which do not return regularly and at stated periods, it follows that the inclination to that conjunction is inconstant and fluctuating with the men.

161. V. CONJUNCTION IS INSPIRED INTO THE MAN BY THE WIFE ACCORDING TO HER LOVE, AND IS RECEIVED BY THE MAN ACCORDING TO HIS WISDOM. That love and consequently conjunction is inspired into the man by the wife, is at this day concealed from the men; yea, it is universally denied by them. The reason is, that wives persuade that the men alone love, and they themselves receive; or, that the men are loves, and themselves obediences; they rejoice also at heart when the men believe it to be so. There are many reasons why they persuade the men of this, which reasons all relate to the prudence and circumspection of wives; respecting which, something shall be said in what follows, and particularly in the chapter on "The Causes of Colds, Separations, and Divorces between Married Partners." The reason why men receive the inspiration or insinuation of love from their wives is, that nothing of conjugial love, or even of the love of the sex, is with men, but only with wives and women. That this is the case, has been shewn me to the life in the spiritual world.

2 * The conversation there once turned on this subject; and the men, in consequence of a persuasion received from their wives, insisted that they, and not the wives, loved, but that the wives received love from them. In order to settle the dispute about this arcanum, all the women, together with the wives, were withdrawn from the men, and at the same time the very sphere of the love of the sex was removed with them. On the removal of this sphere, the men came into a very strange state, such as they had never before perceived, at which they greatly complained. Then, while they were in this state, the women were brought to them, and the wives to the husbands; and both the latter and

* In the original Latin edition, the experience here related is enclosed in inverted commas.

the former addressed them in a caressing manner; but they had become cold to their caresses, and turned away, and said one to another, "What is this? what is a woman?" And when some of the women said that they were their wives, they replied, "What is a wife? we do not know you." But when the wives began to be grieved at this absolutely cold indifference of the men, and some of them to cry, the sphere of the love of the feminine sex, and the conjugial sphere, which had for the time been withdrawn from the men, was restored; and then the men instantly returned into their former state, the lovers of marriage into their state, and the lovers of the sex into theirs. Thus the men were convinced that nothing of conjugial love, nor even of the love of the sex, resided with them, but only with the wives and women. Nevertheless, the wives afterwards from their prudence induced the men to believe, that love resides with the men, and that some small spark of it may pass from them into the wives.

This experience is here adduced, in order that it may be 3
known, that wives are loves and men receptions. That men are receptions according to the wisdom with them, especially according to this wisdom from religion, that the wife only ought to be loved, is evident from this consideration, that when the wife only is loved, the love is concentrated; and because it is also ennobled, it remains in its strength, and is steadfast and permanent; and that otherwise it would be as when wheat from the granary is cast to the dogs, whereby there is want at home.

162. VI. THIS CONJUNCTION IS EFFECTED SUCCESSIVELY FROM THE FIRST DAYS OF MARRIAGE; AND, WITH THOSE WHO ARE IN TRULY CONJUGIAL LOVE, IT IS EFFECTED MORE AND MORE THOROUGHLY TO ETERNITY. The first heat of marriage does not conjoin; for it partakes of the love of the sex, which belongs to the body and thence to the spirit; and what is from the body in the spirit, does not last long; but the love which is from the spirit in the body does last. The love of the spirit, and of the body from the spirit, is insinuated into the souls and minds of married partners together with friendship and confidence. When these two things, [namely, friendship and confidence,] conjoin themselves with the first love of marriage, the love becomes conjugial, which love opens the bosoms and inspires into them the sweetnesses of love, and this more and more inwardly, in proportion as those two things adjoin themselves to the primitive love; and that love enters into them and they into it.

163. VII. THE CONJUNCTION OF THE WIFE WITH THE RATIONAL WISDOM OF THE HUSBAND IS EFFECTED FROM WITHIN, BUT WITH HIS MORAL WISDOM FROM WITHOUT. That wisdom with men (*viri*) is twofold, rational and moral, and that their rational wisdom

belongs to the understanding alone, and their moral wisdom belongs to the understanding and at the same time to the life, may be concluded and seen from mere intuition and examination. But in order that it may be known what is meant by the rational wisdom of men, and what by their moral wisdom, some of their constituents shall be enumerated in detail. Those things which belong to their rational wisdom are designated by various names. In general they are called knowledge, intelligence, and wisdom; but in particular they are called rationality, judgment, cleverness, learning, sagacity. But, since every one has sciences peculiar to his calling, therefore they are manifold; for clergymen have their peculiar sciences, those in authority have theirs; their subordinates in office, again, have theirs; judges theirs, doctors and chemists theirs, soldiers and sailors theirs, artificers and workmen theirs, husbandmen theirs, and so on. To rational wisdom pertain also all the sciences into which youths are initiated in the schools, and by means of which they are afterwards initiated into intelligence; which sciences also are called by various names, as philosophy, physics, geometry, mechanics, chemistry, astronomy, jurisprudence, politics, ethics, history, and many others, through which, as through doors, an entrance is made into rational things, out of which there is formed rational wisdom.

164. But the things which belong to moral wisdom with men are all the moral virtues, which look to the life, and enter it, and also the spiritual virtues which flow out from love to God and love towards the neighbour, and flow again into those loves. The virtues which pertain to the moral wisdom of men are also of various names, and are called temperance, sobriety, probity, benevolence, friendship, modesty, sincerity, obligingness, civility, also assiduity, industry, expertness, alacrity; munificence, liberality, generosity, activity, intrepidity, prudence; besides many others. The spiritual virtues with men are the love of religion, charity, Truth, faith, conscience, innocence, besides many others. The latter and the former virtues may in general be referred to love and zeal for religion, for the public good, for one's country, for one's fellow-citizens, for one's parents, for one's married partner, and for one's children. In all these, justice and judgment bear rule: justice belongs to moral wisdom, and judgment belongs to rational wisdom.

165. The reason why the conjunction of the wife with the man's rational wisdom is from within, is, that this wisdom is peculiar to the understanding of the men, and climbs into a light in which women are not; which is the reason why women do not speak from that wisdom, but in the society of men, when such things are being discussed, they remain silent, and only listen.

That nevertheless such things are with the wives from within, is evident from their listening, and from their inwardly recognizing what had been said, and favouring those things which they hear and have heard from their husbands. But the reason why the conjunction of the wife with the moral wisdom of men is from without, is, that the virtues of that wisdom, for the most part, are akin to similar virtues with women, and partake of the man's intellectual will, with which the will of the wife unites itself and makes a marriage; and since the wife knows those virtues with the man more than the man knows them with himself, it is said that the conjunction of the wife with those virtues is from without.

166. VIII. FOR THE SAKE OF THIS CONJUNCTION AS AN END, THERE HAS BEEN GIVEN TO THE WIFE A PERCEPTION OF THE AFFECTIONS OF THE HUSBAND, AND ALSO THE UTMOST PRUDENCE IN GOVERNING THEM. That wives are cognizant of the affections of their husbands and govern them prudently, is also among the arcana of conjugial love which lie concealed with wives. They become cognizant of those affections by means of three senses, the sight, hearing, and touch, and govern them without their husbands knowing anything about it. Now as these are among the arcana of wives, it does not become me to disclose them circumstantially; but as it is becoming for the wives themselves to do so, therefore four Memorable Relations are added to several of the chapters, in which those arcana are disclosed by them: two of the Relations [nos. 155 and 208] are from the three wives who dwelt in the palace, over which was seen falling as it were a golden shower; and two [nos. 293 and 294] from the seven wives that were sitting in the garden of roses. A perusal of these Relations will unfold this arcanum.

167. IX. THE WIVES CONCEAL THIS PERCEPTION WITH THEMSELVES AND HIDE IT FROM THEIR HUSBANDS, ON ACCOUNT OF CAUSES WHICH AMOUNT TO NECESSITIES, IN ORDER THAT CONJUGIAL LOVE, FRIENDSHIP, AND CONFIDENCE, AND THUS THE BLESSEDNESS OF DWELLING TOGETHER, AND THE HAPPINESS OF LIFE, MAY BE SECURED. The concealing and hiding of the perception of the affections of the husband by the wives, are said to be necessities, because if they were to reveal them, they would estrange their husbands from bed, bed-chamber, and house. The reason is that conjugial cold is deeply seated in most men, from many causes which will be disclosed in the chapter on "The Causes of Colds, Separations, and Divorces between Married Partners." This cold, in case the wives should disclose the affections and inclinations of their husbands, would burst forth from its hiding places, and would first chill the interiors of the mind, afterwards the breast, and thence the ultimates of love which are allotted to genera-

tion; and these being chilled, conjugial love would be banished to such a degree, that there would not remain any hope of friendship, confidence, the blessedness of dwelling together, and thence the happiness of life; when nevertheless wives are continually nourished by this hope. To openly reveal that they know the affections and inclinations of love in their husbands, carries with it a declaration and publication of their own love: and it is known that in proportion as wives open their mouth on the subject of their love, the men grow cold, and desire separation. From these considerations the Truth of this article is evident, that the causes for which wives conceal their perception with themselves, and hide it from their husbands, are necessities.

168. X. THIS PERCEPTION IS THE WISDOM OF THE WIFE; AND THIS WISDOM IS NOT POSSIBLE WITH THE MAN: NEITHER IS THE RATIONAL WISDOM OF THE MAN POSSIBLE WITH THE WIFE. This follows from the difference which exists between the masculine principle and the feminine principle. The masculine consists in perceiving from the understanding, and the feminine in perceiving from love; and the understanding perceives also those things which are above the body and outside of the world; for the rational and spiritual sight reaches thither; whereas love does not go beyond what it feels: when it goes beyond, it does so in consequence of a conjunction, which has been established from creation, with the understanding of the man. For the understanding belongs to light, and love belongs to heat; and those things which belong to light, are seen, and those which belong to heat, are felt. From these facts it is evident, that on account of the universal difference which exists between the masculine and the feminine, the wisdom of the wife is not possible with the man, neither is the wisdom of the man possible with the wife: nor, further, is the moral wisdom of the man possible with women, in so far as it partakes of his rational wisdom.

169 XI. THE WIFE [FROM LOVE] IS CONTINUALLY THINKING ABOUT THE MAN'S INCLINATION TOWARDS HER, WITH THE PURPOSE OF CONJOINING HIM WITH HERSELF [; IT IS OTHERWISE WITH THE MAN]. This agrees with what was explained above, namely, that the inclination to unite the man with herself is constant and perpetual with the wife, but inconstant and fluctuating with the man (see no. 160): hence it follows, that the wife's thought is continually employed about her husband's inclination to her, with the purpose of conjoining him with herself. A wife's thought about her husband is indeed interrupted by the domestic concerns which are under her care; but still it remains in the affection of her love; and this affection does not separate itself

from the thoughts with women, as it does with men. These things, however, I relate from hearsay; see the two Memorable Relations [nos. 293 and 294] from the seven wives sitting in the garden of roses, which are annexed to some of the chapters.

170. XII. THE WIFE CONJOINS HERSELF WITH THE MAN BY MEANS OF APPLICATIONS TO THE DESIRES OF HIS WILL. This being generally known and admitted, it is needless to explain it.

171. XIII. THE WIFE IS CONJOINED WITH HER HUSBAND BY MEANS OF THE SPHERE OF HER LIFE, WHICH GOES OUT FROM HER LOVE. There goes out, yea, pours forth from every human being a spiritual sphere from the affections of his love, which encompasses him, and infuses itself into the natural sphere which is from the body, and the two spheres become conjoined. That a natural sphere is continually flowing forth from the body, not only from man, but also from beasts, yea, from trees, fruits, flowers, and also from metals, is generally known. The case is similar in the spiritual world; but the spheres flowing forth from subjects in that world are spiritual, and those which emanate from spirits and angels are altogether spiritual, because they have affections of love, and thence interior perceptions and thoughts. Everything sympathetic and antipathetic takes its rise thence, and so does all conjunction and disjunction, and, according thereto, presence and absence in that world: for what is homogeneous or concordant causes conjunction and presence, and what is heterogeneous and discordant causes disjunction and absence; wherefore those spheres cause distances in that world. What those spiritual spheres operate in the natural world, is also known to some. The inclinations of married partners towards each other, are from no other origin. They are united by unanimous and concordant spheres, and disunited by adverse and discordant spheres; for concordant spheres are delightful and agreeable, and discordant spheres are undelightful and disagreeable. I have been informed by the angels, who are 2
in a clear perception of those spheres, that there is no part within a man, nor any part without, which does not renew itself; this is effected by dissolutions and reparations; and that hence is the sphere which continually pours forth. They also said that this sphere encompasses man on the back and on the breast, slightly on the back, but more densely on the breast, and that the sphere from the breast conjoins itself with the respiration; and that this is the reason why two married partners who differ in dispositions and disagree in affections, lie in bed back to back, and, on the other hand, why those who agree in dispositions and affections, lie mutually turned towards each other. They also said that these 3
spheres, because they go out from every part of man,

and are abundantly continued around him, conjoin and disjoin the two married partners not only from without, but also from within; and that hence come all the differences and varieties of conjugial love. Lastly they said, that the sphere of love going out from a wife who is tenderly loved, is perceived in heaven as sweetly fragrant, very much more pleasantly [fragrant] than it is perceived in the world by a newly-married husband during the first days after the wedding. From these facts is evident the Truth of the assertion, that the wife is conjoined to her husband by the sphere of her life which goes out from her love.

172. XIV. THE WIFE IS CONJOINED WITH THE HUSBAND BY MEANS OF THE APPROPRIATION OF THE FORCES OF HIS VIRTUE; BUT THIS IS EFFECTED ACCORDING TO THEIR MUTUAL SPIRITUAL LOVE. That this is the case, I have also gathered from the mouth of the angels. They have said that the prolific contributions from the husbands are universally received by the wives, and add themselves to their life; and that thus the wives lead an unanimous, and successively more unanimous life with their husbands; and that hence is effectively produced a union of the souls and a conjunction of the minds. They declared the reason of this was, that in the prolific [element] of the husband is his soul, and also his mind as to its interiors, which are conjoined with the soul. They added, that this was provided from creation, in order that the wisdom of the man, which constitutes his soul, may be appropriated to the wife, and that thus they may become, according to the Lord's words, one flesh; and further, that this was provided, lest the husband *(homo vir)* should, from some caprice, leave the wife after conception. But they added, that the applications and appropriations of the life of the husbands with the wives, take place according to conjugial love, because love, which is spiritual union, conjoins; and that this also has been provided for many reasons.

173. XV. THUS THE WIFE RECEIVES INTO HERSELF THE IMAGE OF HER HUSBAND, AND HENCE PERCEIVES, SEES, AND FEELS HIS AFFECTIONS. From the reasons above adduced it follows as an established fact, that wives receive in themselves those things which belong to the wisdom of their husbands, thus which are characteristic of the souls and minds of their husbands, and thus from virgins make themselves wives. The reasons from which this follows, are, 1. That the woman was created out of the man (*vir*). 2. That hence she has an inclination to unite, and as it were to reunite herself with the man. 3. That by virtue of and for the sake of this union with her consort, the woman is born the love of the man, and becomes more and more the love of him by marriage; because then the love is continually employing

its thoughts to conjoin the man to itself. 4. That the woman is conjoined to her only one by means of applications to the desires of his life. 5. That they are conjoined by the spheres which encompass them, and which unite themselves universally and particularly according to the quality of the conjugial love with the wives, and at the same time according to the quality of the wisdom recipient thereof with the husbands. 6. That they are also conjoined by means of appropriations of the powers (*vires*) of the husbands by the wives. 7. From which reasons it is evident, that there is continually something of the husband being transcribed into the wife, and inscribed on her as her own. From all these considerations it follows, that the image of the husband is formed in the wife; by virtue of which image the wife perceives, sees, and feels the things which are in her husband, in herself, and thus as it were herself in him. She perceives from communication, sees from aspect, and feels from the touch. That she feels the reception of her love by the husband from the touch in the palms of the hands on the cheeks, the shoulders, the hands, and the breasts, was revealed to me by the three wives in the palace, and the seven wives in the garden of roses, spoken of in the Memorable Relations [nos. 155, 208, 293 and 294].

174. XVI. THERE ARE DUTIES PROPER TO THE MAN, AND DUTIES PROPER TO THE WIFE; AND THE WIFE CANNOT ENTER INTO THE DUTIES PROPER TO THE MAN, NOR THE MAN INTO THE DUTIES PROPER TO THE WIFE, AND PERFORM THEM RIGHTLY. That there are duties proper to the man, and duties proper to the wife, has no need of being illustrated by an enumeration of them, for they are many and various: and any one can arrange them numerically according to their genera and species, if only he sets his mind to the task. The duties by means of which wives chiefly conjoin themselves with their husbands, are the education of the little children of both sexes, and of the girls till they are marriageable.

175. The reason why the wife cannot enter into the duties proper to the man, and that, on the other hand, neither can the man enter into the duties proper to the wife, is, that they differ like wisdom and the love thereof, or like thought and the affection thereof, or like understanding and the will thereof. In the duties proper to men, the understanding, thought, and wisdom play the leading part; whereas in the duties proper to wives, the will, affection, and love play the leading part; and the wife from the latter performs her duties, and the man from the former performs his; wherefore their duties are diverse from their very nature, but still conjunctive in a successive series. It 2
is believed by many that women can perform the duties of men, if only they are initiated into them from the earliest age, as

boys are. They may indeed be initiated into the exercise of those duties, but not into the judgment on which the right performance of the duties inwardly depends. Wherefore, such women as have been initiated into the duties of men, are obliged in matters of judgment to consult men, and then, if they are left to their own disposal, they select from the counsels of men
3 that which suits their own love. It is also supposed by some that women are equally capable of elevating the sight of their understanding into the same sphere of light as men, and of viewing things in the same height; and they have been led into this opinion by the writings of certain learned authoresses: but these writings, when examined in the spiritual world in the presence of the authoresses, were found to be works not of judgment and wisdom, but of cleverness and eloquence; and works that proceed from these two qualities, on account of the elegance and neatness of the composition or style, appear as if they were sublime and erudite, but only before those who call all
4 ingenuity wisdom. The reason why neither can men enter into the duties proper to women, and perform them aright, is, that they are not in the affections of women, which are quite distinct from the affections of men. As the affections and perceptions of the masculine sex are thus discriminated by creation, and consequently by nature, [from those of the feminine sex,] therefore among the statutes given to the sons of Israel there was also this one:—"*There shall not be the garment of a man on a woman, nor the garment of a woman on a man; because this is an abomination*" (Deut. xxii. 5). The reason was, that all in the spiritual world are clothed according to their affections; and the two affections, of the woman and of the man, cannot be united except between two, and in no case in one.

176. XVII. These duties, according to mutual aid, also conjoin the two into a one, and at the same time constitute one house. It is known in the world that the duties of the husband conjoin themselves in some way with the duties of the wife, and that the duties of the wife adjoin themselves to the duties of the husband, and that these conjunctions and adjunctions are a mutual aid, and that they are according to it. But the primary duties which confederate, consociate, and gather together into one the souls and lives of two married partners, relate to the common care of educating their children; in relation to which care, the duties of the husband, and the duties of the wife are distinct, and at the same time conjoin themselves. They are distinct, because the care of the suckling and of the education of the little children of both sexes, and also the care of the instruction of the girls till they become marriageable, belongs to the special duty of the wife; whereas the care of the instruction of the boys, after childhood to puberty, and after that till they

become their own masters, belongs to the special duty of the husband: nevertheless the duties of the husband and the wife conjoin themselves by means of counsel and support, and many other mutual aids. It is known that those duties, both conjoined and distinct, or both common and special, combine the lower minds (*animi*) of the married partners into a one, and that this is effected by the love called storge. It is also known that those duties, regarded in their distinction and conjunction, constitute one house.

177. XVIII. MARRIED PARTNERS, ACCORDING TO THE ABOVE-MENTIONED CONJUNCTIONS, BECOME MORE AND MORE ONE MAN. This coincides with what is contained in article VI., where it was explained that conjunction is effected successively from the first days of marriage, and that with those who are in truly conjugial love, it is effected more and more inwardly to eternity; see above. They become one man according to the increase of conjugial love; and as that love in the heavens is genuine in consequence of the celestial and spiritual life of the angels, therefore two married partners are there called two, when they are named husband and wife, but one, when they are named angels.

178. XIX. THOSE WHO ARE IN TRULY CONJUGIAL LOVE, FEEL THEMSELVES TO BE A UNITED MAN, AND AS IT WERE ONE FLESH. That this is the case, must be confirmed not from the testimony of any inhabitant of the earth, but from the testimony of the inhabitants of heaven. For truly conjugial love does not exist with men on earth at the present day: and moreover, men on earth are encompassed with a gross body, which blunts and absorbs the sensation that the two married partners are a united man, and as it were one flesh: and besides, those in the world who love their married partners only outwardly, and not inwardly, do not wish to hear of such a thing: they also think on the subject lasciviously from the flesh. It is otherwise with the angels of heaven, because they are in spiritual and celestial conjugial love, and are not encompassed with so gross a body as the men of the Earth. From those among them who have lived for ages with their married partners in heaven, I have heard it attested, that they feel themselves to be united thus, the husband with the wife, and the wife with the husband, and each in the other mutually and in return, as also in the flesh, although they are separate. The reason why this pheno- 2
menon is so rare on earth, they said was this, that the unition of the souls and minds of married partners on earth is felt in their flesh, because the soul constitutes the inmosts not only of the head, but also of the body; the mind likewise, which is intermediate between the soul and the body, and which, although

it appears to be in the head, is yet actually in the whole body also: and they said that hence it is that the acts, which the soul and mind intend, flow instantly from the body; and that hence also it is, that they themselves, after the casting away of the body in the former world, are perfect men. Now, since the soul and mind adjoin themselves closely to the flesh of the body, in order that they may operate and produce their effects, it follows that the unition of soul and mind with a married partner is felt also in the body as one flesh. When these things had been said by the angels, I heard it asserted by the spirits who were present, that such subjects belong to angelic wisdom, and that they were transcendental; but those spirits were natural-rational, and not spiritual-rational.

179. XX. TRULY CONJUGIAL LOVE CONSIDERED IN ITSELF, IS A UNION OF THE SOULS, A CONJUNCTION OF THE MINDS, AND AN EFFORT FOR CONJUNCTION IN THE BOSOMS, AND HENCE IN THE BODY. That it is a union of the souls and a conjunction of the minds, see above, no. 158. The reason why it is an effort for conjunction in the bosoms is, that the bosom is as it were the forum of assembly, and a royal council-chamber, and the body is as a populous city around it. The reason why the bosom is as it were the forum of assembly, is, that all things, which are determined into the body from the soul and mind, flow in first into the bosom; and the reason why it is as it were a royal council-chamber, is, that in the bosom there is dominion over all things of the body; for in the bosom are the heart and lungs; and the heart reigns everywhere by means of the blood, and the lungs by means of the respiration. That the body is as a populous city around it, is evident. When therefore the souls and minds of married partners are united, and truly conjugial love unites them, it follows that this loving union flows in into their bosoms, and through their bosoms into their bodies, and causes an effort for conjunction; and so much the more, because conjugial love determines the effort to its ultimates, in order to complete its blissful pleasantnesses; and as the bosom is midway [between the body and the mind], it is evident whence it is that conjugial love has fixed therein the seat of its delicate sense.

180. XXI. THE STATES OF THIS LOVE ARE INNOCENCE, PEACE, TRANQUILLITY, INMOST FRIENDSHIP, FULL CONFIDENCE, AND A DESIRE OF THE DISPOSITION AND OF THE HEART TO MAKE ALL GOOD MUTUAL TO EACH OTHER; AND THE STATES ARISING FROM ALL THESE ARE BLESSEDNESS, BLISSFULNESS, DELIGHTSOMENESS, AND PLEASURE; AND FROM THE ETERNAL ENJOYMENT OF THESE IS HEAVENLY FELICITY. The reasons why all these things are in conjugial love, and hence are from it, are, that its origin is from the marriage of good and truth, and this marriage is from the Lord; and, that love

is such that it desires to communicate with another whom it loves from the heart, yea, to confer joys upon him, and thence to derive its own joys. This therefore is the case infinitely with the Divine love which is in the Lord in regard to man, whom He created a receptacle of both love and wisdom proceeding from Himself; and as He has created man (*homo*) for the reception of those principles, the man (*vir*) for the reception of wisdom, and the woman for the reception of the love of the man's wisdom, therefore from the inmosts He has infused into human beings conjugial love, into which love He might bring together all things blessed, blissful, delightful, and pleasurable, which proceed, and flow in, solely from His Divine love through His Divine wisdom together with life; consequently, into those who are in truly conjugial love, for these alone are recipients. Mention is made of innocence, peace, tranquillity, inmost friendship, full confidence, and the desire of the disposition and of the heart to make all good mutual to the other; for innocence and peace belong to the soul, tranquillity to the mind, inmost friendship to the breast, full confidence to the heart, and the desire of the disposition and of the heart to make all good mutual to the other, belongs to the body from them.

181. XXII. These things can by no means exist except in the marriage of one man with one wife. This is a conclusion from all that has been heretofore said, and also from all that remains to be said hereafter; wherefore there is no need of any particular comment for its confirmation.

182. To the above shall be added two Memorable Relations. The first is this:—

*After some weeks, I heard a voice from heaven, saying, "Lo! there is again an assembly on Parnassus: come hither and we will shew you the way."

I accordingly went; and when I was near, I saw a certain person on Helicon with a trumpet, with which he announced and proclaimed the assembly. And I saw the inhabitants of Athens and its suburbs ascending as before; and in the midst of them three novitiates from the world. They were all three from among the Christians; one was a priest, another a politician, and the third a philosopher. They amused these three novitiates on the way by talking on various subjects, especially about the ancient wise men, whom they named. They asked whether they should see them, and were told that they should see them, and that if they liked, they might pay their respects to them, as they were affable.

They inquired about Demosthenes, Diogenes, and Epicurus;

* This Memorable Relation may also be found in the *True Christian Religion*, no. 693.

and were answered, "Demosthenes is not here, but with Plato; Diogenes, with his scholars, dwells beneath Helicon, because he considers worldly things as nothing, and ponders only on heavenly things; Epicurus dwells in the border to the west, and has no intercourse with us, because we distinguish between good affections and evil affections, and say, that good affections are together with wisdom, and evil affections are contrary to it."

2 When they had ascended the hill Parnassus, some guards there brought water in crystal cups from a fountain in the mount, and said, "This is water from the fountain of which the ancients fabled that it was broken open by the hoof of the horse Pegasus, and afterwards consecrated to the nine Virgins: but by the winged horse Pegasus they meant the understanding of truth, by means of which wisdom is procured; by the hoofs of his feet they meant experiences, by means of which natural intelligence is procured; and by the nine Virgins they meant Knowledges and sciences of every kind. These things are now-a-days called fables: but they were correspondences, according to which the primeval people spoke."

Then those who accompanied the three strangers said, "Be not surprised; the guards are instructed to speak thus; but we, by drinking water from the fountain, mean being instructed concerning truths, and, by means of truths, concerning goods, and thus becoming wise."

3 After this, they entered the Palladium, and with them the three novitiates from the world, the priest, the politician, and the philosopher; and then the laureates, who were seated at the tables, asked, "WHAT NEWS FROM THE EARTH?"

They replied, "This is new; that a certain person asserts that he converses with angels, and has his sight opened into the spiritual world, equally as into the natural world; and he brings thence many new facts, among which are the following:—that a man lives a man after death, as he lived before in the world; that he sees, hears, speaks, as before in the world; that he is clothed and adorned, as before in the world; that he hungers and thirsts, eats and drinks, as before in the world; that he enjoys the conjugial delight, as before in the world; that he sleeps and wakes, as before in the world; that in the spiritual world there are lands and lakes, mountains and hills, plains and valleys, fountains and rivers, paradises and groves; also that there are palaces and houses, cities and villages, as in the natural world; and further, that there are writings and books, employments and trades; also precious stones, gold and silver: in a word, that there are all such things there as there are on earth, and that those things in the heavens are infinitely more perfect, with this difference only, that all the things which are in the spiritual world are from a spiritual origin, and thus are spiritual, because they are from the sun of that world, which is pure love:

whereas all things which are in the natural world are from a natural origin, and thus are natural and material, because they are from the sun of that world, which is pure fire; in a word, that a man after death is perfectly a man, yea more perfectly a man than before in the world; for before in the world he was in a material body, but in the spiritual world he is in a spiritual body."

Hereupon the ancient wise men asked, "What do they on the 4
earth think of those things?"

The three strangers replied, "We know that they are true, because we are here, and have examined and explored them all; wherefore we will tell you what has been said and reasoned about them on earth."

Then the PRIEST said, "Those of our order, when they first heard those things, called them visions, then inventions; afterwards they said that the man had seen spectres, and lastly they hesitated, and said, 'Believe them if you will; we have hitherto taught that a man will not be in a body after death until the day of the last judgment.'"

Then they asked, "Are there no intelligent persons among them, who are able to shew and convince them of the Truth, that a man lives a man after death?"

The priest said, "There are indeed some who prove it, but 5
they do not convince others. Those who prove it, say, 'that it is contrary to sound reason to believe, that a man does not live a man till the day of the last judgment, and that in the meanwhile he is a soul without a body. What is the soul, and where is it in the meantime? Is it a breath, or some wind floating in the air, or something hidden in the midst of the earth? Where is its habitat? Have the souls of Adam and Eve, and of all their posterity, for now six thousand years, or sixty ages, been floating about in the universe, or kept shut up in the midst of the earth, waiting for the last judgment? What can be more anxious and miserable than such a waiting? May not their lot be compared with that of prisoners bound hand and foot, in prisons? If such be a man's lot after death, would it not be better to be born an ass than a man? Is it not also contrary to reason to believe, that the soul can be re-clothed with its body? Is not the body eaten up by worms, mice, and fish? And can a bony skeleton that has been parched up by the sun, or that has mouldered into dust, be introduced into a new body? And how could the cadaverous and putrid materials be collected, and re-united to the souls?' When they hear such questions as these, they do not offer any answers from reason, but adhere to their creed, saying, 'We hold reason captive under obedience to faith.' With respect to the collecting of all the parts of the human body from the grave at the day of the last judgment, they say, 'This is a work of omnipotence;' and when they name omnipotence

and faith, reason is banished; and I can say, that sound reason is then as nothing, and by some is regarded as a spectre; yea, they can say to sound reason, 'Thou art unsound, or insane.' "

6 On hearing these things, the Grecian wise men said, "Are not such paradoxes dispersed of themselves, as being contradictory? and yet now-a-days in the world they cannot be dispersed by sound reason. What can be believed more paradoxical than what is told respecting the last judgment; that the universe will then be destroyed, and that the stars of heaven will then fall down upon the earth, which is less than the stars; and that then the bodies of men, whether they be carcases, or mummies eaten by men, or reduced to mere dust, will be united again with their souls? When we were in the world, we believed in the immortality of the souls of men, on account of the inductions with which reason furnished us; and we also assigned regions for the blessed, which we called the Elysian Fields; and we believed that souls were human effigies or appearances, but of a fine and delicate nature, because spiritual."

7 After this, the assembly turned to the other stranger, who in the world had been a POLITICIAN. He confessed that he had not believed in a life after death; and that with regard to the new facts which he had heard about it, he had thought they were figments and inventions. "When meditating on the subject," said he, "I used to say to myself, 'How can souls be bodies?—does not the whole of man lie dead in the grave?—is not the eye there; how can he see?—is not the ear there; how can he hear?—whence can he have a mouth wherewith to speak? If anything of a man were to live after death, must it not resemble a spectre? and how can a spectre eat and drink, or how can it enjoy the conjugial delight? whence can it have clothes, houses, foods, and so on? Besides, spectres, which are aërial effigies, appear as if they really existed; and yet they do not.' These and similar thoughts I used to entertain in the world about the life of men after death; but now, since I have seen all things, and touched them with my hands, I have been convinced by my very senses that I am a man as I was in the world; so that I know no other than that I live now as I lived before; with this difference, that my reason now is sounder. At times I have been ashamed of my former thoughts."

8 The PHILOSOPHER gave much the same account of himself; only differing in this respect, that he had considered the new facts which he had heard about a life after death, as being of the same class as the opinions and hypotheses which he had collected from the ancients and moderns.

The Sophi, on hearing these things, were amazed; and those who were of the Socratic school, said, that from these news from earth, they perceived that the interiors of human minds had been successively closed; and that in the world at the present time the faith of falsity shines as Truth, and a fatuous ingenuity as wisdom; and that the light of wisdom, since their times, has descended from the interiors of the brain into the mouth beneath the nose, where it appears to the eyes as a shining of the lip, while the speech of the mouth proceeding thence appears as wisdom.

Hereupon one of the young scholars said, "How stupid are the minds of the inhabitants of the earth at the present day! I wish we had here the disciples of Heraclitus, who weep at everything, and of Democritus, who laugh at everything; for then we should hear much weeping and much laughter."

When the assembly broke up, they gave the three novitiates from the earth some insignia of their authority, which were thin copper plates, on which were engraved some hieroglyphics; with which they departed.

183. The second Memorable Relation:—

There appeared to me in the eastern quarter a grove of palm-trees and laurels, set in spiral gyres. I approached and entered, and walked in the paths which described several spiral windings, and at the end of the ways I saw a garden, which formed the centre of the grove. There was a little bridge dividing the grove from the garden, and at the bridge was a gate on the side next the grove, and a gate on the side next the garden. I drew near, and the gates were opened by the keeper. I asked him the name of the garden, and he said, "ADRAMANDONI, that is, the delight of conjugial love."

I entered, and lo! there were olive-trees; and between olive-tree and olive-tree there were running and pensile vines, and underneath and among them were little trees in flower. In the midst of the garden was a grassy circus, on which were seated husbands and wives, and young men and maidens, in pairs; and in the midst of the circus was an elevated piece of ground, where there was a little fountain, which, from the strength of its spring, leapt high. When I was near the circus I saw two angels in crimson and scarlet, speaking with those who were seated on the grass. They were speaking about the origin of conjugial love, and about its delights; and as they were speaking about that love, the attention was eager, and the reception full; and hence there was an exaltation as from the fire of love in the conversation of the angels.

I collected the following summary of what was said. They 2
spoke first about the difficult investigation and the difficult perception of the origin of conjugial love; because its origin is Divine celestial, for it is the Divine love, the Divine wisdom, and the Divine use; which three proceed as a one from the Lord, and hence flow in as a one into the souls of human beings, and through their souls into their minds, and there into the

interior affections and thoughts, and through these into the desires next to the body, and from these through the breast into the genital region, where all the things derived from the first origin are together, and, together with their successive things, constitute conjugial love.

After this the angels said, "Let us communicate together by questions and answers; since the perception of a thing, imbibed by hearing only, does indeed flow in, but does not remain, unless the hearer also thinks of it from himself, and asks questions about it."

3 Then some of that conjugial company said to the angels, "We have heard that the origin of conjugial love is Divine celestial, because it is by virtue of influx from the Lord into the souls of men; and as it is from the Lord, that it is love, wisdom, and use, which are the three essentials which together make one Divine essence, and that nothing but what is of the Divine essence can proceed from Him and flow in into the inmost of man, which is called his soul; and that these three essentials are turned into analogous and corresponding things in their descent into the body. We therefore now ask, first, What is meant by the third proceeding Divine essential, which is called use?"

The angels replied, "Love and wisdom, without use, are merely abstract ideas of thought, which also after some continuance in the mind pass away like the winds: but in use they are collected together, and therein become a one, which is called a real thing. Love cannot rest unless it is doing something; for love is the very activity of life: neither can wisdom exist and subsist, except when it is doing something from love and with love, and doing is use: wherefore we define use to be the doing good from
4 love by means of wisdom; use is good itself. As these three, love, wisdom, and use, flow in into the souls of men, it may be manifest whence it is that it is said, that all good is from God; for everything done from love by means of wisdom is called good; and use also is something done. What is love without wisdom but a mere infatuation? and what is love with wisdom without use, but a state of mind? Whereas love and wisdom with use not only constitute man, but also are man; yea, what possibly you will be surprised at, they propagate man; for in the seed of a man (*vir*) is his soul in a perfect human form, covered with substances from the purest things of nature; from which a body is formed in the womb of the mother. This use is the highest and ultimate use of the Divine love through the Divine wisdom."

5 Finally the angels said, "This must be the conclusion, that all fructification, all propagation, and all prolification, are originally from the influx of love, wisdom, and use from the Lord; from immediate influx from the Lord into the souls of men;

from mediate influx into the souls of animals, and from still more mediate influx into the inmosts of plants; and all these effects are wrought in ultimates by the primes. That fructifications, propagations, and prolifications, are continuations of creation, is evident; for creation cannot be from any other source than from Divine love through Divine wisdom in Divine use; wherefore all things in the universe are procreated and formed from use, in use, and for use."

Afterwards those who were sitting on the grassy couches, 6
asked the angels, "Whence are the delights of conjugial love, which are innumerable and ineffable?"

The angels replied, "They are from the uses of love and wisdom, and this may be seen from the fact that in the proportion in which any one loves to be wise for the sake of genuine use, in the same proportion he is in the vein and potency of conjugial love; and in the proportion in which he is in the vein and potency of conjugial love, in the same proportion he is in the delights. Use effects this; because when love acts through wisdom, they are in a state of mutual enjoyment, and as it were sport together like little children; and as they grow up, they become conjoined in marriage, which is effected as it were by betrothals, weddings, marriages, and propagations, and this with continual variety to eternity. These things take place between love and wisdom inwardly in use. But those delights in their beginnings are imperceptible; but they become more and more perceptible as they descend thence by degrees and enter the body. They enter by degrees from the soul into the interiors of a man's mind, from these into its exteriors, from these into the bosom of the breast, and from the bosom into the genital region. Those heavenly nuptial sports in the soul are not at all 7
perceived by man; but they insinuate themselves thence into the interiors of the mind under the appearance of peace and innocence, and into the exteriors of the mind under the appearance of blessedness, blissfulness, and delightsomeness; but into the bosom of the breast under the appearance of the delights of inmost friendship; and in the genital region, in consequence of continuous influx even from the soul with the very sense of conjugial love, as the delight of delights. These nuptial sports of love and wisdom in use in the soul, in proceeding towards the bosom of the breast, become permanent, and make themselves sensible therein under an infinite variety of delights; and on account of the wonderful communication of the bosom of the breast with the genital region, the delights there become the delights of conjugial love, which are exalted above all other delights which exist in heaven and in the world, because the use of conjugial love is the most excellent of all uses; for the procreation of the human race is thence; and the angelic heaven is from the human race."

To this the angels added, "that those who are not in the love 8 of being wise from the Lord for the sake of use, do not know anything about the variety of the innumerable delights of truly conjugial love; for with those who do not love to be wise from genuine truths, but love to be insane from falsities, and by means of this insanity do evil uses from some particular love, the way to the soul is closed; hence it is the heavenly nuptial sports of love and wisdom in the soul, being more and more intercepted, cease, and together with them conjugial love ceases with its vein, potency, and delights."

On hearing this the audience said, "We now perceive that conjugial love is according to the love of being wise from the Lord for the sake of uses."

The angels replied that it was so. And then upon the heads of some of them there appeared chaplets of flowers; and on their asking, "Why is this?" the angels said, "Because they have understood more profoundly." They then departed from the garden, and the latter in the midst of them.

THE CHANGE OF THE STATE OF LIFE [WHICH TAKES PLACE] WITH MEN AND WOMEN BY MEANS OF MARRIAGE.

184. WHAT is meant by states of life, and their changes, is very well known to the learned and the wise, but unknown to the unlearned and the simple; wherefore something shall be prefaced on the subject. The state of a man's life is its quality; and as there are in every man two faculties which constitute his life, and which are called the understanding and the will, the state of a man's life is its quality as to the understanding and the will. Hence it is evident, that by changes of the state of life are meant changes of quality as to the things which belong to the understanding and as to the things which belong to the will. That every man is continually changing as to those two, but with a difference of the varieties before marriage and after it, is the point undertaken to be proved in this section; which shall be done in the following order:—

I. *The state of a man's life from infancy even to the end of his life, and afterwards to eternity, is continually changing.*

II. *A man's internal form, which is that of his spirit, is likewise continally changing.*

III. *These changes are different with men* (viri) *from what they are with women; since men from creation are forms of knowledge, intelligence, and wisdom, and women are forms of the love of those things with men.*

IV. *With men there is an elevation of the mind into a higher light, and with women an elevation of the mind into a higher heat; and the woman feels the delights of her heat in the man's light.*

V. *With both men and women, the states of life before marriage are different from what they are after marriage.*

VI. *With married partners the states of life after marriage are changed and succeed each other according to the conjunctions of their minds by means of conjugial love.*

VII. *Marriage also induces other forms on the souls and minds of married partners.*

VIII. *The woman is actually formed into the wife of the man according to the description in the Book of the Creation.*

IX. *This formation is effected by the wife by secret means; and this is meant by the woman being created while the man slept.*

X. *This formation by the wife is effected by means of the conjunction of her own will with the internal will of the man.*

XI. *This is for the sake of the end that the will of both of them may become one, and that thus they both may become one man* (homo).

XII. *This formation by the wife is effected by means of the appropriation of the affections of the husband.*

XIII. *This formation by the wife is effected by means of the reception of the propagations of the soul of the husband, with the delight originating from the circumstance that she wills to be the love of her husband's wisdom.*

XIV. *Thus a maiden is formed into a wife, and a bachelor into a husband.*

XV. *In the marriage of one man* (vir) *with one wife, between whom there exists truly conjugial love, the wife becomes more and more a wife, and the husband more and more a husband.*

XVI. *Thus also their forms are successively being perfected and ennobled from the Interior.*

XVII. *The offspring born of two who are in truly conjugial love, derive from their parents the conjugial principle of good and truth; whence they have the inclination and faculty, if a son, for perceiving the things which belong to wisdom, and if a daughter, for loving the things which wisdom teaches.*

XVIII. *This happens because the soul of the offspring is from the father, and its clothing from the mother.*

Now follows the explanation of these articles.

185. I. THE STATE OF A MAN'S LIFE, FROM INFANCY EVEN TO THE END OF HIS LIFE, AND AFTERWARDS TO ETERNITY, IS CONTINUALLY BEING CHANGED. The general states of man's life are called infancy, childhood, youth, manhood, and old age. That every man whose life is continued in the world, successively passes from one state into another, thus from the first to the last, is known. The transitions into those ages only become apparent by the intervening spaces of time: that nevertheless they are progressive from one moment to another, thus continual, is seen by reason; for the case is similar with a man as with a tree, which grows and increases every instant of time, even the most minute, from the casting of the seed into the earth. These momentary progressions are also changes of state; for the subsequent adds something to the antecedent, which perfects
2 the state. The changes which take place in a man's internals, are more perfectly continuous than those which take place in his externals; because a man's internals, by which are meant the things which belong to his mind or spirit, are elevated in a higher degree above his externals; and in those things which are in a higher degree, a thousand things take place in the same instant in which one thing takes place in the externals. The

changes which take place in the internals are changes of the state of the will as to the affections, and of the state of the understanding as to the thoughts. The successive changes of state of the latter and of the former are specifically meant in the proposition. The reason why the changes of state of these two 3
lives or faculties are perpetual with every man from infancy even to the end of his life, and afterwards to eternity, is, that there is no end to knowledge, still less to intelligence, and least of all to wisdom; for there are infinity and eternity in the extent of them by virtue of the Infinite and Eternal, from Whom they are. Hence comes the philosophical axiom of the ancients, that everything is divisible to infinity; to which must be added that it is likewise so multiplicable. The angels assert, that they are being perfected in wisdom by the Lord to eternity, which also means to infinity, because eternity is the infinity of time.

186. II. A MAN'S INTERNAL FORM, WHICH IS THAT OF HIS SPIRIT, IS LIKEWISE CONTINUALLY CHANGING. The reason why this form is continually changing as the state of the man's life is changed, is, that nothing exists except in a form; and state induces that form; wherefore it is the same thing whether it be said that the state of a man's life is changed, or that his form is changed. All a man's affections and thoughts are in forms, and therefore are according to forms; for forms are their subjects. If affections and thoughts were not in subjects which were formed, they might exist also in skulls empty of the brain; which would be the same thing as to suppose sight without the eye, hearing without the ear, and taste without the tongue. It is known that these organs are the subjects of these senses, and that these subjects are forms. The reason why the state of life, and thus the form, with a man, is continually changing is, that it is a Truth which the wise have taught and still teach, that there does not exist a sameness, or absolute identity of two things, still less of several; as there are not two human faces the same, and still less several. The case is similar in successive things, in that no subsequent state of life is the same as a preceding one; whence it follows, that there is a perpetual change of the state of life with man, consequently also a perpetual change of form, especially of his internals. But since these considerations do not teach anything about marriages, but only prepare the way for Knowledges concerning them, and since also they are mere philosophical inquiries of the understanding, which, with some persons, are difficult of perception, therefore, after these few remarks, they shall be passed by.

187. III. THESE CHANGES ARE DIFFERENT WITH MEN (*viri*) FROM WHAT THEY ARE WITH WOMEN; SINCE MEN FROM CREATION ARE FORMS OF KNOWLEDGE, INTELLIGENCE, AND WISDOM; AND WOMEN ARE FORMS OF THE LOVE OF THOSE THINGS WITH MEN. That men

have been created forms of the understanding, and that women have been created forms of the love of the understanding of men, may be seen explained above, no. 90. That the changes of state, which succeed both with men and women from infancy to mature age, are for rendering the forms complete or perfect, the intellectual form with men, and the voluntary form with women, follows as a consequence: hence it is clear, that the changes with men are different from those with women; nevertheless with both, the external form which is that of the body, is completed or perfected according to the completion or perfection of the internal form which is that of the mind; for the mind acts upon the body, and not contrariwise. This is the reason why infants in heaven become men of stature and comeliness according to the increase of intelligence with them; it is otherwise with infants on earth, because they are encompassed with a material body like the animals: nevertheless they agree in this, that they first grow in inclination to such things as allure their bodily senses, and afterwards by little and little to such things as affect the internal thinking sense, and by degrees to such things as imbue the will with affection; and when they arrive at an age which is midway between mature and immature age, the conjugial inclination is added, which is that of a maiden for a bachelor, and of a bachelor for a maiden; and, since maidens in the heavens, equally as those on earth, from an innate prudence conceal their inclinations to marriage, the bachelors there know no otherwise than that they affect the maidens with love; and this also appears to them in consequence of their masculine eagerness; but this also they derive from an influx of love from the beautiful sex, which influx will be specially treated of elsewhere. From these considerations is manifest the Truth of the proposition that the changes of state with men are different from those with women; since men from creation are forms of knowledge, intelligence, and wisdom, and women are forms of the love of those things with men.

188. IV. WITH MEN THERE IS AN ELEVATION OF THE MIND INTO A HIGHER LIGHT, AND WITH WOMEN AN ELEVATION OF THE MIND INTO A HIGHER HEAT; AND THE WOMAN FEELS THE DELIGHTS OF HER HEAT IN THE MAN'S LIGHT. By the light into which men are elevated, is meant intelligence and wisdom, because spiritual light, which proceeds from the sun of the spiritual world, which in its essence is love, acts in equality or unity with those two; and by the heat into which women are elevated, is meant conjugial love, because spiritual heat, which proceeds from the sun of that world, in its essence is love, and with women it is love conjoining itself with the intelligence and wisdom in men; which love in its complex is called conjugial
2 love, and by determination becomes that love. It is said, ele-

vation into a higher light and heat, because it is an elevation into the light and heat in which the angels of the higher heavens are. There is also an actual elevation, as from a mist into the air, and from a lower region of the air into a higher one, and from this into the ether; wherefore the elevation into a higher light with men is elevation into a higher intelligence, and from this into wisdom; into which also there is a higher and a still higher elevation. But the elevation into a higher heat with women is an elevation into a chaster and purer conjugial love, and continually towards the conjugial principle, which from
creation is latent in their inmosts. These elevations, considered 3
in themselves, are openings of the mind; for the human mind is distinguished into regions, just as the world is distinguished into regions as to the atmospheres, of which the lowest is watery, the higher is aërial, and still higher one is ethereal, above which there is also the highest; into similar regions the mind of man (*homo*) is elevated as it is opened, with men (*viri*) by means of wisdom, and with women by means of truly conjugial love.

189. It is said, that the woman feels the delights of her heat in the light of the man (*vir*); but this means that the woman feels of the delights of her love in the wisdom of the man, because this wisdom is the receptacle; and wherever love finds a receptacle corresponding to itself, it is in its own delightsomenesses and delights: but it is not meant, that heat with its light is delighted outside of forms, but within them; and spiritual heat is delighted with spiritual light in forms in a greater degree, because those forms by virtue of wisdom and love are vital, and thus susceptible. This may be illustrated to some extent by what are called the sports of heat with light in the subjects of the vegetable kingdom: outside of the subjects of the vegetable kingdom there is only a simple conjunction of heat and light, but within them there is as it were a sporting of the one with the other, because there they are in forms or receptacles; for they pass through them through wonderful windings, and in the inmosts therein they aspire towards the use of bearing fruit, and also breathe forth their pleasantnesses far and wide into the air, which they fill with fragrance. The deliciation of spiritual heat with spiritual light is still more vividly experienced in human forms, in which spiritual heat is conjugial love, and spiritual light is wisdom.

190. V. WITH BOTH MEN AND WOMEN, THE STATES OF LIFE BEFORE MARRIAGE ARE DIFFERENT FROM WHAT THEY ARE AFTER MARRIAGE. Before marriage, there are two states with both sexes, one previous to the inclination towards marriage, and the other subsequent to it. The changes of both these states, and the consequent formations of the minds, proceed in

succedaneous order according to their continual increase; but there is not room here to describe these changes, for they are various and diverse in their several subjects. The inclinations to marriage, previous to marriage, are merely imaginative in the mind, and they become more and more sensible in the body; but the states of those inclinations after marriage are states of conjunction and also of prolification, which, it is evident, differ from the former states as the carrying out into effect differs from the intention.

191. VI. WITH MARRIED PARTNERS THE STATES OF LIFE AFTER MARRIAGE ARE CHANGED AND SUCCEED EACH OTHER ACCORDING TO THE CONJUNCTIONS OF THEIR MINDS BY MEANS OF CONJUGIAL LOVE. The reason why changes of the state and the successions thereof after marriage, with both the man and the wife, are according to conjugial love with them, and thus are either conjunctive or disjunctive of their minds, is, that conjugial love is not only various but also diverse with married partners. It is various with those who love each other inwardly; for with these it has its intermissions, although inwardly in its heat it is regular and permanent. But that love is diverse with those married partners who love each other only outwardly; with these its intermissions do not arise from similar causes, but from alternate
2 cold and heat. The reason of these differences is, that with the latter the body plays the leading part, and its ardour spreads itself around, and forces into communion with itself the lower parts of the mind; but with the former who love each other inwardly, the mind plays the leading part, and draws the body into communion with it. It appears as though love ascends from the body into the soul, because as soon as the body catches the allurement, it enters through the eyes, as through doors, into the mind, and thus through the sight, as through an outer court, into the thoughts, and instantly into the love: but still it descends from the mind, and acts into the lower parts according to their arrangement or disposition; wherefore a lascivious mind acts lasciviously, and a chaste mind chastely; and the latter disposes the body, but the former is disposed by the body.

192. VII. MARRIAGE ALSO INDUCES OTHER FORMS ON THE SOULS AND MINDS OF MARRIED PARTNERS. That marriage induces other forms on the souls and minds, cannot be observed in the natural world, because in that world souls and minds are encompassed with a material body, through which the mind rarely shines. The men also of this age, more than the Ancients, learn from their infancy to induce expressions on their faces, whereby they deeply conceal the affections of the mind; and this is the reason why the forms of the minds as to their quality before marriage,

and as to their quality after it, are not known and distinguished. Nevertheless, that the forms of the souls and the minds differ after marriage from what they were before it, appears manifestly from the same in the spiritual world; for they are then spirits and angels, who are nothing else than minds and souls in a human form, stripped of their outward coverings, which were composed of watery and earthly elements, and of aërial exhalations thence arising; and when these are cast off, the forms of the minds are plainly seen, such as they had been inwardly in their bodies; and then it is clearly seen that those forms are different with those who live in marriage, from the forms with those who do not. In general, married partners have an interior comeliness of face, for the man derives from the wife the lovely redness of her love, and the wife from the man the bright lustre of his wisdom; for two married partners in the spiritual world are united as to their souls; and moreover there appears in both a human fulness. This is the case in heaven, because there are no marriages anywhere else; beneath heaven there are only connubial connections, which are alternately made and broken off.

193. VIII. The woman is actually formed into a wife, according to the description in the Book of the Creation. In this Book it is said, that the woman was created out of the rib of the man (*vir*), and that the man said, when she was brought to him, "This is bone of my bones, and flesh of my flesh; and she shall be called woman (Hebrew *Ishshah*), because she was taken out of man (*Ish*)" (chapter ii. 21–23). By a rib of the breast, in the Word, nothing else is signified, in the spiritual sense, than natural truth. This is signified by the ribs which the bear carried between his teeth (Dan. vii. 5); for bears signify those who read the Word in the natural sense, and see truths therein without understanding. By the breast of the man (*vir*) is signified that essential and peculiar quality which is distinguished from the breast of the woman; that it is wisdom, see above, no. 187; for truth supports wisdom as the ribs support the breast. These things are signified because the breast is that part in which all things of man (*homo*) are as in their centre. From these considerations it is manifest 2
that the woman was created out of the man (*vir*) by the transcription of his own peculiar wisdom, that is, [she was created] out of natural truth; and that the love of this was transferred from the man into the woman, in order that it might become conjugial love; and that this was done in order that in the man there might not be the love of self but the love of his wife. For the wife, by reason of her innate disposition, cannot do otherwise than convert the love of self with the man into his love for herself; and I have been informed, that this is effected

by virtue of the wife's love itself, neither the man nor the wife being conscious of it. Hence it is that no one can ever love his married partner conjugially who is in the conceit of his own
3 intelligence from the love of self. When this arcanum of the creation of the woman from the man is understood, it can then be seen, that the woman is likewise as it were created or formed from the man in marriage; and that this is done by the wife, or rather through the wife by the Lord, who has infused into women the inclinations to do so. For the wife receives into herself the image of the man, by appropriating his affections to herself (see above, no. 173), and by conjoining the man's internal will with her own, of which something shall be said below; and also by appropriating to herself the propagations of his soul, of which also something shall be said below. From these considerations it is evident, that, according to the description in the Book of the Creation, inwardly understood, a woman is formed into a wife by means of such things as she takes out of her husband and his breast, and inscribes on herself.

194. IX. THIS FORMATION IS EFFECTED BY THE WIFE BY SECRET MEANS: AND THIS IS MEANT BY THE WOMAN BEING CREATED WHILE THE MAN SLEPT. It is read in the Book of the Creation that Jehovah God caused a deep sleep to fall upon Adam, so that he fell asleep; and that then He took one of his ribs, and built it into a woman (chap. ii. 21, 22). That by the man's sleep and falling asleep is signified his entire ignorance that his wife is formed and as it were created from him, is evident, from what was shewn in the preceding chapter, and also from the innate prudence and circumspection of wives not to divulge anything about their love or about their assumption of the affections of the man's life, and thus about the transcription of his wisdom into themselves. That this is effected by the wife without the husband's knowledge, and while he is as it were sleeping, thus by secret means, is evident from what was explained above, nos. 166–168; where also it is clearly shewn that the prudence for doing this was implanted in women from creation, and consequently from birth, for reasons which are necessities, in order that conjugial love, friendship, and confidence, and thus the blessedness of dwelling together, and the happiness of life, may be secured; wherefore, in order that this might be properly effected, it was enjoined on the man that he should leave his father and mother and cleave to his wife (Gen. ii. 24; Matt. xix. 4, 5). By the father and mother whom the man (*vir*) is to leave, in the spiritual sense is meant his proprium of will and proprium of understanding; and the proprium of a man's (*homo*) will consists in loving himself, and the proprium of his understanding consists in loving his own wisdom; and by

cleaving [to his wife] is signified devoting himself to the love of his wife. That those two propria are deadly evils to the man (*vir*) if they remain with him; and that the love of those two propria is changed into conjugial love, in proportion as the man cleaves to his wife, that is, receives her love, see above, no. 193, and elsewhere. That by sleeping is signified being in ignorance and unconcern; that by the father and the mother are signified the two propria of a man (*homo*), the one of the will and the other of the understanding: and that by cleaving is signified devoting one's self to the love of any one, can be abundantly confirmed from other passages in the Word; but this is not the place for that purpose.

195. X. THIS FORMATION BY THE WIFE IS EFFECTED BY MEANS OF THE CONJUNCTION OF HER OWN WILL WITH THE INTERNAL WILL OF THE MAN. That with the man (*vir*) there are rational wisdom and moral wisdom, and that the wife conjoins herself with those things which belong to the moral wisdom with the man, see above, nos. 163–165. Those things which belong to rational wisdom constitute the man's understanding, and those which belong to moral wisdom constitute his will. The wife conjoins herself with those things which constitute the man's will. Whether it be said that the wife conjoins herself, or that she conjoins her will with the man's will, it is the same thing, because the wife is born voluntary, or of the will, and, consequently, what she does she does from the will. The reason why it is said that she conjoins herself with the internal will of the man, is, that the will of the man resides in his understanding or intellect; and the Intellectual of the man is the inmost of the woman, according to what was stated above concerning the formation of the woman from the man, no. 32, and in many other subsequent numbers. Men (*viri*) have also an external will; but this frequently derives its quality from simulation and dissimulation. This will the wife sees through; but she does not conjoin herself with it, except feignedly or in sport.

196. XI. THIS IS FOR THE SAKE OF THE END, THAT THE WILL OF BOTH OF THEM MAY BECOME ONE, AND THAT THUS THEY BOTH MAY BECOME ONE MAN (*homo*): for he who conjoins to himself the will of another, also conjoins to himself his understanding; for the understanding considered in itself is nothing else than the minister and servant of the will. That this is the case, appears evidently from the affection of love, which moves the understanding to think as it directs. Every affection of love belongs to the will; for what a man loves that he also wills. From these considerations it follows, that he who conjoins to himself the will of a man, con-

joins to himself the whole man. Hence it is, that it is implanted in the wife's love to unite the will of her husband to her own will; for thus the wife becomes the husband's, and the husband the wife's; thus they both become one man.

197. XII. THIS FORMATION [BY THE WIFE] IS EFFECTED BY MEANS OF THE APPROPRIATION OF THE AFFECTIONS OF THE HUSBAND. This article agrees with the two preceding, because affections belong to the will; for affections, which are nothing else than derivations of the love, form the will, and make and compose it; but these affections with men (*viri*) are in the understanding, whereas with women they are in the will.

198. XIII. THIS FORMATION [BY THE WIFE] IS EFFECTED BY MEANS OF THE RECEPTION OF THE PROPAGATIONS OF THE SOUL OF THE HUSBAND, WITH THE DELIGHT ORIGINATING FROM THE CIRCUMSTANCE THAT SHE WILLS TO BE THE LOVE OF HER HUSBAND'S WISDOM. This coincides with what was explained above, nos. 172, 173, wherefore further explanation is dispensed with. The conjugial delights with wives derive their origin from no other source than the circumstance that they are willing to be one with their husbands, as good is one with truth in the spiritual marriage. That conjugial love descends from this spiritual marriage, has been proved in detail in the chapter on that subject. Hence it may be seen, as in effigy, that the wife conjoins the man with herself, as good conjoins truth with itself; and that the man conjoins himself reciprocally with the wife, according to the reception of her love in himself, even as truth conjoins itself reciprocally with good, according to the reception of good in itself; and that thus the love of the wife forms itself by means of the wisdom of the husband, even as good forms itself by means of truth; for truth is the form of good. From these considerations it is also evident, that conjugial delights exist with the wife, principally on account of her being willing to be one with her husband, consequently on account of her being willing to be the love of her husband's wisdom; for then she is sensible of the delights of her own heat in the man's light, according to what was explained in Article IV. no. 188.

199. XIV. THUS A MAIDEN IS FORMED INTO A WIFE, AND A BACHELOR INTO A HUSBAND. This flows as a consequence from what has been said above in this and the foregoing chapter about the conjunction of married partners into one flesh. A maiden becomes or is made a wife, because in a wife there are elements taken out of the husband, and thus additional, which were not previously in her as a maiden. A bachelor also becomes or is made a husband, because in a husband there are elements taken out of the wife which exalt his capacity for receiving love and

wisdom, and which were not previously in him as a bachelor. But this is the case with those who are in truly conjugial love. That these are among those who feel themselves a united man, and as it were one flesh, may be seen in the preceding chapter, no. 178. From these considerations it is evident, that with females maidenhood is changed into wifehood, and with men (*viri*) the bachelor state is changed into the marital state. That this is the case, was confirmed to me in the spiritual world by the following experience:—Some men (*viri*) asserted, that conjunction with a female before marriage is like conjunction with a wife after marriage. On hearing this, the wives were very indignant, and said, "There is no likeness at all between the two cases. The difference between them is like that between what is fancied and what is real." Hereupon the men retorted, "Are you not females as before?" To this the wives replied with a louder voice, "We are not females, but wives; you are in fancied and not in real love; wherefore you talk fancifully." Then the men said, "If you are not females (*fœminæ*) still you are married women (*mulieres*)": and they replied, "In the first states of marriage we were married women; but now we are wives."

200. XV. In the marriage of one man (*vir*) with one wife, between whom there exists truly conjugial love, the wife becomes more and more a wife, and the husband more and more a husband. That truly conjugial love conjoins two more and more into one man (*homo*), see above, nos. 178, 179; and as a wife becomes a wife from and according to conjunction with the husband, and in like manner the husband with the wife; and as truly conjugial love lasts to eternity, it follows, that the wife becomes more and more a wife, and the husband more and more a husband. The true reason of this is, that in a marriage of truly conjugial love each married partner becomes continually a more interior man (*homo*). For that love opens the interiors of their minds; and in the proportion in which these are opened the man becomes more and more a man: and becoming more a man (*homo*) in the case of the wife means becoming more a wife, and in the case of the husband it means becoming more a husband. I have heard from the angels, that the wife becomes more and more a wife in proportion as the husband becomes more and more a husband, but not contrariwise; because it rarely, if ever, happens that a chaste wife is wanting in love to her husband, but that the husband is wanting in a return of love to his wife; and that this return of love is wanting on account of his having no elevation of wisdom, which alone receives the love of the wife: concerning this wisdom see above, nos. 130, 163–165. These things however they said in relation to marriages on earth.

201. XVI. THUS ALSO THEIR FORMS ARE SUCCESSIVELY BEING PERFECTED AND ENNOBLED FROM THE INTERIOR. The most perfect and noble human form exists when two forms become one form by means of marraige; thus when two fleshes become one flesh, according to the creation. That the mind of the man (*vir*) is then elevated into a higher light, and the mind of the wife into a higher heat, and that then they bud, and bear flowers and fruits, like trees in springtime, see above, nos. 188, 189. That from the ennobling of this form are born noble fruits, which in the heavens are spiritual, and on earth natural, will be seen in the following article.

202. XVII. THE OFFSPRING BORN OF TWO WHO ARE IN TRULY CONJUGIAL LOVE, DERIVE FROM THEIR PARENTS THE CONJUGIAL PRINCIPLE OF GOOD AND TRUTH; WHENCE THEY HAVE THE INCLINATION AND FACULTY, IF A SON, FOR PERCEIVING THE THINGS WHICH BELONG TO WISDOM, AND IF A DAUGHTER, FOR LOVING THE THINGS WHICH WISDOM TEACHES. That the offspring derive from their parents inclinations for such things as had been objects of the love and life of the parents, is a truth perfectly well known from history in general, and experience in particular. But that they do not derive or inherit from their parents the affections themselves, and thus the lives of their parents, but only inclinations and also faculties for those affections, has been demonstrated by the wise in the spiritual world; concerning whom, see the two Memorable Relations adduced above. That the posterity, in consequence of innate inclinations, if they are not broken, are led into affections, thoughts, speech, and lives, similar to those of their parents, is clearly evident from the Jewish nation, who at the present day are like their fathers in Egypt, in the wilderness, in the land of Canaan, and at the time of the Lord; and this likeness is not confined to their minds only, but extends to their faces; for who does not know a Jew by his look? The case is the same with the offspring of others: from which facts it may be concluded, not fallaciously, that the offspring are born with inclinations for such things as their parents were inclined to. But lest the thoughts and the acts should follow the inclinations, it is ordained by the Divine Providence that depraved inclinations should be capable of being corrected; and also that a faculty has been implanted for this purpose, by virtue whereof the morals of children can be efficaciously amended by the parents and masters, and afterwards by the children themselves, when they have arrived at years of discretion.

203. It is said that the offspring derive from their parents the conjugial principle of good and truth, because this is implanted from creation into the soul of every one; for it is that which flows in into man from the Lord, and constitutes his human life. But

this conjugial principle passes from the soul into the succeeding parts even to the ultimates of the body. Yet in both the latter and the former, on the way, it is changed by the man himself in many ways, and sometimes into the opposite, which is called the conjugial or connubial principle of evil and falsity. When this is the case, the mind is closed from below, and is sometimes twisted like a spire into the contrary direction; but with some it is not closed, but remains half-open above, and with some it remains quite open. It is from the latter and the former conjugial principle that the offspring derive inclinations from their parents, a son in one way, and a daughter in another. The reason why this is from the conjugial principle, is that (as was proved above, in no. 65) conjugial love is the fundamental love of all loves.

204. The reason why the offspring born of those who are in truly conjugial love, derive inclinations and faculties, if a son, for perceiving the things which belong to wisdom, and if a daughter, for loving the things which wisdom teaches, is, that the conjugial principle of good and truth is implanted by creation in the soul of everyone, and also in the parts which are derived from the soul. For it was shewn above, that that conjugial principle fills the universe from primes to ultimates, and from a human being even to a worm; and it was also shewn that the faculty to open the lower parts of the mind even to conjunction with its higher parts, which are in the light and heat of heaven, is also implanted in every human being from creation. Hence it is evident, that a greater aptitude and facility for conjoining good with truth, and truth with good, and thus for becoming wise, is inherited at birth by those who are born from such a marriage, than by others; consequently, they have also a greater aptitude and facility than others for imbibing the things which belong to the church and heaven; that conjugial love is conjoined with these things, has been frequently shewn above. From these considerations, reason may clearly see the end for the sake of which the Lord the Creator has provided, and still provides, marriages of truly conjugial love.

205. I have heard from the angels, that they who lived in the Most Ancient eras live at this day in the heavens, in distinct households, families, and nations, as they had lived on earth, and that scarcely any one of a household is wanting: and that the reason of this is, that truly conjugial love was among them; and that hence their offspring inherited inclinations for the conjugial principle of good and truth, and were easily initiated into it more and more inwardly by their parents by means of education, and that afterwards as of themselves, when they became capable of judging for themselves, they were introduced into it by the Lord.

206. XVIII. This happens because the soul of the off-

SPRING IS FROM THE FATHER, AND ITS CLOTHING FROM THE MOTHER. No wise man raises a doubt that the soul is from the father; it is also manifestly perceived from the dispositions, and likewise from the faces, which are the types of the dispositions, in posterities which descend from fathers of families in a regular series; for the father returns as in an effigy, if not in his sons, yet in his grandsons and great-grandsons; and this takes place because the soul constitutes a man's inmost, which may be covered over by the offspring nearest in descent, but nevertheless it comes forth and manifests itself in more remote issue. That the soul is from the father, and its clothing from the mother, may be illustrated by analogous things in the vegetable kingdom. In this kingdom the earth or ground is the common mother, which in itself, as in a womb, receives and clothes seeds, yea, as it were conceives, bears, brings forth, and educates them, as a mother does her offspring from the father.

207. To the above I shall add two Memorable Relations. The First is as follows:—

*After some time I was looking towards the city Athens, of which something was said in a former memorable relation, and I heard thence an unwonted cry. There was in it something of laughter, and in the laughter something of indignation, and in the indignation something of sorrow: still however that cry was not therefore dissonant, but consonant, because one tone was not together with another, but one was within another. In the spiritual world a variety and commixture of affections is distinctly perceived in sound.

I inquired from afar what the matter was; and they said, "A messenger has arrived from the place where the new comers from the Christian world first appear, saying, that he has heard from three persons there, that in the world whence they came they had believed, with the rest there, that the blessed and happy after death enjoy absolute rest from labours; and that, since administrations, offices, and handicrafts are labours, they enjoy rest from these: and as those three persons have now been conducted hither by our emissary, and stand at the gate waiting, a cry was made, and it was deliberately resolved that they should not be introduced into the Palladium on Parnassus, as the former were, but into the great auditory there, to communicate their news from the Christian world: and some deputies have been sent to introduce them in form."

2 As I was in the spirit, and as distances with spirits are according to the states of their affections, and as at that time I had an affection to see and hear them, I seemed to myself to be present there; and I saw them introduced, and heard them speak. The elders or wiser ones of the audience sat at the sides of the

* This Memorable Relation is repeated in the *True Christian Religion* no. 694.

auditory, and the rest in the midst; and before these was an elevated piece of ground. Hither the three strangers, with the messenger, were formally conducted by the younger members, through the middle of the auditory. After silence had been obtained, they were addressed by a certain one of the elders there, and asked, "WHAT NEWS FROM THE EARTH?"

They said, "There is a great deal of news; but pray tell us on what subject you want the news."

The elder answered, "WHAT NEWS IS THERE FROM THE EARTH ABOUT OUR WORLD AND ABOUT HEAVEN?"

They replied, "When we first came into this world, we heard that here and in heaven there are governments, offices, functions, businesses, studies in all branches of learning, and wonderful handicrafts, and yet we had believed that after our removal or translation from the natural world into this spiritual one, we should come into an eternal rest from labours, and what are employments but labours?"

At this the elder said, "By eternal rest from labours did 3
you understand eternal idleness, in which you would be continually sitting and lying down, inhaling delights with the bosom, and sucking in joys with the mouth?"

To this the three strangers said, smiling, that they had thought something of the sort.

They were then answered, "What have joys and delights, and the happiness thence resulting, in common with idleness? By idleness the mind collapses and is not expanded; or, the man is deadened instead of being quickened into life. Suppose a person to be sitting in complete idleness, with his hands hanging down, his eyes cast down, or withdrawn from all objects, and suppose him at the same time to be encompassed by an aura of gladness, would not a lethargy seize both his head and body, and would not the vital expansion of his face shrivel up, and would he not, at length, his fibres being relaxed, totter to and fro, till he fell to the earth? What keeps the system of the whole body in expansion and tension, but the tension of the animus? and whence comes the tension of the animus but from administrations and works, when they are done from delight? Wherefore I will tell you some news from heaven: there are therein governments, offices, higher and lower courts of justice, also arts and handicrafts."

The three strangers, on hearing that there were higher and 4
lower courts of justice in heaven, said, "To what purpose are such proceedings? are not all in heaven inspired and led by God, and do not they know in consequence what is just and right? what need then is there of judges?"

The elder replied, "In this world we are instructed and learn what is good and true, also what is just and fair, just as in the natural world; and these things we learn, not immediately from

God, but mediately through others; and every angel, like every man, thinks what is true, and does what is good, as from himself; and this, according to the state of the angel, is mixed and not pure. Moreover, among the angels also there are those who are simple and those who are wise; and it is the part of the wise to judge, when the simple, from simplicity and ignorance, are doubtful about what is just, or depart from it. But as you are as yet strangers in this world, if it be your good pleasure, follow me into our city, and we will show you everything there."

5 Then they quitted the auditory, and some of the elders also accompanied them. They were first taken into a large library, which was divided into smaller libraries according to the sciences. The three strangers, on seeing so many books, were astonished, and said, "There are books also in this world! whence do you procure parchment and paper, pens and ink?"

To this the elders replied, "We perceive that in the former world you believed that this world is empty, because it is spiritual; and you believed so because you had cherished an idea of what is spiritual abstracted from what is material; and that which is abstracted from what is material appeared to you as nothing, thus as empty; when nevertheless in this world there is a fulness of all things. Here all things are SUBSTANTIAL and not material; and material things derive their origin from substantial things. We who live here are spiritual men, because we are substantial and not material; hence it is, that in this world all things that are in the natural world exist in their perfection, even books and writings, and many other things."

The three strangers, when they heard them talk of SUBSTANTIAL things, thought that it must be so, both because they saw written books, and because they heard it said that matters originate in substances. For their further confirmation about these things, they were taken to the houses of the scribes, who were writing out copies of the writings of the wise ones of the city; and they inspected the writings, and wondered to see them so neat and elegant.

6 After this they were conducted to the museums, high-schools, and colleges, and to the places where they had their literary sports. Some of these were called the sports of the Heliconides, some the sports of the Parnassides, some the sports of the Athenæïdes, and some the sports of the Virgins of the fountain. They said that the latter were so called, because virgins signify affections of sciences, and every one has intelligence according to his affection of sciences. The sports so called were spiritual exercises and trials of skill. Afterwards they were led about the city to see the governors, executive officers, and their subordinates, by whom they were taken to see the wonderful works that are done in a spiritual manner by the artificers.

After these things had been seen, the president again spoke 7
with them about the eternal rest from labour, into which the blessed and happy come after death, and said, "Eternal rest is not idleness; for idleness occasions a languor, listlessness, stupor, and drowsiness of the mind and thence of the whole body; and these things are death and not life, still less eternal life in which the angels of heaven are; wherefore eternal rest is a rest which dispels those mischiefs, and causes a man to live: this also is nothing else than such a thing as elevates the mind; consequently it is some employment and work by which the mind is excited, vivified, and delighted; and this is effected according to the use from which, in which, and for the sake of which, the mind is actively employed. Hence it is, that the universal heaven is regarded by the Lord as containing uses; and every angel is an angel according to use: the delight of use carries him along, as a favourable current does a ship, and causes him to be in eternal peace, and in the rest of peace. This is the meaning of eternal rest from labour. That an angel is alive according to the application of his mind from use is manifestly evident from the fact, that every one has conjugial love with its virtue, potency, and delights, according to the application of the genuine use in which he is."

When the three strangers had been convinced that eternal rest 8
is not idleness, but the delight of some work that is of use, there came some maidens with pieces of embroidery and knitting, the works of their own hands, which they gave to them. When the novitiate spirits were gone, the maidens sang an ode, wherein they expressed with angelic melody the affection of works of use with its pleasantnesses.

208. The Second Memorable Relation:—

When I was meditating on the arcana of conjugial love hidden away with wives, there again appeared the GOLDEN SHOWER described above; and I recollected that it fell over a palace in the east where there lived three conjugial loves, that is, three married pairs, who loved each other tenderly. On seeing it, I, as if invited by the sweetness of the meditation on that love, hastened towards it, and as I approached, the shower from golden became crimson, afterwards scarlet, and when I was near, it was opalescent like dew. I knocked, and the door was opened; and I said to the attendant, "Tell the husbands that he who came before with an angel is come again, and begs that he may be allowed to enter and converse with them." The attendant returned with the assent of the husbands, and I entered.

The three husbands with their wives were together in an open courtyard, and returned my greeting with good-will.

I then asked the wives, whether the white dove in the window had afterwards appeared?

They said, "Yes; and to-day also, and it likewise spread out its wings; from which we surmised that you were near at hand, and were going to beg us to disclose yet one more arcanum of conjugial love."

I asked, "Why do you say one arcanum; when yet I came here to learn several?"

2 They replied, "They are arcana, and some of them transcend your wisdom to such a degree, that the understanding of your thought cannot apprehend them. You glory over us on account of your wisdom; but we do not glory over you on account of ours; and yet ours is eminently above yours, because it enters your inclinations and affections, and sees, perceives, and feels them. You know nothing at all about the inclinations and affections of your own love; and yet these are the things from which and according to which your understanding thinks, consequently from which and according to which you are wise; and yet wives know them so well in their husbands, that they see them in their faces, and hear them from the tones of the speech of their mouth, yea, they feel them on their breasts, arms, and cheeks. But we, from the zeal of love for your happiness, and at the same time for our own, pretend not to know them; and yet we govern them so prudently, that wherever the fancy, good pleasure, and will of our husbands lead, we follow by permitting and suffering it; only bending its direction when it is possible, but never forcing it."

3 I asked, "Whence have you this wisdom?"

They replied, "It is implanted in us from creation and consequently from birth. Our husbands liken it to instinct; but we say that it is of the Divine providence, in order that men (*viri*) may be rendered happy by their wives. We have heard from our husbands, that the Lord wills that the male human being should act from freedom according to reason; and that therefore the Lord Himself from within governs his freedom, which has respect to the inclinations and affections; and that He governs it from without by means of his wife; and that thus the Lord forms the man (*vir*) with his wife into an angel of heaven: and moreover love changes its essence, and does not become that love, if it be forced. But we will speak more openly on this subject: we are moved thereto, that is, to the prudence of governing the inclinations and affections of our husbands, so that they may seem to themselves to act from freedom according to their reason, from this cause, that we are delighted by their love: and we love nothing more than that they should be delighted by our delights, which, if they are lightly esteemed by our husbands, become insipid also to us."

4 Having said this, one of the wives entered her bridal-chamber, and on her return said, "My dove still flutters its wings, which is a sign that we may make further disclosures." They then

said, "We have observed various changes of the inclinations and affections of the men; as, that they become cold towards their wives, when the husbands think vain things against the Lord and the church; that they become cold when they are in conceit from their self-intelligence; that they become cold when they look at other women with concupiscence, that they become cold when the subject of love is adverted to by their wives; besides many other occasions; and that they become cold with different kinds of cold: this we have noticed from a withdrawal of the sense from their eyes, ears, and bodies, at the presence of our senses. From these few observations you may see, that we know better than the men whether it be well or ill with them; if they are cold towards their wives, it is ill with them, but if they are warm towards their wives, it is well with them; wherefore wives are continually devising means in their minds (*animi*) whereby the men may become warm and not cold towards them; and these means they devise with a sagacity inscrutable to their husbands."

As they said this, the dove was heard as it were moaning; 5
and then the wives said, "This is a sign to us that we have a wish to divulge deeper arcana, but that it is not allowable: probably you will reveal to the men what you have heard."

I replied, "I intend to do so: what harm can come from it?"

The wives, after they had spoken together on the subject, said, "Reveal it if you like. We are not unaware of the power of persuasion which wives possess; for they will say to their husbands, 'That man is mocking; he tells idle tales; he is but joking from appearances, and from idle fancies usual with men. Do not believe him, but believe us; we know that you are loves, and we obediences.' Wherefore reveal it if you like; but still the husbands will place no dependence on your lips, but on the lips of their wives which they kiss."

UNIVERSALS RELATING TO MARRIAGES.

209. THERE are so many things relating to marriages that, if they were particularly treated of, they would swell this little work into a large volume: for there might be particularly treated of, the likeness and unlikeness among married partners; the elevation of natural conjugial love into spiritual conjugial love, and the conjunction of those loves; the increase of the one and the decrease of the other; the varieties and diversities of each; the intelligence of wives; the universal conjugial sphere from heaven, and its opposite sphere from hell, and the influx and reception of those spheres; besides many other things, which, if individually enlarged upon, would render this work so bulky as to tire out the reader. For this reason, and to avoid empty prolixity, these things shall be condensed into UNIVERSALS RELATING TO MARRIAGES. But these, like the foregoing subjects, must be distinctly considered under the following articles:

I. *The especial sense of conjugial love is the sense of touch.*

II. *With those who are in truly conjugial love, the faculty of becoming wise increases; but with those who are not in conjugial love, it decreases.*

III. *With those who are in truly conjugial love, the happiness of dwelling together increases; but with those who are not in conjugial love, it decreases.*

IV. *With those who are in truly conjugial love, the conjunction of minds increases, and therewith friendship; but with those who are not in conjugial love, it decreases.*

V. *Those who are in truly conjugial love, continually desire to be one man; but those who are not in conjugial love, desire to be two.*

VI. *Those who are in truly conjugial love, in marriage look to what is eternal; but with those who are not in conjugial love, the case is reversed.*

VII. *Conjugial love resides with chaste wives; but still their love depends on their husbands.*

VIII. *Wives love the bonds of marriage, provided only that the men also love them.*

IX. *The intelligence of women is in itself modest, elegant, pacific, yielding, soft, tender; but the intelligence of men is in itself grave, harsh, hard, daring, fond of licentiousness.*

X. *Wives are in no excitement as men are; but they have a state of preparation for reception.*

XI. *The men have abundance* (copia) *according to the love of propagating the truths of their wisdom, and according to the love of doing uses.*

XII. *The determinations are at the good pleasure of the husband.*

XIII. *There is a conjugial sphere which flows in from the Lord through heaven into each and all things of the universe, even to its ultimates.*

XIV. *This sphere is received by the feminine sex, and through it is transferred into the masculine sex; and not contrariwise.*

XV. *Where there is truly conjugial love, this sphere is received by the wife, and solely through the wife by the husband.*

XVI. *Where the love is not conjugial, this sphere is indeed received by the wife, but not by the husband through her.*

XVII. *Truly conjugial love may exist with one of the married partners, and not at the same time with the other.*

XVIII. *There are various likenesses and unlikenesses, both internal and external, with married partners.*

XIX. *Various likenesses can be conjoined, but not with unlikenesses.*

XX. *The Lord provides a likeness for those who desire truly conjugial love; and if it does not exist on earth, He provides it in the heavens.*

XXI. *According to the defect and loss of conjugial love, man approaches to the nature of the beast.*

Now follows the explanation of these articles.

210. I. THE ESPECIAL SENSE OF CONJUGIAL LOVE IS THE SENSE OF TOUCH. Every love has its own sense. The love of seeing, from the love of understanding, has the sense of sight; and the pleasantnesses of this sense are symmetries and beauties. The love of hearing, from the love of hearkening to and obeying, has the sense of hearing; and the pleasantnesses of this sense are harmonies. The love of cognizing the things which float about in the air, from the love of perceiving, has the sense of smell; and the pleasantnesses of this sense are fragrances. The love of nourishing oneself from the love of imbuing oneself with goods and truths, has the sense of taste; and the delightsomenesses of this sense are delicacies. The love of cognizing objects, from the love of exercising circumspection and protecting oneself, has the sense of touch; and the pleasantnesses of this sense are titillations. The reason why the love of conjunction with a consort, from the love of uniting good and truth, has the sense of touch, is, that this sense is common to all the senses, and hence levies contributions from them. That this love brings all the abovementioned senses into communion with it, and appropriates their pleasantnesses to itself, is known. That the sense of touch is dedicated to conjugial love, and is its especial sense, is evident from all its sports, and from the exaltation of its subtilities to

the utmost exquisiteness. But the further consideration of this subject is left to lovers.

211. II. WITH THOSE WHO ARE IN TRULY CONJUGIAL LOVE, THE FACULTY OF BECOMING WISE INCREASES; BUT WITH THOSE WHO ARE NOT IN CONJUGIAL LOVE, IT DECREASES. The reason why the faculty of becoming wise increases with those who are in truly conjugial love, is, that this love is with married partners from wisdom, and according to it, as has been fully proved in the preceding sections: also that the sense of that love is the touch, and this is common to all the senses, and also is full of delights; consequently it opens the interiors of the minds, as it opens the interiors of the senses, and therewith the organical parts of the whole body. Hence it follows, that they who are in that love, love nothing more than to become wise; for a man becomes wise in proportion as the interiors of his mind are opened; for by means of the opening, the thoughts of the understanding are elevated into a higher light, and the affections of the will into a higher heat; and the higher light is wisdom, and the higher heat is the love of wisdom. The spiritual delights conjoined with natural delights, which are the portion of those who are in truly conjugial love, constitute the faculty of loving and being loved, and hence the faculty of becoming wise. Hence it is that the angels have conjugial love according to wisdom, and the increase of that love and at the same time of its delights is according to the increase of wisdom; and hence also it is that the spiritual offspring which are born from their marriages, are such things as belong to wisdom from the father, and such things as belong to love from the mother, which they love from a spiritual storgë; which love adds itself to their conjugial love, and continually elevates it, and conjoins them.

212. The contrary happens with those who are not in any conjugial love, in consequence of not having any love of wisdom. These enter upon marriage with no other end than that of indulging in lasciviousness, and in this end there is also the love of becoming insane; for every end considered in itself is a love, and lasciviousness in its spiritual origin is insanity. By insanity is meant a delirium of the mind arising from falsities; and a pre-eminent delirium is the delirium of the mind arising from truths which are falsified to such a degree that these [falsifications] are believed to be wisdom. That such persons are opposed to conjugial love, is confirmed or evinced by manifest proof in the spiritual world: in that world, on perceiving the first fragrance of conjugial love, they flee into caverns, and shut the doors; and if these are opened, they rave like madmen in the world.

213. III. WITH THOSE WHO ARE IN TRULY CONJUGIAL LOVE, THE

HAPPINESS OF DWELLING TOGETHER INCREASES; BUT WITH THOSE WHO ARE NOT IN CONJUGIAL LOVE, IT DECREASES. The reason why the happiness of dwelling together increases with those who are in truly conjugial love, is, that they mutually love each other with every sense. The wife sees nothing more lovely than the husband, and the husband nothing more lovely than the wife; yea, neither do they hear, smell, or touch anything more lovely: hence the happiness they enjoy of living together in the same house, bed-chamber, and bed. That this is the case, you that are husbands can convince yourselves from the first delights of marriage, which are in their fulness, because at that time the wife only of all the sex is loved. That the reverse is the case with those who are not in any conjugial love, is known.

214. IV. WITH THOSE WHO ARE IN TRULY CONJUGIAL LOVE, THE CONJUNCTION OF MINDS INCREASES, AND THEREWITH FRIENDSHIP; BUT WITH THOSE WHO ARE NOT IN CONJUGIAL LOVE, IT DECREASES. That the conjunction of minds increases with those who are in truly conjugial love, was proved in the chapter on "The Conjunction of the Souls and Minds by means of Marriage, which is meant by the Lord's words, that they are no longer two but one flesh," see no. 156[*a*]–181. But the reason why that conjunction 2
increases as friendship becomes conjoined with love, is, that friendship is as it were the face, and is also as it were the garment of that love; for it not only adjoins itself to the love as a garment, but also conjoins itself with it as a face. The love which precedes friendship is similar to the love of the sex, which departs after the attainment of its desire; whereas love conjoined with friendship remains after the marriage, and is also rendered stable: it likewise enters more interiorly into the bosom, friendship introducing it, and making it truly conjugial; and then the love makes this its friendship also conjugial, which differs greatly from the friendship of every other love, for it is full. That the contrary takes place with those who are not in 3
conjugial love, is known. With these, the first friendship, which had been insinuated at the time of betrothal, and afterwards during the first days after the wedding, recedes more and more from the interiors of the mind, and from these it successively departs at last to the cuticles; and, with those who think of separations, it goes away entirely; but with those who do not think of separation, love remains in the externals, but it is cold in the internals.

215. V. THOSE WHO ARE IN TRULY CONJUGIAL LOVE, CONTINUALLY DESIRE TO BE ONE MAN; BUT THOSE WHO ARE NOT IN CONJUGIAL LOVE, DESIRE TO BE TWO. Conjugial love in its essence consists in nothing else than the willing of two to be one; that is, in their willing that two lives shall become one life.

This will is the perpetual endeavour of that love, from which flow all its effects. That endeavour is the very essence of motion, and that will is a living endeavour with man, is confirmed by the researches of philosophers, and is also evident to such as take a view of the subject from cultivated reason. Hence it follows, that those who are in truly conjugial love, continually endeavour, that is, will to be one man. That the contrary takes place with those who are not in conjugial love, they themselves know very well; for as they continually think themselves two in consequence of the disunion of their souls and minds, so they do not comprehend what is meant by the Lord's words, that they are no longer two, but one flesh (Matt. xix. 6).

216. VI. THOSE WHO ARE IN TRULY CONJUGIAL LOVE, IN MARRIAGE LOOK TO WHAT IS ETERNAL; BUT WITH THOSE WHO ARE NOT IN CONJUGIAL LOVE, THE CASE IS REVERSED. The reason why those who are in truly conjugial love look to what is eternal, is, that in that love there is eternity; and its eternity is in consequence of that love with the wife, and wisdom with the husband, increasing to eternity; and in the increase or progression the married partners enter more and more interiorly into the blessednesses of heaven, which their wisdom and its love together have stored up in themselves: wherefore if the idea of what is eternal were to be plucked away, or by any chance to escape from their minds, it would be as if they were cast down
2 from heaven. What is the state of married partners in heaven, when the idea of what is eternal falls out of their minds, and the idea of what is temporary takes its place, was made clear to me from the following experience:

Two married partners were once, by permission, present with me from heaven; and at that instant the idea of what is eternal in relation to marriage was taken away from them by a mischievous juggler, who talked cunningly. Hereupon they began to bewail themselves, saying, that they could not live any longer, and that they felt such misery as they had never felt before. When this was perceived by their fellow-angels in heaven, the juggler was removed and cast down; whereupon the idea of what is eternal instantly returned to them, at which they were gladdened in heart, and most tenderly embraced each other.

3 Besides this, I have heard two married partners, who at one moment entertained the idea of what is eternal in relation to their marriage, and the next moment the idea of what is temporary. The reason was, that there was an internal unlikeness between them. When they were in the idea of what is eternal, they were mutually glad; but when in the idea of what is temporary, they said, "There is no longer any marriage between us;" and the wife said, "I am no longer a wife, but a concubine;" and the man, "I am no longer a husband, but an

adulterer (*mœchus*);" wherefore while their internal unlikeness was open to them, the man left the woman, and the woman the man: afterwards, however, since they both had an idea of what is eternal in relation to marriage, they were consociated with suitable consorts.

From these instances it may be clearly seen, that they who 4
are in truly conjugial love look to what is eternal; and that, if this idea from their inmosts drops out of their thought, they are disunited as to conjugial love, although they may not at the same time be disunited as to friendship; for friendship dwells in externals, but conjugial love in internals. The case is similar with marriages on earth, where married partners who tenderly love each other, think of what is eternal in relation to the covenant, and not at all of its end by death; and if this should enter their thoughts, they are grieved; nevertheless they are revived by hope from the thought of its continuation after their decease.

216 [*a*]. VII. CONJUGIAL LOVE RESIDES WITH CHASTE WIVES; BUT STILL THEIR LOVE DEPENDS ON THEIR HUSBANDS. The reason is, that wives are born loves; and hence it is innate to them to will to be one with their husbands; and from this thought of their will they continually suckle their love; wherefore to recede from the endeavour of uniting themselves with their husbands, would be to recede from themselves. It is otherwise with husbands, who are not born loves, but recipients of that love from their wives; and therefore, in proportion as they receive it, in the same proportion the wives enter with their love; but in proportion as they do not receive it, in the same proportion the wives stand outside with their love, and wait. This is the case with chaste wives; but it is otherwise with unchaste ones. From these considerations it is manifest that conjugial love resides with the wives, but that their love depends on their husbands.

217. VIII. WIVES LOVE THE BONDS OF MARRIAGE, PROVIDED ONLY THAT THE MEN ALSO LOVE THEM. This follows from what was said in the foregoing article: add to this, that wives, naturally wish to be, and to be called, wives; this is to them a name of beauty and honour; wherefore they love the bonds of marriage. And as chaste wives wish to be wives, not in name only, but in reality, and this is effected by a closer and closer binding with their husbands, therefore they love the bonds of marriage for the sake of rendering its covenant firm; and this so much the more as they are loved again by their husbands, or, what is the same thing, as the men love those bonds.

218. IX. THE INTELLIGENCE OF WOMEN IS IN ITSELF MODEST,

ELEGANT, PACIFIC, YIELDING, SOFT, TENDER; BUT THE INTELLIGENCE OF MEN IS IN ITSELF GRAVE, HARSH, HARD, DARING, FOND OF LICENTIOUSNESS. That such are the characteristics of women and men, is manifestly evident from the body, the face, the tone of voice, the conversation, the gesture, and the manners of each: from the BODY, in that the skin and flesh of men are hard, and the skin and flesh of women are soft; from the FACE, in that it is harder, stiffer, more rugged, of darker complexion, and also bearded, thus less beautiful, in men; whereas in women it is softer, more yielding, more tender, of fairer complexion, and thus more beautiful; from the TONE OF VOICE, in that it is deep with men, and tender with women; from the CONVERSATION, in that with men it is fond of licentiousness, and daring, but with women it is modest and pacific; from the GESTURE, in that with men it is stronger and firmer, whereas with women it is weaker and feebler; from the MANNERS, in that with men they are more unrestrained, but
2 with women more elegant. How far from the very birth the genius of men differs from that of women, was clearly manifested to me from seeing a number of boys and girls met together. I saw them at times through a window in the street of a great city, where more than twenty assembled every day. The boys, agreeably to the disposition born with them, in their pastimes were tumultuous, vociferous, apt to fight, to strike, and to throw stones at each other; whereas the girls sat peaceably at the doors of the houses, some playing with little children, some dressing dolls, some working on bits of linen, some kissing each other; and, what I was surprised at, they still looked with pleased eyes at the boys who were of such a character. Hence I could see plainly that a man is born understanding, and a woman, love; and also the quality of understanding and of love in their beginnings; and thus what would be the quality of a man's understanding in its progress, without conjunction with female love, and afterwards with conjugial love.

219. X. WIVES ARE IN NO EXCITEMENT AS MEN ARE; BUT THEY HAVE A STATE OF PREPARATION FOR RECEPTION. That men have fecundation, and consequently excitement, and that women have not the latter because they have not the former, is evident; but that women have a state of preparation for reception, and thus for conception, I relate from what I have heard. But what the quality of this state with women is, I am not allowed to describe; and indeed, it is known to them alone: but whether their love, while they are in that state, is in its delight, or in what is undelightful, as some of them say, they have not made known. This only is generally known, that it is not allowed the husband to say to the wife, that he is able and not willing, for thereby the state of reception is grievously hurt, which is prepared according to the state of the husband's potency.

220. XI. THE MEN HAVE ABUNDANCE (*copia*) ACCORDING TO THE LOVE OF PROPAGATING THE TRUTHS OF WISDOM, AND ACCORDING TO THE LOVE OF DOING USES. That this is so, is one of the arcana which were known to the Ancients, and which are now lost. The Ancients knew that each and all things that are done in the body are done from a spiritual origin: as that from the will, which in itself is spiritual, actions flow; and from the thought, which also is spiritual, speech flows; also that natural sight is from spiritual sight, which is that of the understanding; natural hearing from spiritual hearing, which is attention of the understanding and at the same time accommodation of the will; and natural smell from spiritual smell, which is perception; and so forth. The Ancients saw that the virile faculty of secretion of the semen is likewise from a spiritual origin. That it is from the truths of which the understanding consists, they concluded from many proofs both of reason and experience; and they said that nothing is received by males from the spiritual marriage, which is that of good and truth, and which flows in into each and all things in the universe, except truth, and that which has relation to truth; and that this in its progress into the body is formed into seed; and that hence it is, that seeds spiritually understood are truths. As to the formation, they 2
said, that the masculine soul, because it is intellectual, is thus truth; for the Intellectual is nothing else; wherefore when the soul descends, truth also descends: that this is effected by this circumstance, that the soul, which is the inmost of man and of every animal, and which in its essence is spiritual, by reason of an implanted effort for self-propagation, follows in the descent, and wishes to procreate itself; and that when this takes place, the entire soul forms itself, and clothes itself, and becomes seed: and that this can be done thousands of times, because the soul is a spiritual substance, which has not extension but impletion, and from which no part can be taken away, but the whole may be produced, without any loss thereof: hence it is, that it is as fully present in the smallest receptacles, which are seeds, as in its greatest receptacle, which is the body. Since therefore the 3
truth in the soul is the origin of the seed, it follows, that men have abundance according to the love of propagating the truths of their wisdom; it is also according to the love of doing uses, because uses are the goods which truths produce. In the world also it is known to some, that the industrious have abundance, but not the idle. I asked, "How is the feminine [element] propagated from a male soul?" and I received for answer, that it was from intellectual good, because this in its essence is truth: for the intellect can think that this is good, thus that it is true that it is good. It is otherwise with the will: this does not think good and truth, but loves and does them; that therefore by sons in the Word are signified truths, and by daughters goods,

see above, no. 120; and that by seed in the Word is signified truth, may be seen in the *Apocalypse Revealed,* no. 565.

221. XII. THE DETERMINATIONS ARE AT THE GOOD PLEASURE OF THE HUSBAND. The reason is, that with men there is the abundance above mentioned; and this varies with them both according to the states of their minds and according to the states of their bodies. For the understanding is not so constant in its thoughts as the will is in its affections, since it is sometimes carried upwards, sometimes downwards; at one time it is in a serene and clear state, at another in a turbulent and obscure one; sometimes it is among pleasant objects, and then again among unpleasant objects; and as the mind, while it acts, is also in the body, it follows, that the body has similar states. Hence it is, that the husband at times recedes from conjugial love, and at times accedes to it, and that the abundance is removed in the one state, and restored in the other. These are the reasons why the determinations ought to be left to the good pleasure of the husband. Hence also it is that wives, from the wisdom implanted in them, never offer any admonition on such subjects.

222. XIII. THERE IS A CONJUGIAL SPHERE WHICH FLOWS IN FROM THE LORD THROUGH HEAVEN INTO EACH AND ALL THINGS OF THE UNIVERSE, EVEN TO ITS ULTIMATES. That from the Lord proceed love and wisdom, or, what is the same, good and truth, was shewn above in the chapter on that subject. These two in marriage proceed continually from the Lord, because they are Himself, and from Him are all things; and the things which proceed from Him fill the universe; for without Him nothing that exists
2 would subsist. There are several spheres which proceed from Him, as, the sphere of the preservation of the created universe, the sphere of the protection of good and truth against evil and falsity, the sphere of reformation and regeneration, the sphere of innocence and peace, the sphere of mercy and grace, besides many others; but the universal sphere of all is the conjugial sphere, because this is also the sphere of propagation, and thus in a supereminent degree the sphere of the preservation of the
3 created universe through successive generations. That this conjugial sphere fills the universe, and pervades all things from primes to ultimates, is evident from what has been shewn above, that there are marriages in the heavens, and most perfect marriages in the third or highest heaven; and that besides existing with men, there is a [sort of] marriage in all the subjects of the animal kingdom in the earth, even down to worms; and also in all the subjects of the vegetable kingdom, from olive and
4 palm trees even to the smallest grasses. That this sphere is more universal than the sphere of heat and light, which proceeds

from the sun of our world, may be clearly proved to the reason from this consideration, that it operates also in the absence of the sun's heat, as in winter, and in the absence of its light, as at night, especially with human beings. The reason why it so operates is, that it is from the sun of the angelic heaven, and thence there is a constant equalization of heat and light, that is, a conjunction of good and truth; for it is in a continual spring. The changes of good and truth, or of its heat and light, are not variations thereof, like the variations on earth arising from changes of the heat and light from the sun there; but they arise from the recipient subjects.

223. XIV. This sphere is received by the feminine sex, and through this it is transferred into the masculine sex. That there is not any conjugial love with the masculine sex, but only with the feminine sex, and that from this sex it is transferred into the masculine sex, I have seen evidenced by experience, concerning which see above, no. 161. A further proof of it is furnished by this argument, that the masculine form is the intellectual form, and the feminine the voluntary form; and the intellectual form cannot of itself become heated with conjugial heat, but it can be heated by the conjunctive heat of some one into whom this has been implanted by creation; consequently it cannot receive that love except through the voluntary form of woman being adjoined to it, because this also is the form of love. This same position might be further confirmed from the marriage of good and truth; and, before the natural man, from the marriage of the heart and lungs, because the heart corresponds to love, and the lungs to the understanding. But as the generality of mankind are deficient in the knowledge of these subjects, confirmation thereby would obscure rather than enlighten. It is in consequence of the transfer of this sphere from the feminine sex into the masculine sex, that the mind is also inflamed by the mere thought about the sex; that hence also results propagative formation and thus excitement, follows as a consequence; for unless heat is added to light on earth, nothing flourishes there, nor is anything excited to produce fruit.

224. XV. Where there is truly conjugial love, this sphere is received by the wife, and solely through the wife by the husband. That this sphere, with those who are in truly conjugial love, is received by the husband solely through the wife, is an arcanum at the present day; and yet in itself it is not an arcanum, because the bridegroom and newly-married husband may know this: is he not affected conjugially by whatever proceeds from his bride and newly-married wife, but not at that time by what proceeds from others of the sex? The case is similar with those who live together in truly conjugial

love. And since every one, both man and woman, is encompassed by his own sphere of life, densely on the breast, and thinly on the back, it is evident whence it is, that husbands who are very fond of their wives, turn to them, and in the day-time look at them with kindly looks; and why, on the other hand, those who do not love their wives, turn away from them, and in the day-time regard them with a turned-away countenance. By the reception of the conjugial sphere by the husband solely through the wife, truly conjugial love is recognized and distinguished from spurious, false, and cold conjugial love.

225. XVI. WHERE THE LOVE IS NOT CONJUGIAL, THIS SPHERE IS INDEED RECEIVED BY THE WIFE, BUT NOT BY THE HUSBAND THROUGH HER. This conjugial sphere flowing in into the universe is, in its origin, Divine; in its progress in heaven with the angels it is celestial and spiritual; with men it is natural; with beasts and birds animal; with worms merely corporeal; with plants it is devoid of life; and moreover, in all its subjects it is varied according to their forms. Now, since this sphere is received immediately by the feminine sex, and mediately by the masculine sex, and since it is received according to forms, it follows, that this sphere, which is holy in its origin, may in the subjects be turned into what is not holy, yea, may be even inverted into the opposite sphere. The sphere opposite to it is called, with such women, the meretricious sphere, and, with such men, the scortatory sphere; and as such men and women are in hell, this sphere is from thence: but this sphere is also of much variety, and hence there are many kinds of it; and such a kind is attracted and inhaled by a man (*vir*) as is agreeable to him, and conformable to, and correspondent with, his own genius. From these considerations it may be manifest, that the man who does not love his wife, receives that sphere from some other source than his wife; nevertheless it is the fact, that even then, that sphere is inspired by the wife, but without the man's knowing it, and when he becomes heated.

226. XVII. TRULY CONJUGIAL LOVE MAY EXIST WITH ONE OF THE MARRIED PARTNERS, AND NOT AT THE SAME TIME WITH THE OTHER. For one may from the heart long for chaste marriage, while the other knows not what chastity is; one may love the things which belong to the church, but the other those which belong to the world alone: one may be in heaven as to his or her mind, the other in hell; hence there may be conjugial love with the one, and not with the other. The minds of such, since they are turned in contrary directions, are inwardly in collision with each other; and if not outwardly, still the one that is not in conjugial love regards his, or her, covenanted consort as a fulsome old creature; and so in other cases.

227. XVIII. THERE ARE VARIOUS LIKENESSES AND UNLIKENESSES, BOTH INTERNAL AND EXTERNAL, WITH MARRIED PARTNERS. It is known, that between married partners there are likenesses and unlikenesses, and that the external ones appear, but not the internal ones, except after some time of dwelling together, to the married partners themselves, and by indications to others; but it would be useless to enumerate each so that they might be known, since several pages might be filled with an enumeration and description of their varieties. Likenesses may in part be deduced and concluded from the unlikenesses on account of which conjugial love passes away into cold; of which we shall speak in the following chapter. Likenesses and unlikenesses originate in general from connate inclinations, varied by education, the company that is kept, and persuasions that have been imbibed.

228. XIX. VARIOUS LIKENESSES CAN BE CONJOINED, BUT NOT WITH UNLIKENESSES. The varieties of likenesses are very numerous, and differ more or less from each other; but still those which differ may in time be conjoined by various things, especially by accommodations to desires, by mutual offices, by civilities, by abstinence from unchastities, by the common love of infants and the care of children, but especially by conformity in the things of the church; for by means of the things of the church there is effected a conjunction of likenesses differing interiorly, but by the other means there is effected a conjunction of those likenesses only that differ exteriorly. But with unlikenesses no conjunction can be effected, because they are antipathetic.

229. XX. THE LORD PROVIDES LIKENESSES FOR THOSE WHO DESIRE TRULY CONJUGIAL LOVE, AND IF THEY DO NOT EXIST ON EARTH, HE PROVIDES THEM IN THE HEAVENS. The reason is, that all marriages of truly conjugial love are provided by the Lord. That they are from Him, see above, nos. 130, 131; but in what manner they are provided in the heavens, I have heard described by the angels thus:—The Divine providence of the Lord is most singular and most universal in relation to marriages and in marriages, because all the delights of heaven flow from the delights of conjugial love, as sweet waters from the fountain head; and on this account it is provided that conjugial pairs be born; and that they be continually educated for their marriages under the Lord's auspices, neither the boy nor the girl knowing anything of the matter; and after a stated time, when she has become a marriageable maiden, and he a young man fitted for marriage, they meet somewhere as by fate, and see each other, and they then instantly know, as by a kind of instinct, that they are consorts, and by a kind of dictate they think inwardly in

themselves, the young man, that she is mine, and the maiden, that he is mine; and when this thought has been seated some time in the minds of both, they deliberately accost each other, and betroth themselves. It is said, as by fate, by instinct, and by dictate; and the meaning is, by Divine providence, because, while the Divine providence is unknown, it has such an appearance; for the Lord opens internal likenesses, so that they may see themselves.

230. XXI. ACCORDING TO THE DEFECT AND LOSS OF CONJUGIAL LOVE, MAN APPROACHES TO THE NATURE OF THE BEAST. The reason is, that so far as a man is in conjugial love, so far he is spiritual, and so far as he is spiritual, so far he is man. For man is born for the life after death, and attains to that life because he has in him a spiritual soul, and is capable of being elevated thereto by means of the faculty of his understanding; if in this case his will, from the faculty granted to it also, is elevated at the same time, he lives after death the life of heaven. The contrary comes to pass, if he is in a love opposite to conjugial love; for so far as he is in this opposite love, so far he is natural; and a merely natural man is like a beast as to lusts, appetites, and their delights; with this difference only, that he has the faculty of elevating his understanding into the light of wisdom, and also the faculty of elevating his will into the heat of heavenly love. These faculties are never taken away from any man; wherefore the merely natural man although as to concupiscences, appetites, and their delights, he is like a beast, nevertheless lives after death, but in a state corresponding to his past life. From these considerations it may be manifest, that a man, according to the defect of conjugial love, approaches to the nature of a beast. This may seem to be contradicted by the fact, that there is a defect and loss of conjugial love with some who yet are men; but the statement is meant to be confined to those who make light of conjugial love on account of [their being in] scortatory love, and who are thereby in the defect and loss of that love.

231. To the above shall be added three Memorable Relations. The first is as follows:—

* I once heard loud exclamations, which, as it were, bubbled up through waters out of the hells; one to the left hand, "O HOW JUST!" a second to the right, "O HOW LEARNED!" and a third from behind, "O HOW WISE!" and as it occurred to my thought whether there were, even in hell, just, learned, and wise men, I was affected with a desire of seeing whether there were such men there; and it was told me from heaven, "You shall see and hear."

* This Memorable Relation may also be found in the *True Christian Religion*, no. 332.

So I went out of the house in the spirit, and saw before me an opening: I approached this, and looked down, and lo! there was a ladder: by this I descended; and when I was down below, I saw a level country set thick with trees, intermixed with thorns and nettles; and I asked whether this was hell, and they said, "It is the lower earth which is just above hell." I then went on according to the exclamations in order; to the first, "O HOW JUST!" and I saw a company consisting of such as in the world had been judges influenced by friendship and gifts; then to the second exclamation, "O HOW LEARNED!" and I saw a company of such as in the world had been reasoners; and lastly to the third exclamation, "O HOW WISE!" and I saw a company of such as in the world had been confirmers.

But from these I returned to the first, where there were 2
judges influenced by friendship and gifts, and who were proclaimed "Just." On one side I saw as it were an amphitheatre built of bricks, and covered with black tiles; and I was told that they called it a tribunal. There were three entrances to it on the northern side, and three on the western side, but none on the southern and eastern sides; a sign that their judgments were not judgments of justice, but arbitrary judgments. In the middle of the amphitheatre there appeared a fire-place, into which the servants who attended to it threw torches impregnated with brimstone and bitumen; the light whereof, by its flickering on the plastered walls, presented pictured images of birds of evening and night; but both that fire-place, and the flickerings of the light thence into the forms of those images, were representations of their judgments, in that they were able to tinge the matter of any trial with coloured dyes, and give it
a form according to their own interest. In about half an 3
hour I saw some old and young men in robes and cloaks enter, who, laying aside their caps, took their seats at the tables to sit in judgment. I heard and perceived with what skill and ingenuity, according as they noticed friendship, they warped and inverted judgments into appearances of justice, and this to such a degree, that they themselves saw what was unjust no otherwise than what was just, and on the other hand what was just as what was unjust. Such persuasions respecting those things appeared from their faces and were heard from their manner of speaking. There was then given me enlightenment from heaven, from which I perceived whether or not each point was grounded in right; and I saw how industriously they concealed what was unjust, and gave it the semblance of what was just; and how they selected from the laws one which favoured their own side of the question, and by skilful reasonings drew over the rest to the same side. After judgment had been pronounced, the decrees were conveyed to their clients, friends, and patrons, who, to recompense them for

their services, kept shouting during the whole long way, "O HOW JUST, O HOW JUST!"

4 After this I spoke about them with the angels of heaven, and related to them some of the things I had seen and heard. The angels said to me, "Such judges appear to others to be endowed with a most extraordinary acuteness of intellect; when yet they do not see the least of what is just and fair. If you remove the friendship in favour of particular persons, they sit mute in judgment like statues, and only say, 'Yea, I agree to this or to that.' The reason is, that all their judgments are prejudgments; and prejudgment with partiality influences the case from beginning to end. Hence they see nothing but what belongs to their friend's interest; whatever is contrary thereto, they set aside; and when they take it up again, they involve it in reasonings, as a spider does its prey in a web, and make an end of it. Hence it is that unless they follow the thread of their prejudice, they see nothing of what is right. They have been examined whether they were able to see it, and it was discovered that they were not. That this is the case, will seem wonderful to the inhabitants of your world; but tell them it is a Truth that has been investigated by the angels of heaven. As they see nothing of what is just, we in heaven regard them not as men but as monsters, whose heads are constituted of the things which belong to friendship, their breasts of those which belong to injustice, their feet of those which belong to confirmation, and the soles of their feet of those things which belong to justice, which they overturn and trample under foot, if they do not favour their friend. But of what quality they appear to us from heaven, you shall see; for their end is at hand."

5 And lo! at that instant the ground yawned open, and the tables fell one upon another, and the judges were swallowed up, together with the whole amphitheatre, and were cast into caverns, and imprisoned.

It was then said to me, "Do you wish to see them where they now are?" And lo! they appeared as to their faces as of polished steel, as to their bodies, from the neck to the loins, as graven images of stone clothed with leopards' skins, and as to their feet like snakes: and I saw the law books, which they had arranged on the tables, changed into packs of cards: and now instead of sitting in judgment, the office appointed to them is to prepare red lead into rouge, to bedaub the faces of harlots, and thus turn them into beauties.

6 After seeing these things, I wanted to visit the two other companies, one of which consisted of mere reasoners, and the other of mere confirmers: and it was said to me, "Wait awhile, and there shall be given you attendant angels from the society next above them: through these there will be given to you light from the Lord, and you will see wonderful things."

232. The Second Memorable Relation.

* After some time I again heard from the lower earth the voices which I had heard before, "O HOW LEARNED!" and "O HOW WISE!" I looked around to see what angels were then present; and lo! there were present those who were in the heaven immediately above those who cried, "O HOW LEARNED!"

And I spoke with them about the cry, and they said, "Those learned ones are such as only reason *whether a thing be so,* or *whether it be not so,* and seldom think *that it is so;* wherefore they are like winds which blow and pass away, and like the bark around trees which are without pith, or like shells around almonds without a kernel, or like the rind about fruit without pulp; for their minds are devoid of interior judgment, and are united only with the senses of the body, wherefore unless the senses themselves judge, they can conclude nothing; in a word, they are merely sensual, and by us they are called REASONERS. They are called reasoners, because they never conclude anything, but take up whatever they hear, and dispute whether it be so, with perpetual contradiction. They love nothing better than attacking Truths themselves, and thus tearing them to pieces by making them subjects of controversy. These are they who believe themselves learned above all in the world."

On hearing this account, I begged the angels to conduct me 2
to them: so they led me to a cave, from which a flight of steps led to the lower earth. We descended and followed the shout, "O HOW LEARNED!" and lo! there were some hundreds standing in one place, beating the ground with their feet. Being at first surprised at this, I asked why they stood in that manner and beat the ground with the soles of their feet, and said, "They may thus by their feet make holes in the ground."

At this the angels smiled and said, "They appear to stand in this manner, because they never think on any subject that it is so, but only whether it be so, and dispute about it; and when the thought proceeds no further than this, they appear only to tread and trample on a single clod, and not to advance."

I then approached the assembly, and lo! they appeared to me to be men with a face not unbecoming, and in handsome garments; but the angels said, "They appear such in their own light; but if light from heaven flows in, their faces are changed, and so are their garments"; and so it came to pass: they then appeared with dusky faces, and dressed in black sackcloth; but when this light was withdrawn, they appeared as before.

I presently spoke with some of them, and said, "I heard the shout of the crowd about you, '*O how learned!*' may I be allowed therefore to have a little discussion with you on subjects of the highest learning?"

* This Memorable Relation may also be found in the *True Christian Religion*, no. 333.

3 They replied, "Mention whatever you please, and we will give you satisfaction."

I then asked, "What must be the quality of the religion by which man is saved?"

They said, "We will divide this question into several; and we cannot give an answer to it until we have formed conclusions on its subdivisions. The first inquiry shall be, Whether religion be anything; the second, Whether there be such a thing as salvation or not; the third, Whether one religion be more efficacious than another; the fourth, Whether there be a heaven and a hell; the fifth, Whether there be eternal life after death; besides many more inquiries.

Then I asked about the first article,—Whether religion be anything. They began to discuss with abundance of arguments, whether there be any such thing as religion, and whether what is called religion be anything. I requested them to refer it to the assembly, and they did so; and the general answer was, that the proposition required so much investigation that it could not be finished within the evening.

I then asked, "Can you finish it within a year?"

And one of them said, "Not within a hundred years."

So I said, "In the meanwhile you are without religion."

He replied, "Shall it not be first demonstrated whether there be such a thing as religion, and whether what is called religion be anything? If there be such a thing, it must be also for the wise; if there be no such thing, it must be only for the common people. It is known that religion is called a bond: but it is asked, for whom? If it be only for the common people, it is not anything in itself; if it be for the wise also, it is something."

4 On hearing these arguments, I said to them, "There is no character you deserve less than that of being learned; because you can only think whether a thing be, and twist it towards both sides. Who can become learned, unless he know something for certain, and progresses into it, as a man progresses from step to step, and thereby successively progresses into wisdom? Otherwise, you do not so much as touch Truths with your finger-nail, but remove them more and more out of sight. Merely reasoning whether a thing be, is it not like arguing about a cap or a shoe, whether they fit or not, and omitting all the while to try them on? What must be the consequence of such reasoning, except that you will not know whether anything exist, yea, whether there be any such thing as salvation; whether there be any eternal life after death; whether one religion be more efficacious than another, and whether there be a heaven and a hell? On these subjects you cannot possibly think at all, so long as you halt at the first step, and beat the sand there, instead of setting one foot before another and going forward. Take heed to yourselves, lest your minds, thus standing outside

the sphere of judgment, should harden inwardly, and become statues of salt, and yourselves friends of Lot's wife."

Saying thus, I took my leave, and they in their indignation 5
threw stones after me; and then they appeared to me like graven images of stone, with nothing of human reason in them.

I asked the angels about their lot, and they said, "Their lot is, that they are let down into the deep, into a wilderness, where they are forced to carry burdens; and then, because they are no longer capable of uttering anything from reason, they give themselves up to idle chatter and talk, and appear at a distance like asses carrying burdens."

233. The third Memorable Relation.

* After this, one of the angels said, "Follow me to the place where they vociferate, 'O HOW WISE!' and he said, you shall see prodigies of men (*homines*); you shall see faces and bodies, which are the faces and bodies of a man, and yet they are not men."

I said, "Are they beasts then?"

He replied, "They are not beasts, but beast-men; for they are such as are utterly unable to see whether truth be truth or not, and yet are able to make whatever they will to be truth. Such persons among us are called CONFIRMERS."

We followed the vociferation, and came to the place; and lo! there was a company of men (*viri*), and around them a crowd, and in the crowd some of noble descent, who, on hearing that they confirmed whatever they said, and favoured themselves with such manifest consent, turned about, and said, "O HOW WISE!"

But the angel said to me, "Let us not go to them, but call 2
one out of the company." We called one out, and went aside with him, and spoke on various subjects; and he confirmed every one of them, so that they appeared altogether as true.

And we asked him, whether he could also confirm the contrary. He said, "As well as the former." Then he said openly, and from the heart, "What is truth? Is there anything true in the nature of things, except what a man makes true? Make any statement you please, and I will make it to be true."

So I said, "Make this true, That faith is the all of the church."

This he did so dexterously and skilfully, that the learned who were standing by admired and applauded him. I afterwards requested him to make it true, That charity is the all of the church; and he did so: and afterwards, That charity is nothing of the church: and he dressed up each side of the question, and adorned it so with appearances, that the bystanders looked at each other, and said, "Is not this a wise man?"

* This Memorable Relation may also be found in the *True Christian Religion*, no. 334.

But I said, "Do not you know that living well is charity, and that believing well is faith? Does not he who lives well also believe well? and consequently, does not faith belong to charity, and charity to faith? Do you not see that this is true?"

He replied, "I will make it true, and see." He did so, and said, "Now I see it;" but presently he made the contrary to be true, and then said, "I also see that this is true."

At this we smiled, and said, "Are they not contraries? how can two contraries appear true?"

To this he replied with indignation, "You err; each is true; since truth is nothing but what a man makes true."

3 There was standing near a certain person who in the world had been an ambassador of the first rank. He was surprised at this assertion, and said, "I acknowledge that in the world something like this method of reasoning prevails; but still you are out of your senses. Try if you can make it to be true, that light is darkness, and darkness light."

He replied, "I will easily do this. What are light and darkness but states of the eye? Is not light changed into shade when the eye comes out of sunshine, and also when it is kept intently fixed on the sun? Who does not know, that the state of the eye is then changed, and that in consequence light appears as shade; and on the other hand, when the state of the eye is restored, that shade appears as light? Does not an owl see the darkness of night as the light of day, and the light of day as the darkness of night, and also the sun itself as an opaque and dusky globe? If any man had the eyes of an owl, which would he call light, and which darkness? What then is light but a state of the eye? and if it be a state of the eye, is not light darkness, and darkness light? Wherefore each of the propositions is true."

4 Afterwards the ambassador asked him to make this true, That a raven is white and not black.

He replied, "I will do this also with ease;" and he said, "Take a needle or a razor, and lay open the feathers or quills of a raven; are they not white within? Also remove the feathers and quills, and look at the raven's skin; is it not white? What is the blackness then which envelopes it but a shade, which ought not to be made the basis of judgment respecting the raven's colour? That blackness is merely a shade, appeal to those who are skilled in the science of optics, and they will tell you; or do you pound a black stone or glass into fine powder, and you will see that the powder is white."

But the ambassador replied, "Does not the raven appear black to the sight?"

The confirmer answered, "Will you, who are a man, think at all from appearance? You may indeed say from appearance, that a raven is black, but you cannot think so; as for example, you may speak from the appearance and say that the sun rises, advances, and sets; but, as you are a man, you cannot think so, because the sun stands unmoved and the Earth changes its position. The case is the same with the raven; the appearance is an appearance; say what you will, a raven is altogether white: it also grows white as it grows old; this I have seen."

We next requested him to tell us from his heart, whether he 5
was joking, or whether he really believed that nothing is true but what a man makes true? and he replied, "I swear that I believe it."

Afterwards the ambassador asked him, whether he could make it true, that he was out of his senses.

And he said, "I can; but I will not: who is not out of his senses?"

After this, this universal confirmer was sent to the angels, to be examined as to his quality; and after examination they said that he did not possess even a grain of understanding; because all that is above the Rational was closed with him, and that alone which is below the Rational was open. Above the Rational is heavenly light, and below it is natural light; and this light is such that it can confirm whatever it pleases; but if heavenly light does not flow in into natural light, a man does not see whether anything true is true, and consequently neither does he see that anything false is false. Seeing in either case is by virtue of heavenly light in natural light; and heavenly light is from the God of heaven, Who is the Lord; wherefore this universal confirmer is neither a man nor a beast, but a beast-man.

I asked the angel about the lot of such persons, and whether 6
they can be together with the living, since every man has life from heavenly light, and from this light has understanding. He said, "that such persons, when they are alone, can neither think anything, and thence speak, but stand mute like machines, and as in a deep sleep; but that they awake as soon as any sound strikes their ears:" and he added, "that those become such, who are inmostly evil; into these heavenly light from above cannot flow in, but only something spiritual through the world, whence they have the faculty of confirming."

As he said this, I heard a voice from the angels who had 7
examined the confirmer, saying to me, "From what you have now heard make a general conclusion."

I made the following: "That being able to confirm whatever one pleases is not the characteristic of an intelligent man, but being able to see that what is true is true, and what is false is false, and to confirm the same,—that is the characteristic of an intelligent man."

After this I looked towards the company where the confirmers stood, and where the crowd about them shouted, "*O how wise!*" and lo! a dusky cloud covered them, and in the cloud screech-owls and bats were flying about; and it was told me,

"The screech-owls and bats flying about in the dusky cloud are correspondences and consequently appearances of their thoughts; because confirmations of falsities so complete as to make them appear like Truths, are represented in this world under the forms of birds of night, whose eyes are inwardly enlightened by a false light, by virtue of which they see objects in the dark as if in the light. There is such a false spiritual light with those who confirm falsities until they seem as truths, and afterwards are said and believed to be truths: all such are in a vision from below, and not in vision from above.

THE CAUSES OF COLDS, SEPARATIONS, AND DIVORCES, IN MARRIAGES.

234. Here, where the causes of colds in marriages are treated of, the causes of separations, and also of divorces are also treated of at the same time. The reason is, that they cohere; for separations are from no other source than from colds which successively arise after marriage, or from causes discovered after marriage, from which also cold results; but divorces result from adulteries, because these are directly opposite to marriages, and opposites induce cold, if not in both, at least in one. This is the reason why the causes of colds, separations, and divorces are brought together into one chapter. But the coherence of the causes will be more clearly discerned from their being seen in a series. Their series is as follows:

I. *There is spiritual heat and there is spiritual cold; and spiritual heat is love, and spiritual cold the deprivation thereof.*

II. *Spiritual cold in marriages is a disunion of the souls and a disjunction of the minds, whence come indifference, discord, contempt, loathing, and aversion; from which, with many, there at length ensues separation as to bed, bed-chamber, and house.*

III. *There are many causes of cold in their successions, some internal, some external, and some accidental.*

IV. *The internal causes of cold are from religion.*

V. *The first of these causes is, the rejection of religion by both of the married partners.*

VI. *The second is, that one of the married partners has religion, and the other has not.*

VII. *The third is, that one of the married partners has a different religion from the other.*

VIII. *The fourth is, imbibed falsity of religion.*

IX. *These are causes of internal cold, but, with many, not at the same time of external cold.*

X. *There are also many external causes of cold; and the first of them is, an unlikeness of dispositions and manners.*

XI. *The second is, that conjugial love is believed to be one with scortatory love, except that the latter is not allowed by law, but the former is.*

XII. *The third is, a striving for pre-eminence between the married partners.*

XIII. *The fourth is, a want of determination to some employment or occupation, whence comes wandering cupidity.*

XIV. *The fifth is, inequality of state and condition in externals.*

XV. *There are also some causes of separation.*

XVI. *The first of them is, a vitiated state of the mind.*

XVII. *The second is, a vitiated state of the body.*

XVIII. *The third is, impotence before marriage.*

XIX. *Adultery is the cause of divorce.*

XX. *There are also many accidental causes of cold; and the first of these is the commonness* [*of delight*] *which results from* [*its*] *being continually allowed.*

XXI. *The second is, that living with a married partner from covenant and law, seems to be compulsory and not free.*

XXII. *The third is, affirmation by the wife, and a talking about love by her.*

XXIII. *The fourth is, the man's thought by day and night, that his wife is willing; and on the other hand, the wife's thought that the man is not willing.*

XXIV. *In proportion as cold is in the mind, it is in the body also; and according to the increase of that cold, the externals of the body also are closed.*

Now follows the explanation of these articles.

235. I. THERE IS SPIRITUAL HEAT, AND THERE IS SPIRITUAL COLD; AND SPIRITUAL HEAT IS LOVE, AND SPIRITUAL COLD IS THE DEPRIVATION THEREOF. Spiritual heat is from no other source than the sun of the spiritual world; for there is in that world a sun proceeding from the Lord, Who is in the midst of it; and as that sun is from the Lord, it is in its essence pure love. This sun appears fiery before the angels, just as the sun of our world appears before men. The reason why it appears fiery is, that love is spiritual fire. From that sun proceed both heat and light; but as that sun is pure love, the heat thence issuing in its essence is love, and the light thence issuing in its essence is wisdom. Hence it is evident what is the source of spiritual heat, and that spiritual heat is love. But the source of spiritual cold shall also be briefly explained. It is from the sun of the natural world, and its heat and light. The sun of the natural world was created in order that its heat and light might receive into themselves spiritual heat and light, and, by means of the atmospheres, carry them down even to ultimates in the Earth, in order to produce the effects of the ends, which belong to the Lord in His own sun, and also to clothe spiritual things with suitable garments, that is, with materials, to operate ultimate ends in nature. These effects are produced when spiritual heat is joined to natural heat; but the contrary comes to pass when natural heat is separated from spiritual heat, as is the case with those who love natural things, and reject spiritual things: with these,

spiritual heat becomes cold. The reason why these two loves, which from creation are in agreement, become thus opposite, is, that in such a case the dominant heat becomes the servant, and contrariwise; and to prevent this happening, spiritual heat, which from its lineage is the lord, recedes; and in those subjects, spiritual heat then grows cold, because it becomes opposite. From these considerations it is evident that spiritual cold is the deprivation of spiritual heat. In what has here been said, by heat is meant love, because that heat living in subjects is felt as love. I have heard in the spiritual world, that merely natural spirits are chilled with intense cold when they apply themselves to the side of some angel who is in a state of love; and that it is the same with the spirits of hell, when heat flows in unto them out of heaven; and that nevertheless, among themselves, when the heat of heaven is removed from them, they burn with a great heat.

236. II. SPIRITUAL COLD IN MARRIAGES IS A DISUNION OF THE SOULS AND A DISJUNCTION OF THE MINDS; WHENCE COME INDIFFERENCE, DISCORD, CONTEMPT, LOATHING, AVERSION; FROM WHICH, WITH MANY THERE AT LENGTH ENSUES SEPARATION AS TO BED, BED-CHAMBER AND HOUSE. That these effects take place with married partners, while their primitive love is on the decline, and becoming cold, is too well known to need any comment. The reason is that conjugial cold in human minds resides above all other colds; for the conjugial principle itself is inscribed on the soul, to the end that a soul may be propagated from a soul, and the soul of the father into the offspring. Hence it is that this cold begins there, and successively passes thence into the following [parts], and infects them, and thus changes the gladnesses and delights of the primitive love into what is sad and undelightful.

237. III. THERE ARE MANY CAUSES OF COLD IN THEIR SUCCESSIONS, SOME INTERNAL, SOME EXTERNAL, AND SOME ACCIDENTAL. That there are many causes of colds in marriages, is known in the world; also that they arise from many external causes. But it is not known that the origins of the causes lie concealed in the inmosts, and that from these they are derived into the parts that follow in order, until they appear in externals. In order therefore that it may be known that external causes are not causes in themselves, but derivate from causes in themselves, which, as was said, are in the inmosts, therefore the causes shall first be generally distributed into internal and external causes, and afterwards shall be particularly examined.

238. IV. THE INTERNAL CAUSES OF COLD ARE FROM RELIGION. That the very origin of conjugial love resides with man in the

inmosts, that is, in his soul, every one is convinced from the following considerations alone:—that the soul of the offspring is from the father, and that this is known from the likeness of the inclinations and affections, and also from the general character of the countenance derived from the father and remaining even in very remote posterity; also from the propagative faculty implanted in souls by creation; and moreover by what is analogous thereto in the subjects of the vegetable kingdom, in that there lies hidden in the inmost things of germinations the propagation of the seed itself, and thence of the
2 whole, whether it be a tree, a shrub, or a plant. This propagative or plastic force in seeds in the vegetable kingdom, and in souls in the animal kingdom, is from no other source than the conjugial sphere, which is the sphere of good and truth, and which perpetually emanates and flows in from the Lord the Creator and Supporter of the universe (concerning which sphere, see above, nos. 222–225); and from the effort of those two, good and truth, therein [namely, in the seeds and in the souls], to become conjoined into a one. It is from this conjugial effort, which is inherent in souls, that conjugial love originally comes into existence. That that same marriage, from which the above universal sphere is derived, constitutes the church with man, has been abundantly shewn above, in the chapter on "The Marriage of Good and Truth," and frequently elsewhere. Hence it appears with every evidence before the reason, that the origin of the church, and the origin of conjugial love, are in the same seat, and that they are in a continual embrace. But on this subject see further particulars above, in no. 130, where it was proved, that conjugial love is according to the state of the church with man; thus that
3 it is from religion, because religion constitutes this state. Man also has been created with a capacity of becoming more and more interior, and thus of being introduced or elevated more and more nearly towards that marriage, and thus into truly conjugial love, and this even to the extent of perceiving the state of its blessedness. That religion is the only means of introduction and elevation, appears clearly from what was said above, namely, that the origin of the church and the origin of conjugial love are in the same seat, and in a mutual embrace there, and that therefore they cannot but be conjoined.

239. From what has now been said it follows, that where religion is not, there conjugial love does not exist; and that where conjugial love is not, there is cold. That conjugial cold is the deprivation of that love, see above, no. 235; consequently that conjugial cold is also the deprivation of the state of the church, or of religion. Sufficiently evident confirmation of the truth of this may be deduced from the general ignorance that prevails at the present day concerning truly conjugial love.

Who at the present day knows, and who is willing to acknowledge, and who will not be surprised to hear, that the origin of conjugial love is deduced thence? But the only cause and source of this ignorance is, that, notwithstanding there is religion, still there are not the truths of religion; and what is religion without truths? That there are no truths, has been fully shown in the *Apocalypse Revealed;* see also the Memorable Relation in no. 566 of that Work.

240. V. THE FIRST OF THE INTERNAL CAUSES OF COLD IS THE REJECTION OF RELIGION BY BOTH OF THE MARRIED PARTNERS. With those who reject the holy things of the church from the face to the back of the head, or from the breast to the back, there does not exist any good love; if any proceeds apparently from the body, still there does not exist any in the spirit. With such persons goods place themselves outside of evils, and cover them over as clothing glittering with gold covers a corrupt body. The evils which reside within and are covered over, are in general hatreds, and hence intestine combats against everything spiritual; for all the things of the church, which they reject, are in themselves spiritual; and, since truly conjugial love is the fundamental love of all spiritual loves, as was shewn above, it is evident that there is [with such persons] an intrinsic hatred against it, and that there is with them an intrinsic or personal love in favour of the opposite love, which is the love of adultery. Wherefore they, more than others, will ridicule this Truth, that every one has conjugial love according to the state of the church; yea, they will possibly laugh outright at the very mention of truly conjugial love. But be it so; nevertheless they must be excused, because it is as impossible for them to think otherwise of the embraces in marriages than as of those in whoredoms, as it is for a camel to thrust itself through the eye of a sewing-needle. Such persons, as to conjugial love, are chilled with cold more than others. If they cleave to their married partners, it is only on account of some of the external causes enumerated above, no. 153, which check and bind them. With these, the interiors of the soul and thence of the mind are more and more closed up, and in the body are stopped up; and then even the love of the sex becomes cheap, or is insanely lascivious in the interiors of the body, and thence in the lowest things of their thought. It is these also who are meant in the Memorable Relation, no. 79, which they may read if they please.

241. VI. THE SECOND OF THE INTERNAL CAUSES OF COLD IS, THAT ONE OF THE MARRIED PARTNERS HAS RELIGION, AND THE OTHER HAS NOT. The reason is, that their souls cannot help being in

discord, for the soul of one is open to the reception of conjugial love, while the soul of the other is closed against the reception of that love. It is closed with the one that has not religion, and it is open with the one that has. Hence it is not possible for two such married partners to dwell together; and when once conjugial love is banished, there ensues cold; but this is with the married partner that has no religion. This cold is not dissipated except through the reception of a religion agreeing with that of the other, if the latter is a true one. Otherwise, with the married partner who has no religion, there ensues cold, which descends from the soul into the body, even to the cuticles, in consequence of which, he (or she) finally cannot bear to look his (or her) married partner directly in the face, or accost her (or him) in a communion of respirations, or speak to her (or him) except in a distant tone of voice, or touch her (or him) with the hand, and scarcely with the back; not to mention the insanities which, proceeding from that cold, creep into the thoughts, which they do not make known; and this is the reason why such marriages are dissolved of themselves. Moreover, it is known, that an impious person thinks meanly of his married partner; and all who are without religion are impious.

242. VII. THE THIRD OF THE INTERNAL CAUSES OF COLD IS, THAT ONE OF THE MARRIED PARTNERS HAS A DIFFERENT RELIGION FROM THE OTHER. The reason is that with such persons good cannot be conjoined with its own corresponding truth; for, as was shewn above, the wife is the good of the husband's truth, and he is the truth of the wife's good. Hence out of two souls there cannot be made one soul; and hence the fountain of that love is closed, and when this is closed, a conjugial state is entered upon which has a lower place of abode, and which is that of good with another truth, or of truth with another good than its own, between which there does not exist any concordant love: hence with the married partner who is in falsities of religion, there commences a cold, which is intensified in proportion as he (or she) differs from the other. Once in a great city I was wandering through the streets seeking a place of abode, and I entered a house where there dwelled married partners of different religions. As I was ignorant of this fact, the angels spoke to me, and said, "We cannot remain with you in that house, because the married partners there are in discordant religions." This they perceived from the internal disunion of their souls.

243. VIII. THE FOURTH OF THE INTERNAL CAUSES [OF COLD] IS, IMBIBED FALSITY OF RELIGION. The reason is that falsity in spiritual things either takes away religion, or defiles it. It takes it away with those with whom genuine Truths are falsified.

It defiles it with those with whom there are indeed falsities, but not genuine Truths, which therefore could not be falsified. With these latter there may possibly exist goods with which those falsities may be conjoined by the Lord by means of applications; for these falsities are like various discordant tones, which by skilful arrangements and combinations are brought into harmony, whence also comes the pleasantness of harmony. With these some conjugial love is possible. But with those who have falsified with themselves the genuine truths of the church, conjugial love is not possible. The prevailing ignorance concerning truly conjugial love, or the negative doubt whether it can possibly exist, is from these falsified truths; and from the same source also comes the insanity which dwells in the minds of many, that adulteries are not evils of religion.

244. IX. THE ABOVE-NAMED CAUSES ARE CAUSES OF INTERNAL COLD, BUT, WITH MANY, NOT AT THE SAME TIME OF EXTERNAL COLD. If the causes thus far pointed out and confirmed, which are the causes of cold in the internals, were to produce a similar cold in the externals, as many separations would ensue as there are internal colds; and there are as many colds as there are marriages of those who are in falsities of religion, in different religions, and in no religion, which have already been treated of above. And yet it is known, that many such dwell together as if they were loves and mutual friendships; but whence this originates, with those who are in internal cold, will be stated in the following chapter, on "The Causes of apparent Love, Friendship, and Favour, between Married Partners." There are several causes which conjoin the dispositions (*animi*), but still do not conjoin the souls; among these are some of those mentioned above, no. 183; but still cold lies hidden inwardly, and makes itself noticed and felt every now and then. With such married partners the affections depart from each other; but the thoughts, when they go forth into speech and behaviour, approach each other for the sake of apparent friendship and favour; wherefore such persons know nothing of the pleasantness and delightsomeness, and still less of the blissfulness and blessedness of truly conjugial love, accounting them to be little else than fables. These are among those who deduce the origins of conjugial love from the same causes as did the nine companies of wise ones assembled from the several kingdoms of Europe; concerning whom see above in the Memorable Relation, nos. 103–114.

245. To what has been confirmed above, it may be objected, that the soul is nevertheless propagated from the father, although it is not conjoined with the soul of the mother, yea, although cold residing therein causes separation. But the reason why souls or offspring are nevertheless propagated is, that the under-

standing of the man (*vir*) is not closed, but is capable of being elevated into the light in which the soul is; but the love of his will is not elevated into the heat corresponding to the light there, except by the life, which from natural makes him spiritual. Hence it is, that the soul is nevertheless procreated, but, in the descent, when it becomes seed, it is veiled over by such things as belong to his natural love; from this springs hereditary evil. To these statements I will add an arcanum, which is from heaven, namely, that between the disjoined souls of two persons, especially of married partners, there is effected conjunction in a mediate love, and that otherwise no conceptions would be effected among human beings. Besides, what is here said of conjugial cold, and of its place of abode as being in the highest region of the mind, see the last Memorable Relation of this chapter, no. 270.

246. X. THERE ARE ALSO MANY EXTERNAL CAUSES OF COLD; AND THE FIRST OF THEM IS AN UNLIKENESS OF DISPOSITIONS AND MANNERS. There are both internal and external likenesses and unlikenesses. The internal ones derive their origin from no other source than religion; for religion is implanted in souls, and is handed down by the parents, through their souls, to the offspring, as the supreme inclination. For the soul of every human being derives life from the marriage of good and truth, and from this marriage is the church; and as the church is various and diverse in the several parts of the world, therefore also the souls of all human beings are various and diverse; wherefore internal likenesses and unlikenesses are from this source, and according to them
2 are the conjugial conjunctions which have been treated of. But external likenesses and unlikenesses are not of the souls (*animæ*) but of the dispositions (*animi*). By the dispositions are meant the external affections and the consequent external inclinations, which are insinuated after birth chiefly by means of the educations, associations, and the consequent habits; for it is usual to say, "I have a mind or disposition to do this or that," by which is meant an affection and inclination to it. Persuasions conceived respecting this or that kind of life are also wont to form those dispositions; thence come inclinations to enter into marriage even with unequals, and likewise to refuse marriage with equals; but still these marriages, after a certain time of living together, vary according to the likenesses and unlikenesses contracted by heredity and at the same time by education; and unlikenesses
3 give rise to cold. So likewise unlikenesses of manners; as for example, an uncultivated man or woman with a refined woman or man; a clean man or woman with an unclean woman or man; a quarrelsome man or woman with a peaceable woman or man; in a word, an ill-bred man or woman with a well-bred woman or man. Marriages of such unlikenesses are not unlike the conjunctions of diverse species of animals with

each other, as of sheep and goats, of stags and mules, of fowls and geese, of sparrows and the nobler birds, yea, as of dogs and cats, which on account of their unlikenesses do not consociate with each other: but in the human kind these unlikenesses are indicated not by faces, but by habits of life; wherefore external colds are from this source.

247. XI. THE SECOND OF THE EXTERNAL CAUSES OF COLD IS, THAT CONJUGIAL LOVE IS BELIEVED TO BE ONE WITH SCORTATORY LOVE, EXCEPT THAT THE LATTER IS NOT ALLOWED BY LAW, BUT THE FORMER IS. That this is a source of cold, is clearly seen by reason, when it considers that scortatory love is diametrically opposite to conjugial love; wherefore when it is believed that conjugial love is one with scortatory love, both loves become alike in idea; and then the wife is looked upon as a whore, and marriage as uncleanness; the man (*vir*) himself also is an adulterer, if not in body, still in spirit. That hence ensue contempt, disdain and aversion, between the man and his woman, and thereby intense cold, inevitably follows; for nothing stores up in itself conjugial cold more than scortatory love; and as scortatory love also passes into that cold, it may not undeservedly be called conjugial cold itself.

248. XII. THE THIRD OF THE EXTERNAL CAUSES OF COLD IS, A STRIVING FOR PRE-EMINENCE BETWEEN THE MARRIED PARTNERS. The reason is, that conjugial love has chiefly respect to an union of the wills, and a freedom of action resulting thence; both which are cast out from the marriage by a striving for pre-eminence or command; for this divides and tears the wills into pieces, and changes the freedom of action into servitude. While that striving lasts, the spirit of the one meditates violence against the other; if their minds were then to be laid open and viewed by spiritual sight, they would appear like antagonists fighting with daggers, and regarding each other with hatred and favour alternately; with hatred while in the vehemence of rivalry, and with favour while in the hope of dominion, and while in lust. After one has obtained the victory over the other, this contest departs from the externals, and betakes itself into the internals of the mind, and abides there with its restlessness concealed. Hence cold ensues both to the subdued party or servant, and to the victress or mistress. The reason why the latter also suffers cold is, that conjugial love no longer exists, and the deprivation of this love is cold; see no. 235. In the place of conjugial love she has heat from pre-eminence; but this heat is utterly discordant with conjugial heat, yet it can agree with it exteriorly by means of lust. After a tacit agreement between the parties, it appears as if conjugial love had become friendship; but the difference between conjugial and servile friendship in marriages,

is like that between light and shade, between a living fire and an *ignis fatuus*, yea, like that between a well-conditioned man and one consisting only of bone and skin.

249. XIII. THE FOURTH OF THE EXTERNAL CAUSES OF COLD IS, A WANT OF DETERMINATION TO SOME EMPLOYMENT OR OCCUPATION, WHENCE COMES WANDERING CUPIDITY. Man was created for use, because use is the continent of good and truth, from the marriage of which proceeds creation, and also conjugial love, as has been shewn in its own chapter. By employment and occupation is meant every application to uses. While therefore a man is in any employment and occupation, or in any use, his mind is then limited and circumscribed as in a circle, within which it is successively co-ordinated into a truly human form, from which as from a house he sees various concupiscences outside of himself, and by soundness of reason within exterminates them; consequently he also exterminates the wild insanities of scortatory lust. Hence it is that conjugial heat remains better and longer with such than with others. The reverse happens with those who give themselves up to sloth and idleness. The mind of these persons is unlimited and unbounded, and hence the man admits into the whole of it everything vain and nonsensical that flows in from the world and the body, and leads to the love thereof. That then also conjugial love is driven into exile, is evident; for in consequence of sloth and idleness the mind becomes stupid and the body torpid, and the whole man becomes insensible to every vital love, especially to conjugial love, from which as from a fountain issue the activities and alacrities of life. But conjugial cold with such is different from that cold with others; it is indeed the deprivation of conjugial love, but from defect.

250. XIV. THE FIFTH OF THE EXTERNAL CAUSES OF COLD IS, INEQUALITY OF STATE AND CONDITION IN EXTERNALS. There are many inequalities of state and condition, which during the time of dwelling together put an end to the conjugial love which had commenced before the wedding; but they may all be referred to inequalities as to age, dignities, and wealth. That unequal ages induce cold in marriage, as in the case of a lad with an old woman, and of a young maiden with a decrepit old man, needs no proof. That inequality as to dignities has a similar effect, as in the marriage of a prince with a maidservant, or of an illustrious matron with a manservant, is also acknowledged without proof. That the case is similar in regard to wealth, unless a likeness of dispositions and manners, and an application of the one to the inclinations and native desires of the other, consociate them, is evident. But in all such cases, the compliance of the one on account of the pre-eminence of the state and condition of the

other, effects only a servile conjunction; and this conjunction is a cold conjunction; for with such persons the conjugial state is not of the spirit and heart, but only nominal and of the mouth; in consequence of which the inferior party boasts, and the superior blushes with shame. But in the heavens there is no inequality of age, dignities, or wealth. As to age, all there are in the flower of their youth, and in that flower they continue to eternity: as to dignities, all there regard others according to the uses which they perform. The more eminent in condition regard the lower as brethren, neither do they set dignity before the performance of use, but the performance of use before dignity; also when maidens are given in marriage, they do not know from what ancestors they are descended: for no one in heaven knows his earthly father, but the Lord is the Father of all. The case is the same as to wealth, which in heaven consists in the faculty of becoming wise, according to which a sufficiency of wealth is given. How marriages are entered into in heaven, see above, no. 229.

251. XV. THERE ARE ALSO SOME CAUSES OF SEPARATIONS. There are separations from the bed, and separations from the house. There are several causes of separations from the bed, and likewise of separations from the house; but the legitimate causes are here being treated of. As the causes of separation coincide with the causes of concubinage, which are treated of in the latter part of this Work in their own chapter, therefore the reader is referred thereto, in order that he may see the causes in their order. The legitimate causes of separation are the following.

252. XVI. THE FIRST CAUSE OF LEGITIMATE SEPARATION IS A VITIATED STATE OF THE MIND. The reason is, that conjugial love is a conjunction of minds; wherefore if the mind of one goes away from that of the other into what is diverse, that conjunction is dissolved, and with this the love vanishes. What vitiated states separate may be manifest from an enumeration of them; they are therefore as to the greater part these:—unsoundness of mind (*mania*), frenzy (*phrenitis*), insanity (*vesania*), idiocy and imbecility (*actualis stultitia et fatuitas*), loss of memory, severe hysteria (*gravis morbus hystericus*); extreme simplicity (*extrema simplicitas*) so that there is no perception of what is good and true; a high degree of waywardness (*obnixitas*) which refuses to obey what is just and fair; an extraordinary pleasure in gossiping and talking only about insignificant and trivial matters; an unbridled desire to divulge the private matters of the house, also to wrangle, to strike, to revenge, to act wickedly, to steal, to tell lies, to deceive, to blaspheme; neglect of the children, intemperance, luxuriousness, excessive wastefulness, drunkenness, uncleanness, immodesty, engaging in magical practices and sorceries, godlessness, besides many more. By legitimate causes

are not here meant judicial causes, but such as are legitimate in regard to the other married partner: separations from the house are also seldom decreed by a judge.

253. XVII. THE SECOND CAUSE OF LEGITIMATE SEPARATION IS A VITIATED STATE OF THE BODY. By vitiated states of body are not meant accidental diseases, which happen to either of the married partners during their married life, and pass away again; but there are meant permanent or incurable diseases (*morbi inhaerentes*) which do not pass away. Pathology teaches what these are. They are manifold, such as, diseases by which the whole body becomes infected to such a degree that a fatal result ensues from contact with it; of this nature are malignant and pestilential fevers (*febres malignae et pestilentiales*), leprosies, syphilis, gangrenes, cancers, and other similar diseases. Further, diseases by which the body is rendered so loathsome (*ingravatum fit*) that there is no possibility of consociation, and in consequence of which hurtful effluvia and noxious exhalations are generated, either from the surface of the body, or from its inward parts, especially from the stomach and lungs. From the surface of the body there are malignant small-pox, warty growths, pustules, scurvy, virulent itch (*scabies virulenta*); especially if the face has been rendered loathsome (*defœdata est*) by them. From the stomach, risings of foul, stinking, rank, and undigested matters. From the lungs, fetid and putrid breath exhaled from tubercles, ulcers, abscesses, either from vitiated blood, or from vitiated lymph, therein. Besides these, there are also other diseases of various names, as, lipothymy (or fainting), which is an utter debility of the body and failing of strength; paralysis, which is a loosening and relaxation of the membranes and ligaments which serve for motion: certain chronic diseases, arising from a loss of the tensibility and elasticity of the nerves, or from too great a density, toughness, and acridity of the humours; epilepsy; permanent debility from attacks of apoplexy; various wasting diseases, whereby the body is consumed; the iliac passion, the cæliac affection, hernia, and other similar diseases.

254. XVIII. THE THIRD CAUSE OF LEGITIMATE SEPARATION IS IMPOTENCE BEFORE MARRIAGE. The reason why this is a cause of separation is, that the end of marriage is the procreation of offspring, and this cannot be effected by those who are impotent; and as they know this beforehand, they deliberately deprive their wives of the hope of it, which hope, nevertheless, suckles and strengthens their conjugial love.

255. XIX. ADULTERY IS THE CAUSE OF DIVORCE. There are several reasons for this, which are [discernible] in rational light, and yet are hidden at the present day. From rational light it may

be seen that marriages are holy and adulteries profane; and thus that marriages and adulteries are diametrically opposed to each other; and that when opposites act upon each other, the one destroys the other, even to the last spark of its life. This is the case with conjugial love, when a married man commits adultery from confirmation, and thus from set purpose. With those who know something about heaven and hell, these things come more into the clear light of reason; for they know that marriages are in heaven and from heaven, and that adulteries are in hell and from hell, and that the two cannot be conjoined, as heaven cannot be conjoined with hell, and that, if they are conjoined with man, heaven instantly recedes, and hell enters. Hence then it is, that adultery is the cause of divorce; wherefore the Lord saith, "*that whosoever shall put away his wife, except for whoredom, and shall marry another, committeth adultery*" (Matt. xix. 9). He saith, if he shall put away his wife, except for whoredom, and marry another, he committeth adultery; because putting away for this cause is a plenary separation of minds, which is called divorce; whereas, all other cases of putting away, by virtue of their causes, are separations, which have been treated of just above; after these, if another wife is married, adultery is committed; but not after divorce.

256. XX. THERE ARE ALSO MANY ACCIDENTAL CAUSES OF COLD; AND THE FIRST OF THEM IS THE COMMONNESS [OF ENJOYMENT] IN CONSEQUENCE OF ITS BEING CONSTANTLY ALLOWED. The reason why the commonness [of enjoyment] in consequence of its being constantly allowed is an accidental cause of cold is, that it exists with those who think lasciviously about marriage and on the subject of wives, but not with those who think holily about marriage, and tranquilly (*secure*) on the subject of wives. That by reason of the commonness which results from their being continually allowed, even joys become indifferent, and also tiresome, is evident from games and public shows, musical entertainments, dancing, feasting, and the like, which in themselves are agreeable, because they are vivifications. The case is the same with the intimacy and intercourse between married partners, especially between those who have not removed the unchaste love of the sex from the love which they bear to each other, and when they think idly, in the absence of the faculty [for enjoyment], of the commonness [of that enjoyment] arising from its being continually allowed. That that commonness is to such persons a cause of cold, is self-evident. It is called accidental, because it is added to inward cold as a cause, and agrees with it as a reason. To remove the cold arising from this [commonness], wives, from the prudence implanted in them, make what is allowable not allowable, by means of various resistances. But the case is altogether otherwise with those who judge chastely of wives; wherefore

with the angels the commonness [of delight] which results from its being continually allowed, is the very delight of the soul, and is the container of their conjugial love, for they are continually in the delight of that love, and in its ultimates according to the presence of their minds [in that love] uninterrupted by cares, thus according to the decisions of the judgment with the husbands.

257. XXI. THE SECOND OF THE ACCIDENTAL CAUSES OF COLD IS, THAT LIVING WITH A MARRIED PARTNER, FROM COVENANT AND LAW, SEEMS TO BE COMPULSORY AND NOT FREE. This cause exists only with those with whom conjugial love is cold in the inmosts; and since it adds itself to internal cold, it becomes an accessory or accidental cause. With these persons, extra-conjugial love, by reason of its consent and favour, is inwardly in heat; for the cold of the one is the heat of the other, which [heat], if it is not felt, is nevertheless within, yea, in the midst of the cold; and unless it was then also within, there would be no recuperation. This heat is what constitutes the compulsion, which is increased in proportion as, by one of the parties, the covenant resulting from agreement and the law by virtue of its justice, are looked upon as bonds not to be violated; it is otherwise if those bonds are loosened by both. The case is reversed with those who hold extra-conjugial love accursed, and think of conjugial love as of what is heavenly and as heaven; and the more so if they perceive it to be so. With these, that covenant with its articles of agreement, and that law with its obligations, are inscribed on their hearts, and are continually being inscribed thereon more and more. With these, the bond of that love is neither woven by a covenant that has been agreed upon, nor by a law that has been enacted; but both the covenant and the law are by virtue of creation implanted in the love itself in which they are; from the latter [namely, the covenant and the law implanted from creation in the love itself] are derived the former [namely, the covenant and law] in the world, but not contrariwise. Hence it is that everything that belongs to that love is felt as freedom; neither is there any freedom but what belongs to the love: and I have heard from the angels, that the freedom of truly conjugial love is the utmost freedom, because conjugial love is the love of loves.

258. XXII. THE THIRD OF THE ACCIDENTAL CAUSES OF COLD IS, AFFIRMATION BY THE WIFE, AND A TALKING ABOUT LOVE BY HER. With the angels in heaven there is no refusal and resistance on the part of the wives, as there is with some wives on earth: with the angels in heaven also there is a talking by the wives about love, and not such a silence as there is with some wives on earth. But the causes of these diversities I am not allowed

to make known, because it is not becoming for me to do so; nevertheless they may be seen in four Memorable Relations at the close of the chapters as made known by the angels' wives, who freely divulge them to their husbands,—by the three in the palace over which there was seen a golden shower [nos. 155, 208], and by the seven who were sitting in a garden of roses [nos. 293, 294]. These Memorable Relations were adduced, to the end that everything may be disclosed that belongs to conjugial love, which is the subject here treated of both in general and in particular.

259. XXIII. THE FOURTH OF THE ACCIDENTAL CAUSES OF COLD IS, THE MAN'S THOUGHT BY DAY AND NIGHT THAT HIS WIFE IS WILLING, AND ON THE OTHER HAND, THE WIFE'S THOUGHT THAT THE MAN IS NOT WILLING. That the latter circumstance is a cause of the cessation of love with wives, and the former a cause of cold with men, is passed by without comment. For that the man, if he thinks that his wife, when she is in his sight by day, and when at his side by night, desires or is willing, should grow cold to the extremities; and on the other hand that the wife, if she thinks that the man is able and not willing, should lose her love, are among the facts which are well known to husbands who have studied the arcana relating to conjugial love. These circumstances are adduced also, to the end that this Work may be perfected, and that the delights of wisdom relating to conjugial love may be completed.

260. XXIV. IN PROPORTION AS COLD IS IN THE MIND, IT IS IN THE BODY ALSO; AND ACCORDING TO THE INCREASE OF THAT COLD, THE EXTERNALS OF THE BODY ALSO ARE CLOSED. It is believed at the present day that the mind of man is in the head, and nothing of it in the body, when yet both the soul and the mind are both in the head and in the body; for the soul and the mind are the man, since both constitute the spirit which lives after death; and that this spirit is in a perfect human form, has been fully shewn in our treatises. Hence it is that, as soon as a man thinks anything, he can in an instant utter it by means of the mouth of his body, and at the same time effigy it in gesture; and that, as soon as he wills anything, he can in an instant bring it into act and effect by means of the members of the body; which could not be the case unless the soul and the mind were together in the body, and constituted his spiritual man. Since this is so, it may be seen, that while conjugial love is in the mind, it is similar to itself in the body: and since love is heat, that it opens the externals of the body from the interiors: but that, on the other hand, the privation thereof, which is cold, closes up the externals of the body from the interiors. From this appears manifestly the cause why the faculty with

the angels continues to eternity, and the cause why it fails with men who are in a state of cold.

261. To the above I shall add three Memorable Relations. The first is this:—

* In the higher northern quarter near the east in the spiritual world, there are places of instruction for boys, for youths, for men, and also for old men. Into these places are sent all who die infants, and they are educated in heaven: so also are all who are newly come from the world, and desire Knowledges about heaven and hell. This tract is near the east, in order that all may be instructed through influx from the Lord: for the Lord is the east, because He is in the sun there, which from Him is pure love; hence the heat from that sun in its essence is love, and the light from it in its essence is wisdom. These are inspired into them by the Lord out of that sun; and they are inspired according to reception, and reception is according to the love of becoming wise. After the times of instruction, those who have become intelligent are sent forth thence, and are called disciples of the Lord. They are sent forth thence first into the west, and those who do not remain there, into the south; and some through the south into the east; and they are introduced into the societies where their abodes are to be.

2 Once when I was meditating about heaven and hell, I began to desire a universal Knowledge of the state of both; being aware, that whoever knows universals, can afterwards comprehend particulars, because the latter are in the former, as parts in a whole. In this desire I looked to that tract in the northern quarter near the east, where the places of instruction were, and I went there by a way then open to me. I entered one of the colleges, where there were some young men, and addressed the head masters there who gave instruction, and asked them, whether they knew the universals about heaven and hell.

3 They replied, that they knew some little; "but if we look," said they, "towards the east to the Lord, we shall be enlightened and we shall know." They did so, and said, "There are three universals of hell, but they are diametrically opposite to the universals of heaven. The universals of hell are these three loves,—the love of dominion from the love of self, the love of possessing the goods of others from the love of the world, and scortatory love. The universals of heaven opposite to these are these three loves,—the love of dominion from the love of use, the love of possessing the goods of the world from the love of doing uses by means of them, and truly conjugial love.

When they had said this, after wishing [me] peace, I took

* This Memorable Relation is repeated in the *True Christian Religion*, no. 661.

my leave, and returned home. When I was at home, it was said to me from heaven, "Examine those three universals above and beneath, and afterwards we shall see them in thy hand." It was said "in the hand," because everything which a man examines with the understanding, appears to the angels as if inscribed on his hands.

262. After this I examined the first universal love of hell, which was the love of exercising dominion, or of ruling, from the love of self, and afterwards the universal love of heaven corresponding to it, which was the love of exercising dominion from the love of uses; for I was not allowed to examine the one love without the other, because the understanding does not perceive the one love without the other, for they are opposites; wherefore in order that each may be perceived, they must be set in opposition, the one against the other; for a beautiful and handsome face is made apparent as such by contrasting with it an ugly and deformed one. While I was considering the love of exercising dominion from the love of self, it was given me to perceive that this love was in the highest degree infernal, and consequently prevailed with those who are in the deepest hell; and that the love of exercising dominion from the love of uses was in the highest degree heavenly, and consequently prevailed with those who are in the highest heaven. The reason why the 2
love of exercising dominion from the love of self is in the highest degree infernal, is, that exercising dominion from the love of self is exercising it from the proprium, and the proprium of man from birth is evil itself, and evil itself is diametrically opposed to the Lord; wherefore the more those who are evil advance into that evil, the more they deny God and the holy things of the church, and worship themselves and nature. Let those who are in that evil, I entreat them, examine that evil in themselves, and they will see. This love also is such that, in proportion as it is left unchecked, which is the case so long as it is not hindered by impossibilities, in the same proportion it rushes impetuously from step to step, even to the highest, and even there finds no bounds, but sorrows and sighs because there is no higher step for it to ascend. This love with statesmen ascends so high that 3
they want to be kings and emperors, and, if it were possible, to have dominion over all things of the world, and to be called kings of kings and emperors of emperors; and the same love with the clergy ascends so high that they want to be gods, and, as far as is possible, to have dominion over all things of heaven, and to be called gods of gods. That neither of these in heart acknowledge any God, will be seen in what follows. On the other hand, those who desire to exercise dominion from the love of uses, do not desire to exercise dominion from themselves, but from the Lord; since the love of uses is from the Lord, and is the Lord Himself.

These regard dignities no otherwise than as means to perform uses: the latter they set far above dignities; but the former set dignities far above uses.

263. While I was meditating on these things, it was said to me through an angel by the Lord, "You shall presently see, and be convinced by ocular demonstration, what is the quality of that infernal love."

Then suddenly the earth opened on the left, and I saw a devil ascending from hell, having on his head a square cap pulled down over the forehead even to the eyes: his face was full of pustules as of a burning fever, his eyes fierce, his breast swollen immensely; from his mouth he belched smoke like a furnace, his loins were all ablaze, instead of feet he had bony ankles without flesh, and from his body there exhaled a stinking and unclean heat.

2 On seeing him I was terrified, and cried out to him, "Approach no nearer; tell me, whence are you?"

He replied in a hoarse voice, "I am from hell (*ex inferis*), where I am with two hundred in a society which is the most super-eminent of all societies. We in that society are all emperors of emperors, kings of kings, dukes of dukes, and princes of princes; no one in our society is barely an emperor, nor barely a king, duke, or prince. We sit there on thrones of thrones, and despatch thence mandates into the whole world, and beyond it."

I then said to him, "Do you not see that you are insane from the phantasy of super-eminence?"

He replied, "How can you say so, when we absolutely seem to ourselves, and also are acknowledged by our companions, to have such super-eminence?"

On hearing this, I was unwilling to repeat the charge of insanity, because he was insane from phantasy; and it was given me to know that this devil, during his life in the world, had been only a house-steward, and that at that time he was so lifted up in spirit, that he despised all mankind in comparison with himself, and indulged in the phantasy that he was more worthy than a king, and even than an emperor; in consequence of which conceit, he had denied God, and had considered all the holy things of the church as of no concern to himself, but of some to the stupid multitude.

3 At last I asked him, "How long do you two hundred thus glory among yourselves?"

He said, "To eternity; but such of us as torture others for denying our super-eminence, sink down; for we are allowed to glory, but not to do evil to any one."

I asked him again, "Do you know what is the lot of those who sink down?" He said, "They sink down into a certain prison, where they are called viler than the vile, or the vilest; and they work."

I then said to that devil, "Take heed therefore, lest you also sink down."

264. After this the earth again opened, but on the right; and I saw another devil rising up thence, who had on his head a kind of turban, which was wound round spirally like a snake, the head of which stood out from the crown: his face was leprous from the forehead to the chin, and so were both his hands; his loins were naked and black as soot, through which fire as of a furnace shone duskily; and the ankles of his feet were like two vipers.

The former devil, on seeing him, cast himself on his knees, and adored him.

I asked why he did so, and he said, "He is the God of heaven and earth, and is omnipotent."

I then asked the other, "What do you say to this?"

He replied, "What shall I say? I have all Power over heaven and hell; the lot of all souls is in my hand."

Again I enquired, "How can he, who is emperor of emperors, so submit himself, and how can you receive his adoration?"

He answered, "He is nevertheless my servant; what is an emperor before God? the thunder of excommunication is in my right hand."

I then said to him, "How can you be so insane? In the 2
world you were simply a clergyman; and because you laboured under the phantasy that you also had the keys [of heaven], and thus the power of binding and loosening, you have exalted your spirit to such a degree of madness, that you now believe that you are God Himself."

Being indignant at this, he swore that it was so, and said, "The Lord has not any Power in heaven, because He has transferred it all to us. We have only to give the word of command, and heaven and hell reverently obey us. If we send any one to hell, the devils immediately receive him; and so do the angels receive those whom we send to heaven."

I asked further, "How many are you in your society?"

He said, "Three hundred; and we are all gods there; but I am the god of gods."

After this the earth opened under the feet of each, and they 3
sank down deeply into their respective hells; and it was given me to see that under their hells were penitentiaries, into which those who do harm to others would fall; for every one in hell is left to his own phantasy, and is also permitted to glory in it; but he is not allowed to do harm to another. The reason why such are there is, that man is then in his spirit; and the spirit, after it has been separated from the body, comes into the full

liberty of acting according to its own affections and consequent thoughts.

4 It was afterwards given me to look into their hells. The hell where the emperors of emperors and kings of kings were, was full of all uncleanness; and they appeared like various kinds of wild beasts, with fierce eyes. So also it was in the other hell, where the gods and the god of gods were. In this latter hell there appeared the direful birds of night, which are called ochim and ijim, flying about them. The images of their phantasies appeared thus to me. From these circumstances it was evidenced, what is the quality of the political love of self, and what is the quality of the ecclesiastical love of self;—that the quality of the latter is, that they who are in it want to be gods, while the quality of the former is, that they who are in it want to be emperors; and that they cherish such desires, and also strive to gratify them, in proportion as full scope is allowed to those loves.

265. Afterwards a hell was opened, where I saw two men, one sitting on a bench, holding his feet in a basket full of serpents, which seemed to be creeping upwards by his breast even to his neck; and the other sitting on a glowing or red-hot ass, at whose sides red serpents were creeping, raising their heads and necks, and pursuing the rider. I was told that they had been popes who had deprived emperors of their dominion, and had ill-treated them both in word and deed at Rome, whither they went to supplicate and adore them; that the basket in which serpents were seen, and the glowing ass with snakes at his sides, were representations of their love of exercising dominion from the love of self, and that such appearances are seen only by those who look at them from a distance. There were some of the ecclesiastical order present, whom I asked whether those had really been popes? They said, that they were acquainted with them, and knew that they had been such.

266. After beholding these sad and frightful sights, I looked around, and saw two angels standing in conversation not far from me. One wore a woollen robe that shone with flaming crimson, and under it a vest of bright fine linen; the other wore similar garments of scarlet, with a tiara studded on the right side with a few fiery stones. I approached them, and greeted them with a salutation of peace, and respectfully asked them, "For what purpose are you here below?"

They replied, "We have come down from heaven by the Lord's command, to speak with you about the blessed lot of those who desire to have dominion from the love of uses. We are worshippers of the Lord; I am the prince of a society; the other is the high priest there."

2 The prince said, that he was the servant of his society, because

he served it by doing uses: and the other said, that he was the minister of the church there, because in serving them he ministered holy things to the uses of their souls; and that they were both in perpetual joys resulting from the eternal happiness which is in them from the Lord; and that all things in that society were splendid and magnificent; splendid by reason of gold and precious stones, and magnificent by reason of palaces and paradises. "The reason is, that our love of exercising dominion is not from the love of self, but from the love of uses: and as the love of uses is from the Lord, therefore all good uses in the heavens are splendid and refulgent: and as all of us in our society are in this love, therefore the atmosphere there appears golden, by reason of the light there which partakes of the sun's flaming quality, and the flaming quality of the sun corresponds to that love."

As they said this, there appeared to me to be such a sphere 3
around them, from which an aromatic odour issued that was perceivable by the senses. I mentioned this to them, and intreated them to add something more to what they had said about the love of use; and they proceeded thus: "The dignities in which we are, we indeed sought after and solicited, but for no other end than that we might be able to perform uses more fully, and to extend them more widely. We are also encompassed with honour, and we accept it, not for our own sake, but for the sake of the good of the society. For our brethren and associates, who form the commonalty of the society, scarcely know but that the honours of our dignities are in ourselves, and consequently that the uses which we perform are from ourselves. But we ourselves feel otherwise, being sensible that the honours of the dignities are outside of ourselves, and that they are as the garments with which we are clothed; but that the uses which we perform, are, by virtue of the love of them, within us from the Lord: and this love receives its blessedness from communication by means of uses with others; and we know from experience, that so far as we do uses from the love thereof, so far that love increases, and with it wisdom, whereby communication is effected: but that, so far as we retain uses in ourselves, and do not communicate them, so far the blessedness perishes; and in that case use becomes like food stored up in the stomach, which affords no nourishment to the body and its parts, as it would if it were distributed through them, but remains undigested, and thereby causes nausea. In a word, the whole heaven is nothing but a container of use, from primes to ultimates. What is use but the actual love of the neighbour? and what holds the heavens together but this love?"

On hearing this I asked, "How can any one know whether 4
he does uses from the love of self, or from the love of uses? Every man, both good and evil, does uses, and he does uses from

some love. Suppose that in the world there were a society composed of mere devils, and another composed of mere angels; I am of opinion that the devils in their society, from the fire of the love of self, and the splendour of their own glory, would do as many uses as the angels in their society. Who then can know from what love, and from what origin the uses are?"

5 To this the two angels replied, "Devils do uses for the sake of themselves and for the sake of reputation, that they may be raised to honours or may gain wealth; but angels do not do uses from such motives, but for the sake of uses from the love thereof. Man cannot distinguish those uses; but the Lord distinguishes them. Every one who believes in the Lord, and shuns evils as sins, does uses from the Lord: but every one who neither believes in the Lord, nor shuns evils as sins, does uses from himself and for the sake of himself. This is the difference between the uses done by devils and those done by angels."

Having said this, the two angels departed; and were seen from afar carried in a fiery chariot like Elijah, and taken up into their own heaven.

267. The Second Memorable Relation:—

* After a little space of time I entered a certain grove, and walked there meditating on those who are in the concupiscence and thence in the phantasy of possessing the things of the world; and then at some distance from me I saw two angels in conversation, and by turns looking at me; wherefore I went nearer to them, and as I approached they accosted me, and said, "We have perceived in ourselves that you are meditating on what we are conversing about, or that we are conversing about what you are meditating on, which is a consequence of the reciprocal communication of affections."

I asked therefore what they were conversing about? they said, "About phantasy, concupiscence, and intelligence; and just now about those who delight themselves with the vision and imagination of possessing everything in the world."

2 I then asked them to state their opinions on those three subjects—concupiscence, phantasy, and intelligence.

They began by saying, "Every one is inwardly in concupiscence by birth, but outwardly in intelligence by education; and that no one is inwardly, and thus as to the spirit, in intelligence, still less in wisdom, except from the Lord: for everyone is withheld from the concupiscence of evil, and kept in intelligence, according to his looking towards the Lord, and at the same time according to his conjunction with Him. Without this, man is nothing but concupiscence; yet nevertheless in externals, or as to the body, he is in intelligence from education. For man

* This Memorable Relation, as far as the end of no. 268, is repeated in the *True Christian Religion*, no. 662.

lusts after honours and wealth, or eminence and riches, and he cannot attain them, unless he appears to be moral and spiritual, thus intelligent and wise; and he learns so to appear from infancy. This is the reason why, as soon as he comes among men, or into company, he inverts his spirit, and removes it from concupiscence, and speaks and acts from the becoming and honourable maxims which he has learnt from infancy, and retains in the memory of the body: and he is particularly cautious lest anything of the madness of the concupiscence in which his
spirit is, should come forth. Hence every man who is not 3
inwardly led by the Lord, is a pretender, a sycophant, a hypocrite, and thus an apparent man, and yet not a man; of whom it may be said, that his shell or body is wise, and his kernel or spirit insane; also that his external is human and his internal like a wild beast. Such persons, with the back part of the head look upwards, and with the forehead downwards; thus they walk as if oppressed with heaviness, with the head hanging down and the countenance prone to the earth; and when they put off the body, and become spirits, and thus are set at liberty, they become the madnesses of their own concupiscences. For they who are in the love of self desire to domineer over the universe, yea, to extend its limits in order to enlarge their dominion, of which they see no end. Those who are in the love of the world desire to possess everything therein, and are full of grief and envy if any of its treasures are hidden and concealed with others: wherefore, to prevent such persons from becoming mere concupiscences, and thus not men, it is given them in the spiritual world to think from the fear of the loss of reputation, and thereby of honour and gain, and also from a fear of the law and its penalties, and it is also given them to apply their mind to some employment or work, whereby they are kept in externals and thus in a state of intelligence, however raving and insane they may be inwardly."

After this I asked, whether all who are in concupiscence, are 4
also in the phantasy thereof.

They replied, that "those are in the phantasy of their own concupiscence, who think inwardly in themselves, and indulge their imagination too much, by talking to themselves; for these almost separate their spirit from connection with the body, and inundate their understanding with visions, and take a foolish delight as if they were possessed of the universe: into this delirium every man is let after death who has abstracted his spirit from the body, and has not been willing to recede from the delight of the delirium by thinking something from religion about evils and falsities, and least of all something about the unbridled love of self, as being destructive of love to the Lord, and about the unbridled love of the world, as being destructive of love towards the neighbour."

268. After this the two angels and myself also were seized with a desire to see those who from the love of the world are in the visionary concupiscence or phantasy of possessing all wealth; and we perceived that that desire was inspired to the end that such visionaries might be known. Their dwellings were under the earth of our feet, but above hell: wherefore we looked at each other and said, "Let us go." There was seen an opening, and in it a ladder, by which we descended; and we were told that we must approach them from the east, lest we should enter into the mist of their phantasy, and be obscured as to the understanding and at the same time as to the sight.

2 And lo! there appeared a house built of reeds, and consequently full of chinks, standing in a mist, which continually issued like smoke through the chinks of three of the walls. We entered, and saw fifty here and fifty there sitting on benches; they were turned away from the east and south, and were looking towards the west and north. Before each person there was a table, on which were purses filled full, and by the purses a great quantity of gold coin.

We asked them, "Is that the wealth of all the persons in the world?"

They said, "Not of all in the world, but of all in the kingdom." The sound of their speech was hissing; and they appeared to have round faces, which glistened like the shell of a snail, and the pupils of their eyes shot forth lightning as it were, from a green ground, which was an effect of the light of phantasy.

We stood in the midst of them, and said, "You believe that you possess all the wealth of the kingdom."

They replied, "We do possess it."

We then asked, "Which of you?"

They said, "Every one."

So we asked, "How every one? you are many."

They said, "Every one of us knows that all that is his, is also mine. No one is allowed to think, and still less to say, 'Mine are not thine;' but every one may think and say, 'Thine are mine.'"

The coins on the tables appeared, even to us, to be pure gold; but when we let in light from the east, they were little grains of gold, which they had magnified to such a degree by their common united phantasy. They said, that every one that enters ought to bring with him some gold, which they cut into small pieces, and these into little grains, and by the unanimous force of their phantasy they increase them into coins of a larger form.

3 We then said, "Were you not born men of reason? whence have you that visionary infatuation?"

They said, "We know that it is an imaginary vanity; but as it delights the interiors of our minds, we enter here and are delighted as with the possession of all things: we continue in this place, however, only a few hours, at the end of which we depart; and as often as we do so we again become of sound mind; yet still our visionary delight alternately supervenes, and occasions our alternate re-entrance and departure: thus we are alternately wise and insane. We also know that a hard lot awaits those who by cunning rob others of their goods."

We inquired, "What lot?"

They said, "They are swallowed up, and are thrust naked into some infernal prison, where they are obliged to labour for clothing and food, and afterwards for some pieces of coin of trifling value, which they collect, and in which they place the joy of their hearts; but if they do evil to their companions, they are fined a part of their coin."

269. *Afterwards we ascended from these hells to the south where we had been before, and the angels related there many things worthy of mention concerning the concupiscence which is not visionary or fantastic, in which every man is from his birth; namely, that while they are in it, they are like fools, and yet seem to themselves to be wise in the highest degree; and that from this folly they are by turns restored into the Rational, which, with them, is in externals; in which state they see, acknowledge, and confess their insanity, but nevertheless they are very desirous to get out of their rational state into their insane state; and they also do let themselves into it, as from a forced and undelightful state into a free and delightful one; thus it is concupiscence and not intelligence that inwardly pleases them.
There are three universal loves, of which every man has been 2
constituted since the creation; the love of the neighbour, which is also the love of doing uses; the love of the world, which is also the love of possessing wealth; and the love of self, which is also the love of bearing rule over others. The love of the neighbour, or the love of doing uses, is a spiritual love; but the love of the world, or the love of possessing wealth, is a material love; whereas the love of self, or the love of bearing rule over others,
is a corporeal love. A man is a man when the love of the 3
neighbour, or the love of doing uses, constitutes the head, the love of the world the body, and the love of self the feet; whereas if the love of the world constitutes the head, the man is but as a hunch-back; but when the love of self constitutes the head, he is like a man standing, not on his feet, but on the palms of his hands with his head downwards and his haunches upwards. When the love of the neighbour constitutes the head, and the two other loves in order constitute the body and feet, the man appears from heaven of an angelic countenance, with a beautiful rainbow around his head; but if the love of the world constitutes

* The contents of this paragraph are repeated, with slight variations, in the *True Christian Religion*, no. 507.

the head, he appears from heaven of a pale countenance like that of a dead man, with a yellow circle around his head; but if the love of self constitutes the head, he appears from heaven of a dusky countenance, with a white circle around his head."

Hereupon I asked, "What do the circles around the head represent?"

They replied, "They represent intelligence; the white circle around the head of the dusky countenance represents that his intelligence is in externals, or around him, and that insanity is in his internals, or in him. A man also who is such, is wise while in the body, but insane while in the spirit; and no man is wise in the spirit but from the Lord, as is the case when he is regenerated and created again or anew by Him."

4 As they said this, the earth opened to the left, and through the opening I saw a devil rising up with a lucid white circle around his head, and I asked him, "Who art thou?"

He said, "I am Lucifer, the son of the morning: and because I made myself like the Most High, I was cast down." Nevertheless, he was not Lucifer, but believed himself to be him.

I then said, "Since you were cast down, how can you rise up again out of hell?"

He replied, "There I am a devil, but here I am an angel of light: do you not see that my head is surrounded by a lucid sphere? you shall also see, if you wish, that I am superlatively moral among the moral, superlatively rational among the rational, yea, superlatively spiritual among the spiritual: I am also able to preach, and I have also preached."

I asked him, "What have you preached?"

He said, "Against defrauders, against adulterers, and against all infernal loves; yea, I have then called myself, even Lucifer, a devil, and forsworn against myself in that capacity; and therefore I was extolled to heaven with praises. Hence it is that I am called the son of the morning; and, what I myself was surprised at, while I was in the pulpit, I thought no otherwise than that I was speaking rightly and properly; but I discovered that the reason was, that I was in externals, which at that time were separated from my internals; but although I discovered this, still I could not change myself, because on account of my conceit I did not look to God."

5 I next asked him, "How could you so speak, when you are yourself a defrauder, an adulterer, and a devil?"

He answered, "I am one character when I am in externals or in the body, and another when in internals or in the spirit; in the body I am an angel, but in the spirit a devil; for in the body I am in the understanding, but in the spirit I am in the will; and the understanding carries me upwards, whereas the will carries me downwards. When I am in the understanding, my head is surrounded by a white belt, but when the understanding surrenders itself entirely to the will, and becomes its slave, which is our last lot, the belt grows black and perishes; and when this happens, we cannot any longer ascend into this light." Afterwards he spoke about his twofold state, the external and the internal, more rationally than any other person; but suddenly, when he saw the angels with me, his face and voice were inflamed, and he became black, even as to the belt around his head, and he sunk down into hell through the opening through which he had arisen.

The bystanders, from seeing these things, came to this conclusion, that a man is such as his love is, and not such as his understanding is; since the love easily draws over the understanding to its side, and enslaves it.

I then asked the angels, "Whence have devils such 6
rationality?"

They said, "It is from the glory of the love of self; for the love of self is surrounded by glory, and glory elevates the understanding even into the light of heaven. For with every man the understanding is capable of being elevated according to Knowledges, but the will can be thus elevated only by a life according to the truths of the church and of reason. Hence it is that even atheists, who are in the glory of reputation from the love of self, and thence in the conceit of self-intelligence, enjoy a more lofty rationality than many others. This, however, is only when they are in the thought of the understanding, but not when they are in the affection of the will. The affection of the will possesses a man's internal, whereas the thought of the understanding possesses his external." The angel further told the reason why every man is constituted of the three loves above mentioned, namely, the love of use, the love of the world, and the love of self; which reason is, in order that he may think from God, although as from himself. He also said, that the highest things in man are turned upwards to God, the middle outwards to the world, and the lowest downwards to self; and because the latter are turned downwards, man thinks as from himself, when nevertheless he thinks from God.

270. The Third Memorable Relation :—

One morning on awaking from sleep my thought was deeply engaged on some arcana of conjugial love, and at length on this, "*In what region of the human mind does truly conjugial love reside, and consequently in what region does conjugial cold reside?*" I knew that there are three regions of the human mind, one above the other, and that in the lowest region dwells natural love; in the higher, spiritual love; and in the highest, celestial love; and that in each region there is a marriage of good and truth; and since good belongs to love, and truth belongs to wisdom, that in each region there is a marriage of love and wisdom, and that this marriage is the same as the marriage of the will and the understanding, since the will is the receptacle of love, and the understanding the receptacle of wisdom.

2 While I was thus deeply engaged in thought, lo! I saw two swans flying towards the north, and then two birds of paradise flying towards the south, and also two turtledoves flying in the east: as I followed their flight with my eyes, I saw that the two swans bent their course from the north to the east, and so did the two birds of paradise from the south, and that they gathered together with the two turtledoves in the east, and flew together to a certain lofty palace there, about which there were olive-trees, palm-trees, and beeches. The palace had three rows of windows, one above the other; and as I was looking on, I saw the swans fly into the palace through open windows in the lowest row, the birds of paradise through open windows in the middle row, and the turtledoves through open windows in the highest row.

3 When I had observed this, an angel stood by me, and said, "Do you understand what you have seen?"

I replied, "In a small degree."

He said, "That palace represents the habitations of conjugial love, such as they are in human minds. Its highest part, into which the turtledoves betook themselves, represents the highest region of the mind, where conjugial love dwells in the love of good with its wisdom; the middle part, into which the birds of paradise betook themselves, represents the middle region, where conjugial love dwells in the love of truth with its intelligence; and the lowest part, into which the swans betook themselves, represents the lowest region of the mind, where conjugial love dwells in the love of what is just and right with its knowledge.

4 The three pairs of birds also signify these things; the pair of turtledoves signifies the conjugial love of the highest region, the pair of birds of paradise the conjugial love of the middle region, and the pair of swans the conjugial love of the lowest region. Similar things are signified by the three kinds of trees round about the palace, the olive-trees, the palm-trees, and the beeches. We in heaven call the highest region of the mind celestial, the middle spiritual, and the lowest natural; and we perceive them as stories in a house, one above another, and an ascent from one to the other by steps as by stairs; and in each part as it were two chambers, one for love, the other for wisdom, and in front as it were a bed-chamber, where love with its own wisdom, or good with its own truth, or, what is the same thing, the will with its own understanding, consociate in bed. In that palace there exist as in effigy all the arcana of conjugial love."

5 On hearing this, being inflamed with a desire of seeing it, I asked whether any one was permitted to enter and see it, as it was a representative palace?

He replied, "None but those who are in the third heaven, because to them every representative of love and wisdom becomes real: from them I have heard what I have related to you, and also this particular, that truly conjugial love dwells in the highest region in the midst of mutual love, in the bride-chamber or apartment of the will, and also in the midst of the perceptions of wisdom in the bridal-chamber or apartment of the understanding, and that they consociate in bed in the bed-chamber which is in front, and in the east."

I also asked, "Why are there two bride-chambers?"

He said, "The husband is in the bride-chamber of the understanding, and the wife in the bride-chamber of the will."

I then asked, "Since conjugial love dwells there, where does 6
conjugial cold dwell?"

He replied, "It dwells also in the highest region, but only in the bride-chamber of the understanding, the bride-chamber of the will being closed there: for the understanding with its truths, can, as often as it pleases, ascend by a winding staircase into the highest region into its bride-chamber; but if the will with the good of its love does not ascend at the same time into the consociate bride-chamber, the latter is closed, and cold ensues in the other, and this is *conjugial cold.* The understanding, while such cold prevails towards the wife, looks downwards out of the highest region to the lowest region, and also, if not prevented by fear, descends to warm itself there at an illicit fire." Having said this, he was about to recount further particulars respecting conjugial love from its effigies in that palace; but he said, "Enough for this time; inquire first whether these things are above the common understanding; if they are, what would be the use of saying more? but if they are not, more will be disclosed."

THE CAUSES OF APPARENT LOVE, FRIENDSHIP AND FAVOUR IN MARRIAGES.

271. Since the causes of colds and separations have been treated of, it follows in order that the causes of apparent love, friendship and favour in marriages, should also be treated of; for it is known, that although colds separate the dispositions (*animi*) of married partners at the present day, they nevertheless dwell together, and procreate children; which would not be the case, unless there were also apparent loves, alternately similar to or emulous of the heat of genuine love. That these appearances are necessary and useful, and that without them households could not exist, and consequently neither could societies, will be seen in what follows. Moreover, some conscientious persons may be distressed with the idea, that the disagreements of minds between them and their married partners, and the internal alienations thence arising, may be their own fault, and may be imputed to them, and on this account may be grieved at heart; but as it is not in their power to help internal disagreements, it is enough for them, by means of apparent loves and favours, to allay, in accordance with conscience, the disagreeables which may arise: hence, also, friendship is able to return, in which conjugial love lies concealed on the part of such a one, although not on the part of the other. But this section, like the foregoing, by reason of the number of the varieties of its subject, shall be distinguished into articles. These articles are the folowing:—

I. *In the natural world almost all are capable of being conjoined as to the external affections, but not as to the internal affections, if these disagree and appear.*

II. *In the spiritual world all are conjoined according to the internal affections, but not according to the external affections, unless these act as a one with the internal affections.*

III. *It is the external affections according to which matrimonies are generally contracted in the world.*

IV. *But if the internal affections, which conjoin the minds, are not within, the bonds of matrimony are loosened at home.*

V. *Nevertheless matrimonies in the world ought to continue till the end of life.*

VI. *In those matrimonies in which the internal affections do not conjoin, there are external affections which simulate the internal ones, and consociate.*

VII. *Hence there are apparent love, or apparent friendship, and favour between married partners.*

VIII. *These appearances are conjugial simulations, and they are praiseworthy, because useful and necessary.*

IX. *These conjugial simulations, with a spiritual man* (homo) *conjoined with a consort who is natural, derive their quality from justice and judgment.*

X. *These conjugial simulations with natural men derive their quality from prudence for the sake of various reasons.*

XI. *They are for the sake of amendments, and for the sake of accommodations.*

XII. *They are for the sake of preserving order in domestic affairs, and for the sake of mutual help.*

XIII. *They are for the sake of unanimity in the care of the younger and older children.*

XIV. *They are for the sake of peace at home.*

XV. *They are for the sake of reputation outside of the home.*

XVI. *They are for the sake of various favours expected from the married partner, or from his or her relations, and thus for fear of losing such favours.*

XVII. *They are for the sake of excusing blemishes, and consequently for the sake of avoiding disgrace.*

XVIII. *They are for the sake of reconciliations.*

XIX. *If favour does not cease with the wife, when faculty ceases with the man, there may be formed a friendship emulating conjugial friendship, when the consorts grow old.*

XX. *There exist various kinds of apparent love and friendship between married partners, of whom one has been brought under the yoke, and consequently is subject to the other.*

XXI. *In the world there exist infernal marriages between married partners who inwardly are the most inveterate enemies, and outwardly are as the most attached friends.*

Now follows the explanation of these articles.

272. I. In the natural world almost all are capable of being conjoined as to the external affections, but not as to the internal affections, if these disagree and appear. The reason is, that in the world man is possessed of a material body, and this is surcharged with lusts, which are in it as dregs that are precipitated to the bottom, when the must of the wine is clarified. Of such things consist the matters of which the bodies of men in the world are composed. Hence it is that the internal affections, which are of the mind, do not appear; and with many hardly a grain of them shows through; for the body either absorbs them, and involves them in its dregs, or by dissimulation learnt from childhood conceals them deeply from the sight of others; and by this means the man puts himself into the state of every affection that he observes in another, and

allures his affection to himself, and thus they conjoin themselves. The reason why they conjoin themselves is, that every affection has its own delight, and delights tie minds (*animi*) together. But it would be otherwise if the internal affections were to appear before the sight in the face and gesture, and before the hearing in the tone of the speech, as the external affections do; or if their delights were to be made sensible to the nostrils, or to be smelt, as is the case in the spiritual world. In that case, if they disagreed so much as to be discordant, they would separate minds (*animi*) from each other, and according to the perception of antipathy, they would remove to a distance. From these considerations it is evident, that in the natural world, almost all are capable of being conjoined as to the external affections, but not as to the internal affections, if these disagree and appear.

273. II. IN THE SPIRITUAL WORLD ALL ARE CONJOINED ACCORDING TO THE INTERNAL AFFECTIONS, BUT NOT ACCORDING TO THE EXTERNAL AFFECTIONS, UNLESS THESE ACT AS A ONE WITH THE INTERNAL AFFECTIONS. The reason is, that then the material body, which was able to receive and give expression to the forms of all affections, as has been said just above, is cast away, and when man is stripped of that body, he is in his internal affections, which his body had before concealed. Hence it is, that in the spiritual world similarities and dissimilarities, or sympathies and antipathies, are not only felt, but also appear in the face, speech, and gestures; wherefore in that world likenesses are conjoined, and unlikenesses separated. This is the reason why the universal heaven is arranged by the Lord according to all the varieties of the affections of the love of good and truth, and conversely, hell is arranged according to all the varieties
2 of the affections of the love of evil and falsity. Since angels and spirits have internal and external affections, just like men in the world, and since the internal affections cannot, in the spiritual world, be concealed by the external ones, they show through and manifest themselves: hence with angels and spirits both the internal and external affections are reduced into likeness and correspondence; after which their internal affections are effigied in their faces through their external ones, are perceived in the tone of their voice, and also appear in their behaviour and manners. Angels and spirits have internal and external affections, because they have minds and bodies; and affections with the thoughts thence derived belong to the mind, and sensations with the plea-
3 sures thence derived belong to the body. It frequently happens in the world of spirits, that friends meet after death, and recollect their friendships in the former world, and they then believe that they will consociate in a life of friendship as before; but when that consociation, which is of the external affections only,

is perceived in heaven, a separation takes place according to the internal affections; and then some are removed from the place of their meeting into the north, some into the west, and each to such a distance from the other, that they neither see nor know each other any more; for in the places where they tarry, their faces are changed so as to become the effigies of their internal affections. From these considerations it is evident, that in the spiritual world all are conjoined according to the internal affections, and not according to the external ones, unless these act in unity with the internal affections.

274. III. IT IS THE EXTERNAL AFFECTIONS ACCORDING TO WHICH MATRIMONIES ARE GENERALLY CONTRACTED IN THE WORLD. The reason is, that the internal affections are rarely consulted, and even if they are consulted, still the likeness of them is not seen in the woman; for she, by virtue of a native gift, withdraws the internal affections into the inner recesses of her mind. There are many external affections that lead men *(viri)* to contract matrimony. The first affection of this age is the increase of the personal estate by wealth, both for the sake of becoming rich and that there may be a sufficient supply [of necessaries]; the second is a thirst for honours, either for the sake of being held in high estimation, or for the sake of an increase of fortune: besides these, there are various allurements and concupiscences. These leave no room to explore the agreements of the internal affections. From these few considerations it is evident, that matrimonies are generally contracted in the world according to the external affections.

275. IV. BUT IF THE INTERNAL AFFECTIONS, WHICH CONJOIN THE MINDS, ARE NOT WITHIN, THE BONDS OF MATRIMONY ARE LOOSENED AT HOME. It is said at home, because it is done privately between the two consorts; as is the case when the first heats, kindled at the time of betrothal, and blazing up as the wedding approaches, successively cool down afterwards on account of the disagreement of the internal affections, and at length pass off into colds. It is known, that the external affections, which had led on and allured the parties to matrimony, then disappear, so that they no longer conjoin. That colds arise from various causes, internal, external, and accidental, which all derive their source from an unlikeness of the internal inclinations, was proved in the foregoing chapter. From these considerations the Truth is evident, that unless the internal affections, which conjoin minds, are in the external ones, the bonds of matrimony are loosened at home.

276. V. NEVERTHELESS MATRIMONIES IN THE WORLD OUGHT TO CONTINUE TILL THE END OF LIFE. This is adduced in order that

there may be more evidently presented before the reason the necessity, usefulness, and Truth, that conjugial love, where it is not genuine, ought still to be assumed, so that it may appear as if it were. The case would be otherwise if marriages entered into were not contracted for the term of life, but were dissolvable at will, as they were among the Israelitish nation, which arrogated to itself the liberty of putting away wives for any cause whatsoever, as is evident from these words in Matthew: "*The Pharisees came, and said unto Jesus, Is it lawful for a man* (homo) *to put away his wife for every cause? And when Jesus answered, that it is not lawful to put away a wife and marry another, except on account of whoredom, they replied, that nevertheless Moses commanded to give her a bill of repudiation, and to put her away; and the disciples said, If the case of a man* (homo) *with his wife be*
2 *so, it is not expedient to contract matrimony*" (xix. 3–10). Since, therefore, the covenant of marriage is a covenant for life, it follows that the appearances of love and friendship between married partners are necessities. That matrimony, once contracted, must continue even to the end of life in the world, is in accordance with the Divine law, and because it is in accordance with this, it is also in accordance with rational law, and therefore with civil law. It is in accordance with the Divine law, in that, as said above, it is not allowable to put away a wife and marry another, except on account of whoredom; with rational law, because this is founded upon spiritual law, for Divine law and rational law are one law; from both these together, or through the latter from the former, may be seen what a great number of enormities and destructions of societies would result from the dissolutions of marriages, or the putting away of wives at the good pleasure of the husbands, before death. Those enormities and destructions of societies may be seen in some abundance in the Memorable Relation about the origin of conjugial love discussed by those who were assembled from the nine kingdoms, (nos. 103–115); to which there is no need to add further reasons. But these causes do not stand in the way of separations being permitted on account of their own causes, respecting which see above, nos. 252–254; nor in the way of concubinage also being permitted, respecting which see the Second Part of this Work.

277. VI. In those matrimonies in which the internal affections do not conjoin, there are external affections which simulate the internal ones, and consociate. By the internal affections are meant the mutual inclinations which are in the mind of each from heaven; and by the external affections are meant the inclinations which are in the mind of each from the world. The latter affections or inclinations do indeed equally belong to the mind, but they occupy its lower region, while the former occupy its higher one: but since both have their allotted

seat in the mind, it may possibly be believed that they are alike and that they agree together; yet although they are not alike, still they can appear as if they were alike: with some persons they exist as agreements, and with some as courteous simulations. There is a certain communion [between married partners] which is implanted in both from the first covenant of marriage, which, notwithstanding their disagreement in dispositions, still remains implanted; as, a communion of possessions, and in many cases a communion of uses, and of the various necessities of the house, and hence also a communion of thoughts and of certain secrets; there is also a communion of bed, and a communion of the love of children: besides many others, which, because they are inscribed on the conjugial covenant, are also inscribed on their minds. From these [communions] originate especially those external affections which resemble the internal; whereas those which only simulate them are partly from the same origin and partly from another; but both are treated of in what follows.

278. VII. HENCE THERE ARE APPARENT LOVE, APPARENT FRIENDSHIP, AND FAVOUR BETWEEN MARRIED PARTNERS. Apparent loves, friendships, and favours between married partners, are a consequence of the conjugial covenant being made for the term of life, and of the conjugial communion thence inscribed on the covenanters; which communion gives birth to external affections resembling the internal ones, as was just now pointed out. They are moreover a consequence of causes which are usefulnesses and necessities: from which in part exist conjunctive external affections, or counterfeit affections, whereby external love appears like internal love, and external friendship appears as internal friendship.

279. VIII. THESE APPEARANCES ARE CONJUGIAL SIMULATIONS; AND THEY ARE PRAISEWORTHY, BECAUSE USEFUL AND NECESSARY. They are called simulations, because they exist between those who disagree in minds, and who by reason of those disagreements are interiorly in cold: when they nevertheless live harmoniously in externals, as duty and decency require, their mutual kindnesses of married life may be called simulations, but conjugial ones, which, because they are praiseworthy for the sake of uses, are altogether distinguished from hypocritical simulations, for by means of them all those good things are provided for, which are enumerated in order below, from Article XI. to XX. They are praiseworthy for the sake of necessities, because otherwise those good things would be banished; and yet the parties are enjoined by covenant and law to live together, and therefore the fact that they have to live together abides in each of them as a duty.

280. IX. THESE CONJUGIAL SIMULATIONS, WITH A SPIRITUAL MAN (*homo*) CONJOINED WITH A CONSORT WHO IS NATURAL, DERIVE THEIR QUALITY FROM JUSTICE AND JUDGMENT. The reason is, that the spiritual man, in all he does, acts from justice and judgment: wherefore he does not regard these simulations as alienated from their internal affections, but as coupled with them; for he acts seriously, and regards amendment as the end; and if he does not obtain this, he regards accommodation, for the sake of domestic order, mutual aid, the care of the children, and peace and tranquillity. To these things he is led by justice; and from judgment he gives them effect. The reason why a spiritual man so lives with one who is natural is, that a spiritual man acts spiritually, even with one who is natural.

281. X. THESE CONJUGIAL SIMULATIONS WITH NATURAL MEN DERIVE THEIR QUALITY FROM PRUDENCE, FOR THE SAKE OF VARIOUS REASONS. Between two married partners, of whom one is spiritual and the other natural; (—by the spiritual is meant the one who loves spiritual things, and thus is wise from the Lord, and by the natural is meant the one who loves only natural things, and thus is wise from himself)—when they are consociated in marriage, conjugial love with the spiritual married partner is heat, and with the natural one is cold. It is evident that heat and cold cannot be together, and that heat cannot kindle the one who is in cold, unless the cold be first dispelled, and that cold cannot flow in into the one who is in heat, unless the heat be first removed. Hence it is that internal love cannot exist between married partners, one of whom is spiritual and the other natural; but that a love emulating internal love may exist on the part of the spiritual married partner, as was said in the foregoing article. But between two natural married partners no internal love can exist, because both are cold; and if they have any heat, it is from what is unchaste; nevertheless such persons may still dwell together in the same house, with separated dispositions, and also assume looks as of love and friendship towards each other, notwithstanding the disagreement of their minds. With these persons, the external affections, which are for the most part of wealth and possessions, or of honour and dignities, may as it were burn; and as that burning or ardour induces fear for their loss, therefore conjugial simulations are for them necessities, which are chiefly those which are adduced below in Articles XV. to XVII. The rest of the causes enumerated with these may have something in common with the causes with the spiritual man (concerning which, see above, no. 280); but only in case the prudence with the natural man derives its quality from intelligence.

282. XI. THEY ARE FOR THE SAKE OF AMENDMENTS, AND FOR

THE SAKE OF ACCOMMODATIONS. The reason why conjugial simulations, which are appearances of love and friendship between married partners who disagree in minds (*animi*) are for the sake of amendment, is, that a spiritual man, connected by the matrimonial covenant with one who is natural, intends nothing else than amendment of life; which on his (or her) part is brought about by wise and judicious conversations, and by favours shewn to the other, which soothe and please his or her genius; but in case these things prove ineffectual, he or she intends accommodations, for the preservation of order in domestic affairs, for the sake of mutual aid, and for the sake of the younger and older children, and other similar things; for, as was shewn above, no. 280, whatever is said and done by a spiritual man derives its quality from justice and judgment. But with married partners, neither of whom is spiritual, but both natural, similar conduct may exist, but for other ends; if for the sake of amendment and accommodation, the end is, either that the other party may be reduced to a likeness with his (or her) own manners, and be subordinated to his (or her) desires, or in order that some things done by the other may be made of use in the production of those done by himself or herself, or for the sake of peace within the house, of reputation out of it, or for the sake of favours hoped for from the other married partner or his or her relations; not to mention other ends: but with some these ends are from the prudence of their reason, with some from native civility, with some from the delights of cupidities which have been familiar from birth, of which the loss is dreaded; besides many ends, which render the assumed favours as of conjugial love more or less counterfeit. There may also be favours as of conjugial love outside of the house, and none within; these however respect as an end the reputation of both parties; and if they do not respect this, they are empty.

283. XII. THEY ARE FOR THE SAKE OF PRESERVING ORDER IN DOMESTIC AFFAIRS, AND FOR THE SAKE OF MUTUAL HELP. Every household in which there are children, their instructors, and other domestics, is a small society resembling a large one. The latter also consists of the former, as a whole consists of its parts; and further, as the safety of a large society depends on order, so does the safety of this small society; wherefore as it is of importance that those in authority should see and provide that order exist and be preserved in a compound society, so it is of importance that married partners should do likewise in their single society. But this order is not possible if the husband and wife disagree in dispositions; for thereby mutual counsels and helps are drawn different ways, and are divided like their dispositions, and thus the form of the small society is rent asunder. Wherefore, to preserve order, and thereby to take care of them-

selves and at the same time of the household, or of the household and at the same time of themselves, lest they should come to hurt and fall to ruin, necessity requires that the master and mistress should agree and make a one; and if, on account of the difference of their minds, this cannot be done so well as it might, both duty and propriety require that it be done by means of representative conjugial friendship. That thereby concord is established in households for the sake of necessities and consequent usefulnesses, is a known thing.

284. XIII. THEY ARE FOR THE SAKE OF UNANIMITY IN THE CARE OF THE YOUNGER AND OLDER CHILDREN. It is very well known that conjugial simulations, which are appearances of love and friendship resembling truly conjugial love and friendship, exist among married partners for the sake of the infants and children. The common love of infants and children causes each married partner to regard the other with kindness and favour. The love of infants and children with the mother and the father become conjoined as the heart and lungs in the breast. The love of them with the mother is as the heart there, and the love towards them with the father is as the lungs there. The reason of this comparison is, that the heart corresponds to love, and the lungs to the understanding; and love from the will is with the mother, and love from the understanding is with the father. With spiritual men there is conjugial conjunction by means of that love from justice and judgment; from justice, because the mother had carried them in her womb, had brought them forth with pain, and afterwards with unwearied care suckles, nourishes washes, dresses, and educates them.

285. XIV. THEY ARE FOR THE SAKE OF PEACE AT HOME. Conjugial simulations, or external friendships for the sake of peace and tranquillity at home, relate principally to the men, on account of their natural characteristic, which is, to act from the understanding in whatever they do; and the understanding, being the thinking faculty, ponders over a variety of things which disquiet, distract, and disturb the lower mind; wherefore, if there were not tranquillity at home, it would come to pass that the vital spirits of the men would grow faint, and their interior life would as it were expire, and thereby their health of both mind and body would be destroyed. The fear of these and several other dangers would possess the minds of the men, unless they had an asylum with their wives at home for appeasing the disturbances of their understandings. Moreover, peace and tranquillity give serenity to their minds, and dispose them to receive gratefully the kindnesses offered them by their wives, who spare no pains to disperse the mental clouds which they are very quick-sighted to observe in their husbands; and the same peace

and tranquillity make the presence of their wives agreeable. Hence it is evident, that a simulation as of truly conjugial love, for the sake of peace and tranquillity at home, is both a necessity and useful. Add to this, that with the wives simulations are not as with the men; but if they appear to resemble them, they are the effect of real love, because wives are born loves of the understanding of men; wherefore they accept kindly the favours of their husbands, and if not in words, at least with the heart.

286. XV. THEY ARE FOR THE SAKE OF REPUTATION OUTSIDE OF THE HOME. The fortunes of men in general depend on their reputation for justice, sincerity, and uprightness; and this reputation also depends on the wife, who is acquainted with her husband's private life; wherefore, if the disagreements of their minds should break out into open enmities, quarrels, and threats of hatred, and these should be noised abroad by the wife and her friends, and by the domestics, they would easily be turned into tales of scandal, which would bring disgrace and infamy upon the husband's name. To avoid such mischiefs, he has no other alternative than either to simulate affection for his wife, or that they be separated as to the house.

287. XVI. THEY ARE FOR THE SAKE OF VARIOUS FAVOURS EXPECTED FROM THE MARRIED PARTNER, OR FROM HIS OR HER RELATIONS, AND THUS FOR FEAR OF LOSING SUCH FAVOURS. This is the case more especially in marriages of dissimilar state and condition, concerning which see above, no. 250; as when a man marries a wealthy wife who stores up her money in purses, or her treasures in coffers; and the more so if she boldly insists that the husband is bound in duty to support the household out of his own property and income: that hence come forced likenesses as of conjugial love, is generally known. The case is similar where a man marries a wife, whose parents, relations, and friends are in offices of dignity, in lucrative business concerns and manufactures, who have it in their power to better her condition: that simulations of love, as it were conjugial, are also for the sake of these things, is generally known. It is evident that in both cases it is the fear of the loss of those things that is operative.

288. XVII. THEY ARE FOR THE SAKE OF EXCUSING BLEMISHES, AND CONSEQUENTLY FOR THE SAKE OF AVOIDING DISGRACE. There are many blemishes or faults on account of which conjugial partners fear disgrace; some are serious, and some not. There are blemishes of the mind, and blemishes of the body, slighter than those enumerated in the foregoing chapter, nos. 252 and 253, which are causes of separation; wherefore those blemishes are

here meant, which, to avoid disgrace, are buried in silence by the other married partner. Besides these, with some there are incriminatory actions, which, if made public, are subject to penalties of the law; not to mention a defect of that abundance of which the men are accustomed to boast. That excuses of such blemishes, in order to avoid disgrace, are causes of the simulation of love and friendship with a married partner, is evident without further confirmation.

289. XVIII. THEY ARE FOR THE SAKE OF RECONCILIATIONS. That between married partners who disagree in minds from various causes, there are alternate disagreements and confidences, estrangements and conjunctions, yea, quarrels and adjustments of differences, thus reconciliations; and also that apparent friendships promote reconciliation, is known in the world. There are also reconciliations which take place after separations, which are not so alternate and transitory.

290. XIX. IF FAVOUR DOES NOT CEASE WITH THE WIFE, WHEN FACULTY CEASES WITH THE MAN, THERE MAY BE FORMED A FRIENDSHIP EMULATING CONJUGIAL FRIENDSHIP WHEN THE CONSORTS GROW OLD. The primary cause of the separation of dispositions between married partners is a failing of favour on the wife's part in consequence of the cessation of faculty with the husband, and hence a failing of love; for just as heats communicate with each other, so also do colds. That in consequence of a failing of love with both, friendship ceases, and also favour, if not prevented by the fear of domestic ruin, is manifest from reason and experience. If, therefore, the man tacitly imputes the causes to himself, and the wife nevertheless perseveres in chaste favour towards him, there may result thence a friendship which, since it is between married partners, appears like love emulating conjugial love. That a friendship resembling the friendship of that love may exist between aged married partners, is proved by experience, which shows how quietly, harmlessly, lovingly, and courteously they live together, and commune and associate with one another.

291. XX. THERE EXIST VARIOUS KINDS OF APPARENT LOVE AND FRIENDSHIP BETWEEN MARRIED PARTNERS, OF WHOM ONE HAS BEEN BROUGHT UNDER THE YOKE, AND CONSEQUENTLY IS SUBJECT TO THE OTHER. It is well known in the world at the present day, that after the first times of marriage have passed away, there arises rivalry between the married partners respecting right and Power; respecting right, in that according to the statutes of the covenant entered into, there is equality, and each has dignity in the offices of his or her function; and respecting Power, in that it is insisted on by the men, that in

all things at home superiority belongs to them, because they
are men, and inferiority to the women, because they are women.
Such rivalries which are so common at the present day, flow
from no other source than a want of conscience respecting truly
conjugial love, and a want of sensible perception respecting the
blessednesses of that love: in consequence of the absence of
this conscience and perception, lust takes the place of that love,
and counterfeits it. From this lust, when genuine love is
removed, there flows a striving for Power, which is in some
from the delight of the love of domineering; in some it has been
implanted by artful women before marriage; and to some it is
unknown. The men who are in this striving, and after the 2
alternations of the strife obtain the command, reduce their
wives either to become their rightful possession, or to comply
with their arbitrary will, or into slavery, each one according to
the degree and qualified state of that striving implanted and
concealed in himself. But if the wives are in this striving, and
after the alternations of the strife obtain the command, they
reduce their husbands either to an equality of right with themselves, or into compliance with their arbitrary will, or into
slavery: but since, when the wives have obtained the sceptre
of sway, there remains with them a desire which counterfeits
conjugial love, and is restrained by the law and by the fear of
legitimate separation, in case they extend their power beyond
what is lawful into what is unlawful, therefore they lead a
life in consociation with their husbands. But what is the quality 3
of the love and friendship between a ruling wife and an enslaved
husband, and also what is its quality between a ruling husband
and an enslaved wife, cannot be briefly described; yea, if their
differences were to be specifically pointed out and enumerated,
they would fill many pages; for they are various and diverse;—
various according to the nature of the striving for power with
the men, and in like manner with the wives; and diverse with
the men from what they are with the women; for such men
are in no friendship of love except an infatuated friendship, and
such wives are in the friendship of spurious love, from lust. But
by what arts wives procure to themselves Power over the men,
will be stated in the article now following.

292. XXI. IN THE WORLD THERE EXIST INFERNAL MARRIAGES BETWEEN MARRIED PARTNERS WHO INWARDLY ARE THE MOST INVETERATE ENEMIES, AND OUTWARDLY ARE AS THE MOST ATTACHED FRIENDS. I am indeed forbidden by the wives of such a sort, who are in the spiritual world, to present such marriages to public view; for they are afraid lest their art of obtaining Power over their husbands should at the same time be divulged, which yet they are exceedingly desirous should be concealed. But as I am urged by the men in that world to expose the

causes of the intestine hatred and as it were fury excited in their hearts against their wives, in consequence of their clandestine arts, I shall at least adduce the following particulars. The men said, that unwittingly they contracted a terrible fear of their wives, in consequence of which they could not do otherwise than obey their decisions most submissively, and be at their beck more than the lowest menials, so that they became like men of nought; and that this was the case not only with men of low estate, but also with men who were high in office and dignity, yea with brave and famous generals. They also said, that after they had contracted this dread, they did not dare to speak otherwise to their wives than in a friendly manner, nor to do otherwise than was agreeable to them, although they cherished in their hearts a deadly hatred against them; and further, that their wives still behaved courteously to them both in word and deed, and willingly hearkened to
2 some of their requests. Now, as the men themselves greatly wondered whence such an antipathy could arise in their internals, and such an apparent sympathy in their externals, they examined into the causes thereof from some women (*fœminæ*) to whom that secret art was known; and they said that from the mouth of these women they learned, that women (*mulieres*) store up deeply in themselves a knowledge by which they have the skill, if they are disposed, to subject the men to the yoke of their authority; and that this is effected, in the case of uncultured wives by alternate quarrels and kindnesses, with others by constantly harsh and unpleasant looks, and sometimes by other means; but in the case of educated wives, by urgent and unceasing petitions, and by obstinate resistance to their husbands in case they suffer hardships from them, insisting on their right of equality by law, in consequence of which they boldly persist in their obstinacy; yea, insisting that if they were to be turned out of the house, they would return at their pleasure, and harass them as before; for they know that the men, from their nature, are unable to resist the obstinacy of their wives, and that after giving way they submit themselves to their bidding; and that then the wives make a show of kindnesses and caresses to their husbands subjected to their sway. The genuine cause of the domination of wives by means of this cunning is, that a man acts from the understanding and a woman from the will, and that the will can make itself obstinate, but not so the understanding. I have been told, that the worst of this sort of women, who are wholly consumed by the desire for dominion, can stick tenaciously to their obstina-
3 cies even to the death agony. I have also heard the excuses pleaded by such women for entering upon the exercise of this art. They said, that they would not have entered upon it unless they had foreseen supreme contempt and future rejection, and

consequent ruin on their part, if they should be subdued by their husbands; and that thus they had taken up these their arms from necessity. To this they added this admonition for the men, to leave their wives their own rights, and while they are in alternate colds, not to consider them as vile beneath their maid-servants. They said also that many of their sex are not in the state for exercising that art by reason of their connate timidity; but I added, by reason of their connate modesty. From these considerations it may now be known what marriages are meant by infernal marriages in the world between married persons who inwardly are the most inveterate enemies, and outwardly are like the most attached friends.

293. To the above shall be added two Memorable Relations. The first is as follows:—

I was once looking through a window to the east, and I saw seven women sitting on a bed of roses by a certain fountain, and drinking the water. I strained my eyesight greatly to see what they were doing, and this straining of my eyesight affected them; wherefore one of them beckoned me, and I quitted the house and quickly went up to them. When I reached them, I courteously inquired whence they were.

They said, "We are wives, and are conversing here about the delights of conjugial love, and from much confirmation we conclude, that those delights are also the delights of wisdom."

This answer so delighted my mind (*animus*) that I seemed to be in the spirit, and hence in a more interior and brighter perception than ever before; wherefore I said to them, "Permit me to ask a few questions about those pleasantnesses:" and they consented.

So I asked, "How do you wives know that the delights of conjugial love are the same as the delights of wisdom?"

They replied, "We know this from the correspondence of the 2
wisdom in our husbands with the delights of conjugial love in us; for the delights of this love in us are exalted and diminished, and altogether qualified, according to the wisdom in our husbands."

On hearing this, I asked them, saying, "I know that you are affected by the soft words of your husbands, and by their cheerfulness of mind, and that you are delighted with these with the whole bosom; but I am surprised to hear you say, that their wisdom produces this effect; but tell me, what is wisdom, and what wisdom [produces this effect]?"

To this the wives indignantly replied, "Do you suppose that 3
we do not know what wisdom is, and what wisdom [produces that effect], when yet we are continually reflecting upon the wisdom in our husbands, and learn it daily from their mouths? For we wives think of the state of our husbands from morning

till evening; scarcely an intercalary hour passes during the day, in which our intuitive thought is altogether withdrawn from them, or is absent; on the other hand, our husbands think very little in the day about our state; hence we know what wisdom of theirs is being delighted in us. Our husbands call that wisdom rational spiritual wisdom, and moral spiritual wisdom. Rational spiritual wisdom, they say, belongs to the understanding and to Knowledges, and moral spiritual wisdom to the will and to the life; but these two they conjoin and make a one, and declare that the pleasantnesses of this wisdom are transcribed from their minds into the delights in our bosoms, and from our bosoms into theirs, and thus return to wisdom their origin."

4 I then asked, "Do you know anything more about the wisdom of your husbands which delights in you?"

They said, "We do. There is spiritual wisdom, and thence rational and moral wisdom. Spiritual wisdom consists in acknowledging the Lord the Saviour for the God of heaven and earth, and in procuring for oneself from Him the truths of the church, which is done by means of the Word and of preachings thence, whence comes spiritual rationality· and in living from Him according to those truths, whence comes spiritual morality. These two our husbands call the wisdom which in general operates [to produce] truly conjugial love. We have heard from them also that the reason of this is, that by means of that wisdom, the interiors of their minds and thence of their bodies are opened, whence there exists a free passage from primes even to ultimates for the current of love; on the flow, sufficiency, and strength of which current conjugial love depends and lives. The rational and moral spiritual wisdom of our husbands, in particular as to marriage, has for its end and object to love the wife alone, and to put away all concupiscence for other women; and so far as this is effected, so far that love is exalted as to degree, and perfected as to quality; and so far also we feel more distinctly and exquisitely the delights (*delitiae*) in ourselves corresponding to the delights (*jucunda*) of the affections and the pleasantnesses of the thoughts of our husbands."

5 I asked afterwards, whether they knew how the communication is effected.

They said, "In all conjunction by love there must be action, reception, and reaction. The delicious state of our love is the agent or the action, the state of the wisdom of our husbands is the recipient or the reception, and is also the reagent or the reaction according to the reception; and this reaction is perceived by us with delights in the bosom according to the state continually expanded and prepared to receive those things which in any manner cohere with and proceed from the virtue in our husbands, thus also which cohere with and proceed from the extreme state of love in ourselves." They said further,

"Take heed lest by the delights which we have mentioned, you understand the ultimate delights of that love: of these we never speak, but of our bosom delights, of which there is a perpetual correspondence with the state of the wisdom of our husbands."

"After this there appeared at a distance as it were a dove 6
flying with the leaf of a tree in its mouth: but as it approached, instead of a dove there was seen a little boy with a paper in his hand: on coming up to us he held it out to me, and said, "Read that before these Maidens of the fountain." I read these words, "Tell the inhabitants of your earth, that there exists a truly conjugial love, the delights of which are myriads, scarcely any of which are as yet known to the world; but they will be known, when the church betroths herself to her Lord, and is married."

I then asked, "Why did that boy call you Maidens of the fountain?"

They replied, "We are called maidens when we sit by this fountain, because we are affections of the Truths of the wisdom of our husbands, and the affection of truth is called a maiden; moreover, a fountain signifies the truth of wisdom, and the bed of roses, on which we sit, signifies the delights thereof."

Then one of the seven wove a garland of roses, and sprinkled 7
it with water of the fountain, and placed it on the cap of the boy, round his little head, and said, "Receive the delights of intelligence: know that a cap signifies intelligence, and a garland from this rose-bed, the delights." The boy thus decorated departed, and again appeared at a distance like a flying dove, but with a coronet on the head.

294. The Second Memorable Relation:—

After some days I again saw the seven wives in a garden of roses, but not in the same one as before. It was a magnificent garden of roses, the like of which I had never seen before; it was round, and the roses in it formed as it were a rainbow. The roses or flowers of a crimson colour formed its outermost circle, others of a golden yellow colour formed the next inner circle, and within this were others of a bright blue, and the inmost circle was of a prasinous or bright green colour; and within this rainbow of roses was a little lake of limpid water. Those seven wives, who were before called the Maidens of the fountain, were sitting there, and, on seeing me at the window, again called me to them; and when I was come they said, "Did you ever see anything more beautiful upon the earth?"

I replied, "Never."

Then they said, "Such scenery is created in a moment by the Lord, and represents something new on the earth; for everything created by the Lord represents something: but what does this represent? divine, if you can: we divine that it represents the delights of conjugial love."

2 On hearing this, I said, "What! the delights of conjugial love, about which you spoke before with so much wisdom and eloquence? After I had left you, I related your conversation to some wives dwelling in our country, and said, 'I now know from instruction that you have bosom delights arising from your conjugial love, which you can communicate to your husbands according to their wisdom, and that on this account you are continually looking at your husbands with the eyes of your spirit from morning to evening, and studying to bend and lead their dispositions to become wise, to the end that you may secure those delights.' I mentioned also that by wisdom you mean rational and moral spiritual wisdom, and in regard to marriage, the wisdom to love the wife alone, and to put away all concupiscence for other women. But to these things the wives of our country answered with laughter, saying, 'What is all this, but mere idle talk? We do not know what conjugial love is. If our husbands possess any portion of it, still we do not; whence then come its delights with us? Yea, as to the delights which you call the ultimate delights, we sometimes violently refuse them; for they are unpleasant to us, almost like violations; and you will see, if you attend to it, no sign of such love in our faces: wherefore you are trifling or jesting, if you also say, with those seven wives, that we think of our husbands from morning to evening, and continually attend to their will and pleasure in order to obtain such delights from them.' I have retained thus much of what they said, that I might relate it to you; since it is opposed, and also in manifest contradiction, to what I heard from you near the fountain, and which I so eagerly imbibed, and also believed."

3 To this the wives sitting in the garden of roses replied, "Friend, you know not the wisdom and prudence of wives; for they totally hide it from the men, and for no other end than that they may be loved: for in every man, who is not spiritually but only naturally rational and moral, there is cold towards his wife; and the cold lies concealed in his inmosts. This a wise and prudent wife observes exquisitely and acutely, and in the same degree she conceals her conjugial love, and withdraws it into her bosom, and hides it there so deeply that it does not at all appear in her face, in the tone of her voice, or in her behaviour. The reason is, that so far as it appears, so far the conjugial cold of the man pours forth from the inmosts of his mind, where it resides, into its ultimates, and induces a total coldness on the body, and a consequent endeavour to separate from the bed and the bed-chamber."

4 I then asked, "Whence arises such cold as you call conjugial cold?"

They replied, "It is from the insanity of the men in spiritual

things: and every one who is insane in spiritual things, is
inmostly cold towards his wife, and inmostly warm towards
harlots; and since conjugial love and scortatory love are opposite
to each other, it follows that conjugial love becomes cold when
scortatory love is heat; and when cold reigns with a man, he
cannot endure any sense of love, and thus not any breath of it,
from his wife; wherefore the wife so wisely and prudently conceals that love; and in proportion as she conceals it by denying
and refusing, the man is revived and recuperated by the
inflowing meretricious sphere. Hence it is, that the wife of such
a man has no bosom delights such as we have, but only pleasures,
which, on the part of the man, ought to be called the pleasures
of insanity, because they are the pleasures of scortatory love.
Every chaste wife loves her husband, even if he be unchaste; but 5
since wisdom alone is the recipient of her love, therefore she
exerts all her endeavours to turn his insanity into wisdom, that is,
to prevent his lusting after other women besides herself. This she
does by a thousand methods, taking the greatest care lest any
of them should be discovered by the man; for she knows very
well that love cannot be forced, but that it is insinuated in
freedom; wherefore it is given to women to know from the
sight, hearing, and touch, every state of the disposition of their
husbands; but on the other hand it is not given to men to know
any state of the disposition of their wives. A chaste wife can 6
look at her husband with an austere countenance, accost him
with a harsh voice, and also be angry, and quarrel, and yet in
her heart cherish a soft and tender love towards him; but that
anger and dissimulation have for their end wisdom, and thus the
reception of love with the husband, appears manifestly from the
fact, that she can be reconciled in an instant. Besides, wives
possess such means of concealing the love implanted in their
heart and marrows, for the sake of preventing conjugial cold
bursting forth with the man, and extinguishing also the fire of
his scortatory heat, and thus converting him from green wood
into a dry stick."

When the seven wives had spoken these and many more 7
similar things, their husbands came with clusters of grapes in
their hands, some of which were of a delicate flavour, and some
of a disagreeable flavour; and the wives said, "Why have you
also brought bad or wild grapes?"

The husbands replied, "Because we perceived in our souls, with which yours are united, that you were conversing with that man about truly conjugial love, that its delights are the delights of wisdom, and also about scortatory love, that its delights are the pleasures of insanity. The latter are wild grapes, or those of a disagreeable flavour; the former are grapes of a delicate flavour." They confirmed what their wives had said, and added that, "in externals, the pleasures of insanity appear like the delights of wisdom, but not in internals; just like the good grapes and the bad grapes which we have brought; for both the chaste and the unchaste have similar wisdom in externals, but altogether dissimilar in internals."

8 After this the little boy again came with a paper in his hand, and held it out to me, saying, "Read these words;" and I read, "Know, that the delights of conjugial love ascend to the highest heaven, and both on the way thither and also there, conjoin themselves with the delights of all heavenly loves, and thus enter into their happiness, which endures to eternity: the reason is, that the delights of that love are also the delights of wisdom. And know also, that the pleasures of scortatory love descend even to the lowest hell, and, both on the way thither and also there, conjoin themselves with the pleasures of all infernal loves, and thus enter into their unhappiness, which consists in the wretchedness of all the delightsomenesses of the heart: the reason is, that the pleasures of that love are also the pleasures of insanity."

After this the husbands departed with their wives, and accompanied the little boy as far as the way of his ascent into heaven; and they knew that the society from which he had been sent was a society of the new heaven, with which the new church in the earth will be conjoined.

BETROTHALS AND WEDDINGS.

295. THE subject of betrothals and weddings, and also of the rites and ceremonies attending them, is here treated of principally from the reason of the understanding; for the things which are written in this book have for their end that the reader may see Truths from his own Rational, and thereby give his consent, for thus his spirit is convinced; and those things in which the spirit is convinced, are allotted a place above those which, without consulting reason, enter from authority and the faith of authority; for the latter enter the head no further than the memory, and there mix themselves with fallacies and falsities; thus they are beneath the rational things which belong to the understanding. From these things any man can speak as it were rationally, but in reality absurdly; for he then thinks as a crab walks, the sight following the tail. It is otherwise if he thinks from the understanding; for then the rational sight selects from the memory suitable things whereby it confirms Truth viewed in itself. This is the reason why in this 2
chapter many things are adduced which are established customs, as that the choice belongs to the men, that parents ought to be consulted, that pledges ought to be given, that the conjugial covenant ought to be contracted before the wedding, that it [the conjugial covenant] ought to be consecrated by a priest, also that the wedding ought to be celebrated; besides many other things, which are adduced in order that man may see from his Rational that such things are inscribed on conjugial love, as requisite to promote and complete it. The articles into which this section 3
is divided are in their order the following:

I. *The choice belongs to the man and not to the woman.*

II. *The man ought to court and entreat the woman respecting marriage with him, and not the woman the man.*

III. *The woman ought to consult her parents, or those who are in the place of parents, and then deliberate with herself, before she consents.*

IV. *After the declaration of consent, pledges ought to be given.*

V. *The consent ought to be confirmed and corroborated by means of solemn betrothal.*

VI. *By betrothal both are prepared for conjugial love.*

VII. *By means of betrothal, the mind of the one is conjoined with the mind of the other, so that a marriage of the spirit may be effected before the marriage of the body.*

VIII. *This is the case with those who think chastely of marriages; but it is otherwise with those who think unchastely of them.*

IX. *Within the time of betrothal, it is not allowable to be conjoined corporeally.*

X. *When the time of betrothal is completed, the wedding ought to take place.*

XI. *Previous to the celebration of the wedding, the conjugial covenant ought to be ratified in the presence of witnesses.*

XII. *The marriage ought to be consecrated by a priest.*

XIII. *The wedding ought to be celebrated with festivity.*

XIV. *After the wedding, the marriage of the spirit is made also a marriage of the body, and thereby a full marriage.*

XV. *Such is the order of conjugial love with its successive stages from its first heat to its first torch.*

XVI. *Conjugial love hurried on without order and the modes thereof, burns up the marrows and is consumed.*

XVII. *The states of the minds of both parties proceeding in successive order, flow in into the state of marriage; nevertheless in one manner with the spiritual and in another with the natural.*

XVIII. *Because there exist successive order, and simultaneous order, and the latter is from the former and according to it.*

Now follows the explanation of these articles.

296. I. THE CHOICE BELONGS TO THE MAN, AND NOT TO THE WOMAN. This is because the man is born to be understanding, but the woman to be love; also because with men there is generally the love of the sex, but with women the love of one of the sex; and likewise because it is not unbecoming for men to speak about love, and to make it manifest, but it is unbecoming for women. Nevertheless women have the right of choosing one of their suitors. In regard to the first reason, that the choice belongs to the men, because they are born for the understanding, it is because the understanding can clearly see agreements and disagreements, and distinguish them, and from judgment choose what is suitable: it is otherwise with women, because they are born for love, and do not possess the clear-sightedness of that light; and consequently their determinations to marriage would proceed only from the inclinations of their love; if they have the knowledge of how to distinguish between men and
2 men, still their love is carried to appearances. In regard to the second reason, that the choice belongs to the men, and not to the women, because with men there is generally the love of the sex, and with women the love of one of the sex, it is because those who have the love of the sex have the freedom of consideration and also of determination: it is otherwise with women, in whom there is implanted the love for one of the sex. If you wish for a proof of this, ask, if you please, the men you meet, what their

sentiments are respecting monogamous marriage, and respecting polygamous marriage; and you will seldom meet one who will not reply in favour of polygamous marriage, and this also is the love of the sex: but ask the women their sentiments respecting those marriages, and almost all, except prostitutes, will reject polygamous marriages; from which it follows, that with women there is the love of one of the sex, thus conjugial love. In 3
regard to the third reason, that it is not unbecoming for men to speak about love, and to make it manifest, whereas it is for women, it is self-evident; hence also it follows, that the declaration [of love] belongs to the men, and if the declaration does, so also does the choice. That women have the right of choosing from among their suitors, is known; but this kind of choice is confined and limited, whereas that of the men is extended and unlimited.

297. II. THE MAN OUGHT TO COURT AND ENTREAT THE WOMAN RESPECTING MARRIAGE WITH HIM, AND NOT THE WOMAN THE MAN. This naturally follows the choice; and besides, courting and entreating women respecting marriage is in itself honourable and becoming for men, but not for women. If women were to court and entreat men, they would not only be blamed, but, after entreaty, they would be reputed as vile, or after marriage as libidinous, with whom there could be no intercourse but what was cold and fastidious; wherefore marriages would thereby be converted into tragic scenes. Wives also make a merit of the fact that, being conquered as it were, they yielded only to the importunate entreaty of the men. Who does not foresee, that if women courted men, they would seldom be accepted, but that they would either be indignantly rejected, or enticed to lasciviousness, and also would prostitute their modesty? Moreover, as was shown above, men have not any innate love of the sex; and without that love there is no interior pleasantness of life: wherefore to exalt their life by that love, it is incumbent on the men to flatter the women, courting and entreating them with politeness, courtesy, and humility, respecting this sweet addition to their life. The superiority of the female sex over the male in loveliness of countenance, person, and manners, is also an additional motive for this duty.

298. III. THE WOMAN OUGHT TO CONSULT HER PARENTS, OR THOSE WHO ARE IN THE PLACE OF PARENTS, AND THEN DELIBERATE WITH HERSELF, BEFORE SHE CONSENTS. The reason why parents ought to be consulted is, that they deliberate and give advice from judgment, knowledge, and love: from *judgment,* because they are in an advanced age, which excels in judgment, and clearly discerns what is suitable and unsuitable: from *know-*

ledge, both in respect to the suitor and to their daughter; in respect to the suitor they procure to themselves Knowledges, and in respect to their daughter they already know; wherefore they conclude respecting both together with united discernment: from *love,* because to consult the good of their daughter, and to provide for her household, is also to consult and provide for their own and for themselves.

299. The case would be altogether different if the daughter were to consent of herself to her urgent suitor, without consulting her parents or those who are in the place of parents; for she cannot from judgment, knowledge, and love, make a right estimate of the matter which concerns her future welfare: she cannot from *judgment,* because her judgment is as yet in ignorance as to conjugial life, and not in a state of comparing reasons, and of clearly discerning the characters (*mores*) of men from their tastes: nor from *knowledge* or cognition, because she knows few things beyond the domestic affairs of her parents and of some of her companions, and is unqualified to ferret out such things as belong to the habits and peculiarities of her suitor: nor from *love,* because with daughters in their first marriageable age, and also in their second, it obeys the concupiscences originating in the senses, and not as yet the desires originating in a refined mind. The reason why the daughter ought nevertheless to deliberate on the matter with herself before she consents, is, lest she should be led against her will into a connection with an unloved man; for thus consent on her part would be wanting; and yet it is consent that constitutes marriage, and initiates her spirit into that love; and unwilling or extorted consent does not initiate the spirit, although it may the body: and thus it converts chastity, which resides in the spirit, into lust, whereby conjugial love in its first heat is vitiated.

300. IV. After the declaration of consent, pledges ought to be given. By pledges are meant gifts, which, after consent, are confirmations, testifications, first favours, and gladnesses. The reason those gifts are *confirmations* is, that they are tokens of consent on both sides; wherefore, when anything is consented to on both sides, it is said, "Give me a token;" and of two, who have engaged themselves to marriage, and have confirmed their engagement by presents, it is said that they are pledged, thus
2 confirmed. The reason they are *testifications* is, that those pledges are like continual visible witnesses of mutual love: hence they are also memorials thereof; especially if they be rings, scent-bottles, or ribbons, which are worn in sight. In such things there is a sort of representative image of the dispositions of the bridegroom and the bride. The reason those

pledges are *first favours* is, that conjugial love engages for itself everlasting favour; whereof those gifts are the first fruits. That they are the *gladnesses* of love, is known, for the mind is exhilarated at the sight of them; and since love is in them, those favours are dearer and more precious than any gifts whatsoever, it being as if hearts were in them. Since those pledges are 3
securities of conjugial love, therefore presents after consent were in use among the Ancients; and after accepting such presents the parties were declared bridegroom and bride. But it ought to be known that it is at the pleasure of the parties to bestow those presents either before the act of betrothal, or after it; if before, they are confirmations and testifications of consent to the betrothal; if after it, they are also confirmations and testifications of consent to the wedding.

301. V. THE CONSENT OUGHT TO BE CONFIRMED AND CORROBORATED BY SOLEMN BETROTHAL. The reasons for betrothals are these: 1. That after betrothal the souls of the two parties may mutually incline towards each other. 2. That the universal love for the sex may be determined to one man or one woman of the sex. 3. That the interior affections may be mutually known, and by applications in the internal cheerfulness of love, may be conjoined. 4. That the spirits of both parties may enter into marriage, and be more and more consociated. 5. That thereby conjugial love may progress regularly from its first heat even to the nuptial flame. Consequently, 6. That conjugial love may advance and grow up in just order from its spiritual origin. The state of betrothal may be likened to the state of spring before summer; and the internal pleasantnesses of that state to the flowering of trees before fructification. As the initiations and progressions of conjugial love proceed in order for the sake of their influx into the effective love, which commences from the wedding, therefore there are betrothals in the heavens also.

302. VI. BY MEANS OF BETROTHAL, BOTH ARE PREPARED FOR CONJUGIAL LOVE. That the mind or spirit of the one is prepared by betrothing for union with the mind or spirit of the other, or, what is the same thing, that the love of the one is prepared for union with the love of the other, is manifest from the arguments advanced in the foregoing article. Besides which it must be noted, that on truly conjugial love is inscribed this order, that it ascends and descends; it ascends from its first heat progressively upwards towards the souls, with an effort to effect conjunctions there, and this by continually more interior openings of the minds; and there is no love which strives more intensely to effect those openings, or which is more powerful and skilful in opening the interiors of minds, than conjugial love; for the soul of each one intends this: but at the

same moments in which that love ascends towards the souls, it also descends towards the body, and thereby clothes itself. It must, however, be known that conjugial love in its descent is such as it is in the height to which it ascends; if it ascends on high, it descends chaste; but if it does not ascend on high, it descends unchaste; the reason is, that the lower parts of the mind are unchaste, but its higher parts are chaste; for the lower parts of the mind cleave to the body, but the higher separate themselves from them: but on this subject, see more below, no. 305. From these few considerations it may be manifest, that by means of betrothal the mind of each one is prepared for conjugial love, although in a different manner according to the affections.

303. VII. BY MEANS OF BETROTHAL, THE MIND OF THE ONE IS CONJOINED WITH THE MIND OF THE OTHER, SO THAT A MARRIAGE OF THE SPIRIT MAY BE EFFECTED BEFORE THE MARRIAGE OF THE BODY. As this follows logically from what was said above, nos. 301, 302, it is passed by without any further confirmations from reason being adduced.

304. VIII. THIS IS THE CASE WITH THOSE WHO THINK CHASTELY ABOUT MARRIAGES; BUT IT IS OTHERWISE WITH THOSE WHO THINK UNCHASTELY ABOUT THEM. With the chaste, that is, with those who think about marriages in accordance with religion, the marriage of the spirit precedes, and that of the body follows; and these are they with whom love ascends towards the soul, and from its height descends thence; concerning whom, see above, no. 302. The souls of these separate themselves from the unlimited love of the sex, and devote themselves to one man or woman, with whom they look for an everlasting and eternal union and its increasing blessednesses, as the cherishers of the hope which continually recreates their mind. But it is quite otherwise with the unchaste, who are they who do not think from religion about marriages and their holiness. With these there is a marriage of the body, but none of the spirit: if, during the state of betrothal, anything of the marriage of the spirit appears, yet, if it ascends by an elevation of the thoughts concerning it, it nevertheless falls back again to the concupiscences which are from the flesh in the will; and thus from the unchaste [elements] there it casts itself down headlong into the body, and defiles the ultimates of its love with an alluring ardour; and as, in consequence of this ardour, it was in the beginning all on fire, so its fire suddenly goes out, and passes away into the cold of winter; whence the failing [of potency] is accelerated. The state of betrothal with these answers hardly any other purpose than that they may fill their concupiscences with lasciviousnesses, and thereby contaminate the conjugial principle of love.

305. IX. WITHIN THE TIME OF BETROTHAL, IT IS NOT ALLOWABLE TO BE CONJOINED CORPOREALLY; for thus the order which is inscribed on conjugial love, perishes. For in human minds there are three regions, of which the highest is called the celestial region, the middle the spiritual, and the lowest the natural. In this lowest region man is born: but he ascends into his higher region, which is called the spiritual region, by a life according to the truths of religion, and into the highest region by the marriage of love and wisdom. In the lowest region, which is called the natural region, reside all the concupiscences of evil, and lasciviousnesses. But in the higher region, which is called the spiritual region, there are not any concupiscences of evil and lasciviousness; for man is brought into this region by the Lord, when he is re-born. But in the supreme region, which is called the celestial region, there is conjugial chastity in its own love: into this region a man is elevated by the love of uses; and as the most excellent uses are from marriages, he is elevated into it by truly conjugial love. From these considerations, it may be seen, as in a compendium, that conjugial love, from the first beginnings of its heat, must be elevated out of the lowest region into the higher region, in order that it may become chaste, and that thereby from what is chaste it may be let down through the middle and lowest regions into the body; and when this is the case, this lowest region is purified of its unchaste elements by the descent of what is chaste; hence the ultimate of that love also becomes chaste. Now, if the successive order of this love is hurried on by conjunctions of the body before their time, it follows, that the man acts from the lowest region, which by birth is unchaste; and it is known, that thence commences and arises cold for marriage, and neglect with loathing for one's married partner. Nevertheless there are various dangers of events resulting in consequence of premature conjunctions; also in consequence of too great a protraction, and also of too great a hastening, of the time of betrothals; but these, by reason of their number and variety, can hardly be adduced.

306. X. WHEN THE TIME OF BETROTHAL IS COMPLETED, THE WEDDING OUGHT TO TAKE PLACE. There are some customary rites which are merely formal, and others which at the same time are also essential: among the latter are weddings. That weddings are among the essentials, which ought to be manifested in the customary way, and formally celebrated, is confirmed by the following reasons: 1. That the wedding constitutes the end of the foregoing state, which had been inaugurated by the betrothal, which was principally a state of the spirit, and the beginning of the following state, which is to be inaugurated by the marriage, which is a state of the spirit and body together; for the spirit then enters into the body, and acts there: where-

fore on that day the parties put off the state and also the name of bridegroom and bride, and put on the state and name of married partners and bed-consorts. 2. That the wedding is an introduction and entrance into a new state, which is that a maiden becomes a wife, and a bachelor a husband, and both one flesh; and this is effected when love by ultimates unites them. That marriage actually changes a maiden into a wife, and a bachelor into a husband, was proved in a former part of this Work; also that marriage unites two into one human form, so that they are no longer two but one flesh. 3. That the wedding is the commencement of a plenary separation of the love of the sex from conjugial love, which is effected when, by means of the full measure of conjunction, the love of the one devotes itself closely and intimately to the love of the other. 4. It appears as if the wedding were merely an interval between those two states, and thus as if it were a mere formality which may be omitted; but nevertheless there is in it this essential also, that the new state above-mentioned ought then to be entered upon from covenant; and that the consent of the parties ought to be declared in the presence of witnesses, and also to be consecrated by a priest; besides other particulars which establish it. As weddings contain in them essentials, and as marriage is not legitimate till after the wedding, therefore also weddings are celebrated in the heavens; see above, no. 21, and also nos. 27 to 41.

307. XI. Previous to the celebration of the wedding, the conjugial covenant ought to be ratified in the presence of witnesses. It is necessary that the conjugial covenant be ratified before the wedding is celebrated, in order that the statutes and laws of truly conjugial love may be known, and that they may be remembered after the wedding; also that it may be a bond binding the minds of the parties closely together to a just marriage. For after the actual marriage has been entered into in various ways, the state which preceded the betrothal returns at times, in which state remembrance perishes, and forgetfulness of the ratified covenant ensues; yea, it is obliterated by allurements of unchaste [persons] to unchaste [deeds]; and if it is then recalled to the memory, it becomes a subject of reproach: but to avert these transgressions, society has taken upon itself the protection of that covenant, and has denounced penalties on the breakers of it. In a word, the ante-nuptial covenant manifests the sacred obligations of truly conjugial love, and binds libertines to the observance of them. Add to this, that by this covenant, the right of propagating children, and also the right of the children to inherit the goods of their parents, become legitimate.

308. XII. The marriage ought to be consecrated by a priest. The reason is, that marriages, viewed in themselves, are

spiritual, and therefore holy; for they descend from the heavenly marriage of good and truth, and conjugial things correspond to the Divine marriage of the Lord and the church; and hence they are from the Lord Himself, and according to the state of the church with the contracting parties. Now, since the ecclesiastical order on earth administer the things which belong to the priesthood with the Lord, that is, which belong to His love, and thus also the things which belong to blessing, it is needful that marriages should be consecrated by His ministers; and as they are then the chief witnesses, it is needful that the consent to the covenant should also be heard, accepted, confirmed, and thus established by them.

309. XIII. THE WEDDING OUGHT TO BE CELEBRATED WITH FESTIVITY. The reasons are, that the ante-nuptial love, which was the love of the bridegroom and the bride, then descends into their hearts, and by its spreading itself thence in every direction into all parts of the body, the delights of marriage are made sensible, whereby the minds of the parties are led to festive thoughts, and also indulge in the festivities so far as is allowable and becoming; in order to promote this, it is important that the festive feelings of their minds should find expression in the company of others, and that they themselves should be thereby introduced into the joys of conjugial love.

310. XIV. AFTER THE WEDDING, THE MARRIAGE OF THE SPIRIT BECOMES ALSO A MARRIAGE OF THE BODY, AND THEREBY A FULL MARRIAGE. All things which a man does in the body, flow in from his spirit; for it is known that the mouth does not speak of itself, but that it is the thought of the mind which speaks by means of it; also that the hands do not act, and the feet walk, of themselves, but that it is the will of the mind which does so by means of them: consequently, that the mind speaks through its organ, and also that it acts through its organs in the body. Hence it is evident, that such as the mind is, such are the speech of the mouth and the deeds of the body. From these premises it follows as a conclusion, that the mind, through a continual influx, forms the body for concordant and simultaneous actions with itself; wherefore the bodies of men, considered interiorly, are nothing else than forms of their minds organized exteriorly to effect the purposes of the soul. These things are premised in order that it may be perceived whence it is that the minds or spirits ought first to be united as in marriage, before they are united in the body also; namely, that when the marriages become of the body, they may be marriages of the spirit; consequently, that the married partners may mutually
love each other from the spirit, and hence in the body. From these 2
premises let us now take a view of marriage. When conjugial

love conjoins the minds of two persons, and forms them into a marriage, it then also conjoins and forms their bodies for that marriage; for, as has been said, the form of the mind is also interiorly the form of the body, with the sole difference, that the latter form is outwardly organized to give effect to that to which the interior form of the body is determined by the mind. But the mind formed from conjugial love is not only interiorly in the whole body, round about in every part, but moreover is interiorly in the organs allotted to generation, which in their region are situated beneath the other regions of the body, and in which are terminated the forms of the mind with those who are united in conjugial love: consequently the affections and thoughts of their minds are determined thither. The activities of minds arising from other loves differ in this respect, that the latter loves do not reach thither. The conclusion resulting from these considerations is, that such as conjugial love is in the minds or spirits of two persons, such it is interiorly in those its organs. But it is self-evident that the marriage of the spirit after the wedding becomes also a marriage of the body, thus a full marriage; consequently, if the marriage in the spirit is chaste, and partakes of the holiness thereof, it is the same when it is in its fulness in the body; and the reverse is the case if the marriage in the spirit is unchaste.

311. XV. THIS IS THE ORDER OF CONJUGIAL LOVE WITH ITS SUCCESSIVE STAGES FROM ITS FIRST HEAT TO ITS FIRST TORCH. It is said from its first heat to its first torch, because vital heat is love, and conjugial heat or love successively grows, and at length as it were into a flame or torch. It is said, to its first torch, because there is meant the first state after the wedding, when that love burns. But what its quality becomes after this torch in the marriage itself, has been described in the preceding chapters; but in this part of the Work is explained its order from the beginning of its career to this its first goal. That all order proceeds from primes to ultimates, and that the ultimates become the primes of some following order; moreover, that all things of the middle order are the ultimates of the prior and the primes of the following order, and that thus ends proceed continually through causes into effects, may be sufficiently confirmed and illustrated to the reason from what is known and visible in the world. But as the only subject at present being treated of is the order in which love proceeds from its first starting-place to its goal, those confirmations and illustrations shall be passed by, and it shall only be stated on this subject, that such as the order of this love is from its first heat to its first torch, such for the most part it is, and remains, in its progression afterwards; for in this progression it unfolds itself, according to the quality of its first heat: if this heat was chaste,

its chasteness is strengthened in its progressions; but if it was unchaste, its unchasteness increases as it progresses, until it is deprived of all that chasteness in which, from the time of betrothal, it had been from without, but not from within.

312. XVI. CONJUGIAL LOVE HURRIED ON WITHOUT ORDER AND THE MODES THEREOF, BURNS UP THE MARROWS AND IS CONSUMED. So it is said by some in heaven; and by the marrows they mean the interiors of the mind and body. The reason why these are burnt up, that is, consumed, by conjugial love being hurried on is, that that love in such a case begins from a flame which eats up and corrupts those inmost recesses, in which as in its beginnings conjugial love should reside, and from which it should commence. This comes to pass if the man and woman hurry on the marriage without order, by not looking to the Lord, by not consulting reason, by rejecting betrothal, and by obeying the flesh only. If that love commences from the ardour of the flesh, it becomes external and not internal, thus not conjugial; and such love may be said to partake of the shell, not of the kernel; or it may be called fleshly, lean, and dry, because emptied of its genuine essence. See more on this subject above, no. 305.

313. XVII. THE STATES OF THE MINDS OF EACH OF THE PARTIES PROCEEDING IN SUCCESSIVE ORDER, FLOW IN INTO THE STATE OF MARRIAGE; NEVERTHELESS IN ONE MANNER WITH THOSE WHO ARE SPIRITUAL AND IN ANOTHER WITH THOSE WHO ARE NATURAL. That the last state is such as the successive order from which it is formed and exists, is a canon, which from its Truth must be acknowledged in the learned world; for thereby it is discovered what influx is, and what its effects. By influx is meant all that which precedes, and composes that which is subsequent, and by means of things subsequent in order composes what is last; as all that which precedes with a man (*homo*), and composes his wisdom; or all that which precedes with a statesman, and composes his sagacity; or all that which precedes with a theologian, and composes his erudition; in like manner all that which proceeds from infancy, and composes a man (*vir*); also what proceeds in order from a seed and a twig, and makes a tree, and afterwards what proceeds from a blossom, and makes its fruit; in like manner all that which precedes and proceeds with a bridegroom and bride, and makes their marriage. This is the meaning of influx. That all those things which 2
precede in minds form series, and that series are collected together, one beside another, and one after another, and that these together compose what is last or ultimate, is as yet unknown in the world; but as it is a Truth from heaven, it is here adduced: for it explains what influx effects, and what is

the quality of the last or ultimate, in which the above-mentioned series successively formed co-exist. From these considerations it may be seen, that the states of the minds of each of the parties proceeding in successive order flow in into the state of marriage. But married partners after marriage are utterly in ignorance of the successive things which are insinuated into, and exist in their minds from things antecedent; nevertheless it is those things which give form to conjugial love, and constitute the state of their minds, from which
3 state they act with each other. The reason why a different state is formed from a different order with those who are spiritual, from what it is with those who are natural, is, that those who are spiritual proceed in just order, and those who are natural proceed in unjust order; for those who are spiritual look to the Lord, and the Lord provides and leads the order; whereas those who are natural look to themselves, and consequently proceed in inverted order; wherefore with the latter the state of marriage is inwardly full of unchaste elements; and there are as many colds as there are unchaste elements, and there are as many obstructions of the inmost life, whereby its current is closed and its fountain dried up, as there are colds.

314. XVIII. Because there exist successive order, and simultaneous order, and the latter is from the former and according to it. This is adduced as a reason tending to confirm the preceding statements. It is known that there exist what is successive and what is simultaneous; but it is unknown that simultaneous order is from successive order, and according to it; yet how things successive enter into things simultaneous, and what order they form therein, is very difficult to present to the perception, since the learned are not in possession of any idea that serves to elucidate the subject; and as the first idea respecting this arcanum cannot be given in a few words, and to treat it at length would withdraw the mind from a more open view of conjugial love, it may suffice for illustration to quote what has been adduced in a compendium respecting those two orders, the successive and the simultaneous, and respecting the influx of the former into the latter, in the *Doctrine of the New Jerusalem concerning the Sacred Scripture,* where these words occur:—

2 "There exist in heaven and in the world successive order and simultaneous order. In successive order one thing follows after another from the highest things to the lowest; but in simultaneous order one thing is next to another from the inmosts to the outermosts. Successive order is like a column with steps from the top to the bottom; but simultaneous order is like a work cohering from the centre to the surface. Successive order becomes simultaneous in the ultimate, in the following manner:—

The highest things of successive order become the inmost things of simultaneous order, and the lowest things of successive order become the outermost things of simultaneous order; it is comparatively as when the column of steps subsides, it becomes a body cohering in a plane. Thus what is simultaneous is formed from what is successive; and this in each and all things of the spiritual world, and in each and all things of the natural world." See nos. 38 and 65 of that Work; and many more observations on this subject in *Angelic Wisdom concerning the Divine Love and Divine Wisdom*, nos. 205 to 229.

The case is similar with successive order progressing towards 3
marriage, and with simultaneous order in marriage; namely, that the latter is from the former, and according to it. He who is acquainted with the influx of successive order into simultaneous order, can comprehend the reason why the angels are able to see in a man's hand all the thoughts and intentions of his mind, and also why wives, from their husbands' hands on their bosoms, are sensible of their affections; of which circumstance mention has occasionally been made in the Memorable Relations. The reason is, that the hands are the ultimates of man, into which the deliberations and conclusions of his mind are determined, and there constitute what is simultaneous: therefore also it is said in the Word, that a thing is "inscribed on the hands."

315. To the above I shall add two Memorable Relations. The first is as follows:—

"* I once saw not far from me a meteor; I saw a cloud divided into little clouds, some of which were of a blue colour, and some opaque; and I saw them as it were in collision together. They were made translucent in streaks by rays, which at one time appeared sharp like the points of swords, at another, blunt like broken swords. The streaks at times darted forwards, and at times retreated, exactly like combatants: thus those differently coloured little clouds appeared to be fighting together; but they were only sporting. And as this meteor appeared at no great distance from me, I lifted up my eyes, and looked attentively, and I saw boys, young men, and old men, entering a house which was built of marble, on a foundation of porphyry; it was over this house that that phenomenon appeared. Then, addressing one of those who were entering, I asked, "What is going on there?"

He answered, "It is a public school (*gymnasium*), where young persons are initiated into various things relating to wisdom."

On hearing this I went in with them, being then in the 2
spirit, that is, in a state similar to that in which the men of the spiritual world, who are called spirits and angels, are. And behold, in that public school there was seen in the front a chair, in the middle, benches, at the sides round about, seats, and over

* This Memorable Relation is repeated in the *True Christian Religion*, no. 697.

the entrance, an orchestra. The chair was for the young men that were to give answers to the problem at that time to be proposed, the benches were for the audience, the seats at the sides were for those who on former occasions had answered wisely, and the orchestra was for the elders, who were umpires and judges: in the middle of the orchestra was a tribune, where there sat a wise man, whom they called the head master, who proposed the problems, to which the young men were to give their answers from the chair.

When they were assembled, this man arose from the tribune and said, "Pray give an answer to this problem, and solve it if you can, WHAT IS THE SOUL, AND WHAT IS ITS QUALITY?"

3 On hearing this problem all were amazed, and murmured, and some of the company on the benches exclaimed, "What man, from the Saturnian era to the present time, has been able by any thought of reason to see and understand what the soul is, still less what its quality is? Is not this subject above the sphere of all men's understanding?"

But to this they replied from the orchestra, "It is not above the understanding, but within it and before it; only answer."

Then the young men, who had been chosen that day to ascend the chair, and give an answer to the problem, arose. They were five in number, who had been examined by the elders, and found to excel in sagacity, and they were then sitting on couches at the sides of the chair. They afterwards ascended in the order in which they had been seated; and each one when he ascended put on a silken tunic of an opaline colour, and over it a robe of soft wool interwoven with flowers, together with a cap, on the crown of which was a rosette beset with small sapphires.

4 I saw the first one thus clad ascend the desk, and he said: "What the soul is, and what its quality is, has never been revealed to any one since the day of creation: it is an arcanum in the treasuries of the Only God. But this has been disclosed, that the soul resides in man as a queen; yet where her palace is, has been a matter of conjecture among learned authorities. Some have supposed it to be in the small tubercle between the cerebrum and the cerebellum, which is called the pineal gland: in this they have fixed the seat of the soul, because the whole man is ruled from those two brains, and they are regulated by that tubercle; wherefore, whatever regulates the brains at will, regulates also the whole man from the head to the heel." He also said, "Hence this conjecture appeared as true or probable to many in the world; but after this age it was rejected as a figment."

5 When he had said this, he put off the robe, the tunic, and the cap, which the second of the chosen ones put on, and entered the chair. The opinion he expressed in regard to the soul was as

follows: "In the whole heaven and the whole world it is unknown what the soul is, and what its quality is; it is however known that it exists, and that it is in man; but in what part of him, is a matter of conjecture. This is certain, that it is in the head, since the understanding thinks there, and the will intends there; and in front in the face of the head are man's five sensories: both the latter and the former receive life from no other source than the soul which resides within the head. But in what particular part of the head the soul has its seat, I dare not take upon me to say; yet I incline [sometimes] to the opinion of those who fix its abode in the three ventricles of the cerebrum, sometimes to the opinion of those who fix it in the *corpora striata* therein, sometimes to the opinion of those who fix it in the medullary substance of both brains, sometimes to the opinion of those who fix it in the cortical substance, and sometimes to the opinion of those who fix it in the *dura mater;* for there have not been wanting confirmatory arguments [literally, white voting stones] in favour of each of those seats of the soul. The arguments in 6
favour of the three ventricles of the cerebrum have been, that those ventricles are the receptacles of the animal spirits and of all the lymphs of the brain. The arguments in favour of the *corpora striata* have been, that these bodies constitute the marrow, through which the nerves go out, and through which both brains are continued into the spine; and from the spine and the marrow there emanate fibres of which the whole body is interwoven. The arguments in favour of the medullary substance of both brains have been, that that substance is a collection and congeries of all the fibres, which are the initiaments of the whole man. The arguments in favour of the cortical substance have been, that in that substance are contained the prime and ultimate ends, and consequently the beginnings of all the fibres, and thus the beginnings of all the senses and motions. The arguments in favour of the *dura mater* have been, that it is the common covering of both brains, and hence by a certain continuity extends itself over the heart and over the viscera of the body. As for myself, I do not declare in favour of any one of these opinions more than of another; I pray you decide for yourselves, and choose which is preferable."

Having said this, he descended from the chair, and delivered 7
the tunic, the robe, and the cap to the third, who, mounting the chair, spoke as follows: "What shall a young man like myself do with so sublime a problem? I appeal to the learned who are here seated at the sides; I appeal to you wise ones in the orchestra; yea, I appeal to the angels of the highest heaven, whether any one, from his own rational light, is able to form to himself any idea about the soul. Nevertheless I, like others, can conjecture about the place of its abode in man; and my conjecture is, that it is in the heart and hence in the blood; and

this is my conjecture, because the heart by its blood rules both the body and the head; for it sends forth a large vessel called the aorta into the whole body, and vessels called the carotids into the whole head; hence it is universally agreed, that the soul from the heart by means of the blood sustains, nourishes, and vivifies the universal organical system both of the body and the head. As a proof of this position, it may be added, that in the Sacred Scripture frequent mention is made of the 'soul and the heart'; as where it is said, Thou shalt love God 'from the whole soul and the whole heart'; and that God creates in man 'a new soul and a new heart' (Deut. vi. 5; chap. x. 12; chap. xi. 13; chap. xxvi. 16; Jerem. xxxii. 41; Matt. xxii. 35 [37]; Mark xii. 30, 33; Luke x. 27; and in other places): it is also plainly said, that the 'blood is the soul of the flesh' (Levit. xvii. 11, 14)."

On hearing this, some of the assembly lifted up the voice, saying, "Learned! learned!" these were clergymen.

8 After this the fourth put on the garments of the former speaker, and entered the chair, and said: "I also suspect, that there is not a single person of so subtle and refined a genius as to be able to discover what the soul is, and what its quality is; wherefore I am of opinion, that he who attempts to investigate the subject, will exert his subtlety to no purpose. Nevertheless from my childhood I have continued to believe firmly in the opinion of the Ancients, that the soul of man is in the whole of him, and in every part of the whole, and thus that it is in the head and in each of its parts, as well as in the body and in each of its parts; and that it is an idle conceit of the moderns to fix its habitation in any particular part, and not in the body throughout. Besides, the soul is a spiritual substance, of which there cannot be predicated either extension or place, but habitation and impletion. Moreover, when mention is made of the soul, who does not understand life to be meant? and is not life in the whole and in every part?"

These sentiments were favourably received by many of the audience.

9 After him the fifth rose, and, being adorned with the same insignia, thus delivered himself from the chair: "I will not stop to determine where the soul is, whether it be in some particular part of the body, or in the whole throughout; but out of the storehouse of my thoughts I will declare my ideas on the subject of the soul and its quality. No one thinks of the soul but as of a pure something, which may be likened to ether, or air, or wind, in which there is vitality from the rationality which man enjoys above the beasts. This opinion I have founded on the circumstance, that when a man expires, he is said to breathe forth or emit his soul or spirit; hence also the soul which lives after death is believed to be such a breath, in which is the thinking life which is called the soul; what else can the soul be? But

as I heard it declared from the orchestra, that this problem concerning the soul, what it is, and what its quality is, is not above the understanding, but is within it and before it, I entreat and beseech you to disclose this eternal arcanum yourselves."

Then the elders in the orchestra turned their eyes towards 10
the head master, who had proposed the problem, and who understood by their signs that they wished him to descend and teach: so he instantly descended from the tribune, passed through the auditory, and entered the chair, and there, stretching out his hand, he said: "Let me bespeak your attention. Who does not believe the soul to be the inmost and most subtle essence of man? and what is an essence without a form, but an imaginary entity? Wherefore the soul is a form: but the quality of the form shall be stated. It is a form of all things of love, and of all things of wisdom. All things of love are called affections, and all things of wisdom are called perceptions. The latter are derived from the former, and therefore, together with them they constitute one form, in which there are innumerable things in such an order, series, and coherence, that they may be called a one; and they may be called a one because nothing can be taken away from it, or added to it, without changing it. What is the human soul but such a form? are not all things of love and all things of wisdom essentials of that form? and are not these things with man in his soul, and from the soul in his head
and body? You are called spirits and angels, and in the 11
world you believed that spirits and angels are like winds or ethers, and thus minds (*mentes*) and dispositions (*animi*); and now you see clearly that you are truly, really, and actually men, who in the world had lived and thought in a material body, and knew that the material body does not live and think, but the spiritual substance in that body; and this substance you called the soul, whose form you were then ignorant of; and nevertheless you have now seen and continue to see it. You all are souls, of whose immortality you have heard, thought, said, and written so much; and because you are forms of love and wisdom from God, you cannot die to eternity. The soul therefore is a human form, from which the least thing cannot be taken away, and to which the least thing cannot be added; and it is the inmost form of all the forms of the whole body; and since the forms which are without receive from the inmost form both essence and form, therefore you are, as you appear to yourselves and to us, souls. In a word, the soul is the man himself, because it is the inmost man; wherefore its form is fully and perfectly the human form: nevertheless it is not life, but it is the proximate receptacle of life from God, and thus the dwelling-place of God."

When he had said this, many applauded him; but some said, 12
"We will weigh the matter."

I then went home, and lo! over that public school, instead of the former meteor, there appeared a bright white cloud, without streaks or rays that seemed to combat with each other; this cloud, penetrating through the roof, entered, and illuminated the walls; and I heard, that they saw pieces of writing, and among others this, "*Jehovah God breathed into the man's nostrils the* SOUL OF LIVES, *and the man became a* LIVING SOUL" (Gen. ii. 7).

316. The Second Memorable Relation :—

Once as I was walking with my mind (*animus*) at rest, and in a state of delightful peace of mind (*mens*), I saw at a distance a grove, in the midst of which was an avenue leading to a small palace; and I saw maidens and young men, and husbands and wives, entering. I also went thither in spirit, and asked a certain keeper who was standing at the entrance, whether I also might enter.

He looked at me; and I said, "Why do you look at me?"

He replied, "I look at you in order that I may see whether the delight of peace, which is in your face, partakes at all of the delight of conjugial love. Beyond this avenue there is a little garden, and in the midst of it a house, where there are two newly-married consorts, who to-day are visited by their friends of both sexes, coming to wish them happiness. I do not know those whom I admit; but I was told that I should know them by their faces: those in whom I saw the delight of conjugial love, I was to admit, and none else." All the angels can see from the faces of others the delights of their hearts; and he saw the delight of that love in my face, because I was then meditating on conjugial love. This meditation shone forth from my eyes, and thence entered into the interiors of my face; wherefore he told me that I might enter.

2 The avenue through which I entered was formed of fruit trees connected together by their branches, which made on each side a continuous wall of trees. Through the avenue I entered the little garden, which breathed a pleasant fragrance from its shrubs and flowers. The shrubs and flowers were in pairs; and I heard that such little gardens appear about the houses where there are and have been weddings, and that therefore they are called wedding gardens.

I afterwards entered the house, where I saw the two married consorts holding each other by the hands, and conversing together from truly conjugial love; and it was then given me to see from their faces the effigy of conjugial love, and from their conversation the vitality of it.

After I, among many others, had offered them my congratulations, and wished them every happiness, I went out into the lovely wedding garden, and saw on the right side of it a company of young men, to whom all who came out of the house hastened. The reason of their hastening to them was, that they were conversing about conjugial love, and conversation on this subject attracts to it the minds (*animi*) of all by a certain occult power. I then listened to a wise one who was speaking on the subject; and the sum of what I heard is as follows:—

That the Divine providence of the Lord is most particular and 3
consequently most universal in relation to marriages and in marriages in the heavens, because all the felicities of heaven issue from the delights of conjugial love, like sweet waters from the sweet source of a fountain; and that on this account it is provided by the Lord that conjugial pairs be born, and that these pairs be continually educated for marriage, neither the girl nor the lad knowing this; and that after a stated time, when she has become a marriageable maiden, and he a young man fit for marriage, they meet somewhere as by chance, and see each other; and that then they instantly know, as by a kind of instinct, that they are consorts, and by a certain inward dictate think within themselves, the young man, that she is mine, and the maiden, that he is mine: and that when this thought has dwelt for some time in the minds of both, they deliberately accost each other, and betroth themselves. It is said, "as by chance," and "as by instinct," and the meaning is, by the Divine providence; because, when the Divine providence is unknown, it has such an appearance. That conjugial pairs are born and educated for marriage, while both are ignorant of it, he proved by the conjugial likeness visible in the faces of both; also by the intimate and eternal union of the dispositions (*animi*) and minds (*mentes*), which union could not possibly exist, as it does in heaven, without being foreseen and provided for by the Lord.

When the wise one had said this, and had received the applause 4
of the company, he further added, that in the veriest singulars with man, both male and female, there is the conjugial principle or element, but still a different conjugial principle with the male from what there is with the female; also that in the masculine conjugial principle there is conjuctiveness with the feminine conjugial principle, and contrariwise, even in the veriest singulars. This he confirmed by the marriage of the will and the understanding in every individual, which two act together upon the veriest singulars of the mind and of the body; from which considerations it may be seen, that in every substance, even the smallest, there is the conjugial element; and that this is evident from the compound substances which are made up of simple substances; as that there are two eyes, two ears, two nostrils, two cheeks, two lips, two arms with hands, two loins, two feet, and within in man two hemispheres of the brain, two ventricles of the heart, two lobes of the lungs, two kidneys, two testicles; and where there are not two, still they are

divided into two. The reason why there are two is, that the one belongs to the will and the other to the understanding, which act wonderfully into them so as to constitute them a one; wherefore the two eyes constitute one sight, the two ears one hearing, the two nostrils one smell, the two lips one speech, the two hands one labour, the two feet one pace, the two hemispheres of the brain one dwelling-place of the mind, the two chambers of the heart one life of the body through the blood, the two lobes of the lungs one respiration, and so forth. And the masculine and the feminine, united by means of truly conjugial love, constitute one fully human life.

5 While he was saying these things, there appeared red lightning on the right, and bright white lightning on the left; both kinds were mild, and they entered through the eyes into the minds and also enlightened them. After the lightning it also thundered; which was a gentle murmur from the angelic heaven flowing down and increasing. On hearing and seeing these things, the wise one said, "These are to remind and admonish me to add to my discourse the following observations:—that of the above pairs, the right one signifies their good, and the left their truth; and that this is from the marriage of good and truth, which is inscribed on man in general and in every particular; and good has reference to the will, and truth to the understanding, and both together to a one. Hence it is that in heaven the right eye is the good of sight, and the left the truth thereof; also that the right ear is the good of hearing, and the left the truth thereof; and likewise that the right hand is the good of a man's power, and the left the truth thereof; and so likewise with the rest of the above pairs; and since the right and left have such significations, therefore the Lord said, 'If thy right eye cause thee to stumble, pluck it out; and if thy right hand cause thee to stumble, cut it off' [(Matt. v. 29, 30)]; whereby He meant that, if good becomes evil, the evil must be cast out. This is the reason also why He said to His disciples that they should cast the net on the right side of the ship; and that when they did so, they took a great multitude of fishes [(John xxi. 6, 7)]; whereby He meant that they should teach the good of charity, and that thus they would gather men."

6 When he had said these things, the two lightnings again appeared, milder than before; and then it was seen, that the lightning on the left derived its bright whiteness from the ruddy fire of the lightning on the right; on seeing which he said, "This is a sign from heaven confirmative of what I have said, because what is fiery in heaven denotes good, and what is white in heaven denotes truth; and its being seen that the lightning on the left derived its bright whiteness from the ruddy fire of the lightning on the right, is a demonstrative sign

that the bright whiteness of light, or light, is nothing else than the brightness of fire."

On hearing this all went home, inflamed by those lightnings, and by the conversation about them, with the good and truth of gladness.

REPEATED MARRIAGES.

317. It may come to be a matter of question, whether conjugial love, which is that of one man with one wife, can, after the death of one of the consorts, be separated, or transferred, or superinduced; also whether repeated marriages have anything in common with polygamy, and thus whether they may be called successive polygamies; with several other inquiries which are wont to add scruples on scruples with reasoners. In order therefore that those masters in researches, who reason in the shade about these marriages, may see some light, I have thought it would be worth while to present for their judgment the following articles about those marriages:—

I. *After the death of a married partner, again to contract matrimony depends on the preceding conjugial love.*

II. *It depends also on the state of marriage in which they had lived.*

III. *With those who have not been in truly conjugial love, there is no obstacle or hindrance to their again contracting matrimony.*

IV. *Those who had lived together in truly conjugial love are unwilling to marry again, except for reasons separate from conjugial love.*

V. *The state of the marriage of a bachelor with a maiden is different from that of a bachelor with a widow.*

VI. *The state of the marriage of a widower with a maiden is also different from that of a widower with a widow.*

VII. *The varieties and diversities of these marriages as to love and its attributes exceed all number.*

VIII. *The state of a widow is more grievous than the state of a widower.*

Now follows the explanation of these articles.

318. I. After the death of a married partner, again to contract matrimony depends on the preceding conjugial love. Truly conjugial love is like a balance, in which the inclinations for repeated marriages are weighed; so far as the preceding conjugial love had approached to truly conjugial love, in the same proportion the inclination for repeated marriage is weak; but so far as the preceding love had departed from truly conjugial love, in the same proportion the inclination to another marriage usually arises. The reason is obvious, that conjugial love is in a similar degree a conjunction of the minds, which

remains in the life of the body of the one party after the decease of the other; and this holds the inclination as a scale in the balance, and causes a preponderance according to the appropriation of true love. But since the approach to this love is seldom made at the present day, except for a few paces, therefore the scale of the preponderance of the inclination generally rises to a state of equilibrium, and from thence inclines and tends to the other side, that is, to marriage. The 2
contrary is the case with those whose preceding love in the former marriage has receded from truly conjugial love; the reason is, that recession from that love is in a like degree a disjunction of the minds, which also remains in the life of the body of the one party after the decease of the other; and this enters the will that has been disjoined from that of the other, and causes an inclination for a new conjunction; in favour of which the thought arising from the inclination of the will induces the hope of a more united, and thus a more delightful dwelling together. That inclinations to repeated marriages arise from 3
the state of the preceding love, is known, and is also obvious to reason: for in truly conjugial love there is a fear of loss, and loss is followed by grief; and this grief and fear are in the very inmosts of the minds. Hence it is that, in proportion as that love is present, in the same proportion the soul inclines both in will and in thought, that is, in intention, to be in the subject with which and in which it has been. From these considerations it follows, that the mind is kept balancing towards a second marriage, according to the degree of love in which it was in the former marriage. Hence it is that after death the same parties are re-united, and mutually love each other as they did in the world. But, as was said above, that love at the present day is rare, and there are few who come within finger touch of it; and those who do not do so, and still more those who recede far from it, as they were desirous of separation in the preceding married life, which was cold, so after death they are desirous of conjunction with another woman or another man. But respecting both these sorts of persons more will be said in what follows.

319. II. After the death of a married partner, again to contract matrimony depends also on the state of marriage in which the parties had lived. By the state of marriage is not here meant the state of love treated of in the foregoing article, because the latter causes an internal inclination towards marriage or away from it; but there is meant the state of marriage which causes an external inclination towards it or away from it; and this state with its inclinations is manifold; as, 1. If there are little children in the house, and a new mother ought to be provided for them. 2. If there is a desire

for a greater number of children. 3. If the house is large, and full of servants of both sexes. 4. If the continual calls of business abroad divert the mind from domestic affairs, and without a new mistress there is danger of the household going to rack and ruin. 5. If mutual helps and services are required, as is the case in many kinds of employments and handicrafts. 6. Moreover it depends on the genius or disposition of the separated partner, whether after the first marriage he or she can or cannot live alone, or without a consort. 7. The preceding marriage also either gives a fear of married life, or a favour for it. 8. I have been informed that polygamous love, and the love of the sex, also the lust of defloration and the lust of variety, have led the dispositions of some into a desire for repeated marriages: and that the dispositions of some have also been led thereto by a fear of the law and of the loss of reputation, in case they indulge in whoredom: besides many other circumstances which impel the external inclinations towards matrimony.

320. III. WITH THOSE WHO HAVE NOT BEEN IN TRULY CONJUGIAL LOVE, THERE IS NO OBSTACLE OR HINDRANCE TO THEIR AGAIN CONTRACTING MATRIMONY. With those who have not been in conjugial love, there is no spiritual or internal bond, but only a natural or external bond: and if an internal bond does not keep the external in its order and tenor, the external does not hold together any better than does a bundle when the bandage is removed, which is dispersed according as it is scattered or blown about by the wind. The reason is, that what is natural derives its origin from what is spiritual, and in its existence is nothing else than a mass of spiritual things united together; wherefore if the natural be separated from the spiritual which produced and as it were begot it, it is no longer kept together interiorly, but only exteriorly by the spiritual, which encompasses and binds it in general, and does not tie it together and keep it tied together in particular. Hence it is, that the natural separated from the spiritual, in the case of two married partners does not cause any conjunction of minds and thus of the wills, but only a conjunction of some of the external affections, which
2 cohere with the senses of the body. The reason nothing opposes and hinders such persons from again being able to contract matrimony, is, that they have not possessed the essentials of marriage; and consequently no such essentials are present in them after separation by death: therefore they are then at full liberty, whether they be widowers or widows, to bind their sensual affections with whomsoever they please, provided there be no legal impediment. Neither do they themselves think of marriages otherwise than naturally, and from a regard to convenience for the sake of various necessities and ex-

ternal advantages, which after the death of one of the parties
may again be supplied by another person; and possibly, if their
interior thoughts were examined, as in the spiritual world, there
would not be found in them any distinction between conjugial
conjunctions and extra-conjugial copulations. The reason it is 3
allowable for these to contract marriages again and again, is, as
above-mentioned, that merely natural conjunctions are after
death dissolved of themselves, and put an end to; for by death
the external affections follow the body, and are entombed with it;
those only remaining which cohere with the internal affections.
But it ought to be known, that marriages interiorly conjunctive
can scarcely be entered into on earth, because the choice of internal likenesses cannot be provided by the Lord there as in the
heavens; for the choice is limited in many ways, as to equals in
state and condition, within the country, city, and village where
they live; and there, again, the future consorts are bound
together for the most part by externals, and thus not by internals; which internals do not come forth till some time after
marriage, and are only known when they put themselves forth
in the externals.

321. IV. THOSE WHO HAD LIVED TOGETHER IN TRULY CONJUGIAL LOVE ARE UNWILLING TO MARRY AGAIN, EXCEPT FOR REASONS SEPARATE FROM CONJUGIAL LOVE. The reasons why those who
had lived in truly conjugial love are unwilling to marry again,
after the death of their married partners, are as follows: 1. That
they were united as to their souls, and hence as to their minds;
and this union, because it is spiritual, is an actual adjunction of
the soul and mind of the one to those of the other, which cannot possibly be dissolved: that such is the nature of spiritual
conjunction, has been frequently shewn above. 2. That they 2
were also united as to their bodies by the reception of the propagations of the soul of the husband by the wife, and thus by
the insertion of his life into hers, whereby a maiden becomes a
wife; and on the other hand by the reception of the conjugial
love of the wife by the husband, which disposes the interiors of
his mind, and at the same time the interiors and exteriors of his
body, into a state receptible of love and perceptible of wisdom,
which state makes him from a bachelor become a husband;
concerning these particulars see above, no. 198. 3. That the 3
sphere of love from the wife, and the sphere of the understanding
from the husband, is continually flowing forth, and that it perfects
conjunctions, and encompasses them with its pleasant influence,
and unites them; see also above, no. 223. 4. That married 4
partners thus united think of and desire what is eternal in
marriage, and that on this idea their eternal happiness is
founded; see no. 216. 5. From these several considerations it 5
is, that they are no longer two, but one man, that is, one flesh.

6 6. That such a one cannot be destroyed by the death of one of the
7 parties, is manifest to the ocular sight of the spirit. 7. To these
reasons shall be added this new information, that two such married partners are nevertheless not separated by the death of one of them, since the spirit of the deceased continually dwells together with the spirit of the survivor, and this even to the death of the latter, when they again meet and are reunited, and love each other more tenderly than before, because they are then in the spiritual world. Hence flows this indisputable consequence, that those who had lived in truly conjugial love are unwilling to marry again. But if they afterwards contract something like marriage, it is for reasons separate from conjugial love; and these reasons are all external ones; as in case there are little children in the house, and the care of them requires to be provided for; if the house is large and full of servants of both sexes; if the calls of business abroad divert the mind from domestic concerns; if mutual helps and services are necessary; with other similar causes.

322. V. THE STATE OF THE MARRIAGE OF A BACHELOR WITH A MAIDEN IS DIFFERENT FROM THAT OF A BACHELOR WITH A WIDOW. By states of marriage are meant the states of the life of both the husband and the wife, after the wedding, thus in the marriage, as to the quality of the cohabitation at that time, whether it be internal cohabitation of the souls and minds, which is cohabitation in the principal idea, or whether it be only external cohabitation of the dispositions, the senses, and the body. The state of marriage of a bachelor with a maiden is the very initial state to genuine marriage; for between these, conjugial love is able to proceed in its just order, which is from its first heat to its first torch, and afterwards from its first seed with the bachelor husband, and from its first flower with the maiden wife, and thus to germinate, grow, and fructify, and introduce itself into those [states with both parties] mutually; but if otherwise, the bachelor was not a bachelor, nor the maiden a maiden, except in external form. But between a bachelor and a widow there is not such an initiation to marriage from first beginnings, nor a like progression in marriage, since a widow is more independent and at her own disposal than a maiden is; wherefore a bachelor addresses himself differently to his wife, if she has been a widow, from what he would if she were a maiden. But herein there is much variety and diversity; wherefore the subject is here mentioned only in a general way.

323. VI. THE STATE OF THE MARRIAGE OF A WIDOWER WITH A MAIDEN IS ALSO DIFFERENT FROM THAT OF A WIDOWER WITH A WIDOW. For a widower has already been initiated into conjugial life, and a maiden has yet to be; and yet conjugial love perceives

and feels its pleasantness and delight in mutual initiation; a bachelor-husband and a maiden-wife perceive and feel things ever new in whatever occurs, whereby they are in a kind of continual initiation and consequent loving progression. The case is otherwise in the state of the marriage of a widower with a maiden: the maiden-wife has an internal inclination, whereas with the man that inclination has passed away. But in this there is much variety and diversity. The case is similar in a marriage between a widower and a widow; wherefore except this general notion, we may not add anything specifically.

324. VII. THE VARIETIES AND DIVERSITIES OF THESE MARRIAGES AS TO LOVE AND ITS ATTRIBUTES EXCEED ALL NUMBER. There is an infinite variety of all things, and also an infinite diversity. By varieties are here meant the varieties between those things which are of one genus or of one species, also between genera and between species; but by diversities are here meant the diversities between those things which are opposite. Our idea of the distinction of varieties and diversities may be illustrated as follows:—The angelic heaven, which coheres together as a one, is in an infinite variety, no one there being absolutely like another, either as to souls and minds, or as to affections, perceptions, and consequent thoughts, or as to inclinations and consequent intentions, or as to tone of voice, face, body, gesture, and gait, and many other characteristics; and yet, notwithstanding there are myriads of myriads, they have been arranged and are still being arranged by the Lord into one form, in which there is full unanimity and concord; and this would not be possible unless they were all, with their innumerable varieties, universally and individually under the guidance of One: these are what we mean here by varieties. But by diversities 2
we mean the opposites of those varieties, which exist in hell: for each and all there are diametrically opposite to those who are in heaven; and hell, which consists of those, is held together as a one by means of varieties which, in their relation to each other, are absolutely contrary to the varieties in heaven; thus by means of perpetual diversities. From these considerations it is manifest what is perceived by infinite variety and what by infinite diversity. The case is similar in marriages, namely, that there are infinite varieties with those who are in conjugial love, and infinite varieties among those who are in scortatory love; and hence, that there are infinite diversities between the latter and the former. From these premises it follows in conclusion, that the varieties and diversities in marriages of every kind and species, whether of a bachelor and a maiden, or of a bachelor with a widow, or of a widower with a maiden, or of a widower with a widow, exceed all number. Who can divide infinity into numbers?

325. VIII. The state of a widow is more grievous than that of a widower. The reasons are both external and internal. The external reasons are such as all can see, as, 1. That a widow cannot provide for herself and her household the necessaries of life, nor dispose of them when acquired, as a man can, and as she previously could through a man and with a man. 2. That neither can she protect herself and her household as is needful; for, while she was a wife, her husband was her protection, and as it were her arm; and while she herself was her own protection and arm, she still trusted to her husband. 3. That of herself she is devoid of judgment (*consilium*) in such things as belong to interior wisdom and the prudence thence. 4. That a widow is without the reception of love, in which she is as a woman; thus she is in a state alien to that which was innate and induced by
2 marriage. These external reasons, which are natural, derive their origin from internal reasons also, which are spiritual, just as do all other things in the world and in the body; respecting which see above, no. 220. Those natural external reasons are perceived from the spiritual internal reasons which proceed from the marriage of good and truth, and principally from the following:—that good cannot provide or arrange anything but by means of truth; that neither can good protect itself but by means of truth, consequently that truth is the protection and as it were the arm of good; that good without truth is devoid of judgment, because
3 it has judgment, wisdom, and prudence by means of truth. Now since by creation the husband is truth, and the wife the good thereof; or, what is the same thing, since by creation the husband is understanding, and the wife the love thereof, it is evident that the external or natural reasons which aggravate the widowhood of a woman, derive their origin from internal or spiritual reasons. These spiritual reasons are those which, conjoined with natural reasons, are meant by what is said of widows in many passages in the Word; as may be seen in the *Apocalypse Revealed*, no. 764.

326. To the above I shall add two Memorable Relations. The First is as follows:—

* After the problem concerning the soul had been discussed and solved in the public school, I saw them coming out in order: first came the head master, then the elders, in the midst of whom were the five young men who had given the answers, and after these the rest. When they were come out they went apart to the environs of the house, where there were walks enclosed with shrubs; and being assembled, they divided into small crowds, forming so many groups of young men conversing

* This Memorable Relation, as far as the end of no. 328, is repeated, with some variations, in the *True Christian Religion*, no. 280.

together on subjects of wisdom; in each group there was one of the wise men from the orchestra.

As I saw these from my lodging, I became in the spirit, and in the spirit I went out to them, and approached the head master, who had lately proposed the problem about the soul.

On seeing me, he said, "Who are you? I was surprised as I saw you approaching in the way, that at one instant you came into my sight, and the next instant went out of it; or that at one time I saw you, and suddenly I did not see you: assuredly you are not in the same state of life that we are."

To this I replied, smiling, "I am neither a player nor a Vertumnus; but I am alternate, at one time in your light, and at another in your shade; thus both a foreigner and a native."

Hereupon the head master looked at me, and said, "You 2
speak strange and wonderful things: tell me who you are."

I said, "I am in the world in which you have been, and from which you have departed, which is called the natural world; and I am also in the world into which you have come, and in which you are, which is called the spiritual world. Hence it is, that I am in the natural state, and at the same time in the spiritual state; in the natural state with the men of the Earth, and in the spiritual state with you: and when I am in the natural state, you do not see me, but when I am in the spiritual state, you do. That I should be such, has been given me by the Lord. It is known to you, enlightened man, that a man of the natural world does not see a man of the spiritual world, nor contrariwise; wherefore when I let my spirit into the body, you did not see me; but when I let it out of the body, you did see me. You have been teaching in the public school exercises, that you are souls, and that souls see souls, because they are human forms; and you know, that when you were in the natural world, you did not see yourselves or your souls in your bodies; and this is a consequence of the difference between what is spiritual and what is natural."

When he heard of the difference between what is spiritual 3
and what is natural, he said, "What is that difference? is it not like the difference between what is more and less pure? consequently, what is the spiritual but a purer natural?"

I replied, "The difference is not such; but it is like that between what is prior and posterior, between which there is no determinate ratio; for the prior is in the posterior as the cause is in its effect; and the posterior is from the prior as the effect from its cause: hence it is that the one does not appear to the other."

To this the head master said, "I have meditated and ruminated on this difference, but heretofore in vain; I wish I could perceive it."

I said, "You shall not only perceive the difference between what is spiritual and what is natural, but shall also see it." I then proceeded as follows:—"You yourself are in the spiritual state when with your associates, but in the natural state with me; for you speak with your associates in the spiritual language, which is common to every spirit and angel, but with me you speak in my mother tongue; for every spirit and angel, when speaking with a man, speaks the man's own language; thus French with a Frenchman, English with an Englishman, Greek with a Greek, Arabic with an Arab, and so forth. In order, therefore, that you may know the difference between what is spiritual and what is natural in respect to languages, make this experiment: withdraw to your associates, and say something there; then retain the expressions, and return with them in your memory, and utter them before me."

4 He did so, and returned to me with those expressions in his mouth, and uttered them; and he did not understand one of them: they were altogether strange and foreign, such as do not occur in any language of the natural world. By this experiment, several times repeated, it was made very evident, that all in the spiritual world have the spiritual language, which has nothing in common with any language of the natural world, and that every man comes of himself into that language after death. At the same time also he experienced, that the very sound of the spiritual language differs to such a degree from the sound of natural language, that a spiritual sound, although loud, could not be heard at all by a natural man, nor a natural sound by a spiritual man.

5 Afterwards I requested the head master and the bystanders to withdraw to their associates, and write some sentence on a piece of paper, and then return with it to me, and read it. They did so, and returned with the paper in their hand; but when they read it, they could not understand any part of it, because the writing consisted only of some letters of the alphabet, with strokes over them, each of which was significative of some particular meaning: because each letter of the alphabet is significative of some particular meaning there, it is evident whence it is that the Lord is called the Alpha and the Omega. On their repeatedly withdrawing, writing, and returning to me, they found that that writing involved and comprehended innumerable things which no natural writing could possibly express; and they were told that this was because the spiritual man thinks of things which are incomprehensible and ineffable to the natural man, and that these things cannot flow in and be brought into any other writing nor into any other language.

6 Then as the bystanders were unwilling to comprehend that spiritual thought so far exceeds natural thought as to be respectively ineffable, I said to them, "Make the experiment;

withdraw into your spiritual society, and think something, and retain it in your memory, and return, and express it before me."

They did so; they withdrew, thought something, retained their thoughts, and again came forth; but when they wanted to express the thing they had thought, they were unable; for they did not find any idea of natural thought adequate to any idea of spiritual thought, consequently no words expressive of it; for ideas of thought become the expressions of speech.

Then again they withdrew and returned, and they were 7
convinced that spiritual ideas are supernatural, inexpressible, ineffable, and incomprehensible to the natural man; and on account of this their super-eminence, they said, that spiritual ideas or thoughts respectively to natural ones were ideas of ideas, and thoughts of thoughts; and that therefore they were expressive of qualities of qualities, and affections of affections; consequently that spiritual thoughts were the beginnings and origins of natural thoughts. Hence also it was made evident that spiritual wisdom is the wisdom of wisdom, and consequently imperceptible to any wise man in the natural world. It was then told them from the third heaven, that there is a wisdom still more interior and higher, which is called celestial, bearing a proportion to spiritual wisdom like that which spiritual wisdom bears to natural: and that these flow in in order according to the heavens from the Divine wisdom of the Lord, which is infinite.

327. After this I said to the bystanders, "You have seen from these three experimental proofs what is the difference between what is spiritual and what is natural, and also the reason why a natural man does not appear to a spiritual man, nor a spiritual man to a natural one, although they are consociated as to affections and thoughts, and therefore as to presence. Hence it is that, as I was approaching, you—the head master—at one time saw me, and at another you did not."

After this, a voice was heard from a higher heaven, saying to the head master, "Come up hither;" and he went up: and on his return he said that the angels, like himself, had not previously known the differences between what is spiritual and what is natural, because there had not before been given an opportunity of comparing them together, by any man's being in both worlds at the same time; and without comparison those differences are not known.

328. After this we retired, and speaking again on this subject, I said, "Those differences exist from no other source than the fact that you, who are in the spiritual world, and who consequently are spiritual, are in substantial things and not in material things; and substantial things are the beginnings

of material things. You are in principles and thus in singulars; but we are in principiates and composites; you are in particulars, but we are in generals; and as generals cannot enter into particulars, so neither can natural things, which are material, enter into spiritual things which are substantial, any more than a ship's cable can enter into, or be drawn through, the eye of a sewing needle; or than a nerve can enter or be let into one of the fibres of which it is composed, or a fibre into one of the fibrils of which it is composed. This also is known in the world: wherefore the learned are agreed, that there is no influx of what is natural into what is spiritual, but of what is spiritual into what is natural. This now is the reason why a natural man cannot think that which a spiritual man thinks, nor consequently express them; wherefore Paul calls what he heard
2 from the third heaven, unspeakable [2 Cor. xii. 14]. Add to this, that thinking spiritually is thinking apart from space and time, and that thinking naturally is thinking with space and time; for to every idea of natural thought there adheres something from time and space, which is not the case with any spiritual idea; the reason is, that the spiritual world is not in space and time, like the natural world, but in the appearance of space and time. In this respect also spiritual thoughts and perceptions differ from natural ones. Wherefore you are able to think of the essence and omnipresence of God from eternity, that is, of God before the creation of the world, since you think of the essence of God from eternity apart from time, and of His omnipresence apart from space, and thus comprehend such things as transcend the ideas of the natural man."

3 I then related that I had once thought of the essence and omnipresence of God from eternity, that is, of God before the creation of the world; and that because I was not as yet able to remove spaces and times from the ideas of my thought, I became anxious; for there entered the idea of nature instead of God: but it was said to me, "Remove the ideas of space and time, and you will see." It was given me to remove them, and I saw; and from that time I was able to think of God from eternity, and not at all of nature from eternity; because God is in all time apart from time, and in all space apart from space, whereas nature is in all time in time, and in all space in space; and nature, with its time and space, must of necessity have a beginning and an origin, but not God, Who is apart from time and space; wherefore nature is from God, not from eternity, but in time, that is, together with its own time and space.

329. After the head master and the rest had left me, some boys, who also had been in the public school exercises, followed me home, and stood near me for a little while as I was writing: and lo, they then saw a cockroach running upon my paper, and

asked in surprise what the name of that nimble little creature was. I said, "It is called a cockroach; and I will tell you some wonderful things about it. This little living thing contains in itself as many members and viscera as there are in a camel, such as brains, hearts, pulmonary pipes, organs of sense, motion, and generation, a stomach, intestines, and many others; and each of these organs is woven of fibres, nerves, blood-vessels, muscles, tendons, membranes; and each of these of still purer parts, which escape the observation of the keenest eye."

They then said, that this little living thing nevertheless 2
appeared to them as but a simple substance.

To this I said, "There are nevertheless innumerable things within it. I say these things in order that you may know, that the case is similar in regard to every object which appears before you as one, simple, and least, both in your actions and in your affections and thoughts. I can assure you, that every grain of thought, and every drop of your affection, is divisible *ad infinitum:* and that in proportion as your ideas are divisible, so you are wise. Know then, that everything divided is more and more manifold, and not more and more simple; because what is divided again and again approaches nearer and nearer to the infinite, in which all things are infinitely. What I am now telling you is new and heretofore unheard of."

When I had said this, the boys took their leave of me, and 3
went to the chief teacher, and entreated him to propose some time or other in the public school something new and unheard of as a problem.

He inquired, "What?"

They said, "That everything divided is more and more manifold, and not more and more simple; because it approaches nearer and nearer to the infinite, in which all things are infinitely."

So he promised to propose it, and said, "I see this, because I have perceived that one natural idea is the continent of innumerable spiritual ideas; yea, that one spiritual idea is the continent of innumerable celestial ideas. Hence comes the difference between the celestial wisdom in which the angels of the third heaven are, and the spiritual wisdom in which the angels of the second heaven are, and also the natural wisdom in which the angels of the ultimate heaven, and likewise men, are."

330. The Second Memorable Relation :—

I once heard a pleasant discussion between some men about the feminine sex, as to whether any woman who is constantly loving her own beauty, that is, who loves herself on account of her own form, can love her husband. They first agreed among themselves that women have a twofold beauty; one natural, which is that of the face and body, and the other spiritual, which is that of the love and manners. They agreed also, that these two kinds of beauty are very often divided in the natural world, and that they are always united in the spiritual world, for in that world beauty is the form of the love and manners; wherefore after death it very frequently happens that ugly women become beauties, and beautiful women become deformities.

2 While the men were discussing this point, there came some wives and said, "Admit of our presence; because what you are discussing, you have been taught by knowledge, but we are taught it by experience; and you likewise know so little of the love of wives that it scarcely amounts to anything. Do you know that the prudence of the wisdom of wives consists in hiding their love for their husbands in the inmost of their bosoms, or in the midst of their hearts?"

The discussion then began; and the FIRST CONCLUSION drawn by the men was, That every woman wants to appear beautiful in face and beautiful in manners, because she is born an affection of love, and the form of this affection is beauty; wherefore a woman who does not want to be beautiful, is not a woman who wants to love and be loved, and consequently is not truly a woman.

To this the wives said, "The beauty of a woman dwells in soft tenderness, and consequently in exquisite sensation; hence comes the love of woman for man, and the love of man for woman. This possibly you do not understand."

3 The SECOND CONCLUSION of the men was, That a woman before marriage wants to be beautiful for the men, but after marriage, if she be chaste, for one man only, and not for the men.

To this the wives said, "After a husband has sipped the natural beauty of his wife, he no longer sees it, but he sees her spiritual beauty; and from this he loves back again, and recalls her natural beauty, but under a different appearance."

4 The THIRD CONCLUSION of their discussion was, That if a woman after marriage wants to appear beautiful in the same way as before marriage, she loves the men, and not the man: because a woman who loves herself on account of her beauty is continually wanting to have her beauty sipped; and as this no longer appears to her husband, as you said, she wants it to be sipped by the men to whom it does appear. It is evident that such a one has the love of the sex, and not the love of one of the sex.

At this the wives were silent; yet they murmured, "What woman is so devoid of vanity as not to want to seem beautiful to the men also, at the same time that she seems beautiful to her only one?"

Some wives from heaven, who were beautiful, because they were heavenly affections, heard this discussion, and they confirmed the three conclusions of the men; but they added, "Let women only love their beauty, and its adornment, for the sake of their husbands, and from them."

331. Those three wives, being indignant at the three conclusions of the men being confirmed by the wives from heaven, said to the men, "You have inquired whether a woman that loves herself on account of her own beauty, loves her husband; we in our turn will therefore discuss whether a man who loves himself on account of his own intelligence, can love his wife. Be present and hear."

The FIRST CONCLUSION they made was: No wife loves her husband on account of his face, but on account of his intelligence in his occupation and in his general conduct (*mores*): know therefore, that a wife unites herself with the man's intelligence and thus with the man: wherefore if a man loves himself on account of his own intelligence, he withdraws it from the wife into himself, whence comes disunion and not union: moreover, loving his own intelligence is being wise from himself, and this is being insane; wherefore it is loving his own insanity.

To this the men said, "Possibly the wife unites herself with the man's virtue (or virile potency)."

At this the wives smiled, saying, "Virtue does not fail when the man loves the wife from intelligence; but it does fail if he loves her from insanity. Intelligence consists in loving the wife only; and virtue does not fail this love; but insanity consists in not loving the wife but the sex, and virtue does fail this love. Do you comprehend this?"

The SECOND CONCLUSION was: We women are born into the 2
love of the men's intelligence; wherefore if the men love their own self-intelligence, it cannot be united with its genuine love, which is with the wife; and if the man's intelligence is not united with its genuine love, which is with the wife, it becomes insanity from conceit, and conjugial love becomes cold. What woman therefore can unite her love to cold; and what man can unite the insanity of self-conceit to the love of intelligence?

But the men said, "Whence has a man honour from his wife unless he magnifies his intelligence?" The wives replied, "From love, because love honours; and honour cannot be separated from love, but love may be from honour."

Afterwards they came to this THIRD CONCLUSION; "You seem 3
to yourselves as if you loved your wives; and you do not see that you are loved by your wives, and thus that you love them in return; and that your intelligence is a receptacle; if therefore you love your intelligence in yourselves, it becomes the receptacle of your love; and the love of the proprium, since it cannot endure an equal, never becomes conjugial love; but so long as it prevails, so long it remains scortatory."

Hereupon the men were silent; nevertheless they murmured, "What is conjugial love?"

Some husbands in heaven heard this discussion, and they confirmed thence the three conclusions of the wives.

POLYGAMY.

332. THE reason why polygamous marriages are absolutely condemned by the Christian world cannot be clearly seen by any one, with whatever powers of acute and ingenious investigation he may be endowed, unless he be previously instructed, THAT THERE EXISTS A TRULY CONJUGIAL LOVE; THAT THIS LOVE CANNOT POSSIBLY EXIST EXCEPT BETWEEN TWO; THAT NEITHER CAN IT EXIST BETWEEN TWO, EXCEPT FROM THE LORD ALONE; AND THAT ON THIS LOVE IS INSCRIBED HEAVEN WITH ALL ITS FELICITIES. Unless these Knowledges precede, and as it were lay the first stone, the mind busies itself in vain to draw from the understanding any reasons in which it might acquiesce, and on which it may firmly stand as a house upon its stone or foundation, why polygamy is condemned by the Christian world. It is known, that the institution of monogamous marriage is founded on the Word of the Lord, "*That whosoever putteth away his wife, except on account of whoredom, and marrieth another, committeth adultery; and that from the beginning, or from the first establishment of marriages, it was [ordained], that two should become one flesh: and that man should not separate what God hath joined together*" (Matt.
2 xix. 3–9). But although the Lord spoke these words from the Divine law inscribed on marriages, yet if the understanding cannot support that Divine law by some reason of its own, it may nevertheless, by turnings and windings to which it is accustomed, and by sinister interpretations, warp it, and render it obscure and ambiguous, and at length affirmative-negative;—affirmative, because it is also in accordance with the civil law; and negative, because it is not in accordance with their rational sight. Into this the human mind will fall, unless it be previously instructed concerning the above-mentioned Knowledges, which may be serviceable to the understanding as introductory to its reasons. These Knowledges are, that there exists a truly conjugial love; that this love cannot possibly exist except between two; that neither can it between two, except from the Lord Alone; and that on this love is inscribed heaven with all its felicities. But these, and several other particulars concerning the condemnation of polygamy by the Christian world, must be demonstrated in order, according to the following articles:—

I. *Truly conjugial love cannot exist except with one wife, con-*

sequently neither can truly conjugial friendship, confidence, potency, and such a conjunction of the minds that two may be one flesh.

II. *Thus the celestial blessednesses, spiritual blissfulnesses, and natural delightsomenesses, which from the beginning were provided for those who are in truly conjugial love, can only be given with one wife.*

III. *All those things cannot possibly exist except from the Lord Alone; and they do not exist with any others than those who approach Him alone, and at the same time live according to His commandments.*

IV. *Consequently, truly conjugial love, with its felicities, can exist only with those who are of the Christian Church.*

V. *Hence it is that it is not allowable for a Christian to marry more than one wife.*

VI. *If a Christian marries several wives, he commits not only natural adultery, but also spiritual adultery.*

VII. *The Israelitish nation was permitted to marry several wives, because the Christian church was not with that nation, and consequently truly conjugial love could not exist with them.*

VIII. *At the present day, the Mohammedans are permitted to marry several wives, because they do not acknowledge the Lord Jesus Christ to be one with Jehovah the Father, and thus to be the God of heaven and earth; and therefore they cannot receive truly conjugial love.*

IX. *The Mohammedan heaven is outside of the Christian heaven, and is divided into two heavens, a lower and a higher; and no others are elevated into their higher heaven but those who renounce concubines, and live with one wife, and acknowledge our Lord as equal to God the Father, to Whom has been given dominion over heaven and earth.*

X. *Polygamy is lasciviousness.*

XI. *Conjugial chastity, purity, and holiness, cannot possibly exist with polygamists.*

XII. *Polygamists, so long as they remain polygamists, cannot become spiritual.*

XIII. *Polygamy is not sin with those with whom it is in accordance with religion.*

XIV. *Polygamy is not sin with those who are in ignorance about the Lord.*

XV. *Of these, such, although polygamists, are saved as acknowledge a God, and from religion live according to the civil laws of justice.*

XVI. *But none either of the latter or of the former can be consociated with the angels in the Christian heavens.*

Now follows the explanation of these articles.

333. I. TRULY CONJUGIAL LOVE CAN NOT EXIST EXCEPT WITH ONE WIFE, CONSEQUENTLY NEITHER CAN TRULY CONJUGIAL FRIENDSHIP, CONFIDENCE, POTENCY, AND SUCH A CONJUNCTION OF THE MINDS

THAT TWO MAY BE ONE FLESH. That truly conjugial love is at the present day so rare as to be generally unknown, has been occasionally pointed out above; that nevertheless it actually exists, was demonstrated in its own chapter, and occasionally in following chapters. But, apart from such demonstration, who does not know that there exists such a love, which, in excellence and pleasantness, surpasses all other loves, so that all other loves in respect to it are of little account? That it exceeds the love of self, the love of the world, and even the love of life, experience testifies. Have there not been, and are there not still, men who, for the sake of a woman, whom they long for and court as a bride, prostrate themselves on their knees, adore her as a goddess, and submit themselves as the vilest slaves to her will and pleasure? a proof that this love exceeds the love of self. Have there not been, and are there not still, men who, for the sake of a woman, whom they long for and court as a bride, make light of wealth, yea, of treasures, if they happen to possess them, and also lavish them prodigally? a proof that this love exceeds the love of the world. Have there not been, and are there not still, men who, for a woman whom they long for and court as a bride, account their life itself as worthless, and desire to die if she does not agree to their wishes? this also is evidenced by the many fatal combats between rival lovers; a proof that this love exceeds the love of life. Have there not been, and are there not still, men who, for a woman whom they have longed for and courted as a bride, have gone mad in
2 consequence of being rejected? From such a commencement of this love with many, who cannot rationally conclude, that that love, by virtue of its essence, holds supreme dominion over every other love; and that the man's (*homo*) soul in such case is in it, and promises itself eternal blessednesses with the woman whom he longs for and courts? Who can discover, let him make what inquiry he pleases, any other cause of this, than that he has devoted his soul and heart to one woman? for if the lover, while he is in that state, were given the option of choosing out of the whole sex the worthiest, the richest, and the most beautiful, would he not despise the offer, and adhere to her whom he had already chosen, his heart being riveted to her alone? These things are said in order that you may acknowledge, that conjugial love of such super-eminence does exist, and that it comes into existence when one of the sex alone is loved. What understanding which with cultivated acumen attends to a chain of reasons, cannot conclude thence, that if a lover from his soul, or from his inmosts, constantly persisted in love to that one, he would attain those eternal blessednesses which he promised himself before consent, and promises in consent? That he also does attain them if he approaches the Lord, and from Him lives a life of true religion, was shewn above. Who but the Lord enters the

life of man from above, and implants therein internal heavenly joys, and transfers them to the things which follow in order; and the more so, when at the same time He also bestows enduring potency (*virtus*)? The fact that such love does not exist in one's self, or in this or that person, is no proof that it does not exist, or that it cannot possibly exist.

334. Since truly conjugial love conjoins the souls and hearts of two, therefore also it is united with friendship, and through friendship with confidence, and makes both friendship and confidence conjugial; and conjugial friendship and confidence are so pre-eminent above other friendships and confidences, that as that love is the love of loves, so also that friendship is the friendship of friendships, and in like manner that confidence is the confidence of confidences. That this is the case also with the potency, is plain from many reasons, some of which are revealed in the second Memorable Relation that follows this chapter; and from this potency follows the endurance of that love. That by means of truly conjugial love two consorts become one flesh, has been shown in a special chapter, from nos. 156–183.

335. II. Thus the celestial blessednesses, spiritual blissfulnesses, and natural delightsomenesses, which from the beginning were provided for those who are in truly conjugial love, can only be given with one wife. They are called celestial blessednesses, spiritual blissfulnesses, and natural delightsomenesses, because the human mind is distinguished into three regions, of which the highest is called celestial, the second spiritual, and the third natural; and those three regions, with those who are in truly conjugial love, stand open, and influx follows in order according to the openings. And as the pleasantnesses of that love are the most eminent in the highest region, they are perceived as blessednesses, and as in the middle region they are less eminent, they are perceived as blissfulnesses, and lastly, in the lowest region, as delightsomenesses: that those pleasantnesses exist, and are perceived and felt, is manifest from the Memorable Relations in which they are described. The reason why all those happinesses have been from the beginning provided for those who are in truly conjugial love, is, that there is an infinity of all blessednesses in the Lord, and He is Divine love; and it is the essence of love to will to communicate all its goods to another whom it loves; wherefore together with man He created that love, and inscribed on it the faculty of receiving and perceiving those blessednesses. Who is so dull and devoid of reason as not to be able to see, that there is some particular love into which have been collected by the Lord all possible blessednesses, blissfulnesses, and delights?

336. III. ALL THOSE THINGS CANNOT POSSIBLY EXIST EXCEPT FROM THE LORD ALONE; AND THEY DO NOT EXIST WITH ANY OTHERS THAN THOSE WHO APPROACH HIM ALONE, AND [AT THE SAME TIME] LIVE ACCORDING TO HIS COMMANDMENTS. This has been proved above in many places; to which proofs it must be added, that all those blessednesses, blissfulnesses, and delights can only be given by the Lord, and that therefore no one else ought to be approached. Who else can be approached, when through Him all things were made which were made (John i. 3); when He is the God of heaven and earth (Matt. xxviii. 18); when no appearance of God the Father was ever seen, or His voice heard, except through Him (John i. 18; v. 37; xiv. 6–11)? From these and very many other passages in the Word, it is manifest that the marriage of love and wisdom, or of good and truth, from which alone marriages derive their origin, proceeds from Him alone. Hence it follows, that that love with its felicities exists with none but those who approach Him; and the reason it exists with those who live according to His commandments, is, that He is conjoined with them by means of love (John xiv. 21–24).

337. IV. CONSEQUENTLY, TRULY CONJUGIAL LOVE [WITH ITS FELICITIES] CAN EXIST ONLY WITH THOSE WHO ARE OF THE CHRISTIAN CHURCH. The reasons why conjugial love, such as was described in its special chapter, nos. 57–73, and in the following chapters, thus such as it is in its essence, exists only with those who are of the Christian church, are, that that love is from the Lord Alone, and the Lord is not elsewhere so known as that He can be approached as God; and, that that love is according to the state of the church with every one (no. 130), and the genuine state of the church is from no other source than from the Lord, and thus is with none others than those who receive it from Him. That these two [principles] are the first beginnings, the introductions, and the establishments of that love, has been already confirmed by such an abundance of evident and conclusive reasons, that it is altogether needless to say anything more on the subject. The reason why truly conjugial love is nevertheless rare in the Christian world (nos. 58, 59), is, that few in that world approach the Lord, and among those there are some who indeed believe the church, but do not live [according to] it; besides many other circumstances which are unfolded in the *Apocalypse Revealed*, where the state of the Christian church at the present day is fully described. But nevertheless the Truth stands, that truly conjugial love can exist only with those who are of the Christian church; wherefore also from this ground polygamy is absolutely condemned in that church; that this also is of the Divine providence of the Lord, appears very manifest to those who think justly concerning providence.

338. V. Hence it is that it is not allowable for a Christian to marry more than one wife. This follows as confirmed from the confirmation of the preceding articles; to which this must be added, that the genuine conjugial principle is more deeply inscribed on the minds of Christians than on the minds of the nations who have embraced polygamy; and that therefore the minds of Christians are more susceptible of that love than the minds of polygamists; for that conjugial principle is inscribed on the interiors of the minds of Christians, because they acknowledge the Lord and His Divine, and on the exteriors of their minds by civil laws.

339. VI. If a Christian marries several wives, he commits not only natural adultery, but also spiritual adultery. That a Christian who marries several wives, commits natural adultery, is according to the Lord's words, which are, "That it is not lawful to put away a wife, because from the beginning they were created to be one flesh; and that he who putteth away a wife without just cause, and marrieth another, committeth adultery" (Matt. xix. 3–11), thus still more does he commit adultery who does not put away his wife, but retains her, and takes another in addition. This law enacted by the Lord respecting marriages, derives its internal cause from the spiritual marriage; for whatever the Lord spoke was in itself spiritual; which is meant by this declaration, "*The words that I speak unto you are spirit, and they are life*" (John vi. 63). The spiritual [teaching] contained therein is this, that by polygamous marriage in the Christian world, the marriage of the Lord and the church is profaned; likewise the marriage of good and truth; and above all the Word, and with the Word the church; and the profanation of those things is spiritual adultery. That the profanation of the good and truth of the church from the Word corresponds to adultery, and therefore is spiritual adultery; and that the falsification of good and truth likewise corresponds thereto, but in a less degree, may be seen confirmed in the *Apocalypse Revealed*, no.
134. The reason why by polygamous marriages among Chris- 2
tians, the marriage of the Lord and the church is profaned, is, that there is a correspondence between that Divine marriage and the marriages of Christians (concerning which, see above, nos. 83–102); which correspondence utterly perishes, if wife be added to wife; and when it perishes, the married man (*homo*) is no longer a Christian. The reason why by polygamous marriages among Christians, the marriage of good and truth is profaned, is, that from this spiritual marriage are derived marriages on earth; and the marriages of Christians differ from those of other nations in this respect, that, as good loves truth, and truth good, and as they are a one, so a wife and a husband love each other

and are a one; wherefore if a Christian were to add wife to wife, he would rend asunder in himself that spiritual marriage; consequently he would profane the origin of his marriage, and would thus commit spiritual adultery. That marriages on earth are derived from the marriage of good and truth, see nos. 116–131. The reason why a Christian by polygamous marriage would profane the Word and the church, is, that the Word considered in itself is the marriage of good and truth, and the church likewise, so far as this is from the Word; see above, nos.
3 128–131. Now, since a Christian man (*homo*), because he knows the Lord, has the Word, and also has the church from the Lord by means of the Word, it is evident that he, more than a man who is not a Christian, possesses the faculty of being capable of being regenerated, and thus of becoming spiritual, and also of attaining to truly conjugial love: for these things cohere together. Since those Christians who marry several wives, commit not only natural adultery, but also at the same time spiritual adultery, it follows that the damnation of Christian polygamists after death is more grievous than the damnation of those who commit only natural adultery. Upon inquiring about their state after death, I received for answer, that heaven is completely closed in respect to them; that they appear in hell as if lying in warm water in a bath, and that they appear thus at a distance, although they are standing on their feet and walking; and that this lot befalls them in consequence of their internal madness; and that some of them are cast into the chasms which are at the boundaries of the [various] worlds.

340. VII. THE ISRAELITISH NATION WAS PERMITTED TO MARRY SEVERAL WIVES, BECAUSE THE CHRISTIAN CHURCH WAS NOT WITH THAT NATION, AND CONSEQUENTLY TRULY CONJUGIAL LOVE COULD NOT EXIST WITH THEM. There are some at this day who think doubtfully concerning the institution relating to monogamous marriages, or marriages of one man with one wife, and who are distracted by reasonings on the subject; supposing that because polygamous marriages were openly permitted to the Israelitish nation and its kings, and to David and Solomon, they are also in themselves permissible to Christians; but such persons have no distinct knowledge about the Israelitish nation and the Christian, nor about the externals and internals of the church, nor about the change of the church from external to internal by the Lord; consequently they know nothing from interior judgment about marriages. In general it ought to be understood that a man is born natural in order that he may become spiritual; and that so long as he remains natural, he is as it were in the night, and asleep, as to spiritual things; and that in this case he does not even know the difference between the external natural man and
2 the internal spiritual man. That the Christian church was not

with the Israelitish nation, is known from the Word; for they expected the Messiah, as they still expect Him, Who was to exalt them above all the nations and peoples in the world: wherefore if they had been told, and were still to be told, that the Messiah's kingdom is over the heavens, and consequently over all nations, they would have accounted it an idle tale; hence it was, that they not only did not acknowledge Christ or the Messiah, our Lord, when He came into the world, but also cruelly removed Him out of the world. From these considerations it is manifest, that the Christian church was not with that nation, as neither is it at the present day; and those with whom the Christian church is not, are both external natural and internal natural men: to such persons polygamy is not hurtful, for it is inscribed on the natural man; for, in regard to love in marriages, the natural man perceives nothing but what belongs to lust. This is meant by these words of the Lord, "*That Moses, because of the* HARDNESS OF THEIR HEARTS, *permitted them to put away their wives; but that from the beginning it was not so*" (Matt. xix. 8). He says that Moses permitted it, in order that it may be known that it was not the Lord who permitted it.
3 But that the Lord taught the internal spiritual man, is known from His precepts, and from the abrogation of the rituals which served only for the use of the natural man; from His precepts concerning washing, as denoting the purification of the internal man (Matt. xv. 1, 17–20: xxiii. 25, 26; Mark vii. 14–23); concerning adultery, as denoting the cupidity of the will (Matt. v. 28); concerning the putting away of wives, as being unlawful; and concerning polygamy, as not being in harmony with the Divine law (Matt. xix. 3–9). These and many other things which belong to the internal and spiritual man, the Lord taught, because He Alone opens the internals of human minds, and makes them spiritual, and implants these spiritual things in the natural ones, that these also may partake of a spiritual essence: and this takes place if He is approached, and a life is lived according to His commandments; which in a summary are, to believe on Him, and to shun evils because they are of the devil and from the devil, also to do goods, because they are of the Lord and from the Lord; and in both cases for the man to act as from himself, and at the same time to believe that all is done by the Lord through him.
4 The very reason why the Lord Alone opens the internal spiritual man, and implants this in the external natural man, is, that every man thinks and acts naturally, and therefore could not perceive anything spiritual, and receive it in his Natural, unless the Lord had assumed the Human Natural, and had made this also Divine. From these considerations now the Truth is manifest, that the Israelitish nation was permitted to marry several wives, because the Christian church was not with that nation.

341. VIII. AT THE PRESENT DAY, THE MOHAMMEDANS ARE PERMITTED TO MARRY SEVERAL WIVES, BECAUSE THEY DO NOT ACKNOWLEDGE THE LORD JESUS CHRIST TO BE ONE WITH JEHOVAH THE FATHER, AND THUS TO BE THE GOD OF HEAVEN AND EARTH, AND THEREFORE THEY CANNOT RECEIVE TRULY CONJUGIAL LOVE. The Mohammedans, in conformity with the religion which Mohammed gave them, acknowledge Jesus Christ to be the Son of God and a very great prophet, and that He was sent into the world by God the Father to teach mankind; but they do not acknowledge that God the Father and He are one, and that His Divine and His Human are one person, united as the soul and the body, according to the faith of all Christians in conformity with the Athanasian Creed; therefore the followers of Mohammed could not acknowledge our Lord to be any God from eternity, but only to be a perfect natural man; and as this was the opinion entertained by Mohammed, and hence by his disciples, and as they knew that there is One God, and that that God is He Who created the universe, therefore they could do no other than pass by our Lord in their worship; and the more so, because they declare Mohammed also to be a very great prophet; neither do they know what the Lord taught. It is owing to this cause, that the interiors of their minds, which in themselves are spiritual, could not be opened: that the interiors of the mind are opened
2 by the Lord alone, see just above, no. 340. The genuine reason why they are opened by the Lord, when He is acknowledged to be the God of heaven and earth, and is approached, and with those who live according to His commandments, is, that otherwise there is no conjunction, and without conjunction there is no reception. With man there is the presence of the Lord, and there is conjunction with Him. Approaching Him effects presence, and living according to His commandments effects conjunction; His presence alone is without reception, but presence
3 and at the same time conjunction is with reception. On this subject I will relate the following new thing from the spiritual world. Every one in that world, when he is thought of, is brought into view as present; but no one is conjoined with another except from the affection of love, and the affection of love is insinuated by doing his sayings and what is pleasing to him. This circumstance, which is common in the spiritual world, derives its origin from the Lord's being present and conjoined in this same manner. These things are said in order that it may be known that the reason the Mohammedans are permitted to marry several wives, is, that truly conjugial love, which exists only between one man and one wife, was not possible to them, because from their religion they did not acknowledge the Lord to be equal to God the Father, and thus to be the God of heaven and earth. That conjugial love with every

one is according to the state of the church, see above, at no. 130, and in many places in the foregoing pages.

342. IX. THE MOHAMMEDAN HEAVEN IS OUTSIDE OF THE CHRISTIAN HEAVEN, AND IS DIVIDED INTO TWO HEAVENS, A LOWER AND A HIGHER; AND NO OTHERS ARE ELEVATED INTO THEIR HIGHER HEAVEN BUT THOSE WHO RENOUNCE CONCUBINES, AND LIVE WITH ONE WIFE, AND ACKNOWLEDGE OUR LORD AS EQUAL TO GOD THE FATHER, TO WHOM HAS BEEN GIVEN DOMINION OVER HEAVEN AND EARTH. Before anything is said particularly about these points, it is of importance that something should be premised concerning the Divine providence of the Lord in regard to the rise of the Mohammedan religion. That this religion is received by more kingdoms than the Christian religion, may possibly be a stumbling-block to those who think of the Divine providence, and at the same time believe that no one can be saved that is not born a Christian; but the Mohammedan religion is no stumbling-block to those who believe that all things are of the Divine providence. These inquire in what respect [the Divine providence is manifested in the Mohammedan religion]; and they also discover it. It is in this, that the Mohammedan religion acknowledges our Lord to be the Son of God, the wisest of men, and a very great prophet, who came into the world to teach mankind; but since the Mohammedans have made the Alcoran only the book of their religion, and consequently think much of Mohammed who wrote it, and pay him some degree of worship, therefore they think little about our Lord. In order that it may be fully known that the Mohammedan religion was raised up by the Lord's Divine providence to destroy the idolatries of many nations, the matter shall be stated in some order; wherefore, the origin of idolatries shall be first
stated. Previous to the Mohammedan religion, idolatrous 2
worship prevailed throughout the whole world; the reason was, that the churches before the Lord's coming were all representative churches; such also was the Israelitish church, in which the tabernacle, the garments of Aaron, the sacrifices, all things belonging to the temple at Jerusalem, and also the statutes, were representative. With the Ancients, again, there was the science of correspondences, which is also the science of representations. This was the very science of the wise, and was cultivated especially by the Egyptians, whence arose their hieroglyphics. From that science they knew what was signified by animals of every kind, and what by trees of every kind, and likewise what by mountains, hills, rivers, fountains, and also what by the sun, the moon, and the stars. By means of this science also they had a Knowledge of spiritual things; because those things which were represented, which were such things as belong to the spiritual wisdom among the angels, were

3 the origins [of the things which represent]. Now, since all their worship was representative, consisting of mere correspondences, therefore they celebrated it on mountains and hills, and also in groves and gardens. On this account, also, they consecrated fountains, and in adorations turned their faces to the rising sun. Moreover they made graven horses, oxen, calves, and lambs; yea, birds, fishes, and serpents; and they set them in their houses and in other places, in an order according to the spiritual things of the church to which they corresponded, or which they represented. They also set similar things in their temples, as a means of recalling to their remembrance the holy things of worship which they signified. After a time, when the science of correspondences had become obliterated, their posterity began to worship the very graven images as holy in themselves, not knowing that their Ancient forefathers did not see anything holy in them, but that, according to their correspondences, they merely represented and hence signified holy things. Hence arose the idolatries which filled the whole world, both Asia with its
4 islands, and Africa and Europe. In order that all those idolatries might be extirpated, it came to pass of the Lord's Divine providence, that a new religion, accommodated to the genius of the Orientals, should take its rise, in which religion there should be something from both Testaments of the Word, and which should teach that the Lord had come into the world, and that He was a very great prophet, the wisest of all, and the Son of God. This was effected by means of Mohammed, from whom that religion took its name. From these considerations it is evident, that this religion was raised up of the Lord's Divine providence, and accommodated, as has been stated, to the genius of the Orientals, to the end that it might destroy the idolatries of so many nations, and give them some Knowledge of the Lord before they came into the spiritual world, as is the case with every one after death. This religion would not have been received by so many kingdoms, neither could it have extirpated their idolatries, unless it had been made appropriate to their ideas; especially unless polygamy had been permitted; and also for the reason that, without that permission, the Orientals would have blazed out into filthy adulteries more than the Europeans, and would have perished.

343. The reason why the Mohammedans also have a heaven is that all in the universal globe of lands who acknowledge a God, and from religion shun evils as sins against Him, are saved. That the Mohammedan heaven is distinguished into two, a lower and a higher, I have heard from themselves; and that in the lower heaven they live with several wives and concubines as in the world: but that those who renounce concubines and live

with one wife, are elevated into the higher heaven. I have heard also that it is impossible for them to think of our Lord as one with the Father; but that it is possible for them to think of Him as His equal, and also that to Him has been given dominion over heaven and earth, because He is His Son; wherefore this is the faith of those to whom it is given by the Lord to ascend into the higher heaven.

344. It was once given me to perceive the quality of the heat of the conjugial love of polygamists. I was speaking with one who personated Mohammed. Mohammed himself is never present, but some one is substituted in his place, to the end that those who have newly arrived from the world may as it were see him. This substitute, after I had been talking with him at a distance, sent me an ebony spoon, and other things, which were proofs that they came from him; at the same time a communication was opened for the heat of their conjugial love in that place, and it was perceived by me like the foul heat of a bath; on feeling which, I turned away, and the communicating passage was closed.

345. X. Polygamy is lasciviousness. The reason is, that its love is divided among several, and is the love of the sex, and the love of the external or natural man, and thus is not conjugial love, which alone exists chaste. It is known that polygamous love is love divided among several, and divided love is not conjugial love, for this love cannot be divided from one of the sex; hence the former love is lascivious, and polygamy is lasciviousness. Polygamous love is the love of the sex, because it differs from this only in these respects, that it is limited to the number which a polygamist may take, and, that it is bound to the observance of certain laws enacted for the public good; also that it is allowed to take concubines in addition to wives: and thus, as it is the love of the sex, it is the love of lasciviousness. The reason why polygamous love is the love of the external or natural man is, that it is inscribed on that man; and whatever the natural man does from himself is evil, out of which he is not withdrawn except by means of elevation into the internal spiritual man, which is effected solely by the Lord; and evil in regard to the sex, which is within in the natural man, is whoredom; but since whoredom is ruinous to society, instead thereof was induced its likeness, which is called polygamy. All the evil into which man is born from his parents, is implanted in his natural man, but not any in his spiritual man; because into this he is born from the Lord. From what has now been adduced, and also from several other reasons, it may be manifestly seen, that polygamy is lasciviousness.

346. XI. Conjugial chastity, purity, and holiness cannot

POSSIBLY EXIST WITH POLYGAMISTS. This follows from what has just now been proved, and manifestly from what was demonstrated in the chapter on "The Chaste and the Non-Chaste"; especially from these articles of that chapter:—that what is chaste, pure, and holy, is predicated only of monogamous marriages, or of the marriage of one man with one wife (no. 141); also, that truly conjugial love is chastity itself, and that hence all the delights of that love, even the ultimate ones, are chaste (nos. 143, 144); and moreover from what was adduced in the chapter on "Truly Conjugial Love," namely, that truly conjugial love, which is of one man with one wife, on account of its origin, and on account of its correspondence, is celestial, spiritual, holy, and clean above every other love (no. 64). Now, since chastity, purity, and holiness exist only in truly conjugial love, it follows, that they neither do exist nor can possibly exist in polygamous love.

347. XII. A POLYGAMIST, SO LONG AS HE REMAINS A POLYGAMIST, CANNOT BECOME SPIRITUAL. Becoming spiritual means being elevated out of the Natural, that is, out of the light and heat of the world into the light and heat of heaven. No one knows anything about this elevation except he who has been elevated: nevertheless the natural man who is not elevated, perceives no otherwise than that he is elevated; the reason is that the natural man, equally with the spiritual man, is able to elevate his understanding into the light of heaven, and to think and speak spiritually; but if the will does not at the same time follow the understanding into that height, he is nevertheless not elevated; for he does not stay in that elevation, but in a short time lets himself down to his will, and there fixes his abode. It is said the will, but it is the love that is meant at the same time; because the will is the receptacle of the love; for what a man loves, that he wills. From these few considerations it may be manifest, that a polygamist, so long as he remains a polygamist, or what is the same, a natural man, so long as he remains natural, cannot become spiritual.

348. XIII. POLYGAMY IS NOT SIN WITH THOSE WITH WHOM IT IS IN ACCORDANCE WITH RELIGION. All that which is contrary to religion is believed to be sin, because it is contrary to God; and on the other hand, all that which agrees with religion, is believed not to be sin, because it agrees with God; and as polygamy existed with the sons of Israel in accordance with religion, and likewise so exists at the present day with the Mohammedans, it could not, and cannot, be imputed to them as sin. Moreover, to prevent its being sin to them, they remain natural, and do not become spiritual; and the natural man cannot see that there is any sin in such things as belong to the received religion; the

spiritual man alone sees this. It is on this account that, although the Mohammedans are taught by the Koran to acknowledge our Lord as the Son of God, they nevertheless do not approach Him, but Mohammed; and so long they remain natural, and consequently do not know that there is any evil, or indeed any lasciviousness, in polygamy. The Lord also says, "*If ye were blind, ye would not have sin; but now ye say, We see; therefore your sin remaineth*" (John ix. 41). Since polygamy cannot convict them of sin, therefore after death they have their own heavens (see nos. 342, 343); and they enjoy joys there according to their life.

349. XIV. Polygamy is not sin with those who are in ignorance about the Lord. The reason is, that truly conjugial love is from the Lord alone, and cannot be given by the Lord to any others than those who know Him, acknowledge Him, believe on Him, and live the life which is from Him; and those to whom that love cannot be given know no otherwise than that the love of the sex and conjugial love are one thing; consequently also polygamy. Add to this, that polygamists, who know nothing of the Lord, remain natural: for a man is made spiritual by the Lord only; and that is not imputed to the natural man as sin, which is according to the laws of religion and at the same time of society: he also acts according to his reason, and the reason of the natural man is in mere darkness concerning truly conjugial love; and this love in excellence is spiritual. Nevertheless their reason is taught by experience, that both public and private peace require that promiscuous lust in general should be restrained, and be left to every one within his own house: hence comes polygamy.

350. It is known, that man is born viler than a beast. All the beasts are born into the knowledges corresponding to the love of their life; for as soon as they drop from the womb, or are hatched from the egg, they see, hear, walk, know their food, their mother, their friends and foes; and not long afterwards they come to know the sex, and know how to love, and also how to rear their offspring. Man alone, when he is born, knows nothing of this sort; for no knowledge is connate with him: he has only the faculty and inclination to receive those things which belong to knowledge and love; and if he does not receive these from others, he remains viler than a beast. That man is born such, to the end that he may attribute nothing to himself, but to others, and at length everything of wisdom and of the love thereof to God Alone, and may hence become an image of God, see the Memorable Relation, nos. 132 to 136. From these considerations it follows, that a man who does not learn from others that the Lord has come into the world, and that He is God, and

has only imbibed some Knowledges about religion and the laws of his country, is not to blame if he thinks no more of conjugial love than of the love of the sex, and if he believes polygamous love to be the only conjugial love. The Lord leads such persons in their ignorance; and by His Divine auspices He providently withdraws from the imputation of guilt those who, from religion, shun evils as sins, to the end that they may be saved; for every man is born for heaven, and no one for hell; and every one comes into heaven from the Lord, and into hell from himself.

351. XV. Of these, such, although polygamists, are saved as acknowledge a God, and from religion live according to the civil laws of justice. All in the universal globe of lands who acknowledge a God and live according to the civil laws of justice from religion, are saved. By the civil laws of justice are meant such precepts as are contained in the Decalogue, which forbid murder, adultery, theft, and false witness. These precepts are the civil laws of justice in all the kingdoms of the earth;
2 for without them no kingdom could subsist. But some live according to them from fear of the penalties of the law, some from civil obedience, and some also from religion: and those who live according to them from religion, are saved; the reason is, that God is then in them; and a man in whom God is, is saved. Who does not see that among the laws given to the sons of Israel, after they had left Egypt, were those which forbid murder, adultery, theft, and false witness, since without those laws their communion or society could not subsist? And yet the same laws were promulgated by Jehovah God upon Mount Sinai with a stupendous miracle: but the cause of their being so promulgated was, that those same laws might also become laws of religion, and thus that the people might practise them not only for the sake of the good of society, but also for the sake of God, and that when they practised them from religion for the sake of God, they might
3 be saved. From these considerations it may be manifest, that the pagans, who acknowledge a God, and live according to the civil laws of justice, are saved; for it is not their fault that they know nothing of the Lord, consequently nothing of the chastity of marriage with one wife. For it is contrary to the Divine justice to condemn those who acknowledge a God, and from religion live according to the laws of justice, which consist in shunning evils because they are contrary to God, and in doing goods because they are agreeable to God.

352. XVI. But none either of the latter or of the former can be consociated with the angels in the Christian heavens. The reason is, that in the Christian heavens there is heavenly light, which is Divine Truth, and heavenly heat, which is Divine love; and these two discover the quality of truths and goods,

and also of evils and falsities. Hence it is that all communication has been taken away between the Christian heavens and the Mohammedan heavens, and in like manner between the heavens of the Gentiles. If there were a communication, none conld have been saved but those who were in heavenly light and at the same time in heavenly heat from the Lord; yea, neither would these be saved if there were a conjunction of the heavens: for in consequence of conjunction all the heavens would fall to decay to such an extent, that the angels would not be able to subsist; for what is unchaste and lascivious would flow in from the Mohammedans into the Christian heaven, which could not be endured in that heaven; and what is chaste and pure would flow in from the Christians into the Mohammedan heaven, which in its turn could not be endured there. In that case, in consequence of the communication and consequent conjunction, the Christian angels would become natural and thus adulterers; or if they remained spiritual, they would be continually feeling what is lascivious about them, which would intercept all the blessedness of their life. Something similar would take place with the Mohammedan heaven: for the spiritual things of the Christian heaven would continually encompass and torture them, and would take away all the delight of their life, and would moreover insinuate that polygamy is sin, and thus they would be continually rebuked. This is the reason why all the heavens are quite distinct, so that there is no conjunction between them, except through the influx of light and heat from the Lord out of the sun, in the midst of which He is: and this influx enlightens and vivifies every one according to reception; and reception is according to religion. This communication exists, but not a communication of the heavens with each other.

353. To the above I shall add two Memorable Relations. The first is this:—

* I was once in the midst of some angels and heard their conversation. It was about intelligence and wisdom, and was to the effect that a man perceives no otherwise than that both intelligence and wisdom are in him, and thus that whatever he thinks from the understanding and intends from the will, is from himself; when nevertheless not the least portion thereof is from man, but only the faculty of receiving from God the things which belong to the understanding and the will: and as every man (*homo*) by birth inclines to love himself, therefore, to prevent man's perishing in consequence of the love of self and the conceit of self-intelligence, it has been provided from the creation, that that love of the man (*vir*) should be transcribed into the wife, and that there should be implanted in her from birth to love the

* This Memorable Relation is repeated, with some slight variations, in the *True Christian Religion*, no. 663.

intelligence and wisdom of her man, and thus the man himself. Wherefore the wife continually draws to herself her husband's conceit of self-intelligence, and extinguishes it with him, and vivifies it with herself, and thus turns it into conjugial love, and fills it with pleasantnesses beyond measure. This has been provided by the Lord, lest the conceit of self-intelligence should so far infatuate the man (*vir*), as to lead him to believe that he has understanding and wisdom from himself and not from the Lord, and thus to want to eat of the tree of the knowledge of good and evil, and consequently to believe himself like unto God, and also God, as the serpent, which was the love of self-intelligence, said and persuaded him; wherefore man (*homo*) after eating was cast out of paradise, and the way to the tree of life was guarded by a cherub. Paradise spiritually denotes intelligence; eating of the tree of life spiritually denotes being intelligent and wise from the Lord; and eating of the tree of the knowledge of good and evil spiritually denotes being intelligent and wise from self.

354. The angels having finished this conversation departed; and there came two priests together with a man who in the world had been an ambassador of a kingdom, and to them I related what I had heard from the angels.

On hearing it, they began to debate with each other about intelligence and wisdom, and the prudence thence, whether they are from God, or from man. The debate was warm. All three in heart believed alike that they are from man because they are in man, and that the perception and sensation of its being so, confirm it. But the priests, who on this occasion were in theological zeal, said, that there is nothing of intelligence and wisdom, and thus nothing of prudence from man; and when the ambassador retorted, that thus there is nothing of thought from man they said that that was so.

But as it was perceived in heaven, that all the three were in a similar belief, it was said to the ambassador of the kingdom, "Put on the garments of a priest, and believe that you are a priest, and then speak." He did so; and then he declared aloud that nothing of intelligence and wisdom, and consequently nothing of prudence, can possibly exist but from God; and he proved it with his usual eloquence full of rational arguments. It is a peculiar circumstance in the spiritual world, that a spirit thinks himself to be such as he is denoted to be by the garment he wears; the reason is, that in that world the understanding clothes every one.

Afterwards, a voice from heaven said to the two priests, "Put off your own garments, and put on those of political ministers, and believe yourselves to be such." They did so; and then they at the same time thought from their interior self, and spoke from arguments which they had inwardly cherished in favour of self-intelligence. At that moment there appeared a tree near the path; and it was said to them, "It is the tree of the knowledge of good and evil; take heed to yourselves lest ye eat of it." Nevertheless all the three, infatuated by self-intelligence, burned with a desire to eat of it, and said to each other, "Why not? Is not the fruit good?" And they went to it and ate of it. Immediately all the three, as they were in a like faith, became heart friends; and they entered together into the way of self-intelligence, which extended into hell: nevertheless I saw them led back thence, because they were not yet prepared.

355. The second Memorable Relation:—

Once as I was looking out into the spiritual world, I saw in a certain meadow some men (*viri*) clothed in garments like those worn by men (*homines*) of this world; from which circumstance I knew that they had lately come from the world. I approached them and stood beside them, in order that I might hear what they were conversing about. They were conversing about heaven; and one of them who knew something about heaven, said, "In heaven there are wonderful things, such as no one can believe unless he has seen them: there are paradisiacal gardens, magnificent palaces constructed architecturally, because by the art itself, resplendent as of gold; in front of them are columns of silver, and on the columns heavenly forms of precious stones; also houses of jasper and sapphire, in front of which are stately porticos through which the angels enter; and within the houses, decorations which no art or words can describe. As regards the angels 2
themselves, they are of both sexes: there are bachelors and husbands, and there are virgins and wives; virgins so beautiful, that there does not exist in the world any resemblance of such beauty; and wives still more beautiful, who appear like genuine effigies of heavenly love, and their husbands like effigies of heavenly wisdom; and all these are in the full bloom of youth; and what is more, it is not known there that there is any other love of the sex than conjugial love; and, what you will be surprised at, the husbands have a perpetual faculty of enjoying the delights of love."

When the novitiate spirits heard that there was no other love of the sex in heaven than conjugial love, and that they had the perpetual faculty of enjoying the delights of love, they smiled at each other and said, "What you tell us is incredible; there cannot be such a faculty: possibly you are telling idle tales."

But at that instant a certain angel from heaven unexpectedly 3
stood in the midst of them and said, "Pray hear me: I am an angel of heaven, and have now lived a thousand years with my wife, and during all those years in a like flower of age in which you here see me. I have this in consequence of my conjugial love with my wife; and I can asseverate, that I have had and do

have that perpetual faculty; and because I perceive that you believe this to be impossible, I will speak with you on the subject from reasons according to the light of your understanding. You do not know anything of the primeval state of man, which you call the state of integrity. In that state all the interiors of the mind were open even to the Lord, and hence those interiors were in the marriage of love and wisdom, or of good and truth; and as the good of love and the truth of wisdom perpetually love each other, they also perpetually desire to be united; and when the interiors of the mind are open, that spiritual conjugial love flows down freely with its perpetual effort, and causes that
4 faculty to exist. The very soul of man, because it is in the marriage of good and truth, is not only in the perpetual effort for that unition, but also in the perpetual effort for the fructification and production of its own likeness; and when the interiors of a man even from the soul are open by virtue of that marriage, and the interiors continually regard the effect in ultimates to the end that they may come into outward existence, therefore that perpetual effort to fructify and produce its like, which belongs to the soul, becomes also of the body: and since the ultimate of the operation of the soul in the body with two married partners is into the ultimates of love there, and these depend on the state of the soul, it is evident
5 whence they derive this perpetuity. The reason why fructification also is perpetual, is, that the universal sphere of generating and propagating the celestial things which are of love, and the spiritual things which are of wisdom, and thence the natural things which are of offspring, proceeds from the Lord, and fills the whole heaven and the whole world; and that heavenly sphere fills the souls of all human beings, and descends through their minds into the body even to its ultimates, and gives the power of generating. But this cannot be the case with any but those with whom a passage is open from the soul through the higher and lower parts of the mind into the body to its ultimates, as is the case with those who suffer themselves to be led back by the Lord into the primeval state of creation. I can asseverate, that now for a thousand years, I have never wanted faculty, nor strength, nor virtue, and that I have known nothing whatever of any diminution of powers, for they are continually being renewed by the continual influx of the above-named universal sphere, and then also they gladden the lower mind, and do not make it sad, as is the case with those who suffer the loss of those
6 powers. Moreover, truly conjugial love is just like vernal heat, from the influx of which all things aspire to germinations and fructifications, nor is there any other heat in our heaven: wherefore with conjugial partners in that heaven there is spring in its perpetual endeavour; and it is this perpetual endeavour from which that virtue exists. But the fructifications with us

in heaven are different from those with men on earth. With us, the fructifications are spiritual, which are the fructifications of love and wisdom, or of good and truth. The wife from the husband's wisdom receives into herself the love thereof, and the husband from the love thereof in the wife receives into himself wisdom; yea, the wife is actually formed into the love of the husband's wisdom, which is effected by her receiving the propagations of his soul with the delight arising from the circumstance that she wills to be the love of her husband's wisdom: thus from a maiden she becomes a wife and a likeness. Hence also love together with its inmost friendship with the wife, and wisdom together with its happiness with the husband, are perennially growing, and this to eternity. This is the state of the angels of heaven."

When the angel had thus spoken, he looked at those who had 7
lately come from the world, and said to them, "You know that, while you were in the virtue of love, you loved your consorts, and that after the delight you turned away; but you do not know that we in heaven do not love our consorts in consequence of that virtue, but that we have virtue in consequence of love; and that as we perpetually love our consorts, we have perpetual virtue; wherefore, if you can invert the state, you can comprehend this. Does not he who perpetually loves his consort, love her with the whole mind and with the whole body? for love turns all things of the mind and all things of the body to that which it loves; and as this is done reciprocally, it conjoins them so that they become as a one."

He further said, "I will not speak to you of the conjugial 8
love implanted from the creation in males and females, and of their inclination for legitimate conjunction, nor of the faculty of prolification in the males, which makes a one with the faculty of multiplying wisdom from the love of truth; and that in proportion as a man loves wisdom from the love thereof, or truth from good, in the same proportion he is in truly conjugial love and in its attendant virtue."

356. When he had said this, the angel was silent; and from the spirit of the angel's speech the novitiate new-comers comprehended that a perpetual faculty of enjoying the delight of marriage is possible; and as this fact gladdened their minds, they said, "O, how happy is the state of the angels! We perceive that you in the heavens remain for ever in a state of youth, and consequently in the vigour of that age; but tell us how we also may obtain that vigour."

The angel replied, "Shun adulteries as infernal, and approach the Lord, and you will have it."

They said, "We will shun them as such, and we will approach the Lord."

But the angel replied, "You cannot shun adulteries as infernal evils, unless you likewise shun all other evils, because adulteries are the complex of all; and unless you shun them, you cannot approach the Lord; for the Lord receives no others."

After this the angel took his leave, and the new spirits departed sorrowful.

JEALOUSY.

357. JEALOUSY is here treated of, because it also has relation to conjugial love. There is just jealousy and unjust:—just jealousy with married partners who mutually love each other; with these it is a just and prudent zeal lest their conjugial love be violated, and consequently a just grief if it is violated; and unjust jealousy with those who are naturally suspicious, and whose minds are sickly or distempered in consequence of thick and bilious blood. Moreover, all jealousy is by some accounted a vice; which is particularly the case with whoremongers, who censure even just jealousy. The term JEALOUSY *(zelotypia)* is derived from ZELI TYPUS (the type of zeal); and there is a type or image of just zeal and also of unjust zeal; but these differences shall be unfolded in the following series of articles:

I. *Zeal, considered in itself, is like the fire of love blazing up.*

II. *The blazing up or flame of that love, which is zeal, is a spiritual blazing up or flame, arising from the infestation of and assault upon the love.*

III. *The quality of a man's zeal is according to the quality of his love; thus it is different with him whose love is good from what it is with him whose love is evil.*

IV. *The zeal of a good love and the zeal of an evil love are alike in externals, but utterly unlike in internals.*

V. *The zeal of a good love in its internals contains a hidden store of love and friendship; but the zeal of an evil love in its internals contains a hidden store of hatred and revenge.*

VI. *The zeal of conjugial love is called jealousy.*

VII. *Jealousy is like a blazing fire against those who infest the love with the married partner, and it is like a terrible fear for the loss of that love.*

VIII. *There exists spiritual jealousy with monogamists, and natural jealousy with polygamists.*

IX. *Jealousy with those married partners who tenderly love each other, is a just grief arising from sound reason, lest conjugial love be divided, and thus perish.*

X. *Jealousy with married partners who do not love each other, arises from many causes; arising with some from various distempers of the mind.*

XI. *With some there is not any jealousy; and this also is from various causes*

XII. *There is also a jealousy in regard to concubines, but not such as in regard to wives.*

XIII. *Jealousy likewise exists among beasts and birds.*

XIV. *The jealousy with men and husbands is different from that with women and wives.*

Now follows the explanation of these articles.

358. I. ZEAL, CONSIDERED IN ITSELF, IS LIKE THE FIRE OF LOVE BLAZING UP. What jealousy is cannot be known, unless it be known what zeal is; for jealousy is the zeal of conjugial love. The reason zeal is like the fire of love blazing up, is, that zeal belongs to love, and love is spiritual heat, and this in its origin is like fire. In regard to the first position, it is known that zeal belongs to love: nothing else is meant by being zealous, and acting from zeal, than acting from the force of love: but since, when it comes into outward existence, it appears not as love, but as unfriendly and hostile, enraged and fighting against him who hurts the love, therefore it may also be called the defender and protector of love; for all love is such that it breaks forth into indignation and wrath, yea, into fury, when it is thrust out of its delights; wherefore, if a love, especially the ruling love, be touched, there ensues an emotion of the lower mind; and if that touch hurts, there ensues wrath. From these considerations it may be seen, that zeal is not the highest degree of the love, but that it is love blazing up. The love of one, and the corresponding love of another, are like two confederates; but when the love of one rises up against the love of another, they become like enemies; the reason is, that love is the esse of a man's life; wherefore he who assaults the love, assaults the life itself; and then there ensues a state of wrath against the assailant, like the state of every man whose life is attempted by another. Such wrath is attendant on every love, even the most pacific, as is manifestly seen from hens, geese, and birds of every kind, which, without any fear, rise against and fly at those who injure their young, or rob them of their food. That some beasts are seized with anger, and wild beasts with fury, if their young are molested, or their prey taken from them, is known. The reason why love is said to blaze up like fire is, that love is nothing else than spiritual heat, originating in the fire of the angelic sun, which is pure love. That love is heat as it were from fire, is manifestly evident from the heat of living bodies, which is from no other source than from their love; also from the circumstance that human beings grow warm and are inflamed according to the exaltation of their love. From these considerations it is evident, that zeal is like the fire of love blazing up.

359. II. THE BLAZING UP OR FLAME OF THAT LOVE, WHICH IS ZEAL, IS A SPIRITUAL BLAZING UP OR FLAME, ARISING FROM THE

INFESTATION OF AND ASSAULT UPON THE LOVE. That zeal is a spiritual blazing up or flame, is evident from what has been said above. As love in the spiritual world is heat originating in the sun of that world, therefore also love at a distance appears there as flame: it is thus that heavenly love appears with the angels of heaven, and thus also that infernal love appears with the spirits of hell: but it must be known, that that flame does not burn like the flame of the natural world. The reason why zeal arises from an assault upon the love is, that love is the heat of every one's life; wherefore when the life's love is assaulted, the life's heat kindles itself, resists, and bursts forth against the assailant, and acts as an enemy with its own strength and power, which is like flame bursting from a fire upon him who stirs it: that it is like fire, appears from the sparkling of the eyes, from the face being inflamed, also from the tone of the voice, and from the gestures. This is done by love, because it is the heat of life, to prevent its extinction, and with it the extinction of all alacrity, vivacity, and perceptibility of delight, which flow from its own love.

360. It shall be stated how the love is enkindled and set on fire into zeal, by an assault upon it, as fire is into flame. Love resides in man's will; but it is not inflamed in the will itself, but in the understanding: for in the will it is like fire, and in the understanding like flame. Love in the will knows nothing about itself, because there it does not feel anything belonging to itself, neither does it act from itself there: but this is done in the understanding and its thought. Wherefore, when the love is assaulted, it exasperates itself in the understanding, which is done by various reasonings. These reasonings are like pieces of wood, which the fire enkindles, and which consequently blaze up: they are therefore like so much fuel, or so many combustible matters, which feed that spiritual flame, which is of great variety.

361. The very reason why a man is kindled by an assault upon his love, shall be disclosed. The human form in its inmosts is from creation a form of love and wisdom. In man there are all the affections of love, and thence all the perceptions of wisdom, compounded in the most perfect order, so as to make together what is unanimous, and thereby a one. Those affections and perceptions are substantiated; for substances are their subjects. Since therefore the human form is compounded of these, it is evident that, if the love is assaulted, that universal form also, with each and all things therein, is assaulted at the same instant, or simultaneously. And as the wish to continue in its own form is implanted from creation in all living things, therefore this wish operates in every general compound from the singulars of which it is compounded, and in

the singulars from the general compound. Hence, when the love is assaulted, it defends itself by means of its understanding, and the understanding [defends it] by means of the rational and imaginary considerations, by which it represents the event to itself; especially by those which act as a one with the love which is assaulted: and unless this was the case, that form would wholly fall to pieces, in consequence of the deprivation of that love. Hence then it is that love, in order to resist assaults, hardens the substances of its form, and erects them as it were into crests, like so many sharp prickles, that is, ruffles itself. Such is the exasperation of love which is called zeal: wherefore if there is no power (*copia*) of resisting, there arise anxiety and grief, because it foresees the extinction of the interior life with its delights. But on the other hand, if the love is favoured and caressed, that form unbends, softens, and dilates itself; and the substances of the form become soft, caressing, gentle, and alluring.

362. III. THE QUALITY OF A MAN'S ZEAL IS ACCORDING TO THE QUALITY OF HIS LOVE; THUS IT IS DIFFERENT WITH HIM WHOSE LOVE IS GOOD FROM WHAT IT IS WITH HIM WHOSE LOVE IS EVIL. Since zeal belongs to love, it follows that its quality is such as the quality of the love is; and as there are in general two loves, the love of good and thence of truth, and the love of evil and thence of falsity, therefore in general there is a zeal for good and thence for truth, and a zeal for evil and thence for falsity. But it must be known that both loves are of infinite variety. This is manifestly evident from the angels of heaven and the spirits of hell; both the latter and the former in the spiritual world are forms of their own love; and yet there is not one angel of heaven absolutely like another as to face, speech, gait, gesture, and manners; nor any spirit of hell; yea neither can there be to eternity, howsoever they may be multiplied into myriads of myriads. Hence it is evident, that there is an infinite variety of loves, because there is an infinite variety of their forms. The case is similar with zeal, because this belongs to love; namely, that the zeal of one cannot be absolutely like or the same with the zeal of another. In general there is the zeal of a good love, and the zeal of an evil love.

363. IV. THE ZEAL OF A GOOD LOVE AND THE ZEAL OF AN EVIL LOVE ARE ALIKE IN EXTERNALS, BUT UTTERLY ALIKE IN INTERNALS. Zeal in externals, with every one, appears like anger and wrath; for it is love enkindled and inflamed to defend itself against a violator, and to remove him. The reason why the zeal of a good love and the zeal of an evil love appear alike in externals, is, that in both cases the love, when it is in zeal, blazes up; with a good man only in externals, but with an evil man both in ex-

ternals and in internals; and when internals are not perceived, the zeals appear alike in externals; but that they are utterly unlike in internals will be seen in the next article. That zeal appears in externals like anger and wrath, may be seen and heard from all who speak and act from zeal; as for example, from a priest while he is preaching from zeal, in that the tone of his voice is high, vehement, sharp, and harsh; his face is heated and perspires; he exerts himself, beats the pulpit, and calls forth fire from hell against those who do evils: and so in many other cases.

364. In order that a distinct idea may be acquired of zeal with the good, and of zeal with the evil, and of their unlikeness, it is necessary that some idea should be formed of the internals and externals with human beings. For this purpose, let there be taken a common idea on the subject as being adapted to popular apprehension: let it be exhibited by the case of a nut or an almond, and their kernels. With the good, the internals are like the kernels within in their soundness and goodness, encompassed with their usual and natural husk. But the case is utterly unlike with the evil; their internals are like kernels which are either not eatable because of their bitterness, or rotten, or worm-eaten; and their externals are like the shells or husks of those kernels, either like the natural shells or husks, or shining like shell-fish, or variegated like iris stones. Such is the appearance of their externals, within which the above-named internals lie concealed. The case is similar with their zeals.

365. V. THE ZEAL OF A GOOD LOVE IN ITS INTERNALS CONTAINS A HIDDEN STORE OF LOVE AND FRIENDSHIP; BUT THE ZEAL OF AN EVIL LOVE IN ITS INTERNALS CONTAINS A HIDDEN STORE OF HATRED AND REVENGE. It was said, that zeal in externals appears like anger and wrath, both with those who are in a good love and with those who are in an evil love; but as the internals are different, the anger and wrath in each case differs from that of the other, and the difference is as follows: 1. The zeal of a good love is like a heavenly flame, which in no case breaks forth against another, but only defends itself, and it defends itself against an evil person, just as when the latter rushes into the fire and is burnt: but the zeal of an evil love is like an infernal flame, which of itself breaks forth and rushes on, and wants to consume another. 2. The zeal of a good love instantly burns away and is allayed when the assailant ceases to assault; but the zeal of an evil love lasts and is not extinguished. 3. The reason is that the internal of him who is in a good love is in itself mild, soft, friendly, and benevolent; wherefore when his external, for the sake of defending itself, assumes a rough

exterior, ruffles and erects itself, and thus employs harsh measures, it is nevertheless tempered by the good in which his internal is. It is otherwise with the evil; with these the internal is unfriendly, pitiless, harsh, breathing hatred and revenge, and it suckles itself with their delights; and although it is reconciled, those evils nevertheless lie concealed as fires in the embers underneath the ashes; and those fires break forth after death, if not in this world.

366. Since zeal in externals appears alike both with the good and the evil, and since the ultimate sense of the Word consists of correspondences and appearances, therefore in the Word, it is very often said of Jehovah that He is angry and wroth, that He revenges, punishes, casts into hell, besides many other things which are appearances of zeal in externals; hence also it is that He is called zealous; when nevertheless there is not the least of anger, wrath, and revenge in Him; for He is mercy, grace, and clemency itself, thus good itself, in which it is impossible such evil can exist. But on this subject see more particulars in the work on *Heaven and Hell*, nos. 545–550; and in the *Apocalypse Revealed*, nos. 494, 498, 525, 714, 806.

367. VI. THE ZEAL OF CONJUGIAL LOVE IS CALLED JEALOUSY. Zeal for truly conjugial love is the zeal of zeals, because that love is the love of loves, and its delights, for which also zeal is excited, are the delights of delights; for, as was shown above, that love is the head of all loves. The reason is, that that love induces on a wife the form of love, and on a husband the form of wisdom; and from these forms united into one form, nothing else can proceed than what savours of wisdom and at the same time of love. As the zeal of conjugial love is the zeal of zeals, therefore it is called by the new name, Jealousy (*zelotypia*), which is the very type of zeal.

368. VII. JEALOUSY IS LIKE A BLAZING FIRE AGAINST THOSE WHO INFEST THE LOVE WITH THE MARRIED PARTNER, AND IT IS LIKE A TERRIBLE FEAR FOR THE LOSS OF THAT LOVE. The subject here treated of is the jealousy of those who are in spiritual love with their consort; in the following article the subject treated of is the jealousy of those who are in natural love; and afterwards the jealousy of those who are in truly conjugial love. With those who are in spiritual love the jealousy is various, because their love is various; for one love, whether it be spiritual or natural, is never altogether alike with two
2 persons, still less with several. The reason why spiritual jealousy, or jealousy with the spiritual, is like a fire blazing out against those who molest their conjugial love, is, that with them the beginning of love is in the internals of each of them, and

their love from its beginning follows its principiates even to its
ultimates, by virtue of which ultimates and at the same time of
the primes, the intermediates, which are of the mind and body, are
kept in loving connection. These, because they are spiritual, in
their marriage regard union as an end, and in the union spiritual
rest and the pleasantnesses thereof. Now, as they have rejected
disunion from their minds, therefore their jealousy is like a fire
stirred up and darting forth against those who molest. The 3
reason why it is also like a terrible fear is, that their spiritual
love intends that they be a one; wherefore if a chance exists,
or an appearance of separation happens, a fear ensues as terrible
as when two united parts are torn asunder. This description of
jealousy was given me from heaven by those who are in
spiritual conjugial love; for there exist natural conjugial love,
spiritual conjugial love, and celestial conjugial love: concerning
the natural and the celestial conjugial love, and their jealousy,
we shall speak in the two following articles.

369. VIII. There exists spiritual jealousy with monogamists, and natural jealousy with polygamists. The reason why spiritual jealousy exists with monogamists is, that they alone can receive spiritual conjugial love, as has been abundantly shewn above. It is said that it exists; but the meaning is that it is capable of existing with them. That it exists with only a very few in the Christian world, where there are monogamous marriages, but that still it is capable of existing there, has also been confirmed above. That with polygamists conjugial love is natural, may be seen in the chapter on "Polygamy," at nos. 345, 347; jealousy likewise with them is natural, because it follows the love. What the quality of the jealousy of polygamists is, is taught by the relations of those who have been eye-witnesses of it among the Orientals: these relations are, that wives and concubines are guarded as captives in prisons, and are withheld and restrained from all communication with men; that into the women's apartments, or the chambers of their prison, no man is allowed to enter unless attended by an eunuch; and that the strictest watch is set to observe whether any of the women look with a lascivious eye or countenance at a passing man; and that if this be observed, the woman is punished with blows; and in case she indulges her lasciviousness with any man, whether introduced secretly into her apartment, or away from home, she is punished with death.

370. By these relations it is clearly shewn what is the quality of the fire of jealousy into which polygamous conjugial love breaks out,—that it is into anger and revenge; into anger with the meek, and into revenge with the fierce; and this is so, because their love is natural, and does not partake of what is

spiritual. This follows as a consequence from what was demonstrated in the chapter on "Polygamy,"—that polygamy is lasciviousness, no. 345; and that a polygamist, so long as he remains a polygamist, is natural, and cannot become spiritual, no. 347. But the fire of jealousy is different with natural monogamists: their love is inflamed not so much against the women as against the violators: it becomes anger against the latter, and cold against the former. It is otherwise with polygamists, whose fire of jealousy blazes also with the frenzy of revenge: this likewise is one of the reasons why, after the death of polygamists, their concubines and wives are for the most part set free, and are sent to seraglios not guarded, to occupy themselves in the various works proper to women.

371. IX. Jealousy with those married partners who tenderly love each other, is a just grief arising from sound reason, lest conjugial love be divided, and thus perish. In all love there is fear and grief; fear lest it perish, and grief if it perishes. There is also fear and grief in conjugial love; but the fear and grief of conjugial love is called zeal or jealousy. The reasons why this zeal, with married partners who tenderly love each other, is just and from sound reason, are, that it is at the same time a fear for the loss of eternal happiness, not only of its own but also of its married partner's, and, that it is also a protection against adultery. As regards the first consideration, that it is a just fear for the loss of its own eternal happiness and of that of its consort, it follows from everything which has been heretofore adduced about truly conjugial love; and also from this consideration, that married partners derive from that love the blessedness of their souls, the blissfulness of their minds, the delightsomeness of their bosoms, and the pleasure of their bodies; and since these remain with them to eternity, they fear for the eternal happiness of each other. That that zeal is a just protection against adulteries, is evident; hence it is like a fire blazing out against violation, and protecting itself against it. From these considerations it is manifest, that whoever loves his consort tenderly, is also jealous, but is just and sane according to the wisdom of the man (*vir*).

372. It was said that in conjugial love there is implanted a fear lest it be divided, and a grief lest it perish, and that its zeal is like a fire against violation. Once, when meditating on this subject, I asked some zealous angels concerning the seat of jealousy. They said, that it is in the understanding of the man (*vir*) who receives the love of his consort and loves her in return; and that its quality there is according to his wisdom. They said further, that jealousy has in it something in common

with honour, which also resides in conjugial love; for he who loves his wife, also honours her. In regard to zeal's residing with a man in his understanding, they said that the reason was that conjugial love protects itself through the understanding, as good protects itself through truth; so the wife protects those things which are common with the man, through her husband; and that therefore zeal is implanted in the men, and through them, and for their sake, in the women. To the question as to the region of the mind in which jealousy resides with the men, they replied, in their souls, because it is also a protection against adulteries; and because adulteries principally destroy conjugial love, that when there is danger of the violation of that love, the man's understanding grows hard, and becomes like a horn, with which he strikes the adulterer.

373. X. Jealousy with married partners who do not love each other, arises from many causes; arising with some from various distempers of the mind. The causes why married partners who do not mutually love each other are jealous also, are principally the honour of power, the fear of defamation both of his own name and also of that of his wife, and the dread lest domestic affairs should fall into confusion. It is known that the men have the honour of power, that is, that they want to be respected in consequence thereof; for so long as they have this honour, they are as it were of an elevated mind, and not dejected when in the company of men and women: to this honour also is attached the name of bravery; wherefore military officers have it more than others. The fear of defamation, both of his own name and that of his wife, is a cause of jealousy that coheres with the foregoing: to which may be added, that cohabitation with a whore, and debauchery in the house, are infamous. The reason why some are jealous through a dread lest their domestic affairs should fall into confusion, is that, in proportion as this is the case, the husband is made light of, and mutual services and helps are withdrawn; but with some this jealousy in process of time ceases and is annihilated, and with some it is changed into the mere simulation of love.

374. That jealousy with some arises from various sicknesses or distempers of the mind, is not unknown in the world; for there are jealous persons who are continually thinking that their wives are unfaithful, and believe them to be whores, if they merely hear or see them talk in a friendly manner with or about men. There are several vitiated states of the mind which induce this sickness or distemper; the principal of which is a suspicious fancy, which, if it be long cherished, introduces the mind into societies of similar spirits, from whence it can be released only with difficulty; it also strengthens itself in the

body, by rendering the serum, and consequently the blood, sticky, tenacious, thick, slow, and acrid: a failing of the manly powers also increases it; for the consequence of such failing or defect is, that the mind cannot be elevated from its suspicious fancies; for the presence of the manly powers elevates, and their absence depresses, for this absence causes the mind to sink, give way, and become feeble; in which case it immerses itself more and more in that fancy, till it raves, and this passes over into the delight of chiding and reproaching, and, so far as is permitted, of reviling.

375. There are also certain countries which, more than others, labour under the distemper of jealousy. In these countries the wives are imprisoned, tyrannically withheld from conversation with men, prevented from even looking at them through the windows, which are guarded by gratings projecting downwards, and are terrified by threats of death if the cherished suspicion be found well grounded; besides many other hardships which the wives in those countries suffer from their jealous husbands. There are two causes of this jealousy; one is, an imprisonment and suffocation of the thoughts in the spiritual things of
2 the church; the other is, an inward cupidity of revenge. As regards the first cause, which is, the imprisonment and suffocation of the thoughts in the spiritual things of the church, its effect may be concluded from what has been proved above, that every one has conjugial love according to the state of the church with him, and as the church is from the Lord, that that love is solely from the Lord, nos. 130, 131. When therefore, instead of the Lord, living and deceased men are approached and invoked, it follows, that the state of the church is not such that conjugial love can act in unity with it; and the less so when their minds are terrified into that worship by the threats of a dreadful prison. Hence it comes to pass, that the thoughts, together with the expression of them, are violently imprisoned and suffocated; and when they are suffocated, there is an influx of such things as are either contrary to the church, or imaginary in favour of it: in consequence of which there ensues heat towards whores and icy cold towards the married partner; from which two things prevailing together in one
3 subject, such an unconquerable fire of jealousy flows forth. As regards the second cause, which is the inward cupidity of revenge, this altogether checks the influx of conjugial love, absorbs it, and swallows it up, and changes the delight thereof, which is celestial, into the delight of revenge, which is infernal; and the nearest determination of this latter is towards the wife. It seems also as if the malignant character of the atmosphere, which in those regions is impregnated with the poisonous exhalations of the surrounding country, were an additional cause.

376. XI. WITH SOME THERE IS NOT ANY JEALOUSY; AND THIS ALSO IS FROM VARIOUS CAUSES. There are many causes of there being no jealousy, and of the cessation of jealousy. The absence of jealousy is principally with those who make no more account of conjugial than of scortatory love, and at the same time are so devoid of honourable feeling as to slight the reputation of their name: they are not unlike married pimps. There is likewise no jealousy with those who have rejected it from a confirmed belief that it infests the mind (*animus*), and that it is useless to watch a wife, and that to do so serves only to incite her, and that therefore it is better to shut the eyes, and not even to look through the key-hole, lest anything should be discovered. Some have rejected jealousy on account of the reproach attached to the name, thinking that a man who is a man, is afraid of nothing. Some have been driven to reject it lest their domestic affairs should go to ruin, and also lest it should become matter of public scandal if the wife were accused of the disorderly passion of which she is guilty. Moreover, jealousy decreases to nothing with those who grant licence to their wives, on account of their own failure of potency, or for the sake of the procreation of children for the sake of inheritance, also with some for the sake of gain, and so forth. There are also scortatory marriages, in which, by mutual consent, the licence of sexual lust is given to both, and yet they are civil to each other when they meet.

377. XII. THERE IS ALSO A JEALOUSY IN REGARD TO CONCUBINES, BUT NOT SUCH AS IN REGARD TO WIVES. Jealousy in regard to wives flows from the inmosts with man (*homo*); but jealousy in regard to concubines flows from the externals; wherefore they differ in kind. The reason why jealousy in regard to wives flows from the inmosts is, that conjugial love resides there: the reason why it resides there is, that marriage, by virtue of the eternity of its compact established by covenant, and also by virtue of the equality of right in that what belongs to the one belongs also to the other, unites their souls, and binds their minds together more interiorly; this binding together and that union, once implanted, remain inseparable, whatever be the quality of the love that ensues afterwards, whether it be warm or cold. Hence it is that an invitation to love by the wife chills the whole man (*vir*) from the inmosts to the ultimates; whereas an invitation to love by a concubine has not the same effect upon her lover. To jealousy in regard to a wife is added the earnest desire for reputation for the sake of honour; and there is no such accessory to jealousy in regard to a concubine. Nevertheless both kinds of jealousy vary according to the seat of the love received from the wife and from the concubine; and at the same time according to the state of the judgment of the man receiving it.

378. XIII. JEALOUSY LIKEWISE EXISTS AMONG BEASTS AND BIRDS. That it exists among wild beasts, as lions, tigers, bears, and several others, when they have whelps, is known; and also among bulls, although they have not calves. It is most conspicuous among cocks, which on account of their hens fight with their rivals even to death: the reason they have such jealousy is, that they are vain-glorious lovers, and the glory of that love cannot endure an equal; that they are vain-glorious lovers, above every other genus and species of birds, appears from their gestures, nods, gait, and the sounds they make. That the glory of honour with men (*viri*), whether lovers or not, excites, increases, and sharpens jealousy, has been confirmed above.

379. XIV. THE JEALOUSY WITH MEN AND HUSBANDS IS DIFFERENT FROM THAT WITH WOMEN AND WIVES. The differences cannot, however, be distinctly pointed out, since the jealousy of married partners who love each other spiritually, is different from that of married partners who love each other only naturally, and again it is different with those who disagree in dispositions, and also with those who have subjected their consorts to the yoke of obedience to themselves. The jealousies of men and of women, considered in themselves, are diverse, because from different origins. The origin of the jealousies of men is in the understanding, whereas the origin of the jealousies of women is in the will applied to the understanding of the husband: wherefore the jealousy of a man is like a flame of wrath and anger; whereas that of a woman is like a fire restrained, by various fears, by looking upon her husband, and having respect to her own love, in a variety of ways, and by a manifold prudence in not revealing this love to the husbands by jealousy. They differ also because wives are loves, and men recipients thereof; and it is prejudicial to wives to lavish their love upon the men, but it is not prejudicial for the recipients to lavish their love on their wives. With the spiritual, however, it is otherwise: with these the jealousy of the man is transferred into the wife, as the love of the wife is transferred into the husband; wherefore with both it appears like itself against the attempts of a violator; but the jealousy of the wife is inspired into the husband against the attempts of the violating whore, and is like grief weeping and moving the conscience.

380. To the above I shall add two Memorable Relations. The first is as follows:—

*I was once in much amazement at the great multitude of men (*homines*) who ascribe creation, and consequently whatever is under the sun and above it, to nature: saying from the acknow-

* This Memorable Relation may also be found in the *True Christian Religion*, no. 35.

ledgment of their hearts, when they see anything, "Is not this the work of nature?" And when they are asked why they say that it is a work of nature, and not of God, when nevertheless they occasionally join in the general confession, that God created nature, and therefore they might just as well say that the things which they see are works of God as that they are the works of nature, they return for answer, in an internal tone of voice, which is scarcely audible, "What is God but nature?" From this persuasion concerning the creation of the universe by nature, and from this insanity, which has to them the semblance of wisdom, all such persons appear so full of their own importance, that they regard all those who acknowledge the creation of the universe to be from God, as so many ants which creep on the ground and tread a beaten path, and some as butterflies which fly in the air; calling their opinions dreams, because they see what they do not see; and saying, "Who has seen God, and who does not see nature?"

While I was in amazement at the multitude of such persons, 2
there stood at my side an angel, who asked me, "What are you meditating about?"

I replied, "About the multitude of those who believe that nature created the universe."

The angel said to me, "All hell consists of such persons, who are there called satans and devils; satans, if they have confirmed themselves in favour of nature and therefore have denied God; and devils, if they have lived wickedly and thereby rejected all acknowledgment of God from their hearts: but I will lead you to the studies (*gymnasia*), which are in the south-western quarter, where such persons dwell, having not yet departed to hell."

He took me by the hand and led me there. I saw some small houses, in which were studies, and in the midst of them one which served as a principal hall to the rest. It was constructed of pitch-black stones, that were covered with a sort of glazed plates that seemed to sparkle with gold and silver, like those called mica; and here and there were interspersed shells which glittered in a like manner.

We approached and knocked at the door, and presently some 3
one opened it, and said, "Be welcome." He then hastened to the table and fetched four books, and said, "These books are the wisdom which at this day is the admiration of a great many kingdoms: this book or wisdom is the admiration of many in France, this one of many in Germany, this one of some in Holland, and this one of some in Britain." He further said, "If you wish to see, I will cause these four books to shine before your eyes:" he then poured forth and spread around them the glory of his own reputation, and the books presently shone as with light; but this light instantly vanished before our eyes.

We then asked him, "What are you now writing?"

He replied, that he was now bringing forth from his treasures, and publishing, the things which belong to inmost wisdom, and which in a compendium are the following:—I. Whether nature be of life, or life of nature. II. Whether the centre be of the expanse, or the expanse of the centre. III. On the centre and expanse of nature and of life.

4 Having said this, he sat down again on a chair at the table; but we walked about in his study, which was spacious. He had a candle on the table, because the day-light of the sun did not shine in that room, but only the nocturnal light of the moon; and what surprised me, the candle seemed to be carried all round the room, and to illuminate it; but, for want of being snuffed, it gave but little light. While he was writing, we saw images in various forms flying from the table towards the walls, which in that nocturnal moon-light appeared like beautiful Indian birds; but when we opened the door, lo! in the solar day-light they appeared like birds of evening, with wings like network; for they were semblances of truth, which by means of confirmations had been made fallacies which were ingeniously connected together into a series by him.

5 After we had seen these things, we approached the table, and asked him what he was then writing.

He replied, "On the first point, WHETHER NATURE BE OF LIFE, OR LIFE OF NATURE;" and on this subject he said, that he could confirm either side, and cause it to be true; but as something lay concealed within which excited his fears, therefore he durst only confirm this side, that nature is of life, that is, from life, but not that life is of nature, that is, from nature.

We then civilly asked him, what it was that lay concealed within which excited his fears?

He replied, he was afraid lest he should be called a naturalist, and thus an atheist, by the clergy, and a man of unsound reason by the laity; as both the clergy and the laity either believe from a blind faith, or see from the sight of those who confirm that blind faith.

6 But then, being impelled by a kind of indignation of zeal for the Truth, we addressed him, saying, "Friend, you are much deceived; your wisdom, which is only an ingenious talent for writing, has seduced you, and the glory of reputation has led you to confirm what you do not believe. Do you not know that the human mind is capable of being elevated above sensual things, which are things which are derived into the thoughts from the bodily senses, and that when it is so elevated, it sees the things that are of life, above, and those that are of nature, beneath? What is life but love and wisdom? and what is nature but their receptacle, whereby they may produce their effects or uses? Can these possibly be one in any other sense

than as the principal and the instrumental are one? Can light be one with the eye, or sound with the ear? Whence are the senses of the organs but from life, and their forms but from nature? What is the human body but an organ of life? Are not each and all things therein formed organically to produce the things which the love wills and the understanding thinks? Are not the organs of the body from nature, and love and thought from life? And are not those things quite distinct from each other? If you elevate the acumen of your genius yet a little higher, you will see that being affected and thinking belong to life, and that being affected is from love, and thinking is from wisdom, and both are from life; for, as has been said, love and wisdom are life. If you elevate your faculty of understanding yet a little higher, you will see that no love and wisdom exists, unless its origin be somewhere or other, and that its origin is [love itself and] wisdom itself, and consequently life itself, and these are God from Whom is nature."

Afterwards we spoke with him about the second point, 7
WHETHER THE CENTRE BE OF THE EXPANSE, OR THE EXPANSE OF THE CENTRE; and asked him why he discussed this question. He replied, "With a view to conclude concerning the centre and expanse of nature and of life, thus concerning the origin of the one and the other." And when we asked him what were his sentiments on the subject, he answered, as in the former case, that he could confirm either side, but that for fear of losing his reputation, he would confirm that the expanse is of the centre, that is, from the centre; "although I know," said he, "that something existed before the sun, and this in the universe throughout, and that these things flowed together of themselves into order, thus into centres."

But here again we addressed him from indignant zeal, and said, 8
"Friend, you are insane." On hearing these words, he drew his chair aside from the table, and looked timidly at us, and then gave ear to us, but with a smile upon his countenance. And we went on to say: "What is more insane than to say that the centre is from the expanse? By your centre we understand the sun, and by your expanse, the universe; and thus, according to you, the universe existed without the sun. But does not the sun make nature and all its properties, which depend solely on the heat and light proceeding from the sun through the atmospheres? Where were these things previous to the sun's existence? But whence they originated we will state in the following discussion. Are not the atmospheres and all things which exist on the Earth, as surfaces, and the sun their centre? What are they all without the sun? Could they subsist a single moment apart from the sun? Consequently, what were they all before the sun? Could they subsist? Is not subsistence perpetual existence? Since, therefore, the subsistence of all

things of nature is from the sun, it follows that the existence of all things must be from the same origin: every one sees and
9 acknowledges this from personal experience. Does not that which is posterior subsist from what is prior, as it exists from what is prior? Supposing the surface to be prior, and the centre posterior, would not the prior in such case subsist from the posterior, which yet is contrary to the laws of order? How can posterior things produce prior, or exterior things produce interior, or grosser things produce purer? Consequently, how can surfaces, which constitute the expanse, produce centres? Who does not see that this is contrary to the laws of nature? We have adduced these arguments from a rational analysis, to prove that the expanse exists from the centre, and not the centre from the expanse; nevertheless every one who thinks aright, sees it to be so without the help of such arguments. You have asserted, that the expanse flowed together of itself into a centre: did it thus flow by chance into so wonderful and stupendous an order, that one thing exists for the sake of another, and each and all things for the sake of man, and his eternal life? Is it possible for nature, from any love, through any wisdom, to provide such things? And can nature make angels of men, and heaven of angels? Ponder these things, and think, and your idea of the existence of nature from nature will fall to the ground."

10 Afterwards we asked him what he used to think, and now thought, about the third point, THE CENTRE AND EXPANSE OF NATURE AND OF LIFE; whether he believed that the centre and expanse of life are the same with the centre and expanse of nature.

He said, that he was in doubt about it, and that he formerly thought that the interior activity of nature is life; and that love and wisdom, which essentially constitute the life of man, are derived thence; and that the sun's fire, through heat and light, by means of the atmospheres, produce them; but that now, from what he had heard about the eternal life of men, he was in doubt, and that this doubt sometimes carried his mind upwards, sometimes downwards; and that when his mind was carried upwards, he acknowledged a centre of which he had previously known nothing; but when downwards, he saw a centre which he believed to be the only one; and that life is from the centre of which he had previously known nothing, and that nature is from the centre which he previously believed to be the only one; and that each centre has an expanse around it.

11 To this we said, Good, if he would only look at the centre and expanse of nature from the centre and expanse of life, and not contrariwise; and we instructed him, that above the angelic heaven there is a sun which is pure love, in appearance fiery like the sun of the world; and that from the heat which proceeds

from that sun, angels and men derive will and love, and from its light they derive understanding and wisdom; and that the things which belong to life, are called spiritual things, and that those which proceed from the sun of the world, are continents of life, and are called natural things; also that the expanse of the centre of life is called the SPIRITUAL WORLD, which subsists from its own sun, and that the expanse of nature is called the NATURAL WORLD, which subsists from its own sun. Now, since spaces and times cannot be predicated of love and wisdom, but states instead of them, it follows, that the expanse around the sun of the angelic heaven is not an extense, but that nevertheless it is in the extense of the natural sun; and is with the living subjects therein according to their receptions; and their receptions are according to their forms.

But he then asked, "Whence comes the fire of the sun of the 12
world, or of nature?"

We replied, that it is from the sun of the angelic heaven, which is not fire, but the Divine love proximately proceeding from God, Who is love itself. As he was surprised at this, we proved it thus: "Love in its essence is spiritual fire; hence it is, that fire in the Word, in its spiritual sense, signifies love. It is on this account that priests, when officiating in temples, pray that heavenly fire may fill their hearts, by which they mean love. The fire of the altar, and the fire of the candlestick in the tabernacle among the Israelites, represented nothing else than the Divine love. The heat of the blood, or the vital heat of men, and of animals in general, is from no other source than from the love which constitutes their life: hence it is that a man is enkindled, grows warm, and is inflamed, when his love is exalted into zeal, anger, and wrath: wherefore from the fact, that spiritual heat, which is love, produces natural heat with men, even to the kindling and inflaming of their faces and limbs, it may be manifest, that the fire of the natural sun has come into existence from no other source than the fire of the spiritual sun,
which is the Divine love. Now, since the expanse originates 13
from the centre, and not the centre from the expanse, as we said above, and the centre of life, which is the sun of the angelic heaven, is the Divine love proximately proceeding from God, Who is in the midst of that sun; and since the expanse of that centre, which is called the spiritual world, is derived thence; and since from that sun the sun of the world came into existence, and from the latter its expanse, which is called the natural world; it is evident, that the universe was created by the one God."

After this we took our leave; and he accompanied us outside the court of his study, and conversed with us about heaven and hell, and the Divine government, with a new sagacity of genius

381. The second Memorable Relation:—

Once as I was looking around into the world of spirits, I saw at a distance a palace surrounded and as it were besieged by a crowd; I also saw many running towards it. Wondering what this could mean, I speedily left the house, and asked one of those who were running, what was the matter at the palace?

He replied, that three new comers from the world had been taken up into a heaven, and had there seen magnificent things, also maidens and wives of astonishing beauty; and that being let down from that heaven they had entered into that palace, and related what they had seen; especially that they had beheld such beauties as their eyes had never before seen, nor can see, unless enlightened by the light of the heavenly aura. Respecting themselves they said, that in the world they had been orators from the kingdom of France, and had applied themselves to the study of eloquence, and that now they were seized with a desire of making an oration on the origin of beauty. When this was made known in the neighbourhood, the multitude flocked together to hear them.

Upon hearing these particulars, I myself also hastened, and entered the palace, and saw the three men standing in the midst, dressed in long robes of a sapphire colour, which, having threads of gold in their texture, at every movement shone as if they had been golden. They stood behind a kind of pulpit, ready to speak; and presently one of them rose on a step behind the pulpit to deliver an oration on the origin of the beauty of the feminine sex, in the following words:—

382. "What is the origin of beauty but love, which, when it flows in into the eyes of young men and sets them on fire, becomes beauty? wherefore love and beauty are the same thing; for love, from the inmost, suffuses the face of a marriageable maiden with a certain flame, from the transparence of which is derived the dawn and bloom of her life. Who does not know that that flame sends rays into her eyes, and spreads from these as centres into the whole of the face, and also descends into the breast, and sets the heart on fire, and thus affects [a young man], just as a fire with its heat and light affects a person standing near it? That heat is love, and that light is the beauty of love. The whole world agrees in affirming that every one is lovely and beautiful according to his or her love: but nevertheless the love of the male sex is different from the love of the female sex. Male love is the love of becoming wise, and femal love is the love of loving the love of becoming wise in the male; in proportion therefore as a young man is the love of becoming wise, in the same proportion he is lovely and beautiful to a maiden; and in proportion as a maiden is the love of a young man's wisdom, in the same proportion she is lovely and beautiful to the

young man; wherefore as love meets and kisses the love of another, so also do beauties. I conclude therefore that love forms beauty into a resemblance of itself."

383. After him arose a second, in order to reveal the origin of beauty by an elegant speech. He said: "I have heard that love is the origin of beauty; but I cannot agree with this opinion. What human being knows what love is? Who has ever contemplated it with any idea of thought? Who has ever seen it with the eye? Tell me where it is. But I assert that wisdom is the origin of beauty; in women a wisdom which lies inmostly concealed and stored up, in men a wisdom which manifests itself, and is apparent. Whence is a man (*homo*) a man, but from wisdom? Were it not from thence, a man would be a statue or a picture. What does a maiden attend to in a young man, but the quality of his wisdom; and what does a young man attend to in a maiden, but the quality of her affection of his wisdom? By wisdom I mean genuine morality; because this is the wisdom of life. Hence it is, that when the wisdom which lies concealed, approaches and embraces the wisdom which is manifest, which takes place interiorly in the spirit of both, they mutually kiss and become conjoined, and this is called love; and then they both appear beautiful to each other. In a word, wisdom is like the light or brightness of fire, which delicately touches the eyes, and in the act forms beauty."

384. After him the third arose, and spoke as follows;—"Neither love alone, nor wisdom alone, is the origin of beauty, but the union of love and wisdom; the union of love with [its own] wisdom in a young man, and the union of wisdom with its own love in a maiden. For a maiden does not love wisdom in herself but in the young man, and therefore sees him as beauty; and when the young man sees this in the maiden, he then sees her as beauty; wherefore love forms the beauty through the wisdom, and the wisdom receives it from the love. That this is the case, appears manifestly in heaven. I have seen maidens and wives there, and have attentively considered their beauties, and have seen, that beauty in maidens is quite different from beauty in wives; in maidens there is only the brightness, but in wives the resplendescence of beauty. I saw the difference like that between a diamond sparkling with light, and a ruby flashing at the same time with fire. What is beauty but the delight of the sight? In what does this delight originate but in the sporting of love and wisdom? From this sporting the sight glows, and this glowing vibrates from eye to eye, and presents beauty [to the sight]. What constitutes beauty of face, but redness and whiteness, and the lovely intermingling of the one with the other? Is not the redness from love, and the whiteness from wisdom?

for love is red by reason of its fire, and wisdom is white by reason of its light. Both these I have clearly seen in the faces of two married partners in heaven; the redness of whiteness in the wife, and the whiteness of redness in the husband; and I observed that they shone in consequence of their mutually looking at each other."

When the third had thus spoken, the assembly applauded and cried out, "This is the winner." Then on a sudden, a flaming light, which is also the light of conjugial love, filled the house with splendour, and, at the same time, their hearts with pleasantness.

THE CONJUNCTION OF CONJUGIAL LOVE WITH THE LOVE OF CHILDREN.

385. THERE are evidences that clearly shew that conjugial love and the love of children, which is called storgë [στοργή], are conjoined: and there are also evidences which may induce a belief that they are not conjoined; for the love of children exists with married partners who love each other from the heart, and it exists also with married partners who disagree at heart, and likewise with those who are separated from each other, and sometimes it is more tender and stronger with the latter than the former. But that nevertheless the love of children is always conjoined with conjugial love, may be manifest from the origin from which it flows in; for although this origin is varied with the recipients, those loves nevertheless remain inseparable, just as the first end in the last end, which is the effect. The first end of conjugial love is the procreation of offspring, and the last end, which is the effect, is the offspring that is procreated. That the first end enters into the effect, and is therein as in its first origin, and does not withdraw from it, may be seen from a rational view of the progression of ends and causes in their order to effects. But, since the reasonings of the generality commence merely from effects, and from them proceed to some consequences thence resulting, and do not commence from causes, and from them proceed analytically to effects, and so forth; therefore the rational things of light cannot but become the obscure things of cloud, whence come deviations from truth, arising from appearances and fallacies. But in order that it may be seen that conjugial love and the love of children are interiorly conjoined, although exteriorly disjoined, it shall be demonstrated in the following order:—

I. *Two universal spheres proceed from the Lord to preserve the universe in its created state; of which the one is the sphere of procreating, and the other the sphere of protecting the things procreated.*

II. *Those two universal spheres make a one with the sphere of conjugial love and the sphere of the love of children.*

III. *Those two spheres universally and singularly flow in into all things of heaven and all things of the world, from first to last.*

IV. *The sphere of the love of children is a sphere of protection and support of those who are unable to protect and support themselves.*

V. *That sphere affects both the evil and the good, and disposes every one to love, protect, and support his offspring out of self-love.*

VI. *This sphere principally affects the female sex, thus mothers, and the male sex, or fathers, by derivation from them.*

VII. *This sphere is also a sphere of innocence and peace from the Lord.*

VIII. *The sphere of innocence flows in into the children, and through them into the parents, and affects [them].*

IX. *It also flows in into the souls of the parents, and conjoins itself with the same sphere in the children; and it is chiefly insinuated by means of the touch.*

X. *In the degree in which innocence departs from children, affection and conjunction also abate, and this successively even to separation.*

XI. *The state of rational innocence and peace with the parents towards the children is [grounded in the circumstance], that they know nothing and can do nothing from themselves, but from others, especially from the father and mother; and this state also successively departs, in proportion as they know and have ability from themselves and not from others.*

XII. *That sphere progresses in order from the end through the causes into the effects, and makes periods, by means of which creation is preserved in the state foreseen and provided for.*

XIII. *The love of children descends, and does not ascend.*

XIV. *Wives have one state of love before conception, and a different state after conception even to the birth.*

XV. *With parents, conjugial love is conjoined with the love of children by spiritual causes, and thence by natural ones.*

XVI. *The love of little children and older children is different with spiritual married partners from what it is with natural ones.*

XVII. *With the spiritual that love is from what is interior or prior, but with the natural from what is exterior or posterior.*

XVIII. *Hence it is, that that love exists with married partners who mutually love each other, and also with married partners who do not love each other at all.*

XIX. *The love of children remains after death, especially with women.*

XX. *Children are educated under the Lord's auspices by such women, and grow in stature and intelligence as in the world.*

XXI. *It is there provided by the Lord, that with those children the innocence of childhood should become the innocence of wisdom, and that thus the children should become angels.*

Now follows the explanation of these articles.

386. I. TWO UNIVERSAL SPHERES PROCEED FROM THE LORD TO PRESERVE THE UNIVERSE IN ITS CREATED STATE; OF WHICH THE ONE IS THE SPHERE OF PROCREATING, AND THE OTHER THE SPHERE OF PROTECTING THE THINGS PROCREATED. The Divine which pro-

ceeds from the Lord is called a sphere, because it goes forth from Him, encompasses Him, fills both worlds, the spiritual and the natural, and operates the effects of those ends which the Lord predestinated at the creation, and for which He provides ever since the creation. All that which flows forth from a subject, and surrounds and environs it, is called a sphere; as for example, the sphere of light and heat from the sun around it, the sphere of life from man around him, the sphere of odour from a plant around it, the sphere of attraction from the magnet around it, and so forth. But the universal spheres which are here being treated of, are from the Lord around Him; and they proceed from the sun of the spiritual world, in the midst of which He is. From the Lord, by means of that sun, proceeds a sphere of heat and light, or what is the same, a sphere of love and wisdom, to operate ends, which are uses; but that sphere, according to the uses, is distinguished by various names. The Divine sphere which provides for the preservation of the universe in its created state by means of successive generations, is called the sphere of procreating; and the Divine sphere which provides for the preservation of generations in their beginnings, and afterwards in their progressions, is called the sphere of protecting the things procreated. Besides these two spheres, there are many other Divine spheres, which are named according to their uses, consequently variously, see above, no. 222. The operations of uses through those spheres are the Divine providence.

387. II. THOSE TWO UNIVERSAL SPHERES MAKE A ONE WITH THE SPHERE OF CONJUGIAL LOVE AND THE SPHERE OF THE LOVE OF CHILDREN. That the sphere of conjugial love makes a one with the sphere of procreating, is evident; for procreation is the end, and conjugial love the mediate cause by means of which [the end is promoted], and the end and the cause act in unity, because together, in the things to be effected and in the effects. That the sphere of the love of children makes a one with the sphere of protecting the things procreated, is also evident, because it is the end proceeding from the prior end, which was procreation, and the love of children is its mediate cause by which [it is promoted]: for ends progress in a series, one after another, and in their progress the last end becomes the first, and thus [progresses] further, even to the boundary, in which they subsist or cease. But on this subject more will be seen in the explanation of article XII.

388. III. THOSE TWO SPHERES UNIVERSALLY AND SINGULARLY FLOW IN INTO ALL THINGS OF HEAVEN AND ALL THINGS OF THE WORLD, FROM FIRST TO LAST. It is said universally and singularly, because when mention is made of a universal, the singulars of which it is composed are meant at the same time;

for a universal exists from and consists of singulars; thus it takes its name from them, as a whole exists from, consists of, and takes its name from its parts; wherefore, if you take away the singulars, the universal is a mere name, and is like a mere surface within which there is nothing: wherefore, to attribute to God universal government, and to take away the singulars, is vain talk and empty preaching. The comparison with the universal government of the kings of the earth is not to the purpose. From this ground then it is said, that those two spheres flow in universally and singularly.

389. The reason why the spheres of procreating and of protecting the things procreated, or the spheres of conjugial love and the love of children, flow in into all things of heaven and all things of the world, from first to last, is, that all things which proceed from the Lord, or from the sun which is from Him and in which He is, pervade the created universe, even to the last things of all. The reason is, that Divine things, which in progression are called celestial and spiritual, have no relation to space and time. That extension cannot be predicated of spiritual things, because space and time cannot be predicated of them, is known: hence it is, that whatever proceeds from the Lord, is in an instant from first things in last things. That the sphere of conjugial love is thus universal, see above, nos. 222–225. That the sphere of the love of children likewise is universal, is evident from that love's existing in heaven, where there are children from the earths; and from that love's existing in the world with human beings, beasts and birds, serpents and insects. Analogues of this love exist also in the vegetable and mineral kingdoms; in the vegetable, in that seeds are guarded by shells or husks as by swaddling clothes, and moreover are in the fruit as in a house, and are nourished with juice as with milk; that there is something similar in minerals, is plain from the matrices and external coverings, in which noble gems and metals are hidden and guarded.

390. The reason why the sphere of procreating, and the sphere of protecting the things procreated, make a one in a continual series, is, that the love of procreating is continued into the love of what is procreated. The quality of the love of procreating is known from its delight, which is supereminent and transcendent. In this delight is the state of procreation with men, and in an eminent degree the state of reception with women. This highest delight with its love is continued even to the birth, and there attains its fulness.

391. IV. THE SPHERE OF THE LOVE OF CHILDREN IS A SPHERE OF PROTECTION AND SUPPORT OF THOSE WHO ARE UNABLE TO PRO-

TECT AND SUPPORT THEMSELVES. That the operations of uses by the Lord through spheres proceeding from Him, are the Divine providence, was stated above, no. 386; this [Divine providence] therefore is meant by the sphere of protection and support of those who are unable to protect and support themselves: for it is of creation, that the things created must be preserved, guarded, protected, and supported; otherwise the universe would fall to ruin. But since this cannot be done immediately by the Lord with living creatures, who are left to their own choice, it is done mediately through His love implanted in fathers, mothers, and nurses. That their love is love from the Lord with them, they themselves do not know, because they do not perceive the influx, and still less the omnipresence, of the Lord. But who does not see, that this is not of nature, but of the Divine providence operating in nature through nature; and that such a universal principle cannot exist except from God, through a certain spiritual sun which is in the centre of the universe, and whose operation, being apart from space and time, is instant and present from first things in last things? But in what manner that Divine operation, which is the Lord's Divine providence, is received by animate subjects, will be stated in what follows. That mothers and fathers protect and support their children, because they are not able to protect and support themselves, is not the cause of that love, but it is a rational cause derived from that love's falling into the understanding; for man, from this cause alone, without love inspired and inspiring it, or without law and punishment compelling him, would no more provide for his children than a statue.

392. V. THAT SPHERE AFFECTS BOTH THE EVIL AND THE GOOD, AND DISPOSES EVERY ONE TO LOVE, PROTECT, AND SUPPORT HIS OFFSPRING OUT OF SELF-LOVE (*ex proprio amore*). Experience testifies that the love of children, or storgë, exists equally with the evil and the good, and likewise with tame and wild beasts; yea, that sometimes it is stronger and more ardent with evil human beings, and also with wild beasts. The reason is, that all love proceeding from the Lord and flowing in into subjects, is changed in the subject into the love of its life; for every animate subject has no other sensation than that it loves of itself, for it does not perceive the influx; and while also it actually loves itself, it makes the love of children proper to itself, or its own; for it sees as it were itself in them, and them in itself, and itself thus united with them. Hence also it is that that love is fiercer with wild beasts, as with lions and lionesses, he and she bears, leopards and leopardesses, he and she wolves, and others of a like nature, than with horses, deer, goats, and sheep; the reason is, that those wild beasts have dominion over the tame ones, and therefore the love of self is predominant,

and this love loves itself in its offspring; wherefore, as has been stated, the influent love is turned into self-love. Such an inversion of the influent love into self-love, and the consequent protection and support of the offspring and progeny by evil parents, is of the Lord's Divine providence; for otherwise there would remain but few of the human race, and none of the savage beasts, which, nevertheless, are of use. From these considerations it is evident, that every one is disposed to love, protect, and support his offspring, out of self-love.

393. VI. THIS SPHERE PRINCIPALLY AFFECTS THE FEMALE SEX, THUS MOTHERS, AND THE MALE SEX, OR FATHERS, BY DERIVATION FROM THEM. This follows from the same origin that was treated of above, namely, that the sphere of conjugial love is received by the women, and through them is transferred to the men: because women are born loves of the understanding of the men, and the understanding is a recipient. The case is the same with the love of children, because this is originally from conjugial love. It is known that mothers have a most tender love of children, and fathers a less tender love. That the love of children is inscribed on conjugial love, into which women are born, is evident from the amiable and endearing affection of girls towards little children, and towards their dolls, which they carry, dress, kiss, and press to their bosoms: boys do not possess any such affection. It appears as if mothers derived the love of children from nourishing them in the womb out of their own blood, and consequently from the appropriation of their life, and thus from sympathetic union: but nevertheless this is not the origin of that love; for if another child were to be substituted after birth, without the mother's knowledge, in the place of the genuine child, the mother would love it with equal tenderness as if it were her own: moreover, children are sometimes loved by their nurses more than by their mothers. From these considerations it follows, that that love is from no other source than from the conjugial love implanted in every woman, to which is adjoined the love of conceiving, by the delight of which the wife is prepared for reception. This is the first of the above love, which with its delight after the birth passes fully to the offspring.

394. VII. THIS SPHERE IS ALSO A SPHERE OF INNOCENCE AND PEACE [FROM THE LORD]. Innocence and peace are the two inmost things of heaven: they are called inmost because they proceed immediately from the Lord; for the Lord is innocence itself and peace itself. By reason of innocence the Lord is called a Lamb, and by reason of peace He says, "*Peace I leave unto you: My peace I give unto you*" (John xiv. 27); and He is also meant by the peace with which

the disciples were to salute a city or a house which they entered; and of which it is said, that if it were worthy, peace would come upon it, and if not worthy, peace would return (Matt. x. 11–15). Hence also the Lord is called the Prince of peace (Isaiah ix. 5, [6]). A further reason why innocence and peace are the inmost things of heaven, is, that innocence is the esse of all good, and peace is the blessedness of every delight which is of good. See the work on *Heaven and Hell* concerning the state of innocence of the angels of heaven, nos. 276–283; and concerning the state of peace in heaven, nos. 284–290.

395. VIII. THE SPHERE OF INNOCENCE FLOWS IN INTO THE CHILDREN, AND THROUGH THEM INTO THE PARENTS, AND AFFECTS [THEM]. It is known that children are innocences; but it is not known that their innocence flows in from the Lord. It flows in from the Lord, because, as was said just above, He is innocence itself; neither can anything flow in, since it cannot exist, except from its first beginning, which is Very Entity (*Ipsum Illud*). But the quality of the innocence of childhood, which affects the parents, shall be stated in a few words. It shines forth from their face, from some of their gestures, and from their first speech, and affects [them]. They have innocence, because they do not think from the Interior; for they do not as yet know what is good and evil, and what is true and false, as a basis of thought; consequently they do not possess prudence from the proprium; nor any deliberate purpose, and thus no end of evil. They have no proprium acquired from the love of self and the love of the world; they do not attribute anything to themselves; they refer to their parents whatever they receive; they are content with the trifles which are given them as presents; they have no solicitude about food and raiment, nor about the future; they do not look to the world, nor desire many things thence; they love their parents, their nurses, and their child-companions, with whom they play in innocence; they suffer themselves to be guided, they hearken and obey. This is the innocence of childhood, which is the cause of the love called storgë.

396. IX. IT ALSO FLOWS IN INTO THE SOULS OF THE PARENTS, AND CONJOINS ITSELF WITH THE SAME SPHERE IN THE CHILDREN; AND IT IS CHIEFLY INSINUATED BY MEANS OF THE TOUCH. The Lord's innocence flows in into the angels of the third heaven, where all are in the innocence of wisdom, and passes through the lower heavens, but only through the innocences of the angels therein, and thus immediately and mediately into children. These are hardly anything else than graven forms; but nevertheless they are receptible of life from the Lord through the heavens. Yet, unless the parents also received that influx in their souls, and in the inmosts of their minds, they would in vain be affected

by the innocence of the children. There must be something adequate and similar in another, whereby communication may be effected, and which may cause reception, affection, and thence conjunction; otherwise it would be like soft seed falling upon a flint, or a lamb exposed to a wolf. Hence then it is, that innocence flowing in into the souls of the parents, conjoins itself
2 with the innocence of the children. Experience may teach that, with the parents, this conjunction is effected by the mediation of the bodily senses, but especially by means of the touch: as that the sight is inmostly delighted by seeing them, the hearing by their speech, the smell by their odour. That the communication and therefore the conjunction of innocences is chiefly effected by means of the touch, is seen evidently from the pleasantness of carrying them in the arms, from embracing and kissing them, especially with mothers, who are delighted by laying their mouth and face upon their bosoms, and at the same time by their touching the same with the palms of their hands, in general, by their sucking the breasts, and their being fed by their milk, moreover, by stroking their naked body, and by the unwearied pains they take in washing and dressing them on
3 their knees. That the communications of love and of its delights between married partners are effected through the sense of touch, has been proved above in several passages. The reason why communications of the mind are also effected through the same sense is, that the hands are a man's ultimates, and the first things of man, or his primes, are at the same time in his last things, or in his ultimates: by that [sense] also all the intermediate things of the body and mind are kept together in unbroken connection. Hence it is, that Jesus touched little children (Matt. xix. 13–15; Mark x. 13–16); and that He healed the sick by the touch: and that those who touched Him were healed. Hence also it is, that inaugurations into the priesthood are at the present day effected by the laying on of hands. From these considerations it is evident, that the innocence of parents and the innocence of children meet through the touch, especially of the hands, and thereby conjoin themselves as by kisses.

397. That innocence operates similar things with beasts and birds as with human beings, by contact, is known: the reason is, that all that proceeds from the Lord, in an instant pervades the universe (see above, nos. 388–390); and as it proceeds by degrees, and by continual mediations, therefore it passes not only to animals, but also further, to plants and minerals (see no. 389): it also passes into the earth itself, which is the mother of all plants and minerals; for the earth, in spring-time, is in a prepared state for the reception of seeds, as it were in the womb; and when it receives them, it, as it were, conceives, cherishes, carries in the womb, brings forth, suckles, nourishes, clothes,

educates, guards, and, as it were, loves the offspring from them, and so forth. Since the sphere of procreation proceeds thus far, how much more must it not proceed to animals of every kind, even to worms? That as the earth is the common mother of plants, so there is also a common mother of bees in every hive, is a well-established fact.

398. X. In the degree in which innocence departs from children, affection and conjunction also abate, and this successively even to separation. It is known that the love of children, or storgë, departs from parents according as innocence departs from them; and that with human beings it departs even to the separation of the older children from the home, and, with beasts and birds, to a rejection from their presence, and a total forgetfulness that they are of their stock. From this circumstance, as an established fact, it may be further manifest, that innocence flowing in on both sides produces the love called storgë.

399. XI. The state of rational innocence and peace with the parents towards the children, is [on account of the circumstance], that they know nothing and can do nothing from themselves, but from others, especially from the father and mother; and this state [also] successively departs, in proportion as they know and have ability from themselves and not from others. That the sphere of the love of children is a sphere of protection and support of those who are not able to protect and support themselves, was shown above in its proper article, no. 391. That this is only a rational cause with man, but not the very essential cause of that love with them, was also mentioned in the same article. The real original cause of that love is innocence from the Lord, which flows in while the man is ignorant of it, and produces the above rational cause; wherefore as the first cause produces a departure from that love, so also does this second cause at the same time; or, what is the same thing, as the communication of innocence departs, so also the persuading reason accompanies it; but this is the case only with man, to the intent that he may do what he does from freedom according to reason, and that from reason, as from a rational and at the same time moral law, he may support his adult offspring according to necessity and usefulness. This second cause does not influence animals who are devoid of reason, they being influenced only by the prior cause, which to them is instinct.

400. XII. The sphere of the love of procreating progresses in order from the end through the causes into the effects, and makes periods, by means of which creation

IS PRESERVED IN THE STATE FORESEEN AND PROVIDED FOR. All the operations in the universe progress from ends through causes into effects. These three are in themselves indivisible, although in the ideas they appear as if they were divided; but nevertheless the end is not anything there unless the effect which is intended is seen together with it; nor does either of them become anything, unless the cause supports, provides for,
2 and conjoins. Such a progression is inscribed on every man in general, and in every particular, just as the will, the understanding, and the action: every end there belongs to the will, every cause belongs to the understanding, and every effect belongs to the action; in like manner, every end belongs to love, every instrumental cause belongs to wisdom, and every effect thence belongs to use. The reason is, that the receptacle of love is the will, the receptacle of wisdom is the understanding, and the receptacle of use is the action. Since therefore operations in general and in particular with man progress, from the will through the understanding into the act, so also do they progress from love through wisdom into use. By wisdom is here meant all that which belongs to judgment and thought. That these three are a one in the effect, is evident. That they also make a one in ideas before the effect, is perceived from the fact, that determination only intervenes; for in the mind an end goes forth from the will and produces for itself a cause in the understanding, and presents to itself an intention; and an intention is as an act before determination: hence it is, that by a wise man, and also by the Lord, an inten-
3 tion is accepted as an act. What rational person cannot see, or, when he hears, acknowledge, that those three things flow forth from some first cause, and that that cause is, that from the Lord, the Creator and Preserver of the universe, there continually proceed love, wisdom, and use, and these three as a one? Tell, if you can, in what other source they originate.

401. A like progression from the end through the cause into the effect belongs also to the sphere of procreating and of protecting the things procreated. In this case, the end is the will or love of procreating; the mediate cause, through which and into which the end introduces itself, is conjugial love: the progressive series of efficient causes is the loving, conception, gestation of the embryo or offspring to be procreated; and the effect is the procreated offspring itself. But although the end, the cause, and the effect progress successively as three things, yet, nevertheless, in the love of procreating, and inwardly in each of the causes, and in the effect itself, they make a one. It is only the efficient causes that progress through times, because in nature; while the end, or the will, or the love, remains constantly the same: for the ends progress in nature through

times without time; but they cannot come forth and manifest themselves, until the effect or use comes into existence and becomes a subject; before this, that love could love only the progression, but could not secure and fix itself. That there are periods of such progressions, and that by means of them creation is preserved in the state foreseen and provided for, is known. But the series of the love of children from its greatest to its least, thus to the boundary in which it subsists or ceases, is retrograde, since it is according to the decrease of innocence in the subject, and also on account of the periods.

402. XIII. The love of children descends, and does not ascend. That it descends from generation to generation, or from sons and daughters to grandsons and granddaughters, and does not ascend from these to fathers and mothers of families, is known. The cause of its increase in descent is the love of fructifying, or of producing uses, and, in respect to the human race, it is the love of multiplying it; but this derives its origin solely from the Lord, Who, in the multiplication of the human race, regards the preservation of creation, and, as the ultimate end thereof, the angelic heaven, which is solely from the human race; and since the angelic heaven is the end of ends, and thus the love of loves with the Lord, therefore there is implanted in the souls of men, not only the love of procreating, but also of loving the things procreated in their successions: hence also it is, that this love exists only with man, and not with any beast or bird. That this love with man descends increasing, is also in consequence of the glory of honour, which in like manner increases with him according to augmentations. That the love of honour and glory receives into itself the love of children that flows in from the Lord, and makes it as it were its own, will be seen in article XVI.

403. XIV. Wives have one state of love before conception, and a different state after conception, even to the birth. This is adduced to the end that it may be known, that the love of procreating, and the consequent love of what has been procreated, is implanted in the conjugial love with women, and that with them those two loves are divided, when the end, which is the love of procreating, begins its progression. That the love called storgë is then transferred from the wife to the husband, and also that the love of procreating, which, as has been said, with a woman makes one with her conjugial love, is then not alike, is evident from several indications.

404. XV. With parents, conjugial love is conjoined with the love of children by spiritual causes, and thence by natural ones. The spiritual causes are, that the human

race may be multiplied, and from this the angelic heaven enlarged, and that thereby such may be born as will become angels, serving the Lord to do uses in heaven, and by consociation with men also in the earths: for every man has angels associated with him by the Lord; and such is his conjunction with them, that if they were to be taken away, he would instantly die. The natural causes of the conjunction of those two loves are, to effect the birth of those who may promote uses in human societies, and may be incorporated therein as members. That the latter are the natural and the former the spiritual causes of the love of children and of conjugial love, even the married partners themselves think and sometimes declare, saying that they have enriched heaven with as many angels as they have had descendants, and have furnished society with as many servants as they have had children.

405. XVI. THE LOVE OF LITTLE CHILDREN AND OLDER CHILDREN IS DIFFERENT WITH SPIRITUAL MARRIED PARTNERS FROM WHAT IT IS WITH NATURAL ONES. With spiritual married partners the love of children, as to appearance, is like the love of children with natural married partners; but it is more inward, and therefore more tender, because that love exists from innocence, and from a nearer reception of innocence, and thereby a more present perception of it in oneself; for the spiritual are spiritual in proportion as they partake of innocence. But [spiritual] fathers and mothers, after they have sipped the sweetness of innocence in their children, love their older children quite differently from what natural fathers and mothers do. The spiritual love their older children on account of their spiritual intelligence and moral life; thus they love them on account of their fear of God and actual piety, or piety of life, and at the same time on account of their affection for and application to uses which are of service to society, consequently from the virtues and good morals in them. It is chiefly from the love of these things that they provide for, and administer to, their necessities; wherefore if they do not see such things in them, they alienate their mind (*animus*) from them, and only do anything for them from a sense of duty. With natural fathers and mothers the love of children is indeed also from innocence: but when the innocence is received by them, it is entwined around their own self-love, and consequently they love their children from this love, and at the same time from that innocence, kissing, embracing, and dandling them, hugging them to their bosoms, and caressing them beyond all bounds, and they regard them as one heart and soul with themselves; and afterwards, after their state of childhood even to puberty and beyond it, when innocence is no longer operative, they do not love them on account of any fear of God and actual piety, or

piety of life, nor on account of any rational and moral intelligence in them; and they regard very slightly, if at all, their internal affections, and thence their virtues and good morals, but only their externals, which they favour. To these externals their love is adjoined, attached, and cemented: hence also they close their eyes to their faults, excusing and favouring them. The reason is, that with such parents the love of their offspring is also the love of self; and this love cleaves to the subject outwardly, and does not enter into it, as self does not enter into itself.

406. The quality of the love of children and the love of older children with the spiritual, and its quality with the natural, is clearly discerned from them after death; for most fathers, when they come into the other life, remember their children who have died before them; they are also presented to and recognize each other. Spiritual fathers only look at them, and inquire as to their present state, rejoice if it is well with them, and grieve if it is ill; and after some conversation, instruction, and admonition about heavenly moral life, they separate from them, and before separation they teach them that they are no longer to be remembered as fathers, because the Lord is the only Father to all in heaven, according to His words in Matthew xxiii. 9: and that they never remember them as their children. But natural fathers, as soon as they become conscious that they are living after death, and recall to memory their children who have died before them, and when, according to their wish, they are presented to each other, instantly become conjoined with them, and they cleave together like sticks tied up into bundles; and the father is then continually delighted to look at them and talk to them. If the father is told that some of his children are satans, and that they have done injuries to the good, he nevertheless keeps them in a group around him, or in a troop before him; if he himself sees that they inflict injuries and commit evils, he yet pays no attention to it, nor does he dissociate any of them from himself. Wherefore in order to prevent the continuance of such a dangerous company, they are of necessity committed all together to hell; and there the father is shut up in confinement before his children, and the children are separated, and each one is sent away to the place of his own life.

407. To the above I will add this wonderful relation:—in the spiritual world I have seen fathers, who, from hatred, and as it were rage, had looked at children who were presented before their eyes, with a mind (*animus*) so savage, that if they could, they would have killed them; but on its being hinted to them, though without truth, that they were their own children, their

rage and savageness instantly departed, and they loved them to excess. This love and that hatred prevail together with those who in the world had been inwardly deceitful, and had set their minds in enmity against the Lord.

408. XVII. WITH THE SPIRITUAL THAT LOVE IS FROM WHAT IS INTERIOR OR PRIOR, BUT WITH THE NATURAL FROM WHAT IS EXTERIOR OR POSTERIOR. Thinking and concluding from what is interior and prior, is thinking and concluding from ends and causes to effects; but thinking and concluding from what is exterior or posterior, is thinking and concluding from effects to causes and ends. The latter progression is contrary to order, but the former is according to order; for thinking and concluding from ends and causes, is thinking and concluding from goods and truths that are clearly seen in the higher region of the mind, to the effects in the lower region: human rationality itself is such from creation. But thinking and concluding from effects, is making conjectures about causes and effects from the lower region of the mind, where the sensual things of the body, with their appearances and fallacies, are, which in itself is nothing else than confirming falsities and concupiscences, and after confirmation seeing and believing them to be verities of wisdom and goodnesses of the love of wisdom. The case is similar with the love of young and grown-up children with the spiritual and the natural; the spiritual love them from what is prior, thus according to order: but the natural love them from what is posterior, thus contrary to order. These things are adduced merely for the confirmation of the preceding article.

409. XVIII. HENCE IT IS, THAT THAT LOVE EXISTS WITH MARRIED PARTNERS WHO MUTUALLY LOVE EACH OTHER, AND ALSO WITH MARRIED PARTNERS WHO DO NOT LOVE EACH OTHER AT ALL; consequently it exists with the natural equally as with the spiritual; but the latter possess conjugial love, whereas the former possess no conjugial love but what is apparent and simulated. The reason why the love of children and conjugial love nevertheless act in unity, is, that conjugial love is implanted in every woman from creation, and together with it the love of procreating, which is determined to and flows unto the procreated offspring, and from the women is communicated to the men, as was said above. Hence it is, that in households in which there is no conjugial love between the man and his wife, it nevertheless is with the wife, and through it there is some external conjunction with the man. From this same cause it is, that even whores love their offspring; for that which from creation has been implanted in souls, and pertains to propagation, is indelible, and cannot be extirpated.

410. XIX. The love of children remains after death, especially with women. Children, as soon as they are raised up, which happens immediately after their decease, are elevated into heaven, and delivered to angels who are of the female sex, who in the life of the body in the world had loved children and at the same time had feared God. These, since they have loved all children with maternal tenderness, receive them as their own; and the children in this case, as from an innate feeling, love them as their own mothers: as many infants are consigned to them, as they desire from spiritual storgë. The heaven in which children are, appears in front in the region of the forehead, in the line or radius in which the angels look directly at the Lord. That heaven is so situated, because all children are educated under the immediate auspices of the Lord. There also flows in with them the heaven of innocence, which is the third heaven. When they have passed through this first age, they are transferred to another heaven, where they are instructed.

411. XX. Children are educated under the Lord's auspices by such women, and grow in stature and intelligence as in the world. Children in heaven are educated in the following manner:—They learn to speak from their governess: their first speech is merely the sound of affection, in which however there is some beginning of thought, whereby what is human in the sound is distinguished from the sound of an animal; this speech gradually becomes more distinct, as ideas from affection enter the thought: all their affections, which also grow, proceed from innocence. At first, such things are insinuated into them as appear before their eyes, and are delightful; and as these things are from a spiritual origin, there flow in into these things at the same time things which are of heaven, whereby the interiors of their minds are opened. Afterwards, as the children are perfected in intelligence, so they grow in stature, and in this respect also they appear more adult: the reason is, that intelligence and wisdom are essential spiritual nourishment; therefore those things which nourish their minds, also nourish their bodies in heaven. But children in heaven do not grow up beyond their first age, but stop in that age and remain in it to eternity. And when they are in that age they are given in marriage, which is provided by the Lord, and is celebrated in the heaven of the young man, who presently follows his wife into her heaven, or into her house, if they are in the same society. In order that I might know for certain that children grow and mature in stature, as they do in intelligence, it has been given me to speak with some while they were children, and afterwards when they were grown up; and when they were grown up they appeared in a stature like that of grown up young men in the world.

412. Children are instructed especially by means of representatives adapted and suited to their genius; and it can hardly be believed in the world how beautiful and at the same time how full of interior wisdom these representatives are. It is allowed to adduce here two representations, from which a conclusion may be formed in regard to the rest. They once represented the Lord ascending out of the sepulchre, and at the same time the unition of His Human with the Divine. At first they presented the idea of a sepulchre, but not at the same time the idea of the Lord, except so remotely, that it was scarcely, except as it were at a distance, perceived that it was the Lord; because in the idea of a sepulchre there is something funereal, which they thereby removed. Afterwards they discreetly admitted into the sepulchre a sort of atmospheric element, appearing at last as a thin watery element, by which they signified, and this also by a becoming remoteness, spiritual life in baptism. Afterwards I saw represented by them the Lord's descent to those who were bound, and His ascent with them into heaven; and, what was really child-like, they let down small cords that were almost invisible, and very soft and delicate, to aid the Lord in the ascent, being always in a holy fear lest anything in the representative should touch upon something in which there was nothing heavenly. Not to mention other representations, whereby children are introduced at the same time into the Knowledges of truth and the affections of good, as by games adapted to their infant minds (*animi*). To these and similar things children are led by the Lord by means of innocence passing through the third heaven; and thus spiritual things are insinuated into their affections, and thence into their tender thoughts, in order that they may know no otherwise than that they do and think such things from themselves: by means of this their understanding begins to be formed.

413. XXI. It is there provided by the Lord, that with those children the innocence of childhood should become the innocence of wisdom [and that thus the children should become angels]. Many may fancy that children remain children, and become angels immediately after death. But it is intelligence and wisdom that make an angel; wherefore so long as children do not possess intelligence and wisdom, they are indeed among angels, but they are not angels: but they then first become angels, when they have become intelligent and wise. Children therefore are led from the innocence of childhood to the innocence of wisdom, that is, from external innocence to internal innocence: the latter innocence is the end of all their instruction and progression; wherefore when they attain to the innocence of wisdom, the innocence of childhood is adjoined to them, which in the meantime had served them for

a plane. I saw the quality of the innocence of childhood represented by a wooden something almost devoid of life, which is vivified in proportion as they imbibe the Knowledges of truth and the affections of good: and afterwards there was represented the quality of the innocence of wisdom, by a living and naked child. The angels of the third heaven, who are in a state of innocence from the Lord above other angels, appear like naked children before the eyes of spirits who are beneath the heavens; and as they are wiser than all others, they are also more alive: the reason is, that innocence corresponds to childhood, and also to nakedness; wherefore it is said of Adam and his wife, when they were in the state of innocence, that they were naked and were not ashamed; but that when they had lost their state of innocence, they were ashamed of their nakedness, and hid themselves (Gen. ii. 25; iii. 7, 10, 11). In a word, the wiser the angels are, the more innocent they are. The quality of the innocence of wisdom may in some measure be seen from the innocence of childhood described above, no. 395, if only, instead of parents, the Lord be assumed as the Father by Whom they are led, and to Whom they ascribe whatever they have received.

414. On the subject of innocence I have spoken with the angels on various occasions, and they have said that innocence is the esse of every good, and that good is good in proportion as it has innocence in it: and, since wisdom belongs to life and therefore to good, that wisdom is wisdom in proportion as it partakes of innocence: that the like is true of love, charity, and faith; and that hence it is that no one can enter heaven unless he has innocence; and that this is meant by these words of the Lord, "*Suffer the little children to come unto Me, and forbid them not; for of such is the kingdom of the heavens; verily I say unto you, Whosoever will not receive the kingdom of the heavens as a little child, he shall not enter therein*" (Mark x. 14, 15; Luke xviii. 16, 17). In this passage, as well as in other parts of the Word, by little children are meant those who are in innocence. The reason why good is good, in proportion as it has innocence in it, is, that all good is from the Lord, and innocence consists in being led by the Lord.

415. To the above I shall add this Memorable Relation:—

* One morning on awaking out of sleep, while I was meditating, and not yet quite awake, in the early morning and serene light, I saw through the window as it were a flash of lightning, and presently I heard as it were a clap of thunder; and while I was wondering whence this could be, I heard from heaven these

* This paragraph is repeated, with some slight variations, in the *True Christian Religion*, no. 77.

words, "There are some not far from you, who are disputing violently about God and nature. The vibration of light like lightning and the clapping of the air like thunder, are correspondences and consequently appearances of the combat and collision of arguments, on one side in favour of God, and on the other in favour of nature."

The cause of this spiritual combat was as follows:—There were some satans in hell who said among each other: "Would that we might be allowed to speak with the angels of heaven: we will completely and fully demonstrate, that what they call God, from Whom are all things, is nothing but nature; and thus that God is a mere empty expression, unless nature be meant by it." And as those satans believed this with all their heart and soul, and also were desirous to speak with the angels of heaven, it was given them to ascend out of the mire and darkness of hell, and to speak with two angels who were then descending from heaven. They were in the world of spirits,
2 which is intermediate between heaven and hell. The satans, on seeing the angels there, ran swiftly up to them, and cried out with a furious voice, "Are you the angels of heaven with whom we are allowed to engage in reasoning on the subject of God and nature? You are called wise because you acknowledge a God; but, oh! how simple you are! Who sees God? Who understands what God is? Who apprehends that God governs, and can govern the universe, and each and all things thereof? Who, but the vulgar and common herd, acknowledges what he does not see and understand? What is more manifest than that nature is all in all? Who has seen with his eyes anything but nature? Who has heard with his ears anything but nature? Who has smelt with his nostrils anything but nature? Who has tasted with his tongue anything but nature? Who has felt with the touch of his hand and body anything but nature? Are not the senses of our body the only witnesses of Truths? Who cannot swear from them that it is so? Are not your heads in nature? Whence comes the influx into the thoughts of your heads but from nature? Take away nature, and can you think at all?" Not to mention many other arguments of a like kind.

3 On hearing these words, the angels replied, "You speak in this manner because you are merely sensual. All in the hells have the ideas of their thoughts immersed in the senses of the body, neither are they able to elevate their minds above them; wherefore we excuse you. The life of evil and the consequent belief of falsity have closed the interiors of your minds, so that you are incapable of any elevation above sensual things, except in a state removed from evils of life and falsities of faith: for a satan, as well as an angel, can understand truth when he hears it; but he does not retain it, because evil obliterates truth and induces falsity. But we perceive that you are now in a state removed

[from evil], and that thus you can understand the truth which we speak; attend therefore to what we shall say."

They proceeded thus: "You have been in the natural world, and have departed thence, and are now in the spiritual world. Did you know anything till now about the life after death? Did you not till now deny that life, and make yourselves equal with the beasts? Did you know anything heretofore about heaven and hell, or anything about the light and heat of this world? or of the fact that you are no longer within nature, but above it? for this world and all things belonging to it are spiritual, and spiritual things are above natural things, so that not the least of nature can flow in into this world. But you, in consequence of believing nature to be a god or a goddess, believe also the light and heat of this world to be the light and heat of the natural world, when yet it is not at all so; for natural light here is thick darkness, and natural heat here is cold. Did you know anything about the sun of this world, from which our light and heat proceed? Did you know that this sun is pure love, and the sun of the natural world pure fire; and that the sun of the world, which is pure fire, is that from which nature exists and subsists; and that the sun of heaven, which is pure love, is that from which life itself, which is love with wisdom, exists and subsists; and thus that nature, which you make a god or a goddess, is absolutely dead? You can, if a guard be given, ascend with us 4
into heaven; and we also, if a guard be given, can descend with you into hell; and in heaven you will see magnificent and splendid things, but in hell filthy and unclean things. The ground of the difference is, that all in the heavens worship God, and all in the hells worship nature; and the magnificent and splendid objects in the heavens are correspondences of the affections of good and truth, and the filthy and unclean objects in the hells are correspondences of the cupidities of evil and falsity. Conclude now, from all these circumstances, whether God or nature be all in all."

To this the satans replied, "In the state wherein we now are, we can conclude, from what we have heard, that there is a God; but when the delight of evil seizes our minds, we see nothing but nature."

These two angels and the two satans were standing to the right, 5
at no great distance from me; wherefore I saw and heard them: and lo! I saw about them many spirits who had been celebrated in the natural world for their learning; and I was surprised that those learned spirits at one time stood near the angels, and at another near the satans, and that they favoured the sentiments of those near whom they stood; and I was told that the changes of their situation were changes of the state of their minds, which sometimes favoured one side and sometimes the other; for they were Vertumni.

[It was further said to me], "We will tell you a mystery: we have looked down into the earth, to those who were celebrated for learning, and who have thought about God and nature from their own judgment, and we have found six hundred out of a thousand in favour of nature, and the rest in favour of God; and that these were in favour of God, in consequence of having frequently said, not from any understanding, but only from what they had heard, that nature is from God, for frequent speech from the memory and recollection, and not at the same time from thought and intelligence, induces a species of faith."

6 After this, the satans were given a guard, and they ascended with the two angels into heaven, and saw the magnificent and splendid things there: and being then in illustration from the light of heaven, they acknowledged the being of a God, and that nature was created to be serviceable to the life which is in God and from God; and that nature in itself is dead, and consequently does nothing of itself, but is acted upon by life. When they had seen and perceived these things, they descended: and, as they descended, the love of evil returned and closed their understanding above and opened it beneath; and then there appeared above it as it were a veil shining in consequence of infernal fire; and as soon as they touched the earth with their feet, the ground yawned under them, and they returned to their own.

416. *After these things those two angels, seeing me near, said of me to the bystanders, "We know that this man has written on the subject of God and nature: let us hear what he has written."

They therefore drew near and requested that what had been written on the subject of God and nature might be read to them: I therefore read thence as follows:—

"†Those who believe in a Divine operation in each single thing of nature, may confirm themselves in favour of the Divine, from very many things which they see in nature, equally as, yea, more than those who confirm themselves in favour of nature. For those who confirm themselves in favour of the Divine, attend to the wonderful things which are observed in the productions of both vegetables and animals:—in the PRODUCTIONS OF VEGETABLES, that from a little seed sown in the earth there is sent forth a root, by means of the root a stem, and successively buds, leaves, flowers, fruits, even to new seeds: just as if the seed knew the order of succession, or the process by which it was to renew itself. What rational person can think that the sun, which is pure fire, knows this, or that it

* The remainder of this Memorable Relation, as far as the end of no. 421, is repeated, with some variations, in the *True Christian Religion*, no. 12.

† This quotation, as far as the end of no. 421, is from the *Divine Love and Wisdom*, nos. 351 to 357. The quotation in no. 422 is from the *Divine Love and Wisdom*, no. 350.

can impart to its heat and light the power to effect such things; and further, that it can form wonderful things therein, and intend use? When a man who has an elevated Rational sees and considers such things, he cannot think otherwise than that they are from Him Who has infinite wisdom, consequently from God. Those who acknowledge the Divine, also see and think so; but those who do not acknowledge it, do not see and think so, because they are unwilling to; and thus they let down their Rational into the Sensual, which derives all its ideas from the lumen in which the senses of the body are, and confirms their fallacies, saying, 'Do not you see the sun effecting these things by means of its heat and light? What is that which you do
not see? Is it anything?' Those who confirm themselves in 2
favour of the Divine, attend to the wonderful things which are observed in the PRODUCTIONS OF ANIMALS; to mention only what is observed in eggs, that there lies concealed in them a chick in its seed or beginning, with everything requisite even to the hatching, and likewise with everything requisite to its progress after hatching, until it becomes a bird, or winged thing, in the form of its parent. And if he attends to the form, as being such, he cannot, if he thinks deeply, help being astonished [to observe] that in the smallest as in the largest kinds, yea, in the invisible as in the visible, that is, in small insects, as in large birds or great beasts, there are organs of the senses, which are sight, hearing, smell, taste, touch; and also organs of motion, which are the muscles, for they fly and walk; and likewise viscera about the heart and lungs, which are actuated by the brains: that the commonest insects enjoy all these things is known from their anatomy, as described by some writers, especially by SWAMMERDAM in his 'Book of Nature.' Those who 3
ascribe all things to Nature do indeed see such things; but they think only that they exist, and say that nature produces them: and this they say because they have averted their minds from thinking about the Divine; and those who have averted themselves from thinking about the Divine, when they see the wonderful things in nature, cannot think rationally, and still less spiritually, but they think sensually and materially, and in this case they think in nature from nature, and not above it, in like manner as those do who are in hell; differing from beasts only in this respect, that they are possessed of rationality, that is, they are capable of understanding, and thus of thinking
otherwise, if they are willing. Those who have averted them- 4
selves from thinking about the Divine, when they see the wonderful things in nature, and thereby become sensual, do not consider that the sight of the eye is so gross that it sees several small insects as one confused mass; and that nevertheless each of them is organized to feel and to move, and consequently is endowed with fibres and vessels, also with little hearts,

pulmonary pipes, little viscera, and brains; and that these parts are woven together of the purest things in nature, and that their contextures correspond to some life, by virtue of which their minutest parts are distinctly acted upon. Since the sight of the eye is so gross that several such insects, with the innumerable things in each, appear to it as a small confused mass, and yet those who are sensual, think and judge from that sight, it is evident how gross their minds have become, and consequently in what thick darkness they are concerning spiritual things.

417. "Every one is able to confirm himself in favour of the Divine from the visible things in nature, if he is willing to do so; and he also who thinks of God from life, does so confirm himself; for instance, when he observes the flying things of heaven, how each species of them knows its proper food, and where it is to be found; how they can distinguish those of their own kind by the sounds they utter and by their appearance; how also, among other kinds, they can tell which are their friends and which their foes; how they pair together, know the intercourse of the sexes, build their nests with art, lay their eggs therein, hatch them, know the time of hatching, and at its accomplishment hatch their young out of the shell, love them most tenderly, cherish them under their wings, feed and nourish them, until they are able to act on their own account and do the like, and procreate a family in order to perpetuate their kind. Every one who is willing to think of a Divine influx through the spiritual world into the natural, is able to see it in these facts, and he is also able, if he is willing, to say in his heart, 'Such knowledges cannot flow in into those animals from the sun through the rays of its light;' for the sun, from which nature derives its origin and its essence, is pure fire, and consequently the rays of its light are utterly dead; and thus they may conclude, that such effects are derived from an influx of Divine wisdom into the ultimates of nature.

418. "Every one can confirm himself in favour of the Divine from the visible things in nature, when he observes worms, which from the delight of a certain desire, wish and long for a change of their earthly state into a state analogous to a heavenly one; for this purpose they creep into corners, and cast themselves as it were into a womb that they may be born again, and there become chrysalises, aurelias, nymphs, and at length butterflies; and when they have undergone this metamorphosis, and according to their kind are furnished with beautiful wings, they fly into the air as into their heaven, and there sport merrily together, celebrate marriages, lay their eggs, and provide for themselves a posterity; and then they are nourished with sweet

and pleasant food, which they extract from flowers. Who that confirms himself in favour of the Divine from the visible things of nature, does not see some image of the earthly state of man in these animals while they are worms, and of his heavenly state in the same when they become butterflies? Whereas those who confirm themselves in favour of nature, do indeed see such things; but as they have rejected from their mind (*animus*) man's heavenly state, they call them mere instincts of nature.

419. "Every one can confirm himself in favour of the Divine from the visible things in nature, when he attends to the facts that are known about bees—that they know how to gather wax and suck honey from herbs and flowers, and build cells like little houses, and arrange them into the form of a city with streets, through which they come in and go out; that they can smell flowers and herbs at a distance, from which they may collect wax for their home and honey for their food; and that, when laden with these treasures, they can fly back in a straight direction to their hive: thus they provide for themselves food and habitation against the approaching winter, as if they knew and foresaw it. They also set over themselves a mistress as a queen, to be the parent of their posterity, and for her they build as it were a palace above their own cells, and appoint guards about her; and when the time for her to lay eggs is at hand, she goes, accompanied by her guards, from cell to cell, and lays her eggs, which the crowd of bees that follow smear over with a sort of ointment to prevent their receiving injury from the air: hence arises a new generation, which, when old enough to provide in like manner for itself, is driven out from home; and when driven out, it first gathers into a swarm or compact body, to prevent the consociation being dispersed, and then flies forth to seek out a new habitation for itself. About autumn also the useless drones are brought out and deprived of their wings, lest they should return and consume the provisions which they had taken no pains to collect; not to mention many other circumstances; from which it may be manifest that on account of the use which they perform to the human race, they have, by virtue of influx from the spiritual world, a form of government, such as that among men in the world, yea, among angels in the heavens. What man of sound reason does not see that such instincts are not communicated to bees from the natural world? What has the sun, in which nature originates, in common with a form of government which emulates and is analogous to the heavenly government? From these and similar circumstances respecting brute animals, the confessor and worshipper of nature confirms himself in favour of nature, while the confessor and worshipper of God, from the same circumstances, confirms himself in favour of the Divine: for the spiritual man sees spiritual things therein, and

the natural man natural; thus every one according to his quality. With regard to myself, such circumstances have been to me testimonies of an influx of what is spiritual into what is natural, or of an influx of the spiritual world into the natural world; thus of an influx from the Divine wisdom of the Lord. Consider also, whether you can think analytically of any form of government, any civil law, any moral virtue, or any spiritual verity, unless the Divine flows in by virtue of His wisdom through the spiritual world: for my own part, I never could, and am still unable to do so: for I have perceptibly and sensibly observed that influx now for twenty-five years continually: I therefore say this from experience.

420. "Can nature have use for an end, and dispose uses into orders and forms? No one can do this but a Wise Being; and none but God, Who possesses infinite wisdom, can so order and form the universe. Who else can foresee and provide for human beings all things necessary for their food and clothing, producing them from the fruits of the earth and from animals? It is surely a wonderful thing among many others, that those common worms which are called silk-worms, should clothe with silk, and magnificently adorn both women and men, from queens and kings even to maidservants and menservants; and that those common insects, the bees, should supply wax for the candles which light up both temples and palaces. These and many other things are standing proofs that the Lord operates from Himself through the spiritual world, all the things which are in nature.

421. "To this it ought to be added, that I have seen in the spiritual world those who had confirmed themselves in favour of nature from the visible things of this world, so far as to become atheists, and that their understanding in spiritual light appeared open beneath, but closed above, because in thought they had looked downwards to the earth, and not upwards to heaven. Above the Sensual, which is the lowest of the understanding, there appeared as a veil, shining with some, by reason of infernal fire, with some black as soot, and with some livid as a corpse. Let every one therefore beware of confirmations in favour of nature, and let him confirm himself in favour of the Divine; there is no lack of materials.

422. "Some indeed ought to be excused for ascribing certain visible effects to nature, because they have not known anything about the sun of the spiritual world, where the Lord is, and about the influx thence; neither have they known anything about that world and its state, nor yet of its presence with man; and consequently they could think no otherwise than that what is

spiritual was a purer natural; and thus that angels were either in the ether or in the stars; also, that the devil was either man's evil, or, if he actually existed, that he was either in the air or in the deeps; also, that the souls of men after death were either in the inmost part of the earth, or in some nondescript place, till the day of judgment; not to mention other like conceits, which phantasy has brought on in consequence of ignorance of the spiritual world and its sun. This is the reason why those ought to be excused, who have believed that nature has produced its visible effects by virtue of what has been implanted from creation. Nevertheless those who have made themselves atheists by confirmations in favour of nature, ought not to be excused, because they might have confirmed themselves in favour of the Divine. Ignorance indeed excuses, but does not take away confirmed falsity; for this falsity coheres with evil, and evil coheres with hell."

THE PLEASURES OF INSANITY

RELATING TO

SCORTATORY LOVE

THE OPPOSITION OF SCORTATORY LOVE AND CONJUGIAL LOVE.

423. *At this threshold, it must first be explained what is meant in this chapter by scortatory love. The fornicatory love which precedes marriage, is not meant, nor that which follows it after the death of a married partner; nor the concubinage which is engaged in from legitimate, just, and weighty causes; neither are there meant the mild kinds of adultery, nor the grievous kinds of it, which man (*homo*) actually repents of, for the latter do not become opposite, and the former are not opposite, to conjugial love: that they are not opposite, will be seen in the following pages, where each kind will be treated of. But by scortatory love, opposite to conjugial love, is here meant the love of adultery, when it is such, that adultery is not held to be sin, nor to be evil and wrong against reason, but allowable with reason. This scortatory love not only makes conjugial love the same with itself, but it even ruins, destroys, and at length nauseates it. The opposition of this love to conjugial love is treated of in the present chapter. That no other love is treated of [as being in such opposition], may be manifest from the following chapters concerning fornication, concubinage, and the various kinds of adultery.

But in order that this opposition may be evident to the rational sight, it must be demonstrated in the following series:

I. *The quality of scortatory love is not known unless the quality of conjugial love be known.*

II. *Scortatory love is opposed to conjugial love.*

III. *Scortatory love is opposed to conjugial love, as the natural man, considered in himself, is opposed to the spiritual man.*

IV. *Scortatory love is opposed to conjugial love, as the connubial connection of evil and falsity is opposed to the marriage of good and truth.*

V. *Hence scortatory love is opposed to conjugial love, as hell is opposed to heaven.*

VI. *The uncleanness of hell is from scortatory love, and the cleanness of heaven is from conjugial love.*

VII. *The uncleanness and the cleanness in the church are similarly circumstanced.*

VIII. *Scortatory love makes a human being* (homo) *to be more*

* In the original Latin edition, this paragraph is enclosed in inverted commas.

and more not a human being, and a man (vir) *not a man, and conjugial love makes a human being* (homo) *to be more and more a human being and a man* (vir).

IX. *There is a sphere of scortatory love, and a sphere of conjugial love.*

X. *The sphere of scortatory love ascends from hell, and the sphere of conjugial love descends from heaven.*

XI. *Those two spheres mutually meet each other, in both worlds; but they do not become conjoined.*

XII. *Between those two spheres there is an equilibrium, and man is in that equilibrium.*

XIII. *A man is able to turn himself to whichever sphere he pleases; but in the proportion that he turns himself to the one, in the same proportion he turns himself away from the other.*

XIV. *Each sphere bears with it delightsomenesses.*

XV. *The delightsomenesses of scortatory love commence from the flesh, and are of the flesh even in the spirit; but the delightsomenesses of conjugial love commence in the spirit, and are of the spirit even in the flesh.*

XVI. *The delightsomenesses of scortatory love are pleasures of insanity; but the delightsomenesses of conjugial love are delights of wisdom.*

Now follows the explanation of these articles.

424. I. THE QUALITY OF SCORTATORY LOVE IS NOT KNOWN UNLESS THE QUALITY OF CONJUGIAL LOVE BE KNOWN. By scortatory love is meant the love of adultery, which destroys conjugial love; see above, no. 423. That the quality of that scortatory love is not known unless the quality of conjugial love be known, needs no demonstration, but only illustration by similitudes; as for example, who can know what is evil and false, unless he knows what is good and true? and who knows what is unchaste, dishonourable, unbecoming, and ugly, unless he knows what is chaste, honourable, becoming, and beautiful? and who can discern the various kinds of insanity but one who is wise, or who knows what wisdom is? again, who can rightly perceive discordant and grating sounds, but he who by instruction and study has become acquainted with musical harmonies? in like manner, who can clearly discern the quality of adultery, unless he has first clearly discerned the quality of marriage? and who can form a correct judgment of the filthiness of the pleasures of scortatory love, but he who has first formed a correct judgment of the cleanness of conjugial love? As I have now finished *The Delights of Wisdom relating to Conjugial Love,* I am able, by virtue of the intelligence thence acquired, to describe *The Pleasures* [*of Insanity*] *relating to Scortatory Love.*

425. II. SCORTATORY LOVE IS OPPOSED TO CONJUGIAL LOVE.

There does not exist anything in the universe which has not its opposite; and opposites, in respect to each other, are not relatives, but contraries. Relatives are between the greatest and the least of the same thing; but contraries are, by reason of their opposition, against them; and the latter are relatives in respect to each other, just as the former are, wherefore also the relations themselves are opposites. That each and all things have their opposites, is evident from light, heat, the times of the world, affections, perceptions, sensations, and many other things. The opposite of light is darkness; the opposite of heat is cold: of the times of the world the opposites are day and night, summer and winter; of affections the opposites are joys and mourning, also gladnesses and sadnesses; of perceptions the opposites are goods and evils, also truths and falsities; and of sensations the opposites are things delightful and undelightful. Hence, by all evidence, it may be concluded, that conjugial love has its opposite. That this opposite is adultery, every one may see, if he be willing to do so, from all the dictates of sound reason. Tell, if you can, what else is its opposite. It is an additional evidence, that as sound reason, by virtue of its own light, has been able to see this truth clearly, therefore it has enacted laws, which are called the civil laws of justice, in favour of marriages, and against adulteries.
In order that it may appear yet more clearly that marriages 2
and adulteries are opposites, it is allowed to relate what I have very often seen in the spiritual world. When those who in the natural world have been adulterers from confirmation perceive the sphere of conjugial love flowing down from heaven, they instantly either flee away into caverns and hide themselves, or, if they set themselves obstinately against it, they grow mad with rage, and become like furies. The reason why they are so affected is, that all things of the affections, whether delightful or undelightful, are perceived in that world, and sometimes as clearly as an odour is perceived by the smell; for the inhabitants of that world have not a material body which
absorbs such things. But the reason why the opposition of scor- 3
tatory love and conjugial love is unknown to many in the world, is owing to the delights of the flesh, which, in the extremes, apparently emulate the delights of conjugial love; and those who are in delights only, do not know anything about that opposition; and I can venture to affirm that, if you were to say that every thing has its opposite, and were to conclude that conjugial love also has its opposite, adulterers will reply, that that love has not an opposite, because scortatory love cannot be distinguished from it by any sense: from which circumstance it is further evident, that he who does not know of what quality conjugial love is, does not know of what quality scortatory love is; and moreover, that from scortatory love it is not known what

conjugial love is, but from conjugial love it is known what scortatory love is. No one knows good from evil, but evil from good; for evil is in darkness, but good is in light.

426. III. SCORTATORY LOVE IS OPPOSED TO CONJUGIAL LOVE, AS THE NATURAL MAN, CONSIDERED IN HIMSELF, IS OPPOSED TO THE SPIRITUAL MAN. That the natural man and the spiritual are opposed to each other, so that the one does not will what the other wills, yea, that they are at strife together, is known in the church; but still it has not heretofore been explained. It shall therefore be stated what it is that discriminates between the spiritual man and the natural, and excites the latter against the former. The natural man is that into which every one is first introduced as he grows up, and he is introduced into it by means of sciences and Knowledges and by means of the rational things of the understanding; but the spiritual man is that into which he is introduced by means of the love of doing uses, which love is also called charity; wherefore in proportion as any one is in charity, in the same proportion he is spiritual, but in proportion as he is not in charity, in the same proportion he is natural, even if he be clear in his mode of thinking, and wise in judgment. That the latter, which is called the natural man, separate from the spiritual, howsoever he may elevate himself into the light of reason, nevertheless abandons himself to his lusts, and ministers to them, is manifest from his genius alone, in that he is devoid of charity; and whoever is devoid of charity, is prone towards all the lasciviousnesses of scortatory love: wherefore, when he is told that this wanton love is opposed to chaste conjugial love, and is asked to consult his rational lumen, he yet does not consult it, except in conjunction with the delight of evil implanted from birth in the natural man; in consequence whereof he comes to the conclusion that his reason does not see anything opposed to the sweet sensuous allurements of his body; and when he has confirmed himself in those allurements, his reason is in amazement at all those sweetnesses which are predicated of conjugial love: yea, as was said above, he fights against them, and conquers, and, like a conqueror after the enemy's overthrow, he destroys, from the extremes to the inmosts, the camp of conjugial love in himself. These things the natural man does in consequence of his scortatory love. This fact is adduced, in order that it may be known what is the ground of the opposition of those two loves; for, as has been abundantly shown above, conjugial love considered in itself is a spiritual love, and scortatory love considered in itself is a natural love.

427. IV. SCORTATORY LOVE IS OPPOSED TO CONJUGIAL LOVE, AS THE CONNUBIAL CONNECTION OF EVIL AND FALSITY IS OPPOSED TO

THE MARRIAGE OF GOOD AND TRUTH. That the origin of conjugial love is from the marriage of good and truth, was demonstrated above in its own chapter, from nos. 83 to 102; hence it follows, that the origin of scortatory love is from the connubial connection of evil and falsity, and that therefore they are opposed, as evil is opposed to good, and the falsity of evil to the truth of good. It is the delights of each love that are thus opposed; for love without its delights is not anything. That these delights are so opposed, does not at all appear: the reason why it does not appear is, that, in externals, the delight of the love of evil counterfeits the delight of the love of good; but in internals the delight of the love of evil consists of mere concupiscences of evil, evil itself is a round mass or ball of those concupiscences: whereas the delight of the love of good consists of innumerable affections of good, good itself is as a tied bundle of those affections. This bundle and that ball are felt by man as only one delight; and as in externals the delight of evil counterfeits the delight of good, as has been said, therefore also the delight of adultery is as the delight of marriage. But after death, when every one lays aside the externals, and the internals are laid bare, it is manifest to the sensation that the evil of adultery is a ball of the concupiscences of evil, and the good of marriage is a bundle of the affections of good: thus that they are utterly opposed to each other.

428. As regards the connubial connection of evil and falsity, let it be known that evil loves falsity, and wants it to be a one with itself, and they also become conjoined; in like manner as good loves truth, and wants it to be a one with itself, and they also become conjoined: from which it is evident, that as the spiritual origin of marriage is the marriage of good and truth, so the spiritual origin of adultery is the connubial connection of evil and falsity. Hence it is, that this connubial connection is meant by adulteries, whoredoms, and harlotry, in the spiritual sense of the Word; see the *Apocalypse Revealed*, no. 134. It is from this principle that he who is in evil and weds falsity, and he who is in falsity and draws evil into the partnership of his bride-chamber, confirms adultery by the covenant that he has contracted, and commits it so far as he dares and has the strength; he confirms it from evil by means of falsity, and commits it from falsity by means of evil: and on the other hand, it is also from this principle that he who is in good and weds truth, or he who is in truth and draws good into the partnership of the bride-chamber with himself, confirms himself against adultery and in favour of marriage, and attains to a blessed conjugial life.

429. V. HENCE SCORTATORY LOVE IS OPPOSED TO CONJUGIAL

LOVE, AS HELL IS OPPOSED TO HEAVEN. All who are in hell are in the connubial connection of evil and falsity, and all who are in heaven are in the marriage of good and truth; and as the connubial connection of evil and falsity is also adultery (as was shewn just above, nos. 427, 428), hell is also that connubial connection. Hence it is that all who are in hell are in the lust, lasciviousness, and shamelessness of scortatory love, and shun and dread the chastity and modesty of conjugial love; see above, no. 428. From these considerations it may be seen, that those two loves, scortatory love and conjugial love, are opposed to each other, as hell is to heaven, and heaven to hell.

430. VI. THE UNCLEANNESS OF HELL IS FROM SCORTATORY LOVE, AND THE CLEANNESS OF HEAVEN IS FROM CONJUGIAL LOVE. All hell abounds with uncleannesses, and the universal origin of them is shameless and obscene scortatory love: the delights of that love are turned into such uncleannesses. Who can believe that in the spiritual world, every delight of love is presented to the sight under various appearances, to the smell under various odours, and to the view under various forms of beasts and birds? The appearances under which in hell the lascivious delights of scortatory love are presented to the sight, are dung and mire; the odours by which they are presented to the smell, are stinks and stenches; and the forms of beasts and birds under which they are presented to the view, are hogs, serpents, and the birds called ochim and tziim. But it is contrariwise with the chaste delights of conjugial love in heaven. The appearances under which those delights are presented to the sight there, are gardens and flowery fields; the odours whereby they are presented to the smell there, are the sweet smells from fruits and the fragrances from flowers; and the forms of animals under which they are presented to the view, are lambs, kids, turtle-doves, and birds of paradise. The reason why the delights of loves are changed into such and similar things is, that all things which exist in the spiritual world are correspondences: into these correspondences the internals of the minds of the inhabitants are changed when they pass through and become external before the senses. But it must be known, that there are innumerable varieties of uncleannesses, into which the lasciviousnesses of whoredoms are changed when they go forth into their correspondences. These varieties are according to the genera and species of those lasciviousnesses, as may be seen in the following pages, where adulteries and their degrees are treated of. Such uncleannesses however do not proceed from the delights of the love of those who have repented; because they have been washed of them in the world.

431. VII. THE UNCLEANNESS AND THE CLEANNESS IN THE

CHURCH ARE SIMILARLY CIRCUMSTANCED. The reason is, that the church is the Lord's kingdom on the earths, corresponding to His kingdom in the heavens; and the Lord also conjoins them together, that they may make a one; He also distinguishes those who are there, as He distinguishes heaven and hell, and He distinguishes them according to their loves. Those who are in the shameless and obscene delights of scortatory love, associate to themselves similar spirits from hell: but those who are in the modest and chaste delights of conjugial love are associated by the Lord with similar angels from heaven. When these their angels, in their attendance on man, stand near to adulterers who are adulterers from confirmation and set purpose, they become sensible of the horrible stenches mentioned above, no. 430, and recede a little. On account of the correspondence of filthy loves with dung and mire, it was commanded the sons of Israel, "that they should carry with them a paddle with which to cover their excrement, lest Jehovah God walking in the midst of their camp should see the nakedness of the thing, and should turn back" (Deut. xxiii. 14, 15 [13, 14]). This was commanded because the camp of the sons of Israel represented the church, and those unclean things corresponded to the lasciviousnesses of whoredoms, and by Jehovah God's walking in the midst of their camp was signified His presence with the angels. The reason why they were to cover it was, that all those places in hell where troops of such spirits have their abode, are covered and closed up, wherefore also it is said, "lest He see the nakedness of the thing." It has been given me to see that all those places in hell are closed up, and also that when they are opened, as was the case when a new demon entered, such a horrid stench exhaled from them that it sickened my stomach: and what is wonderful, those stenches are as delightful to those who are there as dung is to swine. From these considerations it is evident how it is to be understood, that the uncleanness in the church is from scortatory love, and the cleanness there from conjugial love.

432. VIII. SCORTATORY LOVE MAKES A HUMAN BEING (*homo*) TO BE MORE AND MORE NOT A HUMAN BEING, AND A MAN (*vir*) TO BE NOT A MAN, AND CONJUGIAL LOVE MAKES A HUMAN BEING (*homo*) TO BE MORE AND MORE A HUMAN BEING AND A MAN (*vir*). That conjugial love makes man, is illustrated and confirmed by each and all the propositions which were demonstrated in light before the reason in the First Part of this Work, concerning Love and the delights of its wisdom; as, 1. That he who is in truly conjugial love becomes more and more spiritual; and the more spiritual any one is, so much the more he is a man (*homo*). 2. That he becomes more and more wise; and the wiser any one is, so much the more is he a man. 3. That with such a one

the interiors of the mind are more and more opened, insomuch that he sees or intuitively acknowledges the Lord; and the more any one is in that sight or acknowledgment, so much the more he is a man. 4. That he becomes more and more moral and civil, because a spiritual soul is in his morality and civility; and the more any one is morally civil, so much the more he is a man. 5. Also that after death he becomes an angel of heaven; and an angel is in essence and form a man; and also what is genuinely human in his face shines forth from his speech and manners. From these considerations it is manifest, that conjugial love makes a human being (*homo*) more and more a human being.
2 That the contrary is the case with adulterers, follows as a consequence from the very opposition of adultery and marriage, which is the subject treated of in this chapter; as, 1. That they are not spiritual, but extremely natural; and the natural man separate from the spiritual man, is a man only as to the understanding, but not as to the will: this he immerses in the body and the concupiscences of the flesh, and at those times the understanding also accompanies it. That such a one is but half a man, he himself may see from the reason of his understanding, if he elevates it. 2. That adulterers are not wise, except in their conversation and behaviour when they are in company with such as are high in station or distinguished for their learning and morals; but that when alone by themselves they are insane, holding as of no account the Divine and holy things of the church, and defiling the moralities of life with shamelessness and unchastity, will be shewn in the chapter on "Adulteries." Who does not see that such gesticulators are men only as to the external figure, and not as to the internal form? 3. That adulterers become more and more not men, my own personal observation from seeing them in hell has clearly proved to me; for there they are demons, who when they are seen in the light of heaven, appear with their faces full of pustules, their bodies hunch-backed, their speech grating, and their gestures
3 theatrical. * But it should be known, that such are adulterers from set purpose and from confirmation, but not non-deliberate adulterers: for there are four kinds of adulterers, which are treated of in the chapter on "Adulteries and its Degrees." Adulterers from set purpose are those who are adulterers from the lust of the will; adulterers from confirmation are those who are adulterers from the persuasion of the understanding; deliberate adulterers are those who are adulterers from the allurements of the senses; and non-deliberate adulterers are those who have not the faculty or the liberty of consulting the understanding. The two former kinds of adulterers are those who become more and more not men; but the two latter kinds be-

* The remainder of this paragraph, in the original Latin edition, is enclosed in inverted commas.

come men in proportion as they recede from those errors, and afterwards become wise.

433. That conjugial love makes a man (*homo*) more a man (*vir*), is also illustrated by what was adduced in the preceding part concerning conjugial love and its delights; as, 1. That the faculty and virtue, which is called the virile faculty and virtue, accompanies wisdom, in proportion as this is animated from the spiritual things of the church, and that hence it resides in conjugial love; and that the wisdom of this love opens a vein from its fountain in the soul, and thus invigorates, and also blesses with perpetuity, the intellectual life, which is the masculine life itself. 2. That hence it is, that the angels of heaven are in this faculty to eternity, according to their own declarations in the Memorable Relation, nos. 355, 356. That the Most Ancient men, in the golden and silver ages, were in enduring efficacy, because they loved the caresses of their wives and had a great horror of the caresses of whores, I have heard from their own mouths; see the Memorable Relations, nos. 75, 76. That that spiritual sufficiency, even in the Natural, will not be wanting at the present day to those who approach the Lord and abominate adulteries as infernal, has been told me from heaven. But the contrary happens to adulterers from set purpose and adulterers from confirmation, who were treated of above, no. 432. That with them the faculty and virtue, which is called the virile faculty and virtue, is weakened even till it becomes none, and that after this there commences cold towards the sex; and that this cold is succeeded by a kind of loathing that verges on nausea, is known, although but little talked of. That those adulterers are such in hell, I have heard at a distance from the sirens, who are obsolete venereal lusts, and also from the brothel-keepers there. From these considerations it follows, that scortatory love makes man (*homo*) more and more not human (*homo*) and not a man (*vir*), and that conjugial love makes man (*homo*) more and more human (*homo*) and manly (*vir*).

434. IX. THERE IS A SPHERE OF SCORTATORY LOVE, AND A SPHERE OF CONJUGIAL LOVE. What is meant by spheres, and that they are manifold, and that those which are of love and wisdom proceed from the Lord, and through the angelic heavens descend into the world, and pervade it even to its ultimates, was shewn above at nos. 222–225, and nos. 386–397. That nothing exists in the universe which has not its opposite, see above, no. 425: from this it follows, that since there is a sphere of conjugial love, there must also be a sphere opposite to it, which is called the sphere of scortatory love; for those spheres are opposed to one another as the love of adultery is opposed to the

love of marriage. This opposition has been treated of in the preceding parts of this chapter.

435. X. THE SPHERE OF SCORTATORY LOVE ASCENDS FROM HELL, AND THE SPHERE OF CONJUGIAL LOVE DESCENDS FROM HEAVEN. That the sphere of conjugial love descends from heaven was shewn in the places cited just above, no. 434; but the reason why the sphere of scortatory love ascends from hell, is, that this love is from thence, see no. 429. That sphere ascends thence from the uncleannesses into which are turned the delights of adultery of those of both sexes there; concerning which uncleannesses see above, nos. 430, 431.

436. XI. THOSE TWO SPHERES MUTUALLY MEET EACH OTHER IN BOTH WORLDS, BUT THEY DO NOT BECOME CONJOINED. By both worlds there is meant the spiritual world and the natural world. In the spiritual world those spheres meet in the world of spirits, because this is intermediate between heaven and hell; but in the natural world they meet in the rational plane with man, which also is intermediate between heaven and hell; for from above there flows in into it the marriage of good and truth, and from below there flows in into it the marriage of evil and falsity: the latter marriage flows in through the world, but the former through heaven. Hence it is, that the human Rational can turn to either side it pleases, and receive the influx. If the man turns towards good, he receives the influx from above, and then his Rational is formed more and more for the reception of heaven; but if he turns towards evil, he receives the influx from below, and then his Rational is formed more and more for the reception of hell. The reason why those two spheres do not become conjoined is, that they are opposites; and an opposite acts upon an opposite in no other way than as enemies act upon each other, one of whom, burning with deadly hatred, assaults the other with fury, while the other is in no hatred, but only in the zeal of protecting himself. From these considerations it is evident, that those two spheres only meet one another, but do not become conjoined. The intermediate space which they form between them, consists on the one side of evil which is not of falsity, and of falsity which is not of evil, and on the other side of good which is not of truth, and of truth which is not of good; which two are indeed able to touch one another, but nevertheless cannot be conjoined.

437. XII. BETWEEN THOSE TWO SPHERES THERE IS AN EQUILIBRIUM, AND MAN IS IN THAT EQUILIBRIUM. The equilibrium between them is a spiritual equilibrium, because it is between good and evil; by virtue of this equilibrium man has free will; in and through this [equilibrium] man thinks and wills, and thence

speaks and acts as of himself. His Rational is thus at full liberty to choose whether it will receive good or evil; consequently whether it will rationally from freedom dispose itself to conjugial love or whether it will rationally from freedom dispose itself to scortatory love; if it disposes itself to the latter, the man turns the back of his head and body towards the Lord; if to the former, then he turns his face and breast towards the Lord. If man turns towards the Lord, his rationality and liberty are led by the Lord; but if he turns away from the Lord, his rationality and liberty are led by hell.

438. XIII. A MAN CAN TURN HIMSELF TO WHICHEVER SPHERE HE PLEASES; BUT IN THE PROPORTION THAT HE TURNS HIMSELF TO THE ONE, IN THE SAME PROPORTION HE TURNS HIMSELF AWAY FROM THE OTHER. Man was created so that whatever he does may be done by him from freedom, according to reason, and altogether as of himself. Without these two faculties he would not be a man, but a beast; for he would not receive anything of that which flows in towards him from heaven, and appropriate it to himself as his own, and consequently it would not be possible for anything of eternal life to be inscribed on him; for this must be inscribed on him as his own, in order that it may be his own. And whereas there does not exist any freedom of turning in one direction, unless there is also the freedom of turning in the other direction as well, just as it would be impossible to weigh anything unless the scales by virtue of the equilibrium were able to incline to either side;—so, unless a man were in the freedom from reason of approaching also to evil, consequently of turning from the right to the left, and from the left to the right, likewise, unless he were in the freedom of approaching to the infernal sphere, which is the sphere of adultery, as well as to the heavenly sphere, which is that of marriage.

439. XIV. EACH SPHERE BEARS WITH IT DELIGHTSOMENESSES; that is, both the sphere of scortatory love which ascends from hell, and the sphere of conjugial love which descends from heaven, affects the recipient man with delightsomenesses. The reason is, that the ultimate plane, in which the delightsomenesses of each love terminate, and where they fill and complete themselves, and which presents them in their own proper sense, is the same. Hence it is, that in the extremes, scortatory caresses and conjugial caresses are perceived as alike, although in internals they are utterly unlike; that hence they are also unlike in the extremes is not judged from any sense of the difference; for unlikenesses are not felt from their differences in the extremes, by any others than those who are in truly conjugial love; for evil is cognized from good, but not good from evil, just as neither is a sweet scent perceived by the nostril when a disagreeable one is

present in it. I have heard from the angels, that they distinguish in the extremes what is lascivious from what is not lascivious, as one distinguishes the fire of dung or of burnt horn by its bad smell, from the fire of spices or burnt cinnamon wood by its sweet smell: and that this arises from the difference of the internal delightsomenesses which enter into the external ones and kindle them.

440. XV. THE DELIGHTSOMENESSES OF SCORTATORY LOVE COMMENCE FROM THE FLESH, AND ARE OF THE FLESH EVEN IN THE SPIRIT; BUT THE DELIGHTSOMENESSES OF CONJUGIAL LOVE COMMENCE IN THE SPIRIT, AND ARE OF THE SPIRIT EVEN IN THE FLESH. The reason why the delightsomenesses of scortatory love commence from the flesh is, that the stimulations (*oestra*) of the flesh are their beginnings. The reason why they infect the spirit, and are of the flesh even in the spirit, is, that the spirit, and not the flesh, feels those things which happen in the flesh. The case is the same with this sense as with the rest; as that the eye does not see and discern the various details in objects, but the spirit; neither does the ear hear and discern the harmony of melodies in singing, and the fitness of the articulation of sounds in speech, but the spirit; moreover, the spirit feels everything according to its elevation into wisdom. The spirit that is not elevated above the sensuals of the body, and thus adheres to them, does not feel any other delightsomenesses than those which flow in from the flesh and the world through the senses of the body: these it seizes upon, is delighted with, and makes its own. Now, since the beginnings of scortatory love are only the stimulations and itchings of the flesh, it is evident that these things in the spirit are filthy allurements, which, as they ascend and descend, and are reciprocal, so they excite and inflame. In general, the cupidities of the flesh, considered in themselves, are nothing else than the conglomerated concupiscences of evil and falsity: hence comes this truth in the church, that the flesh lusts against the spirit, that is, against the spiritual man; wherefore it follows, that the delightsomenesses of the flesh, as to the delightsomenesses of scortatory love, are nothing else than the effervescences of lusts, which in the spirit become the ebullitions of shamelessness.

441. But the delightsomenesses of conjugial love have nothing in common with the feculent delightsomenesses of scortatory love: the latter indeed are in the flesh of every man, but they are separated and removed, in proportion as the man's spirit is elevated above the sensuals of the body, and from its elevation sees their appearances and fallacies beneath. It likewise then perceives fleshly delights, first as apparent and fallacious delights, afterwards as libidinous and lascivious ones, which ought to be

shunned, and successively as damnable and hurtful to the soul, and at last it feels them as undelightful, disagreeable, and nauseating; and in the degree that it thus perceives and feels these delights, in the same degree also it perceives the delights of conjugial love as harmless and chaste, and at length as delicious and blessed. The reason why the delightsomenesses of conjugial love become also of the spirit in the flesh, is, that after the delightsomenesses of scortatory love have been removed, as was said just above, the spirit being freed from them enters chaste into the body, and fills the breasts with the delights of its blessedness, and from the breasts fills also the ultimates of that love in the body; in consequence whereof, the spirit with these ultimates, and these ultimates with the spirit, afterwards act in full communion.

442. XVI. THE DELIGHTSOMENESSES OF SCORTATORY LOVE ARE PLEASURES OF INSANITY; BUT THE DELIGHTSOMENESSES OF CONJUGIAL LOVE ARE DELIGHTS OF WISDOM. The reason why the delightsomenesses of scortatory love are pleasures of insanity is, that none but natural men are in that love, and the natural man is insane in spiritual things, for he is contrary to them, and therefore embraces only natural, sensual, and corporeal delightsomenesses. It is said that he embraces natural, sensual, and corporeal delightsomenesses, because the Natural is distinguished into three degrees; in the highest degree are those natural men who from rational sight see insanities, and are nevertheless carried away by the delights thereof, as boats by the current of a river; in a lower degree are the natural men who see and judge only from the senses of the body, and spurn and reject as of no account the rational things which are contrary to appearances and fallacies; in the lowest degree are the natural men who without judgment are carried away by the alluring heats of their body. These last are called corporeal-natural men, the former are called sensual-natural men, but the first, natural men. With these men, scortatory love and its insanities and pleasures are of similar degrees.

443. The reason why the delightsomenesses of conjugial love are delights of wisdom is, that none but spiritual men are in that love, and the spiritual man is in wisdom: and therefore he embraces no other delightsomenesses than such as agree with spiritual wisdom. The quality of the delightsomenesses of scortatory love, and the quality of the delightsomenesses of conjugial love, may be elucidated by a comparison with houses: the delightsomenesses of scortatory love by comparison with a house whose walls glitter outwardly like sea shells, or like the transparent stones of a spurious golden colour called selenites; whereas in the chambers within the walls, are all kinds of filth and refuse:

but the delightsomenesses of conjugial love may be likened to a house, the walls of which are refulgent as with sterling gold, and the chambers within are resplendent as with cabinets full of various precious things.

444. To the above shall be added the following Memorable Relation:—

After I had brought to a conclusion the meditations on conjugial love, and had begun those on scortatory love, suddenly two angels stood by me, and said, "We have perceived and understood what you have heretofore meditated upon; but the things which you are now meditating upon are beyond us, and we do not perceive them. Leave them out, because they are nothing."

But I replied, "This love, on which I am now meditating, is not nothing, because it does exist."

But they said, "How can there exist any love, which is not from creation? Is not conjugial love from creation? Is it not a love between two who are capable of becoming one? How can there exist a love which divides and separates? What young man can love any other maiden than the one who loves him in return? Must not the love of the one know and acknowledge the love of the other, so that when they meet they may become conjoined of themselves? Who can love that which is not love? Is not conjugial love alone mutual and reciprocal? If it is not reciprocal, does it not rebound and become nothing?"

2 On hearing this, I asked the two angels from which society of heaven they were.

They said, "We are from the heaven of innocence; we came when infants into this heavenly world, and were educated under the Lord's auspices; and when I had become a grown-up youth, and my wife, who is here with me, a marriageable girl, we were betrothed and affianced, and united together by wedding: and as we did not know of any other love than truly wedded and conjugial love, therefore, when the ideas of your thought concerning a strange love, directly opposed to our own love, were communicated to us, we did not at all comprehend it; wherefore we have descended in order to ask you the reason why you meditate on things that cannot be perceived. Tell us, therefore, how a love which not only is not from creation, but is also contrary to creation, can possibly exist? We regard things that are opposite to creation as objects of no reality."

3 As they said this, I was glad at heart that it had been given me to speak with angels of such innocence as to be utterly ignorant of what whoredom was; wherefore I opened my mouth and taught them, saying: "Do you not know that there exist both good and evil, and that good is from creation, but not evil? and that nevertheless evil, considered in itself, is not nothing,

although it is nothing of good? From creation there exists good, and also good in the greatest degree and in the least degree; and when this least becomes nothing, there rises up on the other side evil: wherefore there does not exist any relation or progression of good to evil, but a relation and progression of good to a greater and less good, and of evil to a greater and less evil; for there are opposites in each and every particular. And since good and evil are opposites, there exists an intermediate, and in that intermediate there is an equilibrium, in which evil acts against good; but as it does not prevail, it stops in the endeavour. Every man is educated in this equilibrium, which, because it is an equilibrium between good and evil, or, what is the same thing, between heaven and hell, is a spiritual equilibrium, which, with those who are in it, produces freedom. By virtue of this equilibrium the Lord draws all to Himself; and He leads out of evil into good, and thus into heaven, the man who follows from freedom. The case is the same with love, especially with conjugial love, and with scortatory love: the latter love is evil, but the former good. Every man who hears the voice of the Lord, and follows out of freedom, is introduced by the Lord into conjugial love, and into all its delights and blissfulnesses; but he who does not hear and follow, introduces himself into scortatory love, first into its delights, but afterwards into its undelights, and lastly into its joylessnesses."

When I had said this, the two angels asked me, "How could evil exist, when nothing but good had existed from creation? In order that anything may come into existence, it must have an origin. Good could not be the origin of evil, because evil is nothing of good, for it is deprivative and destructive of good; yet, since it exists and is felt, it is not nothing, but something: tell us therefore whence this something came into existence after nothing."

To this I replied, "This arcanum cannot be opened unless it be known that no one is good but God alone, and that there is not anything good which is good in itself, but from God; wherefore he who looks to God, and is willing to be led by God, is in good; but he who turns away from God, and wants to be led by himself, is not in good; for the good which he does is either for the sake of self or for the sake of the world; thus it is either meritorious, or simulated, or hypocritical: from which considerations it is evident, that man himself is the origin of evil; not that that origin was implanted in man from creation; but that he, by turning from God to himself, implanted it in himself. That origin of evil was not in Adam and his wife; but when the serpent said, 'In the day that ye shall eat of the tree of the knowledge of good and evil, ye shall be as God' (Gen. iii. 5); and then because they turned away from God, and turned to themselves, as to a god, they made in themselves the origin of evil. *Eating of that tree, signified believing that they knew good and evil, and were wise, from themselves, and not from God.*"

5 But the two angels then asked, "How could man turn away from God, and turn to himself, when yet man is not able to will, think, and thence do anything except from God? Why did God permit this?"

But I replied, "Man was so created, that everything he wills, thinks, and does, appears to him as in himself, and thus from himself: without this appearance, man would not be man; for he would not be able to receive, retain, and as it were appropriate to himself, anything of good and truth, or of love and wisdom: whence it follows, that without that appearance, as a living appearance, man would not have conjunction with God, and consequently neither would he have eternal life. But if, in conformity with this appearance, he induces in himself the belief that he wills, thinks, and thence does good from himself, and not from the Lord, although in all appearance as from himself, he turns good into evil with himself, and thus makes in himself the origin of evil. This was the sin of Adam.

6 "But I will open this matter somewhat more clearly. The Lord looks at every man in his forehead, and this look passes through into the back of his head. Under the forehead is the cerebrum, and under the back of the head is the cerebellum; the latter is dedicated to love and its goods, and the former to wisdom and its truths; wherefore he who looks with his face towards the Lord, receives from Him wisdom, and through wisdom love; but he who looks backwards from the Lord, receives love and not wisdom; and love without wisdom is love from man and not from the Lord; and this love, since it conjoins itself with falsities, does not acknowledge God, but acknowledges self for a god, and confirms this tacitly by the faculty of understanding and becoming wise implanted in it from creation as from itself: wherefore this love is the origin of evil. That this is the case, can be demonstrated to the eye. I will call hither some evil spirit who turns away from God, and will speak to him from behind, or into the back of the head, and you will see that the things which are said are turned into their contraries."

7 I called one such spirit, and he presented himself, and I spoke to him from behind, saying, "Do you know anything about hell, damnation, and the torment there?" And presently, when he was turned to me, I asked him "What did you hear?"

He replied, "I heard this: 'Do you know anything about heaven, salvation, and the happiness there?'" And afterwards when the latter words were said to him from behind, he said that he had heard the former.

It was next said to him from behind, "Do you know that

they who are in hell are insane from falsities?" and when I asked him about these words, what he had heard, he said, "I heard, 'Do you know that they who are in heaven are wise from truths?'" And when the latter words were said to him from behind, he said that he heard, "Do you know that they who are in hell are insane from falsities?" And so in other instances.

From these examples it evidently appears, that when the mind turns away from the Lord, it turns to itself, and then it perceives the contrary things.

"This is the reason why, as you are aware, in this spiritual world no one is allowed to stand behind another, and to speak to him; for thus there is inspired into him a love, which his self-intelligence favours and obeys for the sake of its delight; but since it is from man, and not from God, it is the love of evil, or
the love of falsity. Besides this, I will relate to you another 8
similar circumstance, namely: I have sometimes heard goods and truths let down from heaven into hell; and they were there progressively turned into their opposites, good into evil, and truth into falsity: the cause of this is the same as above, namely, that all who are in hell turn away from the Lord."

On hearing these things, the two angels thanked me, and said, "As you are now meditating and writing about a love opposite to our conjugial love, and the opposite to that love makes our minds sad, we will depart;" and when they said, "Peace be to you," I begged them not to relate anything about this love to their brethren and sisters in heaven, because it would hurt their innocence.

I can positively asseverate that those who die when infants grow up in heaven, and when they attain the stature which is common in the world to young men of eighteen years, and to maidens of fifteen years, they remain of that stature, and that then marriages are provided for them by the Lord; and further, that both before marriage and after it, they are utterly ignorant what whoredom is, and that such a thing can possibly exist.

FORNICATION.

444 [a]. By fornication is meant the lust of a grown up youth or young man, before marriage, with a woman who is a prostitute (*mœcha*); but lust with a woman who is not a prostitute, that is, with a virgin or with the wife of another man, is not fornication, but with a virgin it is an act of corruption (*stuprum*), and with the wife of another man it is adultery. In what manner these two differ from fornication cannot be seen by any rational being, unless he takes a clear view of the love of the sex in its degrees and diversities, and on the one part of its chaste things and on the other of its unchaste things, and divides each part into genera and species, and thus distinguishes: otherwise, the difference between what is more and less chaste, and between what is more and less unchaste, cannot be clearly visible in any one's idea, and without these distinctions all relation perishes, and therewith clear-sightedness in matters of judgment, and the understanding is involved in such shade, that it does not know how to discriminate fornication from adultery, and still less the milder things of fornication from the more grievous ones, and in like manner those of adultery: thus it mixes evils, and of diverse evils makes one pottage, and of diverse goods one paste. In order therefore that the love of the sex may be distinctly known as to that part by which it inclines and advances to the scortatory love which is utterly opposite to conjugial love, it is expedient that its beginning, which is fornication, should be examined; and this shall be done in the following series:—

I. *Fornication belongs to the love of the sex.*

II. *This love commences when a youth begins to think and act from his own understanding, and the voice of his speech begins to become masculine.*

III. *Fornication belongs to the natural man.*

IV. *Fornication is lust, but not the lust of adultery.*

V. *With some men, the love of the sex cannot, without mischiefs, be altogether coerced from going forth into fornication.*

VI. *Therefore in populous cities brothels are tolerated.*

VII. *The lust of committing fornication is light, in proportion as it looks to conjugial love, and gives this love the preference.*

VIII. *The lust of committing fornication is grievous, in proportion as it looks to adultery.*

IX. *The lust of committing fornication is more grievous, in proportion as it verges to the desire of varieties, and to the desire of defloration.*

X. *The sphere of the lust of committing fornication, such as it is in the beginning, is intermediate between the sphere of scortatory love and the sphere of conjugial love, and makes an equilibrium.*

XI. *Care ought to be taken lest conjugial love be destroyed by inordinate and immoderate fornications.*

XII. *Inasmuch as the conjugial [principle or state] of one man with one wife is the jewel of human life and the interior homestead* (reconditorium) *of the Christian religion.*

XIII. *With those who, for various reasons, cannot as yet enter into marriage, and on account of salacity cannot restrain their lusts, this conjugial principle may be preserved, if the vague love of the sex be confined to one mistress.*

XIV. *Pellicacy (or commerce with a mistress*—pellex) *is preferable to roaming lust, provided only it be entered into with not more than one woman, and not with a virgin or undeflowered woman, nor with a married woman, and it be kept separate from conjugial love.*

Now follows the explanation of these articles.

445. I. FORNICATION BELONGS TO THE LOVE OF THE SEX. It is said that fornication belongs to the love of the sex, because fornication is not the love of the sex, but is derived from it. The love of the sex is like a fountain, from which both conjugial love and scortatory love may be derived; they may be derived by means of fornication, and they can be derived without it: for the love of the sex is in every man (*homo*), and it either manifests itself, or it does not manifest itself: if it manifests itself before marriage with a woman who is a prostitute, it is called fornication; if not until with a wife, it is called marriage; if, after marriage, with another woman, it is called adultery; wherefore, as has been said, the love of the sex is like a fountain from which both chaste love and unchaste love may flow forth. But with what caution and prudence chaste conjugial love can proceed by means of fornication, and by what imprudence unchaste or scortatory love may proceed by means of it, shall be explained in the following pages. Who can draw the conclusion, that he who has committed fornication cannot be more chaste in marriage?

446. II. THE LOVE OF THE SEX, FROM WHICH FORNICATION PROCEEDS, COMMENCES WHEN A YOUTH BEGINS TO THINK AND ACT FROM HIS OWN UNDERSTANDING, AND THE VOICE OF HIS SPEECH BEGINS TO BECOME MASCULINE. This is adduced to the end that the rise of the love of the sex, and thus of fornication, may be known, as taking place when the understanding begins of itself

to become rational, or from its own reason to clearly discern and provide for such things as are for profit and use; in which case that which is retained in the memory from parents and instructors serves it for a plane. At that time a change takes place in the mind: it had previously thought only from things that had been introduced into the memory, meditating upon them, and obeying them; it afterwards thinks from reason exercised upon them, and then, under the guidance of the love, it arranges into a new order the things seated in the memory, and in agreement with this order it begins its own life, and successively thinks more and more according to its own reason, and wills from its own freedom. It is known that the love of the sex follows the commencement of a man's own understanding, and progresses according to its vigour; and this is a proof that that love ascends as the understanding ascends, and descends as the understanding descends. By ascending is meant into wisdom, and by descending is meant into insanity; and wisdom consists in restraining the love of the sex, and insanity consists in allowing it a wide range. If it be allowed to run into fornication, which is the beginning of its activity, the fornication ought to be moderated from the principles of honour and morality that have been implanted in the memory and thence in the reason, and that are afterwards to be implanted in the reason and thence in the memory. The reason why the voice also becomes masculine, together with the commencement of a man's own understanding is, that the understanding thinks and speaks through the thought; a proof that the understanding makes the man (*vir*) and also constitutes his masculinity; consequently that, in proportion as his understanding is elevated, so far he becomes a man (*homo vir*), and also a male man (*masculus vir*), see nos. 432, 433.

447. III. Fornication belongs to the natural man, in like manner as does the love of the sex, which, if it becomes active before marriage, is called fornication. Every human being is born corporeal, becomes sensual, afterwards natural, and successively rational; and, if he does not stop then, he becomes spiritual. The reason why he thus advances step by step, is, in order that planes may be formed, on which the higher [planes] may rest and find support, as a palace on its foundations: the ultimate plane, with those that are formed upon it, may also be compared to ground, in which, when prepared, noble seeds are sown. As to what specifically concerns the love of the sex; it also is first corporeal, for it commences from the flesh; next it becomes sensual, for the five senses are delighted by its general [nature]; afterwards it becomes natural, like the same love with animals, because it is a vague love of the sex; but as man was born in order that he might become spiritual, it afterwards becomes natural-rational, and from natural-rational, spiritual, and lastly,

spiritual-natural; and then that love made spiritual flows into and acts upon rational love, and through this flows into and acts upon sensual love, and lastly through this flows into and acts upon that love in the body and the flesh; and as this is its ultimate plane, it acts upon it spiritually, and at the same time rationally and sensually; and it flows in and acts thus successively when the man is meditating upon it, but simultaneously when he is in its ultimate. The reason fornication belongs to the natural man, is, that it proceeds proximately from the natural love of the sex; and it may exist natural-rational, but not spiritual, because the love of the sex cannot become spiritual until it becomes conjugial; and the love of the sex from natural becomes spiritual, when a man (*homo*) recedes from wandering lust, and devotes himself to one, to whose soul he unites his own soul.

448. IV. Fornication is lust, but not the lust of adultery. The reasons why fornication is lust are:—1. That it proceeds from the natural man, and in everything which proceeds from the natural man there is concupiscence and lust; for the natural man is nothing but an abode and receptacle of concupiscences and lusts, since all the evil propensities inherited from the parents reside therein. 2. That the fornicator has a wandering and promiscuous regard for the sex, and not as yet for one of the sex; and so long as he is in this state, lust excites him to do what he does: but in proportion as he has a regard for one of the sex, and loves to conjoin his life with hers, concupiscence becomes chaste affection, and lust becomes human love.

449. That the lust of fornication is not the lust of adultery, every one sees clearly from common perception. What law, and what judge, imputes the like criminality to the fornicator as to the adulterer? The reason why this is seen from common perception is, that fornication is not opposite to conjugial love as adultery is. In fornication, conjugial love may lie stored up within, as what is spiritual may lie stored up in what is natural; yea, what is spiritual is even actually evolved out of what is natural; and when what is spiritual has been evolved, then what is natural encompasses it, as the bark does the wood, and the scabbard the sword, and it also serves what is spiritual as a protection against violence. From these considerations it is evident, that natural love, which is love for the sex, precedes spiritual love, which is love for one of the sex; but if fornication proceeds from the natural love of the sex, it may also be wiped away, provided only that conjugial love be regarded, wished for, and sought after, as the chief good. It is altogether otherwise with the libidinous and obscene love of adultery, which has been shewn to be opposite to conjugial love, and destructive of it, in

the foregoing chapter concerning "The Opposition of Scortatory and Conjugial Love;" wherefore if an adulterer who is one of set purpose or from confirmation enters for various reasons into the conjugial covenant, the case is reversed: [in this case,] what is natural lies latent within with its lasciviousnesses and obscenities, and an appearance of what is spiritual covers it outwardly. From these considerations reason can see, that the lust of limited fornication in respect to the lust of adultery, is as the first warmth is to the cold of mid-winter in northern countries.

450. V. WITH SOME MEN, THE LOVE OF THE SEX CANNOT, WITHOUT MISCHIEFS, BE TOTALLY COERCED FROM GOING FORTH INTO FORNICATION. It is useless to recount the mischiefs which may be caused and produced by too great a coercion of the love of the sex, with those who, by reason of superabundance, suffer from intense venereal excitement (*oestrum*). From such coercion with such persons are to be traced the origins of certain diseases of the body, and distempers of the mind, not to mention unknown evils, which must not be named. It is otherwise with those whose love of the sex is so moderate that they are able to resist the strivings of its lust; also with those who are at liberty to introduce themselves into a legitimate partnership of the bed at the approach of manhood, without injury to their worldly fortunes, thus under the first favourable circumstances. As this is the case in heaven with children when they have grown up to the conjugial age, therefore it is unknown there what fornication is: but the case is different on earth, where matrimony cannot be contracted till the season of youth is past, as happens to many who live within forms of government where remunerative positions have to be earned by long service, and the property necessary for supporting a house and family must be acquired, and then first a suitable wife must be courted.

451. VI. THEREFORE IN POPULOUS CITIES BROTHELS ARE TOLERATED. This is adduced as a confirmation of the preceding article. It is known that they are tolerated by kings, magistrates, and consequently by judges, the police (*inquisitores*), and the people at London, Amsterdam, Paris, Vienna, Venice, Naples, and also at Rome, besides many other places: among the reasons for this toleration are also those above mentioned.

452. VII. FORNICATION IS LIGHT IN PROPORTION AS IT LOOKS TO CONJUGIAL LOVE, AND GIVES THIS LOVE THE PREFERENCE. There are degrees of the qualities of evil, as there are degrees of the qualities of good; wherefore every evil is lighter and more grievous, as every good is better and more excellent. The case is similar with fornication; which, because it is a lust, and a lust of the natural man not yet purified, is an evil. But, as

every man is capable of being purified, therefore in proportion as he approaches a purified state, in the same proportion this evil becomes a lighter evil; for in the same proportion it is wiped away; thus in proportion as fornication approaches conjugial love, which is a purified state of the love of the sex [in the same proportion it becomes a lighter evil, and in the same proportion also it is wiped away]. That the evil of fornication is more grievous in proportion as it approaches the love of adultery, will be seen in the following article. The reason why 2
fornication is light in proportion as it looks towards conjugial love, is, that it then looks from the unchaste state in which it is, to a chaste state; and in proportion as it prefers the latter, in the same proportion also it is in it as to the understanding; and in proportion as it not only prefers the chaste state, but also loves it better, in the same proportion it is in it as to the will also, thus as to the internal man; and in this case fornication, if the man nevertheless persists in it, is for him a necessity, the causes of which he has ascertained. There are 3
two reasons which make fornication light with those who prefer and love better the conjugial state. The first is, that a conjugial life is their purpose, intention, or end; the second is, that they separate evil from good in themselves. In regard to the FIRST, that the conjugial life is their purpose, intention, or end, it is because a man is such a man as he is in his purpose, intention, or end, and he is also such before the Lord and before the angels, yea, he is also regarded as such by the wise in the world; for intention is the soul of all actions, and causes incriminations and exculpations in the world, and after death imputations. In regard to 4
the SECOND, that those who prefer conjugial love to the lust of fornication, separate evil from good, thus what is unchaste from what is chaste, it is because those who separate those two in perception and intention, before they are in good or in what is chaste, are also separated and purified from the evil of that lust, when they come into the conjugial state. That this is not the case with those who in fornication look to adultery, will be seen in the article now following.

453. VIII. THE LUST OF COMMITTING FORNICATION IS GRIEVOUS, IN PROPORTION AS IT LOOKS TO ADULTERY. All those in the lust of fornication look to adultery who do not believe adulteries to be sins, and who think of marriages as they do of adulteries, with the sole difference of what is allowed and what is not. These also make one evil out of all evils, and mix them together, like dirt with eatable food in one dish, and like offscourings with wine in one cup, and thus eat and drink. Thus they do with the love of the sex, fornication, pellicacy, the milder, grievous, and more grievous kinds of adultery, and even stupration or defloration. Add to this, that they not only mix up all those things to-

gether, but also mix them with marriages, and defile marriages with similar notions. But those who do not distinguish even marriages from those other states, after unrestrained intercourse with the sex, are overtaken by states of cold, loathing, and disgust, first for their married partner, next for other women, and lastly for the sex. It is self-evident that with such persons there is no purpose, intention, or end, of what is good or chaste, in order that they may be exculpated, and no separation of evil from good, or of what is unchaste from what is chaste, in order that they may be purified; as there is with those who from fornication look to conjugial love, and prefer the latter (concerning whom, see the foregoing article, no. 452). The above observations it is allowed to confirm by this new thing from heaven: I have met with many who, in the world, had lived outwardly like others, wearing rich apparel, feasting daintily, trading like others with capital, frequenting theatrical performances, joking about love affairs as from lust, besides other similar things; and yet the angels charged those things upon some as evils of sin, and upon others as not evils, and declared the latter guiltless, but the former guilty. On being questioned why they did so, when the deeds were alike, they replied, that they regard all from purpose, intention, or end, and distinguish accordingly; and that on this account they excuse or condemn those whom the end excuses or condemns, since all in heaven are influenced by a good end, and all in hell by an evil end; and that this, and nothing else, is meant by the Lord's words, "*Judge not, that ye be not condemned*" (Matt. vii. 1).

454. IX. THE LUST OF COMMITTING FORNICATION IS MORE GRIEVOUS, IN PROPORTION AS IT VERGES TO THE DESIRE OF VARIETIES, AND TO THE DESIRE OF DEFLORATION. The reason is, that these two desires are accessories of adultery, and thus make it more grievous; for there are mild adulteries, grievous ones, and more grievous ones, and each kind is estimated according to its opposition to, and consequent destruction of, conjugial love. That the desire of varieties and the desire of defloration, strengthened by being brought into act, lay waste conjugial love, and drown it as it were in the bottom of the sea, will be seen in the following chapters on those subjects.

455. X. THE SPHERE OF THE LUST OF COMMITTING FORNICATION SUCH AS IT IS IN THE BEGINNING, IS INTERMEDIATE BETWEEN THE SPHERE OF SCORTATORY LOVE AND THE SPHERE OF CONJUGIAL LOVE, AND MAKES AN EQUILIBRIUM. The two spheres, of scortatory love and conjugial love, were treated of in the foregoing chapter, and it was shewn that the sphere of scortatory love ascends from hell, and that the sphere of conjugial love descends from heaven (no. 435); that those two spheres meet each other

in both worlds, but do not become conjoined (no. 436); that between those two spheres there is an equilibrium, and that man is in that equilibrium (no. 437); that man can turn himself to whichever sphere he pleases, but that in proportion as he turns himself to the one, in the same proportion he turns himself away from the other (no. 438). What is meant by spheres, see no. 434, and the passages there cited. The reason why the sphere of the lust of committing fornication is intermediate between those two spheres, and makes an equilibrium, is, that while any one is in it, he can turn himself to the sphere of conjugial love, that is, to this love, and also to the sphere of the love of adultery, that is, to the love of adultery. But, if he turns himself to conjugial love, he turns himself to heaven; if to the love of adultery, he turns himself to hell. Both are in the man's freedom of choice, good pleasure, and will, in order that he may act freely according to reason, and not from instinct; consequently in order that he may be a man, and appropriate influx to himself, and not a beast, which appropriates nothing of influx to itself. It is said, the lust of fornication such as it is in the beginning, because at that time it is in a middle state. Who does not know that whatever a man does in the beginning is from concupiscence, because from the natural man? And who does not know that that concupiscence is not imputed, when from natural it becomes spiritual? The case is similar with the lust of fornication, when a man's love becomes conjugial.

456. XI. Care ought to be taken lest conjugial love be destroyed by immoderate and inordinate fornications. By immoderate and inordinate fornications whereby conjugial love is destroyed, are meant fornications by which not only the virile forces are enervated, but also all the delicacies of conjugial love are taken away; for from the unbridled licence of fornications there arise not only weaknesses and consequent impotence, but also uncleannesses and shamelessnesses, by reason of which conjugial love cannot be perceived and felt in its cleanness and chastity, and thus neither in its sweetness nor the delights of its flower; not to mention the mischiefs occasioned to both the body and the mind, and also the forbidden allurements, which not only deprive conjugial love of its blessed delights, but also take it away, and change it into cold, and thereby into loathing. Such fornications are the violent excesses whereby conjugial sports are turned into tragic scenes; for immoderate and inordinate fornications are like burning flames, which arise from the ultimates, and consume the body, parch the fibres, defile the blood, and vitiate the rational powers of the mind; for they burst forth like a fire from the foundation into the house, which consumes the whole. It is the duty of parents to take care lest these mischiefs happen,

for a growing youth, strongly excited by lust, cannot as yet from reason impose a restraint upon himself.

457. XII. Inasmuch as the conjugial principle of one man with one wife is the jewel of human life and the inner homestead (*reconditorium*) of the Christian religion. These two points have been demonstrated universally and particularly in the whole of the preceding part on *Conjugial Love and its Delights of Wisdom.* It is the jewel of human life, because the quality of a man's life is according to the quality of that love with him, for that love consitutes the inmost of his life; for it is the life of wisdom dwelling together with its love, and of love dwelling together with its wisdom, and hence it is the life of the delights of both: in a word, a man is a living soul by means of that love: hence it is, that the conjugial principle of one man (*vir*) with one wife is called the jewel of human life. This is confirmed from the following articles adduced above:—That only with one wife do there exist truly conjugial friendship, confidence and potency, because there is a union of minds (nos. 333, 334): that in and from that [union] there exist celestial blessedness, spiritual blissfulnesses, and thence natural delightsomenesses, which from the beginning have been provided for those who are in truly conjugial love (no. 335). That it is the fundamental love of all celestial, spiritual and consequent natural loves, and that into that love are gathered up all joys and gladnesses from first to last (nos. 65–69): and that, considered in its origin, it is the sporting of wisdom and love, has been fully demonstrated in the *Delights of Wisdom relating to Conjugial Love*, which constitutes the First Part of this Work.

458. The reason why that love is the inner homestead of the Christian religion, is, that this religion makes a one with that love, and dwells together with it; for it was shown, that none others come into that love, or can be in it, except those who approach the Lord, and do the truths of His church and its goods (nos. 70, 71): that that love is from the Lord Alone, and that therefore it exists with those who are of the Christian religion (nos. 131, 335, 336): that that love is according to the state of the church, because it is according to the state of wisdom with man (no. 130). That these things are so, was fully confirmed in the whole chapter on "The Correspondence of that Love with the Marriage of the Lord and the Church" (nos. 116–131); and in the chapter on "The Origin of that Love from the Marriage of Good and Truth" (nos. 83–102).

459. XIII. With those who, for various reasons, cannot as yet enter into marriage, and on account of salacity can-

NOT RESTRAIN THEIR LUSTS, THIS CONJUGIAL PRINCIPLE MAY BE PRE-
SERVED IF THE [VAGUE] LOVE OF THE SEX BE CONFINED TO ONE
MISTRESS. That immoderate and inordinate lust cannot be restrained by those who are salacious, reason sees, and experience
teaches. In order therefore that this immoderation and inor-
dinateness may be curbed, with those who suffer from intense
venereal excitement (*oestrum*), and who for several reasons
cannot precipitate and hurry on marriage, and in order that
it may be reduced to something moderate and ordinate, there
seems to be no other refuge, and as it were asylum, than the
keeping of a mistress, who in French is called a *maîtresse.* It
is known, that in kingdoms where there are forms of government, matrimonies cannot be contracted by many till the
season of youth is past; for appointments must first be
obtained, and property acquired for the support of a house
and family, and then first a worthy wife must be courted;
and yet in the preceding age, the springing fountain of manhood can with but few be kept closed, and reserved for a
wife. It is indeed better that it should be reserved; but if this
cannot be done on account of the unbridled power of lust, an
intermediate means is needed, by which conjugial love
may be prevented from perishing in the meantime. The
following considerations are in favour of pellicacy, or the
keeping a mistress, being such a means:—I. That by this
means promiscuous inordinate fornications are bridled and
limited, and thus a more restricted state is induced,
which has more affinity with conjugial life. II. That 2
the ardour of venery, which in the beginning is glowing hot,
and as it were burning, is allayed and mitigated; and thus the
lasciviousness of salacity, which is filthy, is tempered by something which is as it were an analogue of marriage. III. By 3
this means too the virile forces are not cast away, nor are weaknesses contracted, as they are by roaming and unlimited
venereal lusts (*satyriases*). IV. By this means also venereal 4
diseases of the body, and insanities of the mind, are avoided
V. By this means, likewise, adulteries, which are adulteries
(*mœchationes*) with wives, and rapes (*stuprationes*), which are
violations of virgins, are guarded against; to say nothing of
criminal practices, which must not be named. For a youth
who has arrived at the age of puberty does not think that
adulteries and rapes (*stupra*) are anything else than fornications,
thus to him the one is the same with the other. Nor does he
know how from reason to resist the enticements of certain ones
of the sex, who have assiduously cultivated meretricious arts.
But in pellicacy, which is a more orderly and sane fornication,
he can learn and see the above distinctions. VI. By pellicacy, 6
also, no access is given to the four kinds of lusts which are in the
highest degree destructive of conjugial love, namely, the lust of

defloration, the lust of varieties, the lust of violation, and the lust of seducing innocences, which are treated of in the following pages. But these things are not said to those who are able to coerce the heat of lust; nor to those who are able to enter into marriage as soon as they arrive at manhood, and offer and devote to their wives the first fruits of their manly potency.

460. XIV. Pellicacy is preferable to roaming lust, provided only it be entered into with not more than one woman, and not with a virgin or undeflowered woman, nor with a married woman, and it be kept separate from conjugial love. At what time and with what persons pellicacy is better than roaming lust, has been pointed out just above. I. The reason why pellicacy may not be entered into with more than one, is, that, with more than one, there is what is polygamous within, which induces on a man a merely natural state, and thrusts this down into the Sensual, to such an extent that he cannot be elevated into the spiritual state, in which
2 conjugial love must be (see nos. 338, 339). II. The reason why it must not be entered into with a virgin or undeflowered woman is, that conjugial love with women acts in unity with their virginity, and hence is the chastity, purity, and holiness of that love; wherefore to solemnly promise and surrender that virginity to any man, is to give a pledge that she will love him to eternity: therefore a virgin can from no rational consent bargain it away, except with the solemn promise of the conjugial covenant. It is also the crown of her honour. Wherefore, to snatch it away without the covenant of marriage, and afterwards to discard her, is to make a harlot of some virgin who might have become a bride and a chaste wife, or to defraud some other man, and both of these deeds are damnable. Therefore he who adjoins to himself a virgin as a mistress, may indeed dwell together with her, and thus initiate her into the friendship of love, but still with the constant intention, if she does not commit adultery, that she shall be or become his wife.
3 III. That pellicacy must not be entered into with a married
4 woman, because this is adultery, is evident. IV. The reason why the love of pellicacy must be kept separate from conjugial love is, that those loves are distinct, and therefore ought not to be mixed together: for the love of pellicacy is an unchaste, natural, and external love, whereas the love of marriage is chaste, spiritual, and internal. The love of pellicacy keeps the souls of the two persons distinct, and conjoins only the sensuals of the body; but the love of marriage unites the souls, and from the union of the souls conjoins also the sensuals of the body, until from two they become as a one, which is one flesh.
5 V. The love of pellicacy enters only into the understanding, and into the things which depend on the understanding; but the

love of marriage enters also into the will and the things which depend on the will, consequently into each and all things of man (*homo*); wherefore if the love of pellicacy becomes the love of marriage, a man (*vir*) cannot abandon [his mistress] from any principle of right, without a violation of the conjugial union; and if he abandons [her] and marries another woman, conjugial love perishes in consequence of the breach of it. It should be known, that the love of pellicacy is kept separate from conjugial love by the man's not promising marriage to the mistress, and by his not holding out to her any hope of marriage. Nevertheless it is better that the torch of the love of the sex be first lighted with a wife.

461. To the above shall be added the following Memorable Relation:—

* I once spoke with a novitiate spirit who, when he was in the world, had meditated much about heaven and hell. By novitiate spirits are meant human beings newly deceased, who are called spirits, because they are then spiritual men. As soon as he entered into the spiritual world, he began to meditate in like manner about heaven and hell, and seemed to himself, when meditating about heaven, to be in joy, and when about hell, in sadness. When he observed that he was in the spiritual world, he immediately asked where heaven was, and where hell was, and also what, and of what quality, the one and the other were.

And they answered, "Heaven is above your head, and hell beneath your feet; for you are now in the world of spirits, which is intermediate between heaven and hell; but what and of what quality heaven and hell are we cannot describe in a few words."

And then, as he burned with the desire of knowing, he cast himself upon his knees, and prayed devoutly to God that he might be instructed.

And lo! an angel appeared at his right hand, and raised him, and said, "You have supplicated to be instructed about heaven and hell. INQUIRE AND LEARN WHAT DELIGHT IS, AND YOU WILL KNOW;" and having said this, the angel was taken up.

Then the novitiate spirit said within himself, "What does 2
this mean, '*Inquire and learn what delight is, and you will know what and of what quality heaven and hell are*'?" And leaving that place he wandered about, and accosting those he met, said, "Tell me, I pray you, what delight is."

Some said, "What a strange question! Who does not know what delight is? Is it not joy and gladness? Wherefore delight is delight; one delight is like another; we know no difference."

* This Memorable Relation is repeated in the *True Christian Religion*, no. 570.

Others said, that delight was the laughter of the mind; for when the mind laughs, the face is cheerful, the talk jocular, the behaviour sportive, and the whole man is in delight.

But some said, "Delight is nothing else than feasting and eating delicacies, drinking and getting intoxicated with generous wine, and then talking about different things, especially about the sports of Venus and Cupid."

3 On hearing all this, the novitiate spirit, being indignant, said to himself; "These answers are ill-bred and unbecoming: these delights are neither heaven nor hell; would that I could meet the wise."

He then took his leave of them, and inquired where he might find the wise.

Just then he was seen by a certain angelic spirit, who said, "I perceive that you are inflamed with the desire of knowing what is the universal of heaven and the universal of hell; and since this is DELIGHT, I will conduct you to a hill, where there meet daily those who examine effects, those who investigate causes, and those who explore ends. There are three companies; those who examine effects are called spirits of sciences, and abstractedly sciences; those who investigate causes are called spirits of intelligence, and abstractedly intelligences; and those who explore ends are called spirits of wisdom, and abstractedly wisdoms. Directly above them in heaven are angels, who from ends see causes, and from causes effects: from these angels those three companies have enlightenment."

4 The angelic spirit then taking the novitiate spirit by the hand, led him up the hill to the company which consisted of those who explore ends, and are called wisdoms. To these the novitiate spirit said, "Pardon me for having ascended to you: the reason is, that from my childhood I have meditated about heaven and hell, and lately came into this world, where I was told by some who were then associated with me, that here heaven is above my head and hell beneath my feet; but they did not tell me what and of what quality the one and the other were; wherefore, becoming anxious from my constant thought on these subjects, I prayed to God; and then an angel presented himself, and said, '*Inquire and learn what delight is, and you will know.*' I have inquired, but hitherto in vain: I beg therefore that you will kindly teach me what delight is."

5 To this the wisdoms replied, "Delight is the all of life to all in heaven, and the all of life to all in hell: they who are in heaven have the delight of good and truth, but they who are in hell have the delight of evil and falsity; for all delight belongs to love, and love is the esse of man's life; wherefore as man is man according to the quality of his love, so he is man according to the quality of his delight. The activity of love makes the sense of delight; its activity in heaven is with wisdom, and its activity

in hell is with insanity; each in its own subjects presents delight. But the heavens and the hells are in opposite delights, because in opposite loves; the heavens in the love and therefore in the delight of doing good, but the hells in the love and therefore in the delight of doing evil. If therefore you know what delight is, you will know what and of what quality heaven and hell are. But inquire and learn further what delight is from those who investigate causes, and are called intelligences; they are to the right from hence."

He departed, and came to them, and told them the reason of 6
his coming, and begged that they would instruct him what delight was.

And they, rejoicing at the question, said, "It is true that he who knows what delight is, knows what and of what quality heaven and hell are. The will, by virtue whereof man is man, cannot be moved in the least except by delight; for the will, considered in itself, is nothing but the affect and effect of some love, thus of some delight; for it is something pleasing, agreeable, and pleasurable, which causes willing; and as the will actuates the understanding to think, there does not exist the least of an idea of thought except from the influent delight of the will. The reason of this being so is, that the Lord through influx from Himself actuates all things of the soul and all things of the mind with angels, spirits, and men; and actuates them through the influx of love and wisdom; and this influx is the activity itself, from which is all the delight, which in its origin is called blessed, blissful, and happy, and in its derivation is called delightful, pleasant, and pleasurable, and in the universal sense, GOOD. But the spirits of hell invert all things with themselves; thus they turn good into evil, and truth into falsity, the delight constantly remaining: for without the permanence of delight, they would have neither will nor sensation, thus not life. From these considerations it is evident what, of what quality, and whence, is the delight of hell; also what, of what quality, and whence, is the delight of heaven."

Having heard this, he was conducted to the third company, 7
which consisted of those who examine effects, and are called sciences. These said, "Descend to the lower earth, and ascend to the higher earth: in the latter you will perceive and feel the delightsomenesses of the angels of heaven, and in the former of the delightsomenesses of the spirits of hell."

But lo! at that moment, at a distance from them, the ground gaped open, and through the opening there ascended three devils, who appeared on fire from the delight of their love; and as they who were consociated with the novitiate spirit perceived that those three had ascended out of hell providentially, they said to them, "Do not come nearer; but from the place where you are, tell something about your delights."

Whereupon they said, "Know, that every one, whether he be good or evil, is in his own delight; a good person in the delight of his own good, and an evil one in the delight of his own evil."

They then asked, "What is your delight?"

They said that it was the delight of committing of whoredom, stealing, defrauding, and blaspheming.

Again they asked, "What is the quality of those delights?"

They said that they were smelt by others as stinks from ordure, stenches from dead bodies, and bad smells from stale urine.

They asked, "Are those things delightful to you?"

They said that they were most delightful.

And they said, "Then you are like unclean beasts which wallow in such things."

To which they answered, "If we are, we are; but such things are the delights of our nostrils."

8 And they asked, "What more?"

They said, "Every one is allowed to be in his own delight, even the most unclean, as they call it, provided he does not infest good spirits and angels; but as from our delight we could not do otherwise than infest them, we have been cast into penitentiaries, where we suffer direful things. The restraint and repression of our delights there is what is called the torture of hell; it is also interior pain."

It was then asked them, "Why did you infest the good?"

They said that they could not do otherwise, that it was as if a fury invaded them when they see any angel and perceive the Divine sphere about him.

It was then said to them, "Herein also you are like wild beasts."

And presently, when they saw the novitiate spirit with the angel, the devils were overcome with fury, which appeared like a fire of hatred; wherefore, to prevent them from doing mischief, they were cast back into hell.

After these things, appeared the angels who from ends see causes, and through causes effects, and who were in the heaven above those three companies. They were seen in a bright white light, which, rolling itself spirally downwards, brought with it a round garland of flowers, and placed it on the head of the novitiate spirit; and at the same moment a voice came forth to him thence, saying, "This wreath is given you because from childhood you have meditated about heaven and hell."

CONCUBINAGE.

462. IN the preceding chapter, where fornication was treated of, pellicacy was also treated of, and by pellicacy was meant the conjunction of an unmarried man with a woman, under a definite contract (*pacta*): but by concubinage is here meant the conjunction of a married man with a woman, likewise under a definite contract. Those who do not distinguish genera, use the two terms promiscuously, as if they had one meaning, and thus one signification: but as they are two genera, and the term pellicacy [or keeping a mistress] is suitable to the former, because a kept mistress is a prostitute (*mœcha*), and the term concubinage is suited to the latter, because a concubine is a substituted partner (*succuba*) of the bed, therefore, for the sake of separation, an ante-nuptial contract with a woman is signified by pellicacy, and a post-nuptial contract by concubinage. Concubinage is here treated of for the sake of order; for from order it is discovered what is the quality of marriage on the one part, and of adultery on the other. That marriage and adultery are opposites, has already been shown in the chapter concerning their opposition; and in what degree and in what manner they are opposed cannot be learnt except from their intermediates, of which concubinage is one. But as there are two kinds of concubinage, which ought to be carefully distinguished, therefore this section, like the foregoing, must be arranged into its distinct parts, as follows:—

I. *There are two kinds of concubinage, which differ exceedingly from each other, the one conjointly with the wife, and the other apart from the wife.*

II. *Concubinage conjointly with the wife, is altogether unlawful for Christians, and detestable.*

III. *It is polygamy, which has been condemned, and ought to be condemned, by the Christian world.*

IV. *It is whoredom, whereby the conjugial principle, which is the most precious treasure of the Christian life, is destroyed.*

V. *Concubinage apart from the wife, when it is engaged in from legitimate, just, and truly weighty causes* (causae vere sonticae) *is not unlawful.*

VI. *The legitimate causes of this concubinage are the legitimate causes of divorce, when the wife is nevertheless retained at home.*

VII. *The just causes of this concubinage are the just causes of separation from the bed.*

VIII. *The weighty causes of this concubinage are real, and not real.*

IX. *The really weighty causes are such as are based on what is just.*

X. *The weighty causes which are not real are such as are not based on what is just, although on the appearance of what is just.*

XI. *Those who, from legitimate, just, and really weighty causes, are in this concubinage, may at the same time be in conjugial love.*

XII. *While this concubinage lasts, actual conjunction with the wife is not allowable.*

Now follows the explanation of these articles.

463. I. THERE ARE TWO KINDS OF CONCUBINAGE, WHICH DIFFER EXCEEDINGLY FROM EACH OTHER, THE ONE CONJOINTLY WITH THE WIFE, AND THE OTHER APART FROM THE WIFE. That there are two kinds of concubinage, which differ exceedingly from each other, and that the one kind consists in adjoining an additional partner (*succuba*) to the bed, and living conjointly and at the same time with her and with the wife; and that the other kind consists in taking, after a legitimate and just separation from the wife, a
2 woman in her stead as a partner of the bed. That these two kinds of concubinage are as different from each other as a dirty linen cloth is from one that is washed, may be seen by those who take a careful and distinct view of things, but not by those who take a confused and indistinct view of things. Yea, it may be seen by those who are in conjugial love, but not by those who are in the love of adultery. The latter are in the night concerning all the derivations of the love of the sex, but the former are in day-light concerning them. But still, those who are in adultery, can see those derivations and their distinctions, not, indeed, in themselves from themselves, but from others when they hear them: for there is with an adulterer a similar faculty of elevating the understanding as there is with a chaste married person; but an adulterer, after he has acknowledged the distinctions which he has heard from others, nevertheless forgets them, when he immerses his understanding in his filthy pleasure; for what is chaste and what is unchaste, and what is sane and what is insane, cannot be together; but they can be distinguished by
3 the understanding separated. Once, in the spiritual world, those who had not accounted adulteries sins, were asked by me whether they knew a single distinction between fornication, pellicacy, the two kinds of concubinage, and between the degrees of adultery? They said that one was as the other, and they were asked whether marriage was so too: and they looked around to see whether any of the clergy were present, and as there were not, they said, that in itself it was like the rest. It was otherwise with those who in the ideas of their thought had accounted adulteries sins: these said, that in their interior

ideas which belong to the perception, they saw distinctions, but had not yet studied to discern and know them from one another. This I can asseverate, that those distinctions, as to their minutiæ, are perceived by the angels of heaven. In order, therefore, that it may be manifest, that there exist two kinds of concubinage, which are opposite to each other: one by which conjugial love is abolished, the other by which it is not abolished, therefore the damnable kind shall be described first, and afterwards the other which is not hurtful.

464. II. Concubinage conjointly with the wife, is [altogether] unlawful for Christians, and detestable. It is unlawful, because it is contrary to the conjugial covenant; and it is detestable, because it is contrary to religion; and what is contrary to religion, and at the same time contrary to the conjugial covenant, is contrary to the Lord: wherefore, as soon as any one, without a really weighty cause, adjoins a concubine to the wife, heaven is closed against him, and by the angels he is no longer numbered among Christians. From that time also he despises the things which belong to the church and to religion, and afterwards does not lift up his face above nature, but turns to her as to a deity, who favours his lust, and from whose influx his spirit thenceforward lives. The interior cause of this apostasy will be disclosed in what follows. That this concubinage is detestable, is not seen by the man (*vir*) himself who is guilty of it; because after the closing of heaven he becomes a spiritual insanity: but a chaste wife has a clear view of it, because she is a conjugial love, and this love nauseates that concubinage; wherefore also, many such wives refuse actual conjunction with their husbands afterwards, as that which would contaminate their chastity by the contagion of the lust adhering to the men from the harlots.

465. III. It is polygamy, which has been condemned, and ought to be condemned, by the Christian World. That simultaneous concubinage, or concubinage conjointly with the wife, is polygamy,—although not acknowledged to be such, because it is not so declared, and thus not so called, by any law,—is seen by every person, even if he be not clear-sighted; for the woman is like a wife who is kept for use, and who shares the conjugial couch. That polygamy has been condemned, and ought to be condemned, by the Christian world, has been shown in the chapter on "Polygamy," especially from these articles therein: It is not allowable for a Christian to marry more than one wife (no. 338); If a Christian marries several wives, he commits not only natural adultery, but also spiritual adultery (no. 339): Polygamy was permitted to the Israelitish nation, because the Christian church was not among that nation (no. 340). From

these considerations it is evident, that to adjoin a concubine to the wife, and to share the bed with both, is filthy polygamy.

466. IV. It is whoredom, whereby the conjugial principle, which is the most precious treasure of the Christian life, is destroyed. That it is a whoredom more opposed to conjugial love than common whoredom, which is called simple adultery; and that it is a deprivation of all faculty and inclination for conjugial life, which is in Christians from birth, may be evinced by arguments which will have great weight with the reason of a wise man. In regard to the first proposition,—that simultaneous concubinage, or concubinage conjointly with the wife, is a whoredom more opposed to conjugial love than common whoredom, which is called simple adultery, it may be seen from these considerations: that in common whoredom or simple adultery there is not a love analogous to conjugial love; for it is only a mad desire (*oestrum*) of the flesh, which presently cools down, and sometimes does not leave behind it any trace of love towards its object; wherefore this effervescing lasciviousness, if it is not from purpose or confirmation, and if the adulterer (*mœchus*) repents of it, detracts but very little from conjugial love. It is otherwise with polygamous whoredom: in this there is a love analogous to conjugial love; for it does not cool down, and disperse, and pass off into nothing after effervescence, like the foregoing; but it remains, renews and strengthens itself, and in that proportion takes away from the love for the wife, and in the place thereof induces cold towards her; for it then regards the concubine harlot as lovely in consequence of a freedom of the will, in that it can depart from her if it pleases; which [freedom] is inborn in the natural man, and because this [freedom] is, for that reason, agreeable, it supports that love; and moreover, with a concubine the unition with allurements is nearer than with the wife: but on the other hand, it does not regard the wife as lovely, by reason of the duty of cohabitation with her enjoined by the covenant of life, which it then perceives as far more constrained in consequence of the freedom enjoyed with the other woman. It is manifest that the love for the wife grows cold, and she herself is held cheaply, in the same degree in which the love for a certain
2 prostitute grows warm, and she is held in estimation. In regard to the second proposition—that simultaneous concubinage, or concubinage conjointly with the wife, deprives a man (*vir*) of all faculty and inclination for conjugial life, which is in Christians from birth,—it may be seen from the following considerations: that in proportion as love towards the wife is transcribed into love towards a concubine, in the same proportion the love towards the wife is rent, exhausted, and emptied, as has been shewn just above: that this is effected by a closing up of the interiors of his natural mind, and an opening of its lower parts, may be

manifest from the seat of the inclination with Christians to love one of the sex, as being in his inmosts, and that this seat can be shut up, but cannot be extirpated. The reason why the inclination to love one of the sex, and also the faculty for receiving that love, is implanted in Christians from birth, is, that that love is from the Lord Alone, and has been made a point of religion, and in Christendom the Lord's Divinity is acknowledged and worshipped, and religion is from His Word; hence there is an ingrafting, and also a transplanting thereof, from generation to generation. It was said that that Christian conjugial principle perishes through polygamous whoredom, but there is meant that with the Christian polygamist it is closed up and intercepted; but nevertheless it is capable of being revived in his posterity, as is the case with the likeness of a grandfather or a great-grandfather returning in a grandson or a great-grandson. Hence it is, that that conjugial principle is called the most precious treasure of the Christian life, and (as above, nos. 457, 458) the jewel of human life, and the inner homestead of the Christian religion. That that conjugial principle is destroyed by 3
polygamous whoredom with the Christian who is in the latter, appears manifestly from this consideration, that he cannot, like a Mohammedan polygamist, love a concubine and a wife equally; but that in proportion as he loves a concubine, or grows warm towards her, in the same proportion he does not love his wife, that is, in the same proportion he grows cold towards her; and, what is yet more detestable, in the same proportion he also in heart acknowledges the Lord to be only a natural man, and the son of Mary, and not at the same time to be the Son of God, and in the same proportion also he makes light of religion. But it ought to be well noted, that this takes place with those who add a concubine to the wife, and actually conjoin themselves with both; but not at all with those who, from legitimate, just, and truly weighty causes, separate themselves and keep apart, as to actual love, from the wife, and keep a woman for use. This kind of concubinage now comes to be treated of.

467. V. CONCUBINAGE APART FROM THE WIFE, WHEN IT IS ENGAGED IN FROM LEGITIMATE, JUST, AND TRULY WEIGHTY CAUSES, IS NOT UNLAWFUL. What causes are meant by legitimate, what by just, and what by truly weighty, shall be stated in their order: the bare mention of the causes is here premised, in order that this concubinage, which is about to be treated of, may be distinguished from the former concubinage.

468. VI. THE LEGITIMATE CAUSES OF THIS CONCUBINAGE ARE THE LEGITIMATE CAUSES OF DIVORCE, WHEN THE WIFE IS NEVERTHELESS RETAINED AT HOME. By divorce is meant the abolition of the conjugial covenant, and a consequent plenary separation,

and after this the full liberty to marry another wife. The one only cause of this total separation or divorce, is whoredom, according to the Lord's precept in Matthew xix. 9. To the same cause also belong manifest obscenities, which banish decency, and fill and infest the house with infamous allurements, from which there arises a scortatory shamelessness, into which the whole mind is dissolved. To these things may be added malicious desertion, which involves whoredom, and causes the wife to commit adultery, and thereby to be put away (Matt. v. 32). These three causes, being the legitimate causes of divorce,—the first and third before a public judge, and the middle one before the man as judge,—are also legitimate causes of concubinage; but when the adulterous wife is retained at home. The reason why whoredom is the one only cause of divorce is, that it is diametrically opposite to the life of conjugial love, and destroys it even to extermination (see above, no. 255).

469. The reasons why, by many men, the adulterous wife is nevertheless retained at home, are, 1. That the man is afraid to bring an action against his wife, to accuse her of adultery, and thereby to make the crime public; for unless the evidences of eye-witnesses, or equivalent evidences, were produced to convict her, he would be covertly reproached in companies of men, and openly in companies of women. 2. He is afraid also lest his adulteress should have the cunning to clear her conduct, and likewise lest the judges should show favour to her, and thus his name should be dishonoured. 3. Moreover, there are the conveniences of domestic uses, which make separation from the house unadvisable: as, in case they have children, towards whom also the adulteress has maternal love; in case there exist between them mutual obligations, by which they are conjoined, and which cannot be broken off; in case the wife enjoys favour and patronage on the part of her relatives by marriage, and her blood-relations, and there is prospect of an increase of property from them; in case he had in the beginning encouraged habits of pleasant intimacy with her; and in case, after she has become faithless, she understands how to cunningly appease her husband by captivating speeches and a feigned courteous demeanour, so that she may not be incriminated; besides other cases, which, because in themselves they are legitimate causes of divorce, are also legitimate causes of concubinage; for the causes of retention at home do not take away the cause of divorce, when she has committed whoredom. Who but a vile person can preserve the rights of the marriage bed, and share the couch with a harlot? If this takes place here and there, it proves nothing.

470. VII. THE JUST CAUSES OF THIS CONCUBINAGE ARE THE

JUST CAUSES OF SEPARATION FROM THE BED. There are legitimate causes of separation, and there are just causes: legitimate causes are made by the decisions of judges, and just causes by the decisions come to by the man alone. The causes both legitimate and just of separation from the bed, and also from the house, were briefly enumerated above, nos. 252, 253; among which, the VITIATED STATES OF THE BODY are diseases by which the whole body becomes infected to such a degree that a fatal result ensues from contact with it: of this nature are malignant and pestilential fevers (*febres malignae et pestilentiales*), leprosies, syphilis, cancers. Further, diseases by which the whole body is rendered so loathsome, that there is no possibility of consociation, and in consequence of which hurtful effluvia and noxious exhalations are generated, either from the surface of the body, or from its inward parts, especially from the stomach and lungs. From the surface of the body there arise malignant small-pox, warty growths, pustules, scurvy, virulent itch (*scabies virulenta*), especially if the face has been rendered loathsome (*defaedata est*) by them. From the stomach, constant risings of foul, stinking, and rank matters. From the lungs, fetid and putrid exhalations generated by tubercles, ulcers or abscesses, or by vitiated blood or serum. Besides these, there are also other diseases of various names, as, lipothymy [or fainting], which is an utter debility of the body and a failing of strength; paralysis, which is a loosening and relaxation of the membranes and ligaments which serve for motion; epilepsy; permanent debility caused by attacks of apoplexy; certain chronic diseases; the iliac passion; hernia; besides other diseases, which pathology teaches. VITIATED STATES OF THE MIND, which are just causes of separation from the bed and the house, are unsoundness of mind (*mania*), frenzy (*phrenitis*), insanity (*vesania*), idiocy and imbecility (*actualis stultitia et fatuitas*), loss of memory, and the like. That these are just causes of concubinage, because they are just causes of separation, reason sees without the help of a judge.

471. VIII. THE WEIGHTY CAUSES OF THIS CONCUBINAGE ARE REAL, AND NOT REAL. Since besides the just causes, which are just causes of separation, and consequently become just causes of concubinage, there are also weighty causes, which depend on the judgment and justice with the man, therefore these also must be mentioned: but as the judgments of justice may be perverted, and be turned by confirmations into the appearances of what is just, therefore these weighty causes are distinguished into real and not real, and are described separately.

472. IX. THE REALLY WEIGHTY CAUSES ARE SUCH AS ARE BASED ON WHAT IS JUST. To know these causes, it is sufficient to mention some which are really weighty, such as a want of

love of children (*storgë*), and a consequent rejection of children, intemperance, drunkenness, uncleanness, shamelessness, a desire of divulging family secrets, of disputing, striking, taking revenge, acting wickedly, stealing, deceiving; internal unlikeness, from which comes antipathy; a clamorous demand for the conjugial debt, whereby the man becomes a cold stone; engaging in magical practices and sorcery; extreme godlessness; and other similar things.

473. There are also milder causes, which are really weighty, and which separate from the bed, and yet not from the house; as a cessation of prolification on the part of the wife, in consequence of advanced age, and a consequent refusal and denial of connubial intercourse, while the ardour thereof still continues with the man; besides similar things, in which rational judgment sees what is just, and which do not hurt the conscience.

474. X. THE WEIGHTY CAUSES WHICH ARE NOT REAL ARE SUCH AS ARE NOT BASED ON WHAT IS JUST, ALTHOUGH ON THE APPEARANCE OF WHAT IS JUST. These are known from the really weighty causes above mentioned, and, if not rightly examined, may appear to be just, and yet they are unjust; as, that times of abstinence are required after child-birth; and, the transitory sicknesses of wives; on these grounds and also not on these grounds the waste of the prolific fluid [on the part of the man]; the polygamy permitted to the Israelites; and other like causes of no weight as based on justice. These are fabricated by the men after they have contracted colds, when unchaste lusts have deprived them of conjugial love, and have infatuated them with an idea of its likeness to scortatory love. When such men enter upon concubinage, they, in order to prevent the loss of their reputation, make of such spurious and fallacious causes, real and genuine causes, even as they also very frequently spread lies about their wives, which lies, according to the favour which they enjoy among their befriended fellow-citizens, are approved and applauded by them.

475. XI. THOSE WHO, FROM LEGITIMATE, JUST, AND REALLY WEIGHTY CAUSES, ARE IN THIS CONCUBINAGE, MAY AT THE SAME TIME BE IN CONJUGIAL LOVE. It is said that they may at the same time be in conjugial love; and it is meant, that they may keep this love stored up in themselves; for that love, in the subject in which it is, does not perish, but is quiescent. The reasons why conjugial love is preserved with those who prefer marriage to concubinage, and enter upon the latter from the causes above mentioned, are these:—that this concubinage is not repugnant to conjugial love; that it is

not a separation from it; that it is only a veiling around of it; and that this veil is taken away from them after death. I. That this concubinage is not repugnant to conjugial love, follows from what was proved above,—that that concubinage, when engaged in from legitimate, just, and really weighty causes, is not unlawful (nos. 467–473). II. That this concubinage 2
is not a separation from conjugial love; for when legitimate, or just, or really weighty causes arise, and persuade and compel, conjugial love with marriage is not separated, but only interrupted: and love interrupted, and not separated, remains in the subject. The case in this respect is like that of a person who, being engaged in an employment which he loves, is kept away from it by company, by public sights, or by travelling; still he does not lose the love of his employment. It is also like the case of a person who loves generous wine, and who, when he drinks wine of an inferior quality, does not lose his taste and appetite for the generous wine. III. The reason why that 3
concubinage is only a veiling around of conjugial love, is, that the love of concubinage is natural, and the love of marriage spiritual; and natural love veils over spiritual love, when the latter is interrupted: that this is the case, is unknown to the lover, because spiritual love is not felt apart by itself, but through natural love, and it is felt as delight, in which there is blessedness from heaven: but natural love by itself is felt only as delight. IV. The reason why this veil is taken away after death, is, that then a man from natural becomes spiritual, and instead of a material body enjoys a substantial one, wherein natural delight flowing from spiritual delight is felt in its eminence. That this is the case, I have heard from communication with some in the spiritual world, even from kings there, who in the natural world had been in concubinage from really weighty causes.

476. XII. WHILE THIS CONCUBINAGE LASTS, ACTUAL CONJUNCTION WITH THE WIFE IS NOT ALLOWABLE. The reason is that in such case conjugial love, which in itself is spiritual, chaste, pure, and holy, becomes natural, is contaminated, and becomes obsolete, and thereby perishes; wherefore in order that this love may be preserved, it is expedient that concubinage grounded in really weighty causes (nos. 472, 473), be engaged in with one only, and not with two at the same time.

477. To the above shall be added the following Memorable Relation:—

I heard a certain spirit, a young man, recently arrived from the world, boasting of his whoredoms, and eager to obtain a reputation of being a man of superior masculine powers; and in the insolence of his boasting he thus expressed himself:

"What is more dismal than for a man to imprison his love, and to live only with one woman? and what more delightful than to set the love at liberty? Who does not grow tired of one? and who is not revived by several? What is sweeter than promiscuous liberty, variety, deflorations, the making fools of husbands, and scortatory hypocrisies? Do not those things which are obtained by cunning, deceit, and theft, delight the inmosts of the mind?"

2 On hearing this, the by-standers said, "Speak not so; you know not where you are, and with whom you are; you are but lately come hither. Hell is beneath your feet, and heaven over your head; you are now in the world which is intermediate between those two, and is called the world of spirits. All who depart out of the world come here, and are gathered hither, and examined as to their quality; and here they are prepared, the evil for hell, and the good for heaven. Possibly you still retain what you have heard from priests in the world, that whoremongers and harlots are cast down into hell, and that chaste married partners are raised into heaven."

At this the novitiate laughed, saying, "What is heaven and what is hell? Is not it heaven where one is free; and is not he free who is allowed to love as many as he pleases? and is not it hell where one is a servant; and is not he a servant who is obliged to cleave to one?"

3 But a certain angel, looking down from heaven, heard what he said, and broke off the conversation, lest it should proceed further to profane marriages; and he said to him, "Come up hither, and I will shew you to the life what heaven and hell are, and what the quality of the latter is to confirmed whoremongers. He then shewed him the way, and he ascended.

And after reception he was led first into a paradisiacal garden, where were fruit-trees and flowers, which from their beauty, pleasantness, and fragrance, filled the minds (*animi*) with the delights of life. When he saw these things, he admired them with a great admiration; but he was then in external sight, such as he had been in in the world when he saw similar objects, and in this sight he was rational; but in the internal sight, in which whoredom played the first part, and occupied every point of thought, he was not rational; wherefore the external sight was closed, and the internal sight opened; and when the latter was opened, he said, "What do I see now? is it not straw and dry wood? and what do I smell now? is it not a stench? Where now are those paradisiacal objects?"

The angel said, "They are near at hand and present; but they do not appear before your internal sight, which is scortatory, for it turns heavenly things into infernal things, and sees only opposites. Every man has an internal mind and an external mind, thus an internal sight and an external sight; with the evil the internal mind is insane and the external mind is wise; but with the good the internal mind is wise, and from this also the external mind; and such as the mind is, so a man in the spiritual world sees objects."

After this the angel, by virtue of power which had been given 4
him, closed his internal sight, and opened his external sight, and led him away through gates towards the middle point of the habitations; and he saw magnificent palaces of alabaster, marble, and various precious stones, and beside them arcades, and round about pillars overlaid and encompassed with wonderful ornaments and decorations. When he saw these things, he was amazed and said, "What do I see? I see magnificent objects in their own real magnificence, and architectonic objects in their own real art." At that instant the angel again closed his external sight, and opened his internal sight, which was evil because filthily scortatory: whereupon he exclaimed, saying, "What do I now see? Where am I? Where now are those palaces and magnificent objects? I see only ruins, rubbish, and places full of caverns."

But presently he was brought back again into his external 5
sight, and introduced into one of the palaces; and he saw the decorations of the gates, windows, walls, and ceilings, and especially of the utensils, over and round about which were heavenly forms of gold and precious stones, which cannot be described by any words, nor delineated by any art, for they surpassed the ideas of words and the notions of art. On seeing these things he again exclaimed, saying, "These are wonders of wonders, such as no eye had ever seen." But then his internal sight was opened, the external being closed, as before, and he was asked what he then saw. He replied, "Nothing but decayed piles of bulrushes in this place, of straw in that, and of firebrands in that."

But once again he was brought into the external state of the 6
mind, and some maidens were brought to him, who were beauties, because images of heavenly affection; and they addressed him in the sweet voice of their affection; and instantly, on seeing and hearing them, his countenance changed, and he returned of himself into his internals, which were scortatory; and since such internals cannot endure anything of heavenly love, and neither on the other hand can they be endured by heavenly love, therefore both parties vanished,—the maidens out of the sight of the man, and the man out of the sight of the maidens.

After this, the angel instructed him concerning the origin of 7
the changes of the state of his sights; saying, "I perceive that in the world from which you are come, you had been twofold, having been different in internals from what you were in externals; in externals you were a civil, moral, and rational man; whereas in internals you were neither civil, moral, nor rational, because

a whoremonger and an adulterer: and such men, when they are
allowed to ascend into heaven, and are there kept in their externals, are able to see the heavenly things there; but when
their internals are opened, instead of heavenly things they see
8 infernal things. Know, however, that with every one in this
world, the externals are successively closed, and the internals
are opened, and thereby they are prepared either for heaven or
for hell; and as the evil of whoredom defiles the internals of
the mind more than every other evil, you must needs be conveyed down to the defiled [states] of your love, and these are in
the hells, where the caverns stink of ordure. Who cannot
know from reason, that what is unchaste and lascivious in the
spiritual world is impure and unclean, and thus that nothing
more pollutes and defiles a man, and induces in him what is infernal? Take heed therefore how you boast any more of your
whoredom, that in it you show yourself a more masculine man
than others. I forewarn you that you will become very weak,
so that you will scarce know where your masculine power is.
Such is the lot which awaits those who boast of their power of
whoredom."

On hearing these words he descended, and returned into the world of spirits, and to his former companions, and conversed with them modestly and chastely for a time, but nevertheless not for long.

ADULTERIES: THEIR KINDS AND DEGREES.

478. No one can know that there is any evil in adultery who judges of it only from externals; for in the externals it is like marriage. Such external judges, when internal things are named, and it be said to them that externals derive their good or their evil from the internals, say with themselves, "What are internals? Who sees them? Is not this climbing above the sphere of every one's intelligence?" Such persons are like those who accept all simulated good as genuine voluntary good, and who judge of a man's wisdom from the elegance of his conversation; or who respect the man himself on account of the richness of his dress and the magnificence of his equipage, and not from his internal habit, which belongs to judgment from the affection of good. This also is like judging of the fruit of a tree, and of any other eatable thing, from the sight and touch only, and not of its goodness from its flavour and from science: such is the conduct of all those who are unwilling to perceive any thing relating to man's internals. Hence comes the insanity of many at the present day, in that they see no evil in adulteries, yea, conjoin marriages with adulteries in the same bridal-chamber, that is, make them altogether alike; and this only on account of their appearance of likeness in the externals.

That this is the case, has been clearly proved by the fol- 2
lowing conclusive teaching of experience:—There were once assembled together by the angels, from Europe, some hundreds of those who were distinguished there for their genius, their learning, and their wisdom, and they were questioned about the distinction between marriage and adultery, and intreated to consult the reason of their understandings: and after consultation, all, except ten, replied, that it is only the judicial law that makes a distinction, for the sake of some useful purpose; which [distinction] may indeed be known, but may nevertheless be adapted to circumstances by civil prudence. They were next asked whether they saw any good in marriage and any evil in adultery. They returned for answer, that they did not see any rational evil or any rational good. On being questioned whether they saw any sin in it, they said, "Where is the sin? Is not the deed alike?" At these answers the angels were amazed, and exclaimed, "Oh! how gross and how great is the stupidity of the age!" On hearing this exclamation, the hun-

dreds of the wise ones turned themselves, and said to each other with loud laughter, "Is this gross stupidity? Can there be any wisdom that can bring conviction that loving another man's wife merits eternal damnation?"

3 But that adultery is spiritual evil, and therefore moral evil, and civil evil, and diametrically contrary to the wisdom of reason; also that the love of adultery is from hell and returns to hell, and the love of marriage is from heaven and returns to heaven, has been demonstrated in the first chapter of this part, concerning "The Opposition of Scortatory Love and Conjugial Love." But since all evils, like all goods, partake of breadth and height, and according to breadth have their kinds, and according to height their degrees, therefore, in order that adulteries may be known as to each dimension, they shall first be arranged into their kinds, and afterwards into their degrees; and this shall be done in the following series:—

I. *There are three kinds of adulteries,—simple, twofold, and threefold.*

II. *Simple adultery is that of an unmarried man with the wife of another, or of an unmarried woman with the husband of another.*

III. *Twofold adultery is that of a husband with the wife of another, or of a wife with the husband of another.*

IV. *Threefold adultery is with blood-relations.*

V. *There are four degrees of adulteries, according to which their predications, their charges of blame, and after death their imputations, take place.*

VI. *Adulteries of the first degree are adulteries of ignorance, which are committed by those who cannot as yet, or cannot at all, consult the understanding, and thus check them.*

VII. *Adulteries committed by these persons are mild.*

VIII. *Adulteries of the second degree are adulteries of lust, which are committed by those who indeed are able to consult the understanding, but from accidental causes at the moment are not able to do so.*

IX. *Adulteries committed by these persons are imputatory, according as the understanding afterwards favours them or does not favour them.*

X. *Adulteries of the third degree are adulteries of the reason, which are committed by those who confirm with the understanding that they are not evils of sin.*

XI. *The adulteries committed by these persons are grievous, and are imputed to them, according to confirmations.*

XII. *Adulteries of the fourth degree are adulteries of the will, which are committed by those who make them allowable and pleasing, and who do not think them of such great importance as to make it worth while to consult the understanding about them.*

XIII. *The adulteries committed by these persons are exceedingly grievous, and are imputed to them as evils of set purpose, and remain sealed in them as guilt.*

XIV. *Adulteries of the third and fourth degrees are evils of sin, according to the quantity and quality of the understanding and the will in them, whether they are committed in act, or not committed in act.*

XV. *Adulteries from set purpose of the will, and adulteries from confirmation of the understanding, render human beings natural, sensual, and corporeal.*

XVI. *And this to such a degree that at length they reject from themselves all things of the church and of religion.*

XVII. *Nevertheless they possess human rationality like others.*

XVIII. *But they use that rationality when they are in externals, but abuse it when in their internals.*

Now follows the explanation of these articles.

479. I. THERE ARE THREE KINDS OF ADULTERIES,—SIMPLE, TWOFOLD, AND THREEFOLD. The Creator of the universe has distinguished each and all the things that He has created, into kinds, and each kind into species; and He has distinguished each species, and likewise each distinction, and so forth, to the end that an image of the Infinite may exist in a perpetual variety of qualities. Thus the Creator of the universe has distinguished goods and their truths, and likewise evils and their falsities, after they had arisen. That He has distinguished each and all things in the spiritual world into kinds, species, and differences, and has gathered together into heaven all goods and truths, and into hell all evils and falsities, and has arranged the latter in an order diametrically opposite to the former, may be manifest from what has been disclosed in the Work on *Heaven and Hell*, published in London in the year 1758. That in the natural world He has also thus distinguished and does still distinguish goods and truths, and likewise evils and falsities with men, and thus the men themselves, may be known from their lot after death, in that the good possess heaven, and the evil, hell. Now, since all things which belong to good, and all things which belong to evil, are distinguished into kinds, species, and so forth, therefore marriages are distinguished into the same, and likewise their opposites, which are adulteries.

480. II. SIMPLE ADULTERY IS THAT OF AN UNMARRIED MAN WITH THE WIFE OF ANOTHER, OR OF AN UNMARRIED WOMAN WITH THE HUSBAND OF ANOTHER. By adultery here and in the following pages is meant whoredom opposite to marriage. It is opposite because it violates the covenant of life contracted between married partners, rends asunder their love, and defiles it, and closes up the union which was begun at the time of betrothal, and strengthened in the beginning of marriage; for the con-

jugial love of one man with one wife, after the engagement and the covenant, unites their souls. Adultery does not dissolve this union, because it cannot be dissolved; but it closes it up, like one who blocks up a fountain at its source and thence obstructs its stream, and fills the cistern with filthy and stinking waters: in like manner conjugial love, the origin of which is a union of souls, is befouled and covered over by adultery; and when it is thus befouled there rises up from below the love of adultery; and as this love increases, it becomes fleshly, and rises up against conjugial love, and destroys it. Hence is the opposition of adultery and marriage.

481. In order that it may be further known how gross is the stupidity of this age, in that its wise ones do not see any sin in adultery (as was disclosed by the angels, see just above, no. 478), I will here add the following Memorable Relation:—*

There were certain spirits who, from a habit they had acquired in the life of the body, infested me with peculiar adroitness, and this they did by a very gentle and as it were undulating influx, such as that of well-disposed spirits usually is; but it was perceived that there were cunning, and other like elements, in them, to the intent that they might entrap and deceive.

At length I spoke with one of them who, it was told me, had, while he lived in the world, been the general of an army; and as I perceived that in the ideas of his thought there was what was lascivious, I conversed with him in spiritual speech with representatives, which speech fully expresses the meanings, and many things in a moment.

He said that, in the life of the body in the former world, he had accounted adulteries as nothing.

But it was given me to tell him that adulteries are wicked, although on account of the delight which they have taken in them, and from the persuasion thence resulting, they appear to those who are adulterous to be not wicked, but even allowable; which also he might know from this consideration, that marriages are the seminaries of the human race, and consequently also the seminaries of the heavenly kingdom, and therefore that they ought not to be violated, but to be accounted holy; also from this fact (which he ought to know, being in the spiritual world, and in a state of perception), that conjugial love descends from the Lord through heaven, and that from that love, as a parent, is derived mutual love, which is the main support of heaven; and further from this consideration, that adulterers,

* In the original Latin edition, this Memorable Relation is enclosed in inverted commas. It is also given in the *Arcana Cœlestia*, no. 2733; in *Heaven and Hell*, no. 385; and in the *Spiritual Diary*, no. 4405, in which latter passage it is stated that the general mentioned in this Memorable Relation was Prince Eugene.

whenever they but approach the heavenly societies, are made sensible of their own stench, and cast themselves headlong thence towards hell: at least he might know, that violating marriages is contrary to the Divine laws, to the civil laws of all kingdoms, also to the genuine lumen of reason, and thus to the right of nations, because contrary to order both Divine and human; besides many other considerations.

But he replied, that he entertained no such thoughts in the former life. He wanted to reason whether the case was so.

But he was told, that Truth does not admit of reasonings, for reasonings favour the delights of the flesh against the delights of the spirit, the quality of which latter delights he was ignorant of; and that he ought first to think about the things which I had told him, because they are true; or to think from the principle, which is perfectly well-known in the world, that no one should do to another what he is unwilling another should do to him; and thus that he ought to consider whether, if any one had in such a manner deceived his wife, whom he had loved (as is the case in the beginning of every marriage), and he had then been in a state of wrath on that account, and had spoken from that state,—he himself also would not then have detested adulteries, and whether, being a man of talent, he would not then have confirmed himself against them more than other men, even so far as to damn them to hell: and being the general of an army, and having brave companions, whether he would not, in order to prevent disgrace, either have put the adulterer to death, or have cast the adulteress out of his house.

482. III. Twofold adultery is that of a husband with the wife of another, or of a wife with the husband of another. This adultery is called twofold, because it is committed by two, and on each side the covenant of marriage is violated: wherefore also it is twofold more grievous than the former. It was said above (no. 480), that the conjugial love of one man with one wife, after the engagement and the covenant, unites their souls, and that that union is that very love in its origin; and that this origin is closed up and blocked up by adultery, as the source and stream of a fountain. That the souls of two unite themselves, when love for the sex is restricted to one woman or one man of the sex, which is the case when a maiden engages herself wholly to a young man, and on the other hand a young man engages himself wholly to a maiden, is clearly evident from this consideration, that the lives of both unite themselves, consequently their souls, because the souls are the beginnings of life. This union of souls cannot possibly exist except in monogamous marriages, or those of one man with one wife, but not in polygamous marriages, or those of one man with several wives; because in the latter marriages the

love is divided, in the former marriages it is united. The reason why conjugial love in this supreme abode is spiritual, holy, and pure, is, that the soul of every human being, by reason of its origin, is celestial, wherefore it receives influx immediately from the Lord, for it receives from Him the marriage of love and wisdom, or of good and truth; and this influx makes him a human being, and distinguishes him from the beasts. From this union of souls, conjugial love, which is there in its spiritual holiness and purity, flows down into the life of the whole body, and fills it with blessed delights, so long as its channel remains open; which is the case with those who are made spiritual by the Lord. That nothing but adultery closes up and blocks up this seat, origin, or fountain and its channel, of conjugial love, is evident from the Lord's words, that it is not lawful to put away a wife and marry another, except on account of adultery (Matt. xix. 3–9); and also from what is said in the same passage, that he who marries her that is put away commits adultery (verse 9). When therefore, as was said above, that pure and holy fountain is blocked up, it is clogged about with filthinesses, as a jewel with ordure, or bread with vomit; which things are altogether opposite to the purity and holiness of that fountain, or of conjugial love: from which opposition comes conjugial cold, and according to this cold is the voluptuous lewdness of scortatory love, which consumes itself of its own accord. The reason why this is an evil of sin is, that what is holy is covered over, and thereby its channel into the body is obstructed, and in the place thereof what is profane succeeds, and its channel into the body is opened; hence a man from heavenly becomes infernal.

483. To the above I will add some things from the spiritual world, which are worthy of relation.

* I have heard in that world, that some married men have the lust of committing whoredom with undeflowered women or maidens; some with deflowered women, or whores; some with married women or wives; some with women who are of noble family; and some with such as are not of noble family. That this is the case, I have been confirmed by several instances from the various kingdoms in that world.

While I was meditating about the variety of such lusts, I asked whether there are any who find all their delight with the wives of others, and none with unmarried women? Wherefore, in order that I might know that there are such, several were brought to me from a certain kingdom, who were compelled to speak according to their lustfulness. These said that it was,

* In the original Latin edition, the following Memorable Relation is enclosed in inverted commas. The men who are the subject of this Relation are referred to in the *Spiritual Diary*, nos. 6103[2], 6110[71], and 6110[73], as English Lords.

and still is, their sole pleasure and delight to commit adultery with the wives of others; and that they look out for such as are beautiful, and hire them for themselves at a great price according to their wealth, and generally make arrangements about the price with the wife alone.

I asked why they did not hire for themselves unmarried women.

They said, that this to them would be common, and thus in itself cheap, in which there would be nothing delightful for them.

I asked also, whether those wives afterwards return to their husbands and live with them.

They replied, that they either do not return, or they live coldly with them, because they have become harlots.

Afterwards I asked them seriously, whether they ever thought, or now think, that this is twofold adultery, because they commit it while they are married men, and that such adultery ravages a human being of all spiritual good.

But at this most of those who were present laughed, saying, "What is spiritual good?"

But I persisted, saying, "What is more detestable than for a man to mix his soul with the soul of the husband in his wife? Do you not know that the soul of a man (*vir*) is in his seed?"

Hereupon they turned away, and muttered, "What harm can this do there?"

At length I said, "Although you do not fear Divine laws, do you not fear the civil laws?"

They replied, "No; we only fear certain of the ecclesiastical order; but we conceal this in their presence; and if we cannot conceal it, we keep on good terms with them."

I afterwards saw them divided into companies, and some of these cast into hell.

484. IV. Threefold adultery is with blood-relations. This adultery is called threefold, because it is threefold more grievous than the two former. The blood-relations, or remains of the flesh, which are not to be approached unto, may be seen enumerated in Leviticus xviii. 6–18. The reasons why these adulteries are threefold more grievous than the two above-mentioned kinds, are internal and external; the internal reasons are based on the correspondence of those adulteries with the violation of spiritual marriage, which is the marriage of the Lord and the church, and thus of good and truth; and the external reasons are for the sake of guards, to prevent man becoming a beast. There is not room, however, to proceed to the disclosure of these reasons.

485. V. There are four degrees of adulteries, according

TO WHICH THEIR PREDICATIONS, THEIR CHARGES OF BLAME, AND AFTER DEATH THEIR IMPUTATIONS, TAKE PLACE. These degrees are not genera, but they enter into each genus, and constitute its distinctions between more and less evil or good; in the present case, deciding whether adultery of any given kind, by reason of the circumstances and contingencies, is to be considered milder or more grievous. That circumstances and contingencies vary every thing, is known. Nevertheless things are considered in one way by a man from his rational lumen, in another by a judge from the law, and in another by the Lord from the state of the man's mind: wherefore they are called predications, charges of blame, and after death imputations; for predications are made by a man according to his rational lumen, charges of blame are made by a judge according to the law, and imputations are made by the Lord according to the state of the man's mind. That these three differ exceedingly from each other may be seen without explanation: for a man, from rational conviction according to the circumstances and contingencies, may acquit a person, whom a judge, when he sits in judgment, cannot acquit in accordance with the law; and again, a judge may acquit a person, who after death is damned. The reason is, that a judge gives sentence according to the deeds, whereas after death every one is judged according to the intentions of the will and thence of the understanding, and according to the confirmations of the understanding and thence of the will: these intentions and confirmations a judge does not see. Nevertheless both judgments are just; the one for the sake of the good of civil society, the other for the sake of the good of heavenly society.

486. VI. ADULTERIES OF THE FIRST DEGREE ARE ADULTERIES OF IGNORANCE, WHICH ARE COMMITTED BY THOSE WHO CANNOT AS YET, OR CANNOT AT ALL, CONSULT THE UNDERSTANDING AND THUS CHECK THEM. All evils, and thus also all adulteries, considered in themselves, belong at once to the internal and the external man; the internal man intends them, and the external man does them; such therefore as the internal man is in the deeds done by the external, such are the deeds viewed in themselves. But since the internal man with his intention does not appear before man, every one must be judged in court by his deeds and words according to the law in force and its previsions: the interior sense of the law must also be discerned by the judge. But let examples illustrate the case: if adultery happens to be committed by a youth, who does not as yet know that adultery is a greater evil than fornication; if the like be committed by a man of extreme simplicity; if it be committed by a person who is deprived by disease of the full powers of judgment; or, as is sometimes the case, by a person who is subject to attacks of delirium, and is at the time in a state in which are they who are in reality

delirious: yet again, if it be committed in a fit of insane drunkenness, and so forth; it is manifest that, in such cases, the internal man, or mind, is not present in the external, scarcely any otherwise than in an irrational person. Adulteries in these instances are distinguished by a rational man according to the above circumstances; nevertheless the perpetrator is charged with blame by the same rational man as a judge, and is punished in accordance with the law; but after death those adulteries are imputed according to the presence, quality, and faculty of understanding in the will of the perpetrators.

487. VII. ADULTERIES COMMITTED BY THESE PERSONS ARE MILD. This is manifest from what was said just above, no. 486, without further confirmation; for it is known that the quality of every deed, and in general the quality of every thing, depends upon circumstances, and that these mitigate or aggravate it; but adulteries of this degree are mild at the first times of their commission; and they also remain mild in proportion as the offender of either sex, in the future course of life, abstains from them for these reasons,—that they are evils against God, or against the neighbour, or against the goods of the state, and that in consequence of their being such evils, they are evils against reason; but on the other hand, if they are not abstained from for one of the above-mentioned reasons, they are reckoned among grievous adulteries; thus it is according to the Divine law in Ezek. xviii. 21, 22, 24, and in other places; but they cannot, from the above circumstances, be pronounced either blameless or culpable, or be predicated and judged as mild or grievous, by man, because they do not appear before him; neither is it the province of his judgment to do so: wherefore it is meant that after death they are so accounted or imputed.

488. VIII. ADULTERIES OF THE SECOND DEGREE ARE ADULTERIES OF LUST, WHICH ARE COMMITTED BY THOSE WHO INDEED ARE ABLE TO CONSULT THE UNDERSTANDING, BUT FROM ACCIDENTAL CAUSES AT THE MOMENT ARE NOT ABLE TO DO SO. There are two things which in the beginning with every man who from natural is made spiritual, are at strife together, which are commonly called the spirit and the flesh; and since the love of marriage is of the spirit, and the love of adultery is of the flesh, there takes place then also a combat between those loves. If the love of marriage conquers, it masters and subjugates the love of adultery, and this is effected by its removal; but if it happens that the lust of the flesh is excited to a heat greater than the spirit can control from reason, it follows that the state is inverted, and the heat of lust overcomes the spirit with allurements to such a degree that it is no longer master of its reason, and thus of itself. This is meant by adulteries of the second

degree, which are committed by those who indeed are able to consult the understanding, but by reason of accidental causes at the moment are not able. But the matter may be illustrated by examples; as, if a meretricious wife by her cunning captivates a man's mind (*animus*), enticing him into her bed-chamber, and inflaming him till he loses control of his judgment; and especially if, at the same time, she also threatens to expose him if he does not consent: likewise, if any meretricious wife is skilled in sorceries, or by drugged potions inflames the man to such a degree, that the raging desire (*oestrum*) of the flesh deprives the understanding of the free use of reason: likewise, if a man, by seductive enticements, works upon another man's wife till her inflamed will is no longer master of itself; besides other like cases. That these and similar accidental circumstances lessen the grievousness of adultery, and give a milder turn to the predications of the blame thereof in favour of the party seduced, is agreeable to the dictates and conclusions of reason. The imputation of this degree of adultery comes next to be treated of.

489. IX. Adulteries committed by these persons are imputatory, according as the understanding afterwards favours them or does not favour them. In proportion as the understanding favours evils, in the same proportion the man appropriates them to himself and makes them his own. Favour implies consent; and consent induces in the mind a state of the love of evils. The case is the same with adulteries, which in the beginning were committed without the consent of the understanding, and are favoured: the contrary comes to pass if afterwards they are not favoured. The reason is, that evils or adulteries which are committed in the blindness of the understanding, are committed from the concupiscence of the body; which [evils or adulteries] have a near resemblance to such instincts as beasts have: with man indeed the understanding is present while they are being committed, but in a passive or dead force, and not in an active or living force. From these considerations it follows of itself, that such things are not imputed, except in the proportion in which they are afterwards favoured or not favoured. By imputation is here meant accusation after death, and thence adjudication, which takes place according to the state of the man's spirit: but there is not meant inculpation by a man before a judge; for this does not take place according to the state of the man's spirit, but according to the state of the body in the deed; and unless there was a difference herein, those would be acquitted after death who are acquitted in the world, and those would be condemned who are condemned in the world; and thus the latter would have no hope of salvation.

490. X. ADULTERIES OF THE THIRD DEGREE ARE ADULTERIES OF THE REASON, WHICH ARE COMMITTED BY THOSE WHO CONFIRM WITH THE UNDERSTANDING THAT THEY ARE NOT EVILS OF SIN. Every man knows that there exist the will and the understanding; for in common speech he says, "This I will, and this I understand;" but still he does not distinguish them, but makes the one the same as the other. The reason is that he only reflects upon the things which belong to the thought from the understanding, and not upon those which belong to the love from the will; for the latter do not appear in light as the former do. Nevertheless, he who does not distinguish between the will and the understanding, cannot distinguish between evils and goods, and consequently he cannot know anything at all about the blame of sin. But who does not know that good and truth are two distinct things, like love and wisdom? and who cannot thence conclude, when he is in rational enlightenment (*lumen*), that there are two [faculties] in man, which distinctly receive and appropriate to themselves those principles, and that the one is the will and the other the understanding, by reason that what the will receives and reproduces is called good, and what the understanding receives is called truth? for what the will loves and does, is called good, and what the understanding perceives and thinks, is called truth.
Now, since the marriage of good and truth was treated of in 2
the first part of this Work, and in the same place many propositions were adduced concerning the will and the understanding, and the various attributes and predicates of each, (which, as I imagine, are also perceived by those who had not thought anything distinctly concerning the understanding and the will, for human reason is such, that it understands truths from the light thereof, although it has not heretofore distinguished them;) therefore, in order that the distinctions of the understanding and the will may be more clearly perceived, I will here mention some particulars on the subject, to the end that it may be known what is the quality of adulteries of the reason or the understanding, and afterwards what is the quality
of adulteries of the will. The following propositions may 3
help to distinguish them: 1. The will alone of itself does nothing; but whatever it does, it does by means of the understanding. 2. On the other hand also, the understanding alone of itself does nothing; but whatever it does, it does from the will. 3. The will flows in into the understanding but not the understanding into the will; yet the understanding teaches what is good and evil, and consults with the will, that out of those two it may choose and do what is pleasing to it. 4. After this there is effected a twofold conjunction; one, in which the will acts from within and the understanding from without; the other, in which the

understanding acts from within and the will from without. Thus are distinguished adulteries of the reason, which are here treated of, from adulteries of the will, which are next to be treated of. They are distinguished, because one is more grievous than the other; for adultery of the reason is less grievous than adultery of the will; the reason is, that in adultery of the reason, the understanding acts from within and the will from without; whereas in adultery of the will, the will acts from within and the understanding from without; and the will is the man himself, and the understanding is the man, by virtue of the will [in the understanding]; and that which acts within has dominion over that which acts without.

491. XI. THE ADULTERIES COMMITTED BY THESE PERSONS ARE GRIEVOUS, [AND ARE IMPUTED TO THEM,] ACCORDING TO CONFIRMATIONS. The understanding alone confirms, and when it confirms, it engages the will, and sets it about itself, and thus drives it to compliance. Confirmations are effected by means of reasonings, which the mind seizes either from its higher region or from its lower region: if from the higher region, which communicates with heaven, it confirms marriages, and damns adulteries; but if from the lower region, which communicates with the world, it confirms adulteries and makes light of marriages. Every one can confirm evil just as well as good; likewise falsity and truth; and the confirmation of evil is perceived as more delectable than the confirmation of good, and the confirmation of falsity appears more lucid than the confirmation of truth. The reason is, that the confirmation of evil and falsity derives its reasonings from the delights, pleasures, appearances, and fallacies of the senses of the body; whereas the confirmation of good and truth derives its reasons from the region above the sensuals of the body. Now, since evils and falsities can be confirmed just as well as goods and truths, and since the confirming understanding draws the will over to its own side, and the will together with the understanding forms the mind, it follows, that the form of the human mind is according to confirmations, being turned towards heaven if its confirmations are in favour of marriages, but towards hell if they are in favour of adulteries; and such as the form of a man's mind is, such is his spirit; consequently such is the man. From these considerations then it is manifest, that adulteries of this degree are imputed after death according to confirmations.

492. XII. ADULTERIES OF THE FOURTH DEGREE ARE ADULTERIES OF THE WILL, WHICH ARE COMMITTED BY THOSE WHO MAKE THEM ALLOWABLE AND PLEASING, AND WHO DO NOT THINK THEM OF SUCH GREAT IMPORTANCE AS TO MAKE IT WORTH WHILE TO CONSULT THE UNDERSTANDING ABOUT THEM. These adulteries are distin-

guished from the foregoing by their origins. The origin of these adulteries is from the depraved will connate to man, or from hereditary evil, which a man blindly obeys after he has become capable of exercising his own judgment, not at all judging about them whether they are evils or not; wherefore it is said, that he does not consider them of such great importance as to make it worth while to consult the understanding about them. But the origin of the adulteries which are called adulteries of the reason, is from a perverted understanding; and they are committed by those who confirm that they are not evils of sin. With these adulterers, the understanding plays the leading part; with the former, the will. These two distinctions do not appear to any man in the natural world; but they appear plainly to the angels in the spiritual world. In the latter world all are in general distinguished according to the evils which originally flow from the will or from the understanding, and which are accepted and appropriated. They are also separated in hell according to those evils: in hell, those who are evil from the understanding, dwell in front, and are called satans; but those who are evil from the will, dwell behind, and are called devils. On account of this universal distinction, mention is made in the Word of satan and the devil. With those evil ones, and also with adulterers, who are called satans, the understanding plays the leading part; but with those who are called devils, the will plays the leading part. But it is not possible to explain these distinctions so that the understanding may see them, unless the distinctions of the will and the understanding be first known; and unless a description be given of the formation of the mind by the will through the understanding, and of its formation by the understanding through the will. The Knowledge of these subjects must shed light before, in order that the distinctions above-mentioned may be seen by the reason; but this requires a volume to itself.

493. XIII. The adulteries committed by these persons are exceedingly grievous, and are imputed to them as evils of set purpose, and remain seated in them as guilt. The reason why they are exceedingly grievous, and more grievous than the foregoing, is, that in them the will plays the leading part, whereas in the foregoing the understanding plays the leading part, and a man's life essentially is of his will, and formally is of his understanding: the reason is, that the will acts in unity with the love, and love is the essence of a man's life, and forms itself in the understanding by means of such things as are in agreement with it: wherefore the understanding, considered in itself, is nothing else than the form of the will; and since love is of the will, and wisdom of the understanding, therefore wisdom is nothing else than the form of love; likewise truth is nothing

else than the form of good. That which flows from the very essence of a man's life, thus which flows from his will or his love, is principally called purpose; but that which flows from the form of his life, thus from the understanding and its thought, is called intention. Guilt also is principally predicated of the will: hence comes the common observation, that every one has the guilt of evil from inheritance, but that the evil is from the man. Hence it is, that these adulteries of the fourth degree are imputed as evils of set purpose, and remain seated in them as guilt.

494. XIV. ADULTERIES OF THE THIRD AND FOURTH DEGREES ARE EVILS OF SIN, ACCORDING TO THE QUANTITY AND QUALITY OF THE UNDERSTANDING AND THE WILL IN THEM, WHETHER THEY ARE COMMITTED IN ACT, OR NOT COMMITTED IN ACT. That adulteries of the reason or the understanding, which are of the third degree, and adulteries of the will, which are of the fourth degree, are grievous, consequently evils of sin, according to the quality of the understanding and of the will in them, may be seen from the comment above concerning them, nos. 490–493. The reason is, that man is man by virtue of the will and the understanding; for from these two faculties exist not only all the things which are done in the mind, but also all those which are done in the body. Who does not know that the body does not act of itself, but the will through the body? also that the mouth does not speak of itself, but the thought through the mouth? Wherefore if the will were to be taken away, action would instantly come to a stop, and if thought were to be taken away, the speech of the mouth would instantly cease. Hence it is clearly manifest, that adulteries which are committed in act are grievous according to the quantity and quality of the understanding and will in them. That they are likewise grievous, if the same are not committed in act, is manifest from the Lord's words: "*It was said by them of old time, Thou shalt not commit adultery; but I say unto you, that if any one hath looked at another's woman, so as to lust after her, he hath already committed adultery with her in heart* (Matt. v. 27, 28): committing adultery
2 in the heart means committing it in the will. There are many reasons which prevent an adulterer's being an adulterer in act while he is nevertheless an adulterer in will and understanding: for there are some who abstain from adulteries as to the act through fear of the civil law and its penalties; through fear of the loss of reputation and thence of honour; through fear of diseases thence arising; through fear of quarrels at home on the part of the wife, and the consequent loss of tranquillity of life; through fear of revenge on the part of the husband or relations, and also through fear of being whipped by the servants; through poverty or avarice; through weakness arising from disease, from abuse.

from age, or from impotence, and consequent shame. If any one restrains himself from adulteries in act, for these and like reasons, and yet favours them in his will and understanding, he is still an adulterer; for he believes nevertheless that they are not sins, and he does not make them unlawful before God in his spirit; and thus he commits them in spirit, although not in the body before the world; wherefore after death, when he becomes a spirit, he speaks openly in favour of them.

495. XV. ADULTERIES FROM SET PURPOSE OF THE WILL, AND ADULTERIES FROM CONFIRMATION OF THE UNDERSTANDING, RENDER HUMAN BEINGS NATURAL, SENSUAL, AND CORPOREAL. Man is man, and is distinguished from the beasts, by this circumstance, that his mind is distinguished into three regions, as many as the heavens are; and that he is capable of being elevated out of the lowest region into the higher, and also from this into the highest, and thus of becoming an angel of one of the heavens, and even of the third. For this end, there has been given to man the faculty of elevating the understanding thereunto; but if the love of his will is not elevated at the same time, he does not become spiritual, but remains natural. Nevertheless he retains the faculty of elevating the understanding. The reason why he retains this faculty is, in order that he may be able to be reformed; for he is reformed by means of the understanding: and this is effected by the Knowledges of good and truth, and by means of rational intuition therefrom. If he views those Knowledges rationally, and lives according to them, then the love of the will is elevated at the same time, and in the same degree what is human is perfected, and the man becomes more and
more a man. It is otherwise if he does not live according to 2
the Knowledges of good and truth: in this case the love of his will remains natural, and his understanding by turns becomes spiritual; for it elevates itself alternately, like an eagle, and looks down upon what belongs to its love beneath; and when it sees this, it flies down to it, and conjoins itself with it: if therefore the concupiscences of the flesh belong to its love, it lets itself down to these from its height, and in conjunction with them derives delight to itself from their delights; and again, for the sake of the acquisition of reputation, that it may be believed wise, it lifts itself on high, and thus rises and sinks by turns, as
was just now stated. The reason why adulterers of the third 3
and fourth degree, who are such as from set purpose of the will and confirmation of the understanding have made themselves adulterers, are utterly natural, and progressively become sensual and corporeal, is, that they have immersed the love of their will, and together with it their understanding, in the uncleannesses of scortatory love, and are delighted therewith, as unclean birds and beasts are delighted with decaying and stercoraceous

things as with delicacies and dainties; for the effluvia rising up from their flesh fill the dwelling of the mind with their grossnesses, and cause the will to perceive nothing to be more delicate and dainty. It is these who after death become corporeal spirits, and from whom the uncleannesses of hell and of the church (spoken of above, nos. 430, 431) gush out.

496. There are three degrees of the natural man. In the first degree are those who love only the world, placing their heart on wealth; these are properly meant by the natural. In the second degree are those who love only the delights of the senses, placing their heart on every kind of luxury and pleasure; these are properly meant by the sensual. In the third degree are those who love only themselves, placing their heart on the quest of honour; these are properly meant by the corporeal; the reason is, that they immerse all things of the will, and consequently of the understanding, in the body, and look backwards from others at themselves, and love only what belongs to themselves. But the sensual immerse all things of the will and consequently of the understanding in the allurements and fallacies of the senses, indulging in these alone. Whereas the natural pour forth into the world all things of the will and of the understanding, covetously and fraudulently acquiring wealth, and regarding no other use therein and thence but that of possession. The above-mentioned adulteries turn human beings into these degenerate degrees, one into this, and another into that; each one according to the pleasurable feeling characteristic of his peculiar genius.

497. XVI. AND THIS TO SUCH A DEGREE THAT AT LENGTH THEY REJECT FROM THEMSELVES ALL THINGS OF THE CHURCH AND OF RELIGION. The reason why adulterers from set purpose and adulterers from confirmation reject from themselves all things of the church and religion, is, that the love of marriage and the love of adultery are opposite (no. 425), and the love of marriage acts in unity with the church and religion (see no. 130, and throughout the First Part): hence the love of adultery, because it is opposite, acts in unity with those things which are contrary to the church. Another reason why those adulterers reject from themselves all things of the church and religion, is, that the love of marriage and the love of adultery are opposite, as the marriage of good and truth is opposite to the connubial connection of evil and falsity (see nos. 427, 428): and the marriage of good and truth constitutes the church, whereas the connubial connection of evil and falsity constitutes the antichurch. Yet another reason why those adulterers reject from themselves all things of the church and religion, is, that the love of marriage and the love of adultery are opposite, as heaven

and hell are (no. 429); and in heaven there is the love of all things of the church, whereas in hell there is hatred against them. A further reason why those adulterers reject from themselves all things of the church and of religion, is, that their delightsomenesses commence from the flesh, and are of the flesh even in the spirit (nos. 440, 441), and the flesh is contrary to the spirit, that is, contrary to the spiritual things of the church: hence also the delightsomenesses of scortatory love are called the pleasures of insanity. If you desire demonstration, pray go to those whom you know to be such adulterers, and ask them privately, what they think about God, the church, and eternal life, and you will hear. The genuine reason is, that as conjugial love opens the interiors of the mind, and thus elevates them above the sensuals of the body, even into the light and heat of heaven, so, on the other hand, the love of adultery closes up the interiors of the mind, and thrusts down the mind itself, as to its will, into the body, even into all the lusts of its flesh; and the deeper it thrusts it down, the further it withdraws and removes it from heaven.

498. XVII. NEVERTHELESS THEY POSSESS HUMAN RATIONALITY LIKE OTHERS. That the natural, the sensual, and the corporeal man is equally rational, as to the understanding, as the spiritual man, has been proved to me from satans and devils arising up by leave out of hell, and conversing with angelic spirits in the world of spirits; concerning whom, see the Memorable Relations throughout. But as the love of the will makes the man, and this love draws the understanding into consent, therefore such are not rational except in a state removed from the love of the will; when they return again into this love, they are more dreadfully insane than wild beasts. But man, without the faculty of elevating the understanding above the love of the will, would not be a man, but a beast; for a beast does not enjoy that faculty; consequently neither would he be able to choose anything, and from choice do what is good and expedient, and thus he would not be able to be reformed, and to be led to heaven, and to live to eternity. Hence it is, that adulterers from set purpose and confirmation, although they are merely natural, sensual, and corporeal, still possess, like other men, the gift of understanding, or rationality: but when they are in the lust of adultery, and think and speak from that lust concerning it, they do not enjoy that rationality; the reason is, that at that time the flesh acts on the spirit, and not the spirit on the flesh. It ought however to be known, that these at length after death become stupid; not that the faculty of becoming wise is taken away from them, but that they are unwilling to become wise, because wisdom is undelightful to them.

499. XVIII. But they use that rationality when they are in externals, but abuse it when they are in their internals. They are in externals when they speak abroad and in company, but in their internals when at home or by themselves. If you wish, put the matter to the test. Bring some such person, as, for example, one of the order called Jesuits, and cause him to speak in company, or to teach in a temple, concerning God, the holy things of the church, and heaven and hell, and you will hear him a more rational zealot than any other; perhaps also he will move you to sighs and tears for your salvation. But take him into your house, extol him above the [other] orders, call him the father of wisdom, and make yourself his friend, until he opens his heart, and you will hear what he will then preach concerning God, the holy things of the church, and heaven and hell; namely, that they are mere fancies and delusions, and thus bonds invented for souls, whereby great and small, rich and poor, may be caught and bound, and kept under the yoke of their dominion. Let these observations suffice for illustration of what is meant by the statement that natural men, even down to corporeal men, possess human rationality like others, and that they use it when they are in externals, but abuse it when in their internals. The conclusion to be hence deduced is, that no one ought to be judged of from the wisdom of his mouth, but from the wisdom of his life in union therewith:

500. To the above I will add the following Memorable Relation:—

Once in the spiritual world I heard a great tumult: there were some thousands of people gathered together, who cried out, "Let them be punished, let them be punished."

I went nearer, and asked, "What is the matter?"

One who was separate from this great congregation said to me, "They are enraged with anger against three priests, who go about and preach everywhere against adulterers, saying, that adulterers have no acknowledgment of God, and that heaven is closed up to them, and hell open; and that in hell they are unclean devils, because they appear there from afar like swine wallowing in dung, and that the angels of heaven abominate them."

I inquired, "Where are those priests? and why is there such a vociferation on that account?"

He replied, "The three priests are in the midst of them, guarded by attendants; and those who are gathered together are of those who believe adulteries not to be sins, and who say, that adulterers have an acknowledgment of God equally with those who cleave to their wives. They are all of them from the Christian world; and the angels have been to see how many there were there who

believe adulteries to be sins; and out of a thousand they did not find a hundred." He then told me, that the nine hundred 2
speak about adulteries in the following manner: "Who does not know that the delight of adultery is superior to the delight of marriage; that adulterers are in perpetual heat, and thence in alacrity, industry, and active life, superior to those who live with only one woman; and that, on the other hand, love with a married partner grows cold, and sometimes to such a degree, that at length scarce a single expression of speech or act of endearment with her is alive; that it is otherwise with whores; that the deadness of life with a wife, which arises from a defect of potency, is recruited and vivified by whoredoms? Is not that which recruits and vivifies of more consequence than that which deadens? What is marriage but lawful whoredom? Who knows any distinction between them? Can love be forced? and yet love with a wife is forced by a covenant and by the laws. Is not love with a married partner the love of the sex? and this love is so universal that it exists even among birds and beasts. What is conjugial love but the love of the sex? and the love of the sex is free with every woman. The reason why the civil laws are against adulteries is, that lawgivers have believed that it is required by the public good; and yet lawgivers and judges themselves sometimes commit adultery, and say among themselves, 'Let him that is without sin cast the first stone.' It is only the simple and religious that believe adulteries to be sins: the intelligent think otherwise, who like us view them by the lumen of nature. Are not offspring born of adulteries as well as of 3
marriages? Are not illegitimate children as clever and well qualified for the discharge of offices and employments as legitimate ones? Moreover families, otherwise barren, are provided with offspring; and is not this an advantage and not an injury? What harm does it do a wife if she admits several rivals? And what harm does it do the husband? To say that it brings disgrace upon the husband, is a frivolous opinion based on mere phantasy. The fact that adultery is contrary to the laws and statutes of the church, is owing to the ecclesiastical order for the sake of Power: but what have theology, and spiritual matters, to do with a merely corporeal and carnal delight? Are not there presbyters and monks who are adulterers? and are they on that account incapable of acknowledging and worshipping God? Why therefore do those three priests preach that adulterers have no acknowledgment of God? We cannot endure such blasphemies; wherefore let them be judged and punished."

After this I saw that they called judges, whom they requested 4
to pass sentence of punishment upon them. But the judges said, "This is no part of our duty; for the point in question is

concerning the acknowledgment of God, and concerning sin, and thus concerning salvation and damnation; and judgment on these subjects must be given from heaven: but we will give you counsel how you may know whether these three priests have preached Truths. There are three places known to us as judges, where such points are examined and revealed in a singular manner: ONE place is where a way into heaven is open to all; but when they come into heaven, they themselves perceive their own quality as to the acknowledgment of God: the SECOND place is, where also a way is open into heaven; but no one can enter into that way unless he has heaven in himself: and the THIRD place is, where there is a way to hell; and those who love infernal things enter that way of their own accord, because from delight. We as judges charge you all who require judgment from us concerning heaven and hell, to go to those places."

5 On hearing this, those who were gathered together said, "Let us go to those places."

And while they were going to the FIRST, where a way into heaven is open to all, it suddenly became very dark; wherefore some of them lighted torches and carried them before. The judges who were with them said, "This happens to all who go to the first place: as they approach, the fire of the torches becomes dimmer, and is extinguished in that place by the light of heaven flowing in, which is a sign that they are there: the reason is, that at first heaven is closed to them, and is afterwards opened."

They then came to that place, and when the torches were extinguished of themselves, they saw a way tending obliquely upwards into heaven: this way those entered who were enraged with anger against the priests; among the first, those who were adulterers from set purpose, after them those who were adulterers from confirmation; and as they ascended, the first cried out, "Follow;" and those who followed cried out, "Make haste;" and they pressed forward.

6 After the space of nearly an hour, when they were all within in the heavenly society, there appeared a gulf between them and the angels; and the light of heaven above the gulf flowing in into their eyes, opened the interiors of their minds, whereby they were compelled to speak as they interiorly thought; and then they were asked by the angels, whether they acknowledged that there is a God.

The first, who were adulterers from set purpose of the will, replied, "What is God?" And they looked at each other, and said, "Which of you has seen Him?" The second, who were adulterers from confirmation of the understanding, said, "Are not all things of nature? What is there above nature but the sun?" And then the angels said to them, "Depart from us; now you yourselves perceive that you have no acknowledgment of God: when you descend, the interiors of your mind will be closed, and its exteriors opened, and then you can speak against the interiors, and say that there is a God. Believe, that as soon as a man actually becomes an adulterer, heaven is closed against him; and when heaven is closed, God is not acknowledged. Hear the reason: all the uncleanness of hell is from adulterers, and this stinks in heaven like the stinking mire of the streets."

On hearing these things they turned, and descended by three ways; and when they were below, the first and second groups conversing together said, "The priests have conquered there; but we know that we can speak of God equally with them: and when we say that He is, do not we acknowledge Him? The interiors and exteriors of the mind, of which the angels told us, are inventions. But let us go to the second place pointed out by the judges, where a way is open into heaven to those who have heaven in themselves, thus to those who are about to come into heaven."

When they were come thither, a voice proceeded from that 7
heaven, saying, "Close the gates; there are adulterers at hand." Then suddenly the gates were closed, and guards with rods in their hands drove them away, and delivered out of their custody the three priests, against whom they had raised the tumult, and led them into heaven: and instantly, when the gate had been opened for the priests, there breathed forth from heaven upon the rebels the delight of marriage, which, because it was chaste and pure, almost deprived them of life; wherefore, for fear of fainting from suffocation, they hastened to the third place, concerning which the judges said that thence there was a way to hell; and instantly there breathed forth from thence the delight of adultery, whereby those who were adulterers from set purpose, and those who were adulterers from confirmation were so vivified, that they descended as it were dancing, and there like hogs immersed themselves in uncleannesses.

THE LUST OF DEFLORATION.

501. The lusts treated of in the four following chapters, are not only lusts of adultery, but are more grievous than those, since they exist only from adulteries, for they are taken to after adulteries are loathed; as the lust of defloration, which is first treated of, and which cannot previously arise with any one; likewise the lust of varieties, the lust of violation, and the lust of seducing innocences, which are afterwards treated of. They are called lusts, because according to the quantity and quality of the lust for those things, such and so great is their appropriation. In reference specifically to the lust of defloration, in order that the conviction may be brought home that it is a villainy, it shall be made manifest from the following propositions in order:—

I. *The state of a maiden or undeflowered woman before marriage, and after marriage.*

II. *Virginity is the crown of chastity, and the pledge of conjugial love.*

III. *Defloration, without a view to marriage as the end, is the villainy of a robber.*

IV. *The lot of those who have confirmed themselves in the persuasion that the lust of defloration is not an evil of sin, after death is grievous.*

The explanation of these articles follows.

502. I. The state of a maiden or undeflowered woman before marriage, and after marriage. What is the quality of the state of a maiden, before she has been instructed concerning the various particulars of the conjugial torch, has been made known to me by those wives in the spiritual world, who had departed out of the natural world in their infancy, and have been educated in heaven. They said, that when they had come into the marriageable state, from seeing married partners they began to love the conjugial life, but only for the end that they might be called wives, and might live in friendly and trustful intercourse with one man; and also that, being removed from the house of obedience, they might become independent. They also said, that they thought of marriage only from the blessedness of mutual friendship and trust with a consort,
2 and not at all from the delight of any passion. But that their

maiden state was changed after the wedding into a new one, of
which they had previously known nothing at all; and they
declared, that this state was a state of the expansion of all
things of the life of their body from first things to last, to
receive the gifts of their husband, and to unite these gifts to
her own life, that thus she might become his love and his wife;
and that this state commenced from the moment of defloration
(or first union in ultimates), and that after this the flame of love
burned for the husband alone, and that they felt the delights of
that expansion to be heavenly. And further, that as each wife
was introduced into this state by her own husband, and as it is
from him, and thus his in her, it is quite impossible for her to
love any other than him alone. From this account it was made 3
manifest what is the quality of the state of maidens before
marriage and after marriage in heaven. That the state of
those maidens and wives on earth, who are mated in their first
virginal state, is similar to that of the maidens and wives in
heaven, is no secret. What maiden can know that new state
before she is in it? Inquire, and you will learn. The case is
different with those who, before marriage, long for the allurement in consequence of having been taught.

503. II. VIRGINITY IS THE CROWN OF CHASTITY, AND THE PLEDGE OF CONJUGIAL LOVE. Virginity is called the crown of chastity, because it crowns the chastity of marriage: it is also the badge of chastity, wherefore the bride wears a crown on her head at her wedding: it is also a badge of the holiness of marriage; for the bride, after the virgin flower, gives and devotes herself wholly to the bridegroom, at that time the husband, and the husband in return gives and devotes himself wholly to the bride, at that time the wife. Virginity is also called the pledge of conjugial love, because it belongs to the covenant [of marriage], and the covenant is, that love may unite them into one human being, or into one flesh. The men themselves also regard the virginity of the bride before marriage as the crown of her chastity, and as the pledge of conjugial love, and as the very dainty from which the delights of that love are about to commence and to last for ever. From these and the foregoing considerations, it is manifest, that after the girdle is taken away, and the virginity is tasted, the maiden becomes a wife, and if not a wife, she becomes a harlot; for the new state, into which she is then introduced, is a state of love for her husband, and if it is not a state of love for her husband, it is a state of lust.

504. III. DEFLORATION, WITHOUT A VIEW TO MARRIAGE AS THE END, IS THE VILLAINY OF A ROBBER. Some adulterers are possessed by the desire of deflowering maidens, and thus also of deflowering young girls in their age of innocence; they entice

them to such deeds either by the persuasions of procuresses, or by presents made by themselves, or by promises of marriage; and those men after defloration leave them, and continually seek for others and yet others. Moreover, they are not delighted with the objects they have left, but with a continual supply of new ones; and this lust grows till it becomes the chief of the delightsomenesses of their flesh. They add also to the above this crime, that by various cunning artifices they entice maidens about to be married, or immediately after marriage, to offer them the first-fruits of marriage, which also they thus filthily defile. I have heard also, that when that mad desire (*oestrum*) with its potency has failed, they boast of the number of virginities, as of so many golden fleeces of Jason.
2 This villainy, which is an act of corruption (*stuprum*), since it was begun in the age of strength, and afterwards strengthened by boastings, remains inrooted, and thus infixed, after death. What the quality of this villainy is, appears from what was said above, that virginity is the crown of chastity, the pledge of future conjugial love, and that a maiden devotes her soul and life to him on whom she bestows it; conjugial friendship and the confidence thereof are also founded upon it. Moreover, a woman deflowered by such [adulterers], after this door of conjugial love has been broken through, casts away shame, and becomes a harlot, and for this result also, that robber is re-
3 sponsible. Such robbers, if, after having run through a course of those venereal lusts (*satyriases*) and profanations of chastity, they apply their mind (*animus*) to marriage, have no other object in their mind (*mens*) than the virginity of their future married partner; and when they have sipped this, they loathe both bed and bed-chamber, yea, even the whole female sex except young girls: and as such men are violators of marriage, and despisers of the female sex, and thus spiritual robbers, it is evident that the Divine Nemesis pursues them.

505. IV. THE LOT OF THOSE WHO HAVE CONFIRMED THEMSELVES IN THE PERSUASION THAT THE LUST OF DEFLORATION IS NOT AN EVIL OF SIN, AFTER DEATH IS GRIEVOUS. Their lot is as follows: After they have passed the first time of their stay in the world of spirits, which is a time of [external] modesty and morality on account of their being in company with angelic spirits, they are let from their externals into their internals, and then into the concupiscences which they had been addicted to in the world; and they are let into their concupiscences, to the end that it may appear in what degree they had been [addicted to them]; and if in a lesser degree, that after they have been let into them, they may be let out again, and may be covered with shame.
2 But those who had been in this malignant lust to such a degree that they felt its delight to be eminent, and made a boast of those

thefts as of the choicest spoils, do not suffer themselves to be drawn away from it; wherefore they are let into their freedom, and then they instantly wander about, and inquire after brothels, and also enter them when they are pointed out; these brothels are at the sides of hell. But when they meet with none but prostitutes there, they go away, and inquire where there are maidens; and then they are conducted to whores, who by phantasy can assume super-eminent beauty, and a florid girlish complexion, and boast themselves of being maidens; and on seeing these they burn with desire towards them as in the world: wherefore they bargain with them, but when they are about to realize the bargain, the phantasy that had been cast on them by heaven is taken away, and then those maidens appear in their own deformity, monstrous and dusky, to whom nevertheless they are compelled to cleave for an hour; those whores
are called sirens. But if by such sorcerers' tricks they do not 3
suffer themselves to be drawn away from that insane lust, they are cast down into the hell which is in the confines of the south and west, beneath the hell of the most cunning harlots, and there they are associated with their companions. It has also been given me to see them in that hell; and I have been told that many of noble descent, and of the richer class, are therein; but because they had been such in the world, all remembrance of their descent and of the dignity derived from their wealth is taken from them, and a persuasion is induced on them that they
have been vile slaves, and thus unworthy of all honour. Among 4
themselves indeed they appear as human beings: but in the sight of others who are allowed to look in thither, they appear like apes, with grim instead of pleasant faces, and savage instead of pleasant countenances; they walk with the loins contracted, and bowed in consequence, the upper part of the body leaning forwards as if they were going to fall down, and they emit a bad smell. They loathe the sex, and turn away from those of the sex whom they see, for they have no desire towards them. They appear such when seen near at hand; but when seen from afar, they appear like dogs of indulgences or whelps of delights; and there is also heard something like barking in the tone of their speech.

THE LUST OF VARIETIES.

506. By the lust of varieties which is treated of here, is not meant the lust of fornication, which was treated of in its proper chapter: the latter lust, notwithstanding its being usually promiscuous and wandering, still does not occasion the lust of varieties, except when it exceeds the bounds of moderation, and the fornicator looks to number, and boasts thereof from cupidity: this idea initiates this lust. But of what quality it is in its progression cannot be distinctly perceived, except in some such series as the following:—

I. *By the lust of varieties is meant the utterly dissolute lust of whoredom.*

II. *That lust is love and at the same time loathing for the sex.*

III. *That lust utterly annihilates conjugial love with itself.*

IV. *The lot after death of those [who have been addicted to that lust] is miserable, since they have not the inmost of life.*

The explanation of these articles now follows.

507. I. By the lust of varieties is meant the utterly dissolute lust of whoredom. This lust insinuates itself with those who in youth have relaxed the bonds of modesty, and have had opportunities of associating with many harlots, especially if they have not wanted for the means of satisfying their pecuniary demands. They implant and inroot this lust in themselves by inordinate and unlimited whoredoms, and by shameless thoughts about the love of the female sex, and by confirmations that adulteries are not evils, and not at all sins. This lust grows with them as it advances, to such an extent that they desire all the women in the world, and wish for whole troops, and a new one every day. Since this love casts itself out of the general love of the sex that is implanted in every human being, and altogether out of the love of one of the sex, which is conjugial love, and intrudes itself into the exteriors of the heart as a delight of love separate from those loves, and yet derived from them; therefore it is so thoroughly inrooted in the cuticles that it remains in the touch after the virile forces are decayed. Those [who are addicted to this lust] make nothing of adulteries; wherefore they think of the whole female sex as of a common whore, and of marriage as of a common harlotry, and thus they mix shamelessness with modesty, and from the mixture become

insane. From these considerations it is evident what is here meant by the lust of varieties, [namely,] that it is the utterly dissolute lust of whoredom.

508. II. THAT LUST IS LOVE AND AT THE SAME TIME LOATHING FOR THE SEX. Those [who are addicted to that lust] have a love for the sex, because they derive variety from the sex; and they have a loathing for the sex, because after enjoying a woman they reject her and lust after others. This obscene lust burns towards a new woman, and after burning, it grows cold towards her; and cold is loathing. That that lust is love and at the same time loathing for the sex, may be illustrated as follows: set on the left side a company of the women whom they have enjoyed, and on the right side a company of those whom they have not enjoyed; would they not look at the latter company from love, but at the former from loathing? and yet each company is of the sex.

509. III. THAT LUST UTTERLY ANNIHILATES CONJUGIAL LOVE WITH ITSELF. The reason is, that that lust is utterly opposed to conjugial love, and so opposed, that it not only tears it asunder, but as it were grinds it to powder, and thus annihilates it: for conjugial love is [confined] to one of the sex; whereas that lust does not stop at one, but within an hour or a day is as intensely cold as it was before hot towards her; and since cold is loathing, this, by forced cohabitation and dwelling together, is so augmented as to inspire nausea, and thus conjugial love is consumed to such a degree that nothing of it is left. From these considerations it may be seen that this lust is fatal to conjugial love; and, as conjugial love constitutes the inmost of life with man, that it is fatal to his life; and that that lust, by successive interceptions and closings of the interiors of the mind, at length becomes cuticular, and thus merely alluring; the faculty of understanding, or rationality, nevertheless remaining.

510. IV. THE LOT AFTER DEATH OF THOSE [WHO HAVE BEEN ADDICTED TO THAT LUST] IS MISERABLE, SINCE THEY HAVE NOT THE INMOST OF LIFE. Every one has excellence of life according to his conjugial love; for that excellence conjoins itself with the life of the wife, and by conjunction exalts itself: but as with these there does not remain the least of conjugial love, and consequently not anything of the inmost of life, therefore their lot after death is miserable. After passing a certain period of time in their externals, in which they speak rationally and act civilly, they are let into their internals, and in this case into a similar lust and its delights, in the same degree in which they had been in it in the world: for every one after death is intromitted into the same state of life which he had appropriated to himself, to the in-

tent that he may be withdrawn from it. For no one can be withdrawn from his evil unless he has first been led into it: otherwise the evil would conceal itself, and defile the interiors of the mind, and spread like a pestilence, and would then burst the barriers and destroy the externals which are of the body. For this end, there are opened to them brothels, which are on the side of hell, where there are whores, with whom there is given opportunity of varying their lusts: but this is granted with the restriction of one in a day, and it is forbidden under a penalty
2 to have intercourse with more than one on the same day. Afterwards, when from examination it appears that that lust is so inbred that they cannot be withdrawn from it, they are conveyed to a certain place, which is just above the hell assigned for them, and then they appear to themselves as if they fall into a swoon, and to others as if they sink down with the face turned upward; and also the ground under their backs is actually opened, and they are swallowed up, and sink down into the hell where their like are; thus they are gathered to their own. It has been given me to see them there, and likewise to speak with them. Among themselves they appear as human beings, which is granted them lest they should be a terror to their companions; but at a certain distance they seem to have white faces, consisting as it were only of skin, and this because they have no spiritual life in them, which every one has according to
3 the conjugial principle that is implanted in him. Their speech is dry, parched, and sorrowful; when they are hungry, they lament, and their lamentations are heard as a peculiar snarling sound. Their garments are tattered, and their lower garments are drawn up over the belly round about the breast, because they have no loins, but their ancles commence from the region of the bottom of the belly: the reason is, that the loins with human beings correspond to conjugial love, and this love they do not possess. They said that, on account of their having no potency, they loathe the sex. Nevertheless, among themselves they can reason as from rationality about various things, but because they are cutaneous, they reason from the fallacies of the senses. This hell is in the western quarter towards the north. These same persons, when seen from afar, appear not as human beings, nor as monsters, but as substances of ice. It must, however, be known, that those become such who have imbued themselves with the above lust to such a degree as to rend and annihilate in themselves the human conjugial principle.

THE LUST OF VIOLATION.

511. By the lust of violation is not meant the lust of defloration, which is the violation of virginities, but not of maidens when it is effected from consent; whereas the lust of violation, which is here treated of, retreats in consequence of consent, and is rendered more violent by refusal; and it is the passion of violating all women whatsoever, who altogether refuse, and violently resist, whether they be maidens, or widows, or wives. Those [who are addicted to this lust] are like robbers and pirates, who are delighted with spoil and plunder, and not with what is given and justly acquired; and they are like malefactors, who covet what is unlawful and forbidden, and despise what is allowed and granted. These violators are altogether averse to consent, and are inflamed by resistance, which if they observe to be not internal, the ardour of their lust is instantly extinguished, as fire is by water thrown upon it. It is known, that wives do not spontaneously submit themselves to the disposal of their husbands as to the ultimate effects of love, and that from prudence they resist as they would resist violations, to the end that they may take away from their husbands the cold arising from the commonness that results from the enjoyment being continually allowed, and also from an idea of lasciviousness on their part. These resistances, although they enkindle, are nevertheless not the causes, but only the beginnings of this lust. Its cause is, that after conjugial love and also scortatory love have grown insipid by exercise, they require, in order that they may be recuperated, to be set on fire by absolute resistances. This lust, thus begun, afterwards grows, and as it grows it despises and breaks through all bounds of the love of the sex, and exterminates itself, and from a lascivious, corporeal, and fleshly love, becomes cartilaginous and bony; and then, from the periostea, which enjoy a keen sense, it becomes sharpened. Nevertheless this lust is rare, because it exists only with those who had entered into marriage, and then had practised whoredoms until they became insipid. Besides this natural cause of this lust, there is also a spiritual cause, of which something will be said in what follows.

512. The lot after death of those [who have been addicted to this lust] is as follows: these violators then of their own

accord separate themselves from those who are in the limited love of the sex, and entirely from those who are in conjugial love, thus from heaven: afterwards they are sent away to the most cunning whores, who not only by persausion, but also by a perfectly histrionic imitation, can feign and represent as if they were essentially chastities. These whores clearly discern those who are in that lust: in their presence they speak of chastity and its preciousness; and when the violator comes near and touches them, they are full of wrath, and fly away as through terror into a room, where there is a couch and a bed, and slightly close the door after them, and lie down; and from thence by their art they inspire the violator with an ungovernable desire of breaking down the door, of rushing in, and assaulting them; and when this takes place, the whore, raising herself erect, begins to fight with the violator with her hands and nails, tearing his face, rending his clothes, and with a furious voice crying out to her fellow-whores, as to her maid-servants, for assistance, and opening the window with a loud outcry of thief, robber, and murderer; and when the violator is in her embrace, she wails and weeps: and after violation she prostrates herself, howls, and calls out that she is undone, and then threatens in a serious tone, that unless he expiates the violation by paying a considerable sum, she will attempt his destruction. While they are engaged in this venereal scene, they appear from afar like cats, which nearly in like manner before their conjunctions
2 fight together, rush against each other, and howl. After some such brothel-contests, they are taken away, and conveyed into a cavern, where they are forced to some work; but as they smell offensively, in consequence of having destroyed the conjugial principle, which is the most precious treasure of human life, they are sent to the borders of the western quarter, where at a certain distance they appear lean, as if consisting of bones covered over with skin only; and from afar they appear like panthers. When it was given me to see them nearer, I was surprised that some of them held books in their hands, and were reading; and I was told that this is the case, because in the world they had spoken various things about the spiritual things of the church, and yet had defiled them by adulteries, even to these very extremities of them, and that such was the correspondence of this lust with the violation of the spiritual marriage. But let it be known, that instances of those who are in this lust are rare. Certain it is, that women, because it is unbecoming for them to prostitute love, repeatedly resist, and that resistance strengthens; nevertheless this is not from any lust of violation.

THE LUST OF SEDUCING INNOCENCES.

513. The lust of seducing innocences is neither the lust of defloration nor the lust of violation, but is peculiar to, and stands alone by itself; it exists more especially among the deceitful. The women, who appear to them as innocences, are such as regard the evil of whoredom as an enormous sin, and who therefore strive to acquire a character for chastity, and at the same time for piety: these women they burn after. In Roman Catholic countries they are nuns; and because they believe these maidens to be pious innocences above all the rest of their sex, they view them as the dainties and delicacies of their lust. In order that they may seduce either the latter or the former, they first, because they are deceitful, devise arts, and afterwards, when they have trained themselves well therein, they practise them without shame or compunction, as from nature. These arts are chiefly simulations of innocence, love, chastity, and piety; by these and other cunning arts they enter into the interior friendship of such women, and thence into their love, which they change from spiritual into natural love by various persuasions and at the same time by various blandishments, and afterwards into corporeal-carnal love by irritations, and then they take possession of them at their pleasure; and when they have attained their end, they rejoice at heart, and laugh to scorn those whom they have violated.

514. The lot of these seducers after death is sad, inasmuch as that seduction is not only impiety, but also malignity. After they have passed through their first period, which is in externals, wherein they excel many others in the elegance of their manners and the courteousness of their speech, they are reduced into the second period of their life, which is in internals, in which internals their lust is set free, and begins its sport; and then they are first conveyed to women who had made vows of chastity, and with these they are examined as to the quality of their malignant concupiscence, to the intent that they may not be judged except on conviction: when they feel the chastity of those women, their deceit begins to act, and to attempt its cunning
arts; but as this is in vain, they depart from them. They are 2
afterwards introduced to women of genuine innocence; and when they attempt to deceive these in like manner, they are

grievously punished, by virtue of a power given to those women, for they bring on their hands and feet an oppressive numbness, and likewise on their necks, and at last make them feel as it were a swoon; after undergoing which they hastily flee away from them. After this there is opened to them a way to a certain company of harlots, who have acquired the art of feigning innocence in a cunning manner; and these first expose them to derision among themselves, and at length after various promises
3 suffer themselves to be violated. After some such scenes, the third period takes place, which is that of judgment; when, being convicted, they sink down, and are gathered to their like in the hell which is in the northern quarter, and there they appear from afar, like weasels. But if they had been addicted to deceit, they are carried down from this hell to the hell of the deceitful, which is in the western quarter deep down at the back. In this hell they appear from afar as serpents of various kinds, and the most deceitful as vipers; but in the hell itself into which I was permitted to look, they appeared to me as if they were ghastly pale, with faces of chalk; and as they are mere concupiscences, they do not like to speak; and if they do speak, they only mumble and mutter various things which are understood by none but their companions who are near them; but presently, as they sit or stand, they make themselves invisible, and fly about in the cavern like phantoms; for then they are in phantasy, and phantasy appears to fly: after flying they rest themselves; and then, what is wonderful, one does not know another: the reason of this is, that they are in deceit, and deceit does not believe another, and therefore withdraws itself. When they feel anything [proceeding] from conjugial love, they flee away into vaults and conceal themselves. They are also void of the love of the sex, and are real impotences. They are called infernal genii.

THE CORRESPONDENCE OF WHOREDOMS WITH THE VIOLATION OF THE SPIRITUAL MARRIAGE.

515. I SHOULD here preface something concerning what correspondence is; but the subject does not properly belong to the present Work. But what correspondence is, may be seen in a brief summary above, no. 76, and no. 342; and it may be seen fully in the *Apocalypse Revealed,* from beginning to end, that there is a correspondence between the natural sense and the spiritual sense of the Word. That in the Word there is a natural sense and a spiritual sense, and a correspondence between them, has been demonstrated in the *Doctrine of the New Jerusalem concerning the Sacred Scripture,* and especially in nos. 5–26 of that Work.

516. By the spiritual marriage is meant the marriage of the Lord and the church, spoken of above, nos. 116–131; and hence also the marriage of good and truth, likewise spoken of above, nos. 83–102; and because this marriage of the Lord and the church, and therefore the marriage of good and truth, is in each and all things of the Word, it is the violation of the Word that is meant here by the violation of the spiritual marriage; for the church is from the Word, and the Word is the Lord. The Lord is the Word, because He is the Divine good and Divine truth there. That the Word is that marriage, may be seen fully confirmed in the *Doctrine of the New Jerusalem concerning the Sacred Scripture,* nos. 80–90.

517. Since therefore the violation of the spiritual marriage is the violation of the Word, it is evident that this violation is the adulteration of good and the falsification of truth; for the spiritual marriage, as was said, is the marriage of good and truth; hence it follows, that when the good of the Word is adulterated, and its truth falsified, that marriage is violated. How this violation is effected, and by whom, is in some measure evident from what now follows.

518. Above, in treating of the marriage of the Lord and the church (no. 116 and following numbers) and in treating of the marriage of good and truth (no. 83 and following numbers), it was proved, that that marriage corresponds to marriages on

earth: hence it follows, that the violation of that marriage corresponds to whoredoms and adulteries. That this is the case, is manifestly evident from the Word itself, in that whoredoms and adulteries there signify falsifications of truth and adulterations of good, as may be plainly seen from numerous passages adduced from the Word in the *Apocalypse Revealed*, no. 134.

519. The violation of the Word is effected by those in the Christian church who adulterate its goods and truths; and those do this who separate truth from good, and good from truth; also, who assume and confirm appearances of truth and fallacies as genuine truths; and likewise, who know truths of doctrine from the Word, and live evilly; not to mention other like cases. These violations of the Word and of the church correspond to the prohibited degrees enumerated in Leviticus xviii.

520. Since the Natural and the Spiritual with every man cohere as the soul and the body, for a man without the Spiritual which flows in into and vivifies his Natural, is not a man, it hence follows, that he who is in the spiritual marriage is also in happy natural marriage; and on the other hand, that he who is in spiritual adultery is also in natural adultery, and contrariwise. Now, since all who are in hell are in the connubial connection of evil and falsity, and this is essentially spiritual adultery; and all who are in heaven are in the marriage of good and truth, and this is essentially marriage; therefore hell as a whole is called adultery, and heaven as a whole is called marriage.

521. To the above shall be added this Memorable Relation:—
My eye was opened, and I saw a dark forest, and therein a crowd of satyrs. The satyrs as to their breasts were hairy, and as to their feet some were like calves, some like panthers, and some like wolves, and they had wild beasts' claws instead of toes. They were running to and fro like wild beasts, crying out, "Where are the women?" and then there appeared whores who were waiting for them; and they also were of divers monstrous conformations. The satyrs ran towards them, and laid hold of them, dragging them into a cavern, which was in the midst of the forest deep beneath the earth; and upon the earth round about the cavern lay a great serpent coiled up spirally, breathing poison into the cavern; in the branches of the forest above the serpent dismal birds of night were croaking and screeching. But the satyrs and whores did not see these things, because they were the correspondences of their lasciviousnesses, and therefore their usual appearances from afar.

2 Afterwards they came out of the cavern, and entered a certain cottage of lowly structure, which was a brothel; and then being separated from the whores they spoke together, and I listened;

for speech in the spiritual world may be heard by a distant person as if he were present, since the extent of space in that world is only an appearance. They were speaking about marriages, nature, and religion.

Those who as to the feet appeared like calves, spoke about MARRIAGES, and said, "What are marriages but lawful adulteries? and what is sweeter than scortatory hypocrisies, and the making fools of husbands?" At this the rest clapped their hands with loud laughter.

The satyrs who as to the feet appeared as panthers, spoke about NATURE, and said, "What is there but nature? What distinction is there between a man and a beast, except that a man can speak articulately and a beast sonorously? Does not each derive life from heat, and understanding from light, by the operation of nature?" Hereupon the rest exclaimed, "Admirable! you speak from judgment."

Those who as to the feet appeared like wolves, spoke about RELIGION, saying, "What is God or the Divine but the inmost of nature in operation? What is religion but a device to ensnare and bind the common people?" Hereupon the rest vociferated "Bravo!"

After a few minutes they rushed forth, and in so doing they 3
saw me at a distance looking attentively at them. Being provoked at this, they ran out from the forest, and with a threatening countenance directed their course swiftly towards me and said, "Why are you standing here and listening to our whispers?"

I replied, "Why not? what is to hinder me? you were only talking:" and I related what I had heard from them. Hereupon their minds (*animi*) were quieted: this was through fear lest what they had said should be divulged; and then they began to speak modestly and to act becomingly; from which circumstance I knew that they were not of mean descent but of honourable birth. And then I told them, that I had seen them in the forest as satyrs, twenty as calf-satyrs, six as panther-satyrs, and four as wolf-satyrs: they were thirty in number.

They were surprised at this, because they saw themselves 4
there no otherwise than as men, in like manner as they saw themselves here with me.

I then taught them that they appeared thus from afar by reason of their scortatory lust, and that this satyr-like form was a form of dissolute adultery, and not the form of a person. I said that the reason was that every evil concupiscence exhibits a likeness of itself in a certain form, which is not perceived by those who are in the concupiscence, but by those who are standing at a distance: I also said, "In order that you may believe, send some from among you into that forest, and do you remain here, and look at them."

They did so, and sent away two; and viewing them when near the above brothel-cottage they saw them altogether as satyrs; and when they returned, they saluted them as satyrs and said, "O what ridiculous figures!"

While they were laughing, I joked on various matters with them, and told them that I had also seen adulterers as hogs; and then I recollected the fable of Ulysses and Circe, how she sprinkled the companions and servants of Ulysses with enchanter's herbs, and touched them with a magic wand, and turned them into hogs,—perhaps into adulterers, because she could not by any art turn any one into a hog.

After they had indulged in loud laughter at this and other similar things, I asked them whether they knew from what kingdoms in the world they had come.

They said they had come from various kingdoms, and they named Italy, Poland, Germany, England, Sweden.

I inquired, whether they had seen any one from Holland among them.

And they said, "Not one."

5 After this I gave the conversation a serious turn, and asked them, whether they had ever thought that adultery is sin.

They replied, "What is sin? we do not know what it is."

I then asked, whether they had ever remembered that adultery was contrary to the sixth commandment of the Decalogue.

They replied "What is the Decalogue? Is not it the catechism? What have we men (*viri*) to do with that childish tract?"

I asked them, whether they had ever thought at all about hell.

They replied, "Who ever came up thence to give information about it?"

I asked, whether they had ever thought at all in the world about the life after death.

They said, "Just as much as about the future life of beasts, and at times as about phantoms, that, if they exhale from dead bodies, they float about."

I further asked them, whether they had heard anything from the priests on any of these subjects.

They replied, that they had attended only to the sound of their voices and not to the matter; and what is this latter?

6 Being astonished at these answers, I said to them, "Turn your faces, and direct your glance to the midst of the forest, where the cavern is in which you have been."

So they turned themselves, and saw that great serpent around the cavern coiled up spirally, breathing poison, and also the doleful birds in the branches over the serpent.

I then asked them, "What do you see?"

But being terrified, they did not answer.

Then I said, "Do you see the dreadful sight? Know, that this is a representative of adultery in the flagitiousness of its lust."

At that instant an angel suddenly stood present: he was a priest, and opened the hell in the western quarter, into which such spirits are at length collected; and he said, "Look thither;" and they saw a pool as it were of fire, and they recognized there some who had been their friends in the world, who invited them to themselves.

Having seen and heard these things, they turned away, and rushed out of my sight, and retired from the forest; but I observed their steps, that they pretended to retire, but that by winding ways they returned into the forest.

522. After this I returned home, and the next day, from a recollection of these sad scenes, I looked towards the same forest, and saw that it had disappeared, and in its place there was a sandy plain, and in the midst thereof a pool, in which were some red serpents.

But some weeks after, when I was looking thither again, I saw on its right side some fallow land, and upon it some husbandmen.

And again, after some weeks I saw springing out of that fallow land some tilled land surrounded with little trees.

And I then heard a voice from heaven, "Enter into your bed-chamber, and shut the door, and apply to the work begun on the Apocalypse, and finish it within two years."

THE IMPUTATION OF BOTH LOVES, SCORTATORY AND CONJUGIAL.

523. THE Lord says, JUDGE NOT, THAT YE BE NOT CONDEMNED (Matt. vii. 1); which cannot in any wise mean judgment respecting any one's moral and civil life in the world, but judgment respecting his spiritual and celestial life. Who does not see, that if it were not allowable to judge respecting the moral life of those who live with him in the world, society would perish? What would society be if there were no public judicature, and if every one did not exercise his judgment respecting another? But to judge what is the quality of the interior mind, or soul, thus what is the quality of any one's spiritual state, and thence what his lot after death is, is not allowable; because that is known to the Lord alone: neither does the Lord reveal this till after the person's decease, to the intent that every one may do whatever he does from freedom, and thereby that good or evil may be from him, and thus in him, and that on this ground he may live to eternity by and for himself, and as his own *ego.* The reason why the interiors of the mind, which are kept hidden in the world, are revealed after death, is, that this is of importance and advantage to the societies into which the man then comes; for all there are spiritual. That those interiors are then revealed, is evident from these words of the Lord: "*There is nothing concealed, which shall not be revealed, or hidden, which shall not be known: therefore whatsoever things ye have said in the darkness, shall be heard in the light; and that which ye have spoken into the ear in bedchambers, shall be preached on the house-tops*" (Luke xii. 2, 3). A general judgment, such as this,—"If you are such in internals as you appear to be in externals, you will be saved or condemned," is allowed; but a particular judgment, as this, for instance,—"You are such in internals, therefore you will be saved or condemned," is not allowed. Judgment concerning the spiritual life of a human being, or the internal life of the soul, is meant by the imputation which is here treated of. Can any human being know, who in heart is a whoremonger, and who a [genuinely] married man? And yet the thoughts of the heart, which are the purposes of the will, judge every one. But this subject shall be opened up in the following order:—

I. *The evil in which any one is, is imputed to him after death; likewise the good.*

II. *The transcription of the good of one person into another is impossible.*

III. *Imputation, if by it is meant such transcription, is a frivolous term.*

IV. *Evil is imputed to every one according to the quality of his will, and according to the quality of his understanding; likewise good.*

V. *Thus scortatory love is imputed to every one.*

VI. *Thus conjugial love likewise is imputed to every one.*

Now follows the explanation of these articles.

524. I. THE EVIL IN WHICH ANY ONE IS, IS IMPUTED TO HIM AFTER DEATH; LIKEWISE THE GOOD. To make this proposition in some degree evident, it shall be considered under the following distinct heads:—1. Every one has a life peculiar to himself. 2. Every one's life remains with him after death. 3. To an evil person is then imputed the evil of his life, and to a good person the good of his life. As to the FIRST point,—that every one has a life peculiar to himself, thus distinct from that of another, it is known; for there is a perpetual variety, and there is not anything the same as another; consequently every one has his own peculiarity. This is evident from the faces of human beings, in that the faces of no two persons are absolutely alike, nor can there be two alike to eternity: the reason is, that there are no two dispositions alike, and the faces are from the dispositions; for the face, as it is said, is a type of the disposition, and the disposition derives its origin and form from the life. Unless 2
a man had a life peculiar to himself, as he has a disposition and a face peculiar to himself, he would not have any life after death separate from that of another; yea, neither would there be a heaven, for heaven consists of perpetual others; its form is derived solely from the varieties of souls and minds arranged into such an order as to make a one; and they make a one from the One Whose life is in each and all therein as the soul is in a man: unless this were the case, heaven would be dispersed, because the form would be dissolved. The One from Whom all things have life, and from Whom the form coheres, is the Lord. In general every form consists of various things, and is such as is their harmonious co-ordination and arrangement into a one: such is the human form; hence it is that a man, consisting of so many members, viscera, and organs, does not feel anything in himself and from himself but as a one. As to the SECOND 3
point,—that every one's life remains with him after death, it is known in the church from these passages of the Word: "*The Son of Man will come, and will then render to every one according to his deeds*" (Matt. xvi. 27). "*I saw the books opened; and all were judged according to their works*" (Apoc. xx. 12, 13). "*In the day of judgment God will render to every one according to his*

works" (Rom. ii. 6; 2 Cor. v. 10). The works according to which it will be rendered to every one, are the life, because the life does the works, and they are according to the life. As it has been given me for many years to be together with angels, and to speak with those who have come from the world, I can testify for certain that every one is then examined as to what the quality of his life had been, and that the life which he has contracted in the world remains with him to eternity. I have spoken with those who lived ages ago, with whose life I have been acquainted from history, and I have recognized it to be like the description given of it: and I have learnt from the angels, that no one's life can be changed after death, because it is organized according to his love and consequent works; and that if it were changed, the organization would be torn to pieces, which cannot be done in any case; also that a change of organization is possible only in the material body, and is utterly impossible in the spiritual body, after the former has been cast away.
4 In regard to the THIRD point,—that to an evil person is then imputed the evil of his life, and to a good person the good of his life: the imputation of evil is not accusation, arraignment, incrimination, and the giving of judgment, as in the world, but evil itself produces this effect; for the evil freely separate themselves from the good, since they cannot be together. The delights of the love of evil hold in aversion the delights of the love of good: and delights exhale from every one, as odours do from every plant in the earth: for they are not absorbed and hidden by the material body as before, but flow out freely from their loves into the spiritual aura; and as evil is there felt as in its odour, it is this which accuses, arraigns, incriminates, and judges, not before any judge, but before every one who is in good; and this is what is meant by imputation. Moreover, an evil person chooses companions with whom he may live in his own delight; and because he holds the delight of good in aversion, he spon-
5 taneously betakes himself to his own in hell. The imputation of good is effected in like manner. This takes place with those who in the world have acknowledged that all good in them is from the Lord, and nothing from themselves. These, after they have been prepared, are let into the interior delights of good, and then there is opened to them a way into heaven, to the society where the delights are homogeneous to their own. This is done by the Lord.

525. II. THE TRANSCRIPTION OF THE GOOD OF ONE PERSON INTO ANOTHER IS IMPOSSIBLE. The evidence of this proposition may also be seen from the following points in order: 1. Every human being is born in evil. 2. He is led into good by means of regeneration by the Lord. 3. This is effected by means of a life according to His precepts. 4. Wherefore good, when it is

thus implanted, cannot be transcribed. The FIRST point—that every human being is born in evil, is known in the church. It is said that this evil is derived hereditarily from Adam; but it is from the man's parents. Every one derives from his parents his natural disposition, which is his inclination. That this is the case, is evinced both by reason and experience; for the likenesses of parents as to their faces, geniuses and manners, are exhibited in their immediate offspring and in their posterity: hence families are known by many, and a judgment is also formed concerning their dispositions; wherefore the evils which parents themselves have contracted, and which they have transmitted to their offspring, are the evils in which human beings are born. The reason why it is believed that the guilt of Adam is inscribed on all the human race, is that few reflect upon any evil with themselves, and thence know it; wherefore they suppose that it is so deeply hidden away as to appear only before God. In regard to the SECOND point— 2
that a man is led into good by means of regeneration by the Lord: that there is such a thing as regeneration, and that unless a person be regenerated, he cannot enter into heaven, appears clearly from the Lord's words in John iii. 3, 5. That regeneration consists in purification from evils, and thereby renovation of life, cannot be unknown in the Christian world; for reason also sees this when it acknowledges that every one is born in evil, and that evil cannot be washed and wiped away like filth by soap and water, but by repentance. As to the 3
THIRD point—that a man is led into good by the Lord, by means of a life according to His precepts: there are five precepts of regeneration (which may be seen above, no. 82); among which are these,—That evils ought to be shunned, because they are of the devil and from the devil, and that goods ought to be done, because they are of God and from God; and that men ought to approach the Lord in order that He may lead them to do those things. Let any one consult himself and consider whether a man derives good from any other source; and if he has not good, he has not salvation. In regard to the FOURTH point—that 4
good, when it is thus implanted, cannot be transcribed; (by transcription is meant the transcription of the good of one person into another;) it follows from what has been already said, that a man by regeneration is made altogether new as to his spirit, and that this is effected by means of a life according to the Lord's precepts. Who does not see that this renewal can only be effected from time to time, in nearly the same manner as a tree successively takes root and grows from a seed, and is perfected? Those who have a different idea of regeneration do not know anything about the state of man, or about evil and good, that those two are altogether opposite, and that good can only be implanted in proportion as evil is removed; nor do they

know, that so long as any one is in evil, he holds in aversion the good which in itself is good: wherefore if the good of one were to be transferred into any one who is in evil, it would be as if a lamb were cast before a wolf, or as if a pearl were tied to a swine's snout: from which considerations it is evident that transcription is impossible.

526. III. IMPUTATION, IF BY IT IS MEANT SUCH TRANSCRIPTION, IS A FRIVOLOUS TERM. That the evil in which every one is, is imputed to him after death, and likewise the good, was proved above, no. 524; hence it is manifest what is meant by imputation: but if by imputation is meant the transcription of good into any one who is in evil, it is an empty expression, because such transcription is impossible, as was also proved above, no. 525. In the world, merits may as it were be transcribed (or transferred) by men; that is, good may be done to children for the sake of their parents, or to the friends of any adherent out of favour; but the good of merit cannot be inscribed on their souls, but only outwardly adjoined. The like is not possible with men as to their spiritual life: this, as was shewn above, must be implanted; and if it is not implanted by means of a life according to the Lord's precepts above mentioned, the man remains in the evil in which he was born. Before this is done, it is impossible for any good to reach him, or if it reaches him, it is instantly struck back and rebounds like an elastic ball falling upon a rock, or it is absorbed like a diamond thrown into a bog. A man who has not been reformed as to the spirit, is like a panther, or a horned owl, and may be compared to a brier and a nettle; but a man who has been regenerated is like a sheep or a dove, and may be compared to an olive-tree and a vine. Pray consider, if you are so inclined, how can a panther-man be converted into a sheep-man, or a horned owl into a dove, or a brier into an olive-tree, or a nettle into a vine, by any imputation, if by it is meant transcription? In order that such a conversion may be effected, is it not necessary that the wild-beast element of the panther and the horned owl, or the noxious quality of the brier and the nettle, be first taken away, and thereby what is truly human and harmless be implanted? How this is effected, the Lord also teaches in John xv. 1–7.

527. IV. EVIL IS IMPUTED TO EVERY ONE ACCORDING TO THE QUALITY OF HIS WILL, AND ACCORDING TO THE QUALITY OF HIS UNDERSTANDING; [LIKEWISE GOOD]. It is known that there are two faculties which constitute a man's life, the will and the understanding; and that all things which a man does are done by his will and his understanding; and that without these acting powers a man would have neither action nor speech other than as a machine. Hence it is evident, that such as are a

man's will and understanding, such is the man; and further, that a man's action in itself is such as is the affection of his will which produces it, and that a man's conversation in itself is such as is the thought of his understanding which produces it: wherefore several men may act and speak alike, and yet they act and speak differently; one from a depraved will and thought,
the other from an upright will and thought. From these con- 2
siderations it is manifest what is meant by the deeds or works according to which every one will be judged, namely, that there are meant the will and the understanding; consequently that by evil works are meant the works of an evil will, of whatsoever quality they may have appeared in externals, and that by good works are meant the works of a good will, although in externals they may have appeared like the works done by an evil man. All things which are done by a man's interior will are done from purpose, since that will proposes to itself what it does by its intention; and all things which are done by the understanding are done from confirmation, since the understanding confirms. From these considerations it may be manifest, that evil, or good, is imputed to every one according to the quality of his will in them, and according to the quality of his understanding concerning them. These observations it is allowed to confirm by the 3
following relation: In the spiritual world I have met many who in the natural world had lived like others, dressing splendidly, feasting sumptuously, trading with their capital like others, frequenting stage-plays, jesting on love topics as it were from lust, and doing other like things; and yet the angels charged those things against some as evils of sin, and to others they did not impute them as evils; the latter they declared guiltless, but the former guilty. Being questioned why they did so, when nevertheless all had done alike, they replied that they regard all from their purpose, intention, or end, and distinguish accordingly; and that therefore they excuse or condemn those whom the end either excuses or condemns, since all in heaven have an end of good, and all in hell an end of evil.

528. To the above shall be added the following observation: It is said in the church that no one can fulfil the law, and the less so because he who transgresses against one precept of the decalogue, transgresses against all; but this form of speaking is not such as it sounds; for it ought to be understood thus, that he who, from purpose or confirmation, acts against one precept, acts against the rest; since acting so from purpose or confirmation is altogether denying that it is a sin; and he who denies that it is a sin makes nothing of acting against the rest of the precepts. Who does not know, that he who is an adulterer is not on that account a murderer, a thief, and a false witness, nor wishes to be so? But he who is an adulterer from purpose and

confirmation, makes no account of anything which belongs to religion, thus neither does he make any account of murders, thefts, and false witnesses; and he abstains from these evils, not because they are sins, but because he is afraid of the law and of the loss of reputation. That adulterers from purpose and from confirmation make no account of the holy things of the church and religion, see above, nos. 490–493, and in the two Memorable Relations, no. 500, and nos. 521, 522. It is similar if any one, from purpose or confirmation, acts against any other precept of the decalogue; he also acts against the rest, because he does not regard anything as sin.

529. The case is similar with those who are in good from the Lord: if these from will and understanding, or from purpose and confirmation, abstain from one evil because it is a sin, they abstain from all evils, and still more if they abstain from several; for as soon as any one, from purpose or confirmation, abstains from any evil because it is a sin, he is kept by the Lord in the purpose of abstaining from the rest: wherefore if he does evil from ignorance, or from some prevailing concupiscence of the body, this is, nevertheless, not imputed to him, because he did not purpose it to himself, nor does he confirm it with himself. A man comes into this purpose, if once or twice in a year he examines himself, and repents of the evil which he discovers in himself: it is otherwise with him who never examines himself. From these considerations it evidently appears who he is to whom sin is not imputed, and who to whom it is imputed.

530. V. THUS SCORTATORY LOVE IS IMPUTED TO EVERY ONE; namely, not according to his deeds such as they appear in externals before men, nor either such as they appear before a judge, but such as they appear in internals before the Lord, and from Him before the angels, that is, according to the quality of the man's will and the quality of his understanding in them. Various circumstances exist in the world which mitigate and excuse crimes, also which aggravate them and fix the blame of them on the perpetrator: nevertheless, imputations after death take place, not according to the external circumstances of the deed, but according to the internal circumstances of the mind; and these are viewed according to the state of the church with every one; as for example, a man impious in will and understanding, that is, who has no fear of God or love of the neighbour, and consequently no reverence for any holiness of the church,—he, after death, becomes guilty of all the crimes which he had done in the body; nor is there any remembrance of his good deeds, since his heart, from whence as from a fountain those things had flowed, had been turned away from heaven and turned towards hell; and acts flow from the place of the habitation of

every one's heart. In order that this may be understood, I will 2
relate an arcanum. Heaven is distinguished into innumerable societies, and so is hell, on the principle of opposition; and the mind of every man, according to his will and consequent understanding, actually dwells in some one society, and intends and thinks like those who are in that society. If the mind be in any society of heaven, it then intends and thinks like those who are in that society; if it be in any society of hell, it intends and thinks like those who are in that society. But so long as a man lives in the world, so long he wanders from one society to another, according to the changes of the affections of his will and of the consequent thoughts of his mind: after death, however, his wanderings are collected into one, and a place is accordingly allotted to him, in hell if he is evil, in heaven if
he is good. Now, since all in hell are influenced by a will of 3
evil, all there are viewed from that will; and since all in heaven are influenced by a will of good, all there are viewed from that will; wherefore imputations after death take place according to the quality of every one's will and understanding. The case is similar with whoredoms, whether they be fornications, pellicacies, concubinages, or adulteries; for those things are imputed to every one, not according to the deeds themselves, but according to the state of the mind in the deeds; for the deeds follow the body into the tomb, whereas the mind rises again.

531. VI. THUS CONJUGIAL LOVE IS IMPUTED TO EVERY ONE. There are marriages in which conjugial love does not appear, and yet is; and there are marriages in which conjugial love appears, and yet is not. There are several causes in both cases, which can be known in part from what has been stated concerning truly conjugial love, nos. 57–73; concerning the causes of colds and separations, nos. 234–260; and concerning the causes of apparent love and friendship in marriages, nos. 271–292. But appearances in externals decide nothing in relation to imputation: the only thing which decides is the conjugial principle or state, which is seated in every one's will, and is guarded, in whatsoever state of marriage the man is. That conjugial principle or state is like a pair of scales, in which that love is weighed; for the conjugial state of one man with one wife is the jewel of human life, and the inner homestead of the Christian religion, as was shown above, nos. 457, 458: and because this is so, it is possible that that love may exist with one married partner and not at the same time with the other; it is also possible that it may lie too deeply hidden for the man himself to notice anything in relation to it; and, again, it may be inscribed in the progress of the life. The reason is, that that love in its progress accompanies religion, and religion, because it is the marriage of the Lord and the church, is the beginning

and inoculation of that love; wherefore conjugial love is imputed to every one after death according to his spiritual rational life; and for him to whom that love is imputed, a marriage in heaven is provided after his decease, whatever may have been his marriage in the world. From these considerations then results this conclusion, that no inference must be drawn concerning any one, from the appearances of marriages, nor from the appearances of whoredoms, as to whether he has conjugial love, or not; wherefore *Judge not, lest ye be condemned* (Matt. vii. 1).

532. To the above I will add the following Memorable Relation:—

* I was once raised, as to my spirit, into the angelic heaven, and into a certain one of its societies; and then some of the wise ones there came to me, and said, "What is there new from the earth?"

I said to them, "This is new, that the Lord has revealed arcana which in excellence surpass the arcana that have heretofore been revealed since the beginning of the church."

They asked, "What are they?"

I said that they were the following:—

I. That in the Word, in each and all of its particulars, there is a spiritual sense corresponding to the natural sense; and that by means of that sense there is a conjunction of the men of the church with the Lord, and a consociation with the angels; and that the holiness of the Word resides in that sense.

2 II. That the correspondences, of which the spiritual sense of the Word consists, are unfolded.

The angels asked, "Did the inhabitants of the world not know about correspondences before?"

I said, that they knew nothing at all, and that correspondences had lain concealed now for some thousands of years, namely, ever since the time of Job; and that with those who lived at that time, and before it, the science of correspondences was the science of sciences, from which they had wisdom, because thence they had Knowledge concerning the spiritual things which are of heaven and thence of the church; but that this science, on account of its being turned into an idolatrous science, was, of the Divine providence of the Lord, so obliterated and destroyed, that no one saw any sign of it: but that nevertheless it has now been revealed by the Lord, in order that there may be effected a conjunction of the men of the church with Him, and a consociation with the angels; and that this is effected by means of the Word, in which each and all things are correspondences.

The angels rejoiced exceedingly that it had pleased the Lord

* This Memorable Relation may also be found in the *True Christian Religion*, nos. 846 to 849.

to reveal this great arcanum, which had lain so deeply concealed for some thousands of years; and they said it was for the end that the Christian church, which is founded on the Word, and is now at its end, may again revive and draw breath through heaven from the Lord. They asked whether, by means of that science, it had at this day been disclosed what is signified by Baptism and what by the Holy Supper, about which they had hitherto thought so variously.

I replied, that it had been disclosed.

III. I said further, that a revelation has at this day been 3
made by the Lord concerning the life of men after death.

The angels said, "What concerning the life after death? Who does not know that man lives after death?"

I replied, "They know, and they do not know. They say that it is not the man that lives after death, but his soul, and that this lives a spirit; and of a spirit they cherish an idea as of wind or ether, and that it does not live a man till after the day of the last judgment, and that then the corporeal parts, which they had left in the world, although eaten up by worms, mice, and fish, will be collected together and again fitted together into a body, and that thus men are to rise again."

The angels said, "What is this? Who does not know that a man lives a man after death, with the sole difference, that he then lives a spiritual man; and that a spiritual man sees a spiritual man as a material man sees a material man; and that they do not know one distinction, except that they are in a more perfect state?"

IV. The angels asked, "What do they know about our world, 4
and about heaven and hell?"

I said, that they knew nothing at all; but that at this day it has been disclosed by the Lord, what is the quality of the world in which angels and spirits live, thus what is the quality of heaven and what the quality of hell; and also, that angels and spirits are in conjunction with men; besides many wonderful things about them.

The angels were glad that it had pleased the Lord to disclose such things, so that man from ignorance may no longer be in uncertainty respecting his immortality.

V. I said further, that at this day it has been revealed by the Lord, "that in your world there is a sun, different from ours, and that the sun of your world is pure love, and the sun of our world pure fire; and that therefore all that which proceeds from your sun, because it is pure love, partakes of life, and all that which proceeds from our sun, because it is pure fire, partakes nothing of life; and that hence is the difference between what is spiritual and what is natural, which difference, heretofore unknown, has been also disclosed. From this there has been made known the source of the light which enlightens the human understanding with wisdom, and the source of the heat which kindles the human will with love."

6 VI. Furthermore, that it has been disclosed, that there are three degrees of life, and that hence there are three heavens; and that the human mind is distinguished into those degrees, and that therefore man corresponds with the three heavens.

The angels said, "Did not they know this before?"

I answered that they knew of the degrees between what is more and less, but nothing of the degrees between what is prior and posterior.

7 VII. The angels inquired whether any other things have been revealed besides these?

I said that several more had been revealed; which are, concerning the last judgment; concerning the Lord, that He is God of heaven and earth; that God is one both in person and essence, in Whom is the Divine trinity; and that He is the Lord: also concerning the New church which is to be established by Him, and concerning the doctrine of that church; concerning the holiness of the Sacred Scripture; that the Apocalypse also has been revealed, which could not be revealed even as to a single little verse except by the Lord; moreover concerning the inhabitants of the planets, and concerning the Earths in the universe; besides many memorable and wonderful relations from the spiritual world, by means of which many things which belong to wisdom have been disclosed from heaven.

533. The angels rejoiced exceedingly at hearing this; but they perceived sadness in me, and asked, "Whence is your sadness?"

I said that those arcana that have at this day been revealed by the Lord, although in excellence and worth they exceed the Knowledges hitherto made known, yet on earth are considered as of no value.

The angels wondered at this, and besought the Lord that they might be allowed to look down into the world: and they looked down, and lo! mere darkness was therein. And it was told them, that those arcana should be written on a paper, and the paper let down to the earth, and they would see a marvellous thing. And it was done so; and lo! the paper, on which those arcana were written, was let down from heaven, and in its progress, while it was yet in the spiritual world, it shone as a star; but when it descended into the natural world, the light disappeared, and it was darkened in the degree in which it fell. And when it was let down by the angels into companies where there were learned and erudite men from the clergy and laity, there was heard a murmur from many, in which were these expressions, "What is this? Is it anything? What matters it whether we know those things or do not know them? Are they not the offspring of the brain?" And it appeared as if some took the paper and folded it, rolling and unrolling it with their fingers, in order that they might obliterate the writing; and it appeared as if some tore it in pieces, and some as if they wanted to trample upon it with their feet: but they were withheld by the Lord from that crime, and it was commanded the angels to take it away and keep it safely: and as the angels became sad, and thought how long this was to be, it was said, *Until a time, and times, and half a time* (Apoc. xii. 14).

534. After this I spoke with the angels, and said that something further is being revealed in the world by the Lord.

They asked, "What is it?"

I said, "Concerning truly conjugial love and its heavenly delights."

The angels said, "Who does not know that the delights of conjugial love exceed the delights of all loves? and who cannot see, that into some love are brought together all the blessednesses, blissfulnesses, and delightsomenesses, which can ever be conferred by the Lord, and that the receptacle of them is truly conjugial love, which is capable of receiving and perceiving them to a full sense?"

I replied, that they do not know this, because they have not come to the Lord, and lived according to His precepts, by shunning evils as sins and by doing goods; and truly conjugial love with its delights is solely from the Lord, and is given to those who live according to His precepts; thus that it is given to those who are received into the Lord's New church, which is meant in the Apocalypse by the "New Jerusalem." To this I added, that I am in doubt whether in the world at the present day they are willing to believe that this love in itself is a spiritual love, and consequently from religion, because they entertain only a corporeal idea respecting it.

They then said to me, "Write about it, and follow the revelation; and afterwards the book written about it shall be sent down by us from heaven, and we shall see whether the things contained in it are received; and at the same time whether they are willing to acknowledge that that love is according to religion with man, spiritual with the spiritual, natural with the natural, and merely carnal with adulterers."

535. After this I heard a hostile murmur from hell (*ex inferis*), and at the same time these words, "Do miracles: and we will believe."

And I asked, "Are not those things miracles?"

Answer was made, "They are not."

I again asked, "What miracles then do you want?"

And it was said, "Disclose and reveal things to come; and we will have faith."

But I replied, "Such disclosure and revelation are not given from heaven; since in proportion as a man knows things to come, in the same proportion his reason and understanding, together with his prudence and wisdom, fall into inactivity, grow torpid, and decay."

Again I asked, "What other miracles shall I do?"

And a cry was made, "Do such miracles as Moses did in Egypt."

To this I answered, "Possibly you may harden your hearts against them, as Pharaoh and the Egyptians did."

And reply was made, "We will not."

But again I said, "Assure me of a certainty, that you will not dance about a golden calf and adore it, as the posterity of Jacob did within the space of a month after they had seen the whole Mount Sinai on fire, and heard Jehovah Himself speaking out of the fire, thus after the miracle which was the greatest of all miracles." A golden calf in the spiritual sense denotes the pleasure of the flesh.

And reply was made from hell (*ex inferis*), "We will not be like the posterity of Jacob."

But at that instant I heard it said to them from heaven, "If ye believe not Moses and the prophets,—that is, the Word of the Lord, ye will not believe because of miracles, any more than the sons of Jacob did in the wilderness, nor any more than they believed when they saw with their own eyes the miracles done by the Lord Himself, while He was in the world."

INDEX OF SUBJECTS.

The numbers refer to the paragraphs, not to the pages.

ABOMINATION OF DESOLATION (Matt. xxiv. 15) signifies the falsification and deprivation of all truth, 80[3].

ABSENCE in the spiritual world is caused by what is heterogeneous and discordant, 171.

ABSTRACT AND REAL. Love and wisdom, without use, are merely abstract ideas of thought; but in use they are collected together, and therein become a one, which is called a real thing, 183[3].

ABUNDANCE (*copia*). Men have abundance [*i.e.*, potency], according to the love of propagating the truths of wisdom, and according to the love of doing uses, 220, 221; it varies with them according to the states of their minds and bodies, 221.

The industrious have abundance, but not the idle, 220[3].

ACROBATS. The inhabitants of the Age of Iron and Clay appear to the angels in heaven like acrobats who lie upon their elbows with the body inverted, and advance in that posture, 79[3].

ACTION. In all conjunction by love there must be action, reception, and reaction, 293[5].

A man's action in itself is such as is the affection of his will which produces it, 527.

ACTIONS flow from the will, which in itself is spiritual, 220.

How the acts which the soul and mind intend, flow instantly from the body, 178[2].

ACTIVITY is one of the virtues which pertain to the moral wisdom of men, 164.

The activities and alacrities of life issue from conjugial love as from a fountain, 249.

The activity of love makes the sense of delight; its activity in heaven is with wisdom, and its activity in hell is with insanity, 461[5].

The influx of love and wisdom from the Lord is the activity itself from which is all the delight which, in the universal sense, is called good, 461[6].

ACTORS in heaven, 17[5].

ACTUALLY, 66, 98[2], 178[2], etc.

Note:—This expression is used to distinguish *Actualiter* from *Realiter*, of which the author also makes use; thus, between *actually* and *really*, there is the same distinction as between *actual*, taken in the philosophical sense, and *real*.

ACUTION, see INTENSIFICATION.

ADAM. They are in enormous error who believe that Adam was wise, and did good, from himself, and that this was his state of integrity; when yet Adam himself was cursed on account of that belief, 135[3].

"Adam" and "man" are one expression in the Hebrew language, 156 [a][2].

How Adam and his wife made in themselves the origin of evil, 444[4].

What the sin of Adam was, 444[5].

It is said, that the evil in which every man is born is hereditarily from Adam; but it is from his own parents, 525.

The reason it is believed that the guilt of Adam is inscribed on the whole human race, 525.

ADJUNCTION. The conjunction between married partners is not a conjunction into a one, but an adjunction which is close and near according to the love, and amounting to contact with those who are in truly conjugial love. This adjunction may be called spiritual dwelling together, 158.

The union of the souls and minds of two married partners in truly conjugial love, because it is spiritual, is an actual adjunction of the soul and mind of the one to those of the other, which cannot possibly be dissolved, 321.

ADMINISTRATIVE POSITIONS in heaven, 7[4].

ADORATIONS. Why the Ancients in their adorations turned their faces to the rising sun, 342[3].

ADRAMANDONI, the name of a garden in the spiritual world, 183.

ADULTERERS. Those who are adulterers from set purpose and from confirmation are not spiritual, but extremely natural, 432[2]. They are not wise, *ib.* They become more and more not men, *ib.*

There are four kinds of adulterers, Enum, 432[3].

Reasonings of adulterers, 500[2, 3].

As soon as a man actually becomes an adulterer, heaven is closed against him, 500[6].

All the uncleanness of hell is from adulterers, 500[6].

All those who account adulteries as nothing, that is, who believe and commit them from confirmation and thus from set purpose that they are not sins, are at heart evil doers and impious, 80[2].

Adulterers from confirmation do not believe adulteries to be evils of religion, 152.

With certain classes of adulterers the virile faculty and virtue is weakened till it becomes none, 433.

An adulterer has a similar faculty of elevating the understanding as a chaste married person, yet with a certain difference, 463.

Adulterers, whenever they but approach heavenly societies, are made sensible of their own stench, and cast themselves headlong towards hell, 481.

ADULTERY: See also *Marriage and Adultery.* Adultery is the cause of divorce, 255.

Adulteries are the complex of all evils, 356.

Christian polygamy is not only natural but also spiritual adultery, 339.

It denotes the cupidity of the will, 340[3].

Adulteries principally destroy conjugial love, 372.

It is the opposite of conjugial love, 425.

Adulteries in the Word denote the connubial connection of evil and falsity, 428.

The desire of varieties and the desire of defloration are accessories of adultery, and thus make it more grievous, 454.

There are mild adulteries, grievous ones, and more grievous ones, and each kind is estimated according to its opposition to, and consequent destruction of, conjugial love, 454.

Adultery is spiritual evil, and therefore moral evil and civil evil, 478[3].

There are three kinds of adulteries,—simple, twofold, and threefold, 479–484.

ADULTERY—*continued.*

By adultery is meant whoredom that is opposite to marriage, 480.

The detestable nature of adultery, 483.

Twofold adultery ravages a human being of all spiritual good, 483.

There are four degrees of adulteries, Enum. and des., 485–499; 1st, adulteries of ignorance, 486, 487; 2nd, adulteries of lust, 488, 489; 3rd, adulteries of the reason, 490, 491; 4th, adulteries of the will, 492, 493. The distinction between adulteries of the will and adulteries of the understanding, 490[2, 3]. Adultery of the reason is less grievous than adultery of the will, 490[3].

All adulteries considered in themselves, belong at once to the internal and external man, 486.

Arguments used by adulterers in favour of adultery, 500[2, 3].

Whoredoms and adulteries in the Word signify falsifications of truth and adulterations of good, 518.

Causes of abstinence from adulteries in the body, 153[2], 494[2].

The connubial connection of evil and falsity is spiritual adultery itself, 520.

Why hell as a whole is called adultery, 520.

Whoever is in spiritual adultery is also in natural adultery, 520.

AFFECTION. Affections, which are nothing else than derivations of the love, form the will, and make and compose it; but these affections with men are in the understanding, whereas with women they are in the will, 197.

Every affection has its own delight, 272.

All things of the affections are perceived in the spiritual world, 425[2].

The affections of women are quite distinct from the affections of men, 175[4]; the two affections, of the woman and of the man, cannot be united except between two, and in no case in one, *ib.*

Changes of the inclinations and affections of men towards their wives, 208[4].

— *Internal and external affections.* In the natural world almost all are capable of being conjoined as to the external affections, but not as to the internal affections, if these disagree and appear, 272.

In the spiritual world all are conjoined according to the internal affections, but not according to the external affections, unless these act as a one with the internal affections, 273.

AFFECTION—*continued.*
Since the internal ones cannot, in the spiritual world, be concealed by the external ones, they show through and manifest themselves, 273[2].
Angels and spirits have internal and external affections, because they have minds and bodies ; and affections with the thoughts thence derived belong to the mind, and sensations with the pleasures thence derived belong to the body, 273[2].
It is the external affections according to which matrimonies are generally contracted in the world ; the reason is, that the internal affections are rarely consulted, 274.
The first affection of this age is the increase of the personal estate by wealth ; the second is a thirst for honours, 274.
But if the internal affections, which conjoin the minds, are not within, the bonds of matrimony are loosened at home, 275.
In those matrimonies in which the internal affections do not conjoin, there are external affections which simulate the internal ones, and consociate : by the internal affections are meant the mutual inclinations which are in the mind of each from heaven ; and by the external affections are meant the inclinations which are in the mind of each from the world ; the latter affections or inclinations do indeed equally belong to the mind, but they occupy its lower region, while the former occupy its higher one, 277.
By death the external affections follow the body, and are entombed with it ; those only remaining which cohere with the internal affections, 320[3].
—*Affections and perceptions.* All things of love are called affections, and all things of wisdom, perceptions. The latter are derived from the former, and therefore, together with them they constitute one form, etc., 315[10].
In man there are all the affections of love, and thence all the perceptions of wisdom, compounded in the most perfect order so as to make a one ; these affections and perceptions are substantiated, 361.
—*Affections and thoughts.* As thoughts are expressed by speech, so are affections by song, 55.
Affection belongs to the will, thought to the understanding, 121, 126.
The affection of the will possesses a man's internal, whereas the thought of the understanding possesses his external, 269[6].
Every grain of thought and every drop of affection, is divisible *ad infinitum*, 329[2].
—*Affection of good* is meant by the daughter of Zion, etc., 120.
—*Affection of love.* All angels are affections of love in human form. The ruling affection itself shines forth out of their faces ; and garments are allotted to them, from the affection, and according to it, 42[3].
The affection of the love does not separate itself from the thoughts with women, as it does with men, 169.
Every affection of love belongs to the will ; for what a man loves that he also wills, 196.
—*Affection of the male,* see under MALE.
—*Affection of truth* is called a maiden, 293[6].
—*Affection of wisdom.* Women were created by the Lord affections of the wisdom of the men, and the affection of wisdom is beauty itself, 56[3].
AFFLICTION (THE GREAT) (Matt. xxiv. 15, 21) signifies the state of the church infested by evils and falsities, 80[3].
AFFLUX, 293.
AFRICANS. Their opinion on the subject of conjugial love and its virtue or potency, 113, 114.
AFTERNOON, how spent in heaven, 17[3-5].
AGE (*Aetas*).
The general states of man's life are called infancy, childhood, youth, manhood, and old age, 185.
Unequal ages induce cold in marriage, 250.
In the heavens there is no inequality of age : all there being in the flower of their youth, and in that flower they continue to eternity, 250.
AGE (*Saeculum*).
—*Golden Age.* Description of a married pair of the golden age, 42.
The golden, silver, and copper ages had passed away before the time of written documents, 73.
Conjugial love in the Golden Age, 75.
The men of the Saturnian or Golden Era knew and acknowledged that they were forms receptive of life from God ; and on this account wisdom was inscribed on their souls and hearts, and hence they saw truth

AGE—*continued.*
from the light of truth, and through truths perceived good from the delight of the love of it, 153 [a][2].
The difference of mankind in the subsequent ages, *ib.*
In the first eras they acknowledged in heart and soul that all the good of life and truth of wisdom were from God, and also God's in them, etc., but in the succeeding eras they did not, 153 [a][3].
—*Silver Age*, Conjugial love in, 76.
All those who lived in the silver era had intelligence from spiritual verities, and thence from natural verities, 76[3].
—*Copper Age*, Conjugial love in, 77.
—*Iron Age*, Conjugial love in, 78.
—*Age of Iron and Clay*, Conjugial love in, 79.
—*Present Age*. The men of this age, more than the Ancients, learn from infancy to conceal their affections, 192.

AID (Mutual) of husband and wife, 176.

ALACRITY is one of the virtues which pertain to the moral wisdom of men, 164.

ALCOHOL. Wisdom purified may be compared with alcohol, which is spirit most highly rectified, 145.

ALCORAN, 342.

ALPHA. Why the Lord is called the Alpha and the Omega, 326[5].

ALPHABET. In the spiritual world, each letter of the alphabet is significative, 326[5].

ALTITUDE, see HEIGHT.

AMBASSADOR'S (An) discussion with a confirmer, 233[3-5].
An ambassador in the spiritual world discussing with two priests the subject of intelligence and wisdom, and the prudence thence, whether they are from God or from man, 354.

ANCIENTS. The quality of conjugial love among the Ancient and Most Ancient peoples, 73–78.
Precepts concerning marriages left by the Most Ancient people to their posterity, 77[4].
The Ancient people, who succeeded the Most Ancient, acknowledged the wisdom of reason as wisdom; and they were called *Philosophers*, 130.
They knew that each and all things that are done from the body are done from a spiritual origin, 220.
They had the science of correspondences, 342[2].

ANGEL. Every one who becomes an angel carries his own heaven within

ANGEL—*continued.*
himself, because he carries within himself the love of his own heaven, 10[8].
Every society in heaven is as one common body, and the angels in it are as the like parts, from which the common body co-exists, *ib.*
With the angels, wisdom never has an end or ceases to be, but grows and increases to eternity, 18.
When the eyes of the spirit are opened, angels appear in their own form, which is the human form; but when the eyes of the spirit are closed, then they do not appear, 30.
An angel cannot appear to a man of this world, nor a man of this world to an angel, 31.
Two angels from the third heaven appear to Swedenborg, and describe to him their state as to conjugial love, 42[2].
All angels are affections of love in human form. The ruling affection itself shines forth out of their faces; and garments are allotted to them, from the affection, and according to it, 42[3].
The angels, after the delights [of conjugial love], do not become sad, as some do on earth, but cheerful; the cause of this, 44[9].
All who come into heaven return into their vernal youth, and into the powers of that age, and remain so to eternity, 44[9].
The angelic spirits said, "The Word is inwardly spiritual, and the angels, because they are spiritual, will teach the spiritual understanding of it," 44[10].
There are weddings in the heavens, but for no others there than those who are in the marriage of good and truth; nor are any others angels, 44[10].
All in the heavens are consociated according to affinities and relationships of love, 50.
Conjugial love perfects an angel; for married consorts in heaven are not two, but one angel, 52.
By means of the conjugial unition they become filled with the Human, 52.
They are spiritual, 53.
The angels of the highest heaven are called celestial angels, because they are wisdoms and hence loves, and the angels beneath that heaven are called spiritual angels, because they are wisdoms and thence loves, 64.
They have genuine conjugial love, 64, 69.
What they say about the delights of conjugial love, 69.

ANGEL—*continued.*

They are in a clear perception of spheres, 171².

They are in spiritual and celestial conjugial love, and are not encompassed with so gross a body as the men of the Earth, 178.

Every angel, like every man, thinks what is true, and does what is good, as from himself, 207⁴.

Among the angels there are those who are simple and those who are wise; and it is the part of the wise to judge, when the simple, from simplicity and ignorance, are doubtful about what is just, or depart from it, 207⁴.

Every angel is an angel according to use, 207⁷.

An angel is alive according to the application of his mind from use: this is manifestly evident from the fact that every one has conjugial love with its virtue, potency, and delights, according to the application of the genuine use in which he is, 207⁷.

No one in heaven knows his earthly father, but the Lord is the Father of all, 250.

With angels, the commonness [of delight] resulting from constant permission is the very delight of the soul, and the container of their conjugial love, for they are constantly in the delight of that love, and in its ultimates; when, 256ᵉ.

With the angels there is no refusal and resistance on the part of the wives, . . . and there is also a talking by the wives about love, 258.

All the angels can see from the faces of others the delights of their hearts, 316.

They are of both sexes, bachelors and husbands, virgins and wives, 355².

They do not know in heaven any other love of the sex than conjugial love, 355².

Of a certain angel who had lived one thousand years with his wife in perpetual faculty, 355³.

Their married state, 355⁶.

Every man has angels associated with him by the Lord; and such is his conjunction with them, that if they were to be taken away, he would instantly die, 404.

The angels of the third heaven, who are in a state of innocence from the Lord above other angels, appear like naked children; . . . as they are wiser than all others, they are also more alive, 413.

The wiser the angels are, the more innocent they are, *ib.*

ANGEL—*continued.*

An angel is in essence and form a man, 432.

They are in the faculty of conjugial love to eternity, 433.

They have a clear perception of the distinctions between the different kinds of evils, 463ᵉ.

—*Angels and devils.* The angels of heaven are forms of God, and the angels of hell forms of the devil, and the two forms are opposite to each other, the latter being insanities, the former wisdoms, 153 [a].

Angels are spiritual, but those who go to hell are all natural, 53.

They both do uses, but from opposite motives, 266⁴, ⁵.

They are both forms of their own love; and there is not one angel absolutely like another, nor any spirit of hell, 362.

All in the heavens worship God, and all in the hells worship nature, 415⁴.

All in hell are in the connubial connection of evil and falsity, and all in heaven are in the marriage of good and truth; . . . all in hell are in the lust, lasciviousness and shamelessness of scortatory love, and shun and dread the chastity and modesty of conjugial love, 429.

All in hell are influenced by a will of evil, and all in heaven by a will of good, 529⁵.

—*Angels and spirits* are men, 30.

They are nothing else than minds and souls in a human form, 192.

They have internal and external affections, just like men in the world, . . . with them, both the internal and external affections are reduced into likeness and correspondence, 273².

—*Angelic heaven*, see under HEAVEN.

ANGELIC SPIRITS have all interpretation of the Word, from heaven, 44¹⁰.

ANGER. Why anger is attributed to the Lord in the Word, 366.

ANIMALS. See also BEASTS. Difference between man and animals, 96.

The wonderful things that are observed in the productions of animals, may be used to confirm in favour of of the Divine, 416²⁻⁴.

ANIMUS. *Note:*—This Latin term is sometimes translated "mind," sometimes "lower mind," and sometimes "disposition," according to the context.

External likenesses and unlikenesses are not of the souls but of the dispositions. By the dispositions are meant the external affections and the consequent external inclinations, which are

ANIMUS—*continued.* insinuated after birth chiefly by means of the educations, associations, and the consequent habits, 246[2].

There are no two dispositions alike; . . . the disposition derives its origin and form from the life, 524.

ANTIPATHY. Sympathy and antipathy take their rise from the spiritual spheres that flow forth from the objects, 171.

In the natural world antipathy can be concealed, 272.

In the spiritual world antipathies are not only felt, but they also appear in the face, speech, and gestures, 273.

In infernal marriages in the natural world, the married partners are inwardly antipathetic and outwardly to all appearance sympathetic, 292[2].

ANTIQUITY. Remarkable things of Antiquity itself seen in the heaven of the Copper Age, 77[6].

AORTA, 315[7].

APES. Those who have confirmed themselves in the persuasion that the lust of defloration is not an evil of sin, in hell appear like apes, 505[4].

APOCALYPSE. A voice from heaven commanding Swedenborg to apply to the work begun on the Apocalypse, and to finish it within two years, 522.

The Apocalypse has been revealed, which could not be revealed even as to a single little verse except by the Lord, 532[7].

APOPLEXY. Permanent debility from attacks of apoplexy, a cause of legitimate separation, 253; and a just cause of concubinage, 470.

APPEARANCES in the spiritual world, how circumstanced, 158.

Appearances of spaces in the spiritual world are according to the state of life of those who are there, 50.

Note:—Those things which in the spiritual world are exhibited to the sight of spirits and angels are called *appearances;* those things are called appearances, because, corresponding to the interiors of spirits and of angels, they vary according to the states of those interiors. There are real appearances and unreal appearances; the unreal appearances are those which do not correspond to the interiors. See *Heaven and Hell*, 175.

APPLICATIONS and appropriations of the life of the husbands with the wives take place according to conjugial love, 172[e].

APPROPRIATION of evil, how effected, 489.

ARCHITECTONIC ART (The) in heaven, is in its very art, and from it are derived all the rules of that art in the world, 12.

ARISTIPPUS, 151[a].

ARISTOTLE, 151[a].

"ARMIES of the Lord Jehovih": thus the Most Ancient people call themselves and their habitations, 75[3].

ARTS in the spiritual world, 207.

As from himself, 132, 134, 269, 340.

ASSAULT. How love defends itself when assaulted, 361.

ASSES. Of those who, in the other world, appear at a distance like asses carrying burdens, 232[5].

A pope in hell seated on a glowing or red-hot ass, 265.

ASSIDUITY is one of the virtues that pertain to the moral wisdom of men, 164.

ASSOCIATE, see CONSOCIATE.

ASTRONOMY, its use, 163.

ATHEISTS. Even atheists, who are in the glory of reputation from the love of self, and thence in the conceit of self-intelligence, enjoy a more lofty rationality than many others: the reason why, 269[6].

I have seen in the spiritual world those who had confirmed themselves in favour of nature so far as to become atheists, and that their understanding in spiritual light appeared open beneath, but closed above, 421.

Those who have made themselves atheists by confirmations in favour of nature ought not to be excused; why, 422.

ATHENS. A city in the spiritual world called Athens, 151[a], 182, 207.

Sports of the Athenaeïdes, . . . which are spiritual exercises and trials of skill, 207[6].

ATMOSPHERES. The world is distinguished into regions as to the atmospheres, of which the lowest is watery, the higher is aërial, the still higher one is ethereal, above which there is also the highest, 188[3].

The reason why the atmosphere appears golden in the heaven where the love of ruling is from the love of uses, 266[2].

Use is as the atmosphere which contains heat and light (love and wisdom) in its bosom, 137[4].

AUDITORY (An) in the spiritual world, 207.

AURA. A higher aura is the continent of heavenly light and heat, or of the wisdom and love in which the angels are, 145.

AUTHORESSES. Examination of the writings of certain learned authoresses

BLESSEDNESS—*continued.*
possibly be conferred upon man by the Lord, are collected into conjugial love, 68.

The innermost delights of conjugial love in their descent become more and more perceptible, in the higher parts of the mind as blessednesses, 69.

Blessedness is one of the states arising from the innocence, peace, and other states of conjugial love, 180.

The love of uses receives its blessedness from communication by means of uses with others, 266^3.

Celestial blessednesses, etc., can only be given with one wife, 335.

The pleasantnesses of conjugial love in the highest region of the soul are perceived as blessednesses, *ib.*

There is an infinity of all blessednesses in the Lord, *ib.*

Married partners derive from conjugial love the blessedness of their souls, 371.

BLESSING of marriages by the priests, 308.

BLISSFULNESS (*faustitas*). In the thoughts of the mind, the delights of the soul are perceived as blisssfulnesses, 16^2.

Blissfulness is one of the states arising from the states of truly conjugial love, 180.

The innermost delights of conjugial love in their descent become perceptible in the lower parts of the mind as blissfulnesses, 69.

The pleasantnesses of truly conjugial love, in the middle region of the mind are perceived as blissfulnesses, 335.

BLOOD. The heat of the blood, and also its redness, are from no other source than the love, 34.

BLUE (DARK) COLOUR: its signification, $76^{6,7}$.

BODY. See also *Mind and body; Soul, mind, and body.*

The body blunts and absorbs the sensation that the two consorts are a united man, 178.

Angels, after the casting away of the body, are perfect men, 178^2.

The bosom is as it were the forum of assembly and a royal council chamber, and the body is as a populous city around it, 179.

Arguments against the resurrection of the body, 182^{5-7}.

Each and all things that are done in the body are from a spiritual origin, 220.

The material body of man is surcharged with lusts, which are in it as dregs; the matters of which the bodies

BODY—*continued.*
of men in the world are composed, consist of such things, 272.

The body either absorbs the internal affections, and involves them in its dregs, or by dissimulation conceals them, 272.

The material body is cast away at death, and when man is stripped of that body, he is in his internal affections, which his body had previously concealed, 273.

A change of organization is possible only in the material body, and is utterly impossible in the spiritual body, after the former has been cast away, 524^3.

BOND. Wives love the bonds of marriage, provided only that the men also love them, 217.

Bonds of wedlock, when loosened at home, 275.

Internal and external bonds: their mutual relation, 320.

BOOKS in the spiritual world, 207^5, 380^3.

BORN (To be). Every man, when he is born, is merely corporeal, 59, 94, 102, 447.

"Born of the Lord" signify those who are regenerated by the Lord, 120.

Why man is born without knowledges, 133, 134.

Difference between man and beasts at their birth, and during after life, 133, 134; reason for this difference, 350.

Man is born in the lowest region, the natural, 305.

Every man is born for heaven, and no one for hell, 350.

Why man was born, 447.

BRAINS. The seat of the soul conjectured by some to be in some part of the brain, 315^{4-6}.

The cerebellum is dedicated to love and its goods; and the cerebrum to wisdom and its truths, 444^6.

BREADTH, see HEIGHT AND BREADTH.

BREAST or BOSOM. The sphere which pours forth from every human being encompasses him more densely on the breast than on the back, 171^2, 224; effect of this circumstance on married partners, 171^2.

The bosom is as it were the forum of assembly, and a royal council-chamber; the reason, 179.

The breast of the man (*vir*) signifies wisdom, 193.

The Lord calls those who are of His church, brethren and sisters, 120^e.

BRIDE AND BRIDEGROOM. Description of the dress of a bridegroom and bride in heaven, 20^2, 21.

BRIDE AND BRIDEGROOM—*continued.*
The bridegroom represents the Lord, and the bride the church, 21.
After the wedding, the husband represents wisdom, and the wife the love of his wisdom, 21^2.
After the wedding, both together, the husband and his wife, represent the church, *ib.*
The Lord in the Word is called the bridegroom and husband, and the church the bride and wife, 117.
BRIDECHAMBER. The bride-chambers of the understanding and the will, $270^{5,6}$.
BRIMSTONE. Pools of fire and brimstone, 79^{11}, 80.
Its correspondence, 80.
BROTHELS; why tolerated, 451.
BROTHERS AND SISTERS in the Word mean the offspring from the Lord and the church, 120.
BUTTERFLIES, their metamorphosis, 418.
CALF. A golden calf denotes the pleasure of the flesh, 535.
CAMP (The) of the sons of Israel represented the church, 431.
CANCERS a just cause of concubinage, 470.
CAPS 78^4. A cap signifies intelligence, 293^7.
CAROTID ARTERIES, 315^7.
CASTIGATION (a term in chemistry), 145.
CATS, compared with violators, 512.
CAUSE. See also END. The speech of the angels of the Golden Age is the speech of wisdom, because they speak from causes, 75^6.
CAUSES of colds, separations, and divorces, 234–260.
Causes of concubinage, 467–474.
CELEBRATIONS of the Lord from the Word, 81.
CELESTIAL. In the proportion in which any one loves his own married consort alone, he becomes celestial and internal, 77^4.
CELIBACY. The state of celibates or unmarried persons after death, 54.
The sphere of perpetual celibacy infests the sphere of conjugial love, 54^5.
The relation of celibacy to chastity, 155. Marriage is to be preferred to celibacy, 156.
CENTRE AND EXPANSE of nature and of life, $380^{3, 7-11}$.
CERBERUS, 79^2.
CEREBELLUM } See BRAINS.
CEREBRUM }
CHAMBER, see BRIDE-CHAMBER.
CHANGE. The change of the state of life which takes place with men and women by means of marriage, 841–206.

CHANGE—*continued.*
By changes of the state of life are meant changes of quality as to the things which belong to the understanding and the will, 184.
The changes which take place in a man's internals are more perfectly continuous than those which take place in his externals; why, 185^2.
These changes are different with men from what they are with women, 187.
Object of changes of state, 187.
No one's life can be changed after death; . . . a change of organization is possible only in the material body, 524^3.
CHARGES OF BLAME are made by a judge according to the law, 485.
CHARIOT (A) signifies the doctrine of truth, 76^2.
The angel said, "that chariot is a sign for us to depart," 76^8.
CHARITY is love, 10^7.
It is one of the spiritual virtues with men, 164.
In proportion as any one is in charity, he is spiritual, but in proportion as he is not in charity, he is natural, 426.
Whoever is devoid of charity is prone to all the lasciviousnesses of scortatory love, 426.
CHARITY AND FAITH constitute the life of God in man, and are signified by the tree of life, 135.
Faith belongs to truth, and charity to good, 126.
Living well is charity, and believing well is faith; . . . faith belongs to charity, and charity to faith, 233^2.
CELESTIAL AND SPIRITUAL. Those things which, from their origin, are celestial and spiritual, are not in space but in the appearance of space, 158.
CHASTE; CHASTITY. All novitiates, on ascending into heaven, are explored as to the quality of their chastity, 44^4.
Angelic chastity which is common to both sexes, prevents the passing of the chaste love of the sex beyond the enclosure of the heart, 44^5.
Truly conjugial love is chastity itself, 139, 143.
The purity of conjugial love is what is called chastity, 139.
With those who are chaste each and all things are chaste from the inmosts to the ultimates, and this is effected by the chastity of conjugial love, 140^e.
The chaste is predicated only of monogamous marriages, 141.

CHRISTIAN—*continued.*
Polygamy is not allowable for Christians either in the natural or spiritual world, 47[b].
Conjugial love possible only among Christians, 337.
If a Christian marries several wives he commits not only natural but also spiritual adultery, 339.
A Christian possesses the faculty of being capable of being regenerated, and thus of becoming spiritual, and also of attaining to truly conjugial love; the reason, 339^3.
Concubinage conjointly with the wife is unlawful for Christians, 464.
—*Marriages of*, see under MARRIAGE.
CHRISTIAN CHURCH. Those with whom the Christian church is not, are both external natural and internal natural men: to such persons polygamy is not hurtful, 340^2.
That it may again revive, 532^2.
CHRISTIAN HEAVENS: separation between the Christian heavens and the Mohammedan and Gentile heavens, 352.
CHRISTIAN RELIGION makes a one with conjugial love, and dwells together with it, 458.
Religion in Christendom is from the Word, 466^2.
CHRYSALISES, 418.
CHURCH (The). See also LORD (The) AND THE CHURCH. Consists of both sexes, 21^3.
What constitutes it: the conjunction of good and truth, 63; the truth of faith and the good of life, 72; internal marriage, 76^5; a man and a woman, and still more a husband and wife together, 125; conjunction with the Lord, 126^e, 129^e.
Is the marriage of good and truth, 115^4.
John represented the church as to the goods of charity, which are the church in very effect, 119.
Considered in itself, it is the marriage of good and truth, so far as it is from the Word, 339^2.
Is the Lord's kingdom in the earths, corresponding to His kingdom in the heavens, 431.
If you remove the doctrinals [of the New Church] from the church, you remove from it the Sacred Scripture, and also religion; and when these are removed, the church is not a church, 82^e.
The church is various and diverse in the several parts of the world, 246.
What constitutes the anti-church, 497.
CHURCH—*continued.*
The church and conjugial love are constant companions, 156.
By means of the things of the church there is effected a conjunction of likenesses differing interiorly, 228.
The uncleanness and cleanness of the church, whence, 431.
With whom possible, 76^5.
End of the Church is now, why, 80^3.
—*Its origin.* The church is from the marriage of good and truth, 246.
Is from the Lord, and is with those who approach Him, and live according to His precepts, 129.
The Lord's church in the Christian world is from the Word, 129.
The origin of the church, and the origin of conjugial love, are in the same seat, and in a continual embrace, 238^2.
— *Its formation.* How formed by the Lord with the two married consorts, 63, 125.
It is formed by means of the truth of doctrine, 115^4.
How formed by the Lord with man, 122.
— *Its dwelling-place.* The church in its genuine truths is in the Word, and the Lord is present there in those truths, 142.
The things which belong to the church and are called spiritual things, reside in the inmosts with man, 130^2.
— *Its representation.* The church is meant by the Lord's disciples, 119.
—*Its state.* The genuine state of the Church is from no other source than from the Lord, and thus is with none others than those who receive it from Him, 337.
CHURCHES (The) before the Lord's coming were all representative churches, 342^2.
CIRCE, 521^4.
CIRCLE and progression of conjugial love, 78^8.
What is represented by circles around the head, 269^3.
CIRCUMSTANCES and contingencies vary everything, 485.
The quality of everything depends upon circumstances, 487.
Various circumstances exist in the world that mitigate or aggravate crimes, 530.
CITIES in heaven, 9, 17^{2-5}.
A city of the Silver Age, $76^{3, 4}$.
Cities of the Iron Age, 78^3.
A city of the Age of Iron and Clay, 79^4.
CIVIL THINGS: what they are, and how circumstanced, $130^{2, 3}$.

CIVILITY is one of the virtues that pertain to the moral wisdom of men, 164.

CLAY. The Age of Iron and Clay, 79.

CLEAN. To the clean all things are clean, 140e.

The cleanness of heaven and the uncleanness of hell, and the same in the church, how circumstanced, 430, 431.

COCKROACH, 329.

COHABITATION (Internal) of the souls and minds is cohabitation in the principal idea, 322.

COHOBATION (a term in chemistry), 145.

CLEAVING to one's wife: its signification, 194.

CLEVERNESS belongs to the rational wisdom of men, 163.

Women's writings found to be works not of judgment and wisdom, but of cleverness and eloquence, 175[3].

CLOTHING, see DRESS.

COCKS: their jealousy, 378.

COLD, see also *Heat and Cold.*

—*Conjugial Cold.* When it arises in the marriages of those who love only corporeal natural things, 59[2].

Effect of coldness on conjugial love when divided among several, 147.

What it is, 270[6], 294[3-6].

It is the deprivation of conjugial love; it is also the deprivation of the state of the church, or of religion, 239.

Its cause and occasions, 155[a][3], 167, 208[4], 294[3-6], 331[2], 482e.

It is deeply seated in most men, 167.

In human minds, resides above all other colds, 236.

Causes of, in marriages, 234–250, 256–259.

Cold for marriage, whence it arises, 305e.

The number of colds, 244, 313e.

Intense [conjugial] cold arises from the idea that conjugial love is one with scortatory love, 247.

It is different with the slothful and idle from that cold with others; it is indeed the deprivation of conjugial love, but from defect, 249e.

Its place of abode in the human mind, 270.

Colds arises from various causes, which all derive their source from an unlikeness of the internal inclinations, 275.

Scortatory love may be called conjugial cold itself, 247.

In proportion as cold is in the mind, it is in the body also; and according to its increase, the externals of the body also are closed, 260.

Merely natural spirits are chilled with intense cold, when, 235.

COLD—*continued.*

— *Spiritual,* is the deprivation of love, 235.

Its source, 235.

In marriages, is a disunion of the souls, and a disjunction of the minds, 236.

Cold towards the sex, whence it arises with adulterers, 433.

COLUMN, comparison with, to illustrate successive and simultaneous order, 314[2].

COMMAND, see RULE.

COMMANDMENTS (keeping the Lord's) an essential of the Church, 129, 340, 528; and of conjugial love, 336.

COMMONNESS (The) resulting from constant permission exists with those who think lasciviously about marriage and wives, 256.

With angels, it is the very delight of the soul, and is the container of their conjugial love, 256.

COMMUNICATION, by means of uses, with others, the source of the blessedness of the love of uses, 266[3].

No communication between the Christian and Mohammedan heavens, 352.

Communications of love between married partners, how effected, and why thus, 396[3].

COMMUNION between married partners, 277.

The conjugial communion between married consorts gives birth to external affections resembling the internal ones, 278.

CONATUS, see ENDEAVOUR.

CONCEIT, or the love of one's own intelligence, is an evil love: its origin, 88.

No one can ever love his wife conjugially who is in the conceit of his own intelligence from the love of self, 193[2].

How the Lord provides that man should not perish by reason of the conceit of self-intelligence, 353.

The devil as to the love of self and the conceit of self-intelligence, is meant by the serpent in Gen. iii., 135[3].

The men who are in conceit from the love of self, are the tree of the knowledge of good and evil, and the tree of life, *ib.*

CONCEPTION. Women have a state of preparation for, 219.

Conceptions would not be possible unless conjunction in a mediate love were effected between consorts whose souls are disjoined, 245.

CONCERTS of music in heaven, 6[5], 17.

CONCLUSIONS (Forming), the orderly and disorderly way of, 408.

CONJUGIAL LOVE—*continued.*
mains, in its progression afterwards, 311.
—*Its origin* is from the marriage of good and truth, 60–65, 141.
It is from the Lord, 62[e], 70, 81[e], 131, 458, 534.
There are both internal and external origins of it, 83.
It is the marriage of good and truth, 83.
It is from the influx of the marriage of good and truth from the Lord, 92; why, 93.
It commences from the love of the sex, or rather by means of it, but still it does not originate in it, 98.
Its origin is in the interiors of the mind, 99.
A discussion as to the origin of conjugial love and its potency, 103–114.
It is from the Lord, and corresponds to the marriage of the Lord and the church, 143.
It descends from the marriage of good and truth, *ib.*
Its origin is Divine celestial, for it is the Divine Love, the Divine wisdom, and the Divine use, 183[2].
Its origin is Divine celestial, because it is by virtue of influx from the Lord into the souls of human beings 183[3].
Its very origin resides with man in the inmosts, *i.e.*, in his soul, 238.
It originally comes into existence from the conjugial effort that is inherent in souls, 238[2]
The origin of the church, and of conjugial love, are in the same seat, and in a continual mutual embrace, 238[2, 3].
It is from the Lord alone, 349.
It is from the Lord alone, and has been made a point of religion, 466[2].
Its origin is a union of souls, 480.
It descends from the Lord through heaven, 481.
—*Its appearance and representation.* Its representation in a husband and wife from the third heaven, 42[2–5].
The tone of voice of conjugial love (in a husband and wife of the third heaven) inwardly is simultaneous, and proceeds from the delights of a state of peace and innocence, 42[5].
Its appearance and representation with two married partners from heaven, 137.
—*Conditions of its existence and increase.* It is according to the state of the church with man, 70.
In proportion as a man becomes spiritual, he is in truly conjugial love, 130.
It is according to the state of the

CONJUGIAL LOVE—*continued.*
church, and of wisdom, with man, 130.
It is according to the love of being wise from the Lord for the sake of uses, 183[e].
Every one has conjugial love with its virtue, potency, and delights, according to the application of the genuine use in which he is, 207[7].
The angels have conjugial love according to wisdom, and the increase of that love and at the same time of its delights is according to the increase of wisdom, 211.
Where religion is not, conjugial love does not exist; and where conjugial love is not, there is cold, 239.
Every one has conjugial love according to the state of the church, 240.
It is in the same degree as the conjunction of good and truth, 63.
In proportion as a man loves wisdom from the love thereof, or truth from good, he is in truly conjugial love, 355[8].
—*Its accompaniments.* Conjugial love and vernal heat act as a one in heaven, 137[4].
Truly conjugial love keeps pace with the state of the Church in man, 142.
With women it acts in unity with their virginity, 460[2].
—*Its correspondence.* It corresponds to the marriage of the Lord and the church, 62, 143.
It corresponds to the affection of genuine truth, its chastity, purity, and holiness, 127.
—*Its subjects.* An angel out of the third heaven appears to Swedenborg, and foretells also that no others will appropriate that love to themselves, except those who are received by the Lord into the New Church, which is the New Jerusalem, 43.
Those who love corporeal natural things, and rational things only from them, cannot be conjoined with a consort as into a one; explained, 59[2]; this is the case with most at the present day. It is different with the spiritual: how, *ib.*
It is with the angels of both the higher and the lower heavens, 64.
The angels have genuine conjugial love, 69.
None others can come into it, and be in it, than those who approach the Lord, and love the truths of the church, and do its goods, 70–72, 458.
None others can be in spiritual conjugial love, but those who are such from the Lord, 71[2].

CONJUGIAL LOVE—*continued.*
It is with those who are made spiritual by the Lord through the Word, 81[e].
It exists only with those who earnestly desire wisdom, 98.
Truly conjugial love is known only to those few who are near to God, 113.
Those who do not hold marriages to be holy, do not love their wives from spiritual love, 155 [a][3].
Nothing of conjugial love is with men, but only with wives and women, 161.
No one can ever love his consort conjugially who is in the conceit of his own intelligence from the love of self, 193[2].
Truly conjugial love was among the Most Ancient people, 205.
They who are in it love nothing more than to become wise, 211.
Those who enter upon marriage for the sake of lasciviousness are opposed to conjugial love, 212.
It resides with chaste wives; but still their love depends on their husbands, 216[a].
There is not any conjugial love with the masculine sex, but only with the feminine sex, and from this sex it is transferred into the masculine sex, 223.
Some conjugial love is possible with those who are in falsities yet at the same time in certain goods; but with those who have falsified the genuine truths of the church, no conjugial love is possible, 243.
Truly conjugial love may exist with one consort, and not with the other, 226.
Internal love cannot exist between married partners, one of whom is spiritual and the other natural, 281.
Truly conjugial love can only exist with one wife, 333.
It can exist only with those who are of the church, 337.
It could not exist with the Israelitish nation; why, 340.
The Mohammedans cannot receive it, 341.
It cannot be given by the Lord to any others than those who know Him, acknowledge Him, etc.; and those to whom it cannot be given know no otherwise than that the love of the sex and conjugial love are one, 349.
Monogamists alone can receive spiritual conjugial love, 369.
It is with the spiritual but not with the natural, 409.
It is implanted in every woman from creation, . . . and from the women is communicated to the men, 409.

CONJUGIAL LOVE—*continued.*
In households where there is no conjugial love between the consorts, it nevertheless is with the wife, 409.
It exists with those who are of the Christian religion, 458.
It is preserved with those who prefer marriage to concubinage, 475.
It cannot possibly exist except in monogamous marriages 482.
It is given to those who live according to the Lord's precepts; thus it is given to those who are received into the Lord's New Church, the New Jerusalem, 534.
—*Its effects and blessings.* With the angels in the heavens, especially in the third heaven, heavenly delights are principally from conjugial love, 42.
It perfects an angel, for it unites him with his consort; whence he becomes more and more a human being; . . . wherefore, by means of the conjugial unition they become filled with the Human, 52.
Into it are collected all joys and delights from first to last; the love manifests itself, yea, comes into existence and lives, by means of them, 68.
It expands the innermost parts of the body, as the delicious current of its fountain flows through and opens them, 68.
All delights from primes to ultimates are collected into conjugial love, on account of the surpassing excellence of its use, 68.
It restores man to integrity, 88.
When it has been implanted, the love of the sex inverts itself, and becomes the chaste love of the sex, 99.
With those who are chaste each and all things are chaste from the inmosts to the ultimates, and this is effected by the chastity of conjugial love, 140[e].
Delights constitute the life of that love, 144.
It conjoins two souls, and hence two minds, into a one; . . . especially with married partners who love each other inmostly, 158.
The consorts feel themselves to be a united man, 178.
Truly conjugial love conjoins two more and more into one man, 200.
It opens the interiors of their minds, 200.
With those who are in truly conjugial love the faculty of becoming wise increases, 211; the happiness of dwelling together increases, 213; the conjunction of minds increases, also friendship, 214.
In truly conjugial love there is eter-

CONJUGIAL LOVE—*continued.*
nity; and its eternity is in consequence of that love with the wife, and wisdom with the husband, increasing to eternity, 216.

From conjugial love, as from a fountain, issue the activities and alacrities of life, 249.

While it is in the mind, it is similar to itself in the body; and . . . it opens the externals of the body from the interiors; and the privation of it, which is cold, closes up the externals of the body from the interiors, 260.

Man is elevated into the celestial region of the mind by truly conjugial love, 305.

In truly conjugial love there is a fear of loss, and loss is followed by grief, 318[3].

Truly conjugial love conjoins the souls and hearts of two . . . so that the two consorts become one flesh, 334.

It induces on a wife the form of love, and on a husband the form of wisdom, 367.

From it, married partners derive the blessedness of their souls, the blissfulness of their minds, the delightsomeness of their bosoms, and the pleasure of their bodies, 371.

The cleanness of heaven and in the church is from conjugial love, 430, 431.

— *Its use* is the propagation of the human race, and this use was the end of ends of creation, 68; it is more excellent than the other uses of creation, 143; it is the most excellent of all uses, 183[7], 305.

— *Its end or object.* Conjugial love has chiefly respect to an union of wills, and a freedom of action resulting thence, 248.

The end of marriage is the procreation of offspring, 254.

The first end of conjugial love is the procreation of offspring, and the last end, which is the effect, is the offspring that is procreated, 385.

— *Its vein and potency.* See also under FACULTY.

The vein of potency is the source of the life of conjugial love; when this vein fails, the love fails and grows cold, 44[8].

The delicious current (vein) of its fountain, 68.

A discussion on the virtue or potency of conjugial love, 103–114.

In proportion as any one loves to be wise for the sake of genuine use, he is in the vein and potency of conjugial

CONJUGIAL LOVE—*continued.*
love; and in proportion as he is in this, he is in the delights, 183[6].

Conjugial love depends and lives on the flow, sufficiency, and strength of its current (vein), 293[4].

Its current is closed by obstructions of the inmost life, 313e.

Truly conjugial potency cannot exist except with one wife, 333.

The vein is opened by the wisdom of conjugial love, 433.

How the channel (vein) of conjugial love is obstructed, and how opened, 482e.

— *Its arcana* transcend the wisdom of men to such a degree that the understanding cannot apprehend them, 208[2].

Arcana of wisdom respecting conjugial love now first disclosed, which abound more in the third heaven than in the others, 43.

— *Its place of abode.* With monogamists it does not reside in the natural man, but enters into the spiritual man, and successively opens to itself a way to the spiritual marriage itself, and conjoins itself therewith, for conjugial love enters according to the increase of wisdom, 141.

It dwells in internals, but friendship in externals, 216[4].

In the highest region of the human mind dwells conjugial love in the love of good with its wisdom; in the middle region, it dwells in the love of truth with its intelligence; in the lowest region, it dwells in the love of what is just and right with its knowledge, 270[3].

Truly conjugial love dwells in the highest region in the midst of mutual love, 270[5].

It resides in the inmosts, 377.

—*Its future.* No others will appropriate that love to themselves except those who are received by the Lord into the New Church, 43.

Conjugial love, such as it was among the Ancients, will be raised up again by the Lord after His coming, 81e.

—*Its permanence after death.* It remains after death with those who come into heaven, 37.

Conjugial love remains with man after death, such as it had been interiorly; that is, such as it had been in the man's interior will and thought in the world, 48.

After death, when conjugial love becomes of the spirit, it becomes more interior and pure, and consequently more perceptible, 51.

CONJUNCTION—*continued.*
Conjunction with another, and especially with the Lord, how effected, 341[2, 3].
—*Inclination for*, see under INCLINATION.
—*The conjunction of good and truth* is the church, 63.
It is in the same degree as conjugial love, *ib.*
—*Conjunction of the Lord and the church*, see *Marriage of the Lord and the church.*
—*Conjunction of souls and minds* by marriage (chapter), 156[a]–181.
It is the internal conjunction of the souls that constitutes marriage itself; and this conjunction is not perceptible until after death, 49; these conjunctions are provided on earth with those who from early manhood have loved, wished for, and asked of the Lord, etc., 49.
The conjunction of minds, and not at the same time of bodies, is spiritual love, and consequently chaste love, 55[7].
The conjunction of souls and minds is a kind of re-unition, not a conjunction into a one, but an adjunction, etc., 158.
The conjugial conjunction is that of the will of the wife with the understanding of the man, and *vice versâ*, 159.
There is a very close conjunction of the understanding and will, and it is such that the one faculty can enter into the other, and be delighted from the conjunction and in it, 159.
Conjunction is inspired into the man by the wife according to her love, and is received by him according to his wisdom, 161.
Conjunction is effected successively from the first days of marriage, and with those who are in truly conjugial love, more and more inwardly to eternity, 177.
Conjunction of minds increases with those who are in truly conjugial love, 214.
A thorough conjunction of the minds can exist only with one wife, 333.
CONJUNCTIVENESS. What it is, and how circumstanced, 37, 46, 316[4]. See LOVE OF THE SEX, also INCLINATION.
CONNUBIAL CONNECTION. Beneath heaven there are no marriages, but only connubial connections, that are alternately made and broken off, 192.
—*Connubial principle or connection of evil and falsity* is the opposite of the conjugial principle, 203; what it is, and how circumstanced, 427, 428; it is the anti-church, 497; it is essentially spiritual adultery, 520; all in hell are in it, 520.
CONSCIENCE is one of the virtues that pertain to the moral wisdom of men, 164.
—*Conscientious scruples* with respect to disagreements in marriage, 271.
CONSECRATION of marriages by a priest, a duty, 308.
CONSENT is the essential of marriage; and all the things which follow are its formalities, 21e.
Consent constitutes marriage, and initiates the maiden's spirit into conjugial love, 299.
Extorted consent does not initiate the spirit, though it may the body, *ib.*
Consent ought to be confirmed by solemn betrothal, 300, 301.
Consent [to evils] induces in the mind a state of the love of evils, 489.
CONSOCIATION (Swedenborg's) with angels and spirits, 45.
Principle of consociation in the heavens, 50, 153 [a][2].
CONSORT, see HUSBAND AND WIFE.
CONSUMMATION OF THE AGE signifies the last time and end of the church, 80[3].
CONSULTATION with parents, a duty on the part of the woman, 298.
CONTEMPT between married partners springs from a disunion of the souls and a disjunction of the minds, 236; it also arises from the idea that conjugial love is one with scortatory love, 247.
CONTINGENCIES. See CIRCUMSTANCES.
CONTRARIES, how circumstanced, 425.
CONVERSATION (The) with men and with women; its difference, 218.
CONVICTION is above authority, 295.
COPPER signifies natural good, 77[2].
CORPORA STRIATA, 315[5, 6].
CORPOREAL (The) is like ground, into which natural, rational, and spiritual things are implanted in their order, 59.
Man is born corporeal, and becomes more and more interiorly natural, 59, 447, and remains corporeal unless he learns to know, understand, and be wise, from others, 133.
Who are called corporeal-natural men, 442.
Adulteries render human beings corporeal, 495.
Who become corporeal spirits, 495[e].
Definition of corporeal men, 496.
See also under NATURAL.

DELIGHT (*delitium*)—*continued.*
All joys and delights from primes to ultimates are collected into conjugial love, 68, 69.
All delights belong to love, 155[a][3].
The delight of delirium, 267[4].
— *Paradisiacal delights*, external and internal, their differences, 8[4].
— *Ultimate delights*, see *Delights of conjugial love.*
— *Delights* (*delitiae*) *of conjugial love.* Ultimate delights, in heaven; their nature and use, 44[8, 9].
The innermost delights of conjugial love . . . are imperceptible . . . and at last unite themselves in ultimates into the delight of delights, 69.
Their varieties infinite, 69, 155[a][5].
With those of the Golden Age, they are excellent and eminent according to the worship of the Lord Jehovih, 75[7].
They are all, even the ultimate ones, chaste, 144.
They ascend and enter heaven, and in the way pass through the delights of the heavenly loves; and they conjoin themselves with the delights of the conjugial love in which the angels are, 144.
The angels perceive these delights with themselves to be exalted and fulfilled, when they ascend from chaste consorts on earth, 144.
The sense of the delights of conjugial love, 155[a][2–5].
The wisdom concerning these delights is a wisdom deeply reserved in the hearts of the female sex [in heaven], and is not disclosed to any husband unless he be in truly conjugial love, 155[a][3].
"Adramandoni," 183.
Whence and with whom they are, 183[6–8], 293, 294.
In their beginnings they are imperceptible; but they become more and more perceptible as they descend thence by degrees and enter the body, 183[6].
Their genesis, 183[7].
They are exalted above all other delights which exist in heaven and in the world, 183[7].
Conjugial delights with the wife; their origin and chief *raison d'être*, 198.
The spiritual delights conjoined with natural delights, which are the portion of those who are in truly conjugial love, constitute the faculty of loving and being loved, and hence the faculty of becoming wise, 211.
With wives in heaven, they are exalted and diminished, and altogether

DELIGHT (*delitium*)—*continued.*
qualified according to the wisdom in their husbands, 293[2].
They are myriads, scarcely any of which are as yet known to the world; but they will be known when the church betroths herself to her Lord and is married, 293[6].
Represented by certain beautiful scenery, 294.
Their opposition to the delights of scortatory love, 294.
They are the delights of wisdom, 294[7, 8].
They ascend to the highest heaven, and conjoin themselves with the delights of all heavenly loves, 294[8].
See also below, under *Delights* (*jucunda*) *of conjugial love.*
— *The delights of scortatory love* are the pleasures of insanity, 294[7].
DELIGHT (*jucundum*), DELIGHTSOMENESS (*jucunditas*). *Note:*—This latter term has been adopted in this translation for the sake of distinction.
The delights of infernal and heavenly loves come into collision with each other like enemies, and destroy each other, 10[8].
What are the delights of the body without the delights of the soul? 16[2].
The delights of the soul, what they are: in the sensations of the body they are perceived as delightsomenesses, 16[2].
Spiritual delight is super-eminent in comparison with natural delight, 29[e].
Every delightsomeness grows according to the perception, until its blessedness is discernible in its delightsomeness, 51[e].
All delights whatsoever that are felt by man are of his love, 68.
Delights exalt themselves in the proportion that the love exalts itself, *ib.*
Delights follow the use, and are in man according to the love of use, *ib.*
Each of the senses has delights according to its uses, 68[e].
The innermost delights of conjugial love in their descent become perceptible, in the breast as delightsomenesses, 69.
It is one of the states arising from the states of conjugal love, 180.
Delights tie minds (*animi*) together, 272.
Delights are smelt in the spiritual world, *ib.*
Delightsomenesses, why so called, and where and how perceived, 335, 442.
The delights of the flesh in the extremes apparently emulate the delights of conjugial love; and those who are

DIGNITIES—*continued.*
Dignities and honours are objects of the love of the body, 49.
DINING-HALL of a heavenly palace described, 14[2].
DIOGENES, 182.
DISCIPLES (The Twelve); what they represented, 119.
Who they are that are called disciples of the Lord in the spiritual world, 261.
DISCORD between married partners, its cause, 236.
What is heterogeneous and discordant causes disjunction and absence, 171.
DISDAIN between married partners arises from the idea that conjugial love is one with scortatory love, 247.
DISEASES that are legitimate causes of separation, 253; and just causes of concubinage, 470.
DISHONOURABLE (*dishonestus*), see HONOURABLE.
DISJUNCTION: its origin, 171, 236.
DISPOSITION, see ANIMUS.
DISPUTING (A desire for) is a really weighty cause of concubinage, 472.
DISSIMILARITY, see SIMILARITY AND DISSIMILARITY.
DISSOLUTIONS, see RENEWAL.
DISTANCES in the spiritual world are appearances, 78[2], 158; and are there caused by spheres, 171.
Distances with spirits are according to the states of their affections, 207[2].
DIVERSITIES. Difference between varieties and diversities, 324.
DIVIDED. Everything is divisible to infinity, 185[e], 329[2].
Everything divided is more and more manifold, and not more and more simple; because what is divided again and again approaches nearer to the infinite, 329[2].
DIVINE (The) that proceeds from the Lord is called a sphere, why, 386.
DIVINE ESSENCE, see under ESSENCE.
DIVINE GOOD AND TRUTH. All Divine truth in the heavens gives forth light, 77[2].
The Lord God the Creator is Divine good itself and Divine truth itself, 84.
They proceed as a one from the Lord, 87[4]: this one is, in a certain image, in every created thing, *ib.*
The Divine good is the Esse of the Lord's substance, and the Divine truth is the Existere, 115[3].
The Divine truth in the Word is united with the Divine good, and this also is the Lord, 129.
DIVINE LOVE AND WISDOM are in the Lord the Creator, and they are Himself, 84.

DIVORCE; its causes, 234, 255, 468.
Definition of, 255, 468.
DIVULGING family secrets (A desire for) is a really weighty cause of concubinage, 472.
DOCTRINALS of the New Church, 82.
If you remove these doctrinals from the church, you remove from it the Sacred Scripture, and also religion; and when these are removed, the church is not a church, 82[e].
DOGS: what they represent in the spiritual world, 97[2, 3].
Who those are who appear like dogs of indulgences, 505[4].
DOVE (A), its signification, 155[a][4], 208.
See also TURTLE-DOVES.
DRAGONS: what they represent in the spiritual world, 79[2, 3].
DRAMATIC ENTERTAINMENTS in heaven, 17[5].
DRESS of the prince of a heavenly society, and of his ministers, described, 15.
DRINKS and foods in heaven, 6[5].
Drinking water from the fountain, what it signifies, 182[2].
DRUNKENNESS a legitimate cause of separation, 252; and a really weighty cause of concubinage, 472.
DURA MATER, 315[5, 6].
DUTCH: see HOLLANDERS.
DUTIES, respective, of husband and wife, 174–176.

EAR. In heaven the right ear is the good of hearing, and the left the truth thereof, 316[5].
It is not the ear that hears sounds, but the spirit, 440.
EARTH. *Note:*—Earth (*tellus*) is distinguished from earth (*terra*) by the use of a capital initial E.
The earth or ground is the common mother of all plants, 206, 397; and of all minerals, 397.
See also LOWER EARTH.
EAST. The Lord is the east, because He is the sun there, 261.
EATING of the tree of life, and of the tree of the knowledge of good and evil; what it signifies, 135, 353, 444[4].
ECCLESIASTICAL ORDER: the nature of their love of self, 264, 265.
They administer the things which belong to the priesthood with the Lord, 308.
EDEN, see GARDEN.
EDUCATION. Respective duties of the father and mother with regard to the education of their children, 176.
Education of children in the other world, 261, 411–413.
EFFECT, see *End, Cause, and Effect.*

EFFIGY. In the other world, the faces of spirits become the effigies of their internal affections, 273.

ELEVATION of the mind with men and women, 188.

Conditions of the elevation of the understanding and will, 269^{6}, 347, 495.

The elevation of the judgment of the spirit is effected by withdrawing it from the senses, and exalting it to a higher light, 57.

ELYSIAN FIELDS, 182^{6}.

EMPLOYMENTS in the other world, 207.

END. The end, purpose, or intention of the will, is primarily regarded by the Lord, 146.

Every end considered in itself is a love, 212.

The angelic heaven is the end of ends, 402.

A man is such a man as he is in his purpose, intention, or end, 452, 527^{e}.

All in heaven are influenced by a good end, and all in hell by an evil end, 453^{e}, 527^{e}.

— *The end of marriage* is the procreation of offspring, 254, 387.

— *The end of the Church* is now, because there does not remain a truth which has not been falsified, 80^{3}.

—*The end or purpose of this Work*, 205.

— *End, Cause, and Effect.*

The end and the cause act in unity, because together, in the things to be effected and in the effects, 387.

Ends progress in a series, one after another, and in their progress the last end becomes the first, and thus further, even to the boundary, in which they subsist or cease, 387.

All the operations in the universe progress from ends through causes into effects, 400.

Their mutual relations, 400, 401.

Every end belongs to the will, or the love, every cause to the understanding, or to wisdom, and every effect to the action, or to use, 400^{2}.

Thinking from ends, causes, and effects, 408.

The exploration of ends, causes, and effects, 461$^{3-7}$.

ENDEAVOUR (*conatus*) is the very essence of motion, and will is a living endeavour with man, 215, 238.

ENGLISH. Opinions of five Englishmen on the subject of conjugial love and its potency, 107.

English Lords (adulterers), 483.

ENLIGHTENMENT (*Illustratio*) of the higher ideas of the understanding is from the influx of heaven, 42^{2}.

Enlightenment follows the conjugial delights with the angels, 44^{9}.

ENLIGHTENMENT—*continued.*

In the Christian world there is enlightenment from the Word on the subject of eternal life, 28.

Spiritual things, being in the light of heaven, enlighten by their light the things that follow in order, 130^{3}.

Note:—Enlightenment is an actual opening of the interiors of the mind, *H. D.* 256.

ENUNCIATIONS (or *Utterances*), the name of the prophetic books of the Ancient Word, 77^{2}.

EPICURUS, 182.

EPILEPSY, a cause of legitimate separation, 253 ; and a just cause of concubinage, 470.

EQUILIBRIUM (Spiritual) between the spheres of conjugial and scortatory loves, 437, 444^{3}, 455 ; it produces freedom, *ib.*

ERA : see AGE (*saeculum*).

ESSE and EXISTERE. The Esse of the Lord's substance is Divine good, and its Existere is Divine truth, 115^{3}.

ESSENCE.

— *The Divine Essence* is constituted of love, wisdom, and use, which are its three essentials, 183^{3}.

Nothing but what is of the Divine Essence can proceed from the Lord and flow in into man's soul, *ib.*

—*Essence and form.* There is no essence without a form, nor form without an essence, 87^{3}.

ETERNAL AND TEMPORARY. Effect of the ideas of what is eternal and what is temporary, in relation to marriage, on the minds of two married partners, 216^{3}.

ETERNAL LIFE, see under LIFE.

ETERNAL REST, see under REST.

ETERNITY is the infinity of time, 185^{e}.

ETHICS is one of those sciences through which, as through doors, an entrance is made into rational things, 163.

EUGENE (PRINCE), 481 *note.*

EUNUCHS. Chastity cannot be predicated of eunuchs, 151.

Who are meant by eunuchs in Matt. xix. 12, 156^{e}.

EVENING. No shades of evening in heaven, 137^{5}.

EVIL, see also *Good and evil.*

Whatever the natural man does from himself is evil, 345.

Evil in regard to the sex is whoredom, *ib.*

All the evil into which man is born is in his natural man, *ib.*

Adulteries are the complex of all evils, 356^{e}.

Evil obliterates truth and induces falsity, 415^{3}.

EVIL—*continued.*
Origin of evil, 4444, 5.
All evils belong at once to the internal and the external man, 486.
Evils are appropriated in proportion as the understanding favours them, 489.
In the spiritual world all are in general distinguished according to evils, etc., 492.
No one can be withdrawn from his evil unless he has first been led into it, 510.
Abstinence from evil because it is sin, necessary, 529.
—*Evils and falsities.* Those who are in evils and consequent falsities, have formed in themselves an effigy of hell, 10[8].
A man must either be in good and at the same time in truth, or in evil and at the same time in falsity, 87[e].
Confirmed falsity coheres with evil, and evil coheres with hell, 422.
Connubial connection of evil and falsity, 427, 429.
They are all distinguished into kinds, species, and differences, 479.
Confirmation of evil and falsity, 491.
EVIL PROPENSITIES (*Reatus*) inherited from the parents reside in the natural man, 448.
EVIL SPIRITS love that which is homogeneous to their affection, 71[e].
The spirits of hell are chilled with intense cold when heat flows in unto them out of heaven, 235[e].
The spirits of hell invert all things with themselves, the delight constantly remaining, 461[6].
EXCITEMENT. Wives are in no excitement as men are, 219.
EXISTENCE: How subsistence or preservation is perpetual existence or creation, 86.
EXPANSE, see CENTRE AND EXPANSE.
EXPANSES (Three) seen by Swedenborg (Memorable Relation), 42.
EXPERTNESS is one of the virtues that pertain to the moral wisdom of men, 164.
EXTENSION cannot be predicated of spiritual things, 158; why, 389.
EXTERNALS: see INTERNAL AND EXTERNAL.
EXTRA-CONJUGIAL LOVE, see CONJUGIAL LOVE.
EYE. When the eyes of the spirit are opened, angels appear in their own form; but when the eyes of the spirit are closed, they do not appear, 30.
The eyes of the body derive from the material world all that pertains to them, *ib.*

EYE—*continued.*
In heaven the right eye is the good of sight, and the left the truth thereof, 316[5].
It is not the eye that sees, but the spirit, 440.

FABLES, so called, were correspondences according to which the primeval people spoke, 182[2].
FACES are the types of the loves, 35.
In the heavens the faces are genuine types of the affections of the love, 65.
There are no two faces alike, 186; nor can there be to eternity, 524.
All the angels can see from the faces of others the delights of their hearts, 316.
The faces are from the dispositions, and the face is a type of the disposition, 524.
Difference between the face of the male and female, 218.
FACULTY. Man is born a faculty of knowing, understanding, and becoming wise; and this faculty receives truths, 122.
Man is born faculty and inclination; faculty to know, and inclination to love, 134[2].
The faculty of becoming wise makes a one with conjugial love, 96[e].
From the conjugial principle, both the faculty and inclination to become wise in the things belonging to the church and heaven may become connate, 142.
Inclination and faculty in offspring born from truly conjugial partners, 202.
Faculty of becoming wise increases with those who are in truly conjugial love, 211.
Faculties of elevating the understanding and will, 230.
A faculty has been implanted for the effectual amendment of depraved inclinations, 202.
The faculty to open the lower parts of the mind even to conjunction with its higher parts, is implanted in every human being, 204.
Faculty of understanding and becoming wise was implanted in man from creation, 444[6].
In man and woman there was implanted at creation an inclination and faculty of conjunction as into a one, and these are still in them, 156[a].
Faculty and inclination for conjunction in both sexes from creation, 157.
—*The virile faculty, potency, or virtue* does not fail when the man loves his

FACULTY—*continued.*
wife from intelligence; but it does fail if he loves her from insanity, 331.
Permanence of faculty (*i.e.*, potency) with the angels, 260[e], 355[2, 5].
When the interiors of the mind are open, spiritual conjugial love flows down freely with its perpetual effort, and causes the faculty to exist, 355[3].
Virtue with the angels is the consequence and not the source of love, 355[7].
It accompanies wisdom in proportion as this is animated from the spiritual things of the church, and hence it resides in conjugial love, 433.
Its state with the spiritual man, the angels, the Most Ancient men, and adulterers, 433.

FAITH is truth, 10[7], 24.
Saving faith consists in believing on the Lord Jesus Christ, 82.
Faith is one of the spiritual virtues, 164. See also CHARITY AND FAITH.

FALL (The) described, 153[a].

FALLACIES (The) of the senses are the darkness of Truths, 152[a][e].

FALSIFICATIONS of Truth are spiritual whoredoms, 77[5], 80[3].
The falsification of good and truth corresponds to adultery, but in a less degree than profanation, 339.

FALSIFIED TRUTHS are the cause of the prevailing ignorance of truly conjugial love, and the negative doubt of its possibility; also of the insanity which dwells in the minds of many, that adulteries are not evils of religion, 243.

FALSITY of religion is the fourth of the internal causes of cold in marriages, 243.
Falsity in spiritual things either takes away religion, or defiles it, 243.
Certain falsities are like discordant tones that may be brought into harmony, 243.
Falsities and depraved inclinations to the things which are of worship, represented by dragons and leopards, 79[3].
See also *Evils and falsities.*

FATHER. The Lord, in the Word, is called the father, and the church the mother, 118, 119.
Spiritual and natural fathers: difference in their love towards their children, 406, 407.
—*The father and mother* whom the man is to leave, signify his proprium of will and proprium of understanding, 194.

FAVOUR (Apparent) Causes of between married partners, 278, 287, 290.
Favour implies consent, 489.

FEAR. In truly conjugial love there is a fear of loss, and loss is followed by grief; and this grief and fear are in the very inmosts of the minds, 318[3].
Jealousy is like a terrible fear of the loss of conjugial love, 368.
In all love there is fear and grief; fear lest it perish, and grief if it perishes; the fear and grief of conjugial love is called zeal or jealousy, 371, 372.

FEASTS in heaven, 6[5].

FECUNDATION: see under SEED.

FEMALE. } see MALE AND FEMALE.
FEMININE. }

FEVERS a legitimate cause of separation, 253; and a just cause of concubinage, 470.

FIRE (The) of the angelic sun is pure love, 34.
Fire denotes the love of evil, 80.
What is fiery in heaven denotes good, 316[6].
Love in its essence is spiritual fire; fire in the Word signifies love, 380[12].
The fire of the altar, and the fire of the candlestick in the tabernacle, represent the Divine love, *ib.*
The fire of the natural sun is from the fire of the spiritual sun, which is the Divine love, *ib.*

FIRE-PLACES (The) of the west, denote the loves of evil, 77[5].

FIRST, see PRIMARY.

FISH (Every) corresponds to some quality, 76.

FLAME. The flaming quality of the sun corresponds to the love of uses, 266[2].
Zeal is a spiritual blazing up or flame, 359.
Love at a distance appears in the spiritual world as flame, . . . but that flame does not burn like the flame of the natural world, *ib.*
Difference between heavenly flame and infernal flame, 365.

FLESH. See also *Spirit and flesh.*
"One flesh" signifies one man, 156 [a][2]; "all flesh" means every man, *ib.*
"They are no longer two, but one flesh," meaning of, 50, 156[a], 178.
It is the spirit, and not the flesh, that feels the things that happen in the flesh, 440.
Strife between the spirit and the flesh, 488.
The flesh is contrary to the spirit, that is, contrary to the spiritual things of the church, 497.

FLOW FROM (To). All that which flows from a subject, and surrounds and environs it, is called a sphere, 386.

FLOW IN (To). See INFLUX.

FLOWERS. The delights of conjugial love represented by flowers interwoven in garments, 137[2].

FLOWERY FIELDS and gardens in heaven represent the delights of conjugial love, 430.

FOODS AND DRINKS in Heaven, 6[5].

Heavenly food in its essence is love, wisdom, and use together; that is, use done through wisdom, out of love, 6[6].

Food for the body is given to every one in heaven, according to the use which he performs, 6[6].

FOOL. When men are in their native concupiscence, they are like fools, and yet seem to themselves to be wise in the highest degree, 269.

FORESTS in the other world, described, 75[2], 78[2], 79[2], 522.

FORM, see also *Essence and form* and *Substance and form.*

Every subject receives influx according to its form, 86.

Nothing exists except in a form; state induces form . . . All man's affections and thoughts are in forms, and therefore are according to forms; for forms are their subjects, 186.

Truth is the form of good, 198.

Every form consists of various things, how, 524[2].

The wish to continue in its own form is implanted from creation in all living things, 361.

How man, created the form of God, could be changed into a form of the devil, 153[a].

The soul is a form, 315[10, 11].

The forms which are without receive from the inmost form both essence and form, 315[11].

The form of heaven, whence, 524[2].

—*Human form* (*The*). The human form is a least effigy, image, and type of the great heaven, 10[8].

The form of the angels is the human form, 30.

Difference between male and female forms, 90[3].

A man's internal form, which is that of his spirit, is continually changing, 186.

What the most perfect and noble human form is, 201.

The human form in its inmosts is from creation a form of love and wisdom, 361.

The bodies of men are forms of their minds organized exteriorly, 310.

The form of the mind is also interiorly the form of the body, 310.

Formation of truth into seed, 220.

FORM—*continued.*

Every man is the form of his own love, . . . it is the interior man that is the form of his own love, 35.

Men from creation are forms of knowledge, intelligence, and wisdom; and women are forms of the love of those things with men, 187.

The masculine form is the intellectual form, and the feminine the voluntary form, 223.

The male and female were created to be the very form of the marriage of good and truth, 100.

Two married partners are the very forms and effigies of the marriage of love and wisdom, 66.

Marriage also induces other forms on the souls and minds of married partners, 192.

The woman is actually formed into a wife; how, 193–199.

FORNICATION, 423, 444[a]–459, 463[3].

FORTUNES (The) of men in general depend on their reputation for justice, sincerity and uprightness, 286.

FOUNTAIN (A) signifies the truth of wisdom, 293[6].

Fountain of Parnassus, 182.

FREEDOM. Everything that belongs to conjugial love is felt as freedom . . . the freedom of truly conjugial love is most free, 257[e].

Freedom produced by spiritual equilibrium, 444[3].

—*Freedom and reason.* The wives said, We have heard that the Lord wills that the male human being should act from freedom according to reason, and that therefore He from within governs his freedom; and from without by means of the man's wife, 208[3].

Man was so created that whatever he does may be done by him from freedom, according to reason, 438.

Without freedom and reason, man would not be a man, but a beast, *ib.*

FREE WILL. By virtue of the spiritual equilibrium between good and evil, man has free-will, 437.

FRENCH. Opinion of five Frenchmen on the subject of conjugial love and its potency, 110.

Speeches of French orators on the origin of beauty, 380, 381.

FRENZY a cause of legitimate separation, 252; and a just cause of concubinage, 470.

FRIENDSHIP is one of the virtues that pertain to the moral wisdom of men, 164.

It increases with those who are in truly conjugial love, 214.

FRIENDSHIP—*continued.*
Judges influenced by friendship, 231.
Causes of apparent friendship in marriages, 271–292.
Meeting between friends in the other life, 273[3].
Relation between love and friendship, 214[2].
Friendship dwells in externals, but conjugial love in internals, 216[4].
The chaste love of the sex is interior spiritual friendship, 55[7].
When friendship and confidence conjoin themselves with the first love of marriage, the love becomes conjugial, 162.
Inmost friendship is one of the states of truly conjugial love, 180, and it belongs to the breast, 180[e].
—*Conjugial friendship* differs greatly from the friendship of every other love, for it is full, 214[2].
Difference between conjugial and servile friendship in marriages, 248.
Truly conjugial friendship possible only with one wife, 333; it is the friendship of friendships, 334; its growth in heaven, 355[6].
Conjugial friendship and its confidence are founded upon virginity, 504[2].
FRUCTIFICATION. All fructification is originally from the influx of love, wisdom, and use from the Lord, 183[5].
Fructifications are continuations of creation, *ib.*
Fructifications in heaven, their difference from those on earth, 355[4-6].
FRUITS in a heavenly garden, 13.
The fruit of a tree signifies the good of life, 135.
FUNCTION. Every one has happiness from the use in his own function, 6[5].
Functions in heaven, 207[2].
FUTURE. It is not permitted man to know the future; why, 535.

GAMES in heaven, 17.
GANGRENES a cause of legitimate separation, 253.
GARDENS (Paradisiacal) described, 8, 477[3].
The garden of the prince of a heavenly society described, 13.
The garden in Eden signifies the wisdom of love, 135.
The garden "Adramandoni," 183.
Wedding-gardens in heaven, 316[2].
The delights of conjugial love in heaven are represented by gardens, 430.
GARLANDS signify the delights of conjugial love, 137[2].

GARLANDS—*continued.*
A garland of roses signifies the delights of intelligence, 293[e].
GARMENTS (Heavenly), 10[2], 14, 19[e], 25.
Garments are allotted to the angels, from the affection, and according to it, 42[3], 175[e].
In the spiritual world, a spirit thinks himself to be such as he is denoted to be by the garment he wears, 354.
GENERAL, A certain, who was an adulterer, 481.
GENERALS cannot enter into particulars, 328.
GENEROSITY is one of the virtues that pertain to the moral wisdom of men, 164.
GENII (Infernal). Who those are that are so named, 514[e].
GENTILES. No communication between the Christian heavens and those of the Gentiles, 352.
GENUS, see KIND.
GEOMETRY is one of those sciences through which, as through doors, an entrance is made into rational things, 163.
GERMANS. Opinion of five Germans on the subject of conjugial love and its potency, 109.
GERMINATIONS of the Earth, whence, 137[5].
GESTURES, Difference in, with men and women, 218.
GIANTS, 77.
GLAND (PINEAL), 315[4].
GLORIFICATION OF GOD, what it means, 9[4].
Glorifications of the Lord in heaven, 81.
GLORY elevates the understanding even into the light of heaven, 269[6].
The glory of jealous love cannot endure an equal, 378.
The glory of honour with men (*viri*) excites, increases, and sharpens jealousy, *ib.*
GOD. See LORD, *note.*
The glory of heaven is the Lord, 78[e].
There is one God, in Whom is a Divine Trinity; and He is the Lord Jesus Christ, 82, 532[7].
God is love itself and wisdom itself, 132[5].
Life for man is God in him, 135[4].
No one is good but God alone, 444[4].
—*God and man.* Dependence of man on God, 132[5-7].
—*God and nature.* God is in all time apart from time, and in all space apart from space; whereas nature is in all time in time, and in all space in space; and nature, with its time and space,

GOOD—*continued.*
The male was created to be truth in form; the female, good in form, 100.
The good and truth in the husband and the wife, how circumstanced, *ib.*
All the spiritual things of heaven and the church relate to good and truth, 120.
Truths and goods are the spiritual offspring born from the marriage of the Lord and the church, 121.
By means of truths man has understanding, perception, and all thought, and by means of goods, love, charity, and all affection; why, *ib.*
Good and truth in the Lord are not two but one, 121.
Man receives truth from the good and truth which proceed as a one from the Lord, 122; but not good, this being adjoined by the Lord to the truth appropriated by the man, according to the application of the truth to use, 123, 128; the reason, 122, 123.
Good belongs to charity, and truth to faith, 124.
Truth with man appears as his own, and good is adjoined thereto by the Lord, 127.
Good and truth constitute the life of God in man, and therefore are signified by the tree of life, 135.
Good conjoins truth with itself, . . . truth conjoins itself reciprocally with good, according to the reception of good in itself; . . . good forms itself by means of truth; for truth is the form of good, 198.
Uses are the goods which truths produce, 220[3].
Sons signify truths, and daughters goods, *ib.*
The wife is the good of the husband's truth, and he is the truth of the wife's good, 242.
Good belongs to love and truth to wisdom, 270.
Good has reference to the will, and truth to the understanding, and both together to a one, 316[5].
Good cannot provide or arrange anything but by truth; good cannot protect itself but by truth; truth is the protection and arm of good; good without truth is devoid of judgment, because it has this by means of truth, 325[3].
Why goods and truths are turned into evils and falsities when let down from heaven into hell, 444[8].
The Lord has gathered together into heaven all goods and truths, 479.
What the will receives and reproduces is called good, and what the understanding receives is called truth, 490.
Truth is the form of good, 493.
See also MARRIAGE OF GOOD AND TRUTH.
—*Intellectual good* in its essence is truth; for the intellect can think that this is good, thus that it is true that it is good . . . the will does not think good and truth, but loves and does them, 220[3].
—*Goods of charity.* John represented the church as to the goods of charity, which are the church in very effect, 119.
—*Good of charity, and truth of faith.* The good of charity is the primary of the church. . . . The good of charity is from the Lord, and the truth of faith is with a man as from himself, and these two cause a conjunction of the Lord with man, and of man with the Lord, 126.
—*Good of life, and truth of faith* both constitute the church, and hence heaven, with man. The truth of faith effects the Lord's presence, and the good of life according thereto effects conjunction with Him, and, thus, the church and heaven, 72.
—*Good of love, and truth of wisdom.* From the marriage of good and truth, the male receives the truth of wisdom, and the good of love is conjoined to it by the Lord according to the reception, 90.
The good of love and truth of wisdom perpetually love each other, and perpetually desire to be united, 355[3].
—*Good of truth, and truth of good.* There is a truth of good, or a truth from good, and a good of truth, or a good from truth. The truth of good is in the male, and is the very masculine principle, and the good of truth is in the female, and is the very feminine principle, 61; *illustrated*, 88, 90.
GOOD WORK (A) is a use, 10[7].
GOSSIPING. An extraordinary pleasure in gossiping, etc., a cause of legitimate separation, 252.
GOVERNMENTS and forms of government in heaven, 7[4], 207[2, 3].
GRAPES, good and bad; what they represent in the spiritual world, 294[7].
GREECE. The Sophi of Greece belonged to the Iron Age, 73; some particulars about them, 151[a]; their opinions on the immortality of the soul, 182[6].
GRIEF; see FEAR.
GROUND. The Corporeal is like ground, into which natural, rational, and spiritual things are implanted in their order, 59.

GROUND—*continued.*
Man at birth is like ground not sown, whereas a beast is like ground already sown, 134.
GROVES in the spiritual world, 132, 183, 267, 316.
GUILT (*Reatus*) is chiefly predicated of the will, 493.
GULFS of the west, 79e.
GYMNASIA (Olympic), 151[a].

HAND. Everything that a man examines with the understanding, appears to the angels as if inscribed on his hands, 261e.
The angels are able to see in a man's hand all the thoughts and intentions of his mind, 314[3].
Wives, from their husband's hands on their bosoms, are sensible of their affections, *ib.*
The hands are the ultimates of man, into which the deliberations and conclusions of his mind are determined; therefore it is said in the Word, that a thing is "inscribed on the hands," *ib.*
The sixth sense with wives is in the palms of their hands, 155[a][4].
The right hand denotes the good of a man's power, and the left the truth thereof, 316[5].
HANDICRAFTS in heaven, 207[2, 3].
HAPPINESS. Eternal happiness, 2–25. See also *Joys of Heaven.*
Happiness ought to be within joys, and to flow from them, 6[5].
This happiness within the joys, causes them to be joys; it enriches them, and prevents their becoming worthless and loathsome; and every one has this happiness from the use in his own function, 6[5].
From the reception of the love of use comes heavenly happiness, which is the life of joys, 6[6].
Internal blessedness is eternal happiness, 7[3].
Eternal happiness is derived from the delights of the soul and the delights of the body together; but from the latter alone there results a happiness not eternal but temporary, which comes to an end and passes away, and in some cases becomes unhappiness, 16[2].
Heavenly happiness results from the eternal enjoyment of the states arising from conjugial love, 180.
With those who are in truly conjugial love, the happiness of dwelling together increases, 213.
HARLOTRY in the Word denotes the connubial connection of evil and falsity, 428.
HARMONY: whence its pleasantness arises, 243.
HEAD. The Lord looks at every man in his forehead, and this look passes through into the back of his head, 444[6].
HEALING of the sick by the touch, its cause, 396[3].
HEARING. The perception of a thing, imbibed by hearing only, does indeed flow in, but does not remain, unless the hearer also thinks of it from himself, and asks questions about it, 183[2].
The love of hearing, from the love of hearkening to and obeying, has the sense of hearing, 210.
Natural hearing is from spiritual hearing, which is attention of the understanding and at the same time accommodation of the will, 220.
HEART AND LUNGS. The heart signifies good, and the lungs signify wisdom, 75[5].
The heart cannot produce any sensitive and motory life without the respiration of the lungs; neither can the lungs without the heart. The heart has relation to good, and the respiration of the lungs to truth: there is also a correspondence, 88[3].
The heart reigns everywhere by means of the blood, and the lungs by means of the respiration, 179.
The heart corresponds to love, and the lungs to the understanding, 223, 284.
HEAT. The heat of the blood, and also its redness, are from no other source than the love, 34.
Heat is felt and not seen, 123.
The heat of unchaste love extinguishes conjugial love; for two opposite heats cannot exist together, 147.
The quality of the heat of the conjugial love with polygamists, 344.
HEAT AND COLD. Conjugial love with spiritual married consorts is heat, with natural ones, cold, 281.
As heats communicate with each other, so also do colds, 290.
HEAT AND LIGHT. From heat and light are all the things of the Earth, for they germinate according to their presence and conjunction, 60.
Natural heat corresponds to spiritual heat which is love, and natural light to spiritual light, which is wisdom, 60e.
Spiritual light is the truth of faith, spiritual heat is the good of life, for it is love, 72.
All light, even the light of winter, causes presence, and heat united to light causes conjunction, 72.
Heat in heaven is love, and the light with which it is united, is wisdom, 137[4].

HEAT AND LIGHT—*continued.*
The heat and light proceeding from the spiritual sun cause perpetual spring, 137[5].
Heavenly light and heat are the wisdom and love in which the angels are; for heavenly light acts in unity with wisdom, and heavenly heat with love, 145.
The things that belong to light are seen, and those that belong to heat are felt, 168.
Spiritual light proceeds from the sun of the spiritual world, and acts in equality or unity with intelligence and wisdom; and spiritual heat which also proceeds from that sun, in its essence is love, and with women, conjugial love, 188.
The deliciation of spiritual heat with spiritual light, where and how felt; in human forms spiritual heat is conjugial love, and spiritual light is wisdom, 189.
Spiritual heat in its essence is love, and spiritual light, wisdom, 235, and these are inspired by the Lord out of the spiritual sun, according to reception, 261.
Natural heat is separated from spiritual heat with those who love natural things, and reject spiritual things; with these, spiritual heat becomes cold, 235.
Heavenly light is Divine Truth, and Heavenly heat is Divine love: these two discover the quality of truths and goods, and also of evils and falsities, 352.
In the spiritual world, natural light is thick darkness, and natural heat is cold, 415[3].
HEAVEN. In heaven there are foods and drinks, sports and public shows, and concerts, all in the highest perfection, 6[5].
In the heavens there are lofty administrative positions, and overflowing treasuries, for there are governments, etc., 7[4].
In heaven, the persons of the highest rank are chosen from those whose heart is in the public welfare, 7[4].
Every one who becomes an angel carries his own heaven within himself, because he carries within himself the the love of his own heaven, 7[8].
Days of festivity in heaven, how spent, 17.
In heaven there are all kinds of magnificent and splendid things, and such things as the eye had never seen; there are also maidens and young men, etc., 44[2].
Human forms in heaven, *ib.*
HEAVEN—*continued.*
All things are for the sake of the human race, that from it there may be an angelic heaven through which creation returns to the Creator, 85.
All the spiritual things of heaven and the church relate to good and truth, 120.
The angelic heaven is from the human race, 156, 183[7].
The universal heaven is regarded by the Lord as containing uses, 207[7].
Wonderful things in, 355.
In the third heaven all are in the innocence of wisdom, 396.
The angelic heaven is the end of ends and the love of loves with the Lord, 402.
Heaven of children, its situation, 410.
Heaven of innocence, 444.
Mohammedan heaven, 342–344.
Heaven consists of perpetual others, 534.
At the sides of heaven dwell those who live in extra-conjugial life, 155[2].
—*Heaven and hell.*
Heaven, where all things are honourable and good, has nothing in common with hell, where all things are dishonourable and evil, 17[5].
The universal heaven is arranged in order according to all the varieties of the affections of the love of good, and the universal hell according to all the affections of the love of evil, 36.
Why the universal heaven is arranged by the Lord according to the varieties of the affections of the love of good and truth, and hell according to all the varieties of the affections of the love of evil and falsity, 273.
The angelic heaven, which coheres together as a one, is in an infinite variety, no one there being absolutely like another, in any respect, 324; the opposites to these varieties are the diversities which exist in hell, 324[2].
In heaven there is the love of all things of the church, and in hell there is hatred against them, 497.
Hell as a whole is called adultery, and heaven as a whole is called marriage, 520.
They are both distinguished into innumerable societies, 529[2].
—*Heavenly love.* Infernal love is opposite to heavenly love, 10[8].
HEIGHT AND BREADTH. All evils, like all goods, partake of breadth and height, and according to breadth have their kinds, and according to height their degrees, 478[3].
HELICON, 151[a], 182.
Sports of the Heliconides, 207[6].

HELL. See also *Heaven and hell.*
Those who are in evils and consequent falsities, have formed in themselves an effigy of hell, 10[8].
The hells of the Age of Iron and Clay: their appearance, 79, 80; and the reason of it, 80.
Some hells described, 264[4].
All hell abounds with uncleannesses, 430.
In hell, those who are evil from the understanding (satans) dwell in front; those who are evil from the will (devils) dwell behind, 492.
Hell of the deceitful, 514[3].
HERACLITUS, 182[e].
HEREDITARY EVIL, its source, 245.
Evil is not hereditarily from Adam, but from one's own parents, 525.
HETEROGENEOUS (What is) in the spiritual world causes disjunction and absence, 171.
HIEROGLYPHICS, their origin, 76, 342[2].
HIGHEST AND LOWEST. The highest things of successive order become the inmost of simultaneous order, and the lowest, the outermost, 314[2].
HISTORY is one of those sciences through which an entrance is made into rational things, 163.
HOGS in hell, represent the lascivious delights of scortatory love, 430.
Hogs signify adulterers, 521[4].
HOLLANDERS OR DUTCHMEN. Opinions of five Dutchmen on the subject of conjugial love and its potency, 105.
HOMESTEAD. The conjugial principle of one man with one wife is the jewel of human life and the inner homestead (*reconditorium*) of the Christian Religion, 457.
HOMOGENEOUS (What is) in the spiritual world causes conjunction and presence, 171.
HONOUR. The angels are encompassed with honour, and accept it not for their own sake, but for the sake of the good of the society; *illustrated,* 266[3].
Honours and dignities are objects of the love of the body, 49.
HONOURABLE. Nothing that is honourable and good in any virtue can by successive progressions pass over to what is dishonourable and evil, 17[5].
HOOFS (The) of Pegasus signifies experiences by means of which natural intelligence is procured, 182[2].
HORSE (A) signifies the understanding of truth, 76[2].
HOUSE. In the spiritual world no one can dwell but in his own house, which is provided and assigned him according to the quality of his love, 50.
HUMAN (The) consists in willing to become wise, and in loving that which belongs to wisdom, 52.
—*Human form.* See under FORM.
—*Human race.* All things are for the sake of the human race, how, 85.
In the multiplication of the human race, the Lord regards the preservation of creation, and as its ultimate end, the angelic heaven, 402.
HUNCHBACK. If the love of the world constitutes the head, the man is but as a hunchback, 269[3].
HUSBAND AND WIFE, see also BRIDE AND BRIDEGROOM.
If their minds were in the marriage of good and truth, the husband being truth and the wife the good of it, they would both be in the delights of the blessedness of innocence, and thence in the happiness in which the angels of heaven are; etc., 115[5].
—*Their respective duties,* 174–176.
The husband's reputation depends on the wife, 286.
—*Influence of differing religions on,* 242.
—*Relations between,* in the Golden Age, 75; in the Silver Age, 76; in the Copper Age, 77; in the Iron Age, 78; in the Age of Iron and Clay, 79; in the Future, 80, 81.
—*Their correspondence and representation.*
After the wedding the husband represents wisdom, and the wife the love of his wisdom; and both together represent the church, 21[2].
The representation of conjugial love in a husband and wife of the third heaven, 42[2-5].
The Lord in the Word is called the bridegroom and husband, and the church the bride and wife, 117.
The husband does not represent the Lord, and the wife the church; because both together, the husband and the wife, constitute the church, 125; and therefore there is no correspondence between them, 126.
—*They are forms of the marriage of good and truth.* Two married consorts who are in truly conjugial love, are actually forms of the marriage of good and truth, or of love and wisdom, 66[e].
Two married partners between or in whom at the same time conjugial love is, are an effigy and form of it, 65.
They are the very forms and effigies of the marriage of good and truth, 66; they are that form in their inmosts, in proportion as the interiors of their mind are opened, 101, 102.

HUSBAND AND WIFE—*continued.*
The husband is in the bride-chamber of the understanding, the wife in that of the will, 270[5].
—*The husband is truth; the wife, good.* The husband is truth, and the wife the good thereof, 76[5].
By creation the husband is truth, and the wife the good thereof; or, the husband is understanding, and the wife the love thereof, 325[3].
—*Wives are loves; husbands, receptions.* A wife is the love of a wise man's wisdom, 56[2].
Wives are the receptacles and sensories of the delights of conjugial love, because they are born loves, 155[a][3].
Wives are most tender loves, and as it were burning zeals for the preservation of friendship and confidence, etc., 155[a][3].
Wives are loves and men receptions; men are receptions according to the wisdom with them, especially according to this wisdom from religion, that the wife only ought to be loved, 161[3].
Wives are born loves, and hence it is innate in them to will to be one with their husbands; . . . husbands are not born loves, but recipients of that love from their wives, 216[a].
Wives are born loves of the understanding of men, 285[e].
Wives are loves, and men recipients thereof; and it is prejudicial to wives to lavish their love upon the men, but not for the recipients to lavish their love upon their wives, 379.
—*Their formation and growth in married life.*
The female was created by means of the truth of the male, and is formed into the love thereof more and more after marriage, 122.
Wives receive in themselves those things that belong to the wisdom of their husbands, 171.
How the wife receives into herself the image of her husband, 173, 193.
How the woman is formed into a wife, 193–201.
How the wife becomes the husband's, and the husband the wife's, and both one man, 196.
How a maiden is formed into a wife, and a bachelor into a husband, 199, 321[2].
In a wife there are elements taken out of the husband which were not in her as a maiden; and so with the husband, 199.
In a marriage of truly conjugial love the wife becomes more and more a wife, and the husband more and more a husband; . . each one becomes continually a more interior man; . . and the wife becomes more and more a wife in proportion as the husband becomes more and more a husband, 200.
Chaste wives wish to be wives not in name only but in reality, and this is effected by a closer and closer binding with their husbands, 217.
Married partners after marriage are utterly in ignorance of the successive things that are insinuated into, and exist in their minds from things antecedent, nevertheless it is those things that give form to conjugial love, and constitute the state of their minds, from which state they act with each other, 313[2].
The wife from the husband's wisdom receives into herself the love thereof, and the husband from the love thereof in the wife receives into himself wisdom; yea, the wife is actually formed into the love of the husband's wisdom, how, 355[6].
—*How conjoined* (Chapter), 157–179.
The good which conjoins itself with the truth in the man, is from the Lord immediately; and the good of the wife, which conjoins itself with the truth in the man, is from the Lord mediately through the wife; . . . there are two goods which conjoin themselves with the truth in the husband, and cause him to be constantly in the understanding of truth, and hence in wisdom through truly conjugial love, 100.
The husband's inclination for his wife is according to the ascent of his understanding towards wisdom, 123.
The will of the wife conjoins itself with the understanding of the man, and hence the understanding of the man conjoins itself with the will of the wife, 159.
The inclination for conjunction is constant with the wife, but inconstant with the man, 160.
According to these conjunctions they become more and more one man, 177.
Conjunction is inspired into the man by the wife according to her love, and received by him according to his wisdom, 161.
The wife is continually thinking about the man's inclination towards her, etc.; not so the man, 169.
Influence of spheres on, 171.
The wife perceives, sees and feels the things which are in her husband, in herself, and thus as it were herself in him, 173.

HUSBAND AND WIFE—*continued.* there, than those who are interiorly united or capable of being united as into a one, 50.

Two married partners from heaven seem as little children, 137.

Married partners who had lived to old age, loving each other and shunning adulteries as enormous sins on account of religion, are, in the other world, restored by the Lord to the flower of their age, 137^{7}.

Wives in heaven know all the states of the minds of their husbands, but husbands know nothing of what passes with their wives; the reason, $155[a]^{3}$.

The spiritual delightsomenesses of the husbands [in heaven] put on with their wives a kind of natural embodiment, wherefore the wives are called by their husbands sensory organs of chaste conjugial love, and hence its delights, $155[a]^{4}$.

In heaven, two married partners are called two when they are named husband and wife, but one when they are named angels, 177.

Married partners in heaven have an interior comeliness of face, for the man derives from the wife the lovely redness of her love, and the wife from the man the bright lustre of his wisdom; for they are united as to their souls; and moreover there appears in both a human fulness, 192.

HYPOCRITE. Every man who is not inwardly led by the Lord is a hypocrite, and thus an apparent man, and yet not a man, 267^{3}.

HYSTERIA (Severe) a cause of legitimate separation, 252.

ICE. Those who have been addicted to the lust of varieties appear like substances of ice, 510^{e}.

IDEA. Every idea of man is substantial, 66.

Ideas of thought become expressions of speech, 326^{6}.

Spiritual ideas are supernatural, inexpressible, ineffable, and incomprehensible to the natural man, 326^{7}.

Spiritual ideas, respectively to natural ones, are ideas of ideas, *ib.*

To every idea of natural thought there adheres something from time and space, which is not the case with any spiritual idea; the reason, 328^{2}.

One natural idea is the continent of innumerable spiritual ideas, and one spiritual idea, of innumerable celestial ideas, 329^{e}.

IDENTITY. There does not exist a sameness, or absolute identity of any two things, 186.

IDIOCY a cause of legitimate separation, 252; and a just cause of concubinage, 470.

IDLENESS; its effects on man, $207^{3, 7}$, 249.

IDOLATERS of the Iron Age, in the spiritual world, 78.

IDOLATRY: its origin, 78^{3}, 342.

IGNORANCE indeed excuses, but does not take away confirmed falsity, 422.

IJIM (The) in hell; what they represent, 264^{4}.

IMAGE of the husband, how received by the wife, 173.

IMAGE AND LIKENESS OF GOD, what, 132–134.

IMAGINATION, 4, 7.

IMBECILITY a cause of legitimate separation, 252; and a just cause of concubinage, 470.

IMMODESTY or shamelessness a cause of legitimate separation, 252; and a really weighty cause of concubinage, 472.

All in hell are in the shamelessness of scortatory love, 429.

IMPLANTED. That which from creation has been implanted in souls, and pertains to propagation, is indelible, and cannot be extirpated, 409.

IMPLETION, and not extension, belongs to the soul, 220.

IMPOSITION OF HANDS: its origin, 396^{3}.

IMPURE, see UNCLEAN.

IMPUTATIONS of evil are made by the Lord according to the state of the man's mind, 485.

Imputations of adulteries after death take place according to their degrees, 485, 489, 493.

Imputation means accusation after death, and thence adjudication, which takes place according to the state of the man's spirit, 489.

Chapter on the imputation of good and evil, 523–531.

INCLINATION. See also FACULTY.

Married partners, after death, do not at first know the inclination of each to the other, because this conceals itself in the internals. But afterwards the inclination manifests itself, 47[b].

The inclination for conjunction that has been implanted in the sexes from creation belongs to the spirit and thence to the body; wherefore after death, when man becomes a spirit, the same mutual inclination remains, and this cannot exist without similar intercourse, 51.

INNOCENCE—*continued.*
The Lord's innocence flows in into the angels of the third heaven, where all are in the innocence of wisdom, and passes through the lower heavens, but only through the innocences of the angels therein, and thus into children, 396.
In the degree in which innocence departs from the children, affection and conjunction also abate, and this even to separation, 398.
Children in heaven are first led from the innocence of childhood to the innocence of wisdom, which is the end of all their instruction and progression. Described, 413.
Innocence of childhood and innocence of wisdom, their respective qualities, 413.

INSANITY is a delirium of the mind arising from falsities, 212.
Insanity is a cause of legitimate separation, 252; and a just cause of concubinage, 470.

INSCRIBED on the hands, see HAND.

INSTRUCTION (Places of) in the spiritual world, 261. Instruction of children in heaven, 411, 412.

INTEGRITY, Adam's state of, 135[3].

INTELLECTUAL (The) of the man is the inmost of the woman, 195.
It is nothing else than truth, 220[9].
—*The intellectual life* is the masculine life itself, 433.
—*Intellectual form;* see under *Will and understanding.*

INTELLIGENCE. See also *Knowledge, intelligence, and wisdom.*
Natural intelligence is procured by means of experiences, 182[2].
Every one has intelligence according to his affection of sciences, 207[6].
Difference between the intelligence of men and women, 218.
The characteristic of an intelligent man is, not being able to confirm whatever he pleases, but, being able to see that truth is true and falsity false, and to confirm the same, 233[7].
Every one is outwardly in intelligence by education, 267[2].
Represented by circles around the head, 269[3].
—*Intelligence and insanity.*
Intelligence consists in loving the wife only, but insanity consists in not loving the wife but the sex, 331.
—*Intelligence and wisdom.* No one is inwardly, thus as to his spirit, in intelligence and wisdom, except from the Lord; . . . and he is so according to his looking to the Lord, and conjunction with Him, 267[2].

INTELLIGENCE—*continued.*
They are essential spiritual nourishment, 411.
They make an angel, 413.

INTEMPERANCE a cause of legitimate separation, 252; and a really weighty cause of concubinage, 472.

INTENSIFICATION (a term in chemistry), 145.

INTENTION (The) which is of the will is primarily regarded by the Lord, 71, 146.
An intention is as an act before determination; by a wise man, and also by the Lord, an intention is accepted as an act, 400[2], 452[3].
Intention is the soul of all actions, and causes incriminations, etc., 452[3].
Difference between purpose and intention, 493.

INTERCOURSE between the sexes, why a necessity even in the other world, and why it must be full, and more delightful and blessed, 51.

INTERMEDIATE (The) between good and evil, 444[9].

INTERIORS (The) form the exteriors to their own likeness, 33.
The interiors of the mind are the interiors of the spirit, 39.
The opening of the interiors of the mind cannot be fully effected except with those who have been prepared by the Lord to receive the things which belong to spiritual wisdom, 39.
The interiors of the mind, which in themselves are spiritual, are opened by the Lord alone, 341.

INTERNAL AND EXTERNAL. With every man there is an Internal and an External, which are also called the internal and external man; and hence there is an internal and an external will and thought, 47.
A man, when he dies, leaves his External behind, and retains his Internal; for externals, strictly speaking, belong to his body, and internals, strictly speaking, belong to his spirit, 47.
In the natural world the Internal and External make two, and only make a one with the sincere at heart. But in the spiritual world it is not allowable thus to have a divided mind, but he who has been evil in internals must also be evil in externals; likewise, he who has been good in internals must be good in externals: how this is effected, 48[b][2].
The internal man intends, and the external man does, 486.

INTERNALS AND EXTERNALS. How man after death puts off externals and put on internals, 48[b].

INTERNALS—*continued.*
Relation between the internal and external conjugial principles, 148.
A man's internals, by which are meant the things that belong to his mind or spirit, are elevated in a higher degree above his externals, 185².
Their difference with the good and the evil, 364, 365.
Externals derive their good or evil from the internals, 478.
INTREPIDITY is one of the virtues that pertain to the moral wisdom of men, 164.
IRON (Age of), 78.
ISRAEL signifies the church, 21³.
ISRAELITISH NATION, why permitted polygamy, 340.
ITALIANS. Opinions of five Italians on the subject of conjugial love and its potency, 106.
ITCH (Virulent), a cause of legitimate separation, 252; and a just cause of concubinage, 470.

JAMES the Apostle represents charity, 119.
JEALOUSY (Chapter), 357–379.
It is the zeal of conjugial love, 358, 367.
Reason for its name, 367.
It is like a fire blazing against those who infest the love; and it is like a terrible fear for the loss of the love, 368.
Spiritual jealousy, 368.
There is spiritual jealousy with monogamists, and natural with polygamists, 369, 370.
Its quality with those consorts who tenderly love each other, 371, 372.
The fear and grief of conjugial love is called zeal or jealousy, 371.
It is in the understanding of a man who loves his consort; and its quality there is according to his wisdom, 372.
Its quality and origin with those who do not love each other, 373.
Its distemper in certain countries, 375.
Cause of its absence and cessation, 376.
Difference between jealousy in regard to concubines and that in regard to wives, 377.
It exists also among beasts and birds, 378.
Difference between the jealousy of men and husbands and that of women and wives, 379.
JEHOVAH. The Lord is Jehovah from eternity, 29.
Why Jehovah is said to be zealous, 366.
JERUSALEM signifies the church, 21³.
— *The New Jerusalem* signifies the New Church of the Lord, 1, 43, 534.
JESUITS, mentioned, 499.
JESUS CHRIST. The Divine Trinity is in Jesus Christ, in Whom all the fulness of the Divinity dwells bodily, 24.
JEWEL. The conjugial principle of one man with one wife is the jewel of human life, 457.
JEWISH CHURCH (The) is meant in passages quoted, 119.
JEWISH NATION (The) are still the same as of old, 202.
JOB. Correspondences have lain concealed since the time of Job, 532.
JOHN, the Apostle, represents the church as to the goods of charity, 119.
Represents the works of charity, *ib.*
JOYS (All) and delights from primes to ultimates are collected into conjugial love, 68, 69; they do not exist in any other than genuine conjugial love, 69.
JOYS OF HEAVEN (Chapter), 2–25.
Heavenly joy is the delight of doing something that is useful to oneself and others, 5³.
The delight of use, originating in love through wisdom, is the soul and life of all heavenly joys, 5³.
Heavenly joy, and the eternal happiness flowing thence, do not consist in external paradisiacal delights, unless together with these there are also internal paradisiacal delights, 8⁴.
How joy becomes joy, 8⁵.
The joys of heaven, and eternal happiness, do not belong to a place, but to the state of a man's life, 10⁷.
JUDGES influenced by friendship, their fate in the other life, 231.
Charges of blame or sentences are made by a judge according to the law, 485.
JUDGMENT. See also JUSTICE AND JUDGMENT. Difference between the judgment of the body and the judgment of the spirit, 57.
Judgment belongs to rational wisdom, 163.
Arbitrary judgments; their representation in the other world, 231².
Principle according to which every one is judged after death, 485.
No one ought to be judged of from the wisdom of his mouth, but from the wisdom of his life in union therewith, 499.
Judgment respecting the moral and civil life of another in the world, is allowed, but not judgment respecting his spiritual life, 523.

LIPOTHYMY a cause of legitimate separation, 253 ; and a just cause of concubinage, 470.

LOATHING between married partners results from a disunion of the souls and a disjunction of the minds, 236.

LOINS (The) correspond to conjugial love, 510[3].

LOOK. How the Lord looks at man, and man at the Lord, 444[6].

LORD. *Note:*—In all the Writings of Swedenborg, by the LORD is signified the Lord Jesus Christ, Who is the One only God, because in Him dwelleth the Trinity of Father, Son, and Holy Spirit.

The Lord loves all, and consequently wishes good to all, 7[3].

He does goods or uses mediately through angels and men, *ib.*

He is the Word, that is, the Divine truth itself therein, 81.

He is Divine good itself and Divine truth itself, 84.

He is love itself and wisdom itself, 84, 85.

He is good itself and truth itself, 121.

Nothing can proceed from the Lord but what is in Him, and is Himself, *ib.*

The church is from Him, *ib.*

The Word is from Him, and is Himself, *ib.*

He is the God of heaven and earth, 129.

The Lord alone, when He was in the world, was wise from Himself and did good from Himself; because the Divine Itself from birth was in Him and was His own, 135[3].

He is mercy, grace, and clemency itself, thus good itself, 366.

From Him proceed love, wisdom, and use as a one, 400.

—*The Lord and the church.* The Lord is love, and the church is wisdom, 21[2].

The Lord in the Word is called the bridegroom and husband, and the church the bride and wife; and the conjunction of the Lord with the church, and of the church with the Lord, is called marriage, 117.

The Lord in the Word is called the Father, and the church the mother, 118, 119.

It is the Lord from whom all good and truth proceeds, and it is the church that receives them and puts them into effect; and all the spiritual things of heaven and the church relate to good and truth, 120.

—*The Lord and man.* Man cannot distinguish the uses done by angels and devils, but the Lord can, 266[5].

LOSS OF MEMORY a cause of legitimate separation, 252 ; and a just cause of concubinage, 470.

LOT. A man's lot after death is according to his life in this world, 46.

The blessed lot of those who desire to have dominion from the love of uses, 266.

The lots after death of those who had been addicted to the lust of defloration, 505 ; of varieties, 510 ; of violation, 512 ; of seduction, 514.

LOVE ; see also *Wisdom of love.* Love is the life of man, and hence it is the man himself, 36.

Love is the esse of a man's life, 36, 46, 358.

Love, considered in itself, is nothing else than a desire and a consequent effort towards conjunction, 37.

Every love which proceeds from the form of love itself, is a resemblance of it; wherefore if conjugial love be celestial and spiritual, the loves proceeding from it are also celestial and spiritual, 65.

Love is conjunction, 129.

Love is spiritual union, 172[e].

Love is the very activity of life, 183[3].

Love is spiritual fire, 235.

Spiritual heat is love, 235.

Spiritual heat living in subjects is felt as love, 235.

Love is spiritual heat originating in the fire of the angelic sun, which is pure love, 358, 359.

Love is the heat of life, 359[e].

In its essence it is spiritual fire, 380[12].

It is the esse of man's life, 461[5].

Love is a matter not of light but of heat, 34.

Love is man's very life, not only the general life of his whole body, and of all his thoughts, but also the life of all their particulars, 34.

Love is the heat of man's life, or his vital heat, *ib.*, 359.

Love is continually efficient; it is like heat, flame, and fire, 160.

Love cannot do otherwise than love, and unite itself in order that it may be loved in return, 160.

Love is such that it desires to communicate with another whom it loves, and to confer joys upon him, and thence to derive its own joys. This is the case infinitely with the Divine love, 180.

All love is such that it breaks forth into indignation and wrath when it is thrust out of its delights, especially the ruling love, 358.

LOVE—*continued.*
Love without its delights is not anything, 427.
It is not possible for any love to become perfectly pure either with men or angels, 71, 146.
Love cannot be forced, but is insinuated in freedom, 294[5].
Love belongs properly to the spirit of man, and to the body from the spirit, 46.
Love resides in man's will; but it is not inflamed in the will itself, but in the understanding; for in the will it is like fire, and in the understanding like flame; *illustrated*, 360.
In all love there is fear and grief, 371.
When the love is assaulted, it defends itself by means of its understanding, 361.
Every love has its own delight, for love lives by means of its delight, 18[3].
Wherever love finds a receptacle for itself, it is in its own delightsomenesses and delights, 189.
The interior man, which is the same as his spirit which lives after death, is the form of his own love, but not so the exterior man in the world, 35.
Every one has his own love, or a love distinct from the love of another; *i.e.*, no two men have exactly the same love, 35. The faces are the types of the loves, *ib.*
A man is his own love, yea, the form of his own love, *ib.*
A man is his own love, and love resides in his spirit, 47.
Love from the will is with the mother, and love from the understanding is with the father, 284.
The love of a man and a man, . . . the love of a woman and a woman . . . 55[6]; the love of a man and a woman, 55[7].
Every one's own love remains with him after death, 34.
Every love follows man after death, because it is the esse of his life; and the ruling love, which is the head of all the rest, remains with man to eternity, 46.
—*Apparent love* in marriage; its causes (Chapter), 271–292.
—*The three universal loves* into which every man has been constituted since the creation, 269[2]; their right subordination, and their inversion, 269[3].
—*The love of adultery* is warm with those married partners who are merely natural, 54.
—*The love of the body*, its objects, 49.

LOVE—*continued.*
—*The love of children* corresponds to the protection of truth and good, 127.
The spiritual storgë adds itself to conjugial love, and continually elevates it and conjoins the consorts, 211[e].
The love of children with the mother and father become conjoined as the heart and lungs in the breast, 284.
Its conjunction with conjugial love (Chapter), 385–414.
It exists with consorts who love each other, also with those who disagree at heart, and likewise with those who are separated, and sometimes it is more tender and stronger with the latter, 385.
It is always conjoined with conjugial love, 385.
It is love from the Lord with the parents, 391.
It is originally from conjugial love, 393.
The series of the love of children is retrograde, 401.
It descends, and does not ascend; the reason, 402.
Conjugial love is conjoined with it by spiritual causes, and thence by natural ones, 404.
It is different with spiritual consorts from what it is with natural ones, 405–409.
It remains after death, especially with women, 410.
A want of love of children is a really weighty cause of concubinage, 472.
—*The love of dominion, or of ruling*, from the love of self, is one of the three universals of hell, 261[3]; representations of it, 265.
The love of dominion from the love of use is one of the three universals of heaven, 261[3].
Difference between the heavenly and the infernal love of dominion, 262, 266.
—*Love of good and love of evil.* There are in general two loves, the love of good and the love of evil: both loves are of infinite variety, 362.
—*The love of the Lord*, which is the primary love, is the love of being wise with the husband, 21[2].
—*The love of marriage* is cold with those married partners who are merely natural, 54.
The primitive love of marriage emulates truly conjugial love; why, 58.
—*Masculine and feminine love.* Feminine love is the love derived from the wisdom of the male, and is given by the Lord to the wife through the

LOVE—*continued.*

It belongs to the body and thence to the spirit, 162.

Men have not any innate love of the sex; and without that love there is no interior pleasantness of life, 297.

It has led the dispositions of some into a desire for repeated marriages, 319.

Its beginning is fornication 444[a].

It is like a fountain from which both conjugial love and scortatory love may be derived, 445.

It is in every man (*homo*), and it either does or does not manifest itself, 445.

It follows the commencement of a man's own understanding, and progresses according to its vigour, 446.

Its rise, 446.

If it becomes active before marriage, it is called fornication, 447.

Its nature and progression, *ib.*

It cannot become spiritual until it becomes conjugial, *ib.*

With some men, it cannot, without mischiefs, be totally coerced from going forth into fornication, 450.

—*Spiritual love.* The conjunction of minds and not at the same time of bodies, is spiritual love, and consequently chaste love, 55[7].

—*The love of use.* The satisfaction and calmness resulting from activity of mind, constitute a state of mind capable of receiving the love of use from the Lord; and from the reception of this love comes heavenly happiness, 6[6].

The love of use, and a consequent busying oneself in use, keeps the mind together, etc., 16[3].

It is from the Lord, 262, 266[2], and is the Lord Himself, 262.

Blessed lot of those who desire to rule from the love of uses, 266.

The love of uses, and with it wisdom, increases in proportion to the performance of uses from the love of them, 266[3].

The angels do uses from the love of uses; devils from the love of self, 266[4, 5].

It is the love of the neighbour, 269[2].

It is a spiritual love, *ib.*

By it man is elevated into the celestial region of his mind, 305.

—*The love of wisdom, and the love of becoming wise.* See also *Love and wisdom.* The love of her husband's wisdom is not a primary but a secondary love, which the wife has from the Lord through the wisdom of the husband, 21[2].

The love of wisdom, how formed in man (*vir*); its nature: if it remains in the man it is an evil love, and is called conceit, or the love of one's self-intelligence, 88.

Wisdom cannot exist with man except by means of the love of becoming wise, 88.

Difference between the love of becoming wise and the love of wisdom, 88.

Wisdom was formed from the love of becoming wise, or, truth from good; and the love of wisdom was formed from that wisdom, or, the good of truth from that truth, 89.

The love of the wisdom of the man is transcribed into the wife, 156[a][3], in order that it may become conjugial love, 193[2].

—*The love of the world* is one of the three universal loves of which every man has been constituted since the creation; and it is also the love of possessing wealth, 269[2].

It is a material love, *ib.*

They who are in it desire to possess everything therein, etc., 267[3].

Wealth and possessions especially are its objects, 49.

—*Love and thought.* Love is the Esse or essence of a man's life, and thought is the Existere or existence of his life thence derived; wherefore, speech and action, which flow from the thought, do not flow from the thought, but from the love through the thought, 36.

A man after death is not his own thought, but his own affection and consequent thought; *i.e.*, he is his own love and consequent intelligence, *ib.*

—*The love and the understanding.* A man is such as his love is, and not such as his understanding is; since the love easily draws over the understanding to its side, and enslaves it, 269[5].

—*Love and wisdom:* see also *Good of love and truth of wisdom.*

There are two things which constitute the marriage of the Lord and the church—love and wisdom; the Lord is love, and the church is wisdom, 21[2].

Love has power by means of wisdom, *ib.*

Love and wisdom are the things that are born of marriages in the heavens, 52.

The two things that proceed from the Lord are love and wisdom, because they are Himself, thus from Himself; and all things which are of love are called goods, and all things which are of wisdom, truths, 60.

LUXURIOUSNESS, a cause of legitimate separation, 252.
LYING, a cause of legitimate separation, 252.

MADNESS, see UNSOUNDNESS OF MIND.
MAGICAL PRACTICES, a causes of legitimate separation, 252.
MAIDEN, see VIRGIN.
MALE CHILD (The), what is signified by, 120.
MALE AND FEMALE. Man is male and female, 32.
—*Difference between.* The inmost of the male is love, and its covering is wisdom, *i.e.*, the male is love covered or veiled by wisdom ; and the inmost of the female is that wisdom of the male, and its covering is love thence derived, 32.
The male is the wisdom of love, the female, the love of that wisdom, *ib.*
The male is born intellectual, and the female is born voluntary ; or what is the same thing, the male is born into the affection of knowing, understanding, and growing wise, and the female is born into the love of conjoining herself with that affection in the male, 33.
Differences between male and female as to face, tone of voice, form, 33 ; affection, application, and manners, 90, 91.
The male sex has allurements that actually inflame ; not so the female sex, 98[2].
They make one form, which emulates the conjugial form of good and truth, 100.
The male is born to become understanding, and the female to become will loving the understanding of the male, 159.
—*The masculine and the feminine.*
There is such a distinction between the masculine and the feminine that the one cannot be changed into the other, 32.
The feminine is from the masculine, that is, the woman was taken out of the man, 32.
The masculine form is the form of intellect, and the feminine form is the form of the love of that intellect, 33.
The masculine in the male is masculine in every, even the smallest, part of his body, thought, and affection , so, likewise, the feminine in the female, *ib.*
The masculine in the male is masculine in the whole and in every part thereof ; in like manner the feminine in the female ; and there is a conjunctiveness in all their singulars, yea, even their veriest singulars, 37.
The truth of good is in the male, and is the very masculine principle, and the good of truth is in the female, and is the very feminine principle, 61, 88, 90.
The masculine consists in perceiving from the understanding, and the feminine in perceiving from love, 168.
The feminine principle, how propagated from a male soul, 220[3].
The masculine and the feminine, united by means of truly conjugial love, constitute one fully human life, 316[4].
—*Order of their creation.*
The male human being and the female human being have been so created, that out of two they may become as it were one human being, or one flesh ; and when they become one, then, taken together, they are a human being in his fulness ; but without such conjunction, they are two, and each of them is like a divided or half human being, 37.
The male was created to become wisdom from the love of growing wise, and the female to become the love of the male from his wisdom, and consequently according to that wisdom, 66.
They were created to be the very form of the marriage of good and truth, 100 *seq.*
The male was created to be the understanding of truth, thus truth in form ; and the female to be the will of good, thus good in form, 100.
Man is born a faculty of knowing, understanding, and becoming wise ; . . . the female was created by means of the truth of the male, and is formed into the love thereof more and more after marriage ; and therefore receives her husband's truth in herself, and conjoins it with her own good, 122.
—*Their different reception.* From the marriage of good and truth flowing in from the Lord, the male receives the truth of wisdom, . . . and hence the male is born to become intellectual, 90.
The male receives the universal conjugial sphere according to his form, thus in the intellect, because he is an intellectual form ; and the female according to hers, thus in the will, because she is a voluntary form from the intellectual of the man, 92.
Males receive nothing from the spiritual marriage, except truth, and that which has relation to truth, 220.

MALE AND FEMALE—*continued.*
There is not any conjugial love with the masculine sex, but only with the feminine sex, and from this sex it is transferred into the masculine sex, 223.
—*Their inclination for conjunction.* The one desires and breathes conjunction with the other, 37.
The male and female have been so created, that they have a powerful striving for conjunction, yea, for conjunction so as to become a one, 46.
There has been implanted in each, from their inmosts, an inclination for conjunction, 100.
—*After death* the male lives a male, and the female a female, both being a spiritual man, 32; neither is there anything wanting, 51.
There are in heaven human forms exactly like those in the natural world; nothing is taken away out of the man (*vir*), and nothing out of the woman; in a word, the man (*vir*) is a male, and the woman a woman, in all the perfection of form in which they were created, 44[2].
A man (*vir*) after death is a man, and a woman a woman; and there is nothing in the soul, in the mind, and in the body, which is not masculine in the male and feminine in the female, 46.

MAN, HUMAN BEING. *Note:*—Swedenborg uses in general two terms for "man," viz., *homo* and *vir*, *homo* signifying a human being of either sex, *vir* a male human being. Sometimes however he uses the two terms interchangeably.
—*His nature and constituents.* A man is, by creation, a least effigy, image, or type of the great heaven, 10[8].
A man is his own love; yea, he is the form of his own love, 35.
A man is his own thought, thus his own intelligence and wisdom; but these make a one with his love, 36.
A man is his own love, and love resides in his spirit, 47.
The appearance that love and wisdom are in man as his own, causes him to be man, and makes him capable of being conjoined with God; . . . man is man from this circumstance, that he is able to will good and understand truth altogether as from himself, and yet know and believe that it is from God, 132[5].
Man is a receptacle, that is, an image of God; and also a likeness of God; the reason, 132[7].
A man as to his thoughts and affections, and consequently inwardly as to his bodily actions and behaviour, is according to the conjugial principle, 140.
In proportion as men attribute all the good of charity and truth of faith to the Lord, and not to themselves, they are men, and in the same proportion become angels of heaven, 154[a].
A man is a man when the love of the neighbour, or the love of doing uses, constitutes the head, the love of the world the body, and the love of self the feet: *illustrated*, 269[3].
As man is man according to the quality of his love, so he is man according to the quality of his delight, 461[5].
Man is man by virtue of the will and understanding, 494.
A man is a man, and is distinguished from the beasts by this circumstance, that his mind is distinguished into three regions, as many as the heavens, and that he is capable of being elevated out of the lowest region into the next above it, and from this into the highest, and thus of becoming an angel of heaven, even of the third, 495.
The love of the will makes the man, 498.
The essence of the whole man is from his soul, 46.
With every man there is an Internal and an External, 47. See under *Internal and External.*
Consists of soul, mind, and body, 101, 158; nature of these three, 158.
The highest things in man are turned upwards to God, the middle outwards to the world, and the lowest downwards to self; and because the latter are turned downwards, man thinks as from himself, when nevertheless he thinks from God, 269[e].
In man there are all the affections of love, and thence all the perceptions of wisdom, compounded in the most perfect order, so as to make a one, 361.
—*His association with spirits and angels.* Man, as to the affections and thoughts of his mind, is in the midst of angels and spirits, and he is so consociated with them, that he cannot be separated from them without dying, 28.
—*His quality.* A man thinks, yea, if he be in freedom, speaks and acts, from his love and according to it, 36.
Every man, when he is born, is merely corporeal; how from this he progresses upwards and becomes more and more a man, 59.

MAN—*continued.*
In marriage he becomes a fuller man; why, 59[2].
As he progresses from knowledge into intelligence, and thence into wisdom, his mind changes its form; how, 94.
Every man is born corporeal, and becomes more and more interiorly natural, rational, and spiritual; how, 94.
The more intelligent and wise man becomes, the more internal or spiritual he becomes, and in the same proportion the form of his mind is perfected; and this form receives conjugial love, 95.
Man is born corporeal, and successively becomes rational, and a form of wisdom; how, 102.
In proportion as a man becomes spiritual, in the same proportion he is in truly conjugial love, 130[4].
He becomes spiritual in proportion as his Rational begins to derive a soul from the influx out of heaven, 145.
Every man is such as instruction makes him, — insane from falsities, and wise from truths, 152[a].
Man without instruction is neither a man nor a beast, but a form capable of receiving in itself that which constitutes man, and thus he is not born man, but becomes man; and man is born such a form as to be an organ receptive of life from God; why, 152[a].
So far as a man is in conjugial love, he is spiritual, and so far as he is spiritual, so far he is man, 230.
A man is such as his love is, and not such as his understanding is, 269[5, 6].
Every man thinks and acts naturally, and therefore could not perceive anything spiritual, and receive it in his Natural, unless the Lord had assumed the Human Natural, and made it Divine, 340[4].
The natural man, separate from the spiritual man, is a man only as to the understanding, but not as to the will; this he immerses in the body and the concupiscences of the flesh: such a one is but half a man, 432[2].
A man is such a man as he is in his purpose, intention, or end, 452[3].
The natural, the sensual, and the corporeal man is equally rational, as to the understanding, as the spiritual man, 498.
Every human being is born in evil, but is led into good by means of regeneration by the Lord, 525.
—*End or purpose of his creation.*
Man, at his first creation, was imbued with wisdom and its love, not for the sake of himself, but that he might communicate it to others from himself, 18.
No one is wise, or lives, for himself alone, but for others at the same time; this is the origin of society, which otherwise could not exist, *ib.*
Men were created, and therefore are born, in order that they may become spiritual; wherefore, in the proportion in which a man becomes spiritual, he puts off the love of the sex, and puts on conjugial love, 48.
Man was created to receive love and wisdom from God, and yet to all likeness as from himself, and this for the sake of reception and conjunction: and therefore a man is not born into any love or knowledge, etc., 136.
Man is born for the life after death, and attains to that life because he has in him a spiritual soul, 230.
Man has been created with a capacity of becoming more and more interior, and thus of being introduced or elevated into truly conjugial love, 238[3].
Man was created for use, why, 249.
Man is born natural in order that he may become spiritual, and so long as he remains natural he is as in the night, and asleep, as to spiritual things, 340.
Every man is born for heaven, and no one for hell, 350[e].
Man was so created that everything he wills, thinks, and does, appears to him as in, and thus from, himself: without this appearance man would not be man, 444[5].
—*His capabilities.*
Man is able to grow in wisdom to the end of his life in the world, and afterwards to eternity in heaven; and in proportion as he grows in wisdom, his form is perfected; and this form receives not the love of the sex, but the love of one of the sex, 93.
Man only can become spiritual; the reason, 96.
In man there is the faculty of becoming wise, with which faculty conjugial love makes a one, 96[e].
Every man is capable of being purified, 452.
—*Order of influx with man.* Everything which flows in from the Lord into man, flows in into his inmost, thence into his mind and body, 101.
Man has a common perception, which is the same thing as the influx of heaven into the interiors of his mind,

MAN—*continued.*
by virtue of which he inwardly in himself perceives truths, and as it were sees them, and especially this truth, that he lives a man after death, 28.
—*After death* man lives a man, 28.
It has been provided by the Lord, that the state of the man who conjoins himself with Him by means of a life according to His precepts, becomes more blessed and happy after death than before it in the world, 29.
A spiritual man feels and perceives spiritual delight, 29.
Man after death is not a natural, but a spiritual or substantial man, 31.
A spiritual or substantial man sees a spiritual or substantial man, as a natural or material man sees a natural or material man, *ib.*
An angel cannot appear to a man of this world, nor a man of this world to an angel, *ib.*
The spiritual man is still a perfect man, although he does not appear to the natural man, *ib.*
The interior man, which is the same as his spirit which lives after death, is the form of his own love, but not so the exterior man in the world, 35.
A man after death is not his own thought, but his own affection and consequent thought; *i.e.*, he is his own love and consequent intelligence, 36.
A man after death puts off everything that does not agree with his love; yea, he successively puts on the face, the tone of voice, the speech, gestures, and manners of the love of his life, 36.
A man after death becomes a spirit, and so carries his own love with him, 46.
Such as a man's life has been in the world, such does his lot become after death, 46.
Every one after death is first introduced into the world of spirits, and there he is prepared either for heaven or hell, 48[b].
How man after death puts off his externals and puts on his internals, *ib.*
Every man after death becomes such as he had been interiorly, and not such as he had been exteriorly, 48[b]^{3}.
Man after death is a man as before, 51.
After death a man from natural becomes spiritual, and instead of a material body enjoys a substantial one, 475^{3}.

MAN—*continued.*
—*Detail of differences between the two sexes.* See also MALE AND FEMALE.
Women have an interior perception of love, and men only an exterior perception, 47[b].
The man was created and is born to become understanding; the woman, to become the love of the understanding of a man, 55^{6}, 90, 91.
Women were created by the Lord affections of the wisdom of the men, 56^{3}.
Woman was created by the Lord through the wisdom of the man, because from the man, and hence she is a form of wisdom inspired with the affection of love; . . . the female is the life of wisdom, and the male is wisdom, 56^{3}.
To women there has been given a perception of the delights of conjugial love, *ib.*
The Lord has taken away beauty and elegance of life from the man, and transcribed it into the woman; and hence the man without reunion with the woman is grim, etc., . . . but when reunited with a wife, becomes agreeable, etc., 56^{4}.
Women were created beauties for the sake of the men; the reason, 56^{4}.
In the universe there is nothing more perfect than a woman beautiful in face and graceful in manners . . . in order that man might render thanks to the Lord for this bounty, and repay it by the reception of wisdom from Him, 56^{5}.
The man (*vir*) was born to be wisdom, and the woman to be the love of the man's wisdom, 75^{7}.
Man (*homo*),—a man (*vir*) and a woman,—are a church, 125.
The woman was created out of the man, and both have an inclination and faculty to become reunited into a one, 156[a].
Women are born loves, whereas men are receptions, 160.
Why women do not speak from rational wisdom, but reman silent and only listen while subjects belonging thereto are being discussed by men, 165.
The woman was created out of the man, and hence she has an inclination to unite and as it were re-unite herself with the man, 173.
Women cannot enter into the duties proper to men, nor men into those proper to women, 175.
The Lord has created man a receptacle of both love and wisdom

MAN—*continued.*
proceeding from Himself, the man for the reception of wisdom, and the woman for the reception of the love of the man's wisdom, 180.

Men have been created forms of the understanding, and women forms of the love of the understanding of men, 187.

Men by creation are forms of knowledge, intelligence, and wisdom; and women are forms of the love of those things with men, 187.

The woman is actually formed into a wife according to the description in Genesis, 193.

Difference between females or women, married women, and wives, 199.

Difference between the intelligence, voice, etc., of the sexes, 218.

Woman is able to conceal her internal affections, 274.

Man is born to be understanding, but the woman to be love; with men there is generally the love of the sex, but with women the love of one of the sex; it is not unbecoming for men to speak about love, but it is for women, 296.

Women are born loves of the understanding of the men, 393.

Conjugial love is implanted in every woman from creation, and together with it the love of procreating, which from the women is communicated to the men, 409.

—*Man and beasts,* differences between, 133, 134, 151[a], 152[a], 495.

The state of man compared with that of beasts, 151.

Men like beasts found in the woods, 151.

According to the defect and loss of conjugial love, man approaches to the nature of the beast, 230.

A merely natural man is like a beast as to lusts, appetites, and their delights; with this difference only, that he has the faculty of elevating his understanding and will, 230.

Man is born viler than a beast, and into no knowledge, 350.

Men who worship Nature differ from beasts only in this respect, that they are possessed of rationality, that is, they are capable of understanding, and thus of thinking otherwise, if they are willing, 416[3].

A beast appropriates nothing of influx to itself, as a man can do, 455.

Man, without the faculty of elevating the understanding above the love of the will, would not be a man, but a beast, 498.

MANNERS. A counterfeit grace of manners is an allurement to marriage, 49.

The manners of men are more unrestrained, with women more elegant, 218.

MARRIAGE, MATRIMONY: see also CONJUNCTION; *Love of marriage.*

Note:—The Latin *matrimonium* has in this translation for the sake of uniformity been always rendered *matrimony.* The various meanings intended by the term will be readily perceived from the context.

Marriages in themselves are spiritual, and hence holy, 53.

Marriages, viewed in themselves, are spiritual, and therefore holy, for they descend from the heavenly marriage of good and truth, 308.

Marriages are the seminaries of the human race, and consequently of the heavenly kingdom, and therefore ought not to be violated, but to be accounted holy, 481.

Marriage is preferable to celibacy, 156.

It is the fulness of man; for by means of it man becomes a full man, 156.

When a man marries he becomes a fuller man, because he is conjoined with a consort with whom he acts as one man, 59[2].

Consent is the essential of marriage; and all the things that follow are its formalities, 21[e].

Marriage is not legitimate till after the wedding, 306[e].

The marriage ought to be consecrated by a priest, 308.

Determinations to marriage are delayed from various causes even to middle age, 98[2].

Matrimonies cannot be contracted in some kingdoms till the season of youth is past, 459.

Change of the state of life effected by marriage (Chapter), 184–206.

The conjunctions which are made on earth are seldom made from any internal perception of love, but from an external perception, which hides the internal, 49.

Marriages contracted in the world are for the most part external, and not at the same time internal; when yet it is the internal conjunction of souls that constitutes marriage itself, 49.

Matrimonies are generally contracted in the world according to the external affections, 274.

Merely natural marriages are not

MARRIAGE—*continued.*
that of adultery is the connubial connection of evil and falsity, 428.
The love of adultery is from hell and returns to hell, and the love of marriage is from heaven and returns to heaven, 478[3].
The love of marriage is of the spirit, and the love of adultery is of the flesh, 488.
MARRIED PARTNERS, see HUSBAND AND WIFE.
MARROW (Spinal). From the spine and the marrow there emanate fibres of which the whole body is interwoven, 315[6].
By the marrows in heaven they mean the interiors of the mind and body, 312.
MARY signifies the church, 119.
MATERIAL, see SUBSTANTIAL AND MATERIAL.
MASCULINE AND FEMININE, see MALE AND FEMALE.
MECHANICS, its use, 163.
MEDIA are not primes or first things in themselves, but only conducive to what is first in itself, 98.
MEDULLARY SUBSTANCE (The) of both brains is a collection and congeries of all the fibres which are the initiaments of the whole man, 315[6].
METEOR (A) seen in the spiritual world, 315.
MIND: see also *Soul and mind.*
As a man progresses from knowledge into intelligence, and from this into wisdom, so also his mind changes its form; for it is opened more and more, and conjoins itself more closely with heaven, 94.
If man halts at the threshold in the progression to wisdom, the form of his mind remains natural, 94.
It is successively opened from infancy even to extreme old age, 102.
With men there is an elevation of the mind into a higher light, and with women an elevation into a higher heat, 188.
The human mind is distinguished into regions, which are like the atmospheres, 188[3], 270, 495; nature of conjugial love in each region, 270[3], 335; names of these regions, 270[4], 305, 335.
With some the mind is closed from below, and is sometimes twisted like a spire into the contrary direction; but with some it is not closed, but remains half open above, and with some it remains quite open, 203.
The lower parts of the mind are unchaste, but its higher parts are

MIND—*continued.*
chaste; for the lower parts of the mind cleave to the body, but the higher parts separate themselves from them, 302.
The human mind is capable of being elevated above sensual things, 380[6].
When the mind turns away from the Lord it turns to itself, and then perceives the contrary things, 444[7].
The form of the human mind is according to confirmations, 491.
Such as the form of a man's mind is, such is his spirit, consequently such is the man, *ib.*
Every man has an internal mind and an external mind: with the evil the internal mind is insane and the external wise; but with the good the internal mind is wise, and from this also the external mind, 477[3].
The mind of every man, according to his will and consequent understanding, actually dwells in some one society, in heaven, 530[2].
—*Mind and body.* With the Ancients the science of correspondences conjoined the sensuals of the body with the perceptions of the mind, and procured intelligence, 76[4].
The body is altogether such as the mind or spirit is, 153.
What is from the body in the spirit does not last long, 162.
The external form which is that of the body is perfected according to the perfection of the internal form which is that of the mind; for the mind acts upon the body, but not contrariwise, 187, 191.
The mind rarely shines through the material body, 192.
The body is composed of watery and earthly elements, and of aërial exhalations thence arising; and when these are cast off, the forms of the minds are plainly seen, such as they had been inwardly in their bodies, 192.
As the mind, while it acts, is also in the body, the body has similar states, 221.
Angels and spirits have minds and bodies, 273[2].
The bodies of men, considered exteriorly, are nothing else than forms of their minds organized exteriorly to effect the purposes of the soul, 310.
Marriage of the mind or spirit ought to precede the marriage of the body, *ib.*
All things which a man does in the body flow from his spirit, 310.
Such as the mind is, such are the speech of the mouth and the deeds of

RECEPTACLE—*continued.*
wisdom, and a receptacle of God is an image of God; and a receptacle becomes an image of God in proportion to reception, 132[7].

RECEPTION (The) of influx is according to the form, and therefore causes every species to continue the same species, 86.
The reception of the truth of wisdom by the male takes place in the intellect, 90.
Reception means disposition and willingness to become wise, 90[2].
Reception [of the heat and the light from the spiritual sun] is according to the love of becoming wise, 261.
In all conjunction by love there must be action, reception, and reaction, 293[5].
Without conjunction there is no reception, 341[2].
The influx of light and heat from the Lord out of the spiritual sun enlightens and vivifies every one according to reception; and reception is according to religion, 352[e].

RECIPROCALITY. Without reciprocality no conjunction is possible; what the reciprocality of conjunction [with God] is, 132[6].

RECTIFICATION (a term in chemistry), 145.

REDNESS. The heat and redness of the blood are from no other source than the love, 34.

REFORMATION. Man is reformed by means of the understanding; and this is effected by the Knowledges of good and truth, and by means of rational intuition therefrom, 495.

REFUSAL: see RESISTANCE.

REGENERATION. Those who are regenerated by the Lord are called in the Word sons of God, sons of the kingdom, born of Him, 120.
The birth of the Spiritual is regeneration, 146.
It is a successive separation from the evils which are ingrained in the inclinations from birth, 146.
Man is wise in the spirit from the Lord when he is regenerated and created anew by Him, 269[3].
Man is led into good by means of regeneration by the Lord, 525[2].
It consists in purification from evils, and thereby renovation of life, *ib.*
The five precepts of regeneration, 525[3].
A man by regeneration is made altogether new as to his spirit, and this is effected by means of a life according to the Lord's precepts, 525[4].

REGIONS of the mind; see under MIND.

REIGNING WITH CHRIST means being wise and doing uses, 7[3].

RELATION. There does not exist any relation or progression of good to evil, but of good to a greater and lesser good, and of evil to a greater and lesser evil, 444[3].

RELATIVES (*i.e.*, Relative degrees), 17.
Difference between relatives and contraries, 425.

RELIGION and the human conjugial principle proceed together at the same pace, 80[2].
It belongs to life, 82[e].
If you remove the five doctrinals [of the New Church] from the church, you remove from it the Sacred Scripture, and also religion; and when these are removed, the church is not a church, 82[e].
Religion is formed by means of the good of life according to the truth of doctrine, and among Christians is derived solely from the Sacred Scripture, 115[4].
Without religion man does not become spiritual but remains natural, 149.
The religion with married partners constitutes their chastity, 152.
The internal causes of cold in marriage are from religion, 238–243.
Conjugial love is according to the state of the church with man; thus it is from religion, because religion constitutes this state, 238[2].
Religion is the only means of introducing and elevating man to the marriage of good and truth, 238[3].
Where religion is not, there conjugial love does not exist, 239.
Notwithstanding that there is religion at the present day, still there are not the truths of religion; and what is religion without truths? *ib.*
Influence of differing religions on married partners, 242.
Falsity in spiritual things either takes away religion or defiles it, 243.
Religion is implanted in souls, and is handed down by the parents, through their souls, to the offspring, as the supreme inclination, 246.
Conjugial love in its progress accompanies religion, and religion, because it is the marriage of the Lord and the church, is the beginning and inoculation of that love, 531.

RENEWAL. There is no part within or without a man which does not renew itself; this is effected by dissolutions and reparations, 171[2].

RENUNCIATION (The total) of whoredoms on account of religion gives rise to the chastity of marriage, 147–149.
REPARATIONS, see RENEWAL.
REPRESENT. Everything created by the Lord represents something, 294.
REPRESENTATIONS (The) of verities in forms was, with the Ancients, the study of the senses of their bodies, 76[4].
REPRESENTATIVE. To those who are in the third heaven, every representative of love and wisdom becomes real, 270[5].
Children in the other world are instructed especially by means of representatives, 412.
RESISTANCE. With the angels there is no refusal and resistance on the part of the wives, 258.
RESPIRATION OF THE LUNGS (The) has relation to truth: there is also a correspondence, 87[3].
REST (Eternal) from labour, its meaning, 207[7, 8].
RESURRECTION OF THE BODY, its absurdity and impossibility, 182[5].
REVELATIONS made by the Lord at the present day, 532.
REVENGE. An unbridled desire to revenge, a cause of legitimate separation, 252; and a really weighty cause of concubinage, 472.
The inward cupidity of revenge altogether checks the influx of conjugial love, absorbs it, and swallows it up, and changes its delight, which is celestial, into the delight of revenge, which is infernal, 375[3].
RIB. By a rib of the breast, in the Word, nothing else is signified, in the spiritual sense, but natural truth, 193.
RIGHT AND LEFT. The right signifies good, and the left truth, 316[5].
—*The right hand* signifies power, 21[2].
RITES, see CUSTOMARY RITES.
RIVALRY or striving for pre-eminence, is one of the external causes of cold in marriage, 248.
Rivalry between the married partners respecting right and Power; its nature, source, and results, 291.
ROBBERY. The lot of those who rob others of their goods, 268[3].
ROSES. A bed of roses signifies the delights of wisdom, 293[6].

SABBATH. The life of heaven, by reason of the worship of God, is called a perpetual Sabbath, 9.
How spent in heaven, 23, 24.
SACRED SCRIPTURE: see also WORD.
A sermon in a heavenly temple on the subject of, 24.
SACRED SCRIPTURE—*continued.*
If you remove the doctrinals [of the New Church] from the church, you remove from it the Sacred Scripture and also religion; and when these are removed, the church is not a church, 82[e].
The Sacred Scripture, which has proceeded immediately from the Lord, is in general and particular the marriage of good and truth, 115[4].
The church and religion are, among Christians, derived solely from the Sacred Scripture, *ib.*
SAGACITY belongs to the rational wisdom of men, 163.
SALVATION. All in the universal globe of lands who acknowledge a God, and from religion shun evils as sins against Him, are saved, 343.
What class of polygamists are saved, 351.
SAMENESS, see IDENTITY.
SATAN: see also *Devil and satan.*
A discussion between satans and angels on the subject of nature and God, 415.
SATURNIAN or Golden AGE (The): quality of its men, 153[a].
SATYRS, 44[4], 521: the satyr-like form is a form of dissolute adultery, and not the form of a person, 521[4].
SAVED (To be), see SALVATION.
SCIENCE, see also KNOWLEDGE.
The sciences belong to rational wisdom, 163.
SCIENCE OF CORRESPONDENCES (The), among the Ancients, conjoined the sensuals of their bodies with the perceptions of their minds, and procured them intelligence, 76[4].
It was with the Ancients, 342[2].
Particulars concerning it, 532[2].
SCHOOLS, see PUBLIC SCHOOLS.
SCHOOLS OF WISDOM in the spiritual world, 132.
SCORTATORY LOVE is unchastity itself, 139.
Nothing stores up in itself conjugial cold more than scortatory love; and as scortatory love also passes into that cold, it may be called conjugial cold itself, 247.
It is one of the three universals of hell, 261[3].
Definition of, 423.
Its quality is not known unless the quality of conjugial love be known, 424.
It means the love of adultery, which destroys conjugial love, *ib.*
Its origin, 427.
It is the source of the uncleanness of hell, 430; and of the uncleanness in the church, 431.

SCORTATORY LOVE—*continued.*
Its delightsomenesses commence from the flesh, and are of the flesh even in the spirit, 440.
Its imputation, 523–531.
—*Its opposition to conjugial love:* see under CONJUGIAL LOVE.
SCURVY a cause of legitimate separation, 253; and a just cause of concubinage, 470.
SEDUCING (The Lust of), 513, 514.
The lot of seducers after death, 514.
SEE (To). See SIGHT.
SEED. The virile faculty of secretion of the semen (*seminatio*) is from a spiritual origin; it is from the truths of which the understanding consists, 220.
Seeds spiritually understood are truths, *ib.*
The formation of truth into seed, 220[2].
In the seed of a man (*vir*) is his soul in a perfect human form, covered with substances from the purest things of nature, 183[4].
The soul in its descent, when it becomes seed, is veiled over by such things as belong to the man's natural love: from this springs hereditary evil, 245.
What is meant by the seed of man whereby iron shall be mixed with clay 79.
Fecundation (*seminatio*) corresponds to the potency of truth, 127.
SELF-CONCEIT, see CONCEIT.
SENSATION. Angelic perception and sensation are much more exquisite than human perception and sensation, 44[8].
Sensations with the pleasures thence derived belong to the body, 273[2].
SENSE. Each of the five senses has delights with variations according to its specific uses, 68.
The use of the sense of conjugial love is the complex of all other uses, 68[e].
The senses are the ultimates on which the interior things which belong to the mind, and the inmost things which belong to the soul, as it were sit or rest, 130[2].
The sixth sense of wives, 155[a][4].
Every love has its own sense; explained, 210.
The sense of touch is dedicated to conjugial love, and is its especial sense, *ib.*
The natural senses are from the spiritual senses, 220.
SENSUAL [FACULTY] derives all its ideas from the lumen in which the senses of the body are, and confirms their fallacies, 416.
It is the lowest of the understanding, 421.
SENSUAL [MEN]. Who those are that are meant by the sensual; their difference from the natural and the corporeal, 496.
SEPARATIONS (causes of), 251–254.
They are from no other source than from colds, 234.
SERENITY of peace (The), 155[a][5].
SERIES. All those things which precede in minds form series, and series are collected together, one beside another and one after another, and these together compose what is last or ultimate, in which they coexist, 313[2].
The series of the love of children, from its greatest to its least, is retrograde, 401[e].
SERPENT (The) (Gen. iii.) means the devil as to the love of self and the conceit of self-intelligence, 135[3]: the love of self-intelligence, 353.
Serpents are among the forms under which the lascivious delights of scortatory love are presented to the sight in hell, 430.
SEX. Difference between the love of the male sex and that of the female sex, 382.
The beauty of the female sex, see BEAUTY; also *Love of the Sex.*
SHAMELESSNESS: see IMMODESTY.
SHEEPFOLD (The) signifies the church, 129.
SHOWER (Golden), see GOLDEN SHOWER.
SIGHT. The rational and spiritual sight reaches above the body and outside of the world, 168.
To the love of seeing, from the love of understanding, belongs the sense of sight; the pleasantnesses of this sense are symmetries and beauties, 210.
Natural sight is from spiritual sight, which is that of the understanding, 220.
If heavenly light does not flow in into natural light, a man does not see whether anything true is true, and consequently neither does he see that anything false is false. Seeing in either case is by virtue of heavenly light in natural light, 233[5].
Being able to see that what is true is true, and what is false is false, and to confirm the same, is the characteristic of an intelligent man, 233[7].
How gross the sight of the eye is, 416[4].
Every man has an internal mind and an external mind, thus an internal sight and an external sight: . . . such as the mind is, so a man in the spiritual world sees objects, 477[3].

SILKWORMS, 420.
SILVER signifies intelligence from spiritual verities, and thence from natural verities, 76[3].
The Silver Age, 76.
SIMILARITIES AND DISSIMILARITIES, in in the spiritual world, are not only felt, but also appear in the face, speech, and gestures, 273.
SIMPLE. Everything divided is more and more manifold, and not more and more simple, 329[2].
SIMPLICITY (Extreme) a cause of legitimate separation, 252.
SIMULATIONS (Conjugial), 279–289.
SIMULTANEOUS and successive ORDER, 314[2, 3].
SIN. All that which is contrary to religion is believed to be sin, because it is contrary to God; and all that which agrees with religion is believed not to be sin, because it agrees with God, 348.
SINCERITY is one of the virtues that pertain to the moral wisdom of men, 164.
SINGING (Heavenly) described, 17[2], 19, 155[a].
Heavenly songs are nothing else than sonorous affections, or affections expressed and modified by sounds; for as thoughts are expressed by speech, so affections are expressed by song, 55.
The singing of heaven is nothing else than an affection of the mind sent forth through the mouth as melody, 155[a].
SINGULARS, see *Universals and singulars.*
SIRENS (The) of hell, 505[2]. They are absolete venereal lusts, 433[e].
SISTERS. The Lord calls those who are of His church, brothers and sisters, 120.
SIX. The number six signifies all and what is complete, 21[3].
SLEEP. The man's sleep and falling asleep (Gen. ii.) signifies his entire ignorance that his wife is formed and as it were created from him, 194.
By sleeping is signified being in ignorance and unconcern, 194[e].
SLEEP-WALKERS do what they do from blind knowledge, while the understanding is asleep, 134[4].
SLOTH: its effect on man, 249.
In heaven, no food is given to the slothful, 6[e].
SMALL-POX (Malignant) a cause of legitimate separation, 253; and a just cause of concubinage, 470.
SMELL. To the love of cognizing the things that float about in the air, from the love of perceiving, belongs
SMELL—*continued.*
the sense of smell; and the pleasantnesses of this sense are fragrances, 210.
Natural smell is from spiritual smell, which is perception, 220.
SOBRIETY is one of the virtues that belong to the moral wisdom of men, 164.
SOCIETY. No one is wise, or lives, for himself alone, but for others at the same time: this is the origin of society, which otherwise could not exist, 18.
Uses are the bonds of society, *ib.*
—*Society of heaven.* Every one comes into that society of heaven of whose form he is an effigy in particular, 10[8].
Every society is as one common body, and the angels in it are as the like parts, from which the common body co-exists, *ib.*
Social intercourse in heaven, 5[4].
SOCRATES, 151[a].
SOCRATISTS, 153[a][2].
SOLITARY. There is neither solitary good nor solitary truth, but they are everywhere conjoined, 87.
SONS in the Word mean truths conceived in the spiritual man and born in the natural, 120, 220[3].
Those who are regenerated by the Lord are called in the Word "sons of God," "sons of the kingdom," "born of Him" . . . and the Lord called the disciples "sons," *ib.*
SONS-IN-LAW in the Word denote offspring of the Lord and the church, 120.
SONGS, see SINGING.
SOPHI and Philosophers, Difference between, 130.
SOPHI, see GREECE.
SORCERIES a cause of legitimate separation, 252.
SOUL. It is the soul that enjoys the delights of the senses of the body, 16[2].
The wisdom of the man constitutes his soul, 172.
The soul of the offspring is from the father, and its clothing from the mother, 206, 238 . . . The soul constitutes a man's inmost, which may be covered over by the offspring nearest in descent, but nevertheless comes forth and manifests itself in more remote issue, 206.
The masculine soul, because it is intellectual, is thus truth; . . . wherefore when the soul descends, truth also descends: this is effected by this circumstance, that the soul, which is the inmost of man and

SOUL—*continued.*
animal, and which in its essence is spiritual, by reason of an implanted effort for self-propagation, follows in the descent, and wishes to procreate itself: and when this takes place, the entire soul forms and clothes itself, and becomes seed; and this can be done thousands of times, because the soul is a spiritual substance, which has not extension but impletion, and from which no part can be taken away, but the whole may be produced, without any loss thereof: hence it is as fully present in the smallest receptacles, which are seeds, as in its greatest receptacle, the body, 220[2].

Further particulars as to the propagation of the soul, 245.

How the feminine principle is propagated from a male soul, 220[3].

The soul of every human being derives life from the marriage of good and truth, 246.

As the church is various and diverse in the several parts of the world, therefore the souls of all human beings are various and diverse, 246.

It is in the marriage of good and truth, and not only in the perpetual effort for that unition, but also in the perpetual effort for the fructification and production of its own likeness, 355[4].

The souls are the beginnings of life, 482.

A discussion on the nature and quality of the soul, 315; that it resides in man, and that its precise abode is a matter of conjecture, 315[4]; that it is in the head, either in the three ventricles of the cerebrum, in the *corpora striata*, in the medullary substance, in the cortical substance, or in the *dura mater*, 315[5,6]; that it is in the heart and hence in the blood, and that from the heart by means of the blood it sustains, nourishes, and vivifies the whole system of body and head, 315[7]; that the soul of man is in the whole of him, and in every part of the whole, and thus in the head and in each of its parts, as well as in the body and in each of its parts; that it is a spiritual substance, of which there cannot be predicated extension or place, but habitation and impletion; and that it is life, 315[8]; that it is a pure something, like ether, wind, or air, or breath, 315[9]; that it is the inmost and most subtle essence of man; that it is a form of all things of love, and all things of wisdom, 315[10]; that it is the spiritual substance

SOUL—*continued.*
in the body; that it is a human form from which the least thing cannot be taken away, and to which the least thing cannot be added; that it is the inmost form of all the forms of the whole body; that it is the man himself, because it is the inmost man; that its form is the human form; that it is not life, but the proximate receptacle of life from God, and thus the dwelling-place of God, 315[11].

—*Soul and mind.* Union of the souls and minds by means of marriage, 156[a]–181.

How a union of the souls and a conjunction of the minds, with married consorts, is effected, 172.

In the prolific principle of the husband is his soul, and also his mind as to its interiors, which are conjoined with the soul, *ib.*

The unition of the souls and minds of consorts on earth is felt in their flesh, because the soul constitutes the inmosts not only of the head but also of the body, 178[2].

In the seed of a man (*vir*) is his soul in a perfect human form, covered with substances from the purest things of nature, from which a body is formed in the womb of the mother, 183[4].

The soul of every human being, by reason of its origin, is celestial, wherefore it receives influx immediately from the Lord, 482.

The soul of a man (*vir*) is in his seed, 483.

—*Soul, mind, and body.* Man consists of soul, mind, and body: his inmost is the soul, 101; and it is, from its origin, celestial, 158.

The souls and minds of men are not in space like their bodies; and as they are not in space, they can be conjoined as into a one, although their bodies may not be so conjoined at the time, 158.

The mind is intermediate between the soul and the body, and although it appears to be in the head, is yet actually in the whole body also, 178, 260.

Whence it is that the acts that the soul and mind intend, flow instantly from the body, 178[2].

The soul and mind adjoin themselves closely to the flesh of the body, in order that they may operate and produce their effects, *ib.*

Both the soul and the mind are both in the head and in the body; for the soul and the mind are the man, since

SOUL—*continued.*
both constitute the spirit that lives after death, . . . the soul and mind are together in the body, and constitute his spiritual man, 260.

SOUND. In the spiritual world, a variety and commixture of affections is distinctly perceived in sound, 207.

SPACES. No spaces in the spiritual world, but appearances of spaces, 50.

Those things which, from their origin, are celestial and spiritual, are not in space, but in the appearance of space, 158.

Spaces in the other world are appearances, *ib.*

—*Space and time.* They cannot be predicated of spiritual things, 389.

SPANIARDS. Opinions of five Spaniards on the subject of conjugial love and its potency, 104.

SPECIES. Why the Creator has distinguished everything into species, 479.

SPEECH and action flow not from the thought, but from the love through the thought, 36.

The speech of the angels of the Golden Age is the speech of wisdom, because they speak from causes, 75[6].

The speech is from the thought of the understanding, 140.

Speech flows from the thought, which is spiritual, 220.

Frequent speech from the memory, and not at the same time from thought and intelligence, induces a kind of faith, 415[5].

Spiritual speech fully expresses the meanings, and many things in a moment, 481.

Speech in the spiritual world may be heard by a distant person as if he were present, 521.

Man's speech or conversation is such as is the thought of his understanding which produces it, 527.

— *Speech and song.* Thoughts are expressed by speech, and affections by song, 55.

SPHERE. There goes out, yea, pours forth from every human being a spiritual sphere from the affections of his love, which encompasses him, and infuses itself into the natural sphere which is from the body, and the two spheres become conjoined, 171; origin of that sphere, 171[2].

This sphere encompasses man slightly on the back, but more densely on the breast, and the sphere from the breast conjoins itself with the respiration, 171[2]; these spheres, because they go out from every part of man, and are abundantly continued around him, conjoin and disjoin the two consorts not only from without but also from within; and hence come all the differences and varieties of conjugial love, 171[2].

The sphere of love going out from a wife who is tenderly loved, how perceived in heaven, *ib.*

Every human being is encompassed by his or her own sphere of life, densely on the breast and thinly on the back, 224.

The spheres flowing forth from subjects in the spiritual world are spiritual, and those that emanate from spirits and angels are altogether spiritual; why, 171: why those spheres cause distances in that world, *ib.*; what they operate in the natural world is also known to some, *ib.*; they are the origin of the inclinations of consorts towards each other, *ib.*; consorts are united by unanimous and concordant spheres, and disunited by adverse and discordant spheres; for concordant spheres are delightful and agreeable, and discordant spheres are undelightful and disagreeable, *ib.*; the angels are in a clear perception of those spheres, 171[2].

There are several spheres that proceed from the Lord (enumerated), 222[2], but the universal of all is the conjugial sphere, *ib.* See below, *Universal conjugial sphere.*

The Divine that proceeds from the Lord is called a sphere; why, 386.

All that which flows forth from a subject, and surrounds and environs it, is called a sphere: examples, 386.

From the Lord, by means of the spiritual sun, proceeds a sphere of heat and light, or, of love and wisdom, to operate ends, which are uses; but that sphere, according to the uses, is distinguished by various names, (enumerated), 386.

Spheres are manifold, and those which are of love and wisdom proceed from the Lord, and through the angelic heavens descend into the world, and pervade it even to its ultimates, 434.

—*Sphere of conjugial love.* The sphere of perpetual celibacy infests the sphere of conjugial love, which is the very sphere of heaven: the sphere of conjugial love is the very sphere of heaven, because it descends from the heavenly marriage of the Lord and the church, 54[5].

SPHERE—*continued.*
It makes a one with the sphere of procreating, 387.
It is received by the women, and through them is transferred to the men; why, 393.
Its effects on adulterers, 425[2].
— *The universal conjugial sphere* proceeds from the Lord, and pervades the universe from its primes to its ultimates, thus from angels even to worms, 92, 222[3].
It is also the sphere of propagation, that is, of prolification and fructification; and this sphere is the same with the Divine providence for the preservation of the universe by means of successive generations, 92.
This universal sphere, which is that of the marriage of good and truth, flows in into subjects according to the form of each, *ib.*
It is the source of the love of the sex, 92[e].
It flows in into the form of wisdom with men, and also with angels, 93.
It is the universal sphere of all, because it is also the sphere of propagation, and thus in an eminent degree the sphere of the preservation of the created universe through successive generations, 222[2].
It is more universal than the sphere of heat and light, which proceeds from the sun of our world; proved and explained, 222[4].
This sphere is received by the feminine sex, and through this is transferred into the masculine sex, 223, 225.
Where there is truly conjugial love, this sphere is received by the wife, and solely through the wife by the husband, 224.
By the reception of the conjugial sphere by the husband solely through the wife, truly conjugial love is distinguished from spurious, false, and cold conjugial love, *ib.*
Where the love is not conjugial, this sphere is indeed received by the wife, but not by the husband through her, 225.
This conjugial sphere flowing in into the universe is, in its origin, Divine; in its progress . . . it is varied in all its subjects according to their forms, 225.
It may be inverted into the opposite sphere, which with women is called the *meretricious sphere*, and with men the *scortatory sphere;* and this sphere is from hell, 225 (particulars).
With those who had lived together

SPHERE—*continued.*
in truly conjugial love, the sphere of love from the wife, and the sphere of the understanding from the husband, is continually flowing forth, and perfects conjunctions, and . . . . . unites them, [even when one of them has passed into the other world], 321.
It is the sphere of good and truth, and perpetually emanates and flows in from the Lord, 238[2].
—*The universal spheres of procreating, etc.* Two universal spheres proceed from the Lord to preserve the universe in its created state; the sphere of procreating, and the sphere of protecting the things procreated, . . . they are from the Lord around Him; and they proceed from the sun of the spiritual world, in the midst of which He is, 386.
Those two universal spheres make a one with the sphere of conjugial love and the sphere of the love of children, 387.
The sphere of procreating, and the sphere of protecting the things procreated, make a one in a continual series, 390.
The sphere of the love of procreating progresses in order from the end, through the causes into the effects, and makes periods by means of which creation is preserved in the state foreseen and provided for, 400, 401.
—*The universal sphere of generating and propagating* the celestial things of love and the spiritual things of wisdom, and thence the natural things that are of offspring, proceeds from the Lord, and fills the whole heaven and the whole world; and that heavenly sphere fills the souls of all human beings, and descends through their minds into the body even to its ultimates, and gives the power of generating, 355[5].
—*The sphere of the love of children* makes a one with the sphere of protecting the things procreated, 387: those two spheres universally and singularly flow in into all things of heaven and all things of the world, from first to last, 388, 389.
It is a sphere of protection and support of those who are unable to protect and support themselves; . . . this latter sphere is the Divine providence, 391.
This sphere affects both the evil and the good, and disposes every one to love, protect, and support his offspring out of self-love, 392.
It principally affects the female sex,

SPHERE—*continued.* thus mothers, and the male sex, or fathers, by derivation from them, 393.

It is also a sphere of innocence and peace from the Lord, 394.

The sphere of innocence flows in into the children, and through them into the parents, and affects them, 395; it also flows in into the souls of the parents, and conjoins itself with the same sphere in the children; and it is chiefly insinuated by means of the touch, 396.

—There is a *sphere of scortatory love*, and a *sphere of conjugial love*, . . . those spheres are opposed to one another as the love of adultery is opposed to the love of marriage, 434.

The sphere of scortatory love ascends from hell, from the uncleannesses into which are turned the delights of adultery of those of both sexes there; and the sphere of conjugial love descends from heaven, 435.

Those two spheres mutually meet each other in both worlds, but they do not become conjoined, 436; in the spiritual world they meet in the world of spirits, *ib.*

Between those two spheres there is an equilibrium, and man is in that equilibrium, 437.

A man can turn himself to whichever sphere he pleases; but in proportion as he turns himself to the one, he turns away from the other, 438.

Each sphere bears with it delightsomenesses; that is, it affects the recipient man with delightsomenesses, 439.

—*The sphere of the lust of committing fornication*, such as it is in the beginning, is intermediate between the sphere of scortatory love and the sphere of conjugial love, and makes an equilibrium, 455.

SPINE. From the spine and the marrow there emanate fibres of which the whole body is interwoven, 315[6].

SPIRE. The mind is sometimes twisted like a spire, when, 203.

SPIRIT OF MAN. The interior man is the same as his spirit that lives after death, 35.

The spirit of man, by which is meant his mind as to the affections and thoughts, makes what is chaste and what is unchaste, 153.

The spirit is in a perfect human form, 260.

The spirit, after it has been separated from the body, comes into the full liberty of acting according to its own affections and thoughts, 264[3].

SPIRIT OF MAN—*continued.*

—*The spirit and the flesh.* There are two things which in the beginning with every man who from natural is made spiritual, are at strife together, the spirit and the flesh, 488.

The love of marriage is of the spirit, and the love of adultery is of the flesh, *ib.*

SPIRITS, see also *Angels and spirits*, also *Novitiate spirits.*

In the spiritual world no one can dwell but in his own house, 50.

With those who are in the spiritual world, the third degree, the Natural, is wanting, 52.

All in the spiritual world are clothed according to their affections, 175[e].

Spirits and angels are nothing else than minds and souls in a human form, 192.

Merely natural spirits are chilled with intense cold, when, 235.

Who those are who after death become corporeal spirits, 495.

SPIRITUAL, see *Natural and spiritual.*

SPIRITUAL MAN; see also *Natural and spiritual man.* The Lord taught the internal spiritual man, 340[3].

SPIRITUAL WORLD. In the spiritual world there are not spaces, but appearances of spaces, and these appearances are according to the state of life of those who are there, 50.

All things there appear according to correspondences, 76[2].

There are all such things there as there are on earth, . . . with this difference only, that all the things which are in the spiritual world are from a spiritual origin, and thus are spiritual; whereas all things that are in the natural world are from a natural origin, and thus are natural and material, 182[3].

There is therein a fulness of all things: there, all things are substantial and not material, there, all things that are in the natural world, exist in their perfection, 207[5].

The expanse of the centre of life is called the spiritual world, which subsists from its own sun, and the expanse of nature is called the natural world, which subsists from its own sun, 380[11].

SPORTS and games, etc., in heaven, 6[5], 17[4].

Conjugial love in its origin is the sporting of wisdom and love, 75[7].

Heavenly nuptial sports of love and wisdom, 183[7].

SPORTS—*continued.*
The sixth sense which wives possess is called in the heavens the sporting of wisdom with its love, and of love with its wisdom, 155[a][4].
Literary sports in the spiritual world, 207[6].

SPRING. All who come into heaven return into their vernal youth, and into the powers of that age, and remain so to eternity, 44[9].
The heat and light proceeding from the sun in heaven cause perpetual spring, 137[5].
—*Vernal heat* in heaven, acts as a one with conjugial love, 137[4].
It exists only where heat is equally united with light, or where heat and light are in equal proportion, *ib.*
A perpetual vernal influence breathes into those with whom love is united with wisdom in equal proportion, 137[5].
It affects animals in time of spring, 137[5]; but human beings in all seasons and at all times, 137[6].
In [the highest] heaven there is no other heat except vernal heat; wherefore with conjugial partners in that heaven there is spring in its perpetual endeavour, 355[6].

STABLES signify instructions, 76[2].

STATES. The state of married partners after death (Chapter), 45–54.
There are two states into which man enters after death, an external and an internal state. Described, 47[b].
Nothing exists except in a form, and state induces that form, 186.
The states of the minds of each of the betrothed parties proceeding in successive order, flow in into the state of marriage; nevertheless in one manner with the spiritual and in another with the natural, 313.
The last state is such as the successive order from which it is formed and exists, *ib.*
The quality of the primeval state of man, which is called the state of integrity, 355[3-5].
—*The state of the church* is from the Lord, 142.
—*A state of heavenly life* is derived from love and wisdom; and since use is the containant of love and wisdom, a state of heavenly life is derived from the conjunction of love and wisdom in use, 10[7].

STATESMAN'S (A) account of what he thought about the life of men after death, 182[7].

STATUE (The) seen by Nebuchadnezzar; its signification, 78.

STEALING. An unbridled desire to steal, a cause of legitimate separation, 252; and a truly weighty canse of concubinage, 472.

STENCHES in hell are the correspondences of the lascivious delights of scortatory love, 430; they are as delightful to those there as dung is to swine, 431[e].

STONES signify natural verities, and precious stones spiritual verities, 76[3].

STRIKE. An unbridled desire to strike, a cause of legitimate separation, 252; and a really weighty cause of concubinage, 472.

STRIVING for pre-eminence, see RIVALRY.

STUDY. The chief pursuit of the Silver Age was the study of verities, through which they had intelligence, 76[4].
In the spiritual world and in heaven there are studies in all branches of learning, 207[2].

STUPIDITY (The) of the age, 481.

SUBLIMATION (a term in chemistry), 145.

SUBJECT (A) without predicates is an entity of no reason, 66.
Every subject receives influx according to its form, 86.
All a man's affections and thoughts are in forms, and therefore are according to forms, for forms are their subjects, 186.
See also SUBSTANCE.

SUBSISTENCE is perpetual existence, 86.

SUBSTANCE. There does not exist any good or truth that is not in a substance as in its subject, 66.
Every idea of man, however sublimated, is substantial, that is, affixed to substances, *ib.*
In man all affections of love and all perceptions of wisdom, are substantiated; for substances are their subjects, 361.
—*Substance and form.* There does not exist any substance without a form; an unformed substance is not anything, because nothing can be predicated of it, 66.
—*Substantial and material.* A spiritual or substantial man sees a spiritual or substantial man, as a natural or material man sees a natural or material man, but not contrariwise, 31.
The difference between what is substantial and what is material is like the difference between what is prior and what is posterior, 31.
A man after death is a spiritual or substantial man, because this spiritual or substantial man lay concealed in-

SUBSTANCE—*continued.* wardly in the natural or material man: explained, 31.

In the spiritual world all things are substantial and not material; and material things derive their origin from substantial things: those who live there are spiritual men, because they are substantial and not material, 207[5].

Matters originate in substances, *ib.*

Those who are in the spiritual world are in substantial things and not in material things; and substantial things are the beginnings of material things, 328.

Natural things, which are material, cannot enter into spiritual things, which are substantial, *ib.*

SUCCESSIVE AND SIMULTANEOUS ORDER, 314[2, 3].

SUN. The fire of the angelic sun is pure love, 34.

The sun of the spiritual world does not set and rise like our sun, but remains constantly at an elevation of 45 degrees, 137[5].

The sun of that world is pure love; and the sun of the natural world is pure fire, 182[3], 532[5]; and therefore all that proceeds from the spiritual sun partakes of life, and all that which proceeds from the natural sun partakes nothing of life, 532[5].

Spiritual heat is from no other source than the sun of the spiritual world; for there is in that world a sun proceeding from the Lord, Who is in the midst of it; and as that sun is from the Lord, it is in its essence pure love. This sun appears fiery before the angels, because love is spiritual fire, just as the sun of our world does before men. From that sun proceed both heat and light; but as that sun is pure love, the heat in its essence is love, and the light wisdom, 235.

Spiritual cold is from the sun of the natural world, and its heat and light, *ib.*

Why the sun of the natural world was created, *ib.*

Does not the sun make nature and all its properties, which depend solely on the heat and light proceeding from the sun through the atmospheres? 380[8].

Above the angelic heaven there is a sun which is pure love, in appearance fiery like the sun of the world; and from the heat that proceeds from that sun angels and men derive will and love, and from its light they derive understanding and wisdom, 380[11].

SUN—*continued.*

The spiritual world subsists from its own sun, and the natural world from its own, *ib.*

The sun of the angelic heaven is not fire, but the Divine love proximately proceeding from God, Who is love itself, 380[12], and Who is in the midst of that sun, 380[13].

The fire of the natural sun has come into existence from no other source than the fire of the spiritual sun, which is the Divine love, 380[12].

The centre of life is the sun of the angelic heaven, . . . from that sun the sun of the world came into existence, and from the latter, the universe, 380[13].

The spiritual sun is in the centre of the universe, and its operation, being apart from space and time, is instant and present from first things in last things, 391.

The sun of the spiritual world is pure love, and the sun of the natural world pure fire, 415[3].

SUSPICIOUS FANCY a source of jealousy with some, 374.

SWAMMERDAM'S *Book of Nature*, 416.

SWAN, 155[a][5]. A pair of swans seen flying into the lowest windows of a palace, signified the conjugial love of the lowest region, 270[4].

SWEDENBORG asseverates in truth that the Memorable Relations in this Work are not inventions, but were of a truth done and seen, not in any dozing state of the mind but in a state of full wakefulness, 1; that it had pleased the Lord to manifest Himself unto him, and to send him to teach the things belonging to the New Church, *ib.*; that the interiors of his mind and spirit were opened by the Lord, and that by virtue of that opening it was given him to be in the spiritual world with angels, and at the same time in the natural world with men, *ib.*, 326[2] (particulars). The angels had not previously known the differences between what is spiritual and what is natural, because there had not been given an opportunity of comparing them together, by any man's being in both worlds at the same time, 327.

"I have related thousands of particulars about the departed, . . . I have also written concerning the lot of the English, etc.; and hitherto I have never heard any one say, 'How can such be their lot, when they are not yet risen out of their graves?' etc.," 28.

SWEDENBORG—*continued.*
He states that it had pleased the Lord to prepare him to receive the things that belong to spiritual wisdom, so that the state of heaven and hell, and the state of the life of men after death, might not remain unknown, and be laid asleep in ignorance, and at length buried in denial, 39.
His state on hearing the Glorifications of the Lord by the angels, 81[5].
His conversation with a man on the subject of the New Church, 82.
His intercourse with the spiritual world, and account of it, 182[3], 524[3].
Once in a great city he was wandering through the streets seeking a place of abode, and entered a house where their dwelled married partners of different religions. As he was ignorant of the fact, the angels spoke to him, and said, "We cannot remain with you in that house, because the married partners there are in discordant religions, 242.
State of anxiety into which he once fell on account of not being able to remove spaces and times from the ideas of his thought, when thinking of God before eternity; how removed, 382[3].
He had perceptibly and sensibly observed the influx of the spiritual world for 25 years, 419[e].
SWEDES. Opinions of five Swedes on the subject of conjugial love and its potency, 112.
SWEETNESS. In heaven the chaste love of the sex is called heavenly sweetness, 55[3].
SYCOPHANT. Every man who is not inwardly led by the Lord is a sycophant, and thus an apparent man, and yet not a man, 267[3].
SYMPATHY. Everything sympathetic and antipathetic takes its rise from spiritual spheres, 171.
In the spiritual world sympathies and antipathies are not only felt, but also appear in the face, speech, and gestures, 273.
In infernal marriages in this world there is intense antipathy in internals, and apparent sympathy in externals; the reason, 292[2].
SYPHILIS a just cause of concubinage, 470.

TABERNACLE. The Most Ancient people, while in the world, dwelt in tabernacles; wherefore in heaven they also dwell in tabernacles, 75[3]: the tabernacle of their worship answered exactly to the description of the tabernacle built for the sons of Israel in the wilderness, 75[8].
TABLET. In the sanctuary of the tabernacle of worship of the Golden Age is a tablet with the inscription: *The Covenant between Jehovah and the heavens*, 75[8].
The writings of the Most Ancient people were on tablets of wood and stone, and afterwards on thin tablets of polished wood, 77[6].
TARTARUS, 75[2, 6].
TARTARY. The Ancient Word is now lost in the kingdoms of Asia, and is only preserved in Great Tartary, 77[2].
TASTE. To the love of nourishing oneself from the love of imbuing oneself with goods and truths, belongs the sense of taste; and the delightsomenesses of that sense are delicacies, 210.
TEMPERANCE is one of the virtues that pertain to the moral wisdom of men, 164.
TEMPLE. Description of a temple in heaven, 23.
— *Temple of wisdom* (The) where a discussion was held by the wise men on the causes of the beauty of the feminine sex, 56.
TEMPORARY, see ETERNAL AND TEMPORARY.
THEATRES in heaven, 17[5].
THOUGHT: see also *Affections and thoughts; Love and thought; Will and thought.* There is no idea of natural thought adequate to any idea of spiritual thought, consequently no words expressive of it; for ideas of thought become the expressions of speech, 326[6].
Spiritual ideas or thoughts respectively to natural ones are ideas of ideas and thoughts of thoughts; and therefore they are expressive of qualities of qualities, and affections of affections; consequently spiritual thoughts are the beginnings and origins of natural thoughts, 326[7].
Why a natural man cannot think that which a spiritual man thinks, 328.
Thinking spiritually is thinking apart from space and time, and thinking naturally is thinking with space and time; for to every idea of natural thought there adheres something from time and space . . . Spiritual thoughts and perceptions differ from natural ones in this respect also, that they are not in space and time but in the appearance of space and time, 328[2].
The orderly and disorderly ways of thinking and forming conclusions described, 408.

ULYSSES AND CIRCE, 521^4.

UNCHASTE: see also *Chaste and unchaste.* The quality of those who are unchaste, detailed, 140.

A sphere of lasciviousness issues forth from those who are unchaste, *ib.*

UNCHASTITY, see CHASTITY throughout.

Unchastity is sometimes an allurement to marriage, 49.

With the greatest hypocrites, the unchaste is perceivable from hearing their talk, and is felt also from the sphere issuing from them, 140.

Unless the renunciation of whoredoms be made on account of religion, unchastity still lies hidden within like corrupt matter in a wound that is only outwardly healed, 149.

UNCLEAN. To the unclean all things are unclean, 140^e.

UNCLEANNESS (The) of hell is from scortatory love, 430; from adulterers, 500^6.

All hell abounds with uncleannesses; the origin of these, 430.

The uncleanness in the church is from scortatory love, 431.

There are innumerable varieties of uncleannesses, 430.

Uncleanness is a cause of legitimate separation, 252; and a really weighty cause of concubinage, 472.

UNDERSTANDING: see also *Will and understanding.*

Man alone can elevate his understanding above his natural loves, 96.

Man has understanding from heavenly light, 233^6.

UNHAPPINESS, see HAPPINESS.

UNION (The) between married consorts of the Golden Age; its nature, $75^{5,6,9}$.

Truly conjugial love is a union of the souls, 179: adultery does not dissolve this union, because it cannot be dissolved; but it closes it up with filth, 480, 482: this union of souls cannot possibly exist except in monogamous marriages, 482.

The intimate and eternal union of dispositions and minds could not possibly exist, as it does in heaven, without being foreseen and provided for by the Lord, 316^3.

The union of the souls and minds of married consorts is a spiritual union, and it is an actual adjunction of the soul and mind of the one to those of the other, which cannot possibly be dissolved, 321.

— *Union of love and wisdom:* see *Marriage of good and truth.*

UNIVERSALS. Good and truth are the universals of creation, 84, 92.

UNIVERSALS—*continued.*

There are three universals of heaven, and three opposite universals of hell, 261^3.

—*Universal truth:* see under TRUTH.

—*Universals and particulars.*

Whoever knows universals can afterwards comprehend particulars, because the latter are in the former as parts in a whole, 261^2.

—*Universals and singulars.* When mention is made of an universal, the singulars of which it is composed are meant at the same time; for a universal exists from and consists of singulars, etc., . . . wherefore if you take away the singulars, the universal is a mere name, 388.

UNIVERSE (The) was created by the Lord a most perfect work, 56^5.

All things in the universe have relation to good and truth, 60.

In each and everything of the universe good is conjoined with truth, and truth with good, *ib.*

The universe was created by the Lord God, and thus is as a work proceeding from Him, 85.

The universe, with all its created things, is from Divine love through Divine wisdom; or, from Divine good through Divine truth, 87^4.

All things that proceed from the Lord, or from the sun which is from Him and in which He is, pervade the created universe, even to the last things of all, 389.

UNLIKENESSES: see also *Likenesses and unlikenesses.* Unlikenesses are not felt from their differences in the extremes by any others than those who are in truly conjugial love, 439.

Internal unlikeness a truly weighty cause of concubinage, 472.

UNSOUNDNESS OF MIND a cause of legitimate separation, 252; and a just cause of concubinage, 470.

USE. See also *Delight of use; Love of use; Love, wisdom, and use.*

Every one [in heaven] has happiness from the use in his own function, 6^5.

The Lord does goods or uses mediately through angels, and in the world through men; and to those who do uses faithfully He gives the love of use, and its rewards, which is internal blessedness, 7^3.

It is for the public welfare that every one should be of some use in society, 7^4.

All use is from the Lord, and is done through angels and men, as if by them, 7^4.

Since love and wisdom exist and subsist in use, it is uses that affect the

USE—*continued.*
angels ; and use consists in faithfully, sincerely, and diligently discharging the works of one's own function, 16[3].
Living for others consists in doing uses, 18.
Uses are the bonds of society, and these bonds are as many in number as there are good uses ; and uses are infinite in number, *ib.*
Spiritual, moral and civil, natural, and corporeal uses, specified and described, *ib.*
Delights follow the use, and are in man according to the love of the use, 68.
Use is as the atmosphere which contains both heat and light (love and wisdom) in its bosom, 137[4].
Uses are the goods that truths produce, 220[3].
It is the continent of good and truth, 249.
While a man is in any use, his mind is limited as in a circle, within which it is successively co-ordinated into a truly human form, etc., 249.
All good uses in the heavens are splendid and refulgent, 266[2].
Relations between uses and dignities in heaven, 266[3].
The uses which the angels do are, by virtue of the love of them, within the angels from the Lord, 266[3].
Necessity for the communication of uses, 266[3].
The whole heaven is nothing but a container of use from primes to ultimates. What is use but the actual love of the neighbour? and what holds the heavens together but this love? 266[3].
How one can know whether he does uses from the love of self or from the love of uses, 266[4, 5].
Every one who believes in the Lord and shuns evils as sins, does uses from the Lord ; but every one who neither believes in the Lord nor shuns evils as sins, does uses from and for the sake of himself, 266[5].
The most excellent uses are from marriages, 305.
—*Use of conjugial love:* See under CONJUGIAL LOVE.

VARIETY. Distinction between varieties and diversities, 324.
There is a perpetual variety, and there is not anything the same as another, 524.
The form of heaven is derived solely from the varieties of souls and minds, 524[2].
—*The lust of variety* has led the dispositions of some into a desire for repeated marriages, 319.
It is an accessory of adultery and makes it more grievous, 454 ; it lays waste conjugial love, *ib.*
(Chapter), 506–510.
VEGETABLE KINGDOM. Sports of heat with light in the subjects of the vegetable kingdom, 189.
Wonders seen in the productions of, may be used as confirmations in favour of the Divine, 416.
VEIN. There is a certain vein latent in the affection of the will of every angel which attracts his mind to do something, 6[6].
—*Vein of conjugial love,* see under CONJUGIAL LOVE.
VENERY : its ardour is allayed and mitigated by pellicacy, 459[2].
VENTRICLES (The three) of the cerebrum are the receptacles of the animal spirits and of all the lymphs of the brain, 315[6].
VERNAL HEAT : see under SPRING.
VERTUMNI, 415[5].
VIOLATION (Chapter), 511, 512.
—*Violation of the spiritual marriage,* 515–520 ; it means the violation of the Word, 516, which is the adulteration of good and the falsification of truth, 517 ; it corresponds to whoredoms and adulteries, 518 ; it is effected by those in the Christian church who adulterate its goods and truths, 519.
VIRGIN OR MAIDEN, see also BACHELORS AND MAIDENS.
Virgins signify the Church, 21[3].
The exquisite perception of maidens in heaven, 22.
In heaven there are maidens and young men; . . . and the beauties of the maidens and the moralities of the young men correspond to each other, as forms mutually related to and fitted for each other, 44[2].
All novitiates, on ascending into heaven, are explored as to the quality of their chastity, for they are let into the company of maidens, the beauties of heaven, who perceive from their tone of voice, etc., of what quality they are as to the love of the sex, 44[4].
The nine virgins signify Knowledges and sciences of every kind, 182[2].
How a maiden is formed into a wife, 199, 321.
Virgins signify affections of sciences, 207[6].
Maidens of the fountain, why so called, 293[6].

VIRGIN—*continued.*
A maiden signifies the affection of truth, *ib.*
State of a maiden before and after marriage, 502.
Defloration is the violation of virginities, but not of virgins if effected from consent, 511.
VIRGINITY. The lot after death of those who had vowed perpetual virginity, 155[3].
Conjugial love with women acts in unity with their virginity, and hence is the chastity, purity, and holiness of that love; wherefore to solemnly promise and surrender that virginity to any man, is to give a pledge that she will love him to eternity; therefore a virgin can from no rational consent bargain it away except on promise of marriage. It is also the crown of her honour, 460.
It is the crown of chastity, and the pledge of conjugial love, 503.
VIRTUE: see also FACULTY. No virtue, with its honourable and becoming qualities, can be exhibited to the life except by means of relatives, 17[5].
Nothing that is honourable and good in any virtue can by successive progressions pass over to what is dishonourable and evil, but only to its own least till it perishes; and when it perishes, the opposite commences, *ib.*
Moral and spiritual virtues enumerated, 164.
VISIBLE THINGS (The) in nature can be used as confirmations in favour of the Divine, 416–421.
VISION from above, and vision from below, 233[e].
VISIONARIES, 268.
VITIATED STATES of mind and body that are causes of legitimate separation, 252, 253.
VOICE. The tone of the voice is from the affection of the will, and the voice or speech itself is from the thought of the understanding, 140.
It is the tone of voice, separate from the discourse of the speaker, and flowing from the affection of love, that gives life to the speech, 155[a].
The tone of voice is deep with men, and tender with women, 218.
Why the voice becomes masculine together with the commencement of the man's understanding, 446[e].

WAKEFULNESS (The first) is more internal, peaceful, and sweet than the rest of the day 155[a].
WANDERINGS (Man's) as to his spirit during the life of the body, are after death collected into a one, and a place is accordingly allotted to him, either in hell or heaven, 530[2].
"WARS OF JEHOVAH (The)" are the historical books of the Ancient Word, 77.
WARTY GROWTHS, a cause of legitimate separation, 253, and a just cause of concubinage, 470.
WASHING denotes the purification of the internal man, 340[3].
WASTEFULNESS (Excessive), a cause of legitimate separation, 252.
WATER in the spiritual sense denotes truth, 80.
Drinking water from the fountain signifies being instructed concerning truths and goods, and thus becoming wise, 182[2].
WAYWARDNESS (Extreme), a cause of legitimate separation, 252.
WEALTH and possessions especially are objects of the love of the world, 49.
Inequality of wealth a cause of cold in marriages, 250.
Wealth in heaven consists in the faculty of becoming wise, according to which a sufficiency of wealth is given, 250.
WEASELS. Seducers in hell appear like weasels, 514[3].
WEDDING (*Nuptiae*). Description of a wedding in heaven, 19–25.
Weddings in heaven represent the marriage of the Lord with the church, 21.
It is expedient on earth that a priest should be present and minister at weddings, 21[4].
Spiritual weddings are meant by the Lord's words that "after the resurrection they are not given in marriage," 41.
By spiritual weddings is meant conjunction with the Lord, and this is effected on earth; and when it is effected on earth, it is also effected in the heavens; wherefore in the heavens they are not married again, nor again given in marriage, 41[2].
Making a wedding denotes being conjoined with the Lord, and entering into a wedding denotes being received into heaven by the Lord, 41[3].
There are weddings in the heavens, as on earth; but for no others in the heavens than those who are in the marriage of good and truth; nor are any others angels; wherefore, it is spiritual weddings, which are of the marriage of good and truth, that are meant in the Word. These spiritual weddings take place on earth, but not after death, thus not in the heavens, 44[10].

Weddings are essential rites, and not mere formalities, 306.

WHITE COLOUR signifies the intelligence of the husband, 76[7].

What is white in heaven denotes truth, 316[6].

WHOREDOM (*Scortatio*). In heaven they are utterly ignorant what whoredom is; nor do they know that it exists, or that its existence is possible, 44[7].

The falsifications of truths are spiritual whoredoms, 77[5].

The falsification of truth is spiritual whoredom, which acts in unity with natural whoredom, because they cohere, 80[e].

The total renunciation of whoredoms on account of religion gives rise to the chastity of marriage, 147–149.

Evil in regard to the sex, which is within in the natural man, is whoredom, 345.

It is ruinous to society, *ib.*

Whoredoms in the spiritual sense of the Word signify the connubial connection of evil and falsity, 428.

It is diametrically opposite to the life of conjugial love, and destroys it even to extermination, 468.

Whoredoms in the Word signify falsifications of truth and adulterations of good, 518.

How imputed, 530[3].

WICKEDNESS. An unbridled desire to act wickedly, a cause of legitimate separation, 252; and a really weighty cause of concubinage, 472.

WIDOW AND WIDOWER, relative grievousness of their condition, 325.

WILDERNESS (A) of the Age of Iron and Clay, 79[4].

WILL is a living endeavour with man, 215.

The will is the receptacle of the love, for what a man loves, that he also wills, 347.

—*Will and thought.*

There is an internal and an external will and thought, 47.

—*Will and understanding.*

The will does nothing except through the understanding; nor the understanding except from the will, 87[3].

The will and understanding constitute man; the will is the receptacle of good, and the understanding of truth; love, charity, and affection belong to the will, and perception and thought to the understanding, 121.

The understanding imbibes from the Word only such things as are its own, that is, truths, 128.

The will of the wife conjoins itself

WILL—*continued.*

with the understanding of the man, and hence the understanding of the man conjoins itself with the will of the wife, 159.

The understanding perceives those things also which are above the body and outside of the world, whereas love does not go beyond what it feels, 168.

The understanding belongs to light, and love belongs to heat, 168.

The will of the man resides in his understanding; and the Intellectual of the man is the inmost of the woman, 195.

He who conjoins to himself the will of another, also conjoins to himself his understanding; for the understanding is the servant of the will . . . he who conjoins to himself the will of a man, conjoins to himself the whole man, 196.

The intellect can think that this is good; the will does not think good and truth, but loves and does them, 220[3].

The understanding is not so constant in its thoughts as the will is in its affections, 221.

The understanding of the man is not closed, but is capable of being elevated into the light in which the soul is; but the love of his will is not elevated into the heat corresponding to the light there, except by the life, which from natural makes him spiritual, 245.

With every man the understanding is capable of being elevated according to Knowledges, but the will can be thus elevated only by a life according to the truths of the church and of reason, 269[6].

The will is the receptacle of love, and the understanding, of wisdom, 270.

The understanding, with its truths can, as often as it pleases, ascend by a winding staircase into the highest region into its bride-chamber; but if the will with the good of its love does not ascend . . . 270[6].

The understanding, being the thinking faculty, ponders over a variety of things which disquiet the animus, 285.

The will can make itself obstinate, but not so the understanding, 292[2].

The will and understanding in every individual act together upon the veriest singulars of the mind and of the body, 316[4].

The natural man is able to elevate his understanding into the light of heaven, and to think and speak spiritually; but if the will does not at the same time follow the understanding

WILL—*continued.*
into that height, he is nevertheless not elevated; for he does not stay there, but soon lets himself down to his will, and there fixes his abode, 347, 495.

In the spiritual world the understanding clothes every one, 354.

The understanding is a recipient [of love from the will], 393.

The understanding thinks and speaks through the thought: the understanding makes the man, and also constitutes his masculinity, 446^e.

The will, by virtue whereof man is man, cannot be moved in the least except by delight; for the will, considered in itself, is nothing but the affect and effect of some love, thus of some delight, 461^6.

The will actuates the understanding to think, *ib.*

In proportion as the understanding favours evils, the man appropriates them to himself and makes them his own, 489.

He who does not distinguish between the will and the understanding, cannot distinguish between evils and goods, 490.

These two faculties receive and appropriate to themselves good and truth, 490.

The will alone of itself does nothing; but whatever it does, it does by means of the understanding; and contrariwise, 490^3.

The will flows in into the understanding, but not the understanding into the will; yet the understanding teaches what is good and evil, and consults with the will, that out of those two it may choose and do what is pleasing to it, *ib.*

After this, there is effected a twofold conjunction; one, in which the will acts from within, and the understanding from without; the other, in which the understanding acts from within and the will from without, *ib.*

The will is the man himself, and the understanding is the man by virtue of the will, 490^e.

The understanding alone confirms, and when it confirms it engages the will and sets it about itself, and thus drives it to compliance, 491.

A man's life essentially is of his will, and formally of his understanding; because the will acts in unity with the love, and forms itself in the understanding; the understanding is nothing else than the form of the will, 493.

Man is man by virtue of the will and the understanding; for from these two faculties exist not only all the things which are done in the mind, but also those done in the body, 494.

The will acts through the body, . . . wherefore if the will were to be taken away, action would instantly come to a stop, *ib.*

The love of the will makes the man, and draws the understanding into consent, 498.

These two faculties constitute a man's life: and all things which a man does are done by them; and without them a man would have neither action nor speech other than as a machine, 527.

—*The affection of the will, and thought of the understanding:* see under *Affection and thought.*

—*Intellectual and voluntary forms.*

The masculine form is the intellectual form, and the feminine the voluntary form; and the intellectual form cannot of itself become heated with conjugial heat, but it can be heated by the conjunctive heat of some one into whom this has been implanted by creation; consequently it cannot receive that love except through the voluntary form of woman being adjoined to it, because this also is the form of love, 223.

—*Will, understanding, and action.*

The will is the receptacle of love, the understanding, of wisdom, and the action, of use, 400^2.

Operations in general and in particular with man progress from the will (love) through the understanding (wisdom) into the act (use), 400^2.

WISDOM: see also *Intelligence and wisdom; Knowledge* (scientia), *intelligence and wisdom; Love of wisdom; Love and wisdom.*

With the angels, wisdom never has an end or ceases to be, but grows and increases to eternity, 18.

Those who are in spiritual uses, are also in moral, civil, natural, and corporeal uses, and these persons are wise; but those who are not in spiritual uses, and yet are in the remaining ones, are not so wise, but only appear to be so by virtue of external morality and civility, 18^2.

The man of the church is wise as of himself, and in the proportion in which he is wise he receives love from the Lord, 21^2.

What is a wise man or a wisdom without a woman, or without love? A wife is the love of a wise man's wisdom, 56^2.

WORLD OF SPIRITS—*continued.* and hell, and there he is prepared either for heaven or hell, 48[b].

Into it all mortals are first collected after their departure out of the natural world, 2[2].

In it all are previously prepared, the good for heaven, and the evil for hell; and when they are prepared, they see ways opened for them to societies of their like, with whom they are to remain to eternity; and they then enter these ways with delight, because they are the ways of their love, 10[6].

It is intermediate between heaven and hell, 436, 461, 477[2].

All who depart out of the world come thither, and are gathered thither, and examined as to their quality; and here they are prepared, the evil for hell, and the good for heaven, 477[2].

WORMS, 418.

WORSHIP (The) of God in heaven returns at stated times, and is proclaimed by the priests, 23.

Idolatrous worship prevailed before the Mohammedan religion, 342[2].

The worship of the Ancients was representative, 342[3].

WRANGLE. An unbridled desire to wrangle, a cause of legitimate separation, 252.

WRATH ensues when the love is hurt, 358.

Why attributed to the Lord in the Word, 366.

WRITINGS (The) of the Most Ancient and of the Ancient people are not extant: those which are extant are of writers who lived after those ages, 73.

The Golden, Silver, and Copper Ages had passed away before the time of written documents, 73.

The quality of the writings of women, 175[3].

Writings in the heavens, 182, 326[5].

XENOPHON, 151[a].

YOUNG MAN: see BACHELOR.

YOUTH. All who come into heaven return into their vernal youth, and into the powers of that age, and remain so to eternity, 44[9].

In heaven all are in the flower of their youth, 250.

All in heaven are in the full bloom of youth, 355[2].

Children in heaven do not grow up beyond their first age, but stop in that age and remain in it to eternity, 411: when they attain the stature which is common in the world to young men of eighteen years, and to maidens of fifteen years, they remain of that stature, 444[e].

ZEAL. Wives are as it were burning zeals for the preservation of friendship and conjugial confidence, 155[a][3].

Zeal, considered in itself, is like the fire of love blazing up, 358.

It belongs to love, *ib.*

It is not the highest degree of love, but it is love blazing up, *ib.*

It is a spiritual blazing up or flame, arising from the infestation of and assault upon the love, 359.

The quality of a man's zeal is according to the quality of his love, 362.

In general there is a zeal for good and thence for truth, and a zeal for evil and thence for falsity, *ib.*

In general there is the zeal of a good love and the zeal of an evil love, *ib.;* these zeals are alike in externals, but utterly unlike in internals, 363, 364, 366; their differences, 365.

The zeal of conjugial love is called jealousy, 367. See JEALOUSY.

ZEALOUS. Why Jehovah in the Word is called zealous, 366.

ZION signifies the church, 21[7].

INDEX OF SCRIPTURE REFERENCES.

*** The numbering of chapters and verses is that of the Bibles used by Swedenborg. Where this differs from the numbering used in the Authorized English version of the Bible, the latter is inserted in parentheses.

Heavy type, thus, **1, 2, 3**, indicates that the very words of the verses referred to are quoted.

Thin type, thus, 1, 2, 3, indicates that the substance of the verse is given, but not the very words.

Thin Italic type, thus, *1, 2, 3*, indicates that the verses indicated are merely referred to.

REFERENCES TO THE WORD.

REFERENCES TO THE APOSTOLIC WORD.

TRANSLATOR'S CRITICAL NOTES.

The following readings of the original Latin text have been adopted in the present translation. References are to pages of the present edition. Mere typographical corrections are not recorded.

no.	page	line	
98	101	8	*conjugialis* (conjugial) has been read instead of *conjugalis* (conjugal).
119	116	23	*dimiserim* (*I have put away*) has been read instead of *dimisistis* (*you have put away*).
151	141	11	*neutrum* (of a neuter quality) has been read instead of *mutum* (dumb).
183[4]	172	12 bot.	*status* (state) has been read instead of *flatus* (breath).
203	187	5	*conjugiale* (conjugial principle) has been read instead of *conjugale*.
276	248	28, 29	The text here has been read thus: [*fierent*] *ex dissolutionibus conjugiorum seu dimissionibus etc.* (would result from the dissolutions of marriages, or the putting away etc.), instead of *et dissolutiones conjugiorum seu dimissiones etc.* (and the dissolutions etc.).
355[2]	315	33	*quod alius amor* (that there is any other love) has been read instead of *quid alius amor* (what other love there is).
401	348	2 bot.	*seu amore* (or the love) has been read instead of *et amore* (and the love).
447[2]	386	5 bot.	*sensus* (sense) has been read instead of *sexus* (sex).
458	392	11	70, 71 has been read instead of 58, 59.
465	401	13 bot.	*conjunctim* (conjointly) has been read instead of *conjunctus* (conjoined).
466	402	11	
——[2]	,,	8 bot.	
495	425	24	*cognitiones* (Knowledges) has been read instead of *cogitationes* (thoughts).
521[4]	446	7	*Circe* has been read instead of *Medea*.
522	447	last	*intra* (within) has been read instead of *infra* (below).